RET

E

Organizations: STRUCTURE AND BEHAVIOR

Organizations:

Assistant Professor of Management, University of Illinois, Urbana, Illinois

John Wiley and Sons, Inc.

Structure and Behavior

Joseph A. Litterer

New York and London

Preface

This book is about organizations, primarily large organizations; for example, business corporations, government agencies, or service institutions such as hospitals. This is a large topic which can be approached in many ways. We can, for example, study the subject from a detached, outside point of view where organizations are examined by type, shape, products, inputs; in short, study what is known *about* the topic. Or, the subject can be approached from the point of view of a person planning or operating an organization, who is concerned with what an organization can do, what problems or issues develop relevant to an organization, what alternatives are open in coping with these issues, and what the consequences of these alternatives are. This approach is concerned with *what happens in* an organization; how organization activities are allocated, what makes coordination difficult, and how integration is obtained. We are concerned in this book with the organizational processes about which the manager, actual or potential, will have to make decisions in developing or operating an organization.

The above is a statement of intent but, alas, not of what this book accomplishes. The book falls short of realizing this ideal for several reasons. First, although our knowledge of organizations is growing rapidly, we admittedly have a great deal more to learn. Second, even to present all we do know of the topic would require several volumes. Hence a decision was made about the content of the book. It is intended as an introduction to the basic, well-established material of the field for the reader who has little or no background in this subject.

The book was prepared to be used in advanced undergraduate or graduate level courses, or by the interested business or government executive. The book can be used in a separate, single-semester course with no prerequisite work, or can be used following a course in Human Relations or Administrative Behavior where individual and group behavior have been covered, in which case Part II might be dropped.

One of the things which have made the study of organizations trying is that there is not one but several approaches to, or schools of thought on, the subject. Often the differences have been noted by the adherents of one school, with the implication, and sometimes the direct assertion, that the other school(s) are in error and that the one to which the writer belongs is the only way to salvation. Unfortunately, much energy has been expended in establishing and maintaining these positions, often obscuring the fact that the opposing schools of thought contain elements that could fit together into a concept larger and more inclusive than any of them. Observing these actions, we are reminded of the fable of how the disputes between the blind men examining an elephant kept them from developing a real understanding of what an elephant looked like.

Selections for this book were chosen from the major schools of thought to be representative of the different approaches and are arranged to suggest ways in which they might be integrated. Although differences between these schools of thought are discussed, particular attention is given to areas where they can

v

support or supplement each other. Some elements that enable different schools of thought to be bridged, or linked, are identified. Again, these are intentions and guides to action, illustrated by a few applications of bridging elements, rather than complete accomplishments.

This book has five parts, each of which has a definite place and function. Each part begins with an introductory section that explains the scope and nature of the part and the relation of this part to those which have preceded and will follow. As the introduction to each part is developed, the purpose and place of each selection are identified. The introductory sections then form the basic framework which heightens the meaning of individual selections and integrates them into a meaningful whole.

Such a book is not possible without the kind cooperation of the authors and publishers who permitted these selections to be used.

JOSEPH A. LITTERER

Urbana, Illinois
January, 1963

Contents

Organizations: STRUCTURE AND BEHAVIOR

INTRODUCTION

ONE OF THE dominant characteristics of our era is the existence of large-scale organizations. This prevalence of organizations and their influence on modern life has not always been viewed as an unmixed blessing. There are those who are concerned with the power these large organizations have in our social, political, and economic life. Still another group is concerned with the tremendous, often subtle influence that organizations can have on the individual. They see organizations subverting the individualistic nature of man and molding him into a cog in a large impersonal entity. On the other hand, there are those who view large-scale organizations as one of the primary factors in developing our modern society to its high level of physical wellbeing. Obviously these different points of view deal with very fundamental issues relevant to organizations. We begin with them primarily to dispose of them, for although they are of vital importance, they are outside the scope of this book. The point of view taken here is that organizations do exist, are numerous, and have a very profound impact on our individual and collective lives. It is accepted that the prevalence of organizations will not only continue but in all probability increase in the future. The purpose of this book is to bring about a better understanding of organizations, in order to help make them more fruitful for all concerned. Before leaving this issue completely, we wish to examine both the prevalence and the importance of organizations a bit further, thereby establishing a background against which the rest of the book can be placed.

General Considerations about Organizations

Perhaps the prevalence of organizations can be appreciated by examining the number to which each of us belong and to contrast this situation with that which existed only a few generations earlier. Not too many decades ago large portions of our population lived in rural settings in which the most significant social structures were the family and the immediate community. Only occasionally did the majority of our population come in contact with a large, complex organization, such as the government or the military. Today this has been sharply changed. The bulk of our population lives in the city, where larger organizations have always been more prevalent. Even those portions of the population living in rural areas are influenced by and are members of many more large organizations than were their forefathers.

This brief over-view could be extended greatly, but we have covered the main point that in today's world each individual, throughout his life from the time he enters school, is in at least one and perhaps several large complex organizations. Anything that looms so large in the lives of so many people in today's world is a matter of great importance.

Some Advantages and Requirements of Organizations. It is not the prevalence of organizations alone that makes them important for us to study. We live today in a world of vast

1

abundance. Our material bounty has been cited many times, and it might also be noted that many artistic things are available in larger quantities and to more people than ever before in history. This increase in material abundance has freed us to a considerable degree, in the United States at least, from the fear of want. In addition to freedom from the specter of starvation which haunts much of the world, we have, even at the lowest levels of our society, a relatively large amount of free time. We can use this leisure for hobbies, the pursuit of pleasure, self-improvement, or in any activity which to us as individuals seems desirable. We might describe the life of an individual in today's world of large complex organizations as one of performing his own unique, special task within the organization while expending a relatively small proportion of time. From this he is able to acquire an extraordinarily wide array of goods, services, and also free time. This is indeed a comfortable and attractive picture, but in it there is an element which, although frequently ignored, is of the most fundamental importance.

Perhaps the simplest way to develop this point is to examine certain aspects of the life of a member of a large contemporary organization. Let's look at the proverbial John Q. Smith who works as a quality control engineer. His education and experience have all been directed to increasing his competence in the area of quality control. Such specialization, incorporating high degrees of expertness, is recognized as one of the fundamental characteristics of modern organizations. Let us imagine for a moment that we had at our disposal a time machine and could move our quality control expert back to the time of the frontier in our country. Many things would be different for our hero. One of the most significant would be that from being a person who was quite important in his local organization because of his special knowledge and unique contribution he had suddenly become among the most useless people in his environment. In all likelihood he would not know how to milk a cow, ride a horse, plant a crop, skin a bear, make soap, store food through the winter, or any of the other simple but vitally important things necessary in a frontier community. There would be nothing on which he could use his special knowledge and skill.

He would only have his brawn, and he would have to put it at the disposal of anyone who had the knowledge to direct it.

A vitally important point to recognize is that as a consequence of our large-scale organizations we have been able to develop high degrees of individual specialization. In addition to producing efficiencies, such specialization has also made us highly dependent on our organizations, our society, and each other. While we have looked at an individual and his dependency on others, we should emphasize that the same point could be made for subunits within an organization. For example, the work of the production department is highly interrelated with other departments, such as sales, engineering, and purchasing. Its success in producing goods is only partially dependent on itself and to no small degree dependent on the success with which these other units do their work. To carry this thinking one step further, an organization such as a business firm is highly dependent on other business firms in the economy, as is so dramatically illustrated when there is a steel or railroad strike.

In summary, organizations, as they have increased in size and number, have also tended to bring about much greater specialization, which in turn has produced a much higher order of interdependency among all organizational elements.

Influence of Organizations Not Always Readily Recognized. While it may be easy to recognize the importance and prevalence of organizations in our modern life, even to recognize how highly dependent we are on organizations and therefore on each other as linked by these organizations, it is still surprising how frequently we fail to take into account the impact of organizations on our lives and on events in the world about us. We tend to think in individualistic terms. Hence, when two people are continually having arguments or fighting with each other, their clash is commonly described as a personality conflict. Perhaps it is, but in many instances the root of the difficulty can be more accurately described as an organizational problem. A not uncommon situation occurs when one of two men who are supposed to be on the same level of the organization is dependent on the other for assistance in successfully completing his responsibilities. The likelihood of difficulty increases greatly if the second party receives no credit or has to detract from his own performance to help the first person.

As an illustration of this situation, let us envision a production manager who is plagued by high production costs resulting from high labor costs largely incurred when machines break down and workers sit around idle while repairs are made. He knows that many of these delays are hours long because the maintenance department, which does not report to him, does not have the necessary repair parts in stock, but has to send out to a supplier when they are needed. The production manager feels quite strongly that his high production costs could be sharply reduced if the maintenance department could give him quicker service. On the other hand, the maintenance supervisor believes that to stock the vast number of parts needed for repair of the company equipment would require an enormous inventory which would be very expensive for his department. Since he is probably under continuous pressure to keep costs down, as is the production manager, he is reluctant to keep an inventory on any parts which are not used regularly. In such a situation the production manager is likely to be continually badgering the maintenance supervisor for quicker repairs which the latter will not be able to provide because of his understandable reluctance to provide the inventories which are necessary. Once such a condition is recognized, it is readily understood that the situation is the source of friction. It is not understanding the effects of the condition that makes the study of organizations difficult; but rather seeing the situation at all.

Reasons for Studying Organizations. The importance of organizations more than justifies their study. There is, however, an additional consideration that makes the study of this subject particularly important for today's college student. After graduation the student in all likelihood will not only work within an organization but sooner or later achieve positions in which he will be responsible for directing and planning the organization. One of the fundamental points kept in mind in preparing this book was its potential usefulness to the current or future manager of organizations. Its material was drawn from many sources. Some of it is theoretical, and some presents the results of empirical research. The guiding rule in selecting and arranging that material has been to permit the practitioner, actual or potential, to better understand, plan, and direct the work of organizations.

The Complexity and Diversity of Views about Organizations

The study of organizations is both new and old. Writings about organizations can be traced back for thousands of years. Some sound organizational advice is found, for example, in the Bible. The study of organizations has begun in different places at different times and has been approached from different points of view. As a result, we have a number of different schools of thought and a number of literatures on organizations. One of the difficulties in dealing with the subject today is this multiplicity of literatures. In a book such as this, which attempts to draw together the most pertinent items from several literatures, these different points of view, using different vocabularies on different levels of abstraction, can be confusing to the reader. As we go from one literature to another it sometimes seems that the authors are talking about quite different and unrelated topics. We can even find instances where, thoroughly convinced of the rightness of their own point of view, authors from one school of thought heatedly deny the validity or usefulness of the ideas of another, opposing school of thought. The particular selections have been chosen and edited so as to reduce this source of confusion as much as possible without distorting the real variety and vitality of the literature.

The Classical School of Thought on Organizations. One approach to organizations, and the oldest as far as a continuing systematic literature is concerned, is the so-called classical school. Its modern roots go back at least to the days of Frederick Taylor, Harrington Emerson, and Henry Fayol. The classical point of view holds that work or tasks can be so organized as to accomplish efficiently the objectives of the organization. An organization is viewed as a product of rational thought concerned largely with coordinating tasks through the use of legitimate authority.

It is based on the fundamental and usually implicit assumption that the behavior of people is logical, rational, and within the same system of rationality as that used to formulate the organization. It is an analytical approach developing normative models. That is, on the basis of deduction from some assumptions it attempts to specify what an organization should be.

In the classical point of view, the manager or executive responsible for the organization plans a set of tasks or jobs that presumably include all the activities necessary to accomplish the objective or objectives of the organization. People are thought of as the means through which the objectives are accomplished. They are looked on primarily as individuals, with the only connections between them being provided by the organization. It is presumed that the people who are assigned to these jobs will perform them exactly as specified. As will be noted later, the classical theorists do not necessarily presume that people will do this naturally. They work on the assumption, however, that through selection, training, or indoctrination, or a combination of all three people can be brought to the point of filling the jobs exactly as specified. At this fundamental point we find the weakest part of the classical approach to organizations and the one to which the behavioral or naturalistic school of thought has made its most significant contributions.

In summary, the classical school of organizations has as its main elements objectives, tasks, rational behavior, coordination of effort, and efficiency.

The Naturalistic School of Organizations. Contrasted to the classical point of view is what might be called the behavioral or empirical school, which holds that "organizations spring naturally or spontaneously from the association of people who have common or mutually supportive needs, interests, or objectives.[1] Hence, from this point of view, there need not be anything consciously planned about an organization. Organizations rest instead on the basic needs, both physical and emotional, of people. This approach has received great attention in the last several decades and has developed into a large and rapidly expanding series of studies about the collective behavior of people. They have shown, for example, that people tend to have a much broader and varied set of behavior than is called for, or for that matter anticipated, in the classical point of view. This approach has done much to increase our understanding of the very important fact that many things are done in organizations which are not directly related to the formal goals that the classical approach considers.

The naturalistic or behavioral point of view has taken as its main topic of interest the behavior of people in groups or collectivities. It recognized early that many things influence the behavior of individuals in groups other than the formal specifications laid down by an organizational plan or orders from superiors who have formal authority. Sometimes behavior of individuals in groups is exactly what superiors or job descriptions call for. At other times it may be almost a direct opposite. In many cases, perhaps most, it is to some degree different from what is formally called for. For example, at times we find employees working very hard and exceeding the levels of production standards established by the company executives. In other cases we find them quite consistently flaunting these standards to hold the level of production down. One of the interesting contributions of the behavioral point of view has been the identification of fundamental factors which can explain both the compliance with production standards set by higher management and the consistent violation of the same standards.

The roots of this approach go back for many years. The real bulk of our material, however, has been largely developed since the time of the now famous Hawthorne studies in the 1920's and 1930's. It has been developed by students of management, industrial sociologists and industrial psychologists and now draws heavily on the work of many social psychologists and, more recently, cultural anthropologists.

The development of this approach to the study of organizations, with its rapidly expanding mass of data, has posed a major dilemma for the student of organizations. It would at first glance appear that there are two

[1] For a discussion of this point of view see Alvin W. Gouldner, "Organization Analysis," in Robert K. Merton, Leonard Broom, and Leonard S. Cottrell, *Sociology Today*, Basic Books, New York, 1959, pp. 400–428.

opposing, perhaps even self-canceling, schools of thought which we must choose between. Actually the situation is both more, and less, complicated.

The Systems Concept of Organizations. To make things more complicated there has slowly but gradually emerged yet a third view of organizations. This approach looks on an organization as a system, or perhaps part of a system, of events, activities, and other components which must exist if any objective is to be realized at all. This point of view, in short, does not concern itself particularly with how to accomplish a specific objective but concerns itself instead with identifying the basic factors and the interrelations between them necessary for any task or goal to be accomplished.

These different approaches to organizations are explored in some detail by the first reading in this book (Scott)[2] and appear in total or in part in many later sections.

The new concept of the field of organizations that will eventually make the field less complicated is the realization that there are not just governmental organizations or business organizations, formal organizations or informal organizations, but that there is a general topic of organizations of which these are but parts. One of the fundamental purposes of this book is to draw together, from many areas and diverse points of view, material that will contribute to an overall understanding of organizations. The sum total of the contributions from these many sources does not at the moment yield a complete and fully integrated concept. Many areas, topics, or issues still have to be studied and explored, and the relationships among them must be analyzed much more adequately. This book, then, is only a step in a direction in which much work must still be done. Limited though it may be, the material is now extensive enough for a beginning to be made.

Fortunately, we now have knowledge that enables us to form some bridges between major concepts and research in the field of organizations which until not too long ago had to be treated as separate and somewhat unrelated topics. Some of the items included, therefore, deal with theories and research that link the major schools of thought on organizations, and all of them have been arranged to give a perspective which will heighten the interrelation of the different points of view.

What Are Organizations?

In this book an organization is considered to be a social unit within which people have achieved somewhat stable relations (not necessarily face-to-face) among themselves in order to facilitate obtaining a set of objectives or goals. This brief and general statement leads to a number of points which should be made more explicit.

Let us begin by examining the point that organizations are purposeful social units, that is, they have an objective or goal. It is not uncommon to read or hear assertions that all the members of an organization have, or should have, the same objective as the organization. Although this may be desirable, it is a condition only occasionally reached. For example, in time of war all the members of an army may have the same objective as the organization: to defeat the enemy in battle. Circumstances that promote such singleness of purpose are, however, more the exception than the rule. If the existence of organizations depended on everyone sharing the same goal, there would be far fewer organizations.

Organizations consist of individuals and small groups, as well as an arrangement of these elements into larger collectivities. Each of these elements may have not one but many goals. Further, it is more than likely that these goals are not identical, in many instances dissimilar, and in some, relatively few, cases are actually in opposition. A business firm may have as its objective to make and distribute radios in such a way as to make a profit. The Vice President of the firm may be working hard for the company so that he can be promoted to the Presidency when the present incumbent retires. He may not be at all interested in radios and may only be interested in any firm that will enable him to become a president, because in this position he feels he can obtain the prestige and power he wants. A worker on the assembly line may be equally uninterested in radios and primarily interested

[2] Papers included in the readings portion of this book will be identified by the author's name in parentheses, for example, (Scott), at related places in the introductory material.

in earning some money to support his family. The fact that the goals of the two individuals and the organization are different probably does not interfere with them working together to accomplish all three effectively. The first point, therefore, in this elaboration of the general description of organizations we have given, is that an organization is a means of accomplishing diverse multiple goals of the organization and its elements.

Although the individuals, groups, or departments within an organization may have different goals, it would be wrong to assume that they can have just any goals. There must be some integration and for that matter ordering among them. Perhaps the nature of this interrelation is more easily understood by examining the way different goals can facilitate their collective accomplishment. For example, it may not be too important for the Vice President and the assembly line worker to share a goal of making radios, but it may be important that whatever goals they have encourage them to work hard for their employer and do not distract them from working, for example, by making them primarily interested in carefree fun. From this point of view it is more important that goals of various organizational elements be functionally related than that they be similar, because quite dissimilar goals can have functional unity.

Organization as a Set of Intervening Factors or Variables

So far we have considered some of the things which are to be found in organizations, such as individuals and small groups, and one of its basic characteristics, that of providing a means for mutal goal attainment. There has been little discussion of just what an organization is, beyond stating that it is a set of stable relations. To develop this a little further we consider a highly simplified situation involving just one goal. Let us take a firm which sets as its objective to make and sell washing machines. Second, let us presume that it gathers together several hundred people who are going to be its workers. Obviously there must be a great deal more in the firm than just this objective and the machinery, buildings, and people. Even if all the people there did want to make washing machines, the like-

lihood is that not much would be done, or that, if something were accomplished, it would not be done with any great dispatch and efficiency. We can put it this way. Between the objective and the efforts of the people there must be a set of intervening factors which bring about the coordination of their effort into the efficient accomplishment of the goal. In the broad view of the concept, these sets of intervening factors are the organization.

Perhaps this concept of intervening factors or variables can be clarified by a simple illustration. At the beginning of the Second World War the aircraft industry expanded enormously in order to satisfy the wartime needs for aircraft. Many new people were drawn into these plants from all over the country. A great many people went to work for both monetary and patriotic reasons. To put it another way, the people working in these firms were interested in the same end result, or the overall objective, of the firm, namely, to make airplanes, as were the owners of the firm and the government. We might assume that having this objective would be all that was necessary to have them work hard and remain on the job. Actually, there was a great deal of turnover. Investigation showed that one of the key factors related to this turnover was the highly unstable social relations within certain departments. People were being moved in or moved out of the departments very rapidly, transferred from one job to another within the department, or in some other way prevented from getting acquainted with each other and building up friendship associations. In other departments, on the other hand, where conditions were much more stable, the turnover and absenteeism rate was much lower.

To summarize this in the terms we have just been using, in order to accomplish its objective of making airplanes, the firm needed people who not only worked hard but stayed on the job. To achieve this condition the company had to provide some degree of social stability, which would permit people to get acquainted and develop friendship groups. Hence, in order to accomplish the objective of making large quantities of airplanes it was necessary to provide another factor, namely, stable interpersonal relations. Therefore, the man building an organization would seem to be wise to give effort and attention to building such intervening factors as cohesive, stable work groups in order to accomplish the ends in which he was interested.

Let us explore this matter a little more fully. By intervening factors or variables we mean things which, although they do not directly produce the end objective, are in some way related to producing it. In any business firm, for example, we expect to find a wage payment plan. A wage payment plan does not directly get washing machines made, but it does reward the people within the organization for making the parts or components that go into the end products which are the objectives of the firm. Some of the effort of management, then, has been diverted in setting up this intervening factor, and another portion, although probably smaller, will be continually diverted to keep it functioning.

While a wage payment plan may represent a deflection of managerial efforts from the direct accomplishment of the company's goals, its relation to this goal is nonetheless readily apparent. This obvious relation does not exist, however, for all the intervening factors that comprise an organization. Let us consider a company newspaper. A company newspaper provides information about the company and the people within it. We would hardly expect people to join a company just to receive this information. The influence on employees of giving them information about the company is hardly likely to be as great or, for that matter, as clear-cut as a wage payment scheme. Despite the relation's lack of clarity, many managements and owners of firms have accepted the idea that in some way the provision of a company newspaper is useful for obtaining the basic objectives of the firm even though they do not see exactly how the result follows.

This brings us to the realization that a number of the things we find comprising organizations are there because in some way people have come to know, or at least to accept the idea, that these factors or organizational components and devices are in some way useful for accomplishing organizational ends. There is, at our current level of knowledge, a good deal of pragmatism in our planning of organizations. Although much work is being done to bring more analysis into the planning of organizations, it would be a mistake to think we have reached this objective.

The Scope of Organizations as Covered in This Book

One of the difficulties in discussing the field of organizations is the scope of the subject matter. To some, organization is properly the study of whole cultures or societies. To others it is the study of small groups. Needless to say, between these extremes there are a number of intermediate concepts of how inclusive the study of organizations should be.

To delimit the area we shall cover here it may be useful to draw an analogy to viewing a drop of water under a microscope. If at first the drop is examined under very low power of magnification, we can see the largest bodies or particles contained in the drop of water quite easily. Several things should be noted, however. First, even under low magnification it is probably impossible to see the boundaries of the drop of water itself. This has become too large for our point of view. At the same time, attached to or around the large particles in the drop are small specks or blurs which as yet are too small for us to see clearly. When we change to a higher power of magnification, however, some of these smaller specks become quite sharp and clear and fill a large portion of our viewing area. If we look closely, we note, for example, that some of the little blurs or specks turn out to be legs or feelers on the larger bodies we noticed earlier and that these larger bodies have now become so large that they blur into the background and extend far beyond our range of vision. Similarly, if we look closely, there are now additional, new blurs or specks, invisible at the lower power of magnification, which have now become visible, although hardly large or clear. This illustration is used for two purposes: first, to bring out the fact that something like an organization consists of several "levels" of parts or units; and second, that although the units at one "level" can be examined separately, the different levels are closely related.

Looking along one dimension of human affairs we might consider whole economies as organizations. Hence, we would have a French economy or an English economy or an economy in the metals industry and an economy in the clothing industry. Looking more closely we would find that any one of these economies

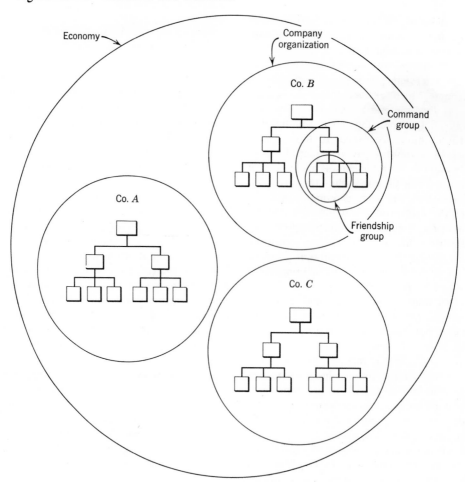

Fig. 1. *Levels at which organizations can be viewed.*

is made up of a collection of companies. (See Fig. 1) At the same time, looking still more closely within each of these companies, we note there are divisions or departments (Fig. 2), which in turn contain command groups (that is, a superior and his immediate subordinates) some members of which have formed into a still different form of unit, a friendship group or clique. If we wanted to carry this even further, of course, we could make our point of examination the individual and look at the things that bear on him. Although it may be desirable to include all these levels in our study of organizations, it is unrealistic to attempt to include them all in one beginning volume. Here we consider a few levels, beginning with the organization at the level of the company or, if you will, the army or the hospital, and the subunits within it down to

and including the small face-to-face group. We shall be quite concerned with studying each of these elements and the interrelations among them. Factors or influences coming from outside the organization, such as those from the industry or the economy at one end, or from the personalities or cultures of the individual at the other, will be recognized and their influence taken into account. They will, however, be considered as "givens" to the system. In short, culture, economy, and personality are exogenous factors, whereas departments, tasks, interpersonal relations, communication systems, and like matters are endogenous variables.

Structure, Process, and Product of Organizations. A number of classes of phenomena can be noted about organizations. Among the more prominent are structure, process, and product. By structure we mean the identification of the elements in an organization and relations between them. Process has two meanings: one, the sequence of events or phases by which organization and its elements, such as structure, develop or change; the other, the sequence of events or interactions between elements and structure when once they are established. By product is meant the outputs of an organization. This could include both the technical accomplishments, such as making a commodity or rendering of service, and the satisfaction of the wants and needs of the organizational members both as individuals and collectivities.

In this book items have been selected to give primary attention to structure and process and relatively less to products of organizations. There are several reasons for this. First, the prosaic but nonetheless essential requirement of keeping the length of the book within some reasonable bounds meant that something had to be omitted. The choice of playing down the products of organizations was encouraged by appreciation of a second point: at the mo-

ment, our knowledge of organizations is such that it is sometimes difficult to state precisely what causal factors bring about a particular result or product. Too many intervening variables, which we either do not fully understand or perhaps at present do not even recognize, influence the outcome of a chain of events. As a result, it seemed more profitable to focus attention on the elements that could be more closely tied together and more assuredly identified.

The Structure of This Book

Part 1. The Formal Organization. The first part of the book examines the formal organization. We begin with the study of the formal organization for several reasons. First, it presents an opportunity of becoming somewhat acquainted with the overall picture of a large, complex organization. Obviously the whole body is not there, but at least a general form and skeleton can be presented. Second, it is the logical starting point if we want to examine an organization from the point of view of the

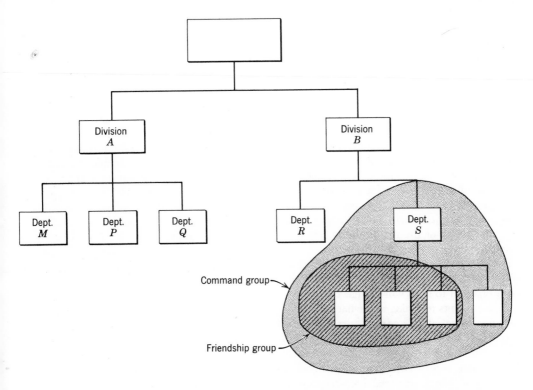

Fig. 2. Different types of social groups within an organization.

actual or potential manager. The formal organization contains many of the elements which the manager can control most directly.

By formal is meant those aspects of organizations which have been, or possibly might be, consciously planned. Hence, much of the classical school of organizations is included in the formal organization area. This category, however, includes more than classical concepts, because we intend to build toward a concept of formal organization that includes any organizational elements which can be planned and specified. Hence, as we learn more about elements of leadership, and these elements reach a state of development where they can be consciously taken into account in planning the organization, they then fall within the province of the formal organization. The formal organization is viewed as a plan by which the efforts of people fit together to accomplish some purpose.

Our study of organizations begins with the purposes or objectives having been chosen. To put it another way, for the organizational designer objectives are given. To accomplish them the work to be done must be broken up or divided into a series of jobs which individuals can perform. One of the early issues centers on just how the work shall be divided, for there are many different ways of dividing work, each with certain advantages and certain disadvantages, or, equivalently, each with certain returns and certain costs. The task of the planner of an organization is not completed when he has decided on a division of labor, because, as noted earlier, the tasks within an organization are interrelated, and if the person filling any one job is to contribute effectively, his efforts must be integrated with those of others. Hence, a formal organization must also include means of integrating the efforts of organizational members. It is at this point that some of the most serious difficulties arise.

Even when people have fairly well defined jobs it is necessary, for example, to inform them of when to start work, what to work on, how many units to make, and what to do with the units when completed. In short, even after a job is defined, we must insure a flow of information and instructions in order to make the position really useful. Some information comes from the managerial hierarchy, other information comes from systems and procedures such as production control. This, however, is but one of the many flows which must be established. Another, for example, is the necessary flow of materials both into and out of a position. This list could be extended, but it hardly seems necessary to do so in order to establish the point that the formal organization planner must establish an elaborate matrix of methods of achieving coordination if his division of labor is to prove useful.

This, however, is only one of the problems in achieving coordination. Even when jobs are specified and systems and procedures and hierarchies of authority are established, we still find that the efforts of people are not always fully coordinated or integrated. This leads us to the second portion of the book.

Part II. The Informal Organization. One of the things noted by numerous early writers and investigators of organizational matters was that people within an organization frequently behaved in a way different from that called for by the formal organization plan. To some this appeared to be erratic, unpredictable behavior but on closer and more intense investigation it was found that much of this behavior followed consistent patterns and was based on recognizable factors. One thing soon appreciated was that if we looked at the individual within an organization we had to recognize that he was actually the member of at least two organizations—the one formally designated, that is, the firm, the agency, etc., and the other—what is often called the informal organization.

The informal organization is conceived of as being the aspects of organization that are not formally planned but that more or less spontaneously evolve from the needs of people. An element of the informal organization then is the small group. The informal organization, however, will also include informal work arrangements, which people develop and perpetuate even though their contacts are so casual as hardly to form a group in the usual sense.

It came as a bit of a shock to some to realize that people within a business firm, for example, frequently had much stronger feelings of loyalty to their informal organization than they did to the firm. At one time this implied that the informal organization was the enemy, or at least the opponent, of the formal. This position has largely changed and its is fairly generally recognized that the informal organization is the basic aspect of social life and we have to accept it just as we have to accept individual personality differences. Even more important has been the understanding that the informal organization need not be in opposition to the objectives of the formal organization. On the contrary, in many ways the informal organization can be supportive of formal organization objectives.

This changed view has come about to a very large extent through our increased knowledge of informal organizations. It has been learned that informal organizations have a structure which has spontaneously arisen, that it has its own rules, usually called norms, for guiding the behavior of its members, and that it has its leaders and its followers. It, too, has its objectives, or perhaps more accurately functions, which it serves. With this knowledge has come the realization that informal organizations are a necessary, vital part of human life and constitute an integral part of a total organization.

Part III. The Effects of the Formal Organization on the Informal. This increased knowledge of the informal organization has not only brought about its acceptance but has identified some of its elements which are most directly influenced by the formal organization. It also enables us to identify some factors which are exceedingly important for organizational stability and individual satisfaction which the concepts of the formal organization have not taken into account. Part III examines some of the elements which serve to tie together or bridge the previous gap between the formal- and the informal organization concepts. Here are the elements that will enable us to make better, more complete organization plans, permitting us to a degree to predict the possible consequences an organization plan will have on group behavior. We are hardly at the point where precise design and prediction is possible, but the links which have been established point to future developments of very great promise.

These three sections—the formal organization, the informal organization, and the elements bridging the two—comprise the heart of the book. The remaining two sections are concerned with matters that build on this foundation.

Part IV. Organizational Adaptation. Existing in much of what has gone before has been the concept that organizations are not fixed or rigid but are instead in a constant state of change. There is, as we noted in our early definition, a stability that characterizes organizations. This is in the short run, however, because over a period of time organizations change or else cease to exist. The reasons are numerous. The objectives of the organization may well change, through an expansion of objectives, as, for example, a business firm changing from making washing machines alone to making a whole array of household products, or by one set of objectives being superceded by another. The recent history of the March of Dimes Association is an interesting illustration of an organization directed to a fairly specific purpose: Developing a means for preventing infantile paralysis. Success in this task made it necessary to develop new objectives. This was done. The organization is now devoted to accomplishing new purposes related to, but nonetheless different from, those it had for so many years.

Even if the objectives of an organization remain stable, we frequently find that the conditions facing an organization, such as the economy or the markets, change and require the organization to modify itself if it is to continue to survive or accomplish its objectives. In addition to external matters, organizations continually have to adjust to internal factors, such as the death or retirement of personnel. Part IV is concerned with identifying some of the changes that require organizations to adapt and also with identifying some of the processes or patterns of adaptation. This is an enormously complex issue. There is no attempt to treat the topic exhaustively. The objective of this section is to emphasize that organizations do change and to point out both some of the ways in which they change and the forces which make these changes necessary or desirable.

Part V. Individual Adjustments to the Formal and Informal Organizations. In Part V we turn our attention to the basic element in an organization—the individual. It is his efforts and behavior, whether viewed as those of an individual, of a member of an informal organization, or of a member of a formal organization, which are really our primary concern.

Earlier it was stated that the individual is for us a given. By this we meant that we do not extend our analysis to include the study of personality. We are, however, concerned with the individual as a member of an organization. Hence, we look at the individual as being under influences and pressures from both the informal organization and the formal organization. Sometimes these may be congruent, but at other times, more frequently than not, they will be divergent and occasionally even conflicting.

In Part V we are concerned with how any individual will be likely or have to behave in certain organizational settings. What happens, for example, when a supervisor sees one of his subordinates violating a company rule? He knows that one of his duties as a member of the managerial hierarchy is to enforce company rules. Yet he may also know that the worker is conforming to one of his group norms in violating the rule. Therefore, to punish the subordinate would be to place himself in conflict not only with the individual but also with the entire group. Or, what hap-

pens with the accountant who knows that company rules state that certain reports must be in by a given time but who is approached by a good golfing friend to permit him to turn it in two days late and to cover up for his tardiness? These are but two of many issues and dilemmas which arise when the individual is caught between the differing demands of the informal and the formal organizations. They are part of the everyday reality of organizational life.

This, the most undeveloped aspect of organizations, may in the long run be of the greatest significance. At the moment, however, this section is concerned with drawing attention to these matters and identifying some of the elements to be considered.

These five sections constitute an approach to analyzing organizations. They represent only one of a number of possible approaches. This particular one, however, seems the most valuable for the person who now is or perhaps will be involved with the direction of affairs in an organization.

Organization Theory: An Overview and an Appraisal

WILLIAM G. SCOTT

Man is intent on drawing himself into a web of collectivized patterns. "Modern man has learned to accommodate himself to a world increasingly organized. The trend toward ever more explicit and consciously drawn relationships is profound and sweeping; it is marked by depth no less than by extension." [1] This comment by Seidenberg nicely summarizes the pervasive influence of organization in many forms of human activity.

Some of the reasons for intense organizational activity are found in the fundamental transitions which revolutionized our society, changing it from a rural culture, to a culture based on technology, industry, and the city. From these changes, a way of life emerged characterized by the *proximity* and *dependency* of people on each other. Proximity and dependency, as conditions of social life, harbor the threats of human conflict, capricious antisocial behavior, instability of human relationships, and uncertainty about the nature of the social structure with its concomitant roles.

Of course, these threats to social integrity are present to some degree in all societies, ranging from the primitive to the modern. But, these threats become dangerous when the harmonious functioning of a society rests on the maintenance of a highly intricate, delicately balanced form of human collaboration. The civilization we have created depends on the preservation of a precarious balance. Hence, disrupting forces impinging on this shaky form of collaboration must be eliminated or minimized.

Traditionally, organization is viewed as a vehicle for accomplishing goals and objectives. While this approach is useful, it tends to obscure the inner workings and internal purposes of organization itself. Another fruitful way of treating organization is as a mechanism having the ultimate purpose of offsetting those forces which undermine human collaboration. In this sense, organization tends to minimize conflict, and to lessen the significance of individual behavior which deviates from values that the organization has established as worthwhile. Further, organization increases stability in human relationships by reducing uncertainty regarding the nature of the system's structure and the human roles which are inherent to it. Corollary to this point, organization enhances the predictability of human action, because it limits the number of behavioral alternatives available to an individual. As Presthus points out:

> Organization is defined as a system of structural interpersonal relations . . . individuals are differentiated in terms of authority, status, and role with the result that personal interaction is prescribed. . . . Anticipated reactions tend to occur, while ambiguity and spontaneity are decreased.[2]

In addition to all of this, organization has built-in safeguards. Besides prescribing acceptable forms of behavior for those who elect to submit to it, organization is also able to counterbalance the influence of human action which transcends its established patterns.[3]

From *Journal of the Academy of Management*, Vol. 4, No. 1, April 1961, pp. 7–26. Reprinted with permission of The Academy of Management.
[1] Roderick Seidenburg, *Post-Historic Man* (Boston: Beacon Press, 1951), p. 1.

[2] Robert V. Presthus, "Toward a Theory of Organizational Behavior," *Administrative Science Quarterly*, June, 1958, p. 50.
[3] Regulation and predictability of human behavior are matters of degree varying with different or-

Few segments of society have engaged in organizing more intensively than business.[4] The reason is clear. Business depends on what organization offers. Business needs a system of relationships among functions; it needs stability, continuity, and predictability in its internal activities and external contacts. Business also appears to need harmonious relationships among the people and processes which make it up. Put another way, a business organization has to be free, relatively, from destructive tendencies which may be caused by divergent interests.

As a foundation for meeting these needs rests administrative science. A major element of this science is organization theory, which provides the grounds for management activities in a number of significant areas of business endeavor. Organization theory, however, is not a homogeneous science based on generally accepted principles. Various theories of organization have been, and are being, evolved. For example, something called "modern organization theory" has recently emerged, raising the wrath of some traditionalists, but also capturing the imagination of a rather elite *avant-garde*.

The thesis of this paper is that modern organization theory, when stripped of its irrelevancies, redundancies, and "speech defects," is a logical and vital evolution in management thought. In order for this thesis to be supported, the reader must endure a review and appraisal of more traditional forms of organization theory which may seem elementary to him.

In any event, three theories of organization are having considerable influence on management thought and practice. They are arbitrarily labeled in this paper as the classical, the neo-classical, and the modern. Each of these is fairly distinct; but they are not unrelated. Also, these theories are on-going, being actively supported by several schools of management thought.

The Classical Doctrine

For lack of a better method of identification, it will be said that the classical doctrine deals almost exclusively with the *anatomy of formal organization*. This doctrine can be traced back to Frederick W. Taylor's interest in functional foremanship and planning staffs. But most students of management thought would agree that in the United States, the first systematic approach to organization, and the first comprehensive attempt to find organizational universals, is dated 1931 when Mooney and Reiley published *Onward Industry*.[5] Subsequently, numerous books, following the classical vein, have appeared. Two of the more recent are Brech's, *Organization* [6] and Allen's, *Management and Organization*.[7]

Classical organization theory is built around four key pillars. They are the division of labor, the scalar and functional processes, structure, and span of control. Given these major elements just about all of classical organization theory can be derived.

1. *The division of labor* is without doubt the cornerstone among the four elements.[8] From it the other elements flow as corollaries. For example, *scalar* and *functional* growth requires specialization and departmentalization of functions. Organization *structure* is naturally dependent upon the direction which specialization of activities travels in company development. Finally, *span of control* problems result

---

ganizations on something of a continuum. At one extreme are bureaucratic type organizations with tight bonds of regulation. At the other extreme are voluntary associations, and informal organizations with relatively loose bonds of regulation.

This point has an interesting sidelight. A bureaucracy with tight controls and a high degree of predictability of human action appears to be unable to distinguish between destructive and creative deviations from established values. Thus the only thing which is safeguarded is the *status quo*.

[4] The monolithic institutions of the military and government are other cases of organizational preoccupation.

[5] James D. Mooney and Alan C. Reiley, *Onward Industry* (New York: Harper and Brothers, 1931). Later published by James D. Mooney under the title *Principles of Organization*.

[6] E. F. L. Brech, *Organization* (London: Longmans, Green and Company, 1957).

[7] Louis A. Allen, *Management and Organization* (New York: McGraw-Hill Book Company, 1958).

[8] Usually the division of labor is treated under a topical heading of departmentation, see for example: Harold Koontz and Cyril O'Donnell, *Principles of Management* (New York: McGraw-Hill Book Company, 1959), Chapter 7.

from the number of specialized functions under the jurisdiction of a manager.

2. *The scalar and functional processes* deal with the vertical and horizontal growth of the organization, respectively.[9] The scalar process refers to the growth of the chain of command, the delegation of authority and responsibility, unity of command, and the obligation to report.

The division of the organization into specialized parts and the regrouping of the parts into compatible-units are matters pertaining to the functional process. This process focuses on the horizontal evolution of the line and staff in a formal organization.

3. *Structure* is the logical relationships of functions in an organization, arranged to accomplish the objectives of the company efficiently. Structure implies system and pattern. Classical organization theory usually works with two basic structures, the line and the staff. However, such activities as committee and liaison functions fall quite readily into the purview of structural considerations. Again, structure is the vehicle for introducing logical and consistent relationships among the diverse functions which comprise the organization.[10]

4. *The span of control* concept relates to the number of subordinates a manager can effectively supervise. Graicunas has been credited with first elaborating the point that there are numerical limitations to the subordinates one man can control.[11] In a recent statement on the subject, Brech points out, "span" refers to ". . . the number of persons, themselves carrying managerial and supervisory responsibilities, for whom the senior manager retains his over-embracing responsibility of direction and planning, co-ordination, motivation, and control."[12] Regardless of interpretation, span of control has significance, in part, for the shape of the organization which evolves

through growth. Wide span yields a flat structure; short span results in a tall structure. Further, the span concept directs attention to the complexity of human and functional interrelationships in an organization.

It would not be fair to say that the classical school is unaware of the day-to-day administrative problems of the organization. Paramount among these problems are those stemming from human interactions. But the interplay of individual personality, informal groups, intraorganizational conflict, and the decision-making processes in the formal structure appears largely to be neglected by classical organization theory. Additionally, the classical theory overlooks the contributions of the behavioral sciences by failing to incorporate them in its doctrine in any systematic way. In summary, classical organization theory has relevant insights into the nature of organization, but the value of this theory is limited by its narrow concentration on the formal anatomy of organization.

Neoclassical Theory of Organization

The neoclassical theory of organization embarked on the task of compensating for some of the deficiencies in classical doctrine. The neoclassical school is commonly identified with the human relations movement. Generally, the neoclassical approach takes the postulates of the classical school, regarding the pillars of organization as givens. But these postulates are regarded as modified by people, acting independently or within the context of the informal organization.

One of the main contributions of the neoclassical school is the introduction of behavioral sciences in an integrated fashion into the theory of organization. Through the use of these sciences, the human relationists demonstrate how the pillars of the classical doctrine are affected by the impact of human actions. Further, the neoclassical approach includes a systematic treatment of the informal organization, showing its influence on the formal structure.

Thus, the neoclassical approach to organization theory gives evidence of accepting classical doctrine, but superimposing on it modifications resulting from individual behavior,

[9] These processes are discussed at length in Ralph Currier Davis, *The Fundamentals of Top Management* (New York: Harper and Brothers, 1951), Chapter 7.

[10] For a discussion of structure see: William H. Newman, *Administrative Action* (Englewood Cliffs: Prentice-Hall, Incorporated, 1951), Chapter 16.

[11] V. A. Graicunas, "Relationships in Organization," *Papers on the Science of Administration* (New York: Columbia University, 1937).

[12] Brech, *op. cit.*, p. 78.

and the influence of the informal group. The inspiration of the neoclassical school was the Hawthorne studies.[13] Current examples of the neoclassical approach are found in human relations books like Gardner and Moore, *Human Relations in Industry*,[14] and Davis, *Human Relations in Business*.[15] To a more limited extent, work in industrial sociology also reflects a neoclassical point of view.[16]

It would be useful to look briefly at some of the contributions made to organization theory by the neoclassicists. First to be considered are modifications of the pillars of classical doctrine; second is the informal organization.

Examples of the Neoclassical Approach to the Pillars of Formal Organization Theory.
1. The *division of labor* has been a long standing subject of comment in the field of human relations. Very early in the history of industrial psychology study was made of industrial fatigue and monotony caused by the specialization of the work.[17] Later, attention shifted to the isolation of the worker, and his feeling of anonymity resulting from insignificant jobs which contributed negligibly to the final product.[18]

Also, specialization influences the work of management. As an organization expands, the need concomitantly arises for managerial motivation and coordination of the activities of others. Both motivation and coordination in turn relate to executive leadership. Thus, in part, stemming from the growth of industrial specialization, the neoclassical school has developed a large body of theory relating to motivation, coordination, and leadership. Much

[13] See: F. J. Roethlisberger and William J. Dickson, *Management and the Worker* (Cambridge: Harvard University Press, 1939).
[14] Burleigh B. Gardner and David G. Moore, *Human Relations in Industry* (Homewood: Richard D. Irwin, 1955).
[15] Keith Davis, *Human Relations in Business* (New York: McGraw-Hill Book Company, 1957).
[16] For example see: Delbert C. Miller and William H. Form, *Industrial Sociology* (New York: Harper and Brothers, 1951).
[17] See: Hugo Munsterberg, *Psychology and Industrial Efficiency* (Boston: Houghton Mifflin Company, 1913).
[18] Probably the classic work is: Elton Mayo, *The Human Problems of an Industrial Civilization* (Cambridge: Harvard University, 1946, first printed 1933).

of this theory is derived from the social sciences.

2. Two aspects of the *scalar and functional* processes which have been treated with some degree of intensity by the neoclassical school are the delegation of authority and responsibility, and gaps in or overlapping of functional jurisdictions. The classical thory assumes something of perfection in the delegation and functionalization processes. The neoclassical school points out that human problems are caused by imperfections in the way these processes are handled.

For example, too much or insufficient delegation may render an executive incapable of action. The failure to delegate authority and responsibility equally may result in frustration for the delegatee. Overlapping of authorities often causes clashes in personality. Gaps in authority cause failures in getting jobs done, with one party blaming the other for shortcomings in performance.[19]

The neoclassical school says that the scalar and functional processes are theoretically valid, but tend to deteriorate in practice. The ways in which they break down are described, and some of the human causes are pointed out. In addition the neoclassicists make recommendations, suggesting various "human tools" which will facilitate the operation of these processes.

3. *Structure* provides endless avenues of analysis for the neoclassical theory of organization. The theme is that human behavior disrupts the best laid organizational plans, and thwarts the cleanness of the logical relationships founded in the structure. The neoclassical critique of structure centers on frictions which appear internally among people performing different functions.

Line and staff relations is a problem area, much discussed, in this respect. Many companies seem to have difficulty keeping the line and staff working together harmoniously. Both Dalton[20] and Juran[21] have engaged in re-

[19] For further discussion of the human relations implications of the scalar and functional processes see: Keith Davis, *op. cit.*, pp. 60–66.
[20] Melville Dalton, "Conflicts between Staff and Line Managerial Officers," *American Sociological Review*, June, 1950, pp. 342–351.
[21] J. M. Juran, "Improving the Relationship between Staff and Line," *Personnel*, May, 1956, pp. 515–524.

search to discover the causes of friction, and to suggest remedies.

Of course, line-staff relations represent only one of the many problems of structural frictions described by the neoclassicists. As often as not, the neoclassicists will offer prescriptions for the elimination of conflict in structure. Among the more important harmony-rendering formulae are participation, junior boards, bottom-up management, joint committees, recognition of human dignity, and "better" communication.

4. An executive's *span of control* is a function of human determinants, and the reduction of span to a precise, universally applicable ratio is silly, according to the neoclassicists. Some of the determinants of span are individual differences in managerial abilities, the type of people and functions supervised, and the extent of communication effectiveness.

Coupled with the span of control question are the human implications of the type of structure which emerges. That is, is a tall structure with a short span or a flat structure with a wide span more conducive to good human relations and high morale? The answer is situational. Short span results in tight supervision; wide span requires a good deal of delegation with looser controls. Because of individual and organizational differences, sometimes one is better than the other. There is a tendency to favor the looser form of organization, however, for the reason that tall structures breed autocratic leadership, which is often pointed out as a cause of low morale.[22]

The Neoclassical View of the Informal Organization. Nothing more than the barest mention of the informal organization is given even in the most recent classical treatises on organization theory.[23] Systematic discussion of this form of organization has been left to the neoclassicists. The informal organization refers to people in group associations at work, but these associations are not specified in the "blueprint" of the formal organization. The informal organization means natural groupings of people in the work situation.

In a general way, the informal organization appears in response to the social need—the need of people to associate with others. How-

ever, for analytical purposes, this explanation is not particularly satisfying. Research has produced the following, more specific determinants underlying the appearance of informal organizations.

1. The *location* determinant simply states that in order to form into groups of any lasting nature, people have to have frequent face-to-face contact. Thus, the geography of physical location in a plant or office is an important factor in predicting who will be in what group.[24]

2. *Occupation* is a key factor determining the rise and composition of informal groups. There is a tendency for people performing similar jobs to group together.[25]

3. *Interests* are another determinant for informal group formation. Even though people might be in the same location, performing similar jobs, differences of interest among them explain why several small, instead of one large, informal organizations emerge.

4. *Special issues* often result in the formation of informal groups, but this determinant is set apart from the three previously mentioned. In this case, people who do not necessarily have similar interests, occupations, or locations may join together for a common cause. Once the issue is resolved, then the tendency is to revert to the more "natural" group forms.[26] Thus, special issues give rise to a rather impermanent informal association; groups based on the other three determinants tend to be more lasting.

When informal organizations come into being they assume certain characteristics. Since understanding these characteristics is important for management practice, they are noted below:

1. Informal organizations act as agencies of *social control*. They generate a culture based on certain norms of conduct which, in turn, demands conformity from group members. These standards may be at odds with the values

---

[22] Gardner and Moore, *op. cit.*, pp. 237–243.
[23] For example: Brech, *op. cit.*, pp. 27–29; and Allen, *op. cit.*, pp. 61–62.

[24] See: Leon Festinger, Stanley Schachter, and Kurt Back, *Social Pressures in Informal Groups* (New York: Harper and Brothers, 1950), pp. 153–163.
[25] For example see: W. Fred Cottrell, *The Railroader* (Palo Alto: The Stanford University Press, 1940), Chapter 3.
[26] Except in cases where the existence of an organization is necessary for the continued maintenance of employee interest. Under these conditions the previously informal association may emerge as a formal group, such as a union.

set by the formal organization. So an individual may very well find himself in a situation of conflicting demands.

2. The form of human interrelationships in the informal organization requires *techniques of analysis* different from those used to plot the relationships of people in a formal organization. The method used for determining the structure of the informal group is called sociometric analysis. Sociometry reveals the complex structure of interpersonal relations which is based on premises fundamentally unlike the logic of the formal organization.

3. Informal organizations have *status and communication* systems peculiar to themselves, not necessarily derived from the formal systems. For example, the grapevine is the subject of much neoclassical study.

4. Survival of the informal organization requires stable continuing relationships among the people in them. Thus, it has been observed that the informal organization *resists change.*[27] Considerable attention is given by the neoclassicists to overcoming informal resistance to change.

5. The last aspect of analysis which appears to be central to the neoclassical view of the informal organization is the study of the *informal leader.* Discussion revolves around who the informal leader is, how he assumes this role, what characteristics are peculiar to him, and how he can help the manager accomplish his objectives in the formal organization.[28]

This brief sketch of some of the major facets of informal organization theory has neglected, so far, one important topic treated by the neoclassical school. It is the way in which the formal and informal organizations interact.

A conventional way of looking at the interaction of the two is the "live and let live" point of view. Management should recognize that the informal organization exists, nothing can destroy it, and so the executive might just as well work with it. Working with the informal organization involves not threatening its existence unnecessarily, listening to opinions expressed for the group by the leader, allowing group participation in decision-making situations, and controlling the grapevine by prompt release of accurate information.[29]

While this approach is management centered, it is not unreasonable to expect that informal group standards and norms could make themselves felt on formal organizational policy. An honestly conceived effort by managers to establish a working relationship with the informal organization could result in an association where both formal and informal views would be reciprocally modified. The danger which at all costs should be avoided is that "working with the informal organization" does not degenerate into a shallow disguise for human manipulation.

Some neoclassical writing in organization theory, especially that coming from the management-oriented segment of this school, gives the impression that the formal and informal organizations are distinct, and at times, quite irreconcilable factors in a company. The formal organizations are distinct, and at times, interaction which takes place between the two is something akin to the interaction between the company and a labor union, or a government agency, or another company.

The concept of the social system is another approach to the interactional climate. While this concept can be properly classified as neoclassical, it borders on the modern theories of organization. The phrase "social system" means that an organization is a complex of mutually interdependent, but variable, factors.

These factors include individuals and their attitudes and motives, jobs, the physical work setting, the formal organization, and the informal organizations. These factors, and many others, are woven into an overall pattern of interdependency. From this point of view, the formal and informal organizations lose their distinctiveness, but find real meaning, in terms of human behavior, in the operation of the system as a whole. Thus, the study of organization turns away from descriptions of its component parts, and is refocused on the system of interrelationships among the parts.

One of the major contributions of the Hawthorne studies was the integration of Pareto's

[27] Probably the classic study of resistance to change is: Lester Coch and John R. P. French, Jr., "Overcoming Resistance to Change," in Schuyler Dean Hoslett (editor) *Human Factors in Management* (New York: Harper and Brothers, 1951) pp. 242–268.

[28] For example see: Robert Saltonstall, *Human Relations in Administration* (New York: McGraw-Hill Book Company, 1959), pp. 330–331; and Keith Davis, *op. cit.*, pp. 99–101.

[29] For an example of this approach see: John T. Doutt, "Management Must Manage the Informal Group, Too," *Advanced Management*, May, 1959, pp. 26–28.

idea of the social system into a meaningful method of analysis for the study of behavior in human organizations.[30] This concept is still vitally important. But unfortunately some work in the field of human relations undertaken by the neoclassicists has overlooked, or perhaps discounted, the significance of this consideration.[31]

The fundamental insight regarding the social system, developed and applied to the industrial scene by the Hawthorne researchers, did not find much extension in subsequent work in the neoclassical vein. Indeed, the neoclassical school after the Hawthorne studies generally seemed content to engage in descriptive generalizations, or particularized empirical research studies which did not have much meaning outside their own context.

The neoclassical school of organization theory has been called bankrupt. Criticisms range from "human relations is a tool for cynical puppeteering of people," to "human relations is nothing more than a trifling body of empirical and descriptive information." There is a good deal of truth in both criticisms, but another appraisal of the neoclassical school of organization theory is offered here. The neoclassical approach has provided valuable contributions to the lore of organization. But, like the classical theory, the neoclassical doctrine suffers from incompleteness, a shortsighted perspective, and lack of integration among the many facets of human behavior studied by it. Modern organization theory has made a move to cover the shortcomings of the current body of theoretical knowledge.

Modern Organization Theory

The distinctive qualities of modern organization theory are its conceptual-analytical base, its reliance on empirical research data and, above all, its integrating nature. These qualities are framed in a philosophy which accepts the premise that the only meaningful way to study organization is to study it as a system.

As Henderson put it, the study of a system must rely on a method of analysis, ". . . involving the simultaneous variations of mutually dependent variables."[32] Human systems, of course, contain a huge number of dependent variables which defy the most complex simultaneous equations to solve.

Nevertheless, system analysis has its own peculiar point of view which aims to study organization in the way Henderson suggests. It treats organization as a system of mutually dependent variables. As a result, modern organization theory, which accepts system analysis, shifts the conceptual level of organization study above the classical and neoclassical theories. Modern organization theory asks a range of interrelated questions which are not seriously considered by the two other theories.

Key among these questions are: (1) What are the strategic parts of the system? (2) What is the nature of their mutual dependency? (3) What are the main processes in the system which link the parts together, and facilitate their adjustment to each other? (4) What are the goals sought by systems? [33]

Modern organization theory is in no way a unified body of thought. Each writer and researcher has his special emphasis when he considers the system. Perhaps the most evident unifying thread in the study of systems is the effort to look at the organization in its totality. Representative books in this field are March and Simon, *Organizations*,[34] and Haire's anthology, *Modern Organization Theory*.[35]

Instead of attempting a review of different writers' contributions to modern organization theory, it will be more useful to discuss the various ingredients involved in system analysis. They are the parts, the interactions, the processes, and the goals of systems.

The Parts of the System and Their Interdependency. The first basic part of the system is the *individual*, and the personality structure he brings to the organization. Elementary

[30] See: Roethlisberger and Dickson, *op. cit.*, Chapter 24.

[31] A check of management human relations texts, the organization and human relations chapters of principles of management texts, and texts on conventional organization theory for management courses reveals little or no treatment of the concept of the social system.

[32] Lawrence J. Henderson, *Pareto's General Sociology* (Cambridge: Harvard University Press, 1935), p. 13.

[33] There is another question which cannot be treated in the scope of this paper. It asks, what research tools should be used for the study of the system?

[34] James G. March and Herbert A. Simon, *Organizations* (New York: John Wiley and Sons, 1958).

[35] Mason Haire (editor) *Modern Organization Theory* (New York: John Wiley and Sons, 1959).

to an individual's personality are motives and attitudes which condition the range of expectancies he hopes to satisfy by participating in the system.

The second part of the system is the formal arrangement of functions, usually called the *formal organization*. The formal organization is the interrelated pattern of jobs which make up the structure of a system. Certain writers, like Argyris, see a fundamental conflict resulting from the demands made by the system, and the structure of the mature, normal personality. In any event, the individual has expectancies regarding the job he is to perform; and, conversely, the job makes demands on, or has expectancies relating to, the performance of the individual. Considerable attention has been given by writers in modern organization theory to incongruencies resulting from the interaction of organizational and individual demands.[36]

The third part in the organization system is the *informal organization*. Enough has been said already about the nature of this organization. But it must be noted that an interactional pattern exists between the individual and the informal group. This interactional arrangement can be conveniently discussed as the mutual modification of expectancies. The informal organization has demands which it makes on members in terms of anticipated forms of behavior, and the individual has expectancies of satisfaction he hopes to derive from association with people on the job. Both these sets of expectancies interact, resulting in the individual modifying his behavior to accord with the demands of the group, and the group, perhaps, modifying what it expects from an individual because of the impact of his personality on group norms.[37]

Much of what has been said about the various expectancy systems in an organization can also be treated using status and role concepts. Part of modern organization theory rests on research findings in social-psychology relative to reciprocal patterns of behavior stemming from role demands generated by both the formal and informal organizations, and role perceptions peculiar to the individual. Bakke's *fusion process* is largely concerned with the modification of role expectancies. The fusion process is a force, according to Bakke, which acts to weld divergent elements together for the preservation of organizational integrity.[38]

The fifth part of system analysis is the *physical setting* in which the job is performed. Although this element of the system may be implicit in what has been said already about the formal organization and its functions, it is well to separate it. In the physical surroundings of work, interactions are present in complex man-machine systems. The human "engineer" cannot approach the problems posed by such interrelationships in a purely technical, engineering fashion. As Haire says, these problems lie in the domain of the social theorists.[39] Attention must be centered on responses demanded from a logically ordered production function, often with the view of minimizing the error in the system. From this standpoint, work cannot be effectively organized unless the psychological, social, and physiological characteristics of people participating in the work environment are considered. Machines and processes should be designed to fit certain generally observed psychological and physiological properties of men, rather than hiring men to fit machines.

In summary, the parts of the system which appear to be of strategic importance are the individual, the formal structure, the informal organization, status and role patterns, and the physical environment of work. Again, these parts are woven into a configuration called the organizational system. The processes which link the parts are taken up next.

The Linking Processes. One can say, with a good deal of glibness, that all the parts mentioned above are interrelated. Although this observation is quite correct, it does not mean too much in terms of system theory unless

---

[36] See Chris Argyris, *Personality and Organization* (New York: Harper and Brothers, 1957), esp. Chapters 2, 3, 7.

[37] For a larger treatment of this subject see: George C. Homans, *The Human Group* (New York: Harcourt, Brace and Company, 1950), Chapter 5.

[38] E. Wight Bakke, "Concept of the Social Organization," in *Modern Organization Theory*, Mason Haire (editor) (New York: John Wiley and Sons, 1959) pp. 60–61.

[39] Mason Haire, "Psychology and the Study of Business: Joint Behavioral Sciences," in *Social Science Research on Business: Product and Potential* (New York: Columbia University Press, 1959), pp. 53–59.

some attempt is made to analyze the processes by which the interaction is achieved. Role theory is devoted to certain types of interactional processes. In addition, modern organization theorists point to three other linking activities which appear to be universal to human systems of organized behavior. These processes are communication, balance, and decision making.

1. Communication is mentioned often in neoclassical theory, but the emphasis is on description of forms of communication activity, i.e., formal-informal, vertical-horizontal, line-staff. Communication, as a mechanism which links the segments of the system together, is overlooked by way of much considered analysis.

One aspect of modern organization theory is study of the communication network in the system. Communication is viewed as the method by which action is evoked from the parts of the system. Communication acts not only as stimuli resulting in action, but also as a control and coordination mechanism linking the decision centers in the system into a synchronized pattern. Deutsch points out that organizations are composed of parts which communicate with each other, receive messages from the outside world, and store information. Taken together, these communication functions of the parts comprise a configuration representing the total system.[40] More is to be said about communication later in the discussion of the cybernetic model.

2. The concept of *balance* as a linking process involves a series of some rather complex ideas. Balance refers to an equilibrating mechanism whereby the various parts of the system are maintained in a harmoniously structured relationship to each other.

The necessity for the balance concept logically flows from the nature of systems themselves. It is impossible to conceive of an ordered relationship among the parts of a system without also introducing the idea of a stabilizing or an adapting mechanism.

Balance appears in two varieties—quasi-automatic and innovative. Both forms of balance act to insure system integrity in face of changing conditions, either internal or external to the system. The first form of balance, quasi-automatic, refers to what some think are "homeostatic" properties of systems. That is, systems seem to exhibit built-in propensities to maintain steady states.

If human organizations are open, self-maintaining systems, then control and regulatory processes are necessary. The issue hinges on the degree to which stabilizing processes in systems, when adapting to change, are automatic. March and Simon have an interesting answer to this problem, which in part is based on the type of change and the adjustment necessary to adapt to the change. Systems have programs of action which are put into effect when a change is perceived. If the change is relatively minor, and if the change comes within the purview of established programs of action, then it might be fairly confidently predicted that the adaptation made by the system will be quasi-automatic.[41]

The role of innovative, creative balancing efforts now needs to be examined. The need for innovation arises when adaptation to a change is outside the scope of existing programs designed for the purpose of keeping the system in balance. New programs have to be evolved in order for the system to maintain internal harmony.

New programs are created by trial and error search for feasible action alternatives to cope with a given change. But innovation is subject to the limitations and possibilities inherent in the quantity and variety of information present in a system at a particular time. New combinations of alternatives for innovative purposes depend on:

(*a*) the possible range of output of the system, or the capacity of the system to supply information.

(*b*) the range of available information in the memory of the system.

(*c*) the operating rules (program) governing the analysis and flow of information within the system.

(*d*) the ability of the system to "forget" previously learned solutions to changed problems.[42] A system with too good a memory

---

[40] Karl W. Deutsch, "On Communication Models in the Social Sciences," *Public Opinion Quarterly*, 16 (1952), pp. 356–380.

[41] March and Simon, *op. cit.*, pp. 139–140.
[42] Mervyn L. Cadwallader, "The Cybernetic Analysis of Change in Complex Social Organization," *The American Journal of Sociology*, September, 1959, p. 156.

might narrow its behavioral choices to such an extent as to stifle innovation. In simpler language, old learned programs might be used to adapt to change, when newly innovated programs are necessary.[43]

Much of what has been said about communication and balance brings to mind a cybernetic model in which both these processes have vital roles. Cybernetics has to do with feedback and control in all kinds of systems. Its purpose is to maintain system stability in the face of change. Cybernetics cannot be studied without considering communication networks, information flow, and some kind of balancing process aimed at preserving the integrity of the system.

Cybernetics directs attention to key questions regarding the system. These questions are: How are communication centers connected, and how are they maintained? Corollary to this question: what is the structure of the feedback system? Next, what information is stored in the organization, and at what points? And as a corollary: how accessible is this information to decision-making centers? Third, how conscious is the organization of the operation of its own parts? That is, to what extent do the policy centers receive control information with sufficient frequency and relevancy to create a real awareness of the operation of the segments of the system? Finally, what are the learning (innovating) capabilities of the system?[44]

Answers to the questions posed by cybernetics are crucial to understanding both the balancing and communication processes in systems.[45] Although cybernetics has been applied largely to technical-engineering problems of automation, the model of feedback, control, and regulation in all systems has a good deal of generality. Cybernetics is a fruitful area which can be used to synthesize the processes of communication and balance.

3. A wide spectrum of topics dealing with types of decisions in human systems makes up

the core of analysis of another important process in organizations. Decision analysis is one of the major contributions of March and Simon in their book *Organizations*. The two major classes of decisions they discuss are decisions to produce and decisions to participate in the system.[46]

Decisions to produce are largely a result of an interaction between individual attitudes and the demands of organization. Motivation analysis becomes central to studying the nature and results of the interaction. Individual decisions to participate in the organization reflect on such issues as the relationship between organizational rewards versus the demands made by the organization. Participation decisions also focus attention on the reasons why individuals remain in or leave organizations.

March and Simon treat decisions as internal variables in an organization which depend on jobs, individual expectations and motivations, and organizational structure. Marschak[47] looks on the decision process as an independent variable upon which the survival of the organization is based. In this case, the organization is viewed as having, inherent to its structure, the ability to maximize survival requisites through its established decision processes.

The Goals of Organization. Organization has three goals which may be either intermeshed or independent ends in themselves. They are growth, stability, and interaction. The last goal refers to organizations which exist primarily to provide a medium for association of its members with others. Interestingly enough these goals seem to apply to different forms of organization at varying levels of complexity, ranging from simple clockwork mechanisms to social systems.

These similarities in organizational purposes have been observed by a number of people, and a field of thought and research called general system theory has developed, dedicated to the task of discovering organizationed universals. The dream of general system theory is to create a science of organizational universals, or if you will, a universal science using com-

---

[43] It is conceivable for innovative behavior to be programmed into the system.

[44] These are questions adapted from Deutsch, *op. cit.*, 368–370.

[45] Answers to these questions would require a comprehensive volume. One of the best approaches currently available is Stafford Beer, *Cybernetics and Management* (New York: John Wiley and Sons, 1959).

[46] March and Simon, *op. cit.*, Chapters 3 and 4.

[47] Jacob Marschak, "Efficient and Viable Organizational Forms" in *Modern Organization Theory*, Mason Haire (editor) (New York: John Wiley and Sons, 1959), pp. 307–320.

mon organizational elements found in all systems as a starting point.

Modern organization theory is on the periphery of general system theory. Both general system theory and modern organization theory study:

1. the parts (individuals) in aggregates, and the movement of individuals into and out of the system.

2. the interaction of individuals with the environment found in the system.

3. the interactions among individuals in the system.

4. general growth and stability problems of systems.[48]

Modern organization theory and general system theory are similar in that they look at organization as an integrated whole. They differ, however, in terms of their generality. General system theory is concerned with every level of system, whereas modern organizational theory focuses primarily on human organization.

The question might be asked, what can the science of administration gain by the study of system levels other than human? Before attempting an answer, note should be made of what these other levels are. Boulding presents a convenient method of classification:

1. The static structure—a level of framework, the anatomy of a system; for example, the structure of the universe.

2. The simple dynamic system—the level of clockworks, predetermined necessary motions.

3. The cybernetic system—the level of the thermostat, the system moves to maintain a given equilibrium through a process of self-regulation.

4. The open system—level of self-maintaining systems, moves toward and includes living organisms.

5. The genetic-societal system—level of cell society, characterized by a division of labor among cells.

6. Animal systems—level of mobility, evidence of goal-directed behavior.

7. Human systems—level of symbol interpretation and idea communication.

8. Social system—level of human organization.

9. Transcendental systems—level of ultimates and absolutes which exhibit systematic structure but are unknowable in essence.[49]

This approach to the study of systems by finding universals common at all levels of organization offers intriguing possibilities for administrative organization theory. A good deal of light could be thrown on social systems if structurally analogous elements could be found in the simpler types of systems. For example, cybernetic systems have characteristics which seem to be similar to feedback, regulation, and control phenomena in human organizations. Thus, certain facets of cybernetic models could be generalized to human organization. Considerable danger, however, lies in poorly founded analogies. Superficial similarities between simpler system forms and social systems are apparent everywhere. Instinctually based ant societies, for example, do not yield particularly instructive lessons for understanding rationally conceived human organizations. Thus, care should be taken that analogies used to bridge system levels are not mere devices for literary enrichment. For analogies to have usefulness and validity, they must exhibit inherent structural similarities or implicitly identical operational principles.[50]

Modern organization theory leads, as it has been shown, almost inevitably into a discussion of general system theory. A science of organization universals has some strong advocates, particularly among biologists.[51] Organization theorists in administrative science cannot afford to overlook the contributions of general system theory. Indeed, modern organization concepts could offer a great deal to those working with general system theory. But the ideas dealt

---

[48] Kenneth E. Boulding, "General System Theory —The Skeleton of a Science," *Management Science*, April, 1956, pp. 200–202.

[49] *Ibid.*, pp. 202–205.

[50] Seidenberg, *op. cit.*, p. 136. The fruitful use of the type of analogies spoken of by Seidenberg is evident in the application of thermodynamic principles, particularly the entropy concept, to communication theory. See: Claude E. Shannon and Warren Weaver, *The Mathematical Theory of Communication* (Urbana: The University of Illinois Press, 1959). Further, the existence of a complete analogy between the operational behavior of thermodynamic systems, electrical communication systems, and biological systems has been noted by: Y. S. Touloukian, *The Concept of Entropy in Communication, Living Organisms, and Thermodynamics*, Research Bulletin 130, Purdue Engineering Experiment Station.

[51] For example see: Ludwig von Bertalanffy, *Problem of Life* (London: Watts and Company, 1952).

with in the general theory are exceedingly elusive.

Speaking of the concept of equilibrium as a unifying element in all systems, Easton says, "It (equilibrium) leaves the impression that we have a useful general theory when in fact, lacking measurability, it is a mere pretence for knowledge." [52] The inability to quantify and measure universal organization elements undermines the success of pragmatic tests to which general system theory might be put.

Organization Theory: Quo Vadis? Most sciences have a vision of the universe to which they are applied, and administrative science is not an exception. This universe is composed of parts. One purpose of science is to synthesize the parts into an organized conception of its field of study. As a science matures, its theorems about the configuration of its universe change. The direction of change in three sciences, physics, economics, and sociology, are noted briefly for comparison with the development of an administrative view of human organization.

The first comprehensive and empirically verifiable outlook of the physical universe was presented by Newton in his *Principia*. Classical physics, founded on Newton's work, constitutes a grand scheme in which a wide range of physical phenomena could be organized and predicted. Newtonian physics may rightfully be regarded as "macro" in nature, because its system of organization was concerned largely with gross events of which the movement of celestial bodies, waves, energy forms, and strain are examples. For years classical physics was supreme, being applied continuously to smaller and smaller classes of phenomena in the physical universe. Physicists at one time adopted the view that everything in their realm could be discovered by simply subdividing problems. Physics thus moved into the "micro" order.

But in the nineteenth century a revolution took place motivated largely because events were being noted which could not be explained adequately by the conceptual framework supplied by the classical school. The consequences

of this revolution are brilliantly described by Eddington:

From the point of view of philosophy of science the conception associated with entropy must I think be ranked as the great contribution of the nineteenth century to scientific thought. It marked a reaction from the view that everything to which science need pay attention is discovered by microscopic dissection of objects. It provided an alternative standpoint in which the centre of interest is shifted from the entities reached by the customary analysis (atoms, electric potentials, etc.) to qualities possessed by the system as a whole, which cannot be split up and located—a little bit here, and a little bit there. . . .

We often think that when we have completed our study of *one* we know all about *two*, because "two" is "one and one." We forget that we have still to make a study of "and." Secondary physics is the study of "and"—that is to say, of organization.[53]

Although modern physics often deals in minute quantities and oscillations, the conception of the physicist is on the "macro" scale. He is concerned with the "and," or the organization of the world in which the events occur. These developments did not invalidate classical physics as to its usefulness for explaining a certain range of phenomena. But classical physics is no longer the undisputed law of the universe. It is a special case.

Early economic theory, and Adam Smith's *Wealth of Nations* comes to mind, examined economic problems in the macro order. The *Wealth of Nations* is mainly concerned with matters of national income and welfare. Later, the economics of the firm, micro-economics, dominated the theoretical scene in this science. And, finally, with Keynes' *The General Theory of Employment Interest and Money*, a systematic approach to the economic universe was re-introduced in the macro level.

The first era of the developing science of sociology was occupied by the great social "system builders." Comte, the so-called father of sociology, had a macro view of society in that his chief works are devoted to social reorganization. Comte was concerned with the inter-

[52] David Easton, "Limits of the Equilibrium Model in Social Research," in *Profits and Problems of Homeostatic Models in the Behavioral Sciences*, Publication 1, Chicago Behavioral Sciences, 1953, p. 39.

[53] Sir Arthur Eddington, *The Nature of the Physical World* (Ann Arbor: The University of Michigan Press, 1958), pp. 103–104.

relationships among social, political, religious, and educational institutions. As sociology progressed, the science of society compressed. Emphasis shifted from the macro approach of the pioneers to detailed, empirical study of small social units. The compression of sociological analysis was accompanied by study of social pathology or disorganization.

In general, physics, economics, and sociology appear to have two things in common. First, they offered a macro point of view as their initial systematic comprehension of their area of study. Second, as the science developed, attention fragmented into analysis of the parts of the organization, rather than attending to the system as a whole. This is the micro phase.

In physics and economics, discontent was evidenced by some scientists at the continual atomization of the universe. The reaction to the micro approach was a new theory or theories dealing with the total system, on the macro level again. This third phase of scientific development seems to be more evident in physics and economics than in sociology.

The reason for the "macro-micro-macro" order of scientific progress lies, perhaps, in the hypothesis that usually the things which strike man first are of great magnitude. The scientist attempts to discover order in the vastness. But after macro laws or models of systems are postulated, variations appear which demand analysis, not so much in terms of the entire system, but more in terms of the specific parts which make it up. Then, intense study of mircocosm may result in new general laws, replacing the old models of organization. Or, the old and the new models may stand together, each explaining a different class of phenomenon. Or, the old and the new concepts of organization may be welded to produce a single creative synthesis.

Now, what does all this have to do with the problem of organization in administrative science? Organization concepts seem to have gone through the same order of development in this field as in the three just mentioned. It is evident that the classical theory of organization, particularly as in the work of Mooney and Reiley, is concerned with principles common to all organizations. It is a macro-organizational view. The classical approach to organization, however, dealt with the gross anatomical parts and processes of the formal organization. Like classical physics, the classical theory of organization is a special case. Neither are es-

pecially well equipped to account for variation from their established framework.

Many variations in the classical administrative model result from human behavior. The only way these variations could be understood was by a microscopic examination of particularized, situational aspects of human behavior. The mission of the neoclassical school thus is "micro-analysis."

It was observed earlier, that somewhere along the line the concept of the social system, which is the key to understanding the Hawthorne studies, faded into the background. Maybe the idea is so obvious that it was lost to the view of researchers and writers in human relations. In any event, the press of research in the microcosmic universes of the informal organization, morale and productivity, leadership, participation, and the like forced the notion of the social system into limbo. Now, with the advent of modern organization theory, the social system has been resurrected.

Modern organization theory appears to be concerned with Eddington's "and." This school claims that its operational hypothesis is based on a macro point of view; that is, the study of organization as a whole. This nobility of purpose should not obscure, however, certain difficulties faced by this field as it is presently constituted. Modern organization theory raises two questions which should be explored further. First, would it not be more accurate to speak of modern organization theories? Second, just how much of modern organization theory is modern?

The first question can be answered with a quick affirmative. Aside from the notion of the system, there are few, if any, other ideas of a unifying nature. Except for several important exceptions,[54] modern organization theorists tend to pursue their pet points of view,[55] suggesting they are part of system theory, but not troubling to show by what mystical means they arrive at this conclusion.

The irony of it all is that a field dealing with systems has, indeed, little system. Modern organization theory needs a framework, and it needs an integration of issues into a common conception of organization. Admittedly, this

---

[54] For example: E. Wight Bakke, *op. cit.*, pp. 18–75.
[55] There is a large selection including decision theory, individual-organization interaction, motivation, vitality, stability, growth, and graph theory, to mention a few.

is a large order. But it is curious not to find serious analytical treatment of subjects like cybernetics or general system theory in Haire's *Modern Organizational Theory* which claims to be a representative example of work in this field. Beer has ample evidence in his book *Cybernetics and Management* that cybernetics, if imaginatively approached, provides a valuable conceptual base for the study of systems.

The second question suggests an ambiguous answer. Modern organization theory is in part a product of the past; system analysis is not a new idea. Further, modern organization theory relies for supporting data on microcosmic research studies, generally drawn from the journals of the last ten years. The newness of modern organization theory, perhaps, is its effort to synthesize recent research contributions of many fields into a system theory characterized by a reoriented conception of organization.

One might ask, but what is the modern theorist reorienting? A clue is found in the almost snobbish disdain assumed by some authors of the neo-classical human relations school, and particularly, the classical school. Re-evaluation of the classical school of organization is overdue. However, this does not mean that its contributions to organization theory are irrelevant and should be overlooked in the rush to get on the "behavioral science bandwagon."

Haire announces that the papers appearing in *Modern Organization Theory* constitute, "the ragged leading edge of a wave of theoretical development." [56] Ragged, yes; but leading no! The papers appearing in this book do not represent a theoretical breakthrough in the concept of organization. Haire's collection is an interesting potpourri with several contributions of considerable significance. But readers should beware that they will not find vastly new insights into organizational behavior in this book, if they have kept up with the literature of the social sciences, and have dabbled to some extent in the esoterica of biological theories of growth, information theory, and mathematical model building. For those who have not maintained the pace, *Modern*

Organization Theory serves the admirable purpose of bringing them up-to-date on a rather diversified number of subjects.

Some work in modern organization theory is pioneering, making its appraisal difficult and future uncertain. While the direction of this endeavor is unclear, one thing is patently true. Human behavior in organizations, and indeed, organization itself, cannot be adequately understood within the ground rules of classical and neo-classical doctrines. Appreciation of human organization requires a *creative* synthesis of massive amounts of empirical data, a high order of deductive reasoning, imaginative research studies, and a taste for individual and social values. Accomplishment of all these objectives, and the inclusion of them into a framework of the concept of the system, appears to be the goal of modern organization theory. The vitality of administrative science rests on the advances modern theorists make along this line.

Modern organization theory, 1960 style, is an amorphous aggregation of synthesizers and restaters, with a few extending leadership on the frontier. For the sake of these few, it is well to admonish that pouring old wine into new bottles may make the spirits cloudy. Unfortunately, modern organization theory has almost succeeded in achieving the status of a fad. Popularization and exploitation contributed to the disrepute into which human relations has fallen. It would be a great waste if modern organization theory yields to the same fate, particularly since both modern organization theory and human relations draw from the same promising source of inspiration—system analysis.

Modern organization theory needs tools of analysis and a conceptual framework uniquely its own, but it must also allow for the incorporation of relevant contributions of many fields. It may be that the framework will come from general system theory. New areas of research such as decision theory, information theory, and cybernetics also offer reasonable expectations of analytical and conceptual tools. Modern organization theory represents a frontier of research which has great significance for management. The potential is great, because it offers the opportunity for uniting what is valuable in classical theory with the social and natural sciences into a systematic and integrated conception of human organization.

[56] Mason Haire, "General Issues," in Mason Haire (editor), *Modern Organization Theory* (New York: John Wiley and Sons, 1959), p. 2.

P A R T   O N E

The Formal

Organization

P A R T   O N E

IF YOU WERE to drive past a factory owned by a large automobile manufacturer and note that the plant made electrical components which were used in the firm's automobiles, you would be observing a tangible manifestation of an organization plan. One part of this plan had determined that part of the work of manufacturing automobiles was to be handled by dividing up the overall task in such a way that people worked on items of a similar nature, in this case electrical components. Another vital part of the plan was concerned with coordinating the work in the various plants and of the people in the plants to make sure that the final result, in this case the automobile, was produced as efficiently as possible. The magnitude of this task can perhaps be appreciated by noting that a number of automobile manufacturers have several hundred thousand employees, and by noting further that any one of the cars made by these companies probably had several thousand employees quite directly involved in its manufacture. To make the task still more difficult these employees were in a number of plants located over a fairly large geographical area. The fact that the efforts of these numerous people resulted pretty efficiently in an automobile rather than in utter chaos and frustration is indeed very remarkable.

A premise on which a formal organization rests is that the sum total of the efforts of people when organized will be greater than the sum of their individual efforts when unorganized. To put it more simply, if each of the several hundred thousand employees working for one of the typical automobile manufacturers was to be put to work on a separate automobile, the likelihood is that very few automobiles would ever be completed and that these few would take a very long time to produce. The same people properly organized can produce hundreds of thousands of automobiles each year. In this section on formal organization we are concerned with the plans used to organize the efforts of people.

Organization Goals

A fundamental characteristic of organizations noted earlier is that they are purposeful entities. Therefore the goals or objectives toward which organizations are directed are of great interest in a very particular way.

28

Organizations Are Shaped by Their Goals.
As mentioned earlier, we are not concerned
with the examination of the particular goals or
objectives which an organization *should* have.
Hence, we are not concerned with whether or
not a company should have an objective of obtaining a certain percentage return on its investment, or that it should have objectives
which are concerned with both the private
advantage of the owners and service to the
community. These are policy decisions made
before planning the organization, or, if you
will, before the formal organization is created.
The relation between goals and an organization is analogous to that between the purpose
of a building and its design; for example, the
architect is told to design a structure that will
serve as a warehouse. His client tells him what
purpose the building is to serve to support his
objectives. The purpose of the building will be
of great importance in determining its size,
appearance, cost, etc. The adequacy of the
building will largely be determined by how
well it serves the purpose for which it was intended. Similarly, with an organization, its
goals or purpose determine many of its characteristics and also serve as a measure of how
adequate the organization is. The initial question before the person establishing a formal
organization is, what type of organization will
satisfy or accomplish the goals or objectives?

An organization, just as a building, is not
created in a vacuum. Along with a set of goals,
the planner of an organization draws on (1)
a set of resources, such as capital and technical
knowledge he can use, and (2) conditions, that
is, a type of competition, an economy, which
the organization must face. All influence the
organization. A second question must therefore be asked; what type of organization can
accomplish the goals we have with the resources available and under the conditions
facing us?

An analysis of these factors in connection
with his knowledge of organizations may well
lead the planner to conclude that a satisfactory
organization is not possible or at least not possible without accepting additional, and perhaps previously unanticipated, "costs," which
may well result in the goals being redefined. In
this way, organizations have an influence on
goals and objectives, by delimiting the possible goals and conditions under which they
are obtainable.

An organization has more than a delimiting
influence on its goals however, in that goal
formation or perhaps more accurately re-
formation can be considered a continuing process of an organization. In this part however,
goals will be considered as "givens." In part
four attention will be given both to the effects
of changes in goals on the organization and,
briefly, some ways in which organizational
goals are changed.

*Coordination of Work on Organization
Goals.* Probably the most commonly cited
characteristic of organizations is that they promote coordination of effort among people.
Definitions of organizational coordination usually identify the factors thought to promote
the unity of action that will accomplish a common purpose or objective (Mooney). How to
bring about such coordination is probably the
most important single issue in the study of organizations. Certainly one important element is
cooperation among organization members. In
turn, necessary cooperation rests on members
of an organization perceiving their actions as
contributing to an organizational goal (Barnard). Hence, although people in an organization may have different private objectives,
there must be a synthesis or a selection of an
encompassing objective to produce an organizational goal to which organization members
can see their actions contributing.

A very simple illustration is a situation where
three men all want to cross a bay for quite
different personal reasons. One may want to see
his girl friend, another to get medical treatment, the third to pay his taxes. To cross the
bay they have to row a boat. Unfortunately
both the distance and weather make it impossible for a person to row himself across. At
least two men will be needed at the oars and
a third to bail. They decide to join forces and
go together, thereby forming an organization.
The organizational objective is to get the boat
across the bay. This is different from, although
closely related to, their individual objectives.
What makes this organization work is that
they see their individual actions contributing
to the organizational goal of getting across
the bay so that they may accomplish their private objectives. Conversely, the more difficult
it is for organizational members to perceive
this relation the more difficult coordination becomes.

Basic Concepts and Problems of Organizations

Thus far we have recognized that formal organizations are characterized by purposefulness and conscious planning. Before going much further it may be useful to consider a definition. For our purposes a formal organization shall be defined as a conscious plan or system of tasks and relations between tasks to coordinate the efforts of people in accomplishing goals effectively and efficiently. Like many technical definitions this one means the most to those who are familiar with the topic and the terms used. Let us consider some of the elements of this definition.

This definition includes two conditions under which an organization may accomplish something. The first is that it accomplishes its goal or objective effectively, or to put it more simply that it gets done what it sets out to do, and that the thing it set out to do could not be accomplished by any other social unit. For example, no individual, small group, or family working by itself could build a Grand Coulee Dam. If an organization gets such a task done it has justified its existence.

As soon as we consider the things that individuals or small groups as well as formal or large organization can accomplish we have to change our basis for evaluating the usefulness of organizations. The second condition is contained in the question: Can the goals or objectives be accomplished more efficiently by an organization? Many things of great importance can be well achieved through a large-scale organization, as so many things in our economic lives bear evidence.

It is not only in our economic lives but frequently in our political lives that large-scale organizations are held to be most efficient (Weber). Weber holds that for many of the administrative tasks of government a bureaucracy is the most efficient of all possible organizational forms. We consider other aspects of this opinion later, but it may be well to pause briefly to consider a few items of definition which may make reading items in this section easier. Weber uses the term "bureaucracy" in the same general way as "organization" was used in the beginning of this volume. By "bureaucracy" Weber means the most extreme form of formal organization wherein every task element is completely and exactly defined by a written set of rules and procedures. Hence, in our terms Weber is saying that a formal organization, and a particularly rigidly defined formal organization at that, is the most efficient of all organizational forms for carrying out administrative tasks. This as we see later is an opinion that does not go entirely unchallenged, but it is a point of considerable importance when studying formal organizations. For it is usually held that in accomplishing tasks or rendering services, large, formal organizations represent a more efficient way of conducting these affairs than the individual or the small group.

Division of Labor. We have in part answered the question of what a formal organization does but we have not really considered what it is. That is, what is this conscious plan or system which coordinates efforts of people?

Probably the single most important aspect of organization is that it provides for a division of labor. By this we mean that in order to accomplish an operating objective a certain amount of work has to be accomplished and rather than have one person do it all himself we divide up the work and allocate it to different individuals or perhaps groups. Carried to its logical conclusion, this gives everyone his own unique job in which he can specialize. As each person does his unique task, the products of his efforts fit together with those of others in the organization to complete the overall objective or goal of the organization. A division of labor which gives each person a small portion of the overall task has many advantages for the organization (Babbage, Weber).

The central concept and advantages of division of labor are rather readily recognized. What may not be so obvious are the many different ways in which work can be divided. One of the real difficulties in applying division of labor is not deciding the question of whether or not it should be used but deciding what form this division should take. One of the things that make this decision difficult is that there are two major forms of division of labor, each of which has many subforms.

The first of the major forms might be classified as a horizontal division of labor, which involves breaking up the task to be handled. An illustration of this might be to look at the job of getting a leaky lifeboat to shore. Some people in the lifeboat may be given the job of bailing out the boat, others may be given the task of rowing, and still others may be given the job of look-out to search for land or any rescue ship which may appear on the horizon. The objective is clear—to use the boat to reach safety—a number of tasks are involved in accomplishing this, and they have been divided among the occupants of the boat.

The other main form of the division of labor may be called a vertical division. We recognize that in almost any group where work is divided there is a central figure, who may be called the foreman, the squad leader, the supervisor, or any one of a number of titles, who is responsible for seeing that a group of people receive task assignments and perform them in the proper fashion. This person has a unique or special job also but it is of a different order from those of bailing the boat or pulling at the oars. His is one of supervision, coordination, direction, and motivation.

In a factory we might have a sheet metal department which makes certain types of metal enclosure, a painting department which paints them, and a shipping department which directs them to the customers. Each of these departments is a work unit, with its own subset of goals and its foreman. In order, however, to tie together the various departments or work units, it is necessary to have higher levels of management to whom the foremen report. These higher levels of management do related, but at the same time quite different work from those at the first, or foreman level, who in turn do work different from those who actually work directly on the company products. There is, in short, a vertical division of the managerial activities of an organization. We will explore this division of labor more fully later. For now let us say it represents the executive hierarchy (Barnard).

Coordination: Control and Communication. In examining the necessity for a vertical division of labor we run into some of the basic limitations or difficulties connected with the horizontal or task division of labor. What this division of labor does is to specify the activities that must be performed and also who will do them. At first glance it might seem enough to know that Pete will bail the boat and John will pull on the right oar and Tom on the left oar,

but is it? Even the simplest boating experience will dramatize the fact that there is more to rowing a boat than just pulling on oars. They must be pulled in unison. In short, there is a need for coordination. In a boat with reasonably skilled rowers, who see where their individual efforts contribute to the organization objective, people may be able, through their willingness to cooperate, to provide the necessary coordination themselves. As noted earlier, however, if these conditions are not met, the coordination may have to come from another source. As organizations grow larger, or as jobs become more specialized, it becomes more difficult for people to see where their efforts contribute the overall objectives, and provided. additional means for coordination must be

Division of labor, then, has many great advantages but it has its cost. It requires the provision of some means of coordinating the different jobs which result from the division of labor. It is important to recognize early that the greater the degree to which this division of labor is carried, and, therefore, the more unique each job becomes, the greater becomes this need of providing some means for coordination. A foreman supervising a group of men digging a ditch, where each of them does the same job with a shovel, has a relatively simple job of coordination and can therefore supervise a fairly large number of men. On the other hand, a foreman supervising people who each have a quite different job that is interrelated with the others in the department has a much more difficult task of coordination and can supervise only a smaller number of people. By the same token the executive who has reporting to him a number of work units all of which are doing the same task and are not very highly interrelated will be able to handle a considerable number of work units each with their own local supervisor. Such is the case, for example, for the regional manager of a shoe store chain in that each of the stores reporting to him handles the same line of products and does the same thing, namely, sell shoes. On the other hand, a manager who has a number of work units that are quite different and are also highly interrelated reporting to him can have far fewer reporting to him.

General Characteristics of Formal Organizations. One thing which implicitly or, many times, explicitly underlies formal-organization thinking is the assumption of a central source of authority within the organization which has some legitimate basis for existence. In government we recognize as a legitimate base the will of the people which, in democratic processes, can elect a president who then becomes the central source of executive authority in a federal government. In a business firm we recognize a legitimate base or source of authority to be the owners or stockholders who appoint through the Board of Directors a president who is the central authority of the firm. This central authority, be it a person or a board, has the prerogative, in fact the necessity, of delegating portions of this authority to subordinates who will carry out their subdivided tasks within the organization. This then extends from the very top of the organization, through various levels, down to the first line supervisor and in fact even to the worker. Each level has a smaller and more narrowly defined sector of authority. We can, therefore, rank positions in an organization on the basis of the authority they possess. This is called a scaler division (Urwick). A legitimate base of authority within an organization, centralized in the hands of a position at the top of the organization, is an essential component for the classical school of organization. It is also a matter that has not gone unchallenged from the behavioral point of view.

Up to now the formal organization has been viewed as the effective or perhaps the most efficient way of accomplishing a goal. A formal organization, however, has another advantage which has not yet been noted. That is, in institutionalizing organizational tasks in positions with specified duties and responsibilities, the organization becomes less dependent on any one individual. This is true whether the institutionalization be at the worker or the managerial level.

Let us put it this way. If someone in a group performs a special job which is very important, a job which he has developed himself through his own interest and which involves skill known only to himself, then the group or organization he is in is highly dependent upon him. When this individual dies or leaves, the service he has been rendering is permanently removed.

If what a person contributes to an organization or group is not completely prescribed by his personal skill, but is to a degree specified as a set of tasks which he is to fill in the form of a job description, rules or procedures, the group or organization becomes less dependent on him as an individual. When the occupant of the position leaves another can be placed in it and trained to do a known set of activities.

Much of what we have considered developed from the examination of a division of labor. It should be obvious that the same can be said for the means of promoting coordination. Hence, in a formal organization where we are consciously planning the efforts of people, we are specifying aspects of positions in the ways in which an organization shall operate, that is, the way tasks will be performed and the way they will be coordinated so that the organization at all levels becomes less dependent on its individual members. A formal organization then represents an impersonal means of coordinating the efforts of people (Barnard). It is this impersonality which raises some serious difficulties in actual organizations.

The Anatomy of Formal Organization

As we consider some of the basic characteristics of formal organizations, it may be well to see what meaning they have for the shape, form, or as we call it here, anatomy of formal organizations. Perhaps the simplest way to begin is to use a symbolic representation of an organization. Probably the most typical portrayal of a formal organization is a chart like that shown in Fig. 3.

Before examining this particular chart in detail, it may be well to say a few words about organization charts in general. First, such a chart represents an attempt to depict some elements of the formal organization. Let us note two things. It is about the formal and not the total organization. Second, it shows only a limited number of things about the formal organization. It is a schematic presentation that identifies positions, their groupings, and their reporting relations. Although it may show which position has authority over another, such as position *a* having authority over position *b* (Fig. 3), it does not tell us very much else about the authority relations which impinge on *b*. For example, it gives us no indica-

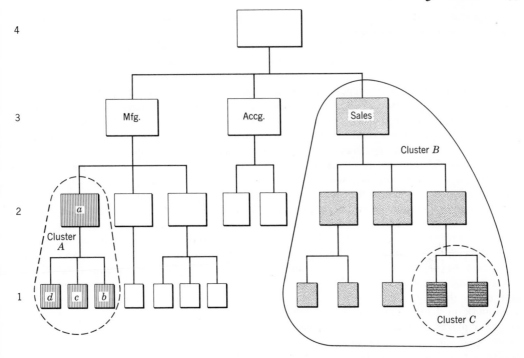

Fig. 3

tion at all of the extent of the authority which position a has over b. Is a, for example, able to fire the occupant of position b, or does his authority only extend to making recommendations for wage increases? The chart does not tell us. Second, it does not show us any of the authority which another position, such as that of a quality control inspector, has over position b. In short, although these schematic representations of the formal organization can be exceedingly useful, we should at the same time always be cognizant of the fact that they contain only limited amounts of information.

Looking at Fig. 3, then, we note a series of rectangles, each representing a position in which the occupant is expected to perform certain tasks or activities. If the organization represented a company making and selling washing machines, we would expect those people at level 1 to be directly involved with the product, making or selling it. The positions above them we recognize as supervisory or managerial positions which are in some way involved in executing the managerial function which makes it possible for those at level 1 to carry out their assignments effectively. We have already noted that as we go from level 1

to 4 the authority in each position increases and the position at the top of the organization is the seat of central authority which ties all the company activities together.

From what has been said up to now, we could obtain the impression that in going from a position on, say, level 2 to one on level 3, we would meet essentially the same type of situation, only with more authority and responsibility attached. This is not entirely the case. As we go from one level to another, not only does the responsibility and authority increase but the nature of the job changes in a very significant way. Those at level 2 are primarily concerned with supervising the day-to-day activities of people in a rather tangible concrete world. As we go higher in the organization the time horizon within which a person works extends further and further into the future and the issues dealt with become far less concrete.

This has been described in a number of ways. One useful distinction is to say that at the top of the organization the occupants of positions are primarily concerned with establishing organizational policy which will guide the overall organization, whereas those at the lower levels are involved with carrying out these top-level decisions. This makes a very distinctive difference in the nature of the work performed at various levels (Holden, Fish, and Smith).

One thing such a chart suggests is that at the top of the organization there is one position which serves as the central or chief executive responsible for the overall affairs of the organization. Although the affairs of the organization do fall into the province of a central authority, there is no reason why this must be invested in one person, and in fact in many cases it consists of a number of people and positions arranged in different ways (Holden, Fish, and Smith).

Another thing we note about Fig. 3 is that positions in the organization have been grouped, as for example happened with cluster *A*. Let us presume that in cluster *A* positions *b*, *c*, and *d* all work on the washing machines which the company makes. It could well be that they are all involved with performing similar operations involved in making parts to be later assembled into washers. If so, we recognize these positions as being grouped because they work on a common process. On the other hand, we might find that position *b* is involved with assembling several parts of the washer into a jig, position *c* is involved with spot welding them, and position *d* is involved with spray painting the items just welded. If this is the case, we find them grouped according to the product on which they work. In short, within an organization positions can be grouped in a number of ways (Dale).

This brings us to the second point that should be noted about the grouping of positions, namely, that within any organization there are very likely to be several different types of groupings used. At one level, as in cluster *B*, it might be by business function, such as selling, and at another level, such as cluster *C*, it might be by geographical area. The question is, what combinations of different types of departments should an organization have? A considerable number of alternatives are open. The real answer lies in determining what purpose the groupings must serve in the organization.

We have covered most of the items shown in Fig. 3. One last grouping remains—the accounting department shown reporting to the top executive. One thing we note about this department is that it is not as directly involved with the purpose of the organization as are the other two principal clusters we have discussed—manufacturing and sales. Because of the more indirect nature of its activities, we recognize this as what is typically called a staff department (Allen). Few areas of organization are under as much constant scrutiny and questioning as is the area of staff. In actual organizations we frequently hear of conflicts between line and staff positions, some of which are examined in later portions of this book. The theory about staff is frequently found at variance with practice, creating demands that it be both re-examined and reconstituted. This is being done, and in the future we shall doubtless have more extended and more adequate theories of staff. For the moment the selection chosen presents a sound statement of current, classical organization theory about staff.

Organizational Style

Up to now we have been considering both the elements and the anatomy of organizations. We are in the position of an architectural student who has learned on one hand that he has to put up with forces of gravity, tension, and stress in beams, the wracking of walls, and the pressure of wind as a set of building elements, and on the other has learned that buildings consist of foundations, walls, roofs, floors, windows, and doors. Once he is aware of these things he is ready to start using these components to design buildings. The components can go together in a wide variety of ways. When designing a house we can make it a Georgian style or a modern contemporary style and still have a house, and so it is with the elements in an organization. They can be combined in a variety of ways which might be called styles.

In the field of organization perhaps the most important differences in style are those which range along a continuum between decentralized and centralized organizations. Although these style differences have many characteristics, probably the most important are those relevant to decision making. In brief, when positions at the lower levels of the organization have a fairly broad array of decision-making authorities, we have a decentralized organization, and when positions at the lower level of the organization are primarily concerned with executing decisions which for the most part are made toward the top of the organization, we have a centralized organization.

Although centering attention on decision making narrows our scope of discussion considerably, it still leaves us with a rather enormous area, because decision making is an exceedingly complex topic. Let us consider some of the differences which can occur in the nature of decision making. We have, for example, the issue of the scope of the decision. Does a person make a decision as to what will be done, how it will be done, and when it will be done; or is he told what will be done and when it will be done, and left with the decision of how? Quite obviously the latter situation has far fewer decision-making prerogatives than the former. Another issue in describing the nature of decision making is the degree of autonomy given the executive. If an executive is given a broad area within which to work and is authorized to make many types of decision, being held accountable for profit and loss results at the end of the year, he has far more autonomy in decision making than another executive who makes decisions about what, when, and how but must obtain clearance for each decision from higher authorities and be accountable for each along the way. Having paid our respects to the complexity of decision making, let us nonetheless draw back and recognize that a given position can have a greater or lesser degree of decision-making prerogatives, because this is the concept we use to discuss decentralization.

The choice of which style to adopt is not an easy one. In truth no organization is ever completely centralized or completely decentralized. Further, most organizations are continually shifting between the two organizational styles. In this book we have chosen two rather detailed examinations of organization style. Drucker discusses in detail how the General Motors Corporation scheme of decentralization operates. In Part IV, Organizational Adaptation, Lawrence takes us through an examination of a firm which at one time was highly centralized and then in response to external conditions planned a change to a more decentralized style of organization. Other ramifications of these style differences are considered in other portions of the book.

Building Organizations

Our overall picture of the formal organization has been pretty well fleshed out. We have identified hierarchies and a number of different ways of setting up divisions and departments and have concerned ourselves with the crucial issue of decision making and related matters. This, however, has been a static view and has largely considered organization as a drafting problem. Once the plans for a house are drawn they are turned over to a contractor to be built. It is now time to consider how to build an operating organization from the static plans considered thus far.

The classical concept of organization views an organization as having a central source of authority and responsibility. At the creation of an organization, then, authority and responsibility may be conceived of as being totally contained in the hands of one person. As he acquires subordinates who will occupy the positions beneath him to carry out their portion of the organization work, he is faced with the task of distributing part of the central authority and responsibility to subordinates. This process is called delegation.

It is usually recognized that although responsibilities can be delegated they can by no means be transferred. By this we mean that when the superior gives some authority and responsibility to a subordinate, he does not relieve himself of the responsibility for the subordinate's performance. Therefore, to the extent that a subordinate fails to live up to his responsibility, the superior proportionately fails to live up to his responsibility. With this realization in mind, superiors are at times reluctant, quite naturally, to delegate to a subordinate, preferring to retain authority and responsibility for themselves using subordinates to execute their instructions. To achieve workable delegation requires more than a statement of its logical necessity; it also calls for an understanding of conditions on which it must rest and the consequences that can result from its ineffective execution (Newman).

The way in which delegation is carried out depends on many factors. Its relation to decentralization is obvious. The more decentralization there is to be the more delegation there must of necessity be. Both reflect some basic assumptions and concepts of the relation between the superior and the subordinate and of the subordinate's role in the organization. In short, both are related to the basic style of leadership which is incorporated into the organization. Consciously or unconsciously a leadership style is adopted in any real organization, and it has a great influence on the way the organization operates. Among the things already discussed that are influenced by the style of leadership is the distribution of decision-making authority (Tannenbaum and Schmidt). The style of leadership is not the only factor which determines how decision making will be distributed, but it is a very important factor.

One of the basic purposes, if not the most important purpose, of organization is to promote coordination. This promotion is an exceptionally complex task; however, it has a central and important place in all approaches to organizations. As noted earlier, some of the steps taken, for example, the dividing of work into departments, divisions, and jobs to promote effective and efficient utilization of effort, at the same time makes coordination a more difficult problem. Jobs, positions, and duties can, however, be grouped in a variety of ways —some of which can aid greatly in promoting coordination. In building an organization, then, one important matter to consider is how to arrange tasks or duties in departments in order to promote coordination (Gulick).

Among the key factors which influence how well an organization functions is the closeness with which the behavior of people within the organization fits the requirements of the organization. As noted in the introduction, one of the difficulties encountered in understanding organizations from a classical point of view is that the behavior of people within real organizations is frequently quite different from that which is called for or predicted. Part of this is because the classical organization concepts are primarily concerned with arrangements of tasks and duties, not with matters of behavior. This is not to suggest that classical organization writers have been oblivious to matters of behavior. Quite to the contrary, they have frequently, as is noted in many of the items already covered, spent no little thought on the real or expected behavior of people in organizations, and their recommendations are based on certain assumptions about human behavior. This matter is explored more fully in a

moment, but first let us turn to one of the common views held by writers of this school.

Writers of the classical organization school have frequently discussed the behavior of organizational members in terms of being either loyal or disloyal. If a person is loyal to an organization or its goals, he willingly does what is expected of him and does not do things which are detrimental to the organization. We are all familiar with issues of loyalty to our nation or loyalty to an army while in military service. It is not surprising to find these ideas being carried over into our thinking about other organizations, such as business firms or service institutions like hospitals. Such a way of looking at behavior is comparatively neat and clean and offers relatively few difficulties for the organization planner and the executive who runs the organization. The basic task is to obtain people who are loyal to an organization or to make them that way and then all behavioral problems evaporate. Some writers assume that if a person joins an organization, he has a moral necessity to support it loyally. Others have adopted a slightly more sophisticated attitude and have recognized that it may be necessary to train or educate people in some way so they will become loyal to the organization. They recognize that people are frequently the most loyal to an organization when they accept the purpose or objective towards which the organization is working. Therefore, establishing a doctrine and inculcating the members of the organization with it becomes a matter of prime importance (Mooney). In short, to promote loyalty and therefore supportive behavior for an organization, it is essential to indoctrinate organizational members with the validity, importance, and desirability of the organization goal. Certainly in our military and governmental institutions such an approach is very commonly followed. We are continually exposed to the idea that the values of freedom, individual worth, and democracy which our government stands for are of primary importance, and therefore we should support our nation at all costs to obtain these goals. This is a powerful approach for obtaining desirable behavior. It is not, however, the only approach, nor may it be the best approach for all organizations.

Some Concluding Points

Having covered the basic elements in this section, it would be worthwhile to look at them as a whole in order to establish some points which will be of great importance later. Perhaps a good place to begin is the assumptions about behavior held by the writers of the classical organization school, who developed so much of our formal-organization theory.

Assumptions of the Classical Organization School. We have recognized that basically a formal organization is an impersonal concept dealing with a definition of duties or positions and the arrangements between these positions both to form superior-subordinate relationships and to combine them into collectivities of departments and divisions. Although the system is not necessarily a behavioral one, it must make assumptions about the behavior of people. We may summarize some common implicit assumptions as follows:

1. When joining an organization people accept the organization and its purposes to the extent of behaving in a way that advances the organizational goal.

2. In order for this objective to be realized people must be educated and indoctrinated in the goal or philosophy or, if you will, the doctrine of an organization.

3. If there is any deviate behavior it must be controlled by some force external to the deviant individual, usually from a hierarchically superior position. This usually involves the superior imposing some penalties or punishments for deviation from desired behavior.

4. In considering people and their behavior it is only necessary to think of them as individuals.

Much of the rest of the book is concerned with aspects of organization where these assumptions are either inadequate or incorrect. Let it be understood clearly that in making this statement there is no intent to condemn classical-organization concepts. We are, however, trying to clearly point out some of their limitations in order that: (1) the ideas can more reliably and profitably be used within their area of legitimacy, (2) knowledge from the behavioral side of the organization can be properly and adequately brought to bear on classical-organization theories.

Summary

The basic elements we have been dealing with and refer to in later sections are summarized in Fig. 4. We begin by recognizing that an organization is set up to accomplish some purpose and that this purpose is not only its reason for existence but also has a pro-

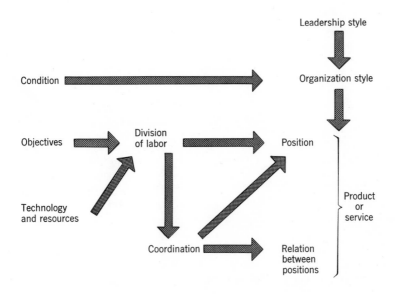

Fig. 4. Relationship of factors influencing and comprising the formal organization.

found influence on the internal arrangement of the organization. In order to accomplish the objective it is necessary to promote a division of labor. This division of labor, however, and the rest of the organization, is influenced not only by the objectives but also by the technology and resources available to the organization and by the social, economic, and political condition which the organization faces.

Once a division of labor begins, the immediate necessity arises of promoting coordination between the parts which are now developing. This necessity is satisfied in part by (1) a hierarchy exercising an executive function, (2) systems and procedures, and (3) arrangements of organizational units. The result is first, a set of positions which are defined by a set of tasks or duties; and second, an arrangement or set of relations between these positions, such as departments and a hierarchy of superior-subordinate relationships.

The content of the job and for that matter the relation between them is influenced not only by the tasks thought necessary to complete the objective but also by other matters, such as organizational style, which may give or deduct duties or authorities from a position on the basis of other factors. Many things may influence organizational style. Two have been noted: one, the more underlying thing which we have called leadership style, which in turn rests on, two, certain assumptions about people and their behavior.

Other factors that influence organization style are the conditions which face the organization. A threatening condition may encourage one style whereas a benign environment may permit a totally different style.

The Coordinative Principle

JAMES MOONEY

Organization begins when people combine their efforts for a given purpose. We have shown this by the simple illustration of two people uniting their efforts to lift and move some weighty object. This combination, however, is not the first principle of organization. It is only an illustration of organization itself.

To find the first principle, let us carry the illustration a step further. The efforts of these two lifters must be coordinated, which means that they must act together. If first one lifted, and then the other, there would be no unity of action, and hence no true organization of effort. Coordination first appeared in organization when one of those hairy, slow-witted ancestors of ours assumed authority and gave the guttural equivalent of "Heave ho!" *Here, then, we find the first principle of organization.*

Coordination therefore, is the orderly arrangement of group effort, to provide unity of action in the pursuit of a common purpose.

When we call *coordination* the first principle, we mean that this term expresses the principles of organization *in toto*; nothing less. This does not mean that there are no subordinated principles; it simply means that all the others are contained in this one of coordination. The others are simply the principles through which coordination operates and thus becomes effective.

As coordination contains all the principles of organization, it likewise expresses all the purposes of organization, in so far as these

From *Principles of Organization*, New York: Harper and Brothers, 1947, pp. 5–8. Reprinted with permission of the publisher.

purposes relate to its internal structure. To avoid confusion we must keep in mind that there are always two objectives of organization, the *internal* and the *external*. The latter may be anything, according to the purpose or interest that calls the group together, but the internal objective is coordinative always.

AUTHORITY. In some spheres of organization the external objective is not continuous. This is true of army organizations in peace-time, when all external objectives are in abeyance, and the army merely waits for mobilization day, for the day of action. In every form of organization, however, the internal objective must be constant. This internal objective is organized efficiency, and everything that is essential to such efficiency is expressed in the single word "coordination." There can be no waiting for "M-day" in coordination. It is a constant necessity in organization, essential to the existence of the organization itself.

As coordination is the all-inclusive principle of organization, it must have its own principle and foundation in *authority*, or the supreme coordinating power. Always, in every form of organization, this supreme authority must rest somewhere, else there would be no directive for any coordinated effort.

The term "authority," as here used, need not imply autocracy. Where true democracy prevails, this authority rests with the group as a whole, as it rests in our government with the people of the United States. In the simplest and most compact forms of democratic organization it is represented in the entire group, assembled at one time, in one place. Examples in secular government are separated as widely in

39

time as the ecclesia of ancient Athens and the present New England town meeting.

In whatever form it may appear, this supreme coordinating authority must be conceived simply as the source of all coordination, and not necessarily as the coordinating directive that runs through the entire organization. In a democracy like our own this authority rests with the people, who exercise it through the leaders of their choice.

The distinction between authority and leadership is such a vital one that it will in due course be considered at greater length. It is sufficient here to observe that the supreme coordinating authority must be prior to leadership in logical order, for it is this coordinating force that makes the organization. Leadership, on the other hand, always presupposes the organization. There can be no leader without something to lead. Leadership, of course, must exercise a derived authority. In absolutist forms of government the supreme coordinating authority usually exercises its own leadership, but this fact does not alter their essential difference.

Just as vital as the distinction between authority and leadership is that between authority and power, two terms so often confused. Power in the psychic sense—that is, ability to do things—is distinctly an individual possession. When we speak of the power of an organization we mean that this power has become collective through coordinated effort.

Authority, on the other hand, is a right. Hence we use the expression "moral authority," and may say of some great teacher, as was said of Jesus, the greatest of all teachers, that he speaks "as one having authority," which means that he has a moral right to speak as he does. In organization, authority is likewise a right, because it inheres legitimately in the structure of the organization. The distinction in the political sphere between de jure and de facto governments is based on the difference between the right of authority, acquired through some procedure recognized as legitimate, and the mere possession of power, however obtained.

The same observations apply to the exercise of authority, a truth that is not altered by the fact that authority rests on *moral right*. Rights cannot be divorced from duties, and if authority does not use its rights with due solicitude relative to these duties, it is sooner or later bound to fall. No organization has any prospect of stability if moral factors are not its basis.

Bureaucracy

MAX WEBER

CHARACTERISTICS OF BUREAUCRACY. Modern officialdom functions in the following specific manner:

✓ I. There is the principle of fixed and official

From *From Max Weber: Essays in Sociology*, edited and translated by H. H. Gerth and C. Wright Mills. Copyright 1946 by Oxford University Press. Reprinted with permission of the publisher.

jurisdictional areas, which are generally ordered by rules, that is, by laws or administrative regulations.

1. The regular activities required for the purposes of the bureaucratically governed structure are distributed in a fixed way as official duties.

2. The authority to give the commands required for the discharge of these duties is distributed in a stable way and is strictly delimited

by rules concerning the coercive means, physical, sacerdotal, or otherwise, which may be placed at the disposal of officials.

3. Methodical provision is made for the regular and continuous fulfilment of these duties and for the execution of the corresponding rights; only persons who have the generally regulated qualifications to serve are employed.

In public and lawful government these three elements constitute "bureaucratic authority." In private economic domination, they constitute bureaucratic "management." Bureaucracy, thus understood, is fully developed in political and ecclesiastical communities only in the modern state, and, in the private economy, only in the most advanced institutions of capitalism. Permanent and public office authority, with fixed jurisdiction, is not the historical rule but rather the exception. This is so even in large political structures such as those of the ancient Orient, the Germanic and Mongolian empires of conquest, or of many feudal structures of state. In all these cases, the ruler executes the most important measures through personal trustees, table-companions, or court-servants. Their commissions and authority are not precisely delimited and are temporarily called into being for each case.

II. The principles of office hierarchy and of levels of graded authority mean a firmly ordered system of super- and subordination in which there is a supervision of the lower offices by the higher ones. Such a system offers the governed the possibility of appealing the decision of a lower office to its higher authority, in a definitely regulated manner. With the full development of the bureaucratic type, the office hierarchy is monocratically organized. The principle of hierachical office authority is found in all bureaucratic structures: in state and ecclesiastical structures as well as in large party organizations and private enterprises. It does not matter for the character of bureaucracy whether its authority is called "private" or "public."

When the principle of jurisdictional "competency" is fully carried through, hierarchical subordination—at least in public office—does not mean that the "higher" authority is simply authorized to take over the business of the "lower." Indeed, the opposite is the rule. Once established and having fulfilled its task, an office tends to continue in existence and be held by another incumbent.

III. The management of the modern office is based on written documents ("the files"), which are preserved in their original or draught form. There is, therefore, a staff of subaltern officials and scribes of all sorts. The body of officials actively engaged in a "public" office, along with the respective apparatus of material implements and the files, make up a "bureau." In private enterprise, "the bureau" is often called "the office."

In principle, the modern organization of the civil service separates the bureau from the private domicile of the official, and, in general, bureaucracy segregates official activity as something distinct from the sphere of private life. Public monies and equipment are divorced from the private property of the official. This condition is everywhere the product of a long development. Nowadays, it is found in public as well as in private enterprises; in the latter, the principle extends even to the leading entrepreneur. In principle, the executive office is separated from the household, business from private correspondence, and business assets from private fortunes. The more consistently the modern type of business management has been carried through the more are these separations the case. The beginnings of this process are to be found as early as the Middle Ages.

It is the peculiarity of the modern entrepreneur that he conducts himself as the "first official" of his enterprise, in the very same way in which the ruler of a specifically modern bureaucratic state spoke of himself as "the first servant" of the state.[1] The idea that the bureau activities of the state are intrinsically different in character from the management of private economic offices is a continental European notion and, by way of contrast, is totally foreign to the American way.

IV. Office management, at least all specialized office management—and such management is distinctly modern—usually presupposes thorough and expert training. This increasingly holds for the modern executive and employee of private enterprises, in the same manner as it holds for the state official.

V. When the office is fully developed, official activity demands the full working capacity of the official, irrespective of the fact that his obligatory time in the bureau may be

[1] Frederick II of Prussia.

firmly delimited. In the normal case, this is only the product of a long development, in the public as well as in the private office. Formerly, in all cases, the normal state of affairs was reversed: official business was discharged as a secondary activity.

VI. The management of the office follows general rules, which are more or less stable, more or less exhaustive, and which can be learned. Knowledge of these rules represents a special technical learning which the officials possess. It involves jurisprudence, or administrative or business management.

The reduction of modern office management to rules is deeply embedded in its very nature. The theory of modern public administration, for instance, assumes that the authority to order certain matters by decree—which has been legally granted to public authorities —does not entitle the bureau to regulate the matter by commands given for each case, but only to regulate the matter abstractly. This stands in extreme contrast to the regulation of all relationships through individual privileges and bestowals of favor, which is absolutely dominant in patrimonialism, at least in so far as such relationships are not fixed by sacred tradition.

THE POSITION OF THE OFFICIAL. All this results in the following for the internal and external position of the official:

I. Office holding is a "vocation." This is shown, first, in the requirement of a firmly prescribed course of training, which demands the entire capacity for work for a long period of time, and in the generally prescribed and special examinations which are prerequisites of employment. Furthermore, the position of the official is in the nature of a duty. This determines the internal structure of his relations, in the following manner: Legally and actually, office holding is not considered a source to be exploited for rents or emoluments, as was normally the case during the Middle Ages and frequently up to the threshold of recent times. Nor is office holding considered a usual exchange of services for equivalents, as is the case with free labor contracts. Entrance into an office, including one in the private economy, is considered an acceptance of a specific obligation of faithful management in return for a secure existence. It is decisive for the specific nature of modern loyalty to an office that, in the pure type, it does not establish a relationship to a *person*, like the vassal's or disciple's faith in feudal or in patrimonial relations of authority. Modern loyalty is devoted to impersonal and functional purposes. Behind the functional purposes, of course, "ideas of culture-values" usually stand. These are *ersatz* for the earthly or supra-mundane personal master: ideas such as "state," "church," "community," "party," or "enterprise" are thought of as being realized in a community; they provide an ideological halo for the master.

The political official—at least in the fully developed modern state—is not considered the personal servant of a ruler. Today, the bishop, the priest, and the preacher are in fact no longer, as in early Christian times, holders of purely personal charisma. The supra-mundane and sacred values which they offer are given to everybody who seems to be worthy of them and who asks for them. In former times, such leaders acted upon the personal command of their master; in principle, they were responsible only to him. Nowadays, in spite of the partial survival of the old theory, such religious leaders are officials in the service of a functional purpose, which in the present-day "church" has become routinized and, in turn, ideologically hallowed.

II. The personal position of the official is patterned in the following way:

1. Whether he is in a private office or a public bureau, the modern official always strives and usually enjoys a distinct *social esteem* as compared with the governed. His social position is guaranteed by the prescriptive rules of rank order and, for the political official, by special definitions of the criminal code against "insults of officials" and "contempt" of state and church authorities.

The actual social position of the official is normally highest where, as in old civilized countries, the following conditions prevail: a strong demand for administration by trained experts; a strong and stable social differentiation, where the official predominantly derives from socially and economically privileged strata because of the social distribution of power; or where the costliness of the required training and status conventions are binding upon him. The possession of educational certificates—to be discussed elsewhere [2]

---

[2] Cf. *Wirtschaft und Gesellschaft*, pp. 73 ff. and part II [German editor's note].

—are usually linked with qualification for office. Naturally, such certificates or patents enhance the "status element" in the social position of the official. For the rest this status factor in individual cases is explicitly and impassively acknowledged; for example, in the prescription that the acceptance or rejection of an aspirant to an official career depends upon the consent ("election") of the members of the official body. This is the case in the German army with the officer corps. Similar phenomena, which promote this guild-like closure of officialdom, are typically found in patrimonial and, particularly, in prebendal officialdoms of the past. The desire to resurrect such phenomena in changed forms is by no means infrequent among modern bureaucrats. For instance, they have played a role among the demands of the quite proletarian and expert officials (the *tretyj* element) during the Russian revolution.

Usually the social esteem of the officials as such is especially low where the demand for expert administration and the dominance of status conventions are weak. This is especially the case in the United States; it is often the case in new settlements by virtue of their wide fields for profit-making and the great instability of their social stratification.

2. The pure type of bureaucratic official is *appointed* by a superior authority. An official elected by the governed is not a purely bureaucratic figure. Of course, the formal existence of an election does not by itself mean that no appointment hides behind the election —in the state, especially, appointment by party chiefs. Whether or not this is the case does not depend upon legal statutes but upon the way in which the party mechanism functions. Once firmly organized, the parties can turn a formally free election into the mere acclamation of a candidate designated by the party chief. As a rule, however, a formally free election is turned into a fight, conducted according to definite rules, for votes in favor of one of two designated candidates.

In all circumstances, the designation of officials by means of an election among the governed modifies the strictness of hierarchical subordination. In principle, an official who is so elected has an autonomous position opposite the superordinate official. The elected official does not derive his position "from above" but "from below," or at least not from a superior authority of the official hierarchy but from powerful party men ("bosses"), who also determine his further career. The career of the elected official is not, or at least not primarily, dependent upon his chief in the administration. The official who is not elected but appointed by a chief normally functions more exactly, from a technical point of view, because, all other circumstances being equal, it is more likely that purely functional points of consideration and qualities will determine his selection and career. As laymen, the governed can become acquainted with the extent to which a candidate is expertly qualified for office only in terms of experience, and hence only after his service. Moreover, in every sort of selection of officials by election, parties quite naturally give decisive weight not to expert considerations but to the services a follower renders to the party boss. This holds for all kinds of procurement of officials by elections, for the designation of formally free, elected officials by party bosses when they determine the slate of candidates, or the free appointment by a chief who has himself been elected. The contrast, however, is relative: substantially similar conditions hold where legitimate monarchs and their subordinates appoint officials, except that the influence of the followings are then less controllable.

Where the demand for administration by trained experts is considerable, and the party followings have to recognize an intellectually developed, educated, and freely moving "public opinion," the use of unqualified officials falls back upon the party in power at the next election. Naturally, this is more likely to happen when the officials are appointed by the chief. The demand for a trained administration now exists in the United States, but in the large cities, where immigrant votes are "corralled," there is, of course, no educated public opinion. Therefore, popular elections of the administrative chief and also of his subordinate officials usually endanger the expert qualification of the official as well as the precise functioning of the bureaucratic mechanism. It also weakens the dependence of the officials upon the hierarchy. This holds at least for the large administrative bodies that are difficult to supervise. The superior qualification and integrity of federal judges, appointed by the President, as over against elected judges in the United States is well known, although both types of officials have been selected primarily in terms of party considerations. The great changes in American metropolitan administrations demanded by reformers have proceeded essentially from elected mayors working with an apparatus of officials who were appointed by them. These reforms have thus come about in a "Caesarist" fashion. Viewed technically, as an organized form of authority, the efficiency of "Caesarism," which often grows out of democracy, rests in general upon the position of the "Caesar" as a free trustee of the masses (of the army or of the citizenry), who is unfettered by tradition. The "Caesar" is thus the unrestrained master of a body of highly qualified military officers and officials whom he selects freely and personally without regard to tradition or to any other considerations. This "rule of the personal genius," however, stands in contradiction to the formally "democratic" principle of a universally elected officialdom.

3. Normally, the position of the official is held for life, at least in public bureaucracies; and this is increasingly the case for all similar structures. As a factual rule, *tenure for life* is presupposed, even where the giving of notice or periodic reappointment occurs. In contrast to the worker in a private enterprise, the official normally holds tenure. Legal or actual life-tenure, however, is not recognized as the official's right to the possession of office, as was the case with many structures of authority in the past. Where legal guarantees against arbitrary dismissal or transfer are developed, they merely serve to guarantee a strictly objective discharge of specific office duties free from all personal considerations. In Germany, this is the case for all juridical and, increasingly, for all administrative officials.

Within the bureaucracy, therefore, the measure of "independence," legally guaranteed by tenure, is not always a source of increased status for the official whose position is thus secured. Indeed, often the reverse holds, especially in old cultures and communities that are highly differentiated. In such communities, the stricter the subordination under the arbitrary rule of the master, the more it guarantees the maintenance of the conventional seigneurial style of living for the official. Because of the very absence of these legal guarantees of tenure, the conventional esteem for the official may rise in the same way as, during the Middle Ages, the esteem of the

nobility of office [3] rose at the expense of esteem for the freemen, and as the king's judge surpassed that of the people's judge. In Germany, the military officer or the administrative official can be removed from office at any time, or at least far more readily than the "independent judge," who never pays with loss of his office for even the grossest offense against the "code of honor" or against social conventions of the salon. For this very reason, if other things are equal, in the eyes of the master stratum the judge is considered less qualified for social intercourse than are officers and administrative officials, whose greater dependence on the master is a greater guarantee of their conformity with status conventions. Of course, the average official strives for a civil-service law, which would materially secure his old age and provide increased guarantees against his arbitrary removal from office. This striving, however, has its limits. A very strong development of the "right to the office" naturally makes it more difficult to staff them with regard to technical efficiency, for such a development decreases the career-opportunities of ambitious candidates for office. This makes for the fact that officials, on the whole, do not feel their dependency upon those at the top. This lack of a feeling of dependency, however, rests primarily upon the inclination to depend upon one's equals rather than upon the socially inferior and governed strata. The present conservative movement among the Badenia clergy, occasioned by the anxiety of a presumably threatening separation of church and state, has been expressly determined by the desire not to be turned "from a master into a servant of the parish." [4]

4. The official receives the regular *pecuniary* compensation of a normally fixed *salary* and the old age security provided by a *pension*. The salary is not measured like a wage in terms of work done, but according to "status," that is, according to the kind of function (the "rank") and, in addition, possibly, according to the length of service. The relatively great security of the official's income, as well as the rewards of social esteem, make the office a sought-after position, especially in countries which no longer provide oppor-

---

[3] *Ministerialen.*

[4] Written before 1914 [German editor's note].

tunities for colonial profits. In such countries, this situation permits relatively low salaries for officials.

5. The official is set for a "*career*" within the hierarchical order of the public service. He moves from the lower, less important, and lower paid to the higher positions. The average official naturally desires a mechanical fixing of the conditions of promotion: if not of the offices, at least of the salary levels. He wants these conditions fixed in terms of "seniority," or possibly according to grades achieved in a developed system of expert examinations. Here and there, such examinations actually form a character *indelebilis* of the official and have lifelong effects on his career. To this is joined the desire to qualify the right to office and the increasing tendency toward status group closure and economic security. All of this makes for a tendency to consider the offices as "prebends" of those who are qualified by educational certificates. The necessity of taking general personal and intellectual qualifications into consideration, irrespective of the often subaltern character of the educational certificate, has led to a condition in which the highest political offices, especially the positions of "ministers," are principally filled without reference to such certificates. . . .

TECHNICAL ADVANTAGES OF BUREAUCRATIC ORGANIZATION. The decisive reason for the advance of bureaucratic organization has always been its purely technical superiority over any other form of organization. The fully developed bureaucratic mechanism compares with other organizations exactly as does the machine with the non-mechanical modes of production.

Precision, speed, unambiguity, knowledge of the files, continuity, discretion, unity, strict subordination, reduction of friction and of material and personal costs—these are raised to the optimum point in the strictly bureaucratic administration, and especially in its monocratic form. As compared with all collegiate, honorific, and avocational forms of administration, trained bureaucracy is superior on all these points. And as far as complicated tasks are concerned, paid bureaucratic work is not only more precise but, in the last analysis, it is often cheaper than even formally unremunerated honorific service.

Honorific arrangements make administrative work an avocation and, for this reason alone, honorific service normally functions more slowly; being less bound to schemata and being more formless. Hence it is less precise and less unified than bureaucratic work because it is less dependent upon superiors and because the establishment and exploitation of the apparatus of subordinate officials and filing services are almost unavoidably less economical. Honorific service is less continuous than bureaucratic and frequently quite expensive. This is especially the case if one thinks not only of the money costs to the public treasury—costs which bureaucratic administration, in comparison with administration by notables, usually substantially increases —but also of the frequent economic losses of the governed caused by delays and lack of precision. The possibility of administration by notables normally and permanently exists only where official management can be satisfactorily discharged as an avocation. With the qualitative increase of tasks the administration has to face, administration by notables reaches its limits—today, even in England. Work organized by collegiate bodies causes friction and delay and requires compromises between colliding interests and views. The administration, therefore, runs less precisely and is more independent of superiors; hence, it is less unified and slower. All advances of the Prussian administrative organization have been and will in the future be advances of the bureaucratic, and especially of the monocratic, principle.

Today, it is primarily the capitalist market economy which demands that the official business of the administration be discharged precisely, unambiguously, continuously, and with as much speed as possible. Normally, the very large, modern capitalist enterprises are themselves unequalled models of strict bureaucratic organization. Business management throughout rests on increasing precision, steadiness, and, above all, the speed of operations. This, in turn, is determined by the peculiar nature of the modern means of communication, including, among other things, the news service of the press. The extraordinary increase in the speed by which public announcements, as well as economic and political facts, are transmitted exerts a steady and sharp pressure in the direction of speeding up the tempo of administrative reaction towards various situations. The optimum of such reaction time is normally attained only by a strictly bureaucratic organization.[5]

Bureaucratization offers above all the optimum possibility for carrying through the principle of specializing administrative functions according to purely objective considerations. Individual performances are allocated to functionaries who have specialized training and who by constant practice learn more and more. The "objective" discharge of business primarily means a discharge of business according to *calculable rules* and "without regard for persons."

"Without regard for persons" is also the watchword of the "market" and, in general, of all pursuits of naked economic interests. A consistent execution of bureaucratic domination means the leveling of status "honor." Hence, if the principle of the free-market is not at the same time restricted, it means the universal domination of the "class situation." That this consequence of bureaucratic domination has not set in everywhere, parallel to the extent of bureaucratization, is due to the differences among possible principles by which polities may meet their demands.

The second element mentioned, "calculable rules," also is of paramount importance for modern bureaucracy. The peculiarity of modern culture, and specifically of its technical and economic basis, demands this very "calculability" of results. When fully developed, bureaucracy also stands, in a specific sense, under the principle of *sine ira ac studio*. Its specific nature, which is welcomed by capitalism, develops the more perfectly the more the bureaucracy is "dehumanized," the more completely it succeeds in eliminating from official business love, hatred, and all purely personal, irrational, and emotional elements which escape calculation. This is the specific nature of bureaucracy and it is appraised as its special virtue.

The more complicated and specialized modern culture becomes, the more its external supporting apparatus demands the personally detached and strictly "objective" *expert*, in

---

[5] Here we cannot discuss in detail how the bureaucratic apparatus may, and actually does, produce definite obstacles to the discharge of business in a manner suitable for the single case.

lieu of the master of older social structures, who was moved by personal sympathy and favor, by grace and gratitude. Bureaucracy offers the attitudes demanded by the external apparatus of modern culture in the most favorable combination. As a rule, only bureaucracy has established the foundation for the administration of a rational law conceptually systematized on the basis of such enactments as the latter Roman imperial period first created with a high degree of technical perfection. During the Middle Ages, this law was received along with the bureaucratization of legal administration, that is to say, with the displacement of the old trial procedure which was bound to tradition or to irrational presuppositions, by the rationally trained and specialized expert. . . .

THE CONCENTRATION OF THE MEANS OF ADMINISTRATION. The bureaucratic structure goes hand in hand with the concentration of the material means of management in the hands of the master. This concentration occurs, for instance, in a well-known and typical fashion, in the development of big capitalist enterprises, which find their essential characteristics in this process. A corresponding process occurs in public organizations.

The bureaucratically led army of the Pharaohs, the army during the later period of the Roman republic and the principate, and, above all, the army of the modern military state are characterized by the fact that their equipment and provisions are supplied from the magazines of the war lord. This is in contrast to the folk armies of argicultural tribes, the armed citizenry of ancient cities, the militias of early medieval cities, and all feudal armies; for these, the self-equipment and the self-provisioning of those obliged to fight was normal.

War in our time is a war of machines. And this makes magazines technically necessary, just as the dominance of the machine in industry promotes the concentration of the means of production and management. In the main, however, the bureaucratic armies of the past, equipped and provisioned by the lord, have risen when social and economic development has absolutely or relatively diminished the stratum of citizens who were economically able to equip themselves, so that their number was no longer sufficient for putting the required armies in the field. They were reduced at least relatively, that is, in relation to the range of power claimed for the polity. Only the bureaucratic army structure allowed for the development of the professional standing armies which are necessary for the constant pacification of large states of the plains, as well as for warfare against far-distant enemies, especially enemies overseas. Specifically, military discipline and technical training can be normally and fully developed, at least to its modern high level, only in the bureaucratic army.

Historically, the bureaucratization of the army has everywhere been realized along with the transfer of army service from the propertied to the propertyless. Until this transfer occurs, military service is an honorific privilege of propertied men. Such a transfer was made to the native-born unpropertied, for instance, in the armies of the generals of the late Roman republic and the empire, as well as in modern armies up to the nineteenth century. The burden of service has also been transferred to strangers, as in the mercenary armies of all ages. This process typically goes hand in hand with the general increase in material and intellectual culture. The following reason has also played its part everywhere: the increasing density of population, and therewith the intensity and strain of economic work, makes for an increasing "indispensability" of the acquisitive strata [6] for purposes of war. Leaving aside periods of strong ideological fervor, the propertied strata of sophisticated and especially of urban culture as a rule are little fitted and also little inclined to do the coarse war work of the common soldier. Other circumstances being equal, the propertied strata of the open country are at least usually better qualified and more strongly inclined to become professional officers. This difference between the urban and the rural propertied is balanced only where the increasing possibility of mechanized warfare requires the leaders to qualify as "technicians."

The bureaucratization of organized warfare may be carried through in the form of private capitalist enterprise, just like any other business. Indeed, the procurement of armies and their administration by private capitalists has been the rule in mercenary armies, especially

[6] *Erwerbende Schichten.*

those of the Occident up to the turn of the eighteenth century. During the Thirty Years' War, in Brandenburg the soldier was still the predominant owner of the material implements of his business. He owned his weapons, horses, and dress, although the state, in the role, as it were, of the merchant of the "putting-out system," did supply him to some extent. Later on, in the standing army of Prussia, the chief of the company owned the material means of warfare, and only since the peace of Tilsit has the concentration of the means of warfare in the hands of the state definitely come about. Only with this concentration was the introduction of uniforms generally carried through. Before then, the introduction of uniforms had been left to a great extent to the arbitrary discretion of the regimental officer, with the exception of individual categories of troops to whom the king had "bestowed" certain uniforms, first, in 1620, to the royal bodyguard, then, under Frederick II, repeatedly.

Such terms as "regiment" and "battalion" usually had quite different meanings in the eighteenth century from the meanings they have today. Only the battalion was a tactical unit (today both are); the "regiment" was then a managerial unit of an economic organization established by the colonel's position as an "entrepreneur." "Official" maritime ventures (like the Genoese *maonae*) and army procurement belong to private capitalism's first giant enterprises of far-going bureaucratic character. In this respect, the "nationalization" of these enterprises by the state has its modern parallel in the nationalization of the railroads, which have been controlled by the state from their beginnings.

In the same way as with army organizations, the bureaucratization of administration goes hand in hand with the concentration of the means of organization in other spheres. The old administration by satraps and regents, as well as administration by farmers of office, purchasers of office, and, most of all, administration by feudal vassals, decentralize the material means of administration. The local demand of the province and the cost of the army and of subaltern officials are regularly paid for in advance from local income, and only the surplus reaches the central treasure. The enfeoffed official administers entirely by payment out of his own pocket. The bureaucratic state, however, puts its whole administrative expense on the budget and equips the lower authorities with the current means of expenditure, the use of which the state regulates and controls. This has the same meaning for the "economics" of the administration as for the large centralized capitalist enterprise.

In the field of scientific research and instruction, the bureaucratization of the always existing research institutes of the universities is a function of the increasing demand for material means of management. Liebig's laboratory at Giessen University was the first example of big enterprise in this field. Through the concentration of such means in the hands of the privileged head of the institute, the mass of researchers and docents are separated from their "means of production," in the same way as capitalist enterprise has separated the workers from theirs.

In spite of its indubitable technical superiority, bureaucracy has everywhere been a relatively late development. A number of obstacles have contributed to this, and only under certain social and political conditions have they definitely receded into the background. . . .

THE PERMANENT CHARACTER OF THE BUREAU-CRATIC MACHINE. Once it is fully established, bureaucracy is among those social structures which are the hardest to destroy. Bureaucracy is *the* means of carrying "community action" over into rationally ordered "societal action." Therefore, as an instrument for "societalizing" relations of power, bureaucracy has been and is a power instrument of the first order—for the one who controls the bureaucratic apparatus.

Under otherwise equal conditions, a "societal action," which is methodically ordered and led, is superior to every resistance of "mass" or even of "communal action." And where the bureaucratization of administration has been completely carried through, a form of power relation is established that is practically unshatterable.

The individual bureaucrat cannot squirm out of the apparatus in which he is harnessed. In contrast to the honorific or avocational "notable," the professional bureaucrat is chained to his activity by his entire material and ideal existence. In the great majority of

cases, he is only a single cog in an ever-moving mechanism which prescribes to him an essentially fixed route of march. The official is entrusted with specialized tasks and normally the mechanism cannot be put into motion or arrested by him, but only from the very top. The individual bureaucrat is thus forged to the community of all the functionaries who are integrated into the mechanism. They have a common interest in seeing that the mechanism continues its functions and that the societally exercised authority carries on.

The ruled, for their part, cannot dispense with or replace the bureaucratic apparatus of authority once it exists. For this bureaucracy rests upon expert training, a functional specialization of work, and an attitude set for habitual and virtuoso-like mastery of single yet methodically integrated functions. If the official stops working, or if his work is forcefully interrupted, chaos results, and it is difficult to improvise replacements from among the governed who are fit to master such chaos. This holds for public administration as well as for private economic management. More and more the material fate of the masses depends upon the steady and correct functioning of the increasingly bureaucratic organizations of private capitalism. The idea of eliminating these organizations becomes more and more utopian.

The discipline of officialdom refers to the attitude-set of the official for precise obedience within his *habitual* activity, in public as well as in private organizations. This discipline increasingly becomes the basis of all order, however great the practical importance of administration on the basis of the filed documents may be. The naive idea of Bakuninism of destroying the basis of "acquired rights" and "domination" by destroying public documents overlooks the settled orientation of *man* for keeping to the habitual rules and regulations that continue to exist independently of the documents. Every reorganization of beaten or dissolved troops, as well as the restoration of administrative orders destroyed by revolt, panic, or other catastrophes, is realized by appealing to the trained orientation of obedient compliance to such orders. Such compliance has been conditioned into the officials, on the one hand, and, on the other hand, into the governed. If such an appeal is successful it brings, as it were, the disturbed mechanism into gear again.

The objective indispensability of the once-existing apparatus, with its peculiar, "impersonal" character, means that the mechanism —in contrast to feudal orders based upon personal piety—is easily made to work for anybody who knows how to gain control over it. A rationally ordered system of officials continues to function smoothly after the enemy has occupied the area; he merely needs to change the top officials. This body of officials continues to operate because it is to the vital interest of everyone concerned, including above all the enemy.

During the course of his long years in power, Bismarck brought his ministerial colleagues into unconditional bureaucratic dependence by eliminating all independent statesmen. Upon his retirement, he saw to his surprise that they continued to manage their offices unconcerned and undismayed, as if he had not been the master mind and creator of these creatures, but rather as if some single figure had been exchanged for some other figure in the bureaucratic machine. With all the changes of masters in France since the time of the First Empire, the power machine has remained essentially the same. Such a machine makes "revolution," in the sense of the forceful creation of entirely new formations of authority, technically more and more impossible, especially when the apparatus controls the modern means of communication (telegraph, et cetera) and also by virtue of its internal rationalized structure. In classic fashion, France has demonstrated how this process has substituted *coups d'état* for "revolutions": all successful transformations in France have amounted to *coups d'état*. . . .

THE POWER POSITION OF BUREAUCRACY. Everywhere the modern state is undergoing bureaucratization. But whether the *power* of bureaucracy within the polity is universally increasing must here remain an open question.

The fact that bureaucratic organization is technically the most highly developed means of power in the hands of the man who controls it does not determine the weight that bureaucracy as such is capable of having in a particular social structure. The ever-increasing "indispensability" of the officialdom, swollen to millions, is no more decisive for this question than is the view of some representatives of the proletarian movement that the economic indispensability of the proletarians is decisive for the measure of their social and political power position. If "indispensability" were decisive, then where slave labor prevailed and where freemen usually abhor work as a dishonor, the "indispensable" slaves ought to have held the positions of power, for they were at least as indispensable as officials and proletarians are today. Whether the power of bureaucracy as such increases cannot be decided *a priori* from such reasons. The drawing in of economic interest groups or other non-official experts, or the drawing in of non-expert lay representatives, the establishment of local, inter-local, or central parliamentary or other representative bodies, or of occupational associations—these *seem* to run directly against the bureaucratic tendency. How far this appearance is the truth must be discussed in another chapter rather than in this purely formal and typological discussion. In general, only the following can be said here:

Under normal conditions, the power position of a fully developed bureaucracy is always overtowering. The "political master" finds himself in the position of the "dilettante" who stands opposite the "expert," facing the trained official who stands within the management of administration. This holds whether the "master" whom the bureaucracy serves is a "people," equipped with the weapons of "legislative initiative," the "referendum," and the right to remove officials, or a parliament, elected on a more aristocratic or more "democratic" basis and equipped with the right to vote a lack of confidence, or with the actual authority to vote it. It holds whether the master is an aristocratic, collegiate body, legally or actually based on self-recruitment, or whether he is a popularly elected president, a hereditary and "absolute" or a "constitutional" monarch.

Every bureaucracy seeks to increase the superiority of the professionally informed by keeping their knowledge and intentions secret. Bureaucratic administration always tends to be an administration of "secret sessions": in so far as it can, it hides its knowledge and action from criticism. Prussian church authorities now threaten to use disciplinary measures against pastors who make reprimands or other admonitory measures in any way accessible to third parties. They do this because the pastor, in making such criticism available, is "guilty" of facilitating a possible criticism of the church authorities. The treasury officials of the Persian shah have made a secret doctrine of their budgetary art and even use secret script. The official statistics of Prussia, in general, make public only what cannot do any harm to the intentions of the power-wielding bureaucracy. The tendency toward secrecy in certain administrative fields follows their material nature: everywhere that the power interests of the domination structure toward *the outside* are at stake, whether it is an economic competitor of a private enterprise, or a foreign, potentially hostile polity, we find secrecy. If it is to be successful, the management of diplomacy can only be publicly controlled to a very limited extent. The military administration must insist on the concealment of its most important measures; with the increasing significance of purely technical aspects, this is all the more the case. Political parties do not proceed differently, in spite of all the ostensible publicity of Catholic con-

gresses and party conventions. With the increasing bureaucratization of party organizations, this secrecy will prevail even more. Commerical policy, in Germany for instance, brings about a concealment of production statistics. Every fighting posture of a social structure toward the outside tends to buttress the position of the group in power.

The pure interest of the bureaucracy in power, however, is efficacious far beyond those areas where purely functional interests make for secrecy. The concept of the "official secret" is the specific invention of bureaucracy, and nothing is so fanatically defended by the bureaucracy as this attitude, which cannot be substantially justified beyond these specifically qualified areas. In facing a parliament, the bureaucracy, out of a sure power instinct, fights every attempt of the parliament to gain knowledge by means of its own experts or from interest groups. The so-called right of parliamentary investigation is one of the means by which parliament seeks such knowledge. Bureaucracy naturally welcomes a poorly informed and hence a powerless parliament—at least in so far as ignorance somehow agrees with the bureaucracy's interests. . . .

Formal Organizations

CHESTER I. BARNARD

An organization comes into being when (1) there are persons able to communicate with each other (2) who are willing to contribute action (3) to accomplish a common purpose. The elements of an organization are therefore

From Chester I. Barnard, *The Functions of the Executive*. Cambridge, Mass.: Harvard University Press, copyright, 1938, by the President and Fellows of Harvard College. Pp. 82–95, 104–113. Reprinted with permission of the publisher.

(1) communication; (2) willingness to serve; and (3) common purpose. These elements are necessary and sufficient conditions initially, and they are found in all such organizations. The third element, purpose, is implicit in the definition. Willingness to serve, and communication, and the interdependence of the three elements in general, and their mutual dependence in specific coöperative systems, are matters of experience and observation.

For the continued existence of an organ-

ization either *effectiveness* or *efficiency* is
necessary;[1] and the longer the life, the more
necessary both are. The vitality of organizations lies in the willingness of individuals to
contribute forces to the coöperative system.
This willingness requires the belief that the
purpose can be carried out, a faith that diminishes to the vanishing point as it appears
that it is not in fact in process of being attained. Hence, when effectiveness ceases, willingness to contribute disappears. The continuance of willingness also depends upon the
satisfactions that are secured by individual
contributors in the process of carrying out
the purpose. If the satisfactions do not exceed
the sacrifices required, willingness disappears,
and the condition is one of organization inefficiency. If the satisfactions exceed the sacrifices, willingness persists, and the condition
is one of efficiency of organization.

In summary, then, the initial existence of
an organization depends upon a combination
of these elements appropriate to the external
conditions at the moment. Its survival depends
upon the maintenance of an equilibrium of
the system. This equilibrium is primarily
internal, a matter of proportions between the
elements, but it is ultimately and basically an
equilibrium between the system and the total
situation external to it. This external equilibrium has two terms in it: first, the effectiveness of the organization, which comprises the
relevance of its purpose to the environmental
situation; and, second, its efficiency, which
comprises the interchange between the organization and individuals. Thus the elements
stated will each vary with external factors,
and they are at the same time interdependent;
when one is varied compensating variations
must occur in the other if the system of which
they are components is to remain in equilibrium, that is, is to persist or survive.

We may now appropriately consider these
elements and their interrelations in some detail, having in mind the system as a whole. In
later chapters we shall consider each element
in greater detail with reference to its variability in dependence upon external factors,
and the interrelations of the elements as deter-

mining the character of the executive functions.

Willingness to Coöperate. By definition
there can be no organization without persons.
However, as we have urged that it is not
persons, but the services or acts or action or
influences of persons, which should be treated
as constituting organizations,[2] it is clear that
willingness of persons to contribute efforts to
the coöperative system is indispensable.

There are a number of words and phrases
in common use with reference to organization
that reach back to the factor of individual
willingness. "Loyalty," "solidarity," "*esprit de
corps*," "strength" of organization, are the
chief. Although they are indefinite, they relate
to intensity of attachment to the "cause," and
are commonly understood to refer to something different from effectiveness, ability, or
value of personal contributions. Thus "loyalty" is regarded as not necessarily related
either to position, rank, fame, remuneration,
or ability. It is vaguely recognized as an
essential condition of organization.

Willingness, in the present connection,
means self-abnegation, the surrender of control of personal conduct, the depersonalization
of personal action. Its effect is cohesion of
effort, a sticking together. Its immediate cause
is the disposition necessary to "sticking together." Without this there can be no sustained personal effort as a contribution to co-
operation. Activities cannot be coördinated
unless there is first the disposition to make a
personal act a contribution to an impersonal
system of acts, one in which the individual
gives up personal control of what he does.

The outstanding fact regarding willingness
to contribute to a given specific formal organization is the indefinitely large range of variation in its intensity among individuals. If all
those who may be considered potential contributors to an organization are arranged in
order of willingness to serve it, the scale gradually descends from possibly intense willingness through neutral or zero willingness to
intense unwillingness or opposition or hatred.
The *preponderance of persons in a modern
society always lies on the negative side* with
reference to any particular existing or poten-

---

[1] See definitions in *The Functions of the Executive*, Chapters II and V, pp. 19 and 55 ff., also
Chapter XVI.

[2] Page 72 [of *The Functions of the Executive*].

tial organization. Thus of the possible contributors only a small minority actually have a positive willingness. This is true of the largest and most comprehensive formal organizations, such as the large nations, the Catholic Church, etc. Most of the persons in existing society are either indifferent to or positively opposed to any single one of them; and if the smaller organizations subordinate to these major organizations are under consideration the minority becomes of course a much smaller proportion, and usually a nearly negligible proportion, of the conceivable total.

A second fact of almost equal importance is that the willingness of any individual cannot be constant in degree. It is necessarily intermittent and fluctuating. It can scarcely be said to exist during sleep, and is obviously diminished or exhausted by weariness, discomfort, etc., a conception that was well expressed by the saying "The spirit is willing, but the flesh is weak."

A corollary of the two propositions just stated is that for any given formal organization the number of persons of positive willingness to serve, but near the neutral or zero point, is always fluctuating. It follows that the aggregate willingness of potential contributors to any formal coöperative system is unstable—a fact that is evident from the history of all formal organizations.

Willingness to coöperate, positive or negative, is the expression of the net satisfactions or dissatisfactions experienced or anticipated by each individual in comparison with those experienced or anticipated through alternative opportunities. These alternative opportunities may be either personal and individualistic or those afforded by other organizations. That is, willingness to coöperate is the net effect, first, of the inducements to do so in conjunction with the sacrifices involved, and then in comparison with the practically available net satisfactions afforded by alternatives. The questions to be determined, if they were matters of logical reasoning, would be, first, whether the opportunity to coöperate grants any advantage to the individual as compared with independent action; and then, if so, whether that advantage is more or less than the advantage obtainable from some other coöperative opportunity. Thus, from the viewpoint of the individual, willingness is the joint

effect of personal desires and reluctances; from the viewpoint of organization it is the joint effect of objective inducements offered and burdens imposed. The measure of this net result, however, is entirely individual, personal, and subjective. Hence, organizations depend upon the motives of individuals and the inducements that satisfy them.

Purpose. Willingness to coöperate, except as a vague feeling or desire for association with others, cannot develop without an objective of coöperation. Unless there is such an objective it cannot be known or anticipated what specific efforts will be required of individuals, nor in many cases what satisfactions to them can be in prospect. Such an objective we denominate the "purpose" of an organization. The necessity of having a purpose is axiomatic, implicit in the words "system," "coördination," "coöperation." It is something that is clearly evident in many observed systems of coöperation, although it is often not formulated in words, and sometimes cannot be so formulated. In such cases what is observed is the direction or effect of the activities, from which purpose may be inferred.

A purpose does not incite coöperative activity unless it is accepted by those whose efforts will constitute the organization. Hence there is initially something like simultaneity in the acceptance of a purpose and willingness to coöperate.

It is important at this point to make clear that every coöperative purpose has in the view of each coöperating person two aspects which we call (1) the coöperative and (2) the subjective aspect, respectively.

1. When the viewing of the purpose is an *act of coöperation*, it approximates that of detached observers from a special position of observation; this position is that of the interests of the organization; it is largely determined by organization knowledge, but is personally interpreted. For example, if five men are coöperating to move a stone from A to B, the moving of the stone is a different thing in the organization view of each of the five men involved. Note, however, that what moving the stone means to each man personally is not here in question, but what he thinks it means to the organization *as a whole*. This includes the significance of his own effort as

an element in coöperation, and that of all others, in his view; but it is not at all a matter of satisfying a personal motive.

When the purpose is a physical result of simple character, the difference between the purpose as objectively viewed by a detached observer and the purpose as viewed by each person coöperating *as an act of coöperation* is ordinarily not large or important, and the different coöperative views of the persons coöperating are correspondingly similar. Even in such cases the attentive observer will detect differences that result in disputes, errors of action, etc., even though no *personal* interest is implicated. But when the purpose is less tangible—for example, in religious coöperation—the difference between objective purpose and purpose as cooperatively viewed by each person is often seen ultimately to result in disruption.

We may say, then, that a purpose can serve as an element of a coöperative system only so long as the participants do not recognize that there are serious divergences of their understanding of that purpose as the object of coöperation. If in fact there is important difference between the aspects of the purpose as objectively and as coöperatively viewed, the divergencies become quickly evident when the purpose is concrete, tangible, physical; but when the purpose is general, intangible, and of sentimental character, the divergencies can be very wide yet not be recognized. Hence, an objective purpose that can serve as the basis for a coöperative system is one that is *believed* by the contributors (or potential contributors) to it to be the determined purpose of the organization. The inculcation of belief in the real existence of a common purpose is an essential executive function. It explains much educational and so-called morale work in political, industrial, and religious organizations that is so often otherwise inexplicable.[3]

2. Going back to the illustration of five men moving a stone, we have noted "that what moving the stone means to each man personally is not here in question, but what he thinks it means to the *organization as a whole*." The distinction emphasized is of first importance. It suggests the fact that every

participant in an organization may be regarded as having a dual personality—an organization personality and an individual personality. Strictly speaking, an organization purpose has directly no meaning for the individual. What has meaning for him is the organization's relation to him—what burdens it imposes, what benefits it confers. In referring to the aspects of purpose as coöperatively viewed, we are alluding to the *organization* personality of individuals. In many cases the two personalities are so clearly developed that they are quite apparent. In military action individual conduct may be so dominated by organization personality that it is utterly contradictory of what personal motivation would require. It has been observed of many men that their private conduct is entirely inconsistent with official conduct, although they seem completely unaware of the fact. Often it will be observed that participants in political, patriotic, or religious organizations will accept derogatory treatment of their personal conduct, including the assertion that it is inconsistent with their organization obligations, while they will become incensed at the slightest derogation of the tenets or doctrines of their organization, even though they profess not to understand them. There are innumerable other cases, however, in which almost no organization personality may be said to exist. These are cases in which personal relationship with the coöperative system is momentary or at the margin of willingness to participate.

In other words we have clearly to distinguish between organization purpose and individual motive. It is frequently assumed in reasoning about organizations that common purpose and individual motive are or should be identical. With the exception noted below, this is never the case; and under modern conditions it rarely even appears to be the case. Individual motive is necessarily an internal, personal, subjective thing; common purpose is necessarily an external, impersonal, objective thing even though the individual interpretation of it is subjective. The one exception to this general rule, an important one, is that the accomplishment of an organization purpose becomes itself a source of personal satisfaction and a motive for many individuals in many organizations. It is rare, however, if ever, and

[3] This will be expanded in Chapter XVII [of *The Functions of the Executive*].

then I think only in connection with family, patriotic, and religious organizations under special conditions, that organization purpose becomes or can become the *only* or even the major individual motive.

Finally it should be noted that, once established, organizations change their unifying purposes. They tend to perpetuate themselves; and in the effort to survive may change the reasons for existence. I shall later make clearer that in this lies an important aspect of executive functions.[4]

Communication. The possibility of accomplishing a common purpose and the existence of persons whose desires might constitute motives for contributing toward such a common purpose are the opposite poles of the system of coöperative effort. The process by which these potentialities become dynamic is that of communication. Obviously a common purpose must be commonly known, and to be known must be in some way communicated. With some exceptions, verbal communication between men is the method by which this is accomplished. Similarly, though under crude and obvious conditions not to the same extent, inducements to persons depend upon communication to them.

The method of communication centers in language, oral and written. On its crudest side, motions or actions that are of obvious meaning when observed are sufficient for communication without deliberate attempt to communicate; and signaling by various methods is an important method in much coöperative activity. On the other side, both in primitive and in highly complex civilization "observational feeling" is likewise an important aspect of communication.[5] I do not think it is generally so

recognized. It is necessary because of the limitations of language and the differences in the linguistic capacities of those who use language. A very large element in special experience and training and in continuity of individual association is the ability to understand without words, not merely the situation or conditions, but the *intention*.

The techniques of communication are an important part of any organization and are the preëminent problems of many. The absence of a suitable technique of communication would eliminate the possibility of adopting some purposes as a basis for organization. Communication technique shapes the form and the internal economy of organization. This will be evident at once if one visualizes the attempt to do many things now accomplished by small organizations if each "member" spoke a different language. Similarly, many technical functions could hardly be carried on without special codes; for example, engineering or chemical work. In an exhaustive theory of organization, communication would occupy a central place, because the structure, extensiveness, and scope of organization are almost entirely determined by communication techniques. To this aspect of communication much of the material in subsequent chapters will be devoted.[6] Moreover, much specialization in organization originates and is maintained essentially because of communication requirements.

Effectiveness of Coöperation. The continuance of an organization depends upon its ability to carry out its purpose. This clearly depends jointly upon the appropriateness of its action and upon the conditions of its environment. In other words, effectiveness is prima-

---

[4] See also Chapters II and III [of *The Functions of the Executive*].

[5] The phrase "observational feeling" is of my coining. The point is not sufficiently developed, and probably has not been adequately studied by anyone. I take it to be at least in part involved in group action not incited by any "overt" or verbal communication. The cases known to me from the primitive field are those reported by W. H. R. Rivers on pages 94–97 of his *Instinct and the Unconscious* (2nd edition Cambridge University Press, 1924), with reference to Polynesia and Melanesia. One case is summarized by F. C. Bartlett, in *Remembering* (Cambridge University Press, 1932), at p. 297. Rivers states in substance

that in some of the relatively small groups decisions are often arrived at and acted upon without having ever been formulated by anybody.

I have observed on innumerable occasions apparent unanimity of decision of equals in conferences to quit discussion without a word to that effect being spoken. Often the action is initiated apparently by someone's rising; but as this frequently occurs in such groups *without* the termination of the meeting, more than mere rising is involved. "Observational feeling," I think, avoids the notion of anything "occult."

[6] Especially in Chapter XII, latter half [of *The Functions of the Executive*].

rily a matter of technological [7] processes. This is quite obvious in ordinary cases of purpose to accomplish a physical objective, such as building a bridge. When the objective is non-physical, as is the case with religious and social organizations, it is not so obvious.

It should be noted that a paradox is involved in this matter. An organization must disintegrate if it cannot accomplish its purpose. It also destroys itself by accomplishing its purpose. A very large number of successful organizations come into being and then disappear for this reason. Hence most continuous organizations require repeated adoption of new purposes. This is concealed from everyday recognition by the practice of generalizing a complex series of specific purposes under one term, stated to be *"the* purpose" of this organization. This is strikingly true in the case of governmental and public utility organizations when the purpose is stated to be a particular kind of service through a period of years. It is apparent that their real purposes are not abstractions called "service" but specific acts of service. A manufacturing organization is said to exist to make, say, shoes; this is its "purpose." But it is evident that not making shoes in general but making specific shoes from day to day is its series of purposes. This process of generalization, however, provides in advance for the approximate definition of new purposes automatically—so automatically that the generalization is normally substituted in our minds for the concrete performances that are the real purposes. Failure to be effective is, then, a real cause of disintegration; but failure to provide for the decisions resulting in the adoption of new purposes would have the same result. Hence the generalization of purpose which can only be defined concretely by day-to-day events is a vital aspect of permanent organization.

Organization Efficiency. It has already been stated that "efficiency" as conceived in this treatise is not used in the specialized and limited sense of ordinary industrial practice or in the restricted sense applicable to technological processes. So-called "practical" efficiency has little meaning, for example, as applied to many organizations such as religious organizations.

Efficiency of effort in the fundamental sense with which we are here concerned is efficiency relative to the securing of necessary personal contributions to the coöperative system. The life of an organization depends upon its ability to secure and maintain the personal contributions of energy (including the transfer of control of materials or money equivalent) necessary to effect its purposes. This ability is a composite of perhaps many efficiencies and inefficiencies in the narrow senses of these words, and it is often the case that inefficiency in some respect can be treated as the cause of total failure, in the sense that if corrected success would then be possible. But certainly in most organization—social, political, national, religious—nothing but the absolute test of survival is significant objectively; there is no basis for comparison of the efficiencies of separate aspects. . . . The emphasis now is on the view that efficiency of organization is its capacity to offer effective inducements in sufficient quantity to maintain the equilibrium of the system. It is efficiency in this sense and not the efficiency of material productiveness which maintains the vitality of organizations. There are many organizations of great power and permanency in which the idea of productive efficiency is utterly meaningless because there is no material production. Churches, patriotic societies, scientific societies, theatrical and musical organizations, are cases where the original flow of *material* inducements is toward the organization, not from it—a flow necessary to provide resources with which to supply material inducements to the small minority who require them in such organizations.

In those cases where the primary purpose of organization is the production of material things, insufficiency with respect to the non-material inducements leads to the attempt to substitute material inducements for the non-material. Under favorable circumstances, to a limited degree, and for a limited time, this substitution may be effective. But to me, at least, it appears utterly contrary to the nature of men to be sufficiently induced by material or monetary considerations to contribute enough effort to a coöperative system to enable it to be productively efficient to the degree necessary for persistence over an extended period.

If these things are true, then even in purely economic enterprises efficiency in the offering

[7] Using "technological" in the broad sense emphasized in Chapter III [of *The Functions of the Executive*].

of non-economic inducements may be as vital as productive efficiency. Perhaps the word efficiency as applied to such non-economic inducements as I have given for illustration will seem strange and forced. This, I think, can only be because we are accustomed to use the word in a specialized sense.

The non-economic inducements are as difficult to offer as others under many circumstances. To establish conditions under which individual pride of craft and of accomplishment can be secured without destroying the material economy of standardized production in coöperative operation is a problem in real efficiency. To maintain a character of personnel that is an attractive condition of employment involves a delicate art and much insight in the selection (and rejection) of personal services offered, whether the standard of quality be high or low. To have an organization that lends prestige and secures the loyalty of desirable persons is a complex and difficult task in efficiency—in all-round efficiency, not one-sided efficiency. It is for these reasons that good organizations—commercial, governmental, military, academic, and others—will be observed to devote great attention and sometimes great expense of money to the non-economic inducements, because they are indispensable to fundamental efficiency, as well as to effectiveness in many cases.[8]

The theory of organization set forth in this chapter is derived from the study of organizations which are exceedingly complex, although it is stated in terms of ideal simple organizations. The temptation is to assume that, in the more complex organizations which we meet in our actual social life, the effect of complexity is to modify or qualify the theory. This appears not to be the case. Organization, simple or complex, is always *an impersonal system of coördinated human efforts;* always there is purpose as the coördinating and unifying principle; always there is the indispensable ability to communicate, always the necessity for personal willingness, and for effectiveness and efficiency in maintaining the integrity of purpose and the continuity of contributions. Complexity appears to modify the quality and form

[8] The economics of coöperative systems and their relation to organizations is presented in Chapter XVI [of *The Functions of the Executive*].

of these elements and of the balance between them; but fundamentally the same principles that govern simple organizations may be conceived as governing the structure of complex organizations, which are composite systems.   . . .

The Growth of Organizations

[I]t will be noted that when the origin of organization is spontaneous, or is the result of the initiative of one man, or is the deliberate creation of a parent organization, the beginning is small. The organization comes into being when two or more persons begin to coöperate to a common end. Where there is division by schism, rebellion, this is likewise true, but is usually not so recognized because attention is given to the final breakup of a large complex organization. What takes place beforehand is the growth of a new counter organization or independent organization supported by the efforts of individuals who may in part still continue to support the older organization. So far as I have learned, this beginning is always small; that is, it results from the spontaneous acceptation of a new purpose, independent of and perhaps definitely conflicting with the older purpose, by a small group; or it is prompted by one individual who associates others with himself. Hence, all organizations of complex character grow out of small, simple organizations.[9] It is impossible for formal organizations to grow except by the process of combining unit organizataions already existing, or the creation of new units of organization to be added to those in an existing complex.

It may, therefore, be said that all large for-

[9] Perhaps this will be clearer if the process is visualized of trying to organize a group of one hundred or five hundred men. Under the most favorable circumstances, i.e., when they are willing to be organized because there has come about some consensus of opinion as to purpose or objective, the mass must be broken up into small groups with group leaders. Only when by this process unit organizations have been created is it possible to combine these units into a complex organization that can manage itself.

In this connection, I should regard a mob not as a formal organization, simple or complex, but a special type of informal organization, until it has formal leaders.

mal organizations are constituted of numbers of small organizations.[10] It is impossible to create a large organization except by combining small organizations.[11]

The basic organization, if measured by the number of persons simultaneously contributing to it, is usually quite small—from two to fifteen or twenty persons, and probably not having an average of more than ten. Certain special types of simple organization, however, are very large, just as in biology some cells, such as birds' eggs, are very large. The largest of such organizations which I have observed are a full orchestra or orchestra and chorus; and a public speaker and his audience, which under radio technique reaches enormous size.[12]

[10] I exclude the very extreme and special case of large audiences as being of limited pertinence to a discussion of the functions of the executive.

[11] The origins of the major organizations being historically so remote, and the processes of reorganization being apparently often directed from central points or by central authority, we are much under the delusion that large mass organizations are subdivided as a secondary process, the mass having first been created. This is the order in which intellectually we approach the understanding of most large complex organizations; it is the method of analysis, of breaking down a whole into parts. Thus, if we wish to study a government organization or a large telephone system, we may often effectively begin with the constitution, the major departments, the parent company, etc. But this procedure is as if we subdivided a trunk of a tree or a piece of flesh into fibres and membranes and finally into cells, being misled into thinking that these subdivisions developed after the existence of an undifferentiated protoplasm of the same mass.

Many theoretical and practical errors arise from employing this analytical approach except for immediate limited purposes. For it is, I think, as true of organization as it is of all living things that they grow by the multiplication of cells and begin with single cells. It is true that quite often a fusion of two existing simple or complex organizations into one complex organization takes place; but fundamentally the growth is from single-cell organizations.

[12] A descriptive catalogue and classification of organizations from the standpoint of unit size would be of interest in a more exhaustive treatment. For example, clubs furnish an illustration of rather units which are partly structured by "working" units (staff, officers, committees and official meetings of members), and temporary "playing" or "social" units.

The clue to the structural requirements of large complex organizations lies in the reason for the limitations of the size of simple organizations. The limitations are inherent in the necessities of intercommunication.[13] In Chapter VII we discussed communication between persons as an essential element of coöperative systems; it is also the limiting factor in the size of simple organizations and, therefore, a dominant factor in the structure of complex organizations. We must now consider why this is true.

Under most ordinary conditions, even with simple purposes, not many men can see what each is doing or the whole situation; nor can many communicate essential information regarding or governing specific action without a central channel or leader. But a leader likewise is limited in time (and capacity) in communicating with many persons contemporaneously, especially if they are widely separated so that he must move about. In practice a limit of usually less than fifteen persons obtains, and for many types of coöperation five or six persons is the practicable limit.

These limits are widely exceeded in certain special cases, chiefly those where the action involved is that of extreme habitual practice within narrow limits, as in military drill and orchestral performance, where there are both individual and collective habituation and a precise special system of language or some other special means of communication; and those where the action is limited substantially to one person, the others being relatively passive, as in an audience. In this case the organization is practically limited (at least for the time being) to communication in one direction only.[14] Moreover, in the case of audiences and speakers, this communication is an end in itself.

Fundamentally, communication is necessary to translate purpose into terms of the concrete action required to effect it—what to do and when and where to do it. This necessitates knowledge of the conditions of the environment, and of the action under way. Under very

[13] These limitations, therefore, arise out of the joint effect of physical, biological, and social factors. See Chapter V [of *The Functions of the Executive*].

[14] Where not limited to one direction, a leader—moderator, chairman, i.e., an executive—is required.

simple and usually temporary conditions and with small numbers of persons the communication problem often appears simple, but under many conditions, even with small numbers, a special channel of communication is required. For if all talk at once there is confusion; and there is indecision particularly as to timing of actions. This creates the necessity for a leader. The size of the unit, therefore, usually is determined by the limitations of effective leadership. These limitations depend upon (1) the complexity of purpose and technological conditions; (2) the difficulty of the communication process; (3) the extent to which communication is necessary; (4) the complexity of the personal relationships involved, that is, of the social conditions.

1. It is clear that when the purpose is not simple—that is, when its requirements are complex and not obvious, or the conditions require precision of coördinated movements, or the nature of the individual action necessary is difficult to grasp by the actor (or by the leader)—much more communication is necessary than under the contrary conditions.

2. It is also evident that the difficulty of the communication process has an important bearing on the size of the organization unit. There are many things that are difficult to communicate by words—in some matters it is impossible. When the difficulty is great it is evident that the time required may limit the number between whom communication may be effectively had; for example, communication perhaps must be accomplished by demonstration.

3. It is apparent that if each actor can see what the other is doing and can see the situation as a whole, the amount of positive communication is reduced. Thus, if five men are working together on a simple task (say pulling a boat into the water) little communication is required; but if five men are coördinating efforts under conditions such that they cannot see each other and the whole situation, constant communication is often necessary. Moreover, if men know what to do from previous experience and can work on the basis of habit and acquired skill, a minimum of communication is required; or if they are accustomed to working together, a special language which they evolve cuts down the time of communication.

4. The complexity of the relationships in any group increases with great rapidity as the number of persons in the group increases. If the simplest possible relationship between two persons is that of "knowing" each other as accomplished by a mutual introduction, then the relational complexity at the very least increases as follows:

NUMBER IN GROUP	NUMBER OF RELATIONSHIPS	INCREASE IN RELATIONSHIPS WITH EACH ADDITION TO GROUP
2	1	—
3	3	2
4	6	3
5	10	4
6	15	5
7	21	6
8	28	7
9	36	8
10	45	9
15	105	—
20	190	—
50	1225	—

The relationships between persons in a group will be "active" in a great variety of subgroupings which may constantly change. If A, B, C, D, and E constitute a group of five, then subgroups may be made as follows: ten pairs, ten triplets, five groups of four, one of five. If only one person be added to the group of five, the possible subgroups become: fifteen pairs, twenty triplets, fifteen groups of four, six groups of five, and one of six.

A person has relationships not only with others individually and with groups, but groups are related to groups. As the number of possible groups increases, the complexity of group relationship increases in greater ratio.[15]

The complexity of relationships within groups is important in two aspects: technologically and socially. Technologically, the burden of coördination, that is, the communication function of a leader, will increase in the proportion that the relationships increase; and the ability of individuals and groups without leadership to coördinate is also quickly outrun with increase in the size of groups. The same

[15] A suggestive exposition of this subject in quantitative terms is given by V. A. Graicunas' "Relationship in Organization," reprinted in *Papers on the Science of Administration*, edited by Gulick and Urwick (New York: Institute of Public Administration, 1937).

is true of the social or informal organization relationships. The capacity of persons to maintain social relationships is obviously limited. If the technological group is larger than is adapted to social limitations, the social organization groupings cannot correspond to the technological requirements. Since a large part of the communication of organizations is informal, the burden on formal channels is thereby increased.[16]

These factors, and probably others also, limit the size of the fundamental organization cell. I shall call the simple basic organization form a "unit" organization. It differs from the ideal organization of Chapter VII in that it is never found isolated from other organizations and is always subordinate to some other formal organization directly or indirectly, being ultimately subordinate to and dependent upon either a church or a state or both.

The size of a unit organization being usually restricted very narrowly by the necessities of communication, it follows that growth of organization beyond the limits so imposed can only be accomplished by the creation of new unit organizations, or by grouping together two or more unit organizations already existing. When an organization grows by the addition of the services of more persons it is compelled, if it reaches the limit of size, to establish a second unit; and henceforward it is a complex of two unit organizations. All organizations except unit organizations are a group of two or more unit organizations. Hence, a large organization of complex character consists not of the services of individuals directly but of those of subsidiary unit organizations. Nowhere in the world, I think, can there be found a large organization that is not composed of small units. We think of them as having descended from the mass, whereas the mass can only be created from the units.[17]

[16] See also discussion on p. 225 [of *The Functions of the Executive*]. I have strongly the opinion that there may be substantial variations in social satisfactions related to disparities between the size of organizations as determined technologically by organization purpose and the size of "natural" social groups. "Natural" would be affected by the personalities involved.

[17] A group of two or more unit organizations may coöperate as a whole without a formal superior organization or leader. Under many conditions

Usually when two and always when several unit organizations are combined in one complex organization, the necessities of communication impose a super-leader, who becomes, usually with assistants, an "overhead" unit of organization. Similarly, groups of groups are combined into larger wholes. The most obvious case of complex structure of this type is an army. The fact that these large organizations are built up of small unit organizations is neglected in the spectacular size that ensues, and we often pass from the whole or major divisions to "men." The resulting dismissal from the mind of the inescapable practice of unit organization often leads to utterly unrealistic attitudes regarding organization problems.

The Executive Organization

In a unit organization there are executive functions to be performed, but not necessarily by a single individual continuously. They may be performed alternately by the several persons who contributed to the organization. In complex organizations, on the other hand, the necessities of communication result almost invariably in the localization of the executive functions of the subordinate unit organizations normally in one person. This is necessary for reasons of formal communication; but it is also necessary to establish executive organizations, that is, those units specializing in the executive functions. The execu-

this is observed, especially where two small organizations (or a large and a small) work together under contract for specified purposes. The method of communication is primarily that of conference. Because of our habit of considering an organization as a group of persons rather than as systems of coöperative services of persons, the usually temporary combinations that are made as a result of contracts or agreements are not recognized as organizations, since they have no name or common officials. Most large building operations are so organized, however; and it will be readily seen that a very large part of the organized activities of today are carried on by temporary limited combinations under contracts without a general coordinating "authority." The state, through the law of contracts and the provisions of courts, is a general formal executive in these cases in limited degree; but the real general executive is custom, etc.

tives of several unit organizations as a group, usually with at least one other person as a superior, form an executive organization. Accordingly, persons specializing in the executive functions in most cases are "members" of, or contributors to, two units of organization in one complex organization—first, the so-called "working" unit, and second, the executive unit. This is clearly seen in practice, it being customary to recognize a foreman, or a superintendent of a shop section, or a captain, at one time or from one point of view as a "member" of his gang, shop crew, or company, at another time or from another point of view as a member of a "district management group," or the "shop executives' group," or the "regimental organization." Under such conditions a single concrete action or decision is an activity of two different unit organizations. This simultaneous contribution to two organizations by a single act appears to be the critical fact in all complex organization; that is, the complex is made an organic whole by it. Here again, it will be noted that the definition of formal organization as an impersonal system of efforts and influences is supported by the facts more closely in accord with concrete phenomena than the "group membership" idea. One person often functions in or contributes services to several different units of the same complex organization, as well as to different external organizations. For payroll, and many other formal purposes, it is convenient to regard every person as being "in" only one unit organization; but this is merely a matter of convenience for certain purposes, and is misleading as to the actual operation of organizations even for many other practical purposes.

The size of executive units of organizations is limited generally by the same conditions that govern the size of unit organizations of other kinds. When there are many basic working units, therefore, there must be several primary executive unit organizations, from the heads of which will be secured the personnel of superior executive units. And so on, in extensive pyramids of executive units in very large complex organizations.[18]

In summary, we may say that historically and functionally all complex organizations are built up from units of organization, and consist of many units of "working" or "basic" organizations, overlaid with units of executive organizations; and that the essential structural characteristics of complex organizations are determined by the effect of the necessity for communication upon the size of a unit organization.

[18] Professor Philip Cabot, in a published address, once quoted my opinion that organizations are best regarded as circular or spherical, with the chief executive positions in the center. This was based on discussions with him and an unpublished manuscript which he was kind enough to examine. I have, however, followed the conventional figures here, because they are well established, and because there appears to be no practicable way to diagram the system of authoritative communication that does not result in a "pyramid" (usually in two-dimensional perspectives, however) which put the chief executive positions at the top. They also are frequently located on top floors. Probably all spatial figures for organization are seriously misleading; but if they are used to cover the functioning of organizations as distinguished from its structural aspects, either the center of a circle or of a sphere better suggests the relationships. The nearest approach to this, I think, is the practice of regarding the location of G.H.Q. in field armies as *behind* the lines centrally.

The Division of Labor

CHARLES BABBAGE

Perhaps the most important principle on which the economy of a manufacture depends, is the *division of labour* amongst the persons who perform the work. The first application of this principle must have been made in a very early stage of society; for it must soon have been apparent, that a larger number of comforts and conveniences could be acquired by each individual, if one man restricted his occupation to the art of making bows, another to that of building houses, a third boats, and so on. This division of labour into trades was not, however, the result of an opinion that the general riches of the community would be increased by such an arrangement; but it must have arisen from the circumstance of each individual so employed discovering that he himself could thus make a greater profit of his labour than by pursuing more varied occupations. Society must have made considerable advances before this principle could have been carried into the workshop; for it is only in countries which have attained a high degree of civilization, and in articles in which there is a great competition amongst the producers, that the most perfect system of the division of labour is to be observed. The various principles on which the advantages of this system depend, have been much the subject of discussion amongst writers on Political Economy; but the relative importance of their influence does not appear, in all cases, to have been estimated with sufficient precision. It is my intention, in the first instance, to state shortly those principles, and then to point out what appears to me to have been omitted by those who have previously treated the subject.

1. *Of the Time Required for Learning.* It will readily be admitted, that the portion of time occupied in the acquisition of any art will depend on the difficulty of its execution; and that the greater the number of distinct processes, the longer will be the time which the apprentice must employ in acquiring it. Five or seven years have been adopted, in a great many trades, as the time considered requisite for a lad to acquire a sufficient knowledge of his art, and to enable him to repay by his labour, during the latter portion of his time, the expense incurred by his master at its commencement. If, however, instead of learning *all* the different processes for making a needle, for instance, his attention be confined to one operation, the portion of time consumed unprofitably at the commencement of his apprenticeship will be small, and all the rest of it will be beneficial to his master: and, consequently, if there be any competition amongst the masters, the apprentice will be able to make better terms, and diminish the period of his servitude. Again, the facility of acquiring skill in a single process, and the early period of life at which it can be made a source of profit, will induce a greater number of parents to bring up their children to it; and from this circumstance also, the number of workmen being increased, the wages will soon fall.

•2. *Of Waste of Materials in Learning.* A certain quantity of material will, in all cases, be consumed unprofitably, or spoiled by every person who learns an art; and as he applies himself to each new process, he will waste some of the raw material, or of the partly manufactured commodity. But if each man commit this waste in acquiring successively every process, the quantity of waste will be much greater than if each person confine his attention to one process; in this view of the subject, therefore, the division of labour will diminish the price of production.

From *On the Economy of Machinery and Manufactures*. London: Charles Knight, 1832, pp. 169–176.

3. Another advantage resulting from the division of labour is, *the saving of that portion of time which is always lost in changing from one occupation to another.* When the human hand, or the human head, has been for some time occupied in any kind of work, it cannot instantly change its employment with full effect. The muscles of the limbs employed have acquired a flexibility during their exertion, and those not in action a stiffness during rest, which renders every change slow and unequal in the commencement. Long habit also produces in the muscles exercised a capacity for enduring fatigue to a much greater degree than they could support under other circumstances. A similar result seems to take place in any change of mental exertion; the attention bestowed on the new subject not being so perfect at first as it becomes after some exercise.

4. *Change of Tools.* The employment of different tools in the successive processes is another cause of the loss of time in changing from one operation to another. If these tools are simple, and the change is not frequent, the loss of time is not considerable; but in many processes of the arts the tools are of great delicacy, requiring accurate adjustment every time they are used; and in many cases the time employed in adjusting bears a large proportion to that employed in using the tool. The sliding-rest, the dividing and the drilling-engine, are of this kind; and hence, in manufactories of sufficient extent, it is found to be good economy to keep one machine constantly employed in one kind of work: one lathe, for example, having a screw motion to its sliding-rest along the whole length of its bed, is kept constantly making cylinders; another, having a motion for equalizing the velocity of the work at the point at which it passes the tool, is kept for facing surfaces; whilst a third is constantly employed in cutting wheels.

5. *Skill Acquired by Frequent Repetition of the Same Processes.* The constant repetition of the same process necessarily produces in the workman a degree of excellence and rapidity in his particular department, which is never possessed by a person who is obliged to execute many different processes. This rapidity is still further increased from the circumstance that most of the operations in factories, where

the division of labour is carried to a considerable extent, are paid for as piece-work. It is difficult to estimate in numbers the effect of this cause upon production. In nail-making, Adam Smith has stated, that it is almost three to one; for, he observes, that a smith accustomed to make nails, but whose whole business has not been that of a nailer, can make only from eight hundred to a thousand per day; whilst a lad who had never exercised any other trade, can make upwards of two thousand three hundred a day.

In different trades, the economy of production arising from the last-mentioned cause will necessarily be different. The case of nail-making is, perhaps, rather an extreme one. It must, however, be observed, that, in one sense, this is not a permanent source of advantage; for, though it acts at the commencement of an establishment, yet every month adds to the skill of the workmen; and at the end of three or four years they will not be very far behind those who have never practised any other branch of their art. Upon an occasion when a large issue of bank-notes was required, a clerk at the Bank of England signed his name, consisting of seven letters, including the initial of his Christian name, five thousand three hundred times during eleven working hours, besides arranging the notes he had signed in parcels of fifty each.

6. *The Division of Labour Suggests the Contrivance of Tools and Machinery to Execute its Processes.* When each process, by which any article is produced, is the sole occupation of one individual, his whole attention being devoted to a very limited and simple operation, improvements in the form of his tools, or in the mode of using them, are much more likely to occur to his mind, than if it were distracted by a greater variety of circumstances. Such an improvement in the tool is generally the first step towards a machine. If a piece of metal is to be cut in a lathe, for example, there is one particular angle at which the cutting-tool must be held to insure the cleanest cut; and it is quite natural that the idea of fixing the tool at that angle should present itself to an intelligent workman. The necessity of moving the tool slowly, and in a direction parallel to itself, would suggest the use of a screw, and thus arises the sliding-rest. It was probably the idea of mounting a chisel in a frame, to

prevent its cutting too deeply, which gave rise to the common carpenter's plane. In cases where a blow from a hammer is employed, experience teaches the proper force required. The transition from the hammer held in the hand to one mounted upon an axis, and lifted regularly to a certain height by some mechanical contrivance, requires perhaps a greater degree of invention than those just instanced; yet it is not difficult to perceive, that, if the hammer always falls from the same height, its effect must be always the same.

When each process has been reduced to the use of some simple tool, the union of all these tools, actuated by one moving power, constitutes a machine. In contriving tools and simplifying processes, the operative workmen are, perhaps, most successful; but it requires far other habits to combine into one machine these scattered arts. A previous education as a workman in the peculiar trade, is undoubtedly a valuable preliminary; but in order to make such combinations with any reasonable expectation of success, an extensive knowledge of machinery, and the power of making mechanical drawings, are essentially requisite. These accomplishments are now much more common than they were formerly; and their absence was, perhaps, one of the causes of the multitude of failures in the early history of many of our manufactures.

Such are the principles usually assigned as the causes of the advantage resulting from the division of labour. As in the view I have taken of the question, the most important and influential cause has been altogether unnoticed, I shall re-state those principles in the words of Adam Smith:

The great increase in the quantity of work, which, in consequence of the division of labour, the same number of people are capable of performing, is owing to three different circumstances: first, to the increase of dexterity in every particular workman; secondly, to the saving of time, which is commonly lost in passing from one species of work to another; and, lastly, to the invention of a great number of machines which facilitate and abridge labour, and enable one man to do the work of many.

Now, although all these are important causes, and each has its influence on the result; yet it appears to me, that any explanation of the cheapness of manufactured articles, as consequent upon the division of labour, would be incomplete if the following principle were omitted to be stated.

*That the master manufacturer, by dividing the work to be executed into different processes, each requiring different degrees of skill or of force, can purchase exactly that precise quantity of both which is necessary for each process; whereas, if the whole work were executed by one workman, that person must possess sufficient skill to perform the most difficult, and sufficient strength to execute the most laborious, of the operations into which the art is divided.**

* I have already stated that this principle presented itself to me after a personal examination of a number of manufactories and workshops devoted to different purposes; but I have since found that it had been distinctly pointed out, in the work of Gioja, *Nuovo Prospetto delle Scienze Economiche*, 6 tom. 4to. Milano, 1815, tom. i. capo iv.

Organisation and Co-ordination:

Principles

L. URWICK

Organisation a Technical Problem. The word "organisation" as it is used here has a strictly limited and technical meaning. In common parlance the word is used very loosely. A man may be described as "a great organiser," because he is energetic and forceful and ruthless so that he secures quick results. In fact, the application of those qualities to a delicate human situation may be calculated to make chaos of the various relationships which have hitherto governed the performance of the undertaking. The man is in fact an eminent disorganiser. When mistakes are made people often say, "there must be something wrong with the organisation." There is no "must" about it. The organisation in the technical sense may be excellent. But one or more people in key positions are nitwits and the chief is either unaware of it or too weak to get rid of them.

This looseness in using the word "organisation" is merely a special case of a general lack of precision in thinking and talking about social groups. The most important fact about all social groups is that each of them consists of human beings, each individual having a highly complex life of his or her own. The correct analogy in considering such groups must be the analogy with the living organism —the biological parallel. But men and women are still, as yet, unaccustomed to thinking scientifically about themselves and one another. For this reason, the mechanistic parallel can be very helpful in discussing organisation. Another name for it, of course, is "the engineering approach."

From *The Elements of Administration*. New York: Harper and Brothers, 1943, pp. 35–55. Reprinted with permission of the publisher.

The Engineering Approach. If a man's automobile stalls he may abuse it and its maker in a first moment of pardonable irritation. But he does not imagine seriously that kissing its radiator or kicking its differential, still less putting it in a concentration camp, will be of great assistance. And if it happens to be a Model T Ford, he will not assume immediately that it is basically different from other kinds of automobiles. The assumption is that it came off much the same kind of assembly line as the rest, and that the only way to make it go is to understand how it works. A universal acceptance of those two simple axioms with reference to human beings would simplify very greatly international and other arrangements. Similarly men distinguish quite clearly between building an automobile and driving it. And they break down the process of building it into design and manufacture. But when they deal with social groups they are very apt to apply the term "organisation" indifferently to *all* the parallel processes.

Here it is used strictly of the first process only—designing the machine. Building the machine, finding and training individuals to fill the various groups of duties and responsibilities which result from the design is part of that aspect of Administration which Fayol calls Command. Driving the machine, holding the individuals who have been selected and trained in constant correlation, is also in part Command and it is the whole of that aspect of Administration which Fayol has called Co-ordination.

Organisation considered strictly in this limited sense may be defined very simply as

determining what activities are necessary to any purpose (or 'plan') and arranging them in groups which may be assigned to individuals.

Manifestly that is a drawing-office job. It is a designing process. And it may be objected with a great deal of experience to support the contention that organisation is never done that way . . . human organisation. Nine times out of ten it is impossible to start with a clean sheet. The organiser has to make the best possible use of the human material that is already available. And in 89 out of those 90 per cent. of cases he has to adjust jobs round to fit the man: he can't change the man to fit the job. He can't sit down in a cold-blooded, detached spirit and draw an ideal structure, an optimum distribution of duties and responsibilities and relationships, and then expect the infinite variety of human nature to fit into it.

The Necessity of Planning. To which the reply is that he can and he should. If he has not got a clean sheet, that is no earthly reason why he should not make the slight effort of imagination required to assume that he has a clean sheet. It is not impossible to forget provisionally the personal facts—that old Brown is admirably methodical but wanting in initiative, that young Smith got into a mess with Robinson's wife and that the two men must be kept at opposite ends of the building, that Jones is one of those creatures who can think like a Wrangler about other people's duties but is given to periodic amnesia about certain aspects of his own.

He should never for a moment pretend that these difficulties don't exist. They do exist: they are realities. Nor, when he has drawn up an ideal plan of organisation, is it likely that he will be able to fit in all the existing human material perfectly. There will be small adjustments of the job to the man in all kinds of directions. But those adjustments can be made without harm, provided they are conscious adjustments, deliberate and temporary deviations from pattern in order to deal with idiosyncrasy. There is a world of difference between such modifications and drifting into an unworkable organisation because Green has a fancy for combining bits of two incompatible functions, or White is "empire building"—a technical term describing smash-and-grab raids on other people's responsibilities—or Black has always looked after the canteen, so when he is promoted to Sales Manager he might just as

well continue to sell buns internally, though the main product of the business happens to be battleships.

What is suggested, is that problems of organisation should be handled *in the right order.* Personal adjustments must be made, in so far as they are necessary. But fewer of them will be necessary and they will present fewer deviations from what is logical and simple, if the organiser first makes a plan, a design—to which he would work if he had the ideal human material. He should expect to be driven from it here and there. But he will be driven from it far less and his machine will work much more smoothly if he *starts* with a plan. If he starts with a motley collection of human oddities and tries to organise to fit them all in, thinking first of their various shapes and sizes and colours, he may have a patchwork quilt; he will not have an organisation.

Human nature is a jig-saw puzzle in any large undertaking. Jig-saw experts view with scorn and derision the weak-minded people who look at the picture first. The wole point of the game is to start with a mixed heap of unrelated pieces and puzzle it out. To know from the beginning what the final design is like, is unsporting, like reading the last chapter of a detective story first. But, treating the organisation of social groups, which means making or marring other peoples' lives, in this lighthearted and childish spirit is illogical, cruel, wasteful and inefficient. Every administrator should have posted up in his office Browning's lines

It's an awkward thing to play with souls,
And matter enough to save one's own.

Lack of Design Is Illogical, Cruel, Wasteful and Inefficient. It is illogical because in good engineering practice design must come first. Similarly in good social practice design should come first. Logically it is inconceivable that any individual should be appointed to a position carrying a large salary, without a clear idea of the part which that position is meant to play in the general social pattern of which it is a component, the responsibilities and relationships attached to it, and the standard of performance which is expected in return for the expenditure. It is as stupid as to attempt to order an expensive piece of machinery without a specification.

It is cruel because the main sufferers from a lack of design in organisation are the individuals who work in the undertaking. If an employer buys a man without any clear idea in his own mind of the exact duties for which he requires him and the kind of qualifications needed to discharge those duties, the chances are that he will blame the man if the results do not correspond with his vague notion of what he wanted him for.

It is wasteful because unless jobs are clearly put together along lines of functional specialisation it is impossible to train new men to succeed to positions as the incumbents are promoted, resign or retire. A man cannot be trained to take over another's special personal experience: and yet if jobs are fitted to men rather than men to jobs that is precisely what the employer must try to do. Consequently, every change in personnel becomes a crisis, an experiment in personalities. It is difficult enough to find suitable individuals to fill positions of responsibility when one half of the equation is "given," that is, when the job is defined. When both the job and the man are uncertain, unknown quantities, hours and days are likely to be expended in fruitless discussion and indecision.

It is inefficient, because if an organisation is not founded on principles, then those directing it have nothing to fall back on but personalities. The personal touch is important. Kindliness, tact, generosity of spirit as between colleagues are invaluable lubricants in any kind of undertaking: from superior to subordinate they are an obvious duty. But the administrator who tries to substitute amiability for definite planning in questions of organisation will find sooner rather than later that "the personal touch" issues in an epidemic of personal touchiness. Unless there are principles on which he can fall back and which are understood by everyone in the undertaking, it is inevitable that in matters of promotion and similar issues men will start "playing politics." And as Mary Follett has observed, within any undertaking "playing politics is a deplorable form of coercion."

Emphasis has been laid on this question of thinking consciously and technically about organisation, of laying out structure first and not thinking about individuals till structure has been determined, because it is still rare to find any general acceptance of this principle. The number of human institutions which do put correct structure first and politics second is very limited. The majority of social groups being left to grow like Topsy find, sooner rather than later, that Topsy has married Turvy.

In short, a very large proportion of the friction and confusion in current society, with its manifest consequences in human suffering, may be traced directly to faulty organisation in the structural sense. A machine will not run smoothly when fundamental engineering principles have been ignored in its construction. Attempts to run it will inevitably impose quite unnecessary and unbearable strain on its components.

The Principle of Continuity. Apart from the effect on the existing situation, there is an important subsidiary principle applicable to organisation as a whole which makes it an imperative responsibility of the administrator that he should have a plan. That is the Principle of Continuity. Institutions in corporate form are usually, at all events in theory, immortal. Their potential life stretches far beyond the brief span of the individuals associated with them at any particular moment. And to provide for that future as well as for the present, is a direct obligation of those who administer them. Thus the structure should be such as to provide, not only for the activities immediately necessary to secure the objects of the enterprise, but for the continuation of such activities for the full period of operation contemplated in its establishment. This involves a continuous supply of the necessary personnel and arrangements for the systematic improvement of every aspect of operation. Such continuity is impossible without a plan of organisation.

The "Practical Man" Fallacy. There is a very general feeling that to be hazy and opportunist about organisation is in some mysterious way "practical," while to try to draw up proper charts and procedures is somehow "theoretical."

For this attitude of mind there are a number of reasons.

In the first place successful administrators, whose example and teaching must necessarily carry great influence, have usually been brought up in the empirical school. And by the time they are successful they are very apt to attribute their achievements to unique personal qualities rather than to adherence to principles. Their performance as organisers seems to them part of the "mystery" of their art, something which can only be conveyed by "experience," not something which can be reduced to writing and discussed by comparative apprentices.

In the early days of machine industry, the engineer was essentially a handicraftsman. He worked with his tools directly on his material. Many inventions and improvements were developed empirically at the bench, long before they were committed to paper. It was only gradually that the drawing office asserted its priority, ceasing merely to record and becoming the source of initiative. At a later stage, with the development of Scientific Management, further elements of the engineer's work were specialised in planning departments and specified for him on instruction cards. At both stages he felt some resentment at the changes in working habits and outlook involved. In the absence of any recognised science of the subject, administration has been hitherto a handicraft job. There is no reason why practical administrators should behave differently, either immediately or in the long run, from the engineer at his bench.

Moreover, in the absence of any general recognition of organisation principles, the successful administrator must perforce spend a great deal of his time "playing politics." It is the only way to get things done, however much he may dislike it. And, quite rightly, the major part of his time and attention as an administrator will be absorbed by personal problems. He cannot escape them by planning his organisation first: he can only facilitate their solution.

Thus, even those, and they are rare, who are sufficiently detached and impersonal to be conscious of the nature of their own experience, are apt to be a little impatient with the structural aspect of organisation. Fayol, for instance, probably of successful industrialists the most advanced thinker of the last fifty years on the general question of administration, wrote on this subject:

> If we could eliminate the human factor, it would be easy enough to build up an organisation; anyone could do it if they had some idea of current practice and had the necessary capital. But we cannot build up an effective organisation simply by dividing

men into groups and giving them functions; we must know how to adapt the organisation to the requirements of the case, and how to find the necessary men and put each one in the place where he can be of most service; we need, in fact, many substantial qualities.[1]

Nevertheless, the effort to work out principles of organisation structure *first*, and apart from the personal problems which arise from them, is not only worth while from the standpoint of the individual, but is of immense social importance. It is also the most difficult of all the aspects of administration.

The Main Concepts. The first task in any such attempt is to define terms. Four concepts are constantly recurring in discussion of organisation. They are:

DUTIES, which are the activities which the individual is required to perform by virtue of his membership in the organisation.

RESPONSIBILITY, which is accountability for the performance of duties.

POWER, which is the ability to get things done: that is to say, it is a function of knowledge, skill and personal qualities.

AUTHORITY, which is the right to require action of others. It may be

1. formal, i.e. conferred by the organisation;
2. technical, i.e. implicit in special knowledge or skill; or
3. personal, i.e. conferred by seniority or popularity.

The principles which should guide the administrator in "determining the activities necessary to any purpose and arranging them in groups which may be allotted to individuals" have been outlined by Mooney and Reiley. They are given in outline in Table 1: It is particularly interesting to note that while Fayol's work was entirely unknown to Mooney and Reiley when they wrote their comparative study of organisation in government, military, ecclesiastical and industrial undertakings,[2] and while Fayol, as has been shown,

[1] *General and Industrial Organisation* (English translation), p. 46.
[2] *Onward Industry.*

Table 1. The Principles of Organization and Co-ordination

The purpose of all organisation is to unify effort—that is, co-ordination. "This term expresses the principles of organisation *in toto;* nothing less. This does not mean that there are no subordinated principles; it simply means that all the others are contained in this one of co-ordination. The others are simply the principles through which co-ordination operates, and thus becomes effective" (p. 19). ("Co-ordinate operations and efforts"—A.D.4.)

1. PRINCIPLE	2. PROCESS	3. EFFECT
		ASSIGNMENT AND INTEGRATION OF FUNCTIONS
1. AUTHORITY Co-ordination finds its principle in authority ("Unity of Command"—A.D.13 and P.4).	THE SCALAR PROCESS Enters into process with the scalar chain, hierarchy or "line" ("The Hierarchy"—P.12).	And takes effect in the assignment and integration of functions ("Division of Labour"—P.1).
	THE SCALAR PROCESS finds its principle in	
2. LEADERSHIP ("Unity of management"—P.3.)	DELEGATION Leadership enters into process with delegation ("Encourage the desire for responsibility"—A.D.8).	FUNCTIONAL DEFINITION And takes effect in functional definition ("Define duties clearly"—A.D.7).

ASSIGNMENT AND INTEGRATION OF FUNCTIONS

"In all forms of organisation three main functions can be distinguished. These are related as principle, process and effect."

3. DETERMINATIVE FUNCTIONALISM (Legislative)	APPLICATIVE FUNCTIONALISM (Executive)	INTERPRETATIVE FUNCTIONALISM (Judicial)
("Make decisions which are clear, distinct and precise"—A.D.5.)	("See that the plan of operations is strictly carried out"—A.D.1.)	("Impose penalties for mistakes and blunders"—A.D.10 and P.2.)

Notes

1. The arrangement used in this table is taken from *Onward Industry,* by James D. Mooney and Alan C. Reiley, and the quotations and references not in brackets are from this book.

2. . . . . [Q]uotations and references in . . . [parentheses] are from Henri Fayol's *General and Industrial Administration.*

3. The logical arrangement adopted by Mooney and Reiley and used in . . . [this table] is founded on *Das Logische, seine Gesetze und Kategorien,* by Louis F. Anderson (Leipzig, 1929).

is impatient of logic in this field, in his aspects of administration and in his empirical lists of Principles and Administrative duties there are statements exactly corresponding to each of Mooney and Reiley's nine principles.

Applying the Principle of the Objective. The first point to remember is the position of Organisation in the general scheme of administration. . . . It comes in the second line. It is the way by which forecasting enters into process. That is to say, it is not an end in itself: it is a means to an end. Because Administration is only one of the six essential functions in any undertaking, forecasting itself postulates a prior decision as to the main objective and general policy of the enterprise. Moreover, forecasting cannot take effect in a plan unless a great deal of detailed precision has been used in defining the objective. That applies also to Organization and to every part of any organisation. The organisation should only exist in order to carry out some specific purpose implicit in the forecast and the plan. Every piece of it should make a definite and authorised contribution to that purpose. Otherwise there is no reason for its existence.

It is important to remember this, especially in examining an organisation already set up. Once an enterprise is in being jobs are created. That is to say, individuals secure emoluments and rank and other advantages from the existence of that piece of the organisation. The whole momentum of their customary habits of work, both individual and collective, is added to these arguments for keeping that particular part of the organisation in action. In short, quite apart from the objectives of the undertaking considered as an entity, all kinds of personal and group incentives come into being internally, all directed positively towards maintaining the *status quo*.

It cannot be too strongly emphasised that these motives may have nothing whatever to do with the objectives of the organisation as such. They constitute a completely separate series of considerations which, if they run counter to the true objectives of the undertaking, should be eliminated or disregarded. To do so demands both vigilance and courage. Which is why little sections are found so commonly in every type of undertaking busily engaged in quite useless tasks—compiling regular statistics, for instance, to answer a question which was asked once five or ten years ago and has never been repeated since. The first questions which every Consultant asks himself in face of every job are: "What does this piece of work contribute towards the main objectives of this undertaking?" "Is it really necessary?"

Co-ordination. The employment of more than one person towards a given end necessarily involves division of labour. The purpose of organisation is to secure that this division works smoothly, that there is unity of effort or, in other words, co-ordination. Mooney and Reiley wrote of co-ordination:

> This term expresses the principles of organisation *in toto*; nothing less. This does not mean that there are no subordinated

principles, it simply means that all the others are contained in this one of co-ordination. The others are simply the principles through which co-ordination operates and becomes effective.[3]

Fayol placed it fourth in his list of Administrative Duties—"Co-ordinate operations and efforts." In so far as co-ordination is a dynamic activity, a process involving principles of its own, it will be discussed later. Here it is sufficient to note that it is the internal objective underlying all organisation. The purpose of the undertaking to which the organisation or a part of the organisation contributes is external. The purpose of organisation itself is co-ordination.

Authority. Mooney and Reiley identified the principle at the root of the process of organisation as authority, by which they meant formal authority. Fayol repeated the same principle twice in his thirteenth Administrative Duty and fourth Principle—"Unity of Command." It is impossible to conceive of the existence of organisation at all unless some person or persons are in a position "to require action of others." The source of that authority is not significant in the study of organisation. It may be authority conferred by the agreement of those over whom it is exercised, as in a democratic State. It may be authority acquired because those over whom it is exercised have accepted a contract of employment, as in business enterprises in a capitalist society. It may be authority which adheres to ownership, as with the institution of slavery. It is interesting to note that Hitler, who has enjoyed a more absolute dictatorship and a more effective apparatus for making things unpleasant for his compatriots who disagree with him than any person in the history of Christendom, had recently to seek from the German people, at all events in form, a reaffirmation and extension of his authority.

It is true that the degree of authority exercised, and particularly the amount of reference required before action is taken, may affect the speed at which any given human organisation can be driven. And a failure to allocate the necessary authority at all at one or other of the essential levels or in respect of a vital function may cause organisation to work very

[3] *Onward Industry*, p. 19.

badly. But that has nothing to do with the political philosophy on which the authority is founded. It is simply an example of ignorance of organisation principles and consequent bad management. As long as the possibility of a correct delegation of authority is provided for and is not inhibited by the constitutional practice, whether written or traditional, of the unit concerned, it is immaterial to the study of organisation whence it is derived.

Authority and Responsibility Must Correspond. An addendum to the principle of authority is provided by F. W. Taylor. He pointed out that it is essential to the conception of authority that authority and responsibility should correspond. Any individual or group to whom is assigned authority for which he is or they are not held accountable to someone will tend to exercise that authority with decreasing effectiveness. That is the root of the old saying that "power corrupts": it is "the Achilles heel" of autocracy in all its forms. To hold a group or individual accountable for activities of any kind without assigning to him or them the necessary authority to discharge that responsibility is manifestly both unsatisfactory and inequitable. It is of great importance to smooth working that at all levels authority and responsiiblity should be coterminous and coequal.

The Scalar Process. Authority enters into process with what Mooney and Reiley have called "the scalar process." Just as "the supreme co-ordinating authority must rest somewhere and in some form in every organisation," so "it is equally essential to the very idea and concept of organisation that there must be a process, formal in character, through which this co-ordinating authority operates from the top throughout the entire structure of the organised body." [4]

They themselves comment that "this is the same form in organisation which is sometimes called hierarchical." Fayol gives as his ninth principle "the Hierarchy." It is unnecessary to comment on this obvious requirement except to utter a warning against the common assumption that the necessity for a scalar chain of authority implies that every action must climb painfully through every link in the chain, whether its course is upwards or downwards.

[4] *Onward Industry*, p. 31.

Provided there is proper confidence and loyalty between superiors and subordinates, and both parties take the trouble to keep the other informed in matters in which they should have a concern, the "scalar process" does *not* imply that there should be no short cuts. It is concerned with authority and, provided the authority is recognised and no attempt is made to evade or to supersede it, there is ample room for avoiding in matters of action the childish practices of going upstairs one step at a time or running up one ladder and down another when there is nothing to prevent a direct approach on level ground.

The correct cure for that kind of nonsense is a healthy and humorous contempt. A brilliant mock military manual called *The Young Officer's Guide to Knowledge*, by "the Senior Major." contains the sage advice: "You are never asked for your reasons in writing unless it is strongly suspected that you have none." And that, in fact, is how, in the last war at all events, a well-led military formation worked. The "proper channels, the official channels," were there and were used to confirm and to record agreement already reached by far quicker and friendlier means of communication. If an officer had to use them before that point was attained, it was rightly regarded as a confession of failure, an admission that his organisational arrangements were not supported by good personal relations.

It is both right and proper that every organisation should have its formal scalar chain, just as every well-built house has its drainage system. But it is as unnecessary to use the formal channels exclusively or primarily as the sole means of communication as it is unnecessary to pass one's time in the drains.

Distinguishing and Correlating Functions. The scalar chain differentiates between different levels or gradations of authority. Authority delegates part of its own authority over others. But always at the end there is the last link in the chain where what is delegated is not authority, but responsibility for the discharge of specific functions. Functionalism is used by Mooney and Reiley in this specific sense to express differentiation or distinction between *different kinds of duties* as contrasted with *different levels of authority*. Always in organisation grouping of activities runs in these two contrary senses; one in which the dividing lines are vertical, indicating kinds or varieties of activity, and the other in which the dividing lines are horizontal, indicating levels of authority. It is impossible to fix any activity accurately in any organisation unless it is placed in *both* these senses, just as it is impossible to fix a point on a map or chart except in terms of both ordinates.

The end and aim of formal co-ordination within any undertaking is simply the correlation of functions, of all the detailed activities necessary to its purpose. The "scalar process" is not an end in itself. It is simply a means to the ultimate end of organisation, which is the assigning and correlation of functional activities. As already noted, wherever more than one person is engaged in any joint undertaking there must be division of labour. And this actual phrase—"Division of Labour"—is used by Fayol as his first principle to express the same truth as is emphasised by Mooney and Reiley. Thus authority moves through the scalar process to the functional effect—assigning and correlating activities.

Specialisation. F. W. Taylor, again, adds a most important subsidiary principle to this one of functional differentiation—the principle of specialisation. "The work of every person in the organisation should be confined as far as possible to the performance of a single leading function." More waste and friction occurs in human organisations through failure to observe this principle, and their is more to be gained by its careful application than in any other single direction. In one sense, it is only immemorial wisdom—"let the cobbler stick to his last."

But its infraction is equally immemorial folly. There is the constant human temptation for men to enlarge their area of responsibility in order to add to their sense of self-importance. There is the equally human tendency to resist like a bulldog the ablation of functions previously performed in a spirit of happy ignorance in order that that performance may be improved by specialisation. The things that the Royal Army Medical Corps said about Florence Nightengale when she pointed out that nursing should be specialised and entrusted to women are unprintable. The change seems commonplace now. The language employed at the time was extravagant. Nevertheless, specialisation is the way of progress in human organisation. It is exactly parallel in the mental sphere to the principle of simplification in the material sphere emphasised in connection with planning. Specialisation enables a man to think about one subject or one group of allied subjects with enormous economy in mental effort and consequent strengthening of the power and reach of his knowledge of his function. If it tempts him to know "more and more about less and less," that is due to faulty leadership or to defects in his basic education.

This consideration leads direct to the second line of the logical square. The Scalar Process has its own Principle, Process and Effect. The principle is Leadership, the process is Delegation and the effect is Functional Definition.

Leadership. As Mooney and Reiley observe, "leadership represents authority, and it must possess all of the authority necessary to the exercise of its leadership."[5] There have been organisations where the supreme co-ordinating authority exercised its own leadership. Cases may be found in the autocratic empires of antiquity, and it may still happen in one-man proprietary businesses. But this is not generally true of any modern form of organisation. Usually the supreme co-ordinating authority appoints, elects or designates its leaders. Thus "leadership becomes the form which authority assumes where it enters into process."[6]

Where, for instance, the supreme co-ordinating authority is in corporate form it cannot lead. Leadership is largely a psychological activity, a matter of personality and example. As a Chief of Staff of the United States Army once observed, "the leader must be everything that he desires his subordinates to be. Men think as their leaders think—and men know unerringly how their leaders think." A Council or Committee cannot by definition exercise this kind of personal inspiration. It is possible to feel enthusiasm for an individual. It is next door to impossible to experience enthusiasm for a collection of individuals, at all events all at the same time.

Failure to recognise this limitation in corporate forms of authority and to provide for subordinate leadership is a common organisational mistake in democratic countries. In

[5] *Op. cit.,* p. 32.
[6] *Op. cit.,* p. 33.

English history the control of the Army in peace never worked well as long as the country was divided into twenty or more military districts. When these districts were reorganised into seven commands, the General Officers Commanding-in-Chief were big enough to supply to leadership which could not be expected of an Army Council. The more recent regionalisation of Post Office administration is another example. The Citrine Report recommended the appointment in each Region of a full-time Regional Director of Production. It was obvious that without provision for executive leadership the Regional Boards could not and would not work. As Boards they could not supply the necessary leadership: the central departments in Whitehall were too remote and were, moreover, in competition with each other for productive facilities.

It is interesting to note that, despite the tremendous concentration of authority in Nazi Germany, great attention has been paid to leadership in the modern German Army. William L. Shirer records from personal observation the sharp distinction between the French and German generals in 1940—the former

> civilised, intellectual, frail, ailing old men, the latter a complete contrast. More than one not yet forty, most of them in the forties, a few at the very top in their fifties. And they have the characteristics of youth —dash, daring, imagination, initiative and physical prowess. General von Reichenau, Commander of a whole army in Poland, was the first to cross the Vistula River. He swam it.[7]

The relations between officers and men have been changed on similar lines.

> In Paris I recall a Colonel who was treating a dozen privates to an excellent lunch in a little Basque restaurant off the Avenue de l'Opéra. When lunch was over, he drew, with all the care of a loving father, a plan for them to visit the sights of Paris. The respect of these ordinary soldiers for their Colonel would be hard to exaggerate. Yet it was not for his rank, but for the man.[8]

This personal equation in leadership emphasises the importance of two subsidiary principles.

The first of these is "fair play." The leader must be sensitive to the rights of all and take measures to ensure that they are maintained for every individual throughout the enterprise. As a corollary, the leaders must ebgin by playing fair with each other. As Mooney and Reiley observe:

> One of the dangers involved in the growth of any industrial organisation is the struggle and lust for power that appears among the leaders themselves with the consequent loss of fine discipline and the subordination of the ambitions of the men at the top to the good of the group. Where such conditions appear it is not alone the subordinates who suffer. The very organisation itself is threatened with disintegration.[9]

The second is the full acceptance by the leader of his own responsibility. The responsibility of a superior for the acts of his subordinates is absolute. This does not mean that a subordinate can never make a mistake or that his chief should never discuss him with his own superiors as a human being, with limitations as well as virtues. It does mean that a chief should never allow a subordinate to be criticised or penalised, except by himself, for any action taken by that subordinate within the chief's area of responsibility. Only with a complete appreciation of and adherence to that principle on the part of the chief can he expect loyalty and confidence from those working under him.

Delegation. Leadership enters into process with delegation. Fayol expresses the same idea in his eighth Administrative Duty—"Encourage the desire for Responsibility." Without delegation no organisation can function effectively. Yet, lack of the courage to delegate properly and of knowledge how to do it, is one of the most general causes of failure in organisation. It is a problem older than history. When Jethro visited Moses, Moses was "staggering under the same problem that has killed many a modern business man." He was wise enough to take his father-in-law's advice.

---

[7] *Berlin Diary*, p. 343.
[8] *Ibid.*, p. 346.

[9] *Onward Industry*, p. 34.

[He] chose able men out of all Israel, and made them heads over the people, rulers of thousands, rulers of hundreds, rulers of fifties, and rulers of tens. And they judged the people at all seasons: *the hard cases they brought unto Moses, but every small matter they judged themselves.*[10]

Two thousand years later it was still fresh enough to call forth F. W. Taylor's formulation of what he called "the exception principle."

As Mooney and Reiley record:

One of the tragedies of business experience is the frequency with which men, always efficient in anything they personally can do, will finally be crushed and fail under the weight of accumulated duties that they do not know and cannot learn how to delegate. Whether this condition is due to egotism which manifests itself in a distrust of the relative capacity of others, or to a training which has always been confined to a narrow horizon, and has thus destroyed the capacity to envisage greater undertakings, the effect is always the same. Under such conditions growth through delegation is absolutely prevented by the character of the leadership.[11]

Sir Ian Hamilton has given a vivid example from personal experience of how failure to delegate creates work:

In 1896 I was Deputy Quartermaster-General at Simla; then, perhaps still, one of the hardest-worked billets in Asia. After a long office day, I used to get back home to dinner pursued by a pile of files three or four feet high. The Quartermaster-General, my boss, was a clever, delightful work-glutton. So we sweated and ran together for a while a neck-and-neck race with our piles of files, but I was the younger, and he was the first to be ordered off by the doctors to Europe. Then I, at the age of forty-three, stepped into his shoes and became officiating Quartermaster-General in India. Unluckily, the Government at that moment was in a very stingy mood. They refused to provide pay to fill the post I was vacating and Sir George White, the C.-in-C., asked

me to duplicate myself and do the double work. My heart sank, but there was nothing for it but to have a try. The day came; the Q.M.G. went home *and with him went the whole of his share of the work.* As for my own share, the hard twelve hours' task melted by some magic into the Socialists' dream of a six hours' day. How was that? Because when a question came up from one of the Departments, I had formerly been forced to compose a long minute upon it, explaining the case, putting my own views, and endeavouring to persuade the Quartermaster-General to accept them. He was a highly conscientious man and if he differed from me he liked to put on record his reasons—several pages of reasons. Or, if he agreed with me, still he liked to agree in his own words and "put them on record." Now, when I became Q.M.G. and D.Q.M.G. rolled into one, I studied the case as formerly, but there my work ended: I had not to persuade my own subordinates; I had no superior except the Commander-in-Chief, who was delighted to be left alone: I just gave an order—quite a simple matter unless a man's afraid: "Yes," I said, or "No!"

The moral of my reminiscence is plain: the higher up the ladder you climb the less you have to do; provided (1) you have some courage; (2) you have some trust; (3) you have your office so organised that you don't have to deal with more than three or four responsible heads. . . . *If big men are overwhelmed with detail it is always their own fault.*[12]

The Span of Control. The quotation emphasises a subsidiary principle bearing on delegation which has been worked out mathematically by Mr. Graicunas. No superior can supervise directly the work of more than five or, at the most, six subordinates whose work interlocks. The reason for this is simple. What is supervised is not only the individuals, but the permutations and combinations of the relationships between them. And while the former increase in arithmetical progression with the addition of each fresh subordinate, the latter increase by geometrical progression. If a superior adds a sixth to five immediate subordinates he increases his opportunity of delegation

[10] *Exod.* xviii.
[11] *Onward Industry*, p. 39.
[12] *The Soul and Body of an Army*, pp. 235, 236.

by 20 per cent. but he adds over 100 per cent. to the number of relationships he has to take into account. Because ultimately it is based on the limitations imposed by the human span of attention, this principle is called *The Span of Control*.[13]

Definition of Duties. Delegation takes effect in functional definition, expressed by Fayol in his seventh Administrative Duty—"define duties clearly." It should be unnecessary to insist on the importance of precision in this matter. But the influence of vagueness in organisation on morale is not always fully appreciated.

To quote Mooney and Reiley once more:

How often do we hear it said of business institutions that the organisations are all "shot through" with politics. . . . Such conditions, when they exist, are really due to inattention on the part of the management to the necessities of formal organisation, and the application of its principles. . . . Management that is inattentive to the definition of subordinate functions is almost sure to be just as disorderly in the exercise of its own. . . . The opposite type of management, which regards the exact definition of every job and every function in its relation to other jobs and functions as of first importance, may sometimes appear excessively formalistic, but in its results it is justified by all business experience.[14]

Legislative, Executive and Judicial Functions. Authority moves through the Scalar Process to the Assignment and Correlation of Functions. But while specific functions may become almost infinite in their variety, dependent on the complexity of the procedure necessary to attain the given purpose, there is no conceivable duty, function or even individual job of any kind which does not belong to one of three broad classes. And these three classes are related as principle, process and effect. They are concerned respectively with one of three things, determining that something shall be done, doing that something and deciding questions that arise in doing it in accordance with predetermined rules and practices. These classes of activities are either determinative, applicative or interpretative, or—to use the terms common in writing of government— they are legislative, executive or judicial.

It may frequently happen that something of all three of these functions is present in the same job. But "the fact that functions may not be segregated in organisation does not in any way destroy their identity as functions."[15] The task of the organiser is to secure the integrated correlation of *all* functions. To do this he must know that these three primary distinctions are present universally in organisation. He must identify them as they appear in every job and make them the basis of his correlation.

This was what F. W. Taylor was doing in his system of functional foremanship. This was based on the distinction between planning and performing, which are merely other terms for "determinative" and "executive." In the Planning Department were the order-of-work man, the instruction card man and the cost and time clerk. On the floor of the shop, i.e. in the Performing Department, were the gang boss, the speed boss, the repair boss and the inspector. An eighth foreman, also in the shop, was the disciplinarian responsible for adjusting grievances and settling disputes, thus representing the judicial function.

Fayol has similar principles. His fifth Administrative Duty reads, "Make decisions which are clear, distinct and precise"—determinative. His first Administrative Duty is "executive" —"See that the plan of operations is strictly carried out." His second Principle and tenth Administrative Duty read: "Impose penalties for mistakes and blunders"—interpretative.

Failure to Isolate the Judicial Function. It will be noted that it is in this last principle that practical writers are least definite. That is merely a reflection of current practice in industry and indeed in public administration, where the judicial function is seldom differentiated from the executive. As Mooney and Reiley comment:

Business executives are about the only present-day counterparts of the governor judges of antiquity. Without intending any sinister implication, they may all be classed

[13] *V.* "Relationship in Organisation," by V. A. Graicunas in *Papers in the Science of Administration.*
[14] *Onward Industry,* pp. 56, 57.
[15] *Onward Industry,* p. 49.

as modern Pontius Pilates, which means that they may initiate, judge and then execute their own sentences.[16]

In this respect the position of the industrial employee is in marked contrast to his rights and privileges considered as a citizen of a democratic community, as a member of his Church, or, as in wartime, temporarily a soldier. As a citizen of the State, he finds one agency, the legislature, determining the rules, a second, the executive or Civil Service, carrying them out, and a third and quite independent body, the judiciary, interpreting them and adjudicating in disputes. In the other two capacities he finds the same people executing and adjudicating.

[16] *Onward Industry*, pp. 204, 205.

But the forms of procedure segregate the two functions very clearly. The members of ecclesiastical and military courts are chosen from among the executive officials. But when they sit in such courts, they cease to be officials and become judges; and they are so recognised in the most formal sense.

It is possible that the backwardness of modern industrial organisation in isolating the judicial function may lie at the root of much discontent with the system, though the cause is unrecognised and the sense of grievance is expressed in other ways. Certainly wider experiment in this direction is desirable, e.g. with such devices as Appeal Committees with an impartial Chairman. Experience of one such experiment gives no ground for any suggestion that it would weaken discipline.

Top-Management Organization

PAUL HOLDEN, LOUNSBURY S. FISH, AND HUBERT L. SMITH

The importance of a sound and clean-cut plan of top-management organization in facilitating and contributing to the effectiveness of corporate administration cannot be overemphasized. In a few of the companies studied this field has obviously been given the attention and study it deserves. In many others it is evident that further clarification and development are needed.

The Three Basic Zones or Levels of Top Management

In order to clarify this stratum of organization, it should be recognized that there are three distinct and separable zones or levels of top management. They differ as to function, and as to the viewpoint, requisite background, and experience of the responsible personnel. These three zones may be characterized as follows:

ZONE 1. THE TRUSTEESHIP FUNCTION is to represent, safeguard, and further the stockholders' interests, determine the basic policies and the general course of the business, appraise the adequacy of over-all results, and in general protect and make the most effective use of the company's assets. This field is the exclusive province of the board of directors.

ZONE 2. THE GENERAL-MANAGEMENT OR ADMINISTRATIVE FUNCTION includes the active

planning, direction, co-ordination, and control of the business as a whole, within the scope of basic policies established and authority delegated by the board. In other words, this function involves the determination of objectives, of operating policies, and of results. This broad co-ordinative function is variously handled (*a*) by the chief executive, (*b*) by the chief executive and a part-time council of divisional executives, (*c*) by a full-time group of general executives, or (*d*) by a managing board of directors.

ZONE 3. THE DIVISIONAL- OR DEPARTMENTAL-MANAGEMENT FUNCTION includes the management of the major divisions or departments of the company by executives fully responsible and accountable to general management for the successful conduct of their respective operations. This zone embraces the topmost level of executives concerned primarily with a particular division of the company rather than with the enterprise as a whole.

In many companies these three fundamental and separable levels of top management appear to be indistinct and confused. In some instances two or even three of these fields are administered by the same identical group of executives, as in the case of some managing boards. This frequently results in the assumption by a single agency of an excessive burden in trying to cover these three distinct functions. It is also difficult for executives steeped in the pressing problems and demands of divisional management to divorce themselves from their divisional interests and assume the broader viewpoint needed in the determination of policies, objectives, and long-range plans for the best interests of the company as a whole.

76

It is believed that a clear conception of the proper functions, responsibilities, and relationships of these three levels of management affords an effective basis (a) for testing the adequacy of any company's plan of top organization, (b) for making sure that each field is entrusted to a "team" whose composition and qualifications are best adapted to do that particular job, and (c) for passing the burden of management detail down to those in the best position to assume it.

Zone 1. Trusteeship Function (Board of Directors)

In this country the stockholders seldom bother, even once a year, to attend personally to the affairs of the corporations they own. As owners these stockholders have definite interests to be considered and protected. The business of a corporation must be conducted in such a way as to preserve its assets. Good judgment must be exercised in setting long-range policies, in selecting the officers, in checking results of operations, and in guiding generally the affairs of the business.

Obviously several thousand stockholders cannot personally manage the business. Therefore, they select a small group upon whom they rely to look after their interests in the enterprise. This group is the board of directors.

The point of view of the board of directors must by the nature of this relationship be identical with that of the stockholders. At all meetings of the board this viewpoint should outweigh any other consideration. In fact, the fundamental concept of the first zone or level of management is management for the benefit of those who own the business.

This point of view is not always easily maintained. Many directors are also full-time executives whose interests as members of management may momentarily be at variance with those of the stockholders.

Functions of the Board of Directors. It may be argued that all transactions of the business are or should be for the interest of the stockholders. At what point, therefore, should the trusteeship of the stockholders' interests, as such, cease and other more direct forms of management begin? In other words, how far should the board of directors enter into the management of the business in order properly to discharge the trusteeship function?

In substantially all the companies reviewed, the board of directors establishes broad basic policies, handles major financial matters, selects the officers and sets their salaries, and takes care of other matters of a similar character. In addition, it receives reports from the management on the company's operation since the last meeting, and passes judgment as to whether, in view of circumstances, the results are satisfactory.

These duties are of such a nature that they can be handled satisfactorily at periodic meetings. Broad policies are not subject to current fluctuation, but stand for relatively long periods. Results of operations are usually shown by monthly statistical and financial reports. Consequently, boards of directors meet at infrequent intervals. Of the thirty-one companies studied, twenty-one have monthly meetings, six meet quarterly, and only four meet oftener than monthly. Some twenty-six of the companies rely upon an executive committee of the board to handle matters requiring board action which cannot await a regular meeting.

In most companies there seems to be an unwritten but well-understood allocation of certain management decisions between the board and general management. But in addition there is a large middle ground within which the chief executive uses his discretion as to whether or not a program shall be decided by general management or presented to the board. In many such instances the action taken by general management is subsequently submitted to the board for ratification.

Any sound plan of management might well begin with the determination and definition of the functions, responsibilities, and limits of authority to be reserved for the board, and those to be delegated to general management. It is only by a clear delineation of functions that each group will know exactly what part it is to play in the management of the company as a whole. In some concerns this separation of functions has been made, and the field and duties of the board have been included as the first section of the organization manual. . . . In such companies top management has been made easier, simply because specific duties have been established, and each level can concern itself with its own particular assignment. . . .

Zone 2. General-Management or Administrative Function

The general-management function may be characterized as the active planning, direction, co-ordination, and control of the business as a whole, within the scope of basic policies established and authority delegated by the board. While both the board of directors and general management are concerned with the interests of the company as a whole, the former performs a judicial and intermittent function, that is, the appraisal and approval of major proposals and results, whereas the latter exercises an active and continuous function, involving the initiation, formulation, co-ordination, and development of those proposals and results.

Among the functions which appear to fall logically within this conception of general management are the following:

1. Maintenance of a sound and effective plan of company organization, with functions, responsibilities, and limits of authority clearly defined and properly allocated.

2. Maintenance of fully qualified personnel in all management positions.

3. Farsighted planning and clarification of general objectives.

4. Maintenance of effective systems of control over such general activities as capital expenditures, operating expenditures and results, manpower, wages, salaries, product line, and prices.

5. Review and approval of major appropriations, budgets, appointments, and salary changes as provided under these systems of control, within the limits delegated to it by the board and above the limits delegated by it to divisional executives.

6. Determination of general operating policies.

7. Recommendation to the board on matters requiring its action.

8. General co-ordination of major operating plans.

9. Appraisal of divisional or departmental performance and results.

Among the thirty-one companies studied, four plans for organizing the general-management function are found: (1) In some companies the chief executive handles this field, calling informally upon his fellow officers and divisional executives for advice and counsel as he may feel the need. (2) In other cases, the chief executive and a council of divisional or departmental executives perform the same function. (3) Other companies have set up a group of general executives to concentrate full time upon the problems of general management. (4) And, finally, in a few companies, a managing board of directors handles this field, as well as performing its natural trusteeship function. These four plans for organizing general management, as they were observed in the different companies, may be characterized and appraised as follows:

General Management through Chief Executive. One-third of the companies rely upon the chief executive, usually the president, to carry the major burden of general management, consulting informally with divisional executives as he deems necessary. Occasionally this amounts to a "one-man show." More frequently there is such close consultation between the chief executive and his fellow officers in regard to all major moves as to approximate council action. Unless the latter condition prevails this arrangement is subject to the following analysis:

ADVANTAGE. Tendency to expedite executive action.

DISADVANTAGES. Possibility that action may be taken without adequate consideration of all important aspects.

Lack of well-rounded experience, viewpoint, and knowledge of all major operations, which are available only through group consideration, and which are valuable aids to and checks upon the chief executive's judgment.

Tendency to overload the chief executive with matters that could be handled satisfactorily by others.

Inability of the chief executive, through lack of time and energy, to accomplish satisfactorily all the important functions and objectives of general management.

Failure to develop fellow officers to major stature through sharing the responsibility of general management with them.

Consequent maximum disruption of the enterprise when the chief executive finally retires or leaves the business.

General Management through Chief Executive and Council of Divisional Executives. Another third of the participating companies look to the chief executive and a part-time but formally constituted and representative council of divisional executives, called together from their divisional duties as necessary, to handle the broad administrative functions of general management. Characteristics of this plan may be summarized as follows:

1. The president (sometimes together with a chairman, vice-chairman, or executive vice-president) is the only executive devoting full time to general management.

2. In a few companies, he makes some of the decisions and exercises some of the functions of general management himself, taking up other matters with the council. In other companies, nearly all the decisions appear to be reached through the council, in order to assure that all aspects of each matter are given adequate consideration.

3. In all cases, the council, variously termed executive council, president's cabinet, officers' board, operating committee or management advisory committee, is a formally constituted agency, with members appointed by the chief executive, holding regular meetings weekly or oftener as required to transact business. Authority of the group is that delegated by the chief executive, who may ordinarily overrule any decision of the cabinet.

4. Council membership ranges from five to seventeen with an average of eight. Besides the chief executive, it usually includes the principal divisional executives whose interests or advice are most often of general concern.

Divisional members of these part-time councils devote their major time and attention to divisional interests, getting together as necessary to advise with the president in regard to general problems. The relative merits of this plan of general management appear to be as follows:

ADVANTAGE. Regular participation of representative divisional executives in council deliberations should assure adequate consideration of divisional interests and points of view. In addition, such participation should result in better understanding of and compliance with council action.

DISADVANTAGES. In the largest companies the problem of general management becomes so complex that it is questionable whether or not the part-time attention of a representative group of divisional executives is sufficient to

find and chart the most profitable course for the business to follow, involving as it does the forecasting of general conditions, formulation of operating policies and objectives, co-ordination of plans, review and approval of major proposals, and appraisal of results.

It is difficult for divisional executives, absorbed in their day-to-day divisional problems and responsibilities. to cast this all aside and take a sufficiently broad company-wide viewpoint to be fully effective in the field of general management during the few hours a week in which they may serve on the council.

Insufficient attention is often devoted to broad planning for and direction of the business as a whole, because these can, without immediately apparent results, be deferred in favor of seemingly more pressing divisional matters.

There is a natural tendency for divisional executives to bring into the council divisional problems which properly need never concern it.

General Management through a Council of General Executives. In one-fourth of the companies studied, particularly those which have devoted the most attention to organization planning, the boards of directors have delegated the field of general management to a full-time group or council of general executives. This group determines operating policies and objectives and concentrates upon the broad direction, co-ordination, and control of the business as a whole. In order that they may devote their full time and energies to this important purpose, council members are usually relieved of direct responsibility for individual divisions or departments through effective delegation to divisional executives.

This arrangement for handling the general-management function, which appears to be particularly effective and toward which there is a discernible trend among the larger concerns, has the following typical characteristics:

1. In all those companies having such a plan, the board confines its sphere to proper trusteeship functions, the intermittent character of which necessitates meeting not oftener than once a month.

2. The executive council usually consists of the three to nine (average six) top active officers of the company, ordinarily the president and ranking vice-presidents, so chosen as to embrace a wide range of experience, back-

ground, and knowledge of the company's principal operations, such as manufacturing, marketing, and finance. As a rule, it is largely the same group that represents management on the board.

3. This group meets daily to weekly as required to transact its business, but the members devote their full time to the broad interests of the company as a whole.

4. While the members are not, as a rule, in charge of any specific phase of the company's operations, this responsibility being effectively delegated to divisional executives, they are usually looked to by the other members of the council and by divisional executives for consultation, co-ordination, and advice within the field of their special experience and background. Thus, particularly in companies which are set up on a product-division basis, council members with a broad manufacturing, marketing, or financial background are able to provide the necessary functional co-ordination between divisions.

5. This is ordinarily done on an advisory basis, however, divisional executives being accountable to the council, not to its individual members. In almost no case would a divisional executive expect to receive a "yes" or "no" decision from an individual council member; such decisions emanate only from the council as a whole. In this connection, it is noteworthy that in companies working under this plan even the president usually takes action through the council rather than as an individual.

6. In the words of one company, the council consists of a president and several "assistant presidents," each of whom has the same company-wide interest and viewpoint as the chief executive, thus multiplying the seasoned consideration of corporate problems.

7. Divisional executives consult members of the council to secure the benefit of their advice on major problems, to enlist their support on specific proposals in advance of council action, and to keep them informed as to what is going on. These contacts are voluntary, not mandatory, and though usually made with a designated council member, divisional executives are free to consult with any of the members at will.

8. Every effort is made to hold divisional executives fully responsible and accountable for successful conduct of their respective operations. They are expected to make their own decisions in regard to strictly divisional matters and to burden council members only with matters whose character or magnitude, as delimited by the council, make them of general concern. Even these matters are presented as well-considered and substantiated proposals for the council's final action.

9. Divisional executives appear frequently before the council, either at their own instigation to present some matter for decision, or upon request to explain or defend proposals or results.

This plan of general management appears to have the following advantages and disadvantages over other plans observed:

ADVANTAGES. Each of the three zones of top management is occupied by a separate agency, designed and constituted to do the most effective job in that particular field. This is broadly true even though usually all members of the general-management group and some members of the divisional-management group may also function as directors at periodic board meetings.

With a small group of top executives concentrating full time on the problems of general management and divorced from the problems and administrative routine of divisional management, the broad planning, direction, and co-ordination so vital to the success of the business as a whole are facilitated and assured.

The small executive group is able to take action easily, effectively, and informally, calling in divisional executives for specialized counsel and advice as necessary.

The time and energy of the top and, presumably, highest-paid officers and executives are devoted to the broad problems of the company as a whole, instead of being dissipated in handling responsibilities which divisional executives with their specialized experience may appropriately assume.

Throwing the full responsibility of divisional management and administration upon divisional executives serves to develop these men to their full potentialities.

DISADVANTAGES. Smaller companies may not feel able to afford a separate group of major executives concentrating on the broad, general aspects of the business as a whole, preferring to call in divisional executives to consult with the chief executive on general problems as necessary.

In such smaller organizations, too, the problems of general direction and co-ordination are less complex and may not require the full time of a general executive group to do them justice.

General Management through the Board of Directors. Two of the thirty-one companies studied rely upon a managing board of full-time executives to handle the entire burden of general management as well as their natural trusteeship function. In comparison with other plans observed, this arrangement is subject to the following appraisal:

ADVANTAGES. Most of the principal functions and activities are directly represented in management deliberations through membership of the responsible executives on the board of directors.

General management is kept thoroughly familiar with all major aspects of the business.

Co-ordination of interdivisional interests and development of a company-wide viewpoint are facilitated.

DISADVANTAGES. Such a large group (the full board of directors) is unwieldy in taking management action.

It is necessary to involve the whole board for frequent and extended periods in deliberation over problems that affect and are of prime interest to only a few members.

With the divisional management so heavily represented there is a natural tendency to burden the general group with the consideration of purely divisional problems which properly need never concern it.

Zone 3. Divisional- or Departmental-Management Function

Divisional management provides the active direction and management of the respective parts or divisions of the company within the scope of operating policies and authority delegated by general management. These parts may be operating departments, such as manufacturing and marketing, or staff departments, product divisions, regional divisions, or subsidiary companies.

Divisional executives are therefore defined as the topmost executives directly in charge of one or more of these divisions or departments, whether they be called vice-presidents, directors, general managers, managers, or presidents (as in the case of some subsidiaries). They are all directly accountable to the chief executive or to general management for the successful conduct of their respective parts of the business.

Divisional executives are distinguished from general executives in that they are immediately concerned with divisional or departmental rather than company-wide interests. A thorough knowledge of divisional operations and problems is therefore of greater moment than a wide knowledge, experience, and viewpoint of the company as a whole which are so important in the zone of general management.

The following considerations are of primary importance in the successful functioning of divisional management:

LOGICAL DIVISIONS. Whatever the nature of the division assigned to each divisional executive, whether a functional division, like manufacturing or marketing, a staff department, a product division, or a subsidiary company, sound organization requires that it be a logical, separable, clean-cut part of the whole. This facilitates the clear conception and definition of functions, objectives, and relationships, and, through the fact that records of performance naturally follow the same channels, makes it possible to measure divisional results effectively.

In some companies, certain divisional executives appear to have an unrelated hodgepodge of activities under their direction. In other companies, the primary divisions are confined to single major functions, product divisions, departments, or logical groups of closely related activities. This appears to facilitate their effective management by permitting concentration and specialization of executive attention.

NUMBER OF DIVISIONS. The number of divisions reporting directly to general management varies widely. In one well-organized company practically all activities head up to four divisional vice-presidents in charge of manufacturing, marketing, financial, and purchasing activities, respectively. The other extreme is reached in the case of a company set up on a product-division basis, where there are ten product-division managers and fourteen staff and service department heads, all report-

Table 1. Four Basic Types of Top-Management Organization

This chart illustrates the four general methods found among the participating companies for organizing the three levels of top management. It will be observed that the principal point of difference relates to the arrangement for handling the general-management function.

THE THREE ZONES OF TOP MANAGEMENT	TYPE A	TYPE B	TYPE C	TYPE D
ZONE 1 **TRUSTEESHIP MANAGEMENT** Representing, safeguarding, and furthering stockholders' interests; determining basic policies and broad course of the business; reviewing and appraising over-all results	*Board of Directors* Meeting usually monthly or quarterly	*Board of Directors* Meetings usually monthly or quarterly	*Board of Directors* Meeting usually monthly or quarterly	*Board of Directors* Meeting weekly or oftener as necessary
ZONE 2 **GENERAL MANAGEMENT** Planning, directing, co-ordinating, and controlling the business as a whole—determining objectives, establishing operating policies, and securing results—within the scope of basic policies established and authority delegated by the board	*Chief Executive* Consulting informally with individual departmental executives as necessary	*Chief Executive* Working in conjunction with a formally constituted *Council of Divisional Executives* Who are called together as necessary from their departmental duties Meeting weekly or oftener as occasion demands	*Council of General Executives* Consisting of the chief executive and a few other top officers who devote full time to the interests of the business as a whole, delegating to departmental or divisional executives wide responsibility for management of specific operations Meeting several times a week	*Board of Directors* Meeting several time a week
ZONE 3 **DIVISIONAL MANAGEMENT** Standing fully accountable to general management for the successful conduct of the respective departments, divisions, or subsidiaries of the company	*Divisional Executives* Including all executives, regardless of rank or title, who are directly responsible to general management for their respective departments, divisions, or subsidiaries	*Divisional Executives* Including all executives, regardless of rank or title, who are directly responsible to general management for their respective departments, divisions, or subsidiaries	*Divisional Executives* Including all executives, regardless of rank or title, who are directly responsible to general management for their respective departments, divisions, or subsidiaries	*Individual Directors* Devoting major attention to the management of their respective departments, divisions, and subsidiaries.

82

ing to the president. It appears that under this latter arrangement, unless some special provision is made to the contrary, the demands upon the president's time for maintaining necessary contacts with such a large number of divisional executives might prove burdensome. There is a prevalent conviction that the number of subordinates reporting to a single executive should be definitely limited in order that each may get the attention he needs without overburdening his principal.

RESPONSIBILITY, AUTHORITY, AND ACCOUNTABILITY. General management, whether it consists of the president or a full-time group of general executives, should keep itself free of divisional detail, concentrating its full time and energy upon the larger problems of overall direction and control. Divisional executives should be expected to handle their strictly divisional problems without burdening their principals, assuming as nearly full proprietary responsibility and accountability for the successful conduct of divisional operations as is consistent with the need for over-all coordination and control. The most effective steps found among the participating companies for insuring and furthering this objective are:

Clear-cut delineation of the functions, responsibilities, and relationships of each divisional executive through job specifications in the organization manual.

Delegation to divisional executives of adequate authority, commensurate with these responsibilities, within limits specifically defined.

The establishment of definite objectives and suitable measures of what constitutes the divisional job well done. This may take the form of budgetary planning, standards of performance, or other devices of control.

Effective current comparison and appraisal of actual results against the preplanned objectives, and the taking of necessary action to stimulate improvement where it is needed.

A conscious effort on the part of general executives to render advice and counsel as requested, but to give no decisions, as individuals, within the field delegated to divisional executives. The latter are expected to make up their own minds, take appropriate action, and stand accountable for results.

Insistence that matters presented for the action of general management be submitted in the form of well-substantiated proposals or recommendations.

Effective use of staff agencies to analyze and digest proposals as a preliminary to general management's consideration.

The Division of Basic Company Activities

ERNEST DALE

General Analysis

The Division of Basic Company Activities. The alternative methods for dividing the work of a company toward the accomplishment of its objectives are numerous. They include, tra-

From *Planning and Developing the Company Organization Structure*. New York: American Management Association, 1952, pp. 25–38. Reprinted with permission of the publisher.

ditionally, function, product, location, customers, process, equipment, and time. It should be noted that in many companies these various bases of division are combined, and coordinated by checks and balances. But there is usually one predominant type of subdivision of the major company activities, made by the chief executive officer himself, called "basic subdivision," "basic delegation," or "departmentation."

The first step in the division of work is the

determination of the primary responsibilities of the enterprise—that is, the purpose of the enterprise, and the major functions necessary to accomplish it. Thus, in a manufacturing enterprise, production is one basic responsibility; in merchandising, it may be advertising; in public utilities, the maintenance of equipment; in the liquor business, the determination of credit risk; in flour milling, the purchase of flour.

The principal or primary subdivision of the activities of an enterprise may then be divided on the following bases:

1. FUNCTION. Major subdivision by function, subject-matter or principal activities is found in many enterprises where actual control throughout all hierarchies and over all locations is exercised by the heads of managerial functions—such as finance; production (including plant design, construction and maintenance, purchasing); manufacture; engineering (product design or research, possibly quality control); law (claims, tax laws, corporate affairs); human relations (relations to stockholders, employees, community, government); sales (marketing, advertising). Many companies are so subdivided at the top. This arrangement has the advantages of specialization. More importantly, it should make possible adequate time for basic long-run planning and major decision-making and consultation for those in charge of the major management functions. But it may result in inter-departmental jealousies and conflicts over the limits of authority. It is also subject to considerable conflict among the local plant managers in multi-plant organizations. An example of a functional type of organization setup is shown in the organization chart of the Dictaphone Corporation (Fig. 1).

There appears to be a certain degree of uniformity in basic managerial functions of the top organization structure, at least in very large companies, as is shown in the accompanying illustrations of abbreviated organization charts (Figs. 2–4). Of particular interest is the abbreviated organization chart of Standard Oil Company of California (Fig. 2), which employs the use of the conventional line and staff organization plan and, in addition, identifies in vertical arrangement the following basic functional groups: Policy Making, Adminis-

tration and Coordination, Staff and Service, and Operations.

2. PRODUCT. Management activities may be grouped on the basis of the major types of products or services marketed, and sold separately. This kind of grouping is used by some large companies manufacturing a diverse product line.

At General Foods Corporation and International Harvester Company, the major subdivisions of work are on a product basis. Other examples are found in merchandising, automobile, chemicals and meat packing. Grouping by product has the advantage of bringing together and coordinating in one place major activities required to make a particular product (purchasing, engineering, production, distribution, etc.). Such an arrangement provides a particularly sound basis for decentralization. It may also make possible close control and accounting comparability through central staff agencies.

Even in the "mono-product plants" (as General R. Johnson, President of Johnson & Johnson, describes them) it may be wise to make "little ones out of big ones." For example, at the General Electric Company the refrigerator cabinet is made separately from refrigerator compressor units. Or in the production of locomotives, the cabs and running gear are made in separate sections, erected and assembled in another section; the rotating units are made in another shop; and control gadgets in still another. In making control gadgets of infinite variety, the necessity for a multi-product plant really arises.

Figure 5 shows the product organization at The Kendall Company, a medium-sized company which is famous for its work in scientific management. It shows a basic organization built about three major products. It also shows in an interesting way the provision of staff services to these line divisions, the operation of which is decentralized, while coordination and control are centralized.

3. LOCATION (also called territorial or geographical division or departmentation). Under this type of arrangement, all activities performed in a particular area are brought together. It is found in companies serving customers on a national or international scale—e.g., the liquor business, railroads, chain stores,

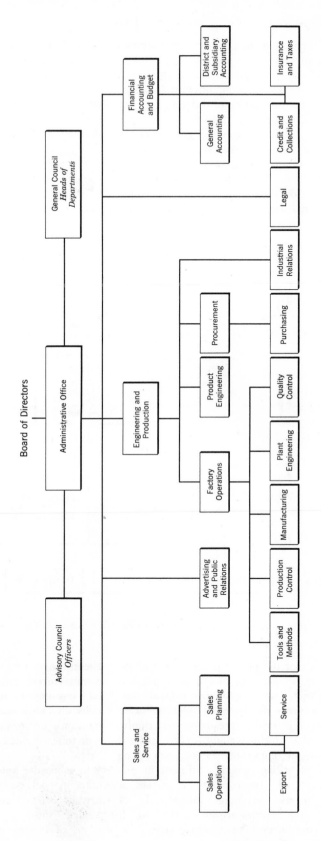

Fig. 1. A functional organization (the Dictaphone Corporation).

life insurance companies, the overseas branches of motor car and oil companies. The product and locational principles may be combined, with different factories in different locations devoted to the production of different types of products (e.g., General Motors).

The major subdivisions of oil companies are often on a regional basis, since the natural unit of work centers around the major oil-producing fields. Production and selling or the selling function alone may often be subdivided on a regional basis. The advantage of such a

It facilitates operation in times of emergency or war. Finally, it provides opportunity for training of lower executives in a wide range of activities so that qualified men will be available to fill vacancies in higher jobs.

Figure 6 illustrates territorial or geographical division of company activities.

4. CUSTOMERS. Major subdivision on a customer basis occurs in certain fields—radio and television, for example. Here emphasis is principally on selling programs to individual

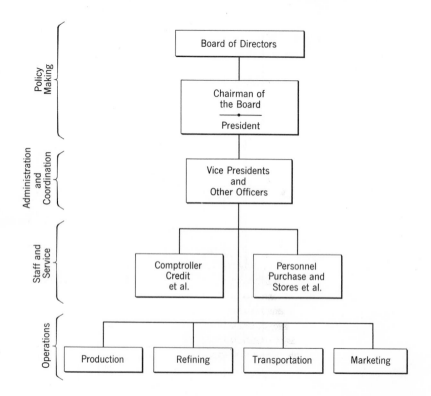

Fig. 2. Abbreviated organization chart (Standard Oil Company of California).

division is that the power of decision-making is concentrated near the source of origin and is all-inclusive, with functional central control. It prevents the losses of efficiency that arise when a company spreads out too thinly. It ensures that careful account is taken of local conditions—an important factor, since the problems of selling may be different in different parts of the country. It makes it possible to take advantage immediately of favorable opportunities arising on the spot. It permits coordination on a manageable scale.

clients, such as a cigarette company, a soap manufacturer, etc. Lower level subdivisions on a customer basis are found, for example, on railroads (Pullman and Coach travellers), and insurance companies (type of policy-holders, sometimes divided by groups of serial numbers).

In a broader sense, not only customers, but other parties connected with the enterprise may be represented on the organization chart. Figure 7 shows such a division of functions in terms of management communications to its

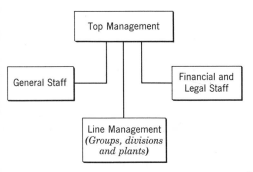

Fig. 3. Abbreviated organization chart (General Motors Corporation).

own people at all levels—stockholders, suppliers, financiers, the consumer audience and the general audience. While the usual organization chart shows the structure of the management hierarchy, this chart shows the inter-relationships (and their absence) between the various "publics" connected with the enterprise. It shows the functions which fall into natural groupings and the combinations of functions which are possible in various managerial activities. For instance, in preparing the company annual report, its uses and the varying interests of the different groups may be indicated by such a chart. (This chart was prepared by A. F. Arnold, designer and management consultant to industry.)

5. PROCESS. In integrated textile concerns, major divisions may be made on the basis of operational sequence—e.g., spinning, weaving, bleaching, dyeing, inspection, boxing, shipping. In steel and men's and women's clothing subdividing is often based on the process.

6. EQUIPMENT. In certain fields, equipment determines major subdivisions. In a secretarial school, for example, the subdivisions may be determined by the chief instruments whose operation is taught, such as the typewriter, the stenotyping machine, the comptometer, etc. (often identical with process).

7. TIME. Division of work may be based on time sequences, with the work broken down under the categories of planning, execution and control. Thus the first major business division would be devoted to the formulation of objectives, methods of accomplishing them, forecasts and budgets. The second major division would be devoted to the execution of the plans, and would correspond roughly to

the major operating group in a business. The third major division is devoted to the control of the results of execution in the light of the objectives and plans of the business.

To present an illustration, at one prominent company the general manager has three principal assistants, each of whom is responsible to him for one of the three main aspects of management, i.e., planning, execution, and control. There are three aspects of planning. In order to do a job one must analyze it carefully and study the available resources. Next, one must balance resources against the job, and design the job to fit the resources. The program must be scheduled on a time basis, and must meet certain set standards of quality and quantity. All these activities are found under the First Vice President. In another corporation this might be a continuing function of the secretariat of a general policy or planning committee. Although the committee may be made up of certain heads of subordinate departments, the permanent secretariat is in fact the Office of the Vice President. Second, general management is supplied with a Vice President for Operations, charged with the execution of the company's program. He is responsible for the day-to-day coordination, direction and supervision of the company's affairs. To his desk come the thousand and one issues which demand prompt decisions to expedite the efficient execution of any large and complex program. And, finally, in the jurisdiction of the Third Vice President is the function of controllership. His is the job of keeping the progress of the company under scrutiny, comparing it constantly with its program. One might say that this Third Vice President serves the other two. He serves the

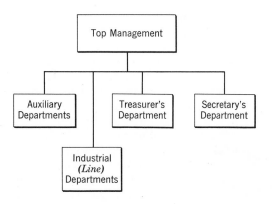

Fig. 4. Abbreviated organization chart (Du Pont).

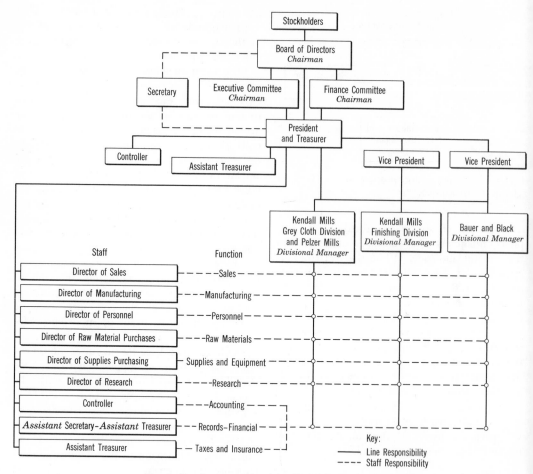

Fig. 5. Product organization (Kendall Company).

planner by making prognosticative analyses, and by analysis of past performance which can serve as the basis for future program activities. Obviously, he is a most valuable aid to the General Manager, because he is able to make decisions on the basis of *all* the facts—not merely those which happen to come to him in connection with specific problems.

8. THE "HARMONIOUS OVERLAP." Another method of work division may be useful, particularly in research work which must be speedily completed to meet competition or fulfill an urgent customer requirement. It can sometimes be applied to a variety of rush jobs.

This method of work division may be best explained by recounting Dr. Alexander Sachs' conference with the late President F. D. Roosevelt in 1939 on dividing the work on the atomic bomb construction:

F.D.R. was worried whether an atomic weapon could be ready in time to decide the outcome of the war. Dr. Sachs had estimated the project might cost two billions, and honestly told the President that, ordinarily, it would take 25 years to do the job. He explained to F.D.R. that he had searched the history of human thought for an example of how time could be telescoped.

He found the example in music, he says. The composer of music has ways of making time three-layered. Remember the old round you used to sing: "Are you sleeping, etc?" Three tunes going at once, harmoniously overlapping each other. This, he advised, was what must be done with the atomic project.

"When you start one part of the project, assume you have finished it successfully, and start the next as if you had." That is exactly what was done, probably for the first time with such a huge undertaking. It worked.[1]

9. COORDINATION AND BALANCE. An attempt has been made to bring together the various factors of organizational planning in such a way that each acts as a check or balance on the others. In his *Design for Industrial Co-ordination*,[2] Robert W. Porter set out a technique for coordinating the basic functions in the field of industrial organization. He set up seven major categories for classifying industrial activities, with three subsidiary classifications for each:

1. The problems of policy, performance and compensation, identified as technical problems.

2. The problems of planning, production and inspection, identified as functional problems.

3. The problems of administration, management and operation, identified as jurisdictional problems.

4. The problems of communication, cooperation and control, identified as organizational problems.

5. The problems of executive capacity dealing with intellect, volition and ethics, identified as leadership problems.

6. The problems of employee stimulation, application and discipline, identified as institutional problems.

7. The problems of expectancy, efficiency and economy, identified as measurement problems.

The author attempts, on the basis of wide practical experience, to bring out the inter-operation and relationships of the 21 elements of performance, so that staff needs can be reduced, while the coordination process is improved. It is claimed that this plan of division has the advantages of economizing staff services, improving communication, cutting down jurisdictional problems, and providing better balance in general.

The foregoing are some general guides for determining how the work of the organization may be subdivided, and what consequences may follow. Their specific application will depend upon the special needs of the enterprise. There is no indication from this list that any one way of grouping activities is better than another. If one basis is adopted, then other bases will have to be intermixed. Even when a proper primary basis of dividing work has been decided on, its specific limits must be determined. For example, suppose it has been decided that it will be best to divide

[1] From "How F. D. R. Planned to Use the A-Bomb," by Nat S. Finney, *Look Magazine*, March 14, 1950, page 25, copyright 1950 by Cowles Magazines, Inc.

[2] Harper & Brothers, New York, 1941.

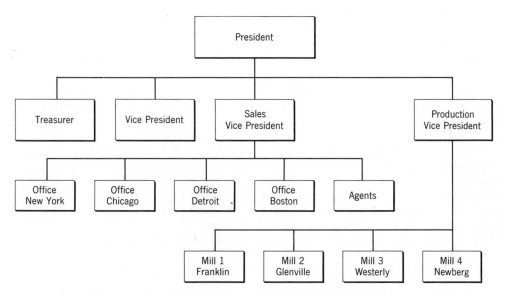

Fig. 6. Territorial division of activities (American Felt Company).

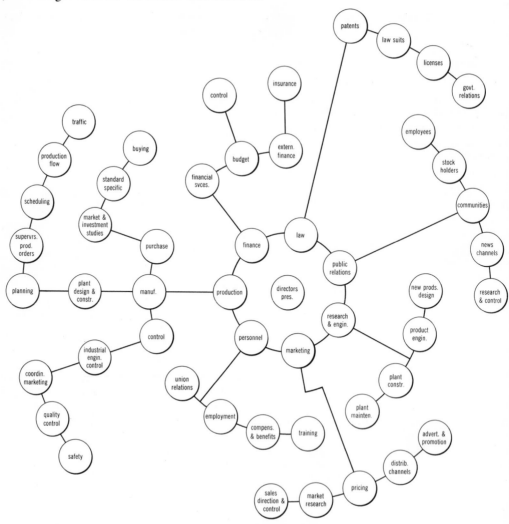

Fig. 7. Division of functions shown in terms of management communication.

sales activities on a territorial basis. This still leaves open the question as to how the territories are to be split up. It is not always practical to determine sales territories by geographical boundaries. The problem must be solved in terms of selling a particular article in a particular situation.

For these reasons it is necessary to develop criteria which are helpful in deciding which method of grouping to use. That method should then be chosen which satisfies best the criteria under consideration, and is best adapted to individual needs.

Criteria for Determining the Division of Basic Activities

In general, the various functions which must be performed to accomplish the objectives of the enterprise should be so assigned as to obtain the greatest possible advantage from the division of labor:

1. Work should be so divided that the incumbent of a position should be able to become a specialist and increase his knowledge on the particular job assigned to him.

2. Special abilities should be used to the full.

3. Groups of people (divisions, departments) should comprise a workable, homo-

geneous and separate field of activity. The nature of their work should be similar or complementary (the former is probably more important in the lower executive ranks, the latter more important in the upper ranks).

Three major criteria may be distinguished for dividing work—economic and non-economic criteria and the size of the company.

Economic Efficiency. Economic criteria relate to business efficiency. These in turn may be evaluated in terms of saving money, contributing more to the company's revenue, in the speed or accuracy of transacting business.

That particular grouping of activities should be chosen which will make the greatest contribution to the profitability of the enterprise. This may take many different forms, some of which are discussed below.

1. MAJOR CONTRIBUTIONS TO SURVIVAL AND PROFITABILITY. In the early stages of a company's growth the fundamental problem is that of economic survival. This may require improvement of the production process so that goods will be turned out on time and within the proper cost limits. It may require successful acquisition of sources of raw materials, as in the timber industry and mining. Or, most commonly, it may require acquisition of cash through sales to meet current expenses and to build up a reserve of working capital. These basic objectives tend to become the major function in the business, with the executive in charge becoming in fact the most important official in the business.

Once production or sales have reached satisfactory levels and have become more or less stabilized, they may well lapse into secondary activities, while research and control become dominant. The primary aim at this point may be technical superiority. If this is under pressure by competitors, or the company itself is forging ahead, this very instability will greatly increase the importance of the technical function—especially if the firm's competitive superiority rests on it. The development by the research or style department of innovations which will accelerate the growth of the company are likely to be primary functions. Or the primary activity, from the standpoint of profits, may be that of integration, consolidation and establishment of central control. Once the firm has reached its final stage of growth and is at the point of defending its share of

the market, sales may again become predominant.

2. The company may wish to take full advantage of *specialization* and therefore may group together similar functions or specialties. Thus the selling function is often divided into groups of closely related products—in a food company, confectionery products, for example, may be grouped together so that salesmen can devote themselves to selling one product group well rather than dissipate their efforts over many products. Similarly, activities which serve the same purpose may be most efficiently grouped together—e.g., recruitment, interviewing, testing, hiring and induction may be handled by the employment department, while the employee benefit activities are handled separately by a welfare department.

3. LINES OF COMMUNICATION may be shortened by a particular type of grouping. Thus specific functions in subsidiary plants may communicate directly with the corresponding headquarters function without going through the local plant manager—e.g., control and auditing.

4. DUPLICATION may be reduced or abolished by consolidating a particular function which was previously widely scattered, e.g., the consolidation of the personnel function into a headquarters department.

5. BALANCE may be improved and better operating results attained by combining different parts of a job under several men into one complete job under one man. Joseph B. Hall, President of The Kroger Company, describes such a change in operations as follows:

Until the past few years, we operated on a functional basis with one man responsible for buying and another man responsible for selling. Sometimes there was friction between these men. If, for instance, merchandise failed to sell, the sales promotion man claimed that the merchandise was inferior; whereupon the buyer would intimate that the sales promotion man had missed his true vocation and should be farming or cleaning the streets. The situation was somewhat like that between the meat managers and the grocery managers; in both cases it was difficult to hold men responsible when each man handled only a part of the complete job.

Railroads have experienced similar cleavages between different parts of the system.

6. The extent of delegated authority may be widened so that lower executives have a greater *power of decision-making*. This has the advantage that people on the spot who are most familiar with the problems can make better and speedier decisions.

7. UNIFORMITY AND CONSISTENCY of policy may be brought about. For example, if a personnel department is set up, there is likely to result greater uniformity in pay for similar jobs, more consistent policies with regard to merit rating and promotion, hiring and training.

8. CONTROL may be improved. Work may be so divided that similar units are created so that there is better comparability of selling and production efforts. On the other hand, control may be improved by separating inspection activities from the group—e.g., separation of the financial or auditing function from a subsidiary plant, separating credit from sales for fear salesmen will be too easy on the creditors.

9. Activities may be grouped in the department which makes the *most effective use* of them. For example, a company might consider having the production department take over the training function from the personnel department if this is the best way to gain acceptance from foremen and hourly-rated employees.

10. COMPETITION may be the criterion for dividing activities. Accordingly, the work may be split up into different departments or factories so that the results are fairly comparable. For example, in cement companies the work is distributed to different plants which are usually highly comparable. Sometimes it may be necessary to proceed on the opposite line of reasoning and join two types of work in order to suppress competition which hurts the total effort of the company.

11. JOB INTEREST may be severely impaired by over-specialization of individual jobs as well as of whole departments. Where work is divided too finely, with little variation or

change, the monotony may obscure the meaning of the job and its relation to the end product, and give rise to job dissatisfaction and quits. Over-specialization is likely to require extra supervision (to deal with the resulting discontent) and an elaborate system of formal controls.

Non-economic Factors. There may be important *non-economic* factors to consider in the division of work. These frequently make for *autonomy* in a particular activity. Thus a special division may be set up to look after special interests connected with the enterprise, e.g., a division on stockholder relations or local community relations. Or the division is created to arouse *attention* to the particular activity—defense work, governmental relationships, safety (Central Maine Power Company), executive health, or salary evaluation. At the National Biscuit Company, for example, the head of the Sanitation Department reports directly to the president because the company attaches primary importance to the maintenance of sanitary conditions. Or a special division may be created for a *particular man*—to feather his ego, to "kick him upstairs," to take account of reduced abilities, or to retain some of his services on retirement (e.g., the position of Honorary Chairman of the Board). Division of work may have to be fitted to traditional arrangements within the company. For example, both the production and sales manager may have equal standing in a subsidiary and be given equal powers, but there may be no plant manager. Or the office manager may take over personnel work because there may not be enough of it to justify a full-time division. Or a particular division may continue to occupy an important position within the company simply because it has existed for a long time—e.g., in one company the engineer in charge of bridge-building (the oldest activity in the company) headed up a major division and reported to the president long after bridge-building had become a minor activity. *Preconceived ideas* and principles, and excessive reliance on formality may also be powerful factors in structuring a business enterprise.

Finally, the *personal interests* or hobbies of the chief executive may play a role. For example, Mac Fisheries were originally added to the Lever soap business in order to facilitate sale of the catch of fishermen of some islands on the West Coast of Scotland in whose development the first Lord Leverhulme took a private interest.

Obviously, not all the factors mentioned above are either rational or desirable determinants of the division of work within an enterprise. However, their existence should be taken into account and the reasons for their existence understood before any attempt is made to change the status quo.

Size of Company. The final major criterion for dividing the work of the organization is the size of the company. The importance of the chief problems faced by the top management varies as the company grows. Hence the major functions exercised and supervised

3. The most important ability on the part of heads of large companies in managerial ability or skills, and the more important the company the greater the place occupied by this ability.

4. Commercial and financial ability play a relatively more important part in the case of heads of small and middle-sized companies than they do in the case of larger companies.

5. As one goes up the scale of industrial concerns the managerial coefficient increases at the expense of the rest, which tend to even out, approximating up to one-tenth of the total evaluation.

It is clear that the larger the size of the business the greater the emphasis on broad managerial functions, such as planning, forecasting, organizing, commanding, coordinating and controlling.

Relative Importance of Requisite Abilities of Personnel in Industrial Concerns

	REQUISITE ABILITIES						
	MAN- AGERIAL %	TECH- NICAL %	COM- MERCIAL %	FINAN- CIAL %	SE- CURITY * %	ACCOUNT- ING %	TOTAL EVALUA- TION %
One-man business	15	40	20	10	5	10	100
Small firm	25	30	15	10	10	10	100
Medium-sized firm	30	25	15	10	10	10	100
Large firm	40	15	15	10	10	10	100
Very large firm	50	10	10	10	10	10	100
State enterprise	60	8	8	8	8	8	100

* Safeguarding property, avoiding social disturbances in the broad sense and any influence endangering the life of the business.

by the chief executive are likely to change also. This may be illustrated by the Work Table which the great French industrialist, Henri Fayol, drew up.[3]

From this table the following conclusions may be drawn:

1. The most important ability of the head of the small industrial company is technical ability.

2. As one goes up the chain of command, the relative importance of managerial ability increases and that of technical ability declines. Equilibrium between these two obtains in medium-sized companies.

[3] From Henri Fayol, *General and Industrial Management*, Sir Isaac Pitman & Sons, Ltd., London, 1949, pp. 10–11. Translator Constance Storres.

Conclusion

The most important criterion for the division of work is that of economic efficiency. This should lead to specialization, full utilization of abilities and homogeneity between groups.

Where this criterion is paramount, the basic functions (i.e., those supervised by the chief executive) are those which make the greatest contribution toward profitability. However, the economic criterion, it should be remembered, must usually be modified in the light of non-economic needs. Both need to be fitted to the particular stage of the growth and the special requirements of the company.

Identifying Line and Staff

LOUIS A. ALLEN

The line constitutes the framework for the organization structure. Line functions are those which have direct responsibility for accomplishing the objectives of the enterprise. It follows, therefore, that only line functions have the power, or authority, to initiate and carry through the primary activities which are necessary to reach the stated goals of the

From "Improving Staff and Line Relationships," *Conference Board Reports, Studies in Personnel Policy,* No. 153. National Industrial Conference Board, 1956, pp. 12–14, 38–44. Reprinted with permission of the publisher.

company. This is a cardinal point that distinguishes line from staff.

How can the "line" be further identified? In business practice, it emerges as "the chain of command" that is formed by a succession of delegations from the top to bottom of the organization. For example, in most business enterprises, the Board of Directors delegates to the chief executive officer responsibility for managing the business so it will accomplish the objectives established by the Board. The chief executive officer reserves over-all responsibility and authority for running the business. He delegates most of his work to

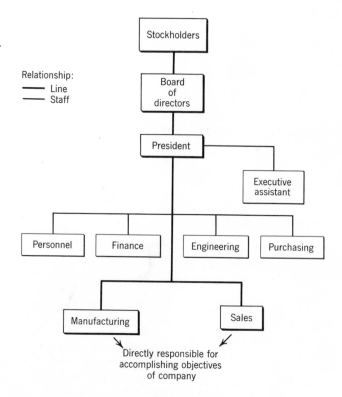

Fig. 1. *Typical line organization.*

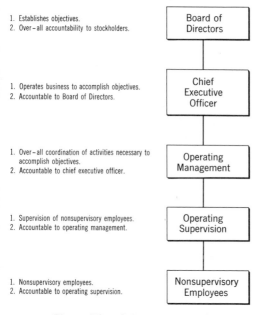

1. Establishes objectives.
2. Over-all accountability to stockholders.

Board of Directors

1. Operates business to accomplish objectives.
2. Accountable to Board of Directors.

Chief Executive Officer

1. Over-all coordination of activities necessary to accomplish objectives.
2. Accountable to chief executive officer.

Operating Management

1. Supervision of nonsupervisory employees.
2. Accountable to operating management.

Operating Supervision

1. Nonsupervisory employees.
2. Accountable to operating supervision.

Nonsupervisory Employees

Fig. 2. The chain of command.

supposed, but in what kind of work is necessary to accomplish the goals of the enterprise.

Production a Line Function

In some companies, production or manufacturing alone is the line function. Where this is the case, the greatest emphasis is on production because, for one reason or another, marketing and other objectives are secondary. Sales, for example, may be under contract, or the product may be manufactured on government order, or the item may be in chronic short supply and require relatively little sales effort.

Production and Sales as Line

In many companies, production and sales are equally important objectives. For example, the Jones & Laughlin Steel Corporation, a company of 43,000 employees, has its primary objectives those of manufacturing quality steel products and selling them at a profit. In Jones & Laughlin, the line functions are production and sales.

Columbia-Geneva Steel Division of the United States Steel Corporation has the basic objective of producing and selling metal and related products and services. The line organization in this company consists of the sales and production functions.

Objective
Columbia-Geneva Steel Division
(United States Steel Corporation)

To make and sell quality products competitively, and to perform those functions at the lowest attainable cost consistent with sound management policies, so as to return an adequate profit after taxes for services rendered. As a corollary objective, the Division must be the low cost producer of the products it offers for sale.

Other "Line" Functions

Many other functions may be classified as "line," depending upon what the company must do to reach its goals. For example, the

subordinates, who, in turn, redelegate to successively lower levels. This continues until the point is reached where the primary objective of the organization is accomplished; that is, a product or service is developed, manufactured, sold, and so forth.

It bears repeating that this line of direct delegation and redelegation is the chain of command; the relationship of one level in this chain to the next is a "line" relationship. (See Fig. 2.)

Line Identified by Objectives

Since the line is directly responsible for accomplishing the company objectives, it follows that the line elements of the organization can be identified most accurately in terms of these objectives. To the extent that the objectives of companies differ, the nature of line activities will also differ.

In some companies the manufacturing function is line. In others, both manufacturing and sales are line. In still others, such functions as engineering, research, finance and transportation may be identified as line. The answer to "What is line?" does not lie in the degree of importance of the work done by individual departments of the company, as is commonly

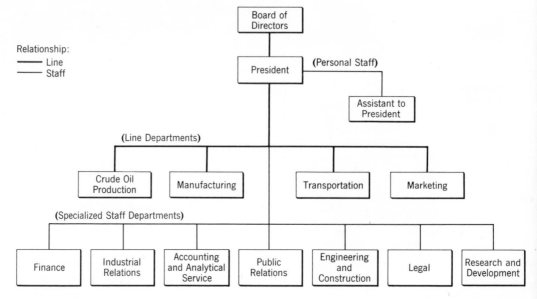

Fig. 3. Atlantic Refining Company. Line departments. This chart outlines the basic relationship established between line and staff in the Atlantic Refining Company. It is reproduced, with permission, from the Organization Manual *of the Atlantic Refining Company.*

basic objective of the Atlantic Refining Company, which has 18,500 employees, is to engage, as an integrated company, in the various phases of the petroleum business, striving for such balance between these phases as may achieve a reasonable profit for the company. In carrying out its basic objective, the company seeks to make the most effective use of capital, people, and other resources as follows:

1. Explore for and develop sources of crude oil, natural gas or other petroleum product raw materials (in those areas where these materials can be made economically available) and produce in maximum quantities consistent with economy and sound conservation.

2. Manufacture petroleum products and by-products at the lowest possible cost consistent with quality that will assure public acceptance.

3. Market, with the maximum economy of distribution, petroleum products and by-products and related merchandise; provide associated services.

4. Operate, or secure the use of, all facilities necessary to meet company transportation requirements; utilize to the best advantage any excess of such facilities.

5. Conduct its operations ethically, in accordance with its Charter and the law, and in a manner which will ensure: protection of investors' funds; a profit sufficient to provide a fair return to stockholders; customer con-

fidence; equitable rewards to and good working conditions for employees, fulfilment of governmental and civic obligations.

The line departments responsible for direct accomplishment of these objectives are production, manufacturing, transportation, and marketing.

Another variation is seen in Cleveland Electric Illuminating Company which defines as predominantly line elements those which usually have the responsibility for decision or action in the achievement of the objectives of the enterprise. The over-all objective of The Cleveland Electric Illuminating Company, which has 5,000 employees, is to provide adequate service to its customers at the lowest cost consistent with the necessity of providing an adequate return to investors for use of their funds, and adequate compensation to employees for their services. The predominantly line functions in the company are distribution, electrical operations and engineering, power production and engineering, finance, and marketing.

The Line in Service Organizations

The line organization may be responsible for the accomplishment of service, rather than production objectives. For example, the objectives of the Nationwide Insurance Company are:

1. To develop and maintain financially sound insurance companies which provide high quality insurance services at the lowest possible cost, and to do this insofar as possible through cooperation with, and sponsorship of, groups of people joined together for their mutual effort and benefit.

2. To further insurance practices which are fair and equitable to the companies' policyholders, agents and employees, and to the public. . . .

Specialized Staff

As indicated at the outset, the foregoing discussion has pertained primarily to staff designated as personal staff. There is another kind of staff that is designated as specialized staff.

The specialized staff advises, counsels, assists, and serves all line and other staff components in a functional capacity. The specialized staff thus becomes a reservoir of special knowledge, skills, and experiences which the entire organization can use. The specialized staff has two identifying characteristics:

1. It has no authority over other parts of the organization. The specialized staff advises and serves; it does not direct.

2. It is available to and can be used by all units of the organization, within the limts of company policy or practice. This character-

istic differentiates it from the personal staff, which exists primarily to advise and help one executive in carrying out his reserved responsibilities.

As Nationwide Insurance Company visualizes the specialized staff, for instance, it aids the line organization by giving it the benefit of its experience on small segments of the work to be performed. The staff in Nationwide Insurance is not responsible for execution of any of the line functions and, therefore, operates solely in an advisory capacity. It never issues orders to the line.

In American Enka, specialized staff acts in an advisory capacity. It conducts special studies, gathers pertinent facts, and develops plans, programs, policies, and procedures which it recommends to the responsible line official. These plans, programs, policies, and procedures may be company-wide in scope.

The American Enka specialized staff official not only assists his superior, but also helps and advises other line and staff officials throughout the organization.

In Armco Steel Corporation, the staff organization furnishes line managers with specialized assistance and counsel. The staff organization is called upon to determine needs and formulate controls in conjunction with line management, to give opinions upon proposed plans and policies, to keep line management informed of significant developments, and to carry out special functions requiring specialized knowledge and experience.

In Armco, line management delegates certain tasks or functions to specialized staff departments, but it does not in the process relinquish its accountability for the execution of these functions. For example, the safety department is charged with certain specialized responsibilities for establishing and promoting the Armco standards of accident prevention, plant cleanliness and order, and fire prevention and control. The safety department is not held responsible, however, for the safety of the crews, for plant cleanup, nor for the cause of fires. These are the responsibility of line management.

In Ford Motor Company, specialized staff units among other basic activities help the line manager in his duties by planning, studying, analyzing, investigating, and making recommendations to him. . . .

In the Atlantic Refining Company, operating departments carry out the basic functions of

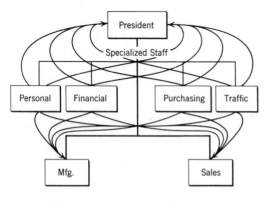

Flow of advice and service

1. Provides help in specialized fields to all parts of the organization.
2. Has no authority over the line.

Fig. 4. Specialized staff.

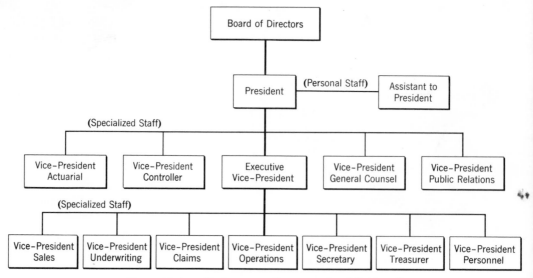

Fig. 5. Nationwide Insurance Company. Specialized staff.

the company, while specialized staff departments perform auxiliary functions. This includes the responsibility for providing advice, counsel, information, and research.

In Koppers Company, Inc., the specialized staff is considered an agency of management, delegated the responsibility to assist management in the determination of what to do and how to do it, and to assist in controlling how the "doing" is actually being done. The specialized staff does the things that the manager himself would do if he had unlimited time and energy. . . .

In Koppers Company, specialized staff performs these functions not only for the line principal, but for his operating or line units as well. In other words, staff may talk to and advise line just as the principal would if he were an expert in every function and had unlimited time.

In Radio Corporation of America, specialized staff works for line management. The principal job of the staff executive in RCA is to help line management develop, produce, and sell new or improved goods and services, better and more profitably. To this end, the specialized staff departments in RCA inform and advise line management on a variety of topics requiring specialized knowledge or skills. . . .

Is Specialized Staff Necessary?

Are specialized staff departments really necessary? Why cannot the work they do be integrated with that of the line so that a separate relationship does not have to be established? There would be obvious advantages if delegation could be entirely within the chain of command. Authority and responsibility would be easier to define, accountability would be clear and direct, the organization would be simpler because there would be no need to establish and define the usually difficult staff relationships. However, from a practical standpoint, virtually all companies of any size have found it desirable to create supporting "staff" departments and not to delegate entirely to the line organization.

Staff as a Service Agency

The chief objective in establishing a staff service department is usually to relieve each of the operating departments of the necessity of performing some function common to all and, through assignment to a single well-qualified agency, to secure the advantages of specialized attention, better service, closer coordination and control, and usually lower costs. The extent and cost of such effort, scattered through many departments and consequently hidden from view, are frequently very great. It is only when they are brought out into the open and assigned to a single agency that their magnitude is appreciated and control measures can be undertaken. Then, too, a central agency can often justify a higher caliber and wider diversity of specialized talent than would be feasible for any single department.

By permission from *Top Management Organization and Control*, by Paul E. Holden, Lounsbury S. Fish, and Herbert L. Smith, 1951, McGraw-Hill Book Company, Inc.

Reliance on a purely line organization would mean that there would be few opportunities for cutting across organizational lines. As a result, there would be little exchange of findings on new and more economical manufacturing processes, changes in customer needs, better marketing methods, or research findings. This kind of information would tend to stay within the channels within which it originated.

If delegation were limited to the line, there would be few people with company-wide interests. It would be difficult to arrange for the selection of technical and executive talent, for the education and development of that talent, and for the rotation of personnel on a company-wide basis.

More than this, the line organization by itself would limit the advantages of a system of checks and balances. There would be no objective agency to question the use of inefficient methods or processes. Growth of technology within the company would be hampered. Uneconomical and inefficient processes would be perpetuated on the basis of precedence and tradition.

For these reasons, line managers need to secure help from other than their own line subordinates. This help should make available to the line manager expert knowledge and depth of experience in such specialized fields as personnel administration, finance, law, public relations, purchasing, and engineering. With this kind of assistance, the line man can do a better rounded and more complete management job than would be possible if he depended exclusively upon line subordinates with their relatively more restricted field of operations and interests.

Advantages of Specialized Staff

Establishment of a specialized staff brings two primary advantages to the company:

1. Provides specialized help.
2. Makes an objective viewpoint available.

Specialization. Staff can handle the specialized portions of the line manager's job that otherwise would not likely be handed effectively by the line organization. There are several reasons why the line manager needs this specialized help:

1. Modern business has become so complex that it is impossible for one individual to have all the knowledge or all the skills necessary to successful administration. More than this, some of these specialties require different mental and personality traits from those which would be most desirable in a competent supervisor.

2. Certain specialized operations may require physical absence from the scene of line operations for long periods of time. Recruitment of college graduates, for example, keeps the staff personnel man on college campuses for weeks or months at a stretch. The purchasing agent may be required to make many trips in interviewing vendors, selling obsolete and scrap materials, and following up delayed shipping promises.

3. Some specialized activities are not worth the line manager's time. For example, the president of the company usually has a great many routine responsibilities. If he is receiving, say, $30 to $50 an hour, it hardly pays him to interview secretarial candidates when this could be done as well by a personnel interviewer receiving $3 or $4 an hour.

4. Use of specialized staff departments auxiliary to the line makes it possible to make specialized skills available at minimum expense to all parts of the organization. Instead of requiring that each line manager have his own lawyer, accountant, or personnel administration expert, all line managers can share the use of one or a few of these specialists.

For example, a training specialist can help a dozen or more line departments carry out their training responsibilities. Because he does work with many units, he can carry the best ideas developed in one department to all the others. He is able to improve his own skills to the utmost, while still providing adequate service to all who need him. This division of labor makes best use of specialization and results in lower total labor costs.

Objectivity. Specialized staff makes it possible for the line manager to bring a fresh and objective viewpoint to his problems. The person who has operating responsibilities is not always in the best position to be objective about his actions. There is almost certain to be some bias or self-interest either conscious or subconscious. For instance, an operating manager may unknowingly distort an organization plan in terms of his personality and his needs, rather than develop it in terms of the best interests of the organization as a whole. It is a truism that the person who is responsible for signing checks should not also cash them. The individual who assembles electric motors should not also inspect them.

The person doing the work needs to plan his own activities and he should have an effective means of self-regulation. However, he needs an objective viewpoint, not wedded to the execution of the work, for most effective control of results.

Role of Specialized Staff

The specialized staff manager generally assists the line and other staff functions in two ways:

1. By performing advisory activities—that is, he provides advise, counsel, suggestions, guidance, and consultation.

2. By performing service activities—that is, he performs work *for* the line and may make certain decisions which the line has asked him to make.

Advisory Activities of Specialized Staff. Specialized staff managers are, by definition, the best-informed and qualified individuals in their particular specialties. The advice offered by staff may be of several different kinds.

PLANNING ADVICE. Planning refers to the groundwork which must be laid before action can take place successfully. As Pullman-Standard Car Manufacturing Company defines it, planning is the thinking that precedes the actual performance of work. It is the determination of a course of action that will lead to a desired result. This being the case, plan-

ning should precede any activity undertaken by the line organization. However, planning in itself is a specialized skill. It requires study, investigation, and research to gather facts and information, analysis and evaluation of the data secured, development of alternatives, and final decision as to a specific plan of action. In a great many instances, this can be done most thoroughly and effectively by utilizing staff specialists.

The staff exercises functional guidance over the operating components. This does not mean that staff members issue orders, supervise activities, or control any position of the operating groups. Each staff man recommends policies to the head of the enterprise for his approval. Once these policies are approved, procedures in line with the policies are established—in some cases by the staff member concerned, and in other cases by the top position upon recommendation of the staff member.

After establishment of a procedure, the staff men within whose province the particular procedure falls furnish the appropriate operating component chief with technical or specialized advice and assistance in the application of the procedure. The staff member is responsible for furnishing this functional guidance, and is accountable to his principal for the fulfillment of his responsibility. In no case is the chief of the operating component subject to the orders, supervision, or control of the staff man; nor can he ever be held accountable to the staff member for fulfillment of his responsibilities.

The Management Guide, Standard Oil Company of California

Provision of advice in all stages of planning is a basic responsibility of the staff man. He is responsible for devising and recommending procedures and methods of operation in his specialty that can be followed throughout the company. After acceptance by the appropriate executive, the staff specialist also helps to interpret and explain these plans to line and other staff departments and offers advice on the implementation of the plans.

Policy planning is an important area in which staff operates in an advisory capacity. A basic responsibility of the specialized staff manager at the corporate level is that of studying the needs of the company so far as his specialty is concerned and recommending to his line principal appropriate policy.

The staff departments in Creole Petroleum Corporation, a company of 14,000 employees, develop and approve, or secure approval of, policies, plans, and procedures which, in their judgment, are required to achieve objectives and standards.

To do this, the staff departments in Creole study and analyze alternative policies, procedures, methods, and forms related to their specialized functions. They present proposals based on these studies and analyses to other departments and those committees concerned for their review and comment.

When necessary, the Creole Petroleum staff departments submit proposals to the board of directors or executive committee for approval. In other cases where the staff department has already been delegated authority by the president, it may determine and establish policies, systems, plans, or procedures. Having participated in their formulation, line departments are expected in these instances to support and actively carry out the policies and procedures which are originated by the staff departments.

INTERPRETING PLANS AND POLICIES. Objectives, plans, programs, policies, and procedures are effective only to the extent that they are understood and properly used. Because of his specialized knowledge and participation in the development of plans and policies, the staff specialist is in an excellent position to explain the meaning and application of specific plans to line and other staff components. It is to the staff specialist that the line manager will turn when he has a question or is seeking advice. Therefore, it is appropriate for the staff manager to explain these plans and policies to the line and how they can be adapted to special conditions.

In Creole Petroleum, the staff departments have a specific responsibility concerning the interpretation of plans. In practice the staff department manager transmits approved instructions for execution through the line departments. He also provides recommendations as to effective date, method of installation, or other advice.

When the approved proposal requires an addition or change to a published manual or guide, the staff department in Creole may transmit the revision directly to the holders of the manual or guide. However, they do this only after the department managers responsible for execution have issued instructions to make the revision effective.

Staff departments in Creole may also transmit other communications of an interpretative or explanatory nature to the field organizations, provided the same information is furnished concurrently to the line department which administers the field organization.

ADVICE ON IMPLEMENTING PLANS. In most companies, specialized staff departments are available in a consulting capacity to advise and guide the line in putting plans into operation. This is particularly true when operating problems occur in the area of the staff man's specialty. He can then provide technical and professional counsel which will help the line do a more effective job.

The specialized staff manager is in constant touch with departments within the company. He is thus in a particularly favorable position to note and evaluate any new methods or techniques that are developed in his area of specialization. When these developments have general application, the specialized staff man can give them wider currency by bringing them to the attention of others who might be interested.

In the New York Telephone Company, which has nearly 80,000 employees, the staff manager is responsible for obtaining a wide and comprehensive knowledge of the operation of the business in other divisions, areas, or companies and to pass the information on, thereby multiplying the knowledge of the line organization.

Staff managers often travel a good deal among the operating units of the company. This places them in a favorable position to note and disseminate information about new developments in their specialty. For example, in the Food Machinery and Chemical Corporation, which manufactures food and agricultural machinery and chemicals and has 13,000 employees, the central staff coordinator of management development travels extensively among the plants and offices of the company. He systematically notes and records any new developments in management development that might be of general value and passes this information along in his visits to other locations.

ADVISING ON PERFORMANCE. A major responsibility of the specialized staff department in many companies is that of advising line on how well plans are being carried out. This may include advice on the establishment of standards, the measurement of work in progress against these standards, and the reporting of variances or exceptions to the proper executive.

In a food company, specialized staff heads assist the line and other staff departments in setting up controls in their area of specialization. They help the line organization to identify hazards and opportunities and suggest appropriate action to them. The staff head also advises the line executive on ways and means to improve the effectiveness and efficiency of the various operating divisions in respect to the specialized staff activity for which he is responsible.

In Johns-Manville Corporation, specialized staff departments observe the manner in which the operating divisions carry on the work of their particular specialty. This observation gives the staff man an opportunity to evaluate the effectiveness of the plans which he has helped develop and to determine what revisions and extensions are necessary. Each specialized staff manager also reports to his principal the more important things which he observes in his specialty. This aids the line executive to improve and supplement his own performance.

The Atlantic Refining Company assigns to staff units the responsibility for reviewing the implementation of certain company policies. This responsibility may involve conducting investigations, making reviews and reporting findings to appropriate supervision.

Specialized staff departments in Standard Oil Company (Ohio) have a definite role in advising on performance. In this company, which has 11,000 employees, the staff may review and inspect operations through personal visits.

Staff may also request reports on current conditions, trends and other evidences of performance. To make his work effective, the staff man may render his own report to the operating executive as to the degree of performance in his specialty, indicating how well approved policies, plans and procedures are being followed and how objectives are being met.

The staff manager in Lockheed Aircraft Corporation, a company of 52,000 employees, has the responsibility for observing operating conditions related to his speciality. When he detects potential trouble spots, he advises the line manager concerned so as to keep things operating smoothly. He does this, however, without giving orders to the line.

In the New York Telephone Company, the staff manager is responsible for establishing methods and studying the conditions of the business. The staff manager helps the heads of operating units to analyze results and to determine weaknesses. He also suggests remedies or alternative methods of operation.

DANGERS IN STAFF CONTOLS. There are obvious dangers in having the staff man operate as an appraiser of the performance of line units, even on an advisory basis. He may arouse a good deal of resentment and even excite active opposition to his activities. Humble Oil & Refining Company, which has 19,000 employees, has given this problem serious consideration. Humble feels that if a staff man is to be used for control, it should be presumed that he will act impersonally, as objectively and as impartially as the recording meter. He simply gathers facts and presents them to his chief, but in so doing he does not infringe upon the functions of the line organization or other staff groups. As a competent staff man serving the entire organization, he will call a supervisor's attention to the facts he has collected before making them known to the supervisor's superior.

The control section of Koppers Company, Inc., in carrying out its functions, operates purely in an advisory capacity. If discrepancies are found in the operations of a line or staff unit of the company, the head of the unit is advised. The responsible head may take corrective action on his own initiative. If not, the president is advised of the control section's findings. The president then takes whatever action he considers desirable.

Service Activities of Specialized Staff. Staff may provide service by performing specified activities *for* the line. For example, the personnel department may recruit, select and, on occasion, actually employ people for the line and other staff departments. The purchasing department may buy materials and supplies for the line. Finance installs accounting, budgetary, and reporting systems. These activities usually involve highly specialized skills that are best developed apart from the line organization for the reasons given earlier.

It is to be noted that in each case where the staff performs a service activity for the line, authority for performing that service and final decision as to whether it will be done and how it will be done rests with the line. For example, the standard accounting procedures necessary to compile a consolidated balance sheet are not authorized by the finance department, if it is a staff department. They are authorized by the president, who gives either explicit or implied authority to the accounting department to install *for him* the accounting system which will best serve the objectives of the company.

As another example, the personnel manager who recruits college graduates, and who may even hire them, is acting only at the express request of the line departments he serves. He recruits and employs the number and kind of people the line departments specify.

Service activities may be performed by specialized staff at several levels in the company. For example, in one company, the president has a specialized staff purchasing department which formulates policies, procedures, and controls on a company-wide basis governing the purchase of materials and services required in operating the company's business. This department prepares plans and recommendations concerning the type and extent of procurement to be performed by other units. It also coordinates purchases between operating divisions with respect to materials, quantities, and procedures.

In an operating division of this company, the manager of the specialized staff purchasing department reports to the division manager. This staff department is responsible for the purchase of materials, supplies, equipment, and services for the division's plants and offices upon requisition by proper authority.

The buyers in the purchasing department are technically trained. They are informed regarding the technicalities of the materials for which they are responsible. The purchasing department has been delegated authority to decide for the line where materials and supplies can be best procured, as to price, quality, and availability, and the purchasing department actually makes the purchase.

The inspection or quality control function often has many responsibilities which are predominantly service in character. However, here again, there is also a definite advisory activity.

The quality control specialized staff may prepare specifications and standards for products, for purposes of both purchasing and production. It may study and report upon complaints regarding quality of products. The quality control staff may have the authority to inspect and reject the product when it does not conform to the standards of quality established for it. It also acts in an advisory capacity to the line production head in any problem he may have concerning the control of quality in the product.

Variations in Advice and Service Needed. In most companies, at all levels, specialized staff provides both advice and service to the line. The relative proportion of advice and service rendered frequently varies with the level within the company at which it takes place. For example, most staff activities at the top management level are advisory in character. Little service, or *doing for* the line is required. The personnel administration department is largely *advisory* to the president; yet the extent of its *service* to him may be that of finding a new secretary or writing a speech to be read at the annual picnic. At the plant manager level, staff takes over proportionately more service or *doing* activities. For example, the purchasing staff actually purchases *for* the plant manager and his departments; the traffic department arranges shipments for the plant manager and plant departments. Advice at this level may be confined almost entirely to interpretation and implementation of company policy and programs in the specialized staff areas. (See Fig. 6.)

At the lowest level of management, staff activities may be largely "doing" and only to a very small extent advisory. For example, in many companies the training specialist leads conferences for the foreman, the payroll de-

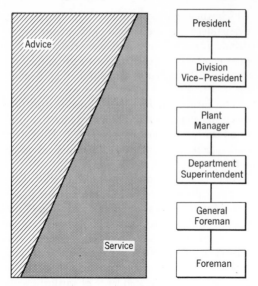

President

Division
Vice–President

Plant
Manager

Department
Superintendent

General
Foreman

Foreman

Fig. 6. Variations in advice and service provided by staff at different company levels.

partment makes out the payrolls for the people who work for the foreman, the inspectors from the quality control department inspect subassemblies and unit assemblies for the foreman.

Making Specialized Staff Available to All Levels

Managers at all levels need staff assistance. However, the amount needed varies at different levels in the company. For instance, the foreman has a much simpler management job than the plant manager. His responsibilities are likely to be less complex and more limited in scope. Instead of being responsible for the whole range of costs in the plant, he is concerned only with direct and indirect labor and materials and burden costs allocable to his job. His need for the specialized services of the cost accountant is relatively small compared to that of the plant manager.

Staff assistance is usually provided in the amount that each level of management needs and can afford. In many companies, the specialized staff is organized so that its services are available to all levels of management. If the foreman needs help from the engineering department for only one hour a day, he is charged this proportion of the total cost of the engineer's services. Relatively higher proportions of the total cost are allocated to other levels, in keeping with the amount of use they make of the staff provided.

Decentralization

PETER DRUCKER

In this study General Motors is considered only as an example of the social structure and of the institutional problems of the big-business corporation. No attempt will be made to give a description of General Motors as such, or of its history—let alone of its products and results. However, an elementary knowledge of the main outlines of the organization and of its policies will be useful.

The domestic manufacturing properties of General Motors can be classed in three groups according to their main peace-time products. First in employment and volume of business comes the automobile and truck group: Chevrolet, Buick, Oldsmobile, Pontiac, Cadillac and General Motors Truck. To this group belongs also the Fisher Body Division, which produces the bodies for all automobile divisions and which works in closest contact with them. Most of the Fisher plants, though managed separately by the Body Division, are physically combined with the assembly plants of the automobile producers.

The second group consists of the manufacturers of automobile accessories who produce most of the accessory needs of the automobile plants. A good many of the accessory producers sell also outside of General Motors. In addition to the spare parts and replacement business which is very important for practically all accessory divisions, some of them, notably the producers of spark plugs, roller bearings, ball bearings and electrical motors, sell directly to other industrial producers who

From *Concept of the Corporation*. Boston: Beacon Press, 1960, pp. 41–71. Copyright 1946 by Peter Drucker. Reprinted with permission of the author.

in some cases account for more than fifty per cent of total sales. To this group also belongs Frigidaire—both historically and according to its manufacturing and engineering problems—which sells exclusively to the public.

The third group of manufacturing properties consists of three Diesel engine producers in Cleveland, Detroit and La Grange, Illinois, whose products comprise small Diesel engines for trucks, marine Diesel engines, and the huge Diesel-electric locomotives which pull America's stream-lined trains. The Allison engine division producing aircraft engines also belongs in this group of non-automotive engine producers.

During the war General Motors added to these three main foci of activities a number of aircraft producing plants located on the Eastern seaboard; these plants which were under one management and organized in the Eastern Aircraft Division presented a special reconversion problem.

These three groups of manufacturing properties are organized in about thirty divisions ranging in size from Chevrolet and Fisher Body, which would be among the largest American businesses by themselves, to small one-plant appliance divisions, employing in peacetime less than a thousand men. Each of these divisions has its own divisional manager who is served by almost as complete a staff as if he were heading an independent business: production manager, chief engineer, sales manager, comptroller, personnel manager, etc.; in other words, each division is organized as an autonomous unit. The three largest of these divisions: Chevrolet, Fisher Body and Buick, are represented in the top management by their own divisional managers. The other divisions are organized in groups according to their products, each under a group executive who, as a vice-president of General Motors, acts as representative of his group in the central management of the corporation and as adviser and representative of central management for the divisional managers of his group.

Side by side with this organization according to products there is, as a part of central management, a set of functional service staffs: manufacturing, engineering, sales, research, personnel, finance, public relations, law, etc., each under its own vice-president. These staff organizations advise both central management and the divisional managers, act as liaison between the divisions and formulate corporation policies.

The "line organization"—the manufacturing divisions—is headed by the President and his two Executive Vice-Presidents; the "staff work" is headed by the Chairman of the Board who is the Chief Executive Officer of General Motors, and by the Vice-Chairman of the Board. These five officials form a team. They work through and with two closely co-ordinated committees, one on policy, one on administration. In addition to top management these committees contain the senior administrative and staff officers of the company, former officers now on the Board of Directors, and representatives of the major stockholders.

These two committees are the central organ of co-ordination, decision and control, and may well be called the government of General Motors. They pass on all major decisions in the fields of policy and administration. They hear periodic reports on conditions, problems and achievements in all branches of the business. And they are the court of last appeal should there be serious disagreements on policy within the organization. Hence all members of these committees—whether departmental executives in charge of service staffs or divisions, or members of top management—are almost automatically informed at all times about the work of all divisions, about all important problems and decisions in all fields, and also about the great line and, the over-all policies of the company. These functions, integration of "staff" and "line," combination of a variety of experiences and special backgrounds into one policy, presentation of the over-all picture to all the senior men, may well be more impor-

tant in the normal course of affairs than the decision-making power of the committees.

Each of these two top committees meets regularly to discuss and to decide. The actual executive work is, however, done by a number of specialized sub-committees, each in charge of a field such as engineering, labor, finance, public relations, distribution, etc. These sub-committees are very much smaller. They are built around a number of men from the field in question. The vice-president in charge of the appropriate service staff usually acts as the chairman. The membership includes experts in the field both from central management and from the divisions. But on each sub-committee there sit also several members of the top-management team and senior executives from other fields to balance the sectional viewpoint of the experts, to bring in a broader background of experience, and to relate the work of the sub-committee to the corporation as a whole. These sub-committees, in monthly meetings, actually work out the recommendations and presentations on which the two top committees act.*

Neither this sketch nor an organization chart can, of course, show the outsider how the organization actually functions. But it should give some impression of the administrative and organizational problems that have to be solved in order to make it run efficiently. There is the sheer size of the business—250,000 workers in peacetime, twice that number during the war. There is a problem of diversity: not only do the finished products—over two hundred in

---

* I have not come across much evidence that theories of governmental organization or historical examples had any considerable influence on the development of General Motors' managerial organization. The impetus seems to have been supplied mainly by experience and needs. Yet, there is a remarkably close parallel between General Motors' scheme of organization, and that of the two institutions most renowned for administrative efficiency: that of the Catholic Church and that of the modern army as first developed by the Prussian General Staff between 1800 and 1870 and later adopted everywhere. I tend to think that this scheme represents one of the basic solutions to the problem of institutional organization for survival and efficiency—the other one being the system of checks and balances between organs constructed upon contrasting principles of rule, for instance the one-man executive, committee-judiciary and many-men legislature of the American Constitution.

peacetime—range from a Diesel-electric loco-motive costing $500,000 to a bolt costing a frac-tion of a cent; the production units required range from gigantic plants with 40,000 em-ployees to machine shops. There is a problem in autonomy: the five hundred men of ability, experience and ambition who are needed in major executive jobs in order to turn out all these different finished products of General Motors could not possibly be organized and managed from the top. There is also a prob-lem of unity: with the bulk of the company's products focused on one final utility, the auto-mobile, and therefore directed towards the same market, the divisions could not be left to their own devices but must be one in spirit and in policy. Divisional management must be both autonomous and directed; central man-agement must at the same time give effective, unifying leadership and be confined to regula-tion and advice.

General Motors could not function as a holding company with the divisions organized like independent companies under loose finan-cial control. Central management not only has to know even minor details of divisional man-agement but the top officials have to exercise the power, the prestige and the influence of real bosses. On the other hand General Motors could not function as a centralized organiza-tion in which all decisions are made on the top, and in which the divisional managers are but little more than plant superintendents. Di-visional managers too must have the authority and standing of real bosses.

Hence General Motors has become *an essay in federalism*—on the whole, an exceedingly successful one. It attempts to combine the greatest corporate unity with the greatest di-visional autonomy and responsibility; and like every true federation, it aims at realizing unity through local self-government and vice versa. This is the aim of General Motors' policy of decentralization.

Decentralization, as the term is usually un-derstood, means division of labor and is noth-ing new. In fact, it is one of the prerequisites of any management whether that of a business or of any army. But in General Motors usage, decentralization is much more than that. In over twenty years of work, first from 1923 to 1937 as President, since then as Chairman of the Corporation, Mr. Alfred P. Sloan, Jr., has developed the concept of decentralization into a philosophy of industrial management and into a system of local self-government. It is not a mere technique of management but an outline of a social order. Decentralization in General Motors is not confined to the relations between divisional managers and central man-agement but is to extend in theory to all man-agerial positions including that of foreman; it is not confined in its operation within the com-pany but extends to the relations to its partners in business, particularly the automobile dealers; and for Mr. Sloan and his associates the ap-plication and further extension of decentraliza-tion are the answer to most of the problems of modern industrial society.

THE AIMS OF DECENTRALIZATION. Because General Motors considers decentralization a basic and universally valid concept of order, I asked several General Motors executives—particularly men well below the top—what in their opinion decentralization seeks to achieve. The following is a summary of the views of a good many different people. One man gave an unusually full statement of what he believed to be the aims and achievements of the policy of decentralization that was of particular in-terest because he himself had joined General Motors only two years earlier after a distin-guished career in another big business organ-ized on radically different lines; his statement —completely unrehearsed as my question was sprung at him in the course of an informal chat—has therefore been regarded as particu-larly valuable.

We shall have occasion later to discuss the question how much of its program decentrali-zation actually realizes; here are the advantages claimed for it:

1. The speed with which a decision can be made, the lack of any confusion as to who makes it and the knowledge of the policies on which the decision is based by everybody con-cerned.

2. The absence of any conflict between the interests of the divisions and those of General Motors.

3. The sense of fairness in dealing among executives, the certainty that a good job will be appreciated, the confidence and feeling of security that comes when personality-issues, intrigues and factionalism are kept under con-trol.

4. The democracy of management and its

informality. Nobody throws his weight around, yet there is never any doubt where the real authority lies. Everybody is free to criticize, to talk and to suggest; yet once the decision is taken, nobody tries to sabotage it.

5. The absence of a gap in the executive group between the "privileged few" and the "great many." "Mr. Wilson (the President) could not arrogate to himself any right he does not accord to his associates."

6. There is a very large management group. Thus there is always a supply of good and experienced leaders, able to take top responsibility.

7. Decentralization means that weak divisions and weak managers cannot ride for any length of time on the coat tails of successful divisions, or trade on their own past reputation.

> At the company I came from [this from the informant mentioned above] nobody ever knew whether the foundry was run efficiently or not, whether our foundry manager was a good or a bad manager; the foundry costs were centrally merged in the general costs. In General Motors, this foundry would be a division, so that the costs and the results of foundry operations would at once be visible to everybody.

8. Decentralization means the absence of "edict management" in which nobody quite knows why he does what he is ordered to do. Its place is taken by discussion and by policies which are public and which are arrived at as a result of the experiences of all the people concerned.

> Perhaps my greatest surprise when I joined General Motors [so again the above-mentioned informant] came when I attended my first 'Sloan meeting' [see below] and saw the extent to which even minor executives are informed of the reasons for company policies, and are encouraged to speak their mind freely and to express their opinions, however much they disagree with central management. In. . . . [the company where my informant had spent twenty years and where he had risen from apprentice to chief engineer] even senior executives were never told the reason for any central management decision.

It is obvious from this summary—as indeed it was obvious in my talks—that the executives of General Motors do not only consider decentralization to be the correct concept for the organization of a big business but that they feel that, at least on the level of top management, the concept has been realized and its aims achieved.

CENTRAL AND DIVISIONAL MANAGEMENT. Decentralization, as said above, is not considered as confined to top management but a principle for the organization of all managerial relationships. It was developed, however, out of the problems of co-ordinating central and divisional management into one whole. It has been tested most thoroughly on the top level of General Motors; and it has been most generally accepted and most successful on this level. Hence we shall study the meaning and the effects of the policy of decentralization by analyzing the relationships between central and divisional managements.

Central management has twofold functions under a system of decentralization. It is at the same time the servant of the divisional managers, helping them to be more efficient and more successful in their autonomy, and the boss of the corporation. And in this role it has to weld several hundred aggressive, highly individual and very independent divisional top executives into one team. These two jobs are apparently contradictory but actually interdependent. Their solution is attempted in various ways: (1) through the power of central management to set the goals for each division and for the whole corporation; (2) through its power to define the limits of authority of the divisional manager and through the power to appoint and remove divisional managers; (3) through its constant check on divisional problems and progress; (4) through relieving the divisional manager of all concern with problems that are not strictly part of the process of production and selling; (5) and finally through offering him the best obtainable advice and help through the service staffs of central management.

1. The manufacturing program of the various divisions has to be approved by central management, particularly as far as the car divisions are concerned; central management sets the price range within which Chevrolet, Buick, etc. operate. Beyond this range they cannot go without specific authorization. But no attempt is made to prevent Oldsmobile, for instance,

from trying to displace the low-priced Buick car. No attempt is made to tell Chevrolet what prices to pay the Fisher Body Division for its bodies. No attempt is made to force any of the car divisions to buy its accessories, such as lamps, from one of the General Motors divisions if the manager of a car division can show that he can get better value elsewhere.

Similarly in respect to the Diesel divisions, it is central management that will have to decide whether the overlapping production programs of two of these divisions—the result of historical developments antedating their acquisition by General Motors—are to be maintained or whether each division is to specialize on one type of engine.

Central management not only delimits the divisions against each other, it fits them into a general pattern as part of the unified corporation. It establishes the general over-all aim and allots to each division its role on the team. It establishes a total production goal on the basis of an analysis of the economic situation and assigns to each division its minimum quota. It determines how much capital to allot to each division.

Above all, central management thinks ahead for the whole Corporation. It is thus differentiated from divisional management not only in power and function but in time. A good divisional manager is fully as much concerned with the future as with the present; indeed one way to distinguish a divisional manager from divisional employees—some of whom, such as the managers of a few large plants owned by the big divisions, have many more people working for them than the manager of a small division—is by the divisional manager's responsibility for the long-term future of the business he runs. But it is not his responsibility to decide in what direction his division should develop; that is the responsibility of central management however much it may rely on the advice of divisional management. It is also the responsibility of central management to foresee problems and to work out solutions in advance. Central management furthermore works out major policy decisions applicable to problems common to all divisions. Finally, it decides on expansion into new lines—for instance on the expansion into the Diesel field, on the acquisition of new properties and the establishment of new divisions. *Of all the functions of central management, this responsibility to think ahead is perhaps the most important as it more than anything else makes General Motors a unified institution with but one purpose.*

2. Central management determines the limits within which the divisional manager operates. Within General Motors this is usually expressed by saying that central management makes policy decisions, while the divisional manager is in charge of administration. This is, of course, a misunderstanding. Every executive down to the lowliest assistant foreman makes policy decisions; and every executive, up to the Chairman of the Board, has administrative duties. But central management determines both the areas of decision for the divisional manager, and the general rules to which his decisions have to adhere. To phrase it in terms of constitutional law, policy decisions of a divisional manager must rest on an explicit or implicit delegation of policy-making power and must conform to implicit or explicit commands or be *ultra vires*.

And behind this, as an ultimate recourse, there is the absolute power of central management to remove a divisional manager and to appoint a new man in his stead. Obviously it is a rare and grave decision to dismiss the manager of a division, and it is regarded as most important by central management that it should be taken not on the basis of a personal impression regarding the man's ability and achievement, but on the basis of objective records. But this is voluntary self-restraint on the part of central management which does not affect its unquestioned final power of removal.

3. More in evidence in every day business conduct is the control through contact which central management exercises over divisional managers. Largely this is informal and a question of advice, discussion or mutual respect built up over years of collaboration. The vice-president in charge of a group of divisions, for instance, has a very real power; but it is rarely, if ever, exercised in the form of orders. Rather it makes itself felt through suggestions made in discussing problems or achievements of the division, in discussing central-management decisions, or as a result of the respect the divisional manager has for a man who, as is usually the case, has successfully been a divisional manager himself. The same kind of informal but very real control is exercised by the subcommittees of the Policy and Administration Committees with whom managers discuss their

problems, plans and policies, and, as will be discussed later, by the service staffs.

However there is a formal safeguard of central-management control, a formal veto power on all capital investments beyond a certain limit and on the hiring of executive personnel beyond a certain salary. This veto power is rarely exercised as a divisional manager is unlikely to make such a proposal without the support of his group-executive and of the appropriate service-staff. But it has the important result that practically every major policy decision of the divisions has to be discussed extensively with central management.

Equally important is central management's role in helping the divisional manager to be as effective as possible.

4. To this end the divisional manager is relieved of all worry over financial matters. As president of an independent company, he would have to spend a great deal of his time in obtaining the capital necessary for expansion. This worry is taken off his shoulders completely. It is the job of central management to obtain the capital for him for any program that has been decided upon as desirable. The same holds for legal matters. Also, General Motors has a uniform accounting system supervised and managed centrally. Finally, most union contracts and all negotiations in labor matters are handled centrally by a staff of the Corporation under a vice-president; this is, however, not the result of a decision to relieve the divisional manager of a worry only incidental to the business such as underlies the centralized handling of financial, legal and accounting matters, but is the result of the demand of the United Automobile Workers Union for a uniform contract for the company; and the wisdom of such a centralized labor policy is hotly debated within the Corporation.

5. Finally, the divisional managers are served through the service staffs of central management. Their first function is to advise the divisional manager whenever he feels in need of such advice. It is, for instance, quite customary for a newly appointed divisional manager to come to the Detroit office to obtain advice on the distribution of the bonus (see below) within his division. During the war the manufacturing staff at Central Office worked out the basic manufacturing processes for many war products upon the request of the

divisions; it is typical however of the way these staff agencies work that the final details of production and improvements in working methods were left entirely to the division.

Another important function of the staff agencies is to act as liaison between the various divisions, and particularly as centers of information on new or improved methods. If, for instance, one division has worked out a new way of treating cast aluminum which cuts down costs by five per cent, the other divisions interested in this or similar problems will at once be informed by the service staff. In this way, the service staffs attempt to make sure that all over General Motors the most advanced methods are used. In the same way, information about new problems that have arisen in one division and about difficulties to be encountered with a new product, a new method or a new labor policy is collected and transmitted to all the other divisions to save time and avoid costly errors. Similarly, the staff experts make available to the divisions the most up-to-date methods developed outside of General Motors, whether in research, in merchandising, in the handling of public relations, etc. This service function of central management alone probably is worth considerably more to the divisions than the one-half of one per cent of turnover that is charged by General Motors for the upkeep of the entire central management.

It should be emphasized that the staff agencies in their relations with the divisions rely on suggestions and advice, and that they have no direct authority whatsoever over the divisional manager and his policies. Of course they might appeal to top management in a last attempt to force an obstructionist divisional manager into line; this, however, is a theoretical rather than a practical recourse. In the normal course of events the service staffs have to "sell themselves" to the divisional manager, and have to rely on their ability to convince the divisional management and on their reputation and achievements. No divisional manager is under compulsion to consult the service staff or to take their advice. Yet the relationship between service staffs and divisional managers is on the whole quite frictionless.

Just as the service staffs apprise the divisional management of all important developments outside of his own division, they inform central management of all important developments within the divisions. To the service staffs—though not exclusively to them—central management owes its knowledge of the details of production, engineering, distribution and personnel management throughout the business, which is one of the most important factors in the teamwork between the policy-makers at the top and the administrators in the division.

Finally, it is the job of the service staff to formulate future policies in closest collaboration with both divisional managers and central management. The staff agencies themselves cannot lay down policies; they can only recommend. They must convince both the central management dealing with broad problems of corporation policy and the divisional managers with their concrete tasks, before any of their recommendations will be accepted as general Corporation policy.

Like any formal analysis of a functioning organization this description fails to convey what is really the most important thing: the way in which the organs of central management work. It gives only an outline of the frame within which central management operates, and not the picture itself. When we turn to the *divisional manager*, we cannot give even the frame. The nearest description of his status and operations might be to say that within the limits of policy and decision set for him by central management, he operates on his own as the boss of his outfit. He is in complete charge of production and sales. He hires, fires and promotes; and it is up to him to decide how many men he needs, with what qualifications and in what salary range—except for top executives whose employment is subject to a central-management veto. The divisional manager decides the factory layout, the technical methods and equipment used. He works out the capital requirements of his division and plans for expansion and for new plants—though central management must approve of major investments. The divisional manager is in charge of advertising and public relations for his division. He buys his supplies independently from suppliers of his own choice. He determines the distribution of production within the several plants under his jurisdiction, decides which lines to push and decides on the methods of sale and distribution. He makes contracts with dealers and gives or cancels their franchises. In everything pertaining to operations he is as much the real head as if his division were indeed an independent business. According to the estimate of several divisional managers—corroborated by members of the central management—ninety-five per cent of all decisions fall within his jurisdiction.

But this description, while correct, fails to convey one intangible though very significant fact: the atmosphere of a team of which the divisional manager is a member. There is no "General Motors atmosphere" and very definitely no "General Motors type." In fact I am greatly struck by the difference of atmosphere between divisions, and by the variety of personality and background between individual divisional managers. This variety is not only permitted, it is definitely encouraged by central management; for it is held that every man will do his best job when he does it his own way, and that each division will do its best job when it feels a pride in its tradition, manners and social climate. Hence central management refrains as much as possible from telling a division how to do its job; it only lays down what to do. Yet the divisional manager, though left alone as long as he does a good job, is conscious of his place on a team.

This is largely the result of two broad policies which will be discussed later in some detail: the system of impersonal yardsticks by which the performance of divisional managers is measured objectively in terms of their contribution to the team, and the interchange of factual and personal knowledge by which the divisional managers are kept informed of their place in the team, and of the work of the team. But the dual position of the divisional manager as being at one and the same time the autonomous boss of his division and a member of a unified team shows best in the administration of the General Motors Bonus Plan—which in itself is an important reason why this dualism works without too much tension.

General Motors sets aside each year a considerable part of its net profit for bonuses to executive employees, to be paid in General Motors shares (during the last years a cash alternative has been offered for part of the bonus to enable the recipients to pay wartime income taxes on the bonus without having to sell General Motors stock; this is, however, considered a temporary expedient). Top management decides how much bonus each divisional manager is to receive as his own personal compensation. It also decides the total to be allotted to each division for distribution among the employees below the rank of divisional manager. While guided by a formula expressing both the total results of the corporation and an appraisal of the results of the division, central management is independent in these decisions. Who is eligible for participation in the bonus is also decided centrally for all divisions; participation is usually confined to men above the income level of a general foreman. Finally there is a definite and strongly recommended pattern of bonus distribution. The more important a man's position the greater should be his stake in the profit; while bonuses in the lower ranks of management should be a relatively unimportant "extra," bonuses of higher executives should be a major source of income though very elastic.

But within these general rules and recommendations the divisional manager decides how the bonus is to be distributed among his subordinates. He may single out one department for a special award or penalize another. He may reward or penalize individuals. To safeguard against arbitrary or partisan decisions he has to obtain the approval of central management before he can make radical departures from precedent, and has to explain his reasons. Once approved, however, his decision is final.

For General Motors executives, particularly for the senior men, the bonus is in normal years a very important part of their income. Hence the power of the divisional manager to decide on its distribution makes him the boss in a very real sense though the general rules and the veto power of central management over the plans of the divisional manager make it difficult for him to be arbitrary or spiteful or to play favorites. At the same time the stake the divisional manager himself has in a bonus which represents both the results of his own division and the results of the whole business, tends to give him a strong incentive to do his best in running his division and to play a cooperative part on the team that is General Motors.

The bonus enables the divisional manager to be both independent and a member of the group. Under normal business and tax conditions the divisional manager even of a small division should become in a few years a moderately wealthy man, if he keeps his bonus stock as he is strongly urged to do. Thus he will soon be financially independent. He need not hesitate to express his own opinion, to object to corporation policy, or to run his own division his own way; for he does not have to keep his job at all costs, nor does he regard himself as in any way inferior to the men in central management; they may be much wealthier than he is but the difference is one of degree rather than one of kind. At the same time his prosperity is directly bound up with the prosperity of General Motors, the shares of which are usually his major asset. It is not a decisive factor in the working of the system of decentralized management that the executives of the company are the largest individual (that is non-corporate) shareholders as a result of the bonus plan, and that General Motors shares are the major assets of most of its executives; but it is important.

A TWO-WAY FLOW. Division of powers and of functions, unity in action—this definition of a federal union would be a fairly accurate description of the aim of General Motors' policy of decentralization. Such a union cannot rest on blind obedience to orders. It must be based on an understanding of each other's problems, policies, approaches, mutually between central management and divisional managers. Every one must not only know what is expected of him but also how his neighbor will act and why. It is a problem which all large organizations have to solve. Concretely, General Motors could not function if every decision had to be approved by a few overworked men in New York or Detroit. At the same time, it could not function if these men at the helm did not know of every major move within the business. Similarly, it could not function if the divisional managers had to determine basic policy at every step; and it could not function if they did not know and understand policy decisions and the reasons behind them. The first requirement of General Motors' management is, therefore, that as many of its executive employees as possible understand the policies, the problems and the program of the company and of its divisions. Both information and decision must flow continually in two directions: from central management to the divisions, from the divisions to central management.

We have already mentioned some of the devices used. The vice-president in charge of a group of divisions acts as a constant liaison on policy and performance between head office and division. The service staffs provide liaison in the technical fields not only between central management and divisions but between the divisions themselves. The sub-committees through which top management works have members from the divisions and call in divisional executives all the time to advise and be advised. In addition, there are special meetings to create common understanding, which are being held twice a year in Detroit under the chairmanship of Mr. Sloan, and at which important or acute problems are discussed. At these meetings the results of the various divisions are also shown and reasons for success and failure are discussed. Suggestions from the divisions or from central management are brought up for debate and unplanned but effective personal contacts are established between central management and divisional personnel. About two to three hundred people attend these meetings regularly; an equal number is invited in rotation. Thus practically every senior employee—beginning perhaps at the level of plant superintendent—has an opportunity to see the business as a whole, to see his place in it and to familiarize himself with the basic policies and the program of the company.

These meetings have been held for more than ten years and have been singularly successful. However, the group was felt to be too large to establish the personal contact between central office and divisional personnel that is necessary for the general understanding of policies and problems on which General Motors depends. Therefore the "Sloan meetings" in Detroit are now being supplemented by smaller meetings in the various centers of production in which members of the central management meet for several days with local executives of the divisions. The attendants at these meetings include all the people who are invited to the "Sloan meetings" and a number of lesser employees from the local plants and offices. Similar meetings are being held with dealers.

By these means managerial employees of the corporation are kept informed on policies and problems: they are also constantly brought into the determination of policies. No important policy decision is made without consulting the divisional executives affected by it. It is the right as well as the duty of every managerial employee to criticize a central man-agement decision which he considers mistaken or ill-advised. In fact, the one definition I could obtain of who is considered an executive in General Motors was: "A man who would be expected to protest officially against a policy decision to which he objects." Such criticism is not only not penalized; it is encouraged as a sign of initiative and of an active interest in the business. It is always taken seriously and given real consideration.

Central management does not of course base its decisions on the votes of the divisional personnel. It may completely disregard the opinions of divisional management. But in turning down a divisional executive it will attempt to explain to him its reasons. It is a standing rule that central management is to rely on persuasion and on rational proof rather than on an order. In debatable matters central management often prefers to wait until the divisional managers have themselves come and requested a policy decision rather than dictate from the top.

An example may illustrate the nature of this relationship. Several years ago, it was laid down as a general policy that all foremen should be on a salary basis rather than on hourly pay, and should enjoy seniority in layoffs over all hourly workers. During the war the number of foremen doubled. The new foremen were given the same status as the old foremen, lest they feel deprived of the relative security of seniority and thus in a worse position than the hourly workers in the event of a postwar depression. This decision was seriously attacked by several divisional managers who felt that it demoralized the old foremen who should be distinguished in some way as the permanent supervisory force of the company. The divisional managers brought their argument before the central management which at once agreed to reconsider the whole matter.

On the other hand central management does not hesitate to interfere directly and even ruthlessly whenever the interests or policies of the business are at stake. There is perhaps no greater contrast than that between the consideration shown to a divisional manager in all matters pertaining to the management of his division, and the co-operation expected of him in all matters where his conduct and policies directly affect the company as a whole. It is precisely here that the General Motors concept of central management functions pays its highest dividends. Because policy matters are usually discussed well in advance of the time when they become pressing, they can be handled leisurely and discussed freely and carefully. This, it is claimed, makes it possible to give all concerned a chance to think things through and to speak their minds without causing dangerous delay. Above all it makes it possible for central management to acquaint itself with the views of divisional management and vice versa. As a result when the time comes to put the policy into action everybody should know what he is supposed to do and why; every divisional manager should not only know where general policy begins and his autonomy stops but he should also accept the general policy as something he has helped formulate. Thus the question whose responsibility a certain decision is, will arise rarely, if ever.

FREEDOM AND ORDER. The impression that emerges from an analysis of the aims of General Motors' policy of organization is one of great individual liberty in which every man— at least among the three to five hundred first- and second-line executives—is to be allowed as much responsibility as he is willing to assume. There is little emphasis on title, rank or formal procedure. Indeed, the one thing that is most stressed by all executives is the "informality" that exists in the relationships among the members of this group and in the division of their work. This raises the question how General Motors avoids the dangers which according to age-old experience threaten every federal and especially every committee form of government: the danger of a deadlock between co-ordinated organs, the danger of a break-up of the organization in factionalism, intrigues and fights for power. It has always been a basic axiom of political theory that freedom such as General Motors accords to the members of its top management group is only possible within a clearly defined order with a strict division of authority and responsibility. General Motors, however, seems to lack largely what might be called a clear division of powers. Yet decisions must obviously be arrived at without too much delay or uncertainty as to who is entitled to make them, so as to enable the corporation to function in a highly competitive market. The question thus arises what it is that makes this "informality" possible. Can it be based solely on good will

and on good intentions? Or does it require a strict frame of objective policy as a condition of individual freedom? This, needless to say, is not a new but a very old question of politics —known in this country perhaps best as it appears in the conflict between Jeffersonian and Hamiltonian ideas of politics.

There is a tendency within General Motors to explain its functioning as owing to human individual good will rather than to institutional structure. There is a good deal to back up such an explanation. There can be no doubt that the informality, the reliance on information and persuasion, and the absence of "edict management" reflect accurately the personality of the man who developed General Motors to its present position—Alfred P. Sloan, Jr., for more than twenty years its active head. It is also certain that without Mr. Sloan's personality the system could never have grown up and established itself. Yet the tendency which underlies this "personality" explanation, to seek the basis of a political order in the personality of the ruler or in the good will of the citizens, is actually a very dangerous one. That it is current within General Motors is a potential weakness as it implies a lack of understanding by the organization of the factors from which it derives its strength. If it were true that the General Motors' system rested on individual good will, it could hardly survive the life span of one man. It would also have validity only for an organization headed by one particular type of personality and could not be regarded as a general model of industrial organization, which is precisely what General Motors aspires to be. Finally—and this is probably the most dangerous point for General Motors itself— such a belief might lead to a false sentimentalism, which evaluates executives according to the lip-service they pay to humanitarian principles, rather than according to their achievements.

Actually, General Motors' decentralization does not rest on the good will of the men in top management positions. It could, if necessary, function without the personal qualities which Mr. Sloan has shown in his long administration. Indeed it has been functioning with senior executives whose personalities were the very opposite of his, and who had nothing of the informality and of the respect for their fellow workers which would seem to be required. There must thus be an objective, impersonal frame of reference to make possible if not mandatory the freedom of decentralized management. This objective frame is given in the use of modern methods of cost accounting and market analysis as an impersonal yardstick to measure achievement of both policy-makers and production men.

This objective yardstick is comprised of two sets of measurements which apply equally to divisional management and its subordinates and to central management and its policy decisions: (1) Base pricing which gives an objective measure of the efficiency of the Corporation and of its subdivisions as a producer; (2) Competitive market standing which shows automatically and immediately the efficiency of the Corporation as a seller. Together these two gauges are supposed to show over-all efficiency and supply an immediate and objective check on decisions and policies.

The function of the system of base pricing is to measure the productive efficiency of all units of the business and also to eliminate from the measurement of productive costs all extraneous and transient factors, particularly those introduced by the fluctuations of the business cycle. Its core is that careful analysis of all the cost factors that enter into production at various rates of capacity which is the basis of modern accounting. This makes it possible to determine at one glance whether a certain division —or a department within a division—is producing with greater or lesser efficiency than the norm, and why. It also shows whether a good result is attributable to an increase in efficiency or to an improvement in methods, or whether it is the result of purely accidental factors for which management cannot claim credit. Above all, it makes it impossible to be deceived by a high profit in boom years if such profit is actually purchased at the expense of productive efficiency, that is at the risk of a permanent impairment of the company's strength. Conversely, it prevents a divisional manager from being blamed for the disappointing returns of a depression year when actually the result was caused by factors over which he had no control. Thus, a divisional manager will be held accountable for a deterioration of productive efficiency even when it is concealed by an increase in total profits; and he will get the credit for any strengthening of managerial efficiency, even when as the result of bad business conditions, his division operates at a loss. The cost analysis of base pricing thus gives an objective standard of manufacturing efficiency.

The instrument of base pricing also furnishes a yardstick for policy decisions—both before they are taken and afterwards. It shows the factors of productive efficiency that are likely to be affected by a policy decision, thus substituting facts for personal differences of opinion in policy arguments. It shows how costs will be affected by policy decisions deemed necessary or advisable not for reasons of productive efficiency but for such reasons as labor policy, merchandising, public relations, etc.

Base pricing also shows the use made of General Motors' capital. It measures the rate of return on capital invested and the factors: rate of capacity at which the plants operate, lifetime of the productive equipment, etc., on which this rate depends. The assumptions under which any given investment is made can thus be isolated and checked against actual economic developments all the time. It thus furnishes a basis for policy decisions on expansion and measures the advisability of proposed new capital investments.

It is indicative of the concept of management that is embodied in General Motors organization that the cost analysis underlying base pricing is made by the divisions—just as it is customary in a good many divisions to have the department heads such as superintendents and foremen make the cost analysis for their jobs. The necessary check is supplied by a comparison of the cost analysis of each division with those of other divisions within the company making comparable products or using comparable methods—one reason for the company's insistence on uniform accounting practices throughout all divisions.

Efficient production is only one element in the success of a business in a free-enterprise economy, and has to be complemented by ability to sell one's products in the market. Hence, in General Motors an objective analysis of the market and of the competitive standing of the products is used as the second measurement. The consumer's decisions and preferences are combined with the facts of the engineer to give an impersonal basis for decisions and for the evaluation of performance. Again the problem is how to eliminate purely extraneous fluctuations in measuring performance. This is done for the car-producing divisions by measuring their achievement and competitive standing not in terms of total sales but according to the ratio of their sales to total automobile sales in their price range. A car division which would show a loss in percentage of its potential market would be considered as losing ground even though—as a result of prosperous business conditions—it might roll up high absolute sales figures. On the other hand, it is generally understood that the management of Cadillac has been doing an outstanding job over the last fifteen years, even though the dollar volume of sales has gone down sharply. The share of the division in the total sales of high-priced cars has risen; the fall in absolute sales volume is thus not chargeable to Cadillac but to a shrinkage of the market for higher priced cars over which the Cadillac management has had no control and for which it can not be blamed.

Since the accessory divisions produce largely for use within General Motors their efficiency could not be measured in terms of their competitive standing on the consumer's market. Hence they are measured by a different—and perhaps even a more severe—standard, their ability to supply the car divisions at lower cost than any outsider. As mentioned above, no car division is under compulsion to buy from the accessory divisions, or under compulsion to pay the prices demanded by them. To obtain the custom of the car divisions, each accessory division must be able to meet the lowest prices of outside accessory manufacturers and to satisfy the quality and styling requirements of the car divisions. Most of them are therefore subjected to the test of competition as much as the car divisions. And while individual car buyers will often decide on the basis of habit or advertising appeal, that is on economically non-rational grounds, the accessory producers have to satisfy a buyer who is interested only in tangible and provable economic factors.

The yardstick of market performance is based on the assumption that consumers' buying preferences and even their prejudices are as much objective facts for the producer as are the facts and figures of engineering and accounting which underlie base pricing. It is as necessary to analyze the consumer's preferences as it is to analyze cost factors. Without knowledge of the elements which make up the consumer's decision, it would be impossible to find the causes of faulty selling performance or

to plan rationally for improvements in the competitive position of a division, or of the business as a whole. Hence, General Motors has built up a comprehensive consumer research organization.

The combination of these two elements of objective analysis, base pricing and competitive market standing, has made possible a considerable degree of production planning. Annually each division submits estimated schedules for the next year in which it gives tentative figures for sales, costs and expected capital requirements on the assumption of a good, an average, and a bad year for the industry as a whole. It also indicates which of these three estimates it considers most likely on the basis of its knowledge of business conditions, trends in the used-car market, etc. By correlating the estimates of the various divisions, central management obtains a fairly representative picture of conditions in the industry as a whole. By closely checking this composite judgment of the producing and selling personnel against the analysis of the consumer research staff and of the company's economists, a result is obtained which should not only be fairly reliable but which also is comprehensible to the executives, thus setting an objective frame for the work of the members both of central and of divisional management.

Through measuring the efficiency and achievement of both policy decision and administration against the objective criteria of cost and efficiency, of return on the invested capital, and of competitive standing in the market, General Motors aims at the elimination of personal and subjective elements in the relationship between boss and subordinate, central management and divisional management. The questions, how efficient is a man, how successful is he, and how important is he to the company, do not have to be decided on the basis of subjective preference. In fact, they should not have to be decided at all; they should be answered clearly by the objective yardstick that records efficiency and achievement immediately and automatically. The President of the company does not have to tell a divisional manager that he is not satisfied with him; the divisional manager knows it anyhow by looking at the figures based on his own cost and market analysis. Similarly, the President does not have to justify a promotion to the colleagues of the promoted man;

he has the man's record which is known within the company. Also the objective yardstick should limit the personal element in policy decisions. If a man's opinion or suggestion are overruled it should be not because of the higher rank of the boss, but because the facts are against him. That would make it possible for superiors freely to admit mistakes to their subordinates—perhaps the most important thing in human relations. In fine, this objective yardstick should not only make possible informal and friendly personal relations, a spirit of teamwork and a free and frank discussion. It should also—at least, that is what the people in General Motors claim—make the organization of management as a team on a federal basis natural and almost inevitable by erecting strong barriers of fact against action based on nothing but seniority and rank.

Overcoming Obstacles to Effective Delegation

WILLIAM H. NEWMAN

"Go West, young man!" was Horace Greeley's counsel for success a century ago. Today, in management circles, the common advice is: "Delegate. Decentralize."

Why is this advice so often disregarded? Many management practices are open to uncertainty and debate, but there is substantial agreement in this country on the desirability of delegation. Experience, especially during the last war, has shown a remarkable capacity in people down the line to shoulder responsibility and get results. We also know that wise delegation is an important training device and helps build morale. Yet, in company after company, executives frankly admit that they do not delegate as much as they can and should.

The malady is not universal, of course. The production achievements of American business would not have been possible without assignment of tasks—and accompanying freedom of action—to literally millions of individuals. Still, in large companies and small ones, we hear:

He's overworked but he won't let go.

There's a good man if only his boss would turn him loose.

Everybody agrees it's a one-man show but we can't seem to break the pattern.

If we could overcome the obstacles to delegation in such cases as these, the resulting resiliency and flexibility would add further strength to the company and our business

---

From *Management Review*, January 1956, pp. 36–41. Reprinted with permission of American Management Association.

structure. What, then, is the nature of the difficulty?

To sharpen the problem, let us set aside the cases where the boss, at any level—president, district manager, superintendent, or first-line supervisor—does not want to delegate. Some bosses are little Napoleons who can satisfy their egos only by keeping all the authority to make decisions within their own hands. Also, the boss's boss may hold such a tight rein that the junior man does not dare delegate further. Then, there are some men in executive positions who haven't given enough thought to management *per se* to recognize the advantages of decentralization. A lack of desire to delegate for such reasons as these is a problem in itself.

But what of the cases where effective delegation is lacking even though it is recognized as desirable? All too often the boss may give lip-service to delegation and sincerely agree that it is desirable, but for some reason the right to decide—with corresponding responsibility and initiative—does not pass down the line.

Effective delegation centers around a personal relationship between two individuals: The boss and his immediate subordinate. The boss, who is accountable for achieving certain results, looks to the subordinate for the performance of parts of the job, and toward this end gives him permission to take certain action. The greater the freedom of action, the higher the degree of delegation. The subordinate, on the other hand, accepts an obligation to use his talents to accomplish the mission.

In practice, this is typically a growing and shifting relationship between the two men. The freedom and initiative which the subordinate is expected to exercise can rarely be spelled out in detail; the substance of the delegation takes on real meaning in the working habits which are developed from day to day. These habits and attitudes, in turn, are shaped by the subtle interplay of the two personalities involved.

The personal adjustments involved in effective delegation cannot be created by an order from the president or a page in the organization manual. Formal statements regarding organization have an influence, of course, as does company tradition. An organization plan, however, does not become reality until it is incorporated into the behavior pattern of the specific individuals involved. This is the point where delegation so often breaks down.

A closer look at some of the tugs and pulls on the two people involved in delegation may reveal blocks to desired behavior. The following list suggests some of the common pitfalls. An executive who is plagued with a failure of real delegation to occur at a specific point in his organization may well find the root of the trouble among these stumbling blocks. At the least the analysis gives an approach which can profitably be applied to such weak spots.

Let us look first at some of the reasons why executives are loath to delegate and then turn our attention to common reasons why subordinates hesitate to take responsibility.

REASONS FOR RELUCTANCE TO DELEGATE. 1. Some executives get trapped in the *"I can do it better myself" fallacy*. A man who is both conscientious and has high standards of performance is naturally tempted to perform himself any activity that he can do better than his subordinates. This may be anything from writing advertising copy to directing repair work when a machine breaks down. Assuming that the executive really can do the job better (which is not true quite so often as he thinks it is), the executive must nevertheless reconcile himself to turning the job over to someone whose performance will be "good enough." The choice the executive has to make is not between the quality of work he or his assistant will do on the specific task; instead, he should compare the improvement in performance resulting from doing the work himself against the benefits to the total operation which will arise from devoting his attention to planning and supervision, which only he is in a position to per-

form. Only after an executive accepts emotionally and intellectually the idea that his job requires getting the most things done through other people will full use be made of delegation.

2. *Lack of ability to direct* is another barrier to successful delegation. The executive must be able to communicate to his subordinate, often far in advance, what is to be done. This means that the executive must (*a*) think ahead and visualize the work situation, (*b*) formulate objectives and general plans of action, and then (*c*) communicate these to his subordinate. After the two men have worked together for a period of time, this process may be extremely informal, but it is still important that the three key elements be present.

All too often executives have not cultivated this ability to direct. The author remembers well one of his first bosses, a very friendly individual with shrewd business judgment, who simply could not tell a man working for him what he wanted done more than a few hours ahead of time. Life for subordinates was a bit precarious because success depended upon guessing how the boss's mind would work before the boss himself had formulated his ideas. Here was a man who wanted desperately to delegate, but could do so only for repetitive situations because he was unable to identify and communicate the essential features of his long-range plans.

3. A third possible block to effective delegation is *lack of confidence in subordinates*. Here, the executive hesitates to turn things over to his subordinate because:

He'll take care of the details all right but miss the main point.

I'm not sure of his judgment in a pinch.

He has ideas but doesn't follow through.

He's too young to command the respect of the other men.

—or some other doubt about the ability to get the job done.

When this kind of a situation is open and recognized, the remedy is clear. Either training should be started immediately or, if this is impractical, a new subordinate found. Often the situation is by no means so clear-cut, however. The lack of confidence may be subjective and almost unconscious. Where this is so, the executive is likely to give lip-service to delegation but in the actual working relationship won't let go.

4. A related obstacle to delegation is *absence of selective controls which give warning of impending difficulties*. Problems beyond those covered by the delegation may arise, and the executive naturally wants to avoid being caught with no warning. Consequently, the executive needs some "feedback" on what is going on. Such information is also useful for counseling and for appraising final results. While care must be taken that the control system does not undermine the very essence of delegation, it is also true that the executive cannot completely abdicate his responsibilities. Unless the executive has confidence in the adequacy of the controls set up he probably will be very cautious about delegating.

5. Finally, the executive may be handicapped by *a temperamental aversion to taking a chance*. Even with clear instructions, proper subordinates and selective controls, there still remains the possibility that something will go wrong. The greater the number of subordinates and the higher the degree of delegation, the more likely it is that sooner or later there will be trouble. The executive who delegates takes a calculated risk. Over a period of time, he expects that the gains from delegation will far offset the troubles that arise. Until the executive sees this characteristic of his job, and adjusts to it emotionally as well as intellectually, he is likely to be reluctant to delegate.

These five obstacles to effective delegation are all related to the attitudes of the boss—the man who is doing the delegating. Fortunately, the attitudes of most men can be modified, at least in intensity. So, when you are faced with a specific situation where authority is in fact not being delegated as it should be, look first for reasons why the executive may be reluctant to turn over authority to someone else.

WHY SUBORDINATES AVOID RESPONSIBILITY. Delegation, as noted above, is a two-sided relationship. Even when the boss is ready and able to turn over authority, there may be reasons why the subordinate shrinks from accepting it. Something within the subordinate himself or in the relationship with his boss may become a block. Let us look at some likely difficulties on the part of the subordinate.

1. Often the subordinate finds it *easier to ask the boss* than decide for himself how to deal with a problem. Making a wise decision is usually hard mental work, and men are perpetually seeking formulas or short cuts to avoid this labor. If a man finds that he can take a half-baked idea or a problem to his boss and get an answer, it is natural for him to do so. In addition, making one's own decisions carries with it responsibility for the outcome. Asking the boss is a way of sharing, if not shifting, this burden. Over a period of time, asking the boss becomes a habit and the man develops a dependence upon his boss rather than on himself.

A habit of taking all the non-routine and tough decisions to the boss can best be broken by an agreement between the two men concerned to mend their ways. If the practice is of long standing, perhaps the executive will have to resort to stubborn refusal even to give advice. Then, after a period of "throw him in the water and let him swim," a more healthy coaching relationship can be established. The distinction between advice, decision and orders will, however, remain slippery and the boss must constantly be on his guard that his advice does not undercut the attitudes of initiative and responsibility he is striving to build.

2. A second factor which deters a man from embracing greater responsibility is the *fear of criticism* for mistakes. Much depends upon the nature of the criticism. Negative criticism is often resented where constructive review might be accepted. "The old man sure raised the roof, but I swear I don't know what I'd do differently if it happened again."

"Unreasonable" criticism is likely to evoke even sharper reactions. Unreasonableness, in this situation, must be defined in terms of the feeling of the subordinate. If he feels that unfavorable results were beyond his control, that his duties and authority were not clear, that his actions were wise in terms of the situation as he knew it at the time, or that he has not been given an opportunity to explain his side of the story, the criticism will have a cowing effect.

Negative or unreasonable criticism given publicly in a way which embarrasses a man before fellow workers adds salt to the wound. The impact of such criticism on a man's willingness to take on new responsibility is direct. He naturally will be inclined to be cautious and play it safe, if he has learned from experience that taking on more risk may result in an embarrassing and unwarranted bawling out. The subordinate's feeling is, "Why should I stick my neck out for that guy?"

3. Most men hesitate to accept responsibility when they believe they *lack the necessary information and resources* to do a good job. The enthusiasm of a newly appointed training director in an industrial company, for example, was dampened when he found he had virtually no equipment and very poor secretarial help. Then, when top management officials not only were too busy to see him, but also failed to keep him advised of changes in company planning which affected training needs, he lost most of his remaining initiative. Here again, much depends upon attitudes and expectations. It is possible for a person reared in a restraining web of budgetary and personnel limitations to accept responsibility knowing full well he will have to battle for each step he takes. Generally, however, the frustrations that go along with inadequate information and resources create in the man an attitude which rejects further assignments. Such a barrier makes effective delegation difficult indeed.

4. A fourth obstacle to accepting responsibility is simply that the subordinate may already have *more work than he can do.* True, such an overload may be the man's own fault; for example, he may make poor use of his own time or fail to hire trained, competent assistants even though he has the authority to do so. But, from the point of view of his willingness to accept responsibility, the cause of the overwork is not the critical point. If he already feels overburdened, he will probably shy away from new assignments which call for thinking and initiative.

5. *Lack of self-confidence* stands in the way of some men's accepting responsibility. The boss believes the man can do the job and is willing to take the risk of the outcome, but the man is unsure of himself and doesn't like to take the plunge. Ordering the man to have self-confidence will have little effect. In many cases, however, self-confidence may be developed by carefully providing experience with increasingly difficult problems to help the man sense his own potentialities. To be sure, some men may not have the psychological make-up to carry heavy responsibilities—but here, again, World War II provided us with many examples of far greater latent ability than appeared on the surface.

6. Finally, *positive incentives may be inadequate.* As already noted, accepting additional responsibility usually involves more mental work and emotional pressure. In the lower ranks of some companies, there is some social stigma on the "eager beaver" who is pushing to get ahead. Also, there is more or less risk of failure; failure is unpleasant and may result in embarrassing removal from the job. For these reasons, there should be positive inducements for accepting delegated responsibility. These inducements may take all sorts of forms, such as pay increases, better opportunity for promotion, fancier title, recognized status in the organization, more pleasant working conditions, additional power, personal recognition and approval by respected members of the enterprise, and other rewards both tangible and intangible. The important point is that the specific subordinate affected by delegation should be provided with a positive incentive which is important to him.

CONCLUSIONS. We see, then, a variety of possible reasons why a subordinate may hesitate to accept new responsibilities. These and other points which might be added to the list emphasize the need to think about the specific individuals involved and the factors which will affect their reactions to a change in delegation of authority.

Fortunately, many delegations encounter none of these obstacles, and in other situations there may be only one or two points which interfere with effective delegation. In any case, the list of common reasons for reluctance on the part of the boss and of the subordinate suggests potential difficulties to look for, and provides a frame of analysis that should be useful even when the specific points don't happen to fit a given situation.

The main thing that all of us who are enthusiastic about delegation and decentralization ought to remember is that the carrying out of such plans requires the adjustment of atttiudes and behavior patterns of specific individuals and a workable adjustment in their relationships. Such adjustments are a normal occurrence in a dynamic society, but we must recognize that they take time and that some individuals are more adaptable than others. Our best plans will come to naught until these personal adjustments have been made.

How to Choose a Leadership Pattern

ROBERT TANNENBAUM AND WARREN H. SCHMIDT

Should a leader be democratic or autocratic in dealing with his subordinates—or something in between?

I put most problems into my group's hands and leave it to them to carry the ball from there. I serve merely as a catalyst, mirroring back the people's thoughts and feelings so that they can better understand them.

It's foolish to make decisions oneself on matters that affect people. I always talk things over with my subordinates but I make it clear to them that I'm the one who has to have the final say.

Once I have decided on a course of action, I do my best to sell my ideas to my employees.

I'm being paid to lead. If I let a lot of other people make the decisions I should be making, then I'm not worth my salt.

I believe in getting things done. I can't waste time calling meetings. Someone has to call the shots around here, and I think it should be me.

Each of these statements represents a point of view about "good leadership." Considerable experience, factual data, and theoretical principles could be cited to support each statement, even though they seem to be inconsistent when placed together. Such contradictions point up the dilemma in which the modern manager frequently finds himself.

From *Harvard Business Review*, Vol. 36, No. 2, March–April 1958, pp. 95–101. Reprinted with permission of the publisher.

New Problem

The problem of how the modern manager can be "democratic" in his relations with subordinates and at the same time maintain the necessary authority and control in the organization for which he is responsible has come into focus increasingly in recent years.

Earlier in the century this problem was not so acutely felt. The successful executive was generally pictured as possessing intelligence, imagination, initiative, the capacity to make rapid (and generally wise) decisions, and the ability to inspire subordinates. People tended to think of the world as being divided into "leaders" and "followers."

New Focus. Gradually, however, from the social sciences emerged the concept of "group dynamics" with its focus on *members* of the group rather than solely on the leader. Research efforts of social scientists underscored the importance of employee involvement and participation in decision making. Evidence began to challenge the efficiency of highly directive leadership, and increasing attention was paid to problems of motivation and human relations.

Through training laboratories in group development that sprang up across the country, many of the newer notions of leadership began to exert an impact. These training laboratories were carefully designed to give people a first-hand experience in full participation and decision making. The designated "leaders" deliberately attempted to reduce their own power and to make group members as responsible as possible for setting their own goals and methods within the laboratory experience.

It was perhaps inevitable that some of the people who attended the training laboratories regarded this kind of leadership as being truly "democratic" and went home with the determination to build fully participative decision making into their own organizations. When ever their bosses made a decision without convening a staff meeting, they tended to perceive this as authoritarian behavior. The true symbol of democratic leadership to some was the meeting—and the less directed from the top, the more democratic it was.

Some of the more enthusiastic alumni of these training laboratories began to get the habit of categorizing leader behavior as "democratic" or "authoritarian." The boss who made too many decisions himself was thought of as an authoritarian, and his directive behavior was often attributed solely to his personality.

New Need. The net result of the research findings and of the human relations training based upon them has been to call into question the stereotype of an effective leader. Consequently, the modern manager often finds himself in an uncomfortable state of mind.

Often he is not quite sure how to behave; there are times when he is torn between exerting "strong" leadership and "permissive" leadership. Sometimes new knowledge pushes him in one direction ("I should really get the group to help make this decision"), but at the same time his experience pushes him in another direction ("I really understand the problem better than the group and therefore I should make the decision"). He is not sure when a group decision is really appropriate or when holding a staff meeting serves merely as a device for avoiding his own decision-making responsibility.

The purpose of our article is to suggest a framework which managers may find useful in grappling with this dilemma. First we shall look at the different patterns of leadership behavior that the manager can choose from in relating himself to his subordinates. Then we shall turn to some of the questions suggested by this range of patterns. For instance, how important is it for a manager's subordinates to know what type of leadership he is using in a situation? What factors should he consider in deciding on a leadership pattern? What difference do his long-run objectives make as compared to his immediate objectives?

Range of Behavior

Figure 1 presents the continuum or range of possible leadership behavior available to a manager. Each type of action is related to the degree of authority used by the boss and to the amount of freedom available to his subordinates in reaching decisions. The actions seen on the extreme left characterize the manager who maintains a high degree of control while those seen on the extreme right characterize the manager who releases a high degree of control. Neither extreme is absolute; authority and freedom are never without their limitations.

Now let us look more closely at each of the behavior points occurring along this continuum:

The Manager Makes the Decision and Announces It. In this case the boss identifies a problem, considers alternative solutions, chooses one of them, and then reports this decision to his subordinates for implementation. He may or may not give consideration to what he believes his subordinates will think or feel about his decision; in any case, he provides no opportunity for them to participate directly in the decision-making process. Coercion may or may not be used or implied.

The Manager "Sells" His Decision. Here the manager, as before, takes responsibility for identifying the problem and arriving at a decision. However, rather than simply announcing it, he takes the additional step of persuading his subordinates to accept it. In doing so, he recognizes the possibility of some resistance among those who will be faced with the decision, and seeks to reduce this resistance by indicating, for example, what the employees have to gain from this decision.

The Manager Presents His Ideas, Invites Questions. Here the boss who has arrived at a decision and who seeks acceptance of his ideas provides an opportunity for his subordinates to get a fuller explanation of his thinking and his intentions. After presenting the ideas, he invites questions so that his associates can better understand what he is trying to accomplish. This "give and take" also enables the manager and the subordinates to explore more fully the implications of the decision.

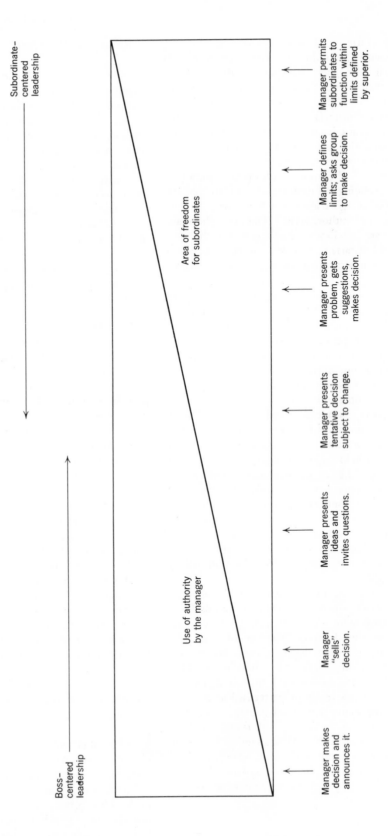

Fig. 1. Continuum of leadership behavior.

The Manager Presents a Tentative Decision Subject to Change. This kind of behavior permits the subordinates to exert some influence on the decision. The initiative for identifying and diagnosing the problem remains with the boss. Before meeting with his staff, he has thought the problem through and arrived at a decision—but only a tentative one. Before finalizing it, he presents his proposed solution for the reaction of those who will be affected by it. He says in effect, "I'd like to hear what you have to say about this plan that I have developed. I'll appreciate your frank reactions, but will reserve for myself the final decision."

The Manager Presents the Problem, Gets Suggestions, and Then Makes His Decision. Up to this point the boss has come before the group with a solution of his own. Not so in this case. The subordinates now get the first chance to suggest solutions. The manager's initial role involves identifying the problem. He might for example, say something of this sort: "We are faced with a number of complaints from newspapers and the general public on our service policy. What is wrong here? What ideas do you have for coming to grips with this problem?"

The function of the group becomes one of increasing the manager's repertory of possible solutions to the problem. The purpose is to capitalize on the knowledge and experience of those who are on the "firing line." From the expanded list of alternatives developed by the manager and his subordinates, the manager then selects the solution that he regards as most promising.[1]

The Manager Defines the Limits and Requests the Group to Make a Decision. At this point the manager passes to the group (possibly including himself as a member) the right to make decisions. Before doing so, however, he defines the problem to be solved and the boundaries within which the decision must be made.

An example might be the handling of a parking problem at a plant. The boss decides that this is something that should be worked

on by the people involved, so he calls them together and points up the existence of the problem. Then he tells them:

There is the open field just north of the main plant which has been designated for additional employee parking. We can build underground or surface multilevel facilities as long as the cost does not exceed $100,000. Within these limits we are free to work out whatever solution makes sense to us. After we decide on a specific plan, the company will spend the available money in whatever way we indicate.

The Manager Permits the Group to Make Decisions within Prescribed Limits. This represents an extreme degree of group freedom only occasionally encountered in formal organizations, as, for instance, in many research groups. Here the team of managers or engineers undertakes the identification and diagnosis of the problem, develops alternative procedures for solving it, and decides on one or more of these alternative solutions. The only limits directly imposed on the group by the organization are those specified by the superior of the team's boss. If the boss participates in the decision-making process, he attempts to do so with no more authority than any other member of the group. He commits himself in advance to assist in implementing whatever decision the group makes.

Key Questions

As the continuum in Fig. 1 demonstrates, there are a number of alternative ways in which a manager can relate himself to the group or individuals he is supervising. At the extreme left of the range, the emphasis is on the manager—on what *he* is interested in, how *he* sees things, how *he* feels about them. As we move toward the subordinate-centered end of the continuum, however, the focus is increasingly on the subordinates—on what *they* are interested in, how *they* look at things, how *they* feel about them.

When business leadership is regarded in this way, a number of questions arise. Let us take four of especial importance:

Can a Boss Ever Relinquish His Responsibility by Delegating It to Someone Else? Our

[1] For a fuller explanation of this approach, see Leo Moore, "Too Much Management, Too Little Change," *Harvard Business Review*, January–February 1956, p. 41.

view is that the manager must expect to be held responsible by his superior for the quality of the decisions made, even though operationally these decisions may have been made on a group basis. He should, therefore, be ready to accept whatever risk is involved whenever he delegates decision-making power to his subordinates. Delegation is not a way of "passing the buck." Also, it should be emphasized that the amount of freedom the boss gives to his subordinates cannot be greater than the freedom which he himself has been given by his own superior.

Should the Manager Participate with His Subordinates Once He Has Delegated Responsibility to Them? The manager should carefully think over this question and decide on his role prior to involving the subordinate group. He should ask if his presence will inhibit or facilitate the problem-solving process. There may be some instances when he should leave the group to let it solve the problem for itself. Typically, however, the boss has useful ideas to contribute, and should function as an additional member of the group. In the latter instance, it is important that he indicate clearly to the group that he sees himself in a *member* role rather than in an authority role.

How Important Is It for the Group to Recognize What Kind of Leadership Behavior the Boss Is Using? It makes a great deal of difference. Many relationship problems between boss and subordinate occur because the boss fails to make clear how he plans to use his authority. If, for example, he actually intends to make a certain decision himself, but the subordinate group gets the impression that he has delegated this authority, considerable confusion and resentment are likely to follow. Problems may also occur when the boss uses a "democratic" façade to conceal the fact that he has already made a decision which he hopes the group will accept as its own. The attempt to "make them think it was their idea in the first place" is a risky one. We believe that it is highly important for the manager to be honest and clear in describing what authority he is keeping and what role he is asking his subordinates to assume in solving a particular problem.

Can You Tell How "Democratic" a Manager Is by the Number of Decisions His Subordinates Make? The sheer *number* of decisions is not an accurate index of the amount of freedom that a subordinate group enjoys. More important is the *significance* of the decisions which the boss entrusts to his subordinates. Obviously a decision on how to arrange desks is of an entirely different order from a decision involving the introduction of new electronic data-processing equipment. Even though the widest possible limits are given in dealing with the first issue, the group will sense no particular degree of responsibility. For a boss to permit the group to decide equipment policy, even within rather narrow limits, would reflect a greater degree of confidence in them on his part.

Deciding How to Lead

Now let us turn from the types of leadership that are possible in a company situation to the question of what types are practical and *desirable*. What factors or forces should a manager consider in deciding how to manage? Three are of particular importance:

1. Forces in the manager.
2. Forces in the subordinates.
3. Forces in the situation.

We should like briefly to describe these elements and indicate how they might influence a manager's action in a decision-making situation.[2] The strength of each of them will,

[2] See also Robert Tannenbaum and Fred Massarik, "Participation by Subordinates in the Managerial Decision-Making Process," *Canadian Journal of Economics and Political Science*, August 1950, pp. 413-418.

of course, vary from instance to instance, but the manager who is sensitive to them can better assess the problems which face him and determine which mode of leadership behavior is most appropriate for him.

Forces in the Manager. The manager's behavior in any given instance will be influenced greatly by the many forces operating within his own personality. He will, of course, perceive his leadership problems in a unique way on the basis of his background, knowledge, and experience. Among the important internal forces affecting him will be the following:

1. HIS VALUE SYSTEM. How strongly does he feel that individuals should have a share in making the decisions which affect them? Or,

how convinced is he that the official who is paid to assume responsibility should personally carry the burden of decision making? The strength of his convictions on questions like these will tend to move the manager to one end or the other of the continuum shown in Fig. 1. His behavior will also be influenced by the relative importance that he attaches to organizational efficiency, personal growth of subordinates, and company profits.[3]

2. HIS CONFIDENCE IN HIS SUBORDINATES. Managers differ greatly in the amount of trust they have in other people generally, and this carries over to the particular employees they supervise at a given time. In viewing his particular group of subordinates, the manager is likely to consider their knowledge and competence with respect to the problem. A central question he might ask himself is: "Who is best qualified to deal with this problem?" Often he may, justifiably or not, have more confidence in his own capabilities than in those of his subordinates.

3. HIS OWN LEADERSHIP INCLINATIONS. There are some managers who seem to function more comfortably and naturally as highly directive leaders. Resolving problems and issuing orders come easily to them. Other managers seem to operate more comfortably in a team role, where they are continually sharing many of their functions with their subordinates.

4. HIS FEELINGS OF SECURITY IN AN UNCERTAIN SITUATION. The Manager who releases control over the decision-making process thereby reduces the predictability of the outcome. Some managers have a greater need than others for predictability and stability in their environment. This "tolerance for ambiguity" is being viewed increasingly by psychologists as a key variable in a person's manner of dealing with problems.

The manager brings these and other highly personal variables to each situation he faces. If he can see them as forces which, consciously or unconsciously, influence his behavior, he can better understand what makes him prefer to act in a given way. And understanding this, he can often make himself more effective.

[3] See Chris Argyris, "Top Management Dilemma: Company Needs vs. Individual Development," *Personnel*, September 1955, pp. 123–134.

Forces in the Subordinate. Before deciding how to lead a certain group, the manager will also want to consider a number of forces affecting his subordinates' behavior. He will want to remember that each employee, like himself, is influenced by many personality variables. In addition, each subordinate has a set of expectations about how the boss should act in relation to him (the phrase "expected behavior" is one we hear more and more often these days at discussions of leadership and teaching). The better the manager understands these factors, the more accurately he can determine what kind of behavior on his part will enable his subordinates to act most effectively.

Generally speaking, the manager can permit his subordinates greater freedom if the following essential conditions exist:

If the subordinates have relatively high needs for independence. (As we all know, people differ greatly in the amount of direction that they desire.)

If the subordinates have a readiness to assume responsibility for decision making. (Some see additional responsibility as a tribute to their ability; others see it as "passing the buck.")

If they have a relatively high tolerance for ambiguity. (Some employees prefer to have clear-cut directives given to them; others prefer a wider area of freedom.)

If they are interested in the problem and feel that it is important.

If they understand and identify with the goals of the organization.

If they have the necessary knowledge and experience to deal with the problem.

If they have learned to expect to share in dcision making. (Persons who have come to expect strong leadership and are then suddenly confronted with the request to share more fully in decision making are often upset by this new experience. On the other hand, persons who have enjoyed a considerable amount of freedom resent the boss who begins to make all the decisions himself.)

The manager will probably tend to make fuller use of his own authority if the above conditions do *not* exist; at times there may be no realistic alternative to running a "one-man show."

The restrictive effect of many of the forces will, of course, be greatly modified by the general feeling of confidence which subordinates have in the boss. Where they have learned to respect and trust him, he is free to vary his behavior. He will feel certain that he will not be perceived as an authoritarian boss on those occasions when he makes decisions by himself. Similarly, he will not be seen as using staff meetings to avoid his decision-making responsibility. In a climate of mutual confidence and respect, people tend to feel less threatened by deviations from normal practice, which in turn makes possible a higher degree of flexibility in the whole relationship.

Forces in the Situation. In addition to the forces which exist in the manager himself and in his subordinates, certain characteristics of the general situation will also affect the manager's behavior. Among the more critical environmental pressures that surround him are those which stem from the organization, the work group, the nature of the problem, and the pressures of time. Let us look briefly at each of these:

TYPE OF ORGANIZATION. Like individuals, organizations have values and traditions which inevitably influence the behavior of the people who work in them. The manager who is a newcomer to a company quickly discovers that certain kinds of behavior are approved while others are not. He also discovers that to deviate radically from what is generally accepted is likely to create problems for him.

These values and traditions are communicated in many ways—through job descriptions, policy pronouncements, and public statements by top executives. Some organizations, for example, hold to the notion that the desirable executive is one who is dynamic, imaginative, decisive, and persuasive. Other organizations put more emphasis upon the importance of the executive's ability to work effectively with people—his human relations skills. The fact that his superiors have a defined concept of what the good executive should be will very likely push the manager toward one end or the other of the behavioral range.

In addition to the above, the amount of employee participation is influenced by such variables as the size of the working units, their geographical distribution, and the degree of inter- and intra-organizational security required to attain company goals. For example, the wide geographical dispersion of an organization may preclude a practical system of participative decision making, even though this would otherwise be desirable. Similarly, the size of the working units or the need for keeping plans confidential may make it necessary for the boss to exercise more control than would otherwise be the case. Factors like these may limit considerably the manager's ability to function flexibly on the continuum.

GROUP EFFECTIVENESS. Before turning decision-making responsibility over to a subordinate group, the boss should consider how effectively its members work together as a unit.

One of the relevant factors here is the experience the group has had in working together. It can generally be expected that a group which has functioned for some time will have developed habits of cooperation and thus be able to tackle a problem more effectively than a new group. It can also be expected that a group of people with similar backgrounds and interests will work more quickly and easily than people with dissimilar backgrounds, because the communication problems are likely to be less complex.

The degree of confidence that the members have in their ability to solve problems as a group is also a key consideration. Finally, such group variables as cohesiveness, permissiveness, mutual acceptance, and commonality of purpose will exert subtle but powerful influence on the group's functioning.

THE PROBLEM ITSELF. The nature of the problem may determine what degree of authority should be delegated by the manager to his subordinates. Obviously he will ask himself whether they have the kind of knowledge which is needed. It is possible to do them a real disservice by assigning a problem that their experience does not equip them to handle.

Since the problems faced in large or growing industries increasingly require knowledge of specialists from many different fields, it might be inferred that the more complex a problem, the more anxious a manager will be to get some assistance in solving it. However, this is not always the case. There will be times when the very complexity of the problem calls for one person to work it out. For example, if the manager has most of the background and factual data relevant to a given issue. it may be easier for him to think it through himself than to take the time to fill in his staff on all the pertinent background information.

The key question to ask, of course, is: "Have I heard the ideas of everyone who has the necessary knowledge to make a significant contribution to the solution of this problem?"

THE PRESSURE OF TIME. This is perhaps the most clearly felt pressure on the manager (in spite of the fact that it may sometimes be imagined). The more that he feels the need for an immediate decision, the more difficult it is to involve other people. In organizations which are in a constant state of "crisis" and "crash programming" one is likely to find managers personally using a high degree of authority with relatively little delegation to subordinates. When the time pressure is less intense, however, it becomes much more possible to bring subordinates in on the decision-making process.

These, then, are the principal forces that impinge on the manager in any given instance and that tend to determine his tactical behavior in relation to his subordinates. In each case his behavior ideally will be that which makes possible the most effective attainment of his immediate goal within the limits facing him.

Long-Run Strategy

As the manager works with his organization on the problems that come up day by day, his choice of a leadership pattern is usually limited. He must take account of the forces just described and, within the restrictions they impose on him, do the best that he can. But as he looks ahead months or even years, he can shift his thinking from tactics to large-scale strategy. No longer need he be fettered by all of the forces mentioned, for he can view many of them as variables over which he has some control. He can, for example, gain new insights or skills for himself, supply training for individual subordinates, and provide participative experiences for his employee group.

In trying to bring about a change in these variables, however, he is faced with a challenging question: At which point along the continuum *should* he act?

Attaining Objectives. The answer depends largely on what he wants to accomplish. Let

us suppose that he is interested in the same objectives that most modern managers seek to attain when they can shift their attention from the pressure of immediate assignments:

1. To raise the level of employee motivation.
2. To increase the readiness of subordinates to accept change.
3. To improve the quality of all managerial decisions.
4. To develop teamwork and morale.
5. To further the individual development of employees.

In recent years the manager has been deluged with a flow of advice on how best to achieve these longer-run objectives. It is little wonder that he is often both bewildered and annoyed. However, there are some guidelines which he can usefully follow in making a decision.

Most research and much of the experience of recent years give a strong factual basis to the theory that a fairly high degree of subordinate-centered behavior is associated with the accomplishment of the five purposes mentioned.[4] This does not mean that a manager should always leave all decisions to his assistants. To provide the individual or the group with greater freedom than they are ready for at any given time may very well tend to generate anxieties and therefore inhibit rather than facilitate the attainment of desired objectives. But this should not keep the manager from making a continuing effort to confront his subordinates with the challenge of freedom.

Conclusion

In summary, there are two implications in the basic thesis that we have been developing. The first is that the successful leader is one who is keenly aware of those forces which are most relevant to his behavior at any given time. He accurately understands himself, the individuals and group he is dealing with, and the company and broader social environment in which he operates. And certainly he is able

[4] For example, see Warren H. Schmidt and Paul C. Buchanan, *Techniques that Produce Teamwork* (New London, Arthur C. Croft Publications, 1954); and Morris S. Viteles, *Motivation and Morale in Industry* (New York, W. W. Norton & Company, Inc., 1953).

to assess the present readiness for growth of his subordinates.

But this sensitivity or understanding is not enough, which brings us to the second implication. The successful leader is one who is able to behave appropriately in the light of these perceptions. If direction is in order, he is able to direct; if considerable participative freedom is called for, he is able to provide such freedom.

Thus, the successful manager of men can be primarily characterized neither as a strong leader nor as a permissive one. Rather, he is one who maintains a high batting average in accurately assessing the forces that determine what his most appropriate behavior at any given time should be and in actually being able to behave accordingly. Being both insightful and flexible, he is less likely to see the problems of leadership as a dilemma.

Structure and Co-ordination

LUTHER GULICK

Interrelation of Systems of Departmentalization. Students of administration have long sought a single principle of effective departmentalization just as alchemists sought the philosophers' stone.[1] But they have sought in vain. There is apparently no one most effective system of departmentalism.

Each of the four basic systems of organization [2] is intimately related with the other three, because in any enterprise all four elements are

present in the doing of the work and are embodied in every individual workman. Each member of the enterprise is working for some major purpose, uses some process, deals with some persons, and serves or works at some place.

If an organization is erected about any one of these four characteristics of work, it becomes immediately necessary to recognize the other characteristics in constructing the secondary and tertiary divisions of the work. For example, a government which is first divided on the basis of place will, in each geographical department, find it necessary to divide by purpose, by process, by clientele, or even again by place; and one divided in the first instance by purpose may well be divided next by process and then by place. While the first or primary division of any enterprise is of very great significance, it must none the less be said that there is no one most effective pattern for determining the priority and order for the introduction of these interdependent principles. It will depend in any case upon the results which are desired at a given time and place. . . .

The major purpose of organization is co-ordination, as has been pointed out above. It should therefore be noted that each of the four principles of departmentalization plays a

From "Notes on the Theory of Organization" in *Papers on the Science of Administration* by L. Gulick and L. Urwick, pp. 31–37. Reprinted with permission of the publisher, The Institute of Public Administration, copyright 1937 by The Institute of Public Administration.
[1] Charles A. Beard, "The Administration and Politics of Tokyo." Macmillan, New York, 1923, Ch. 3; A. E. Buck, "Administrative Consolidation in State Governments," 5th ed. National Municipal League, New York, 1930; Great Britain, Ministry of Reconstruction, Report of the Machinery of Government Committee. H. M. Stationery Office, London, 1918; Luther Gulick, "Principles of Administration," *National Municipal Review*, vol. 14, July, 1925, pp. 400–403; W. F. Willoughby, "Principles of Public Administration." John Hopkins Press, Baltimore, 1927, Part I, Ch. 5.

[2] Purpose, Process, Clientele or Material, Place [ed.].

different rôle in co-ordination. In each case the highest degree of co-ordination takes place within the departments set up, and the greatest lack of co-ordination and danger of friction occurs between the departments, or at the points where they overlap.

If all of the departments are set up on the basis of purpose, then the task of the chief executive in the field of co-ordination will be to see that the major purposes are not in conflict and that the various processes which are used are consistent, and that the government as it touches classes of citizens or reaches areas of the community is appropriate, rational, and effective. He will not have to concern himself with co-ordination within the departments, as each department head will look after this.

If all of the departments are set up on the basis of process, the work methods will be well standardized on professional lines, and the chief executive will have to see that these are co-ordinated and timed to produce the results and render the services for which the government exists, and that the service rendered actually fits the needs of the persons or areas served.

If place be the basis of departmentalization, that is, if the services be decentralized, then the task of the chief executive is not to see that the activities are co-ordinated locally and fit the locality, but to see that each of these services makes use of the standard techniques and that the work in each area is part of a general program and policy.

If the work of the government be departmentalized in part on the basis of purpose, in part on the basis of process, in part on the basis of clientele, and in part on the basis of place, it will be seen that the problems of co-ordination and smooth operation are multiplied and that the task of the executive is increased. Moreover, the nature of his work is altered. In an organization in which all of the major divisions follow one philosophy, the executive himself must furnish the inter-departmental co-ordination and see that things do not fall between two stools. In an organization built on two or more bases of departmentalization, the executive may use, for example, the process departments as a routine means of co-ordinating the purpose departments. None the less the task of the executive is extraordinarily complicated. There is also great danger in such an organization that one department may fail to aid or actually proceed to obstruct another department. When departments cross each other at right angles, the danger of collision is far greater and far more serious than when their contacts are along parallel lines at their respective outer limits.

THE HOLDING COMPANY IDEA. A large enterprise engaged in many complicated activities which do not require extensive or intimate co-ordination may need only the loosest type of central co-ordinating authority. Under such conditions, each activity may be set up, on a purpose basis, as virtually independent, and the central structure of authority may be nothing more than a holding company. In practice various industrial holding companies, particularly in the power field, require little or no co-ordination whatsoever. They have no operating services in common, and seem to have few interrelations except in finance. It has been suggested that the larger governmental units are in comparable position, and that they may well be looked upon not as single enterprises like the Ford Motor Company, but rather as if they were each holding companies like the American Telephone and Telegraph Company, or General Motors. From this point of view, the government of the United States would be the parent company, and each department would be an independent subsidiary. While the parent company would give certain central services and require conformity to certain central plans and policies, each subsidiary, that is each department, would be given extensive freedom to carry on as it saw fit, and the President at the center of the parent company would not pretend to do more than prevent conflict and competition.

This point of view is helpful to the student of administration in that it brings out two important factors:

1. It makes clear the important difference between the operating functions and departments, such as agriculture, war, and labor, and the co-ordinating and central services, such as the budget, planning, and personnel. In the holding company analogy, the former would be subsidiaries, while the latter would be functions of the parent company; and

2. It directs attention to the kind of service to which the central agencies, including the President and the Cabinet, should limit themselves in any case. If the co-ordinating agencies

of the government would look upon themselves as holding company officials and staff, they would devote their energies to the larger problems of co-ordination, and would leave to the departments and their staffs the internal problems of operation.

While this attitude toward the respective functions of the operating and the co-ordinating services of the government may be valuable for certain purposes, it cannot be accepted as the sound theoretical foundation for the consideration of the federal government, or of any of the governments of the states or larger cities. It is not a satisfactory analogy for four important reasons:

1. There is but one board of directors in the governmental set-up, and a single avenue of democratic responsibility;

2. The interrelations between the various departments are many and intimate, requiring extensive and continuous co-ordination;

3. In government there must be highly developed uniform standards and methods, particularly in finance and personnel; and

4. There is in government no simple, final measure of successful operation of subsidiaries like the profit and loss statement in business. Supervisory relations must be intimate and complete, not distant and limited.

In the actual operation of the larger American governmental units we are, as a matter of fact, confronted at the same time by too much activity by the co-ordinating authorities, and by too little co-ordination. This anomalous situation seems to come about because of the lack of understanding both by experts and by laymen of the true function of the chief executive; because of the lack of proper managerial staffs attached to the chief executive; and because of the tendency of legislative bodies to step over the line into administration and to meddle with appointments. It must be recognized that the chief executive of any enterprise has but a limited amount of time and energy at his command. These he can use either in participating in detail in the administration of a few activities, or in dealing broadly with the policies and problems of many activities. If the task of the executive is first of all co-ordination, it would seem that the latter is his true function. But in any large enterprise, the executive cannot perform this function intelligently or skillfully unless he has adequate assistance. Where he is denied

such assistance, he must act either tardily or ruthlessly, and an executive who recoils from either course is immediately drawn down into the minutiae of administration and fails to perform his main job.

In public administration the holding company concept is helpful if it is used to emphasize the need of broad co-ordination and the methods of achieving it. It must be recognized, however, that government is actually not a holding company at all.

OTHER MEANS OF INTERDEPARTMENTAL CO-ORDINATION. In the discussion thus far it has been assumed that the normal method of interdepartmental co-ordination is hierarchical in its operation. That is, if trouble develops between a field representative (X) of one department and the field representative (A) of another department, that the solution will be found by carrying the matter up the line from inferior to superior until the complaint of Mr. X and the complaint of Mr. A finally reach their common superior, be he mayor, governor or President. In actual practice, there are also other means of interdepartmental co-ordination which must be regarded as part of the organization as such. Among these must be included planning boards and committees, interdepartmental committees, co-ordinators, and officially arranged regional meetings, etc. These are all organizational devices for bringing about the co-ordination of the work of government. Co-ordination of this type is essential. It greatly lessens the military stiffness and red tape of the strictly hierarchical structure. It greatly increases the consultative process in administration. It must be recognized, however, that it is to be used only to deal with abnormal situations and where matters of policy are involved, as in planning. The organization itself should be set up so that it can dispose of the routine work without such devices, because these devices are too dilatory, irresponsible and time-consuming for normal administration. Wherever an organization needs continual resort to special co-ordinating devices in the discharge of its regular work, this is proof that the organization is bad. These special agencies of co-ordination draw their sanction from the hierarchical structure and should receive the particular attention of the executive authority. They should not be set up and forgotten,

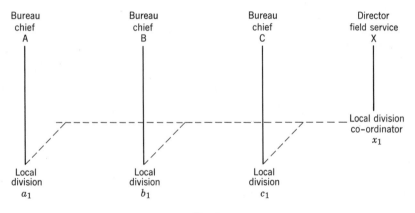

Fig. 1

ignored, or permitted to assume an independent status.

The establishment of special regional co-ordinators to bring about co-operation in a given region between the local representatives of several central agencies presents special difficulties. There are three chief plans which have been tried. One is the device of propinquity, the juxtaposition of offices in the same building or city, and reliance on ordinary daily contact. Another is the establishment of a loose committee, or "conference," meeting locally from time to time to discuss local problems of co-ordination, under a local chairman who is actually nothing but a presiding officer and formulator of agenda. A third plan is the establishment of such groups under the chairmanship of a regional co-ordinator designated by and responsible to a central office of co-ordination of field service. When this is attempted, to whom should the head of the field service be subordinate? For example, in the accompanying diagram [Fig. 1] to whom should X report? Certainly not to A, or to B, or to C. The central director of a co-ordination field service must be on a par with the central directors of the services which are being co-ordinated in the field, or possibly even on a higher plane.

In the devices of co-ordination, one must recognize also joint service contracts and co-incident personnel appointments. Independent agencies may be pulled together in operation through such use of the same staff or service. There are many illustrations of the former, especially in engineering services. The county agent who is at the same time a county, a state, and a federal official is an example of the latter.

A great obstacle in the way of all of these plans of co-ordination is found in the danger of introducing confusion in direction through the violation of the principle of unity of command, and also in the difference in the level of authority of those who are brought together in any interdepartmental or intergovernmental co-ordinating arrangement. The representatives of the Department of Agriculture, for example, may have a large measure of responsibility and power, and may therefore be in a position to work out an adjustment of program through conference and to agree to a new line of conduct, but the representatives of the Army, coming from an entirely different kind of an organization, are sure to be in a position where they cannot make any adjustments without passing the decision back to headquarters.

Doctrine

JAMES MOONEY

Mutual Service. Community of interest is the legitimate basis of every organization. In searching for its psychic fundaments we find that it can mean only *mutuality of interest.* This in turn implies mutual duties, which means the obligation to *mutual service.* This obligation is universal, transcending, therefore, the sphere of organization. As expressed in the ancient Roman juridical maximum *do ut des* (I give that thou mayest give), it is the manifest basis of all human relations.

In a special sense, however, it has an application within the sphere of organization. Here it is the moral phase of the principle of coordination. It is for this reason that organizations of all kinds, whether governmental, religious, military, or industrial, furnish our best human examples of the spirit of mutual service.

Although the formal technique of organization has, until recent years, received but scant attention, the humanistic phases of organization have an extensive literature. In this literature the obligation to mutual service is called by various names, among them cooperation, integration, functional relating, and integrated functioning. All these terms suggest the formal as well as the human side of coordination, which shows how impossible it is to separate them. We must keep in mind that organizations are the creations of people, and hence that everything that is formal in organized forms must rest on psychic fundaments.

A true coordination must be based on a real community of interest in the attainment of the desired object. It is equally true that a community of interest that is real, not only in the objective sense but likewise in everybody's consciousness, can come only through a real

From *The Principles of Organization*. New York: Harper and Brothers, 1947, pp. 8–13. Reprinted with permission of the publisher.

community of understanding. This means not merely that administration and members must understand each other, but that each and all must understand what the real purpose is and, furthermore, that every group represented in the organization must understand how and why the attainment of this purpose is essential to the welfare of all.

The reason, we think, is obvious. Mutuality of interest or, let us say, a common interest, does not, so far as human consciousness is concerned, constitute an *identity* of interest. The only conceivable means of attaining a true integration of all group interests in organization is through administrative policies that will make this community of interest a more tangible reality to every member of the group.

It is evident that every element of psychic coordination is a necessity in the establishment of harmony in all internal relations. Even this statement, however, does not include everything necessary in a truly coordinated efficiency. Before we leave this subject of coordination, therefore, let us consider one more element, especially conspicuous in church and military organization, which has its lessons for organizers in every sphere.

Doctrine. Coordination implies an aim or objective. But it does not follow, even where there is a true mutual interest, a mutual understanding, and a degree of mutual participation, that each and every member of the organization does in fact carry in his mind a deep understanding of the objective and how it may be attained. Among the higher officials, those who are responsible for results, this understanding should be ever present. They should know, furthermore, that the more this understanding seeps down through all ranks and grades, until all are permeated with it, the greater will be the coordinated effort and the greater the strength of the organization for the accomplishment of its purpose. It is the necessary means to this end that brings us in contact with the significant word "doctrine."

To most people this word has a religious favor, and well it may, for, of all forms of organization, religious associations are the ones that are most deeply imbued with its spirit. But the word itself has a broader meaning. We see this illustrated in the various applications of the title "doctor," which means simply the teacher, representative, or practitioner of a doctrine. There is, indeed, a doctrine for every conceivable form of collective human effort.

Doctrine in the primary sense means the *definition of the objective*. In religious associations this doctrine is based on faith, as formally stated in the *creed*. In industrial organizations it is the attainment of a *surplus through service*. In governmental organization we find different and constantly changing doctrines, but always a doctrine of some sort, however varied its interpretations by the leaders and statesmen of history. In this primary sense doctrine is synonymous with the objective.

When we consider, however, the *procedure necessary to attain the objective* we encounter the secondary meaning of the word, which it seems a misnomer to call secondary, for it often transcends the primary meaning in practical importance. This fact the following examples will show.

With a physician or surgeon the doctrine of the objective is obvious. It is to make the patient well. But the doctrine of procedure and its application call for a thorough training and wide experience. Likewise, the doctrine of the military objective is simple. According to the school of Foch and Napoleon, it is the forcing of a decision through the overthrow of the adversary. The necessary procedure, however, constitutes a highly technical art, in which all the principles of military strategy and tactics are involved.

This point is vital in all forms of coordinated effort. Always there is sure to be a doctrine of procedure of some kind, but it is not enough to have such a doctrine, nor is it sufficient for the doctrine to be a sound one. Above all, it is essential that this doctrine shall, in the popular phrase, be "sold" to everyone concerned. Every member of an organization should not only know its doctrine, but he should feel it and absorb it until he lives in its atmosphere and makes it the guide of all his acts.

A doctrine of procedure does not mean a body of set rules that must be accepted as though they were articles of faith. We shall presently discuss more broadly the distinction between rules and principles in organization. "Indoctrination" in the military sense means simply the inculcation of those principles which serve as the guide of the military man, whatever the situation he is compelled to face.

To find a simpler illustration of unity of doctrine, and its necessity in the attainment of any group objective, we may turn to the field of sports, such as our national games of baseball and football, where groups are competing and where success in the attainment of the purpose depends on coordinated effort. In these sports there is a real functional differentiation of duties. In the formal sense, however, the problems of organization are all predetermined by the rules of the game. The primary objective also is so simple that the shortest word will state it. It is to *win*.

When we come, however, to procedure, in other words, to the means necessary to win, we find emerging in each case a real doctrine which accounts for the high importance of the baseball manager and the football coach. Tracing each doctrine through all the intricacies of baseball and football strategy we find that it rests, as it must, on the first principle of organization, namely, coordination of effort. This coordination, so essential to victory in any sport where a number of players combine their efforts for a common purpose, has given us the splendid word "teamwork."

Another illustration in a different sphere is the coordination of a symphony orchestra. Here the purpose is the production of a collective harmony, not as a means to an end but as an end in itself. To attain this end each individual musician merges himself in the common purpose. Functionalism in an orchestra is as varied as the nature of the different instruments. In the orchestra these individual functions derive their importance solely from their contribution to the common purpose, and the relation of each musician's function to this purpose is ever present in the instant result. This fact of the objective resulting instantly from the initial coordination makes the orchestra the supreme symbol and the simplest illustration of a coordinated effort.

Discipline. One other factor essential to organized efficiency must not be overlooked. Organized efficiency in the pursuit of any objective demands a doctrine, but the efficient application, even of the soundest doctrine, demands in turn an organized *discipline*. By this we mean something more vital than the discipline imposed by command. That is essential, but even more vital is the discipline which command must impose on itself, for such discipline is the first necessity to ensure a truly organized efficiency. Without such self-discipline at the top it would be useless to expect it anywhere else down the line. The commander of a battleship is subjected to a greater de-

gree of discipline than a bluejacket. Even the pope must every year wash the feet of a beggar and must go to confession twice a week. Discipline by example we may call it, but such examples are essential to the discipline of any organization.

The sum of these observations is that the strength of an organization is determined by its spirit, that the spirit must be determined by the purpose and the means necessary to its attainment, and that these means imply a doctrine out of which the spirit of an organization grows and on which it lives. On the other hand, no organization can live on its spirit alone. Coordination must have its formalism, which means its technique or method by which its power is directed to the attainment of the purpose.

The Informal

Organization

PART TWO

THE FORMAL ORGANIZATION as discussed in Part I was viewed as an arrangement of tasks or duties to promote the efficient accomplishment of a goal. It was assumed that when people were given these tasks or positions they would perform their assigned duties efficiently and in doing so would contribute to the completion of organizational goals.

The difficulty is that when we look at a total operating organization such as a business firm, hospital, or governmental agency, we see that some of the activities going on are called for by the formal organization but that a great many others are not. Some activities, although not called for in the formal organization plan, are quite necessary to accomplish the organization goal and represent activities which people in the organization have informally added to further the organization's progress. Many other activities neither support nor hinder the work on organization goals; they are, from the formal point of view, neutral activities. Still other activities, either because they work toward opposing goals or because they drain off so much effort, can be considered detrimental to the formal organization.

A person who takes only the formal organ-

ization plan and its assumptions as a measure of what should be going on within an organization will be applying an unfair and for that matter incomplete standard of organizational performance. We can draw a simple analogy to a ship owner who believes that all the fuel on the ship should be totally devoted to propelling the ship from one port to another and that no fuel should be burned to heat the crew's quarters, cook food, and heat water for bathing. The concepts of thermodynamics and studies of fuel consumption in propelling a ship are of vital importance, but they are an incomplete concept with which to examine the overall performance of a ship.

Unfortunately, in years past people have tried to apply concepts of the formal organization as measures for the total organization. In trying to apply them there was a pronounced tendency to look on any behavior by organization members which was not specifically and completely directed to accomplishing organizational goals or assignments as something wrong or wasteful and therefore to be eliminated. Members of the organization who deviated from these standards and goals were at the least lazy, shiftless, and irresponsible, and at the worst disloyal and rebellious. From such a point of view they were led to place great emphasis on such things as selecting people who would be loyal to the organization, training them once they had been hired, and disciplining them should they not follow orders and directions.

This point of view was severely shaken a number of decades ago by a series of studies which examined various aspects of organizational behavior. Perhaps the most famous of these were the Hawthorne studies conducted by Elton Mayo, Fritz Roethlisberger, and other associates at Harvard University, but the field has received major additions from the fields of social psychology, industrial sociology, and more recently anthropology.

One thing soon apparent from these studies was that within large organizations a great deal of effort is expended by organizational members on activities which do not directly support organizational goals. Investigators found, for example, that people spent a lot of time in social activities which had nothing directly to do with the task they were supposed to be accomplishing. Investigators also spent a good deal of time examining the activities of people who resisted or thwarted organization objectives. The well-known practice of work restrictions, by which employees establish a maximum amount they will produce, probably below the standards established by management, is only one of these phenomena.

Investigations went considerably beyond a mere classification of different types of nongoal behavior. It was rapidly established that the behavior was not something capricious, necessarily disloyal, random, or unpredictable, but that instead it fell into regular and consistent patterns which might persist over long periods of time and serve very definite functions. What should be noted is that the functions were important not necessarily for the formal organization but for the people within the organization as individuals and particularly as members of groups or informal organizations.

Up until this point the tendency had been to think primarily of people either as individuals or as occupants of positions in large, impersonal structures. Much behavior in an organization, however, is only understandable when we examine it as a manifestation of group life. Hence, these researches added a neglected but exceedingly important factor to our thinking about organizations.

When probing deeper into the patterns and functions of group behavior, the investigators found that much of it actually was conforming with rules or standards, that other portions of it were under the direction of people who occupied informal superior or leadership positions and that the people in groups knew full well that deviations from these rules or standards, or violation of the directions from the informal superiors, would result in some disciplinary action. In short, much of the behavior on investigation turned out to be controlled behavior.

Here was what organization theorists had been concerned with all along, people behaving according to rules and standards or following orders within a system of control. The point which is exceedingly important, however, is that investigators showed that the rules and standards, the orders and control which influence a very large portion of the behavior of the organization members were not established by the formal organization or the members of the managerial hierarchy. Instead, these organizational elements were components of what has now come to be called the informal organization. They are not formally prescribed by a central, "legitimate" authority, but, rather, spring up out of the situation and have their roots in the needs and requirements of people. The nature of informal organizations is explained more thoroughly in a moment, but first a digression is necessary.

Some Problems with Terms

One of the difficulties with this area is the problem of deciding which words to use to cover the ideas considered. Already we have been using "small groups" and "informal organizations" in an almost completely interchangeable fashion. Many of the investigations in this area have focused on the small group in an attempt to understand what it is, how it operates, and why it operates as it does. The term "informal organizations," as used here, includes something larger and more inclusive than one group. It has among other implications the idea that a person can be, and in fact is, a member of more than one small group. Hence, if we are to study the totality of influences on him other than those coming from the formal organization, we have to include the influences of several small groups, not all equal, perhaps, but all in some way significant.

There are other influences that properly belong to the topic of informal organizations but extend beyond any one small group, or for that matter collection of small groups, which may be included within one organizational unit. For example, status can be discussed relevant to one group, or it can be discussed relevant to a collection of groups within a formal organization, or it can be discussed relevant to a whole social system or culture. This multiplicity and looseness in the use of such terms makes it difficult to talk with precision about what should be included in a discussion of the informal organization. For our purposes we consider the informal organization to be those aspects of the total organization not included in the formal-organization area. Such a view of informal organization will include certain structural properties, processes, and products, and it will quite properly consist of a number of related, perhaps overlapping, small groups. For purposes of exposition, however, we follow the convention adopted by many writers in the field and discuss these matters as if there were just one group. This short cut is taken in order to reduce the cumbersomeness of always talking about a multiplicity of small groups. It would be erroneous to suggest that this approach or convention does not inject some distortion into our thinking about organizations. It certainly limits the things we include, for it tends to exclude conceptually the very difficult problem, faced by an organizational member, of reconciling the multiplicity of pressures placed on him by the formal organization and the different small groups of which he is a member. Such considerations are deferred, however, until Part V.

Properties of the Informal Organization

Norms. One of the most conspicuous items in the literature is the organization members' practice of establishing quota restrictions. Here are definite standards of how much a person should produce. Typically we think of a quota restriction as a ceiling on the amount of work a person will be permitted to produce. Such a ceiling may be considerably below the level of output which management or the time study engineers have specified. It is not as frequently noted that some minimum levels of production are established informally. The circumstances under which these minimums exist can be quite revealing.

Quota restrictions on production are one of the many different types of standards that are established by the informal organization for the behavior of organizational members. They are usually called norms. The processes by which these are established and the purposes they fill are far from simple; in fact, on investigation, they turn out to be exceedingly complex (Roy, 1952). The wide variety of norms, or informal standards, not only guide the behavior of the individual in his relation with management or the formal organization but also guide his relations with other members of the informal organization.

A point perhaps not stressed frequently enough is that many of these norms pertain to the relations people have in getting their work done. We have earlier noted that few formal organizations take into account everything necessary to complete the technical aspects of a task or position assignment. Consequently, in order to do the work assigned to him, a person frequently has to add many things that are not called for in the formal organization plan, additions which may require him to obtain the support and assistance of other people. (Roy, 1954).

The norms of the informal group, like the rules of the formal organization, have connected with them means for enforcement that both reward behavior which conforms to the standard and discipline or penalize behavior which deviates. There are a great many different ways in which member behavior is controlled by the informal organization. A variety of illustrations are contained in the selections in this book (Roy, Sayles, Selznick).

Leader-Follower Relations. At one time there was a tendency to consider workers on the job as a more or less homogeneous group in which everyone was on the same level. Few ideas could be more misleading, for a number of different structural arrangements have been uncovered. Within a small group investigators have found those who fill the leadership functions of pointing to new directions, coordinating the work of others, and holding the group together. Others can be classified as being in follower positions. Such leaders are not formally appointed but are accepted by the members of the group. Several things should be noted about leadership in a small group or informal organization. First, the leadership function may actually be carried out by a number of individuals. Within a group there may be a multiplicity of leaders, each functioning in a different aspect of group activity. One person may serve as leader when it comes to setting new directions or making plans or specifying the steps to be followed in accomplishing group objectives. These are the informal task leaders. Another leader may be concerned with the social activities within the group, making it a pleasant place to be by his wit or personality and thereby helping to hold it together. He is the informal social leader.

Communications. One fact which has been repeatedly observed in investigations and which we all are likely to see in our daily experiences is that people who are in groups, cliques or gangs tend to reach an understanding on things very quickly. To put it briefly, they communicate easily and well among themselves. Once a piece of information enters a group it usually is not too long before everyone within the group knows it. This perhaps comes about because of a common fund of interest, common experiences, and a shared vocabulary which enables members of a group to communicate easily and precisely with each other.

Communications, or the need for information about the world, is perhaps one of the basic reasons for the existence of small groups. People want to belong to groups in order, among other things, to obtain information about the world around them. By going to our friends, our cliques, our lodges, or our fraternities we pick up information which we otherwise might not obtain. We also obtain interpretations of facts which have come to us but whose meanings we perhaps find difficult to ascertain.

This is exceedingly important to have in mind, because we would have an extremely restricted view of the small group if we merely looked on it as an instrument for controlling member behavior. Since an informal organization is so important in getting information to people and interpreting information, it serves a very important role in forming people's opinions and impressions of what the world around them is really like.

The suspicions which workers may have about management when a system of work standards is established may be based on the fact that management does engage in rate-cutting practices. On the other hand, management may not have had any such intentions at all. It may only have engaged in activities which people have interpreted as possibly leading to rate-cutting practices. Many times these interpretations are formed and perpetuated by groups. As far as the final behavior of the individuals is concerned, it does not matter whether management had the intention or not as long as people think it did. If anything is to be done about their behavior, we must be aware of its real basis. For management merely to protest its innocence will do little more than clear its conscience about a frustrating situation. Such statements of innocence will not be likely to eliminate the suspicions of the workers. Management must instead take into account the view of the work standard which their employees have developed in their group and work with it.

Values. This leads us to one of the phenomena very frequently noted both by scientific investigators and lay observers, namely that members of groups, cliques, or gangs frequently share or hold in common certain values, opinions, or beliefs. In fact, some people define groups in this way. Regardless of what they are, we can always be sure that an informal group will have shared values. Understanding the group values will be very important for understanding how the group operates and the influence it has on the behavior of its individual members. Some of these values people have probably had for a long time. We find people who hold similar values coming together to form a group composed on the basis of their shared values. At other times we can find that values are developed among people who are already in a group, and that the values are then a product rather than an antecedent of group life.

Status. One use of values is in ranking things such as positions and the people who occupy them into what are called status hierarchies. Status appears in one way or another in many of the items included in this book (Roy, Homans, Whyte), but only one deals directly with the topic (Gardner and Moore). For this reason it is necessary to consider the topic at some length here.

In a general way we consider status as the social ranking of people. We recognize and frequently use ranking terms of people in our community or on the job or in our church; some people are "upper class," others are perhaps "middle class," and there are also those who are "low class." We all have some idea of what the overall social order is and a pretty good idea of where people fit in this ranking. We understand without too much difficulty that physicians rank very high in social status and that street cleaners rank low in status. Status structures, however, are important not only in understanding where people fit within a community but also where they fit within a work-group. For example, in a restaurant, we find that the people who work on fish are thought to be in a lower status position than those who work on beef.

Status structures define not only where categories of occupations fit, such as cooks and physicians, but also may define an individual's position within any category. Hence, a person will have a position first because he is in the category of a cook, which he knows is somewhere beneath a physician but above a street cleaner. Within the cook's category, however, this position may be more specifically defined by the type of material on which he works. This opens up several important issues. First, there are a number of status structures. Some are general, applying to large categories or groupings of people, and others are quite special and specific. As a result it is frequently possible to define not only the class of a person but also his position within the class.

A second issue is that whereas some of us may understand well the overall and common types of status structure, we are frequently unacquainted with the rather special ones that may exist within different categories. Consequently, the management of a restaurant may fully understand that the cooks rank somewhere between physicians and street cleaners but may not understand that within the category of cooks there are sharp status distinctions. Hence a careless or innnocent grouping

of jobs by the management on the presumption that all cooks are the same could run into serious problems by disturbing some of the status hierarchies which people in this class of work consider quite important. Therefore, the organization planner who will group tasks and assign people to the tasks so that they will do an adequate job must take into account not only the way the jobs and skills will fit together to accomplish the task, but what the arrangements will mean to the occupants of the positions.

A third consideration is of considerable importance. We have noted that there are a great many status structures. Some, as we have seen, dovetail nicely, enabling each person to be placed in a rather definite niche. This, however, is usually on an occupational basis. There are many status hierarchies which do not fit in this neat fashion and in fact may not fit at all. For example, in many situations seniority in the company or in the department or age are matters of status ranking. At the same time the community in which a person lives gives him a certain status. Further, education, parentage, wealth, and many other factors also define a person's status. In short, each of us have positions in a number of status hierarchies. It is possible, therefore, for a person to find himself rather high on one status hierarchy, in a middle position on another, and in a rather low position on still a third hierarchy. As we might suspect, this can and frequently does cause problems. No one will ever occupy the same relative position on all the status hierarchies, and most of us seem to have accepted and adjusted to some incongruities. On the other hand, when a person occupies highly different positions on status hierarchies which are important to him, we may find serious morale problems and behavior that evidences either considerable frustration or an attempt to bring about some reconciliation of his highly different positions.

From the position of the organization planner, it is necessary first to understand the different types of status that exist, and second to recognize that these status relations will, in the minds of people within an organization, define certain types of relation as proper. When the formal organization sets up jobs or job relations that seem incompatable with these informally proper relations, some behavioral consequences can be expected.

An Overall Framework for the Analysis of Social Behavior

The study of informal organization has grown rapidly in the last thirty years or so and is continuing to grow. As a result we have been able to do little more than touch on a few of the more important aspects of behavior and group properties. Important and invaluable as these properties are, they do have some limitations from the point of view taken in this book. We need more fundamental or underlying concepts, both fewer in number and more inclusive in scope. They must be able to take into account that, as has been partially noted, at times the informal organization is a product of the formal. Further, these new concepts must account for the fact that the formal organization is continually modified by the informal (Selznick). This new approach will have to account for these reciprocal influences. One model of social phenomena that meets these requirements is proposed by George Homans in his book *The Human Group*.[1]

Homans begins by suggesting that we look at the total social system which constitutes the small group. Within this total social system he claims most things can be classified into one of three categories: (1) the activities of the group members, by which he means the individual's physical motions; (2) the interactions of the group members, by which he means any transaction whereby two or more members of the group come together; and (3) sentiments. This is a broad and exceedingly slippery dimension, but essentially it includes all the feelings, the beliefs, the hopes which the people within the group have.

In Homans' view these three factors are intimately linked together and therefore a change in one will be expected to produce a change in at least one other. For example, he makes the supposition that if two people interact frequently, they will develop positive sentiments (feelings of friendship) toward each other. The model would also hold that two people who share a common activity or who perform similar activities will likely seek each other out because they presume that people who do the same thing must be somewhat

similar to themselves. Hence, common activities will lead to interaction, which in turn will result in an increase in the strength of sentiments, presumably positive. Lastly, of course, to complete this system, it follows that people who like each other will interact frequently and therefore work well together on common activities (Van Zelst). Obviously this is an exceedingly general system. It does, however, help us relate three things in a useful fashion: the things people do; the interactions between people; and the things they feel, believe, or hold important.

Homans goes one step further and makes another distinction. He says that the total social system in which people find themselves can be divided into two parts: the internal system and the external. The external system is set up by the forces or environment outside the individual or the group. In many instances this is the company or the organization, which as part of its job assignments requires that people do certain activities and in doing these activities interact with certain other people.

The external system, then, brings people together with certain relations, although hardly all, established and assigns them activities in the form of jobs or duties. At first they may be strangers but soon they become acquainted and may become friends forming strong social ties. Their life together now has a meaning which includes a social base, an internal system, in addition to the technical base. The nature of, in fact the very existence of, their social life springs from the technical arrangements of the external system. Once their social life is established, the internal system will, or at least can, have a significant influence on the external system. Homans' model of a social system gives us a very useful tool for analyzing what effect the formal organization will have on the social life of people. In turn, it enables us to explore the effects the informal organization will have on the behavior the formal organization specifies, but may not be receiving. Needless to say, this gives us a most useful tool for bridging the formal and the informal organizations. It also permits us to talk about organizational elements, such as jobs, in a more inclusive, precise manner, without being restricted to dealing with these elements in just formal or informal organization terms.

In the discussion on Homans' model one element was left undeveloped, namely, the senti-

[1] Harcourt Brace, New York, 1950.

ments coming from the external system. Homans identifies these sentiments as those which a person brings into a particular situation from his previous environment or background. Needless to say, this one element of the complete system could have great influence on the small group. It explains in part why taking a collection of people and putting them into the same work situation in which they are interacting does not guarantee that they will all grow to like each other. Bringing people together who have different, perhaps opposing, values may result in bitter hostility rather than friendship. We see in a later section the importance of this possibility.

Homans' concepts have been discussed at considerable length. First, they provide us with an exceedingly useful tool for relating a number of informal and formal organization concepts. The Homans model, however, is also difficult to understand in that its variables are exceedingly broad, frequently contain slippery elements, and the interrelations are very complex. It does require us to recognize that a social system can only be understood when all the elements are considered at the same time in relation to all the other elements. The elements of Homans' concept will be repeatedly referred to in later sections, and even when not specifically noted, they will provide a useful framework for incorporating material from later papers into an overall concept of what is actually happening within an organization.

Summary and Conclusions

In Part I of this book we considered some of the direct and positive effects of organizational decisions. It is necessary to consider the less

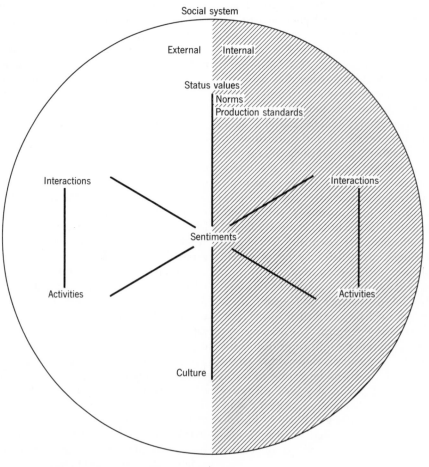

Fig. 5

obvious, and perhaps negative, consequences of these decisions. To do this we need a knowledge of the informal organization and the ways it can be influenced by the formal. On examination the informal organization was found to have a leadership structure, rules, standards, or norms, and ways of rewarding compliance with, or punishing deviations from, norms, thereby controlling people. In short, the informal organization meets with our general definition of an organization quite well, for it presents a set of relations among people. These relations, however, are products of social life and not the results of a central, rational plan based on some legitimate source of authority.

Many things were noted about informal organizations; many more could be noted. To simplify our examination of this part of the organization and also to provide a base for relating it to the formal organization, attention was given to a scheme for classifying elements of the social situation we were examining and also for relating the various classes of phenomena. The major variables were identified as sentiments, interactions, and activities, all mutually related. It was further recognized that some activities, interactions, and sentiments could be considered as coming from without a particular social situation. These would include the beliefs and values people bring with them into a situation, the activities assigned as part of a formal job, and the interactions required in the execution of these duties. On the other hand, another set could be considered as springing from the social situation where people interact with those whose company they enjoy and perhaps share activities with them. The former grouping we called the external system, the latter the internal system. These elements are shown in Fig. 5.

These first two sections, dealing with the formal and the informal organization, cover what has been our traditional ways of viewing an organization. For purposes of investigation or explanation it is frequently necessary to break a large topic into pieces and deal with one piece at a time. As long as the parts are recognized as a division based to a degree on expediency, this is not a particularly dangerous step. Nevertheless, when we lose sight of the fact that we are dealing with pieces of a larger whole and begin to consider the parts as wholes in themselves, serious difficulties arise. This seems to have happened to some who have been studying organizations. Therefore, as these two parts have been developed, particular attention has been given to identifying certain elements that will be particularly useful in developing links or bridges between the two approaches to organizations in order to join them eventually into a larger picture of an organization. This is the task of Part III.

The Informal Organization

PHILIP SELZNICK

This analysis will consider bureaucracy as a special case of the general theory of purposive organization. Recent sociological research has made explicit several conceptions which must serve as essential background for any analysis such as that to follow. Based upon that research, three hypotheses may be introduced here:

1. Every organization creates an informal structure.

2. In every organization, the goals of the organization are modified (abandoned, deflected, or elaborated) by processes within it.

3. The process of modification is effected through the informal structure.

Three recent sociological studies have elucidated these hypotheses.

1. In an intensive examination of a shop department, Roethlisberger and Dickson found clear evidences of an informal structure. This structure consisted of a set of procedures (binging, sarcasm, ridicule) by means of which control over members of the group was exercised, the formation of cliques which functioned as instruments of control, and the establishment of informal leadership. "The men had elaborated, spontaneously and quite unconsciously, an intricate social organization around their collective beliefs and sentiments." [1]

The informal structure of the worker group grew up out of the day-to-day practices of the men as they groped for ways of taking care of their own felt needs. There was no series

of conscious acts by which these procedures were instituted, but they were no less binding on that account. These needs largely arose from the way in which the men defined their situation within the organization. The informal organization served a triple *function:* (*a*) it served to control the behavior of the members of the worker group; (*b*) within the context of the larger organization (the plant), it was an attempt on the part of the particular group to control the conditions of its existence; (*c*) it acted as a mechanism for the expression of personal relationships for which the formal organization did not provide. Thus the informal structure provided those avenues of aggression, solidarity, and prestige-construction required by individual members.

The *consequence* of the activity of the men through the informal organization was a deleterious effect upon the professed goal of the organization as a whole: it resulted in the restriction of output. In asserting its control over the conditions of the job, the group wanted above all to protect itself from outside interference, exhibiting a strong resistance to change.

Thus the facts in this empirical investigation illustrate the hypotheses noted above: the creation of an informal organization, the modification of the professed goal (maximum output), and the effectuation of this modification through the informal structure. In addition, three important characteristics of the informal structure were observed in the study: (*a*) it arises spontaneously; (*b*) the bases of the relationships are personal, involving factors of prestige, acceptance within the group, friendship ties, etc.; and (*c*) the relationships are *power* relationships, oriented toward techniques of *control.* These characteristics are general, and they are important for conceiving of the theory of bureaucratic behavior as a

---

From "An Approach to a Theory of Bureaucracy," *American Sociological Review*, Vol. 8, 1943, pp. 47–48. Reprinted with permission of the author and the publisher, American Sociological Association.
[1] F. J. Roethlisberger, and W. J. Dickson, *Management and the Worker*, Cambridge: Harvard University Press, 1941, 524.

special case of the general theory of organization.

2. C. I. Barnard, in his theoretical analysis of organizational structure, concerned mainly with the problems of the executive, discusses explicitly the character and function of informal structures which arise out of the attempts to solve those problems. By informal structures he means "the aggregate of the personal contacts and interactions and the associated groupings of people" which do not have common or joint purposes, and which are, in fact, "indefinite and rather structureless." [2] He says, further, that "though common or joint purposes are excluded by definition, common or joint results of an important character nevertheless come from such organization." [3]

Barnard lists three functions of informal structures as they operate in formal organizations: (*a*) as a means of communication, establishing norms of conduct between superordinates and subordinates; (*b*) "maintenance of cohesiveness in formal organizations through regulating the willingness to serve and the stability of objective authority"; (*c*) "the maintenance of the feeling of personal integrity, of self-respect, of independent choice." [4] The last mentioned function means simply that the individual's "integrity" is protected by the *appearance* of choice, at the same time that subtle group pressures guarantee control of his actions. Barnard's view of the functions of the informal structure is primarily in terms of the needs of the executive (control through friendship ties, personal authority, a "grape-vine" system, etc.), but it is clear that his analysis agrees with the hypothesis that the informal organization is oriented essentially toward the techniques of control. In the Roethlisberger and Dickson study, it was the worker group which was attempting to control the conditions of its existence; in this case, it is the executive who is doing the same thing.

3. A discussion by Waller and Henderson [5] based on the study of institutions of segregative care, gives further evidence for the theses presented here. The general hypotheses about organizational processes are confirmed by the examination of such structures as private schools, transient camps, prisons, flop-houses, reformatories and military organizations. The authors set the problem in this way:

> Each of our institutions has an idea or purpose—most of them have several purposes more or less compatible with one another—and this idea or purpose gives rise to an institutional structure. The institutional structure consists of a system of organized groups. The interaction of these elements is a principal clue to the understanding of institutions of segregative care. Without a structure, the purpose of an institution would be an empty form of words, and yet the process of translating the purpose into an institutional structure always somehow deflects and distorts it.

It is thus the iron necessity of an organizational structure for the achievement of group goals which creates the paradox to which we have referred. The ideals of those who construct the organization are one thing; the "facts of life" operating independently of and often against those ideals are something else again.

PROFESSED AND OPERATIONAL GOALS. Running an organization, as a specialized and essential activity, generates problems which have no necessary (and often an opposed) relationship to the professed or "original" goals of the organization. The day-to-day behavior of the group becomes centered around specific problems and proximate goals which have primarily an internal relevance. Then, since these activities come to consume an increasing proportion of the time and thoughts of the participants, they are—from the point of view of actual behavior—*substituted* for the professed goals.

The day-to-day activity of men is ordered by those specific problems which have a direct relevance to the materials with which they have to deal. "Ultimate" issues and highly abstract ideas which do not specify any concrete behavior have therefore little direct influence on the bulk of human activities. (The general ideas, of course, may influence action by setting its context and, often, defining its limits.) This is true not because men are evil or un-

[2] C. I. Barnard, *The Functions of the Executive*, Cambridge: Harvard University Press, 1940, p. 115.

[3] *Ibid.*

[4] *Loc. cit.*, pp. 122–123.

[5] W. Waller and W. Henderson, "Institutions of Segregative Care and the Organized Group" (unpublished manuscript), 1941.

intelligent, but because the "ultimate" formulations are not *helpful* in the constant effort to achieve that series of equilibria which represent behavioral solutions to the specific problems which day-to-day living poses. Besides those professed which do not specify any concrete behavior, which are analogous to nonprocedural formulations in science, there are other professed goals which require actions which conflict with what must be done in the daily business of running an organization. In that conflict the professed goals will tend to go down in defeat, usually through the process of being extensively ignored. This phenomenon may be introduced as a fourth hypothesis in the general theory of organization.

Selections from Quota Restriction and Goldbricking in a Machine Shop

DONALD ROY

QUOTA RESTRICTION. It is "quota restriction" which has received the most attention. The Mayo researchers observed that the bank-wiring group at Western Electric limited output to a "quota" or "bogey." [1] Mayo inferred that this chopping-off of production was due to lack of understanding of the economic logics of management, using the following chain of reasoning: Insistence by management on purely economic logics, plus frequent changes in such logics in adaptation to technological change, results in lack of understanding on the part of the workers. Since the latter cannot understand the situation, they are unable to develop a nonlogical social code of a type that brought social cohesion to work groups prior to the Industrial Revolution. This inability to develop a Grade-A social code brings feelings of frustration. And, finally, frustration results in the development of a "lower social code" among the workers in opposition to the economic

logics of management. And one of the symptoms of this "lower social code" is restriction of output. [2]

Mayo thus joins those who consider the economic man a fallacious conception. Now the operators in my shop made noises like economic men. Their talk indicated that they were canny calculators and that the dollar sign fluttered at the masthead of every machine. Their actions were not always consistent with their words; and such inconsistency calls for further probing. But it could be precisely because they were alert to their economic interests—at least to their immediate economic interests—that the operators did not exceed their quotas. It might be inferred from their talk that they did not turn in excess earnings because they felt that to do so would result in piecework price cuts; hence the consequences would be either reduced earnings from the same amount of effort expended or increased effort to maintain the take-home level.

When I was hired, a personnel department clerk assured me that the radial-drill operators were averaging $1.25 an hour on piecework. He was using a liberal definition of the term

From *American Journal of Sociology*, Vol. 57, No. 5, March 1952, pp. 430–432, 436–437. Reprinted with permission of the publisher, The University of Chicago Press; copyright 1952 by the University of Chicago Press.
[1] Fritz Roethlisberger and J. Dickson, *Management and the Worker* (Cambridge: Harvard University Press, 1939).

[2] Elton Mayo, *Human Problems of an Industrial Civilization* (New York: Macmillan Co., 1938), pp. 119–21.

"averaging." Since I had had no previous machine-shop experience and since a machine would not be available for a few days, I was advised to spend some time watching Jack Starkey, a radial-drill man of high rank in seniority and skill.

One of Starkey's first questions was, "What have you been doing?" When I said I had worked in a Pacific Coast shipyard at a rate of pay over $1.00 an hour, Starkey exclaimed, "Then what are you doing in this place?" When I replied that averaging $1.25 an hour wasn't bad, he exploded:

"Averaging, you say! Averaging?"

"Yeah, on the average. I'm an average guy; so I ought to make my buck and a quarter. That is, after I get onto it."

"Don't you know," cried Starkey angrily, "that $1.25 an hour is the *most* we can make, even when we *can* make more! And most of the time we can't even make that! Have you ever worked on piecework before?"

"No."

"I can see that! Well, what do you suppose would happen if I turned in $1.25 an hour on these pump bodies?"

"Turned in? You mean if you actually did the work?"

"I mean if I actually did the work and turned it in!"

"They'd have to pay you, wouldn't they? Isn't that the agreement?"

"Yes! They'd pay me—once! Don't you know that if I turned in $1.50 an hour on these pump bodies tonight, the whole God-damned Methods Department would be down here tomorrow? And they'd retime this job so quick it would make your head swim! And when they retimed it, they'd cut the price in half! And I'd be working for 85 cents an hour instead of $1.25!"

From this initial exposition of Starkey's to my last day at the plant I was subject to warnings and predictions concerning price cuts. Pressure was the heaviest from Joe Mucha, day man on my machine, who shared my job repertoire and kept a close eye on my production. On November 14, the day after my first attained quota, Mucha advised:

"Don't let it go over $1.25 an hour, or the time-study man will be right down here! And they don't waste time, either! They watch the records like a hawk! I got ahead, so I took it easy for a couple of hours."

Joe told me that I had made $10.01 yesterday and warned me not to go over $1.25 an hour. He told me to figure the set-ups and the time on each operation very carefully so that I would not total over $10.25 in any one day.

Jack Starkey defined the quota carefully but forcefully when I turned in $10.50 for one day, or $1.31 an hour.

Jack Starkey spoke to me after Joe left. "What's the matter? Are you trying to upset the apple cart?"

Jack explained in a friendly manner that $10.50 was too much to turn in, even on an old job.

"The turret-lathe men can turn in $1.35," said Jack, "but their rate is 90 cents, and ours 85 cents."

Jack warned me that the Methods Department could lower their prices on any job, old or new, by changing the fixture slightly, or changing the size of drill. According to Jack, a couple of operators (first and second shift on the same drill) got to competing with each other to see how much they could turn in. They got up to $1.65 an hour, and the price was cut in half. And from then on they had to run that job themselves, as none of the other operators would accept the job.

According to Jack, it would be all right for us to turn in $1.28 or $1.29 an hour, when it figured out that way, but it was not all right to turn in $1.30 an hour.

Well, now I know where the maximum is —$1.29 an hour.

Starkey's beliefs concerning techniques of price-cutting were those of the shop. Leonard Bricker, an old-timer in the shop, and Willie, the stock-chaser, both affirmed that management, once bent on slashing a piecework price, would stop at nothing.

"Take these $1.25 jobs. One guy will turn in $1.30 an hour one day. Then another fellow will turn in, say, $1.31 or $1.32. Then the first fellow will go up to $1.35. First thing you know they'll be up to $1.50, and bang! They'll tear a machine to pieces to change something to cut a price!"

In the washroom, before I started work,

Willie commented on my gravy job, the pedestals.

"The Methods Department is going to lower the price," he said. "There was some talk today about it."

"I hope they don't cut it too much," I said. "I suppose they'll make some change in the jigs?"

"They'll change the tooling in some way. Don't worry, when they make up their minds to lower a price, they'll find a way to do it!" [3]

The association of quota behavior with such expressions about price-cutting does not prove a causal connection. Such a connection could be determined only by instituting changes in the work situation that would effect a substantial reduction of "price-cut fear" and by observing the results of such changes.

Even if it should be thus indicated that there is a causal relationship, testing of alternative hypotheses would still be necessary. It may be, but it is not yet known, that "economic determinism" may account for quota restriction in the shop investigated. It may also be, but it is not known, that factors such as Mayo's "failure to understand the economic logics of management" are influential. . . .

PIECEWORK GOLDBRICKING. On "gravy jobs" the operators earned a quota, then knocked off. On "stinkers" they put forth only minimal effort; either they did not try to achieve

[3] John Mills, onetime research engineer in telephony and for five years engaged in personnel work for the Bell Telephone Company, has recently indicated the possibility that there were factors in the bank-wiring room situation that the Mayo group failed to detect: "Reward is supposed to be in direct proportion to production. Well, I remember the first time I ever got behind that fiction. I was visting the Western Electric Company, which had a reputation of never cutting a piece rate. It never did; if some manufacturing process was found to pay more than seemed right for the class of labor employed on it—if, in other words, the rate-setters had misjudged—that particular part was referred to the engineers for redesign, and then a new rate was set on the new part. Workers, in other words, were paid as a class, supposed to make about so much a week with their best efforts and, of course, less for less competent efforts" (*The Engineer in Society* [New York: D. Van Nostrand & Co., 1946], p. 93).

a turn-in equal to the base wage rate or they deliberately slowed down. Jobs were defined as "good" and "bad" jobs, not in terms of the effort or skill necessary to making out at a bare base-rate level, but of the felt attainability of a substantial premium, i.e., 15 cents an hour or more. Earnings of $1.00 an hour in relation to a $1.25 quota and an 85-cent base rate were considered worth the effort, while earnings of 95 cents an hour were not.

The attitude basic to the goldbricking type of restriction was expressed succinctly thus: "They're not going to get much work out of me for this pay!"

Complaints about low piecework prices were chronic and universal in the shop.

> The turret lathe men discussed the matter of making out, one man stating that only half the time could a man make 84 cents day rate on a machine. It was agreed: "What's the use of pushing when it's hard even to make day rate?"

His 50-50 estimate was almost equal to my own experience of 49.6-50.4. Pessimistic though it was, it was less so than usual statements on the subject:

> I asked Jackson if he was making out, and he gave me the usual answer, "No!"
>
> "They ask me how I'm making out, and I always say, 'O.K.' As far as I'm concerned, I'm making out O.K. If they start asking me further, I'll tell them that this place stinks.
>
> "The day man isn't making out either. We get a lot of little jobs, small lots. It's impossible to make out when you're getting small jobs all the time."
>
> Joe was working on a new job, time study on some small pieces tonight. I asked him, "Something good?" and he replied, "Nothing is good any more!"

There seemed to be no relation between a man's ability to earn and his behavior on a "stinker." That the men who most frequently earned the quota goldbricked like the rest on poor jobs appears in the following extracts:

> Al McCann (the man who made quota most often) said that he gives a job a trial, and if it is no good he takes his time. He didn't try to make out on the chucks tonight.
>
> Joe Mucha, my day man, said of a certain

job: "I did just one more than you did. If they don't like it they can do them themselves. To hell with them. I'm not going to bust my ass on stuff like this."

Old Peter, the multiple drill man, said "I ran some pieces for 25 minutes to see how many I could turn out. I turned out 20 at 1½ cents apiece (72 cents an hour). So I smoke and take it easy. I can't make out; so ——— it."

I notice that when Ed Sokolsky, one of the better operators on the line, is working on an operation he cannot make out on, he does not go at his task with vigor. He either pokes around or leaves his machine for long periods of time; and Paul (set-up man) seems always to be looking for him. Steve (supt.) is always bellowing, "Where in hell is Ed?" or "Come on, Ed, let's have some production around here!" Tonight I heard him admonishing Ed again, "Now I want you to work at that machine 'til three o'clock, do you understand?"

Mike Koszyk, regarded as a crack operator: The price was a poor one (a few cents a hundred) and the job tough. Mike had turned out only 9 pieces in 3 hours. When Mike takes his time, he really takes his time!

According to Al, Jack Starkey turned in 40 cents an hour today on his chuck parts. Al laughed, saying, "I guess Jack didn't like this job."

Gus Schmidt, regarded as the best speed-drill operator on the second shift, was timed early in the evening on a job, and given a price of $1.00 per 100 for reaming one hole, chamfering both sides of three holes, and filing burrs on one end of one hole. All that for one cent!

"To hell with them," said Gus.

He did not try to make out.

The possibility of covering "day rate" was ordinarily no spur to the machine operator to bestir himself on a job. A remark of Mucha's was characteristic: "I could have made out," he said, "but why kill yourself for day rate?"

Average hourly earnings of less or even a little more than $1.00 an hour were usually thrown into the "day-rate" category.

Joe Mucha drilled 36 of the bases (at $8.80 per 100) today. "The most I'll ever do until they retime this job is 40," he said. "Do you know, they expect us to do 100? Why, I wouldn't bust my ass to do 50, for $8.00, when day rate is almost that!"

McCann was put to drilling some pieces at $6.50 per 100. I noticed him working furiously and walked over to see what he was doing. He asked me to figure out how many pieces at 6½ cents he had to turn out per hour to make $1.20. When I told him 18 or 19 he said, "I give up," and immediately slowed down.

A few minutes later I met him in the washroom, and he said, "I wouldn't work that hard for eight or ten hours even if I could make out. I thought I'd try it for an hour or so and see what I could do."

He figures that he was making 95 cents an hour. At lunch time he said that he had averaged $1.00 an hour for the two hours and thought maybe he would try to make out.

Efficiency and "the Fix": Informal Intergroup Relations in a Piecework Machine Shop [1]

DONALD ROY

As part of a broader examination and appraisal of the application of piecework incentive to the production line of an American factory this paper essays the simple but largely neglected task of exploring the network of intergroup relations in which the work activity of machine operatives is imbedded. Exploration will be restricted to a limited sector of the total web of interaction in one shop; description will center upon those relationships that provide support to the operator group in its resistance to and subversion of formally instituted managerial controls on production. It is hoped that observations reported here not only will bear upon the practical problem of industrial efficiency but will also contribute to the more general study of institutional dynamics.

This could be considered the third in a series of attempts to make more careful discriminations in an area of research that has been characteristically productive of sweeping generalizations, blanket conceptualizations, or algebraic gymnastics that tend to halt inquiry at the same time that they lay a fog over otherwise easily discerned reality. Data for all three papers were acquired in an investigation of a single work situation by a single technique of social inquiry, participant observation. The writer was employed for nearly a year as radial-drill operator in one of the machine shops of a steel-processing plant, and he kept a daily record of his observations and experiences relating to work activity and social interaction in the shop. His major interest lay in the phenomenon of restriction of output, or "systematic soldiering," the practice of which various sociological soundings have revealed in the lower depths of our industrial organization. To complete the analogy: the writer donned a diving suit and went down to see what it looked like on the bottom.

One conclusion has already been set forth,[2] namely, that the usual view of output restriction is grossly undifferentiating. Different kinds of "institutionalized underworking" were practiced, each with its characteristic pattern of antecedents and consequences. The blanket term "restriction" was found to cloak all-important contrarieties of work behavior. Machine operatives not only held back effort; sometimes they worked hard. The very common failure to note such contrarieties has tended, of course, to impede the progress of research by checking consideration of the specific conditions under which differences in behavior occur.

A second finding was the discovery of complexity where simple lines of relationship had generally been assumed to exist.[3] When inconsistencies in the operator's behavior seemed

From *American Journal of Sociology*, Vol. 60, No. 3, 1954, pp. 255–266. Reprinted with permission of the publisher, The University of Chicago Press; Copyright 1954 by the University of Chicago Press.
[1] This report is drawn from materials presented in the writer's doctoral dissertation, "Restriction of Output in a Piecework Machine Shop" (University of Chicago, 1952), under the direction of Everett C. Hughes.

[2] Donald Roy, "Quota Restriction and Goldbricking in a Machine Shop," *American Journal of Sociology*, LVII (March, 1952), 427–42.
[3] Donald F. Roy, "Work Satisfaction and Social Reward in Quota Achievement: An Analysis of Piecework Incentive," *American Sociological Review*, XVIII (October, 1953), 507–14.

to contradict the hypothesis that variations in application of economic incentive could account for the variations in work effort, a more intensive examination of response to piecework was undertaken. This disclosed that piecework incentive was not equivalent to economic incentive and that attainment of piecework "quotas" afforded machine operators a complex of rewards in which the strictly economic might or might not play a part.

The third set of observations, to be here discussed, again exhibits complication in a picture that has come to be accepted as simple in design. Here the focus of interest is the structure of "informal" intergroup connections that bear directly upon work behavior at the machine level. The material will not deny the hypothesis that the willingness of operatives to put forth effort is a function of their relationship with management or the widely held affirmation that this relationship is mediated by the organization of operatives into "informal groups." It will indicate, however, that further advances in the understanding of work behavior in the factory may involve attention to minor as well as major axes of intergroup relations. It will show that the relevant constituents of problematic production situations may include "lateral" lines of interaction between subgroups of the work force as well as "vertical" connections between managerial and worker groups.

It will be seen, in other words, that the interaction of two groups in an industrial organization takes place within and is conditioned by a larger intergroup network of reciprocal influences. Whyte has called attention to the limitations of studying groups in "isolation," without regard for the "perspectives of large institutional structures."[4] A second warning might be: The larger institutional structures form networks of interacting groups.

As a bona fide member of an informal group of machine operatives the writer had an opportunity to observe and experience management-work group conflict in its day-to-day and blow-by-blow particulars. Also, he participated in another kind of social process, intergroup co-operation. Not only did workers on the "drill line" co-operate with each other as fellow-members of a combat team at war with management; they also received considerable aid and abetment from other groups of the shop. This intergroup co-operation was particularly evident when operators were trying to "make out," or attain "quota" production, on piecework jobs.

It has been noted in another connection that machine operators characteristically evinced no reluctance to put forth effort when they felt that their group-defined piecework quotas were attainable.[5] It might seem, at first glance, that the supporting of operators during intensive application to "getting the work out" would represent co-operation *with* and not *against* management. However, the truth is that operators and their "allies" joined forces in certain situations in a manner not only unmistakably at variance with the carefully prepared designs of staff experts but even in flagrant violation of strongly held managerial "moral principles" of shop behavior. In short, machine operators resorted to "cheating" to attain their quotas; and since this often involved the collusion of other shop groups, not as mere "accessories after the fact" but as deeply entangled accomplices, any managerial suspicion that swindling and conniving, as well as loafing, were going on all the time was well founded. If the workers' conviction that the echelons of management were packed with men addicted to the "dirty deal" be additionally considered, it might appear that the shop was fairly overrun with crooks. Since a discussion of "contrast conceptions"[6] cannot find a place within the limited scope of this paper, it must suffice at this point merely to declare that the kind of effort made by operators and their aids to expedite production, when they did try to expedite it, was actually in many respects conflict with management.

One belief, universally accepted in the work group, may be phrased thus: "You can't 'make out' if you do things the way management

---

[4] William F. Whyte, "Small Groups and Large Organizations," in *Social Psychology at the Crossroads*, ed. John R. Rohrer and Muzafer Sherif (New York: Harper & Bros., 1951), pp. 297–312.

[5] Roy, "Work Satisfaction and Social Reward in Quota Achievement," *op. cit.*

[6] See L. Copeland, "The Negro as a Contrast Conception," in *Race Relations and the Race Problem*, ed. E. T. Thompson (Durham: Duke University Press, 1939), and S. Kirson Weinberg, "Aspects of the Prison's Social Structure," *American Journal of Sociology*, XLVII (March, 1942), 717–26.

wants them done." This gem of shop wisdom thus negatively put is hardly a prescription for action, but its obverse, "You've got to figure the angles," gave all hands plenty to do.

According to Al McCann (all names used are fictitious), the "Fagan" of the drill line, "They time jobs to give you just base rates. It's up to you to figure out how to fool them so you can make out. You can't make any money if you run the job the way it's timed."

We machine operators did "figure the angles"; we developed an impressive repertoire of angles to play and devoted ourselves to crossing the expectations of formal organization with perseverance, artistry, and organizing ability of our own. For instance, job timing was a "battle all the way" between operators and time-study men. The objective of the operators was good piecework prices, and that end justified any old means that would work. One cardinal principle of operator job-timing was that cutting tools be run at lower speeds and "feeds" than the maximums possible on subsequent production, and there were various ways of encouraging the institution of adequate differentials. Also, operators deemed it essential to embellish the timing performance with movements only apparently functional in relation to the production of goods: little reachings, liftings, adjustings, dustings, and other special attentions to conscientious machine operation and good housekeeping that could be dropped instanter with the departure of the time-study man.

However, the sophistication of the time-study men usually matched the strategy employed against them. The canniest operators often gave of their best in timing duels only to get "hopeless prices" for their pains:

Gus Schmidt was timed early in the evening on a job, and given a price of $1.00 per 100 for reaming one hole, chamfering both sides of three holes, and filing burrs on one end of one hole. All that for one cent!

"To hell with them," said Gus.

This is not to say that the "hopeless price" was always truly hopeless. Since the maintenance of an effective control over job-timing and hence price-setting was an uncertain, often disheartening matter, operators were forced to develop skills for turning bad into good. Under the shaping hands of the "angle-applicators" surprising metamorphoses sometimes took

place. Like the proverbial ugly duckling that finally feathered out into a beautiful swan, piecework jobs originally classified in operator vernacular as "stinkers" came to give off the delightful aroma of "gravy." Without going into the particulars of the various types of operation, one might say that jobs were "streamlined." This streamlining was, of course, at times "rough on the tools" and adverse in its effects on the quality of output. The jettisoning of quality called, necessarily, for a corresponding attention to ways and means of shielding supervisors and inspectors from discovering the sacrifices and consequently brought into further play the social graces of equivocation, subterfuge, and prestidigitation.

Still, the adroitness of the machine operators, inventing, scheming, and conniving unto themselves to make quotas attainable, was not enough. Many "stinkers" would not yield before the whitest heat of intelligence or the most cavalier disregard for company property. An appreciable incidence of failure should not be surprising when it is kept in mind that the black arts of "making out" were not only responses to challenge from management but also stimulations, in circular interaction, to the development of more effective countermagic in the timing process. It would be hard to overestimate the wizardry of the time-study men with pencil and paper in computing "angle-tight" piecework prices. During the latter months of his employment, months that marked the peak of his machine performance, the writer was able to achieve quota earnings approximately half the time that piecework jobs were offered. If this experience is roughly representative of the fortunes of the drill-line group, the battle with the stopwatch men was nip and tuck.

It is to be expected that a group of resourceful operatives, working with persistent intent to "make out" at quota levels, and relying heavily upon illegal practices, would be alert to possibilities of assistance from groups that were able and willing to give it and would not hesitate at further flouting the rules and regulations in cultivating it. It is also to be expected that the upholders of a managerial rational and moral order would attempt to prevent corruptive connections and would take action to stamp out whatever subversive organization did develop. During the eleven-month study, machine operators, including the drill-line men, were enjoying the co-operation of several other shop groups in an illegal facilitation of the "make-out" process. This intergroup network effectively modified certain formally established shop routines, a too close attachment to which would handicap the operators. The "syndicate" also proved adequate in circumventing each of a series of "new rules" and "new systems" introduced by management to expurgate all modifications and improvisations and force a strict adherence to the rules.

The shop groups that conspired with the operators were, namely, the inspectors, the tool-crib men, the time-checkers, the stockmen, and the setup men. With a single exception, these "service" groups stemmed from lines of authority distinct from the one for which the operators formed the base. The one exception was the setup group; it was subordinate to the same set of officials in the "production" line of authority that controlled the operators. A brief description of the duties of each of these service groups and a rough tracing of the sequences of interaction involved in the prescribed work routine of the drill men will indicate the formal pattern of intergroup relations within which informally instituted variations were woven.

THE SETUP MEN. A chief function of the setup men was to assist machine operators in the "setting-up" of jigs and fixtures preparatory to operation of machines in the processing of materials. It included the giving of preliminary aid and advice at the beginning of the production process, at which time the setup men would customarily "run the first piece" to show operators how to do it and to indicate that the setup was adequate to meet work specifications. The duties of the setup men also included "trouble-shooting" on occasions when operators encountered difficulties that effected a lowering of the quality of output below inspection standards or a reduction of the rate of output unsatisfactory to operators or supervisors.

THE INSPECTORS. The chief function of the inspectors was to pass judgment on the quality of the output of the machine operators, either accepting or rejecting work turned out, according to blueprint specifications. Their appraisals came at the beginning of operations, when especially thorough examinations of the first pieces processed were made, and subsequently at varying intervals during the course of a job.

THE TOOL-CRIB MEN. The tool-crib attendants served the operators as dispensers of jigs, fixtures, cutting tools, blueprints, gauges, and miscellaneous items of equipment needed to supplement basic machinery and operator-owned hand tools in the processing of materials. They worked inside a special inclosure conveniently located along one of the main arterials of shop traffic and did most of their dispensing across the wide sill of a "window," an aperture which served, incidentally, as locus of various and sundry transactions and communications not immediately relevant to tool-dispensing. There were two other openings into the crib, a door, two steps from the window, and a wide gate, farther down the corridor.

THE STOCKMEN. The stockmen were responsible for conducting a steady flow of materials to the machines for processing. Their work called for the removal of finished work as well as the moving-up of fresh stock and involved a division of labor into two specializations: "stock-chasing" and "trucking." The chief duties of the stock-chasers were to "locate" unprocessed materials in the various storage areas, when operators called for stock, and to direct the activities of the truckers, who attended to the physical transportation.

THE TIME-CHECKERS. The time-checkers worked in another special inclosure, a small "time cage," from which they distributed to the operators the work orders "lined up" by the schedulemen of the Planning Department and within which they registered the starting and completion times of each job. There were four time-registering operations for every work order. First, upon presenting an operator with a work-order slip, the checker would "punch" him "on setup" by stamping a separate order card with a clocking mechanism that registered the hours in tenths. Later, when the operator would call at the cage window to announce completion of all preparatory arrangements for the actual processing of materials, the checker would punch him "off setup" and "on production." Finally, following another operator announcement, the checker would clock the termination of the machining process with a fourth punch. At the time of his terminal punch the operator would report the number of "pieces" completed on the job just concluded and would receive a new work order to start the cycle over again. And, since the terminal punch on the completed job would be registered at the same time as the initial punch on the new one, hours on shift would be completely accounted for.

OPERATOR INTERACTION WITH SERVICE GROUPS. The machine operator's performance of each individual job or order assigned to him involved formal relationships with service groups in well-defined sequences or routines.

First, the operator would receive his work order from the time-checker. Next, he would present the work order to a tool-crib attendant at the crib window as a requisite to receiving blueprints, jigs, cutting tools, and gauges. At the same time, that is, immediately before or after approaching the crib attendant, sometimes while waiting for crib service, the operator would show his work order to a stock-chaser as a requisite to receiving materials to work on. The stock-chaser, after perusing the order slip, occasionally with additional reference to the blueprint, would hail a trucker to bring the necessary stock to the operator's machine. If there were no delay in contacting a stock-chaser or in locating and moving up the stock, a load of materials would await the operator upon his arrival at his machine with equipment from the tool crib.

Upon returning to his machine, the operator would proceed with the work of "setting up" the job, usually with the assistance of a setup man, who would stay with him until a piece was turned out whose quality of workmanship would satisfy an inspector. In appraising a finished piece, the inspector would consult the blueprint brought from the crib for work specifications and then perform operations of measurement with rules, gauges, micrometers, or more elaborate equipment. The inspector might or might not "accept" the first piece presented for his judgment. At any rate, his approval was requisite to the next step in the operator's formal interactional routine, namely, contacting the time-checker to punch "off setup" and "on production."

The operator would ordinarily have further "business" contact with a setup man during the course of production. Even if the job did not "go sour" and require the services of a

"trouble-shooter," the setup man would drop around of his own accord to see how the work was progressing. Likewise, the operator would have further formal contact during the course of his job with inspectors and tool-crib attendants. Each inspector would make periodic "quality checks" at the machines on his "line"; and the operator might have to make trips to the tool crib to get tools ground or to pick up additional tools or gauges. He might also have to contact a stock-chaser or truckers for additional materials.

Upon completion of the last piece of his order the operator would tear down his setup, return his tools to the tool crib, and make a final report to the time-checker. Should the job be uncompleted at the close of a shift, the operator would merely report the number of pieces finished to a checker, and the latter would register a final punchout. The setup would be left intact for the use of the operator coming in to work the next shift.

MAJOR JOB CATEGORIES. Certain variations in types of jobs assigned to operators are pertinent to a discussion of intergroup collusion to modify formal work routines. These variations could be classified into four categories: (1) piecework; (2) time study; (3) rework; and (4) setup.

Each piecework job carried a price per 100 pieces, determined by the timing operations mentioned earlier. Time-study and rework jobs carried no prices. The time-study category included (a) new jobs that had not yet been timed and (b) jobs that had once carried a piecework price. As the label indicates, rework jobs involved the refinishing of pieces rejected either by inspectors or in the assembly process but considered salvageable by reprocessing.

Since time-study and rework jobs carried no piecework prices, operators engaged in these two types of work were paid "day rate," that is, according to an hourly base rate determined in collective bargaining. The base rates represented minimal wage guaranties that not only applied to "day work" but also covered piecework as well. If an operator on piecework failed to exceed his base rate in average hourly earnings on a particular job on a particular day, he would be paid his base rate. Failure to produce at base rate or above on the first day of a piecework job did not penalize an operator in his efforts to earn premium pay on the second day; nor did failure to attain base rate on one piecework job on a given day reduce premiums earned on a second job performed that day.

Not a fourth type of job, but measured separately in time and payment units, were the setup operations. Piecework jobs always carried piecework setups; failure to equal or exceed base rate on setup did not jeopardize chances to earn premium on "production," and vice versa. Time-study jobs frequently carried piecework setups; rework never.

Obviously, these formal work routines may easily be modified to fit the perceived needs of machine operators. Possibilities for the development of "make-out angles" should be immediately apparent in a work situation characterized by job repertoires that included piecework and day-work operations; minimum-wage guaranties uniform for all work done; and separate payment computations by jobs and days worked. If, for instance, time formally clocked as day work could be used to gain a "head start" on subsequent piecework operations, such a transferral might mean the difference between earning and not earning premiums on doubtful piecework jobs. Similarly, time on "hopeless" piecework jobs might be applied to more promising operations; and the otherwise "free time" gained on "gravy" jobs might be consumed in productive anticipation of the formal receipt of ordinarily unrewarding piecework. Especially lush "gravy" jobs might even contribute extra time enough to convert "stinkers" into temporary "money-makers." Realization of such possibilities in any given case would necessarily involve obtaining, without a work order, the following: (1) identification of future operations as listed in sequence on the schedule board inside the time cage; (2) jigs, blueprints, and cutting tools appropriate to the work contemplated; (3) stock to work on; (4) setup help and adivce; (5) inspection service; and (6) "trouble-shooting" assistance as needed. Obviously, this sequence of accomplishments would call for the support of one or more service groups at each step. That the required assistance was actually provided with such regularity that it came to be taken for granted, the writer discovered by observation and personal experience.

The following diary recording of interaction between the writer and a time-checker may be indicative of the extent to which service-group collaboration with the operators in perverting the formal system of work routine had become systematized:

> When I came to punch off the rework, the time-cage girl said, "You don't want to punch off rework yet, do you?"—suggesting that I should get a start on the next job before punching off rework.

Even line foremen, who, in regard to intergroup collusion preferred the role of silent "accessory after the fact," became upset to the point of actual attempted interference with formal rules and regulations when the naïve neophyte failed to meet the expectations of his own informal system.

> Art [foreman] was at the time cage when I punched off the day work of rereaming and on to the piecework of drilling. He came around to my machine shortly after.
> "Say," he said, "when you punch off day work onto piecework, you ought to have your piecework already started. Run a few; then punch off the day work, and you'll have a good start. You've got to chisel a little around here to make money."

Acceptance of such subversive practices did not extend, however, to groups in management other than local shop supervision. The writer was solemnly and repeatedly warned that time-study men, the true hatchet men of upper management, were disposed to bring chiselers to speedy justice.

> Gus went on to say that a girl hand-mill operator had been fired a year ago when a time-study man caught her running one job while being punched in on another. The time-study man came over to the girl's machine to time a job, to find the job completed and the girl running another.

NEW RULES AND NEW SYSTEMS. During the near-year that he spent in the shop the writer felt the impact of several attempts to stamp out intergroup irregularities and enforce conformity to managerial designs of procedure. He coincidentally participated in an upholding of the maxim: "Plus ça change, plus c'est la même chose."

Attempts to tighten controls came in a series of "new rules" or "new systems" promulgated by bulletin-board edicts. How far the beginning of the series antedated the writer's arrival is not known. Old-timers spoke of a "Golden Age" enjoyed before the installation of the "Booth System" of production control; then operators "kept their own time," turning in their work orders as they saw fit and building "kitties" on good jobs to tide them over rainy days on poor jobs.

The first new rule during this study went into "effect" less than two months after the writer was hired. It was designed to tighten controls in the tool-crib sector, where attendants had not only been passing out setups ahead of time but allowing operators or their setup men to enter the toolroom to make the advance pickups themselves. An aim of the new rule was also to curb the operators' practice of keeping "main setups" at the machines instead of turning them in at the completion of operations.

A new crib ruling went into effect today. A memorandum by Bricker [superintendent] was posted on the side of the crib window. Those who check out tools and jigs must sign a slip in triplicate, keeping the pink one and turning it in with the tools in exchange for the white original, which would constitute proof that the tools had been returned. No new setups would be issued until the old ones had been turned in.

An optimistic perception of the new procedures was expressed by young Jonesy, a tool-crib attendant and otherwise willing conniver with the operators: "Tools are scattered all over the shop. This way we'll have them all in order in the crib, and the fellows can get them anytime they need them."

But multiple-drill operator Hanks, old-timer on the line, drew upon his lengthy experience with managerial efficiency measures and saw the situation differently:

Hanks commented unfavorably on the new ruling. He and the day man [his machine partner on the other shift] had been keeping the tools for their main setups at their bench, or, rather, under it. This practice, according to Hanks, was to insure their setting up promptly without inordinate waste of time and to insure their having all the tools needed. Hanks said that on a previous occasion he was told to turn

in one of his main setups, which included over a dozen drills, reamers, taps, etc., of varying sizes. He did so, but, when he needed this setup again, the crib man couldn't locate all the tools. He asked Hanks to come back in the crib and help him find them. Hanks refused. After several hours of futile search, Hanks was finally induced to "come back and find his tools." He did so on condition that it would not be on his own time. The foreman agreed to this.

"The same thing is going to happen again," predicted Hanks. "And I'm not going back there to find my tools they scatter all over, on my own time."

Though the operators went through the formality of an exchange of slips when they exchanged setups, the new procedures did not modify the practice of getting setups from the crib ahead of time. Appreciable effects of the new ruling included making more paper work for crib attendants at the same time that more work at assembling setups was thrust upon them. Jonesy's happy prediction did not materialize: the tools were not "always in order." Subsequent events confirmed Hanks's gloomy forebodings:

It took Paul [setup man] and me several hours to get set up for the sockets, as the setup given was incomplete.

Some time was spent in looking for an angle plate that was specially made for the job. Both Paul and Steve [superintendent] were irritated because the crib men could not find the plate.

We spent an hour setting up because we could not find the jig.

Included in the new ruling was a stipulation that blueprints and gauges be turned in by the operators at the end of each shift, though setup paraphernalia other than prints and gauges were to be left at the machines as long as jobs were in operation. Calling for prints and gauges at the beginning of the shift, waiting at the crib window in the line that naturally formed, even when these items were "located" immediately, consumed operator time.

Owing to the new crib ruling, he [Joe Mucha, the writer's machine partner on another shift] turned in the tap gauge. I spent 20 minutes trying to get it back again. The crib man could not find it and claimed that Joe had not turned it in. Joe stayed after three o'clock to help me get it, countering the arguments of the crib with the slip that he retained as evidence. Finally the gauge was located in the crib.

I started out a half-hour late on operation 55 on the pedestals, due to delay at the crib waiting to check out the print and gauge that Joe had just turned in.

Four months later the new crib ruling was modified by another that canceled the stipulation regarding the turning-in of blueprints and gauges and called for changes in the paper work of operator–crib-attendant relations. These changes were featured by a new kind of work order, duplicates of which became involved in tool-crib bookkeeping. The change reduced the waste of operator time at the start of shifts, but to the burden of the crib attendants paper-work irritations were now added.

When I punched in on the rework and asked Walt [crib attendant] for a print, he fumed a bit as he sought a duplicate of my new-type yellow work order in a new file of his.

"I haven't been able to find more than one in five duplicates so far," he said. "And there's supposed to be a duplicate for every one."

Walt said tonight, when I presented him with a work-order card for tools, "That makes the twelfth card I've had and no duplicate!"

The tool crib under the new system is supposed to have duplicate work orders in their file of all jobs given operators. These duplicates are to be put in the toolroom files as soon as they are put on the board; and the operators are to sign these duplicates when checking out setups.

The "new system" did operate to handicap operators in that they were not to receive new setups from the crib until they received the new yellow work orders from the time cage to check with the duplicates in the crib. However, setup men roamed at will in the toolroom, grinding tools and fixing jigs, and were able to help the operators by picking up setups ahead of time for them. Their detailed knowledge of the various setups made it possible for them to assemble the necessary tools without the use of setup cards.

"This is a good job," I said to McCann [now setup man]. "I wish I could get it set up ahead of time, but I guess it's no use trying. I can't get the setup now from the toolroom until I get the new work order from the time girls."

McCann thought a moment. "Maybe I can get the jig and tools out of the crib for you."

McCann did get the jig and tools, and I got a half-hour's head start on the job.

The writer had found Ted, a stock-chaser, and his truckers, George and Louie, willing connivers in the time-chiseling process. They moved up stock ahead of time, even after the new system made presentation of the new work order to the stock-chaser a prerequisite to getting stock. Contrary to first impressions, for all practical purposes the situation was unchanged under the new system.

I could not go ahead with the next order, also a load of connecting rods, because the new ruling makes presentation of a work order to the stock-chaser necessary before materials can be moved up. So I was stymied and could do nothing the rest of the day.

About an hour before I was to punch off the connecting rods, I advised Ted that I would soon be needing another job. He immediately brought over a load of reservoir casings.

The new system also included complication of operator-inspector relations. Inspectors were now to "sign off" operators from completed jobs before new work orders could be issued at the time booth. The "signing-off" process included notation by the inspector of the time of operation completion, a double check on the time-checker's "punch out." This added, of course, to the paper work of inspectors.

Drill-man Hanks's first response to this feature of the new system was "individualistic":

Hanks commented on the new system tonight. He thinks that its chief purpose is to keep the operators from getting ahead on an operation and starting the next job on saved time. He said that the inspector checked him off a job tonight at 4:40, and he was not due to punch in on the next one until 6:10. He changed the time recorded by the inspector on his work slip to 6:10 and went ahead as usual. If he had not done so, there would have been a "gap" of an hour and a half unaccounted for in the records.

The writer found himself "stymied" at first but soon discovered that the new obstacle could be overcome without engaging in such a hazardous practice as "forging."

> It was ten o'clock when we were ready to punch off setup, and Johnny [setup man] asked Sam [inspector] to sign me off setup earlier, so that I could make out on setup.
> "Punch me off at nine o'clock," I said, not expecting Sam to check me off earlier, and purposely exaggerating Johnny's request.
> Sam refused. "I can't do that! If I do that for you, I'll have to do it for everybody!"
> Sam seemed somewhat agitated in making the refusal.
> A few minutes later he said to Johnny, "Why did you ask me to do that when Hanks was standing there?"
> Hanks had been standing by my machine, watching us set up.
> "I can't take you off an hour back. Go find out when you punched in on this job in the first place."
> Johnny consulted the time-cage girl as to the time I punched on the job, later talked to Sam at Sam's bench while I was working, and came to me with the announcement that it was "fixed up" so that I made out on setup and was credited with starting production at 9:30. This gave me an hour and a half of "gravy."

By the time the "new system" was a month old, Sam was not only doing this for everybody but actually taking the initiative:

> When I punched off setup for the eight pieces, Sam asked me if I wanted him to take me off setup at an earlier time in order that I might make out on the setup. I refused this offer, as it wasn't worth the trouble for me to stop to figure out the time.

Instead of looking at the clock when an operator asks to be taken off setup, Sam usually asks the operator, "When do you want to be taken off?"

No sooner had the shop employees adjusted to this "new system" and settled down to normal informal routine than they were shocked by a new pronunciamento that barred admittance to the toolroom to all save superintendents and toolroom employees:

> A new crib ruling struck without warning today. Typewritten bulletins signed by Faulkner [shop manager] were posted on the toolroom door, barring admittance to all save the toolroom employees and the two departmental foremen [superintendents], Bricker and Steve. Other foremen and setup men are not to be admitted without permission from Milton, toolroom supervisor.
> Hanks predicts that the new ruling won't last out the week.

Stimulated by Hanks's prediction, the writer kept an eye on the toolroom door. The rule seemed to be enforced.

> On one occasion tonight Paul [setup man] asked Jonesy to let him into the crib; he was in a hurry about something. But Jonesy shook his head, and Paul had to wait at the crib window with the rest of us.

Johnny, the setup man, predicted that the new ruling would be "tough on" the tool-crib employees, not on setup men.

> Johnny says that the new rule is going to be tough on grinders and crib attendants, because setup men and foremen have been doing much of the grinding and have made it easier for them by coming in to help themselves to tools, jigs, etc.
> Johnny says that the new rule suits him fine. Now he can just stand at the window and holler and let the toolroom employees do the work.

The line foremen seemed to take offense at the new "exclusion act" and threatened reprisals to the crib attendants.

> At quitting time I noticed Gil [line foreman] talking to Walt at the crib window. Gil seemed very serious; Walt was waving his arms and otherwise gesturing in a man-

ner indicating rejection of responsibility. I didn't catch any words but gathered that Gil was voicing disapproval or warning, and after Gil left I said to Walt, "Looks like you're behind the eight-ball now!"

I noticed that Walt's hair was mussed, and he looked a little wild. He denied that he was in any trouble whatsoever; nor was he worried about anything whatsoever.

"I'm just working here!" he exclaimed. "I just go by the cards, and beyond that I've got no responsibility!"

I was curious as to what Gil had told him and asked Johnny later, on the way home. I had noticed that Johnny was standing nearby when Gil was talking to Walt. Johnny said that Gil was telling Walt that from now on the crib was going to be charged with every minute of tool delay to the operators—that, if there was any waiting for tools, Gil was going to make out allowance cards charging these delays to the crib.

Contrary to Hanks's prediction, the new rule did "last out the week," and crowds milled around the crib window.

The boys seemed very much disgusted with the slow service at the tool crib. They crowd around the window (always a crowd there) and either growl or wisecrack about the service.

It was at this time that Jonesy, erstwhile optimist and regarded by shop employees as the most efficient of the crib attendants, decided that he had "had enough." He transferred to the quiet backroom retreat of tool-grinding. But several days later, just ten days since the new rule was promulgated, the sun began to break through the dark clouds of managerial efficiency. Hanks's prediction was off by four days.

While I was waiting for tools at the crib window tonight, I noticed the jockey [turret-lathe man] dash into the tool crib through a door that was left ajar; he was followed soon after by Gil. Later, when the door was closed, Paul shook it and shouted to the attendant, "Let me in!" He was admitted.

Steve [superintendent] called out, "Hey!" when he saw the jockey go into the crib.

When the jockey came out, he spoke to him, and the jockey joshed him back. Steve did not seem to be particularly put out about it.

Soon the boys were going in and out of the crib again, almost at will, and setup men were getting setups ahead of time for operators, ignored by the crib attendants.

I noticed that Johnny and others seemed to be going in and out of the crib again, almost at will.

I noticed tonight that Johnny got into the tool crib by appearing at the door and saying to the attendant, "Let me in!"

So much for Faulkner's order—until he makes a new one!

When I asked Walt for some jaws to fit the chuck I had found, he said, "We've got lots of jaws back here, but I wouldn't know what to look for. You'd better get the setup man to come back here and find you some."

Walt said to me, "I break the rules here, but not too much—just within reason to keep the boys on production."

Faulkner's order still hangs at eye level on the crib door.

"So much for Faulkner's order!" The "fix" was "on" again, and operators and their service-group allies conducted business as usual for the remaining weeks of the writer's employment.

CONCLUSIONS. This rough sketch of the operation of one shop "syndicate" has been no more than indicative of the existence of intergroup co-operation in the lower reaches of factory social structure. No attempt has been made here to account for the aid extended by service groups, though suggestion that this assistance might be part of a larger system of reciprocal obligations has been implicit. It is apparent, for instance, that tool-crib attendants benefited from their practice of admitting operators and setup men to the toolroom to seek and pick up equipment.

A more complete picture of intergroup relations would include conflict, as well as co-operation, between operators and the various service groups. It could be shown, if space permitted, that changes in relationship accompanied, in cyclical fashion, changes in basic conditions of work.

Furthermore, attention has not been drawn to intragroup role and personality variations in intergroup relations. Such additional discriminations and the questions that they might raise in regard to the study of institutional dynamics must be left for future discussion.

As for their possible bearing on practical industrial administration, materials presented here seem to challenge the view held in some research circles that the "human" problem of industrial efficiency lies in faulty communication between an economically "rational" or "logical" management and "nonrational" or "nonlogical" work groups. While nothing has been offered to deny linkage between communication and efficiency, observations reported here suggest examination of the stereotypes of the two parties.[7] And questioning the fitness of the stereotypes may lead to a more fruitful conceptualization of the process that is reputedly in need of attention: communication.

Do we see, in the situation studied, an economically "rational" management and an economically "nonrational" work group? Would not a reversal of the labels, if such labels be used, find justification? Does it not appear that operatives and their allies resisted managerial "logics of efficiency" because application of those "logics" tended to produce something considerably less than "efficiency"? Did not worker groups connive to circumvent managerial ukase in order to "get the work out"? Did not Walt, for instance, break the rules "to keep the boys on production"? May not the common query of industrial workers, "What in the hell are they trying to do up there?" be not merely reflective of faulty communication but also based on a real managerial inadequacy, quite apart from a failure in "explanation"? May it not be assumed that managerial inefficiency is and has been for some time a serious problem to those who labor?

If managerial directives are not the guides to efficient action that they are claimed to be, then, perhaps, "logics of efficiency" would be better designated as "sentiments of efficiency." When failure to "explain" is additionally considered, perhaps bulletin-board pronunciamentos might properly be classified with the various exorcisms, conjurations, and miscellaneous esoteric monkey-business of our primitive contemporaries.

If we conceive of "logical" behavior not as self-contained ratiocinative exercises but as intellectual operations in continuous reciprocal interplay with concrete experience, machine operators and their service-group allies would appear the real holders of "logics of efficiency." Like big-city machine politicians, they develop plans for action that, under given conditions of situational pressures, "work."

But this rejection of commonly held stereotypes cannot lead to mere reversal of invidious distinctions; the situation is far too complex for that. The group life that the writer shared was by no means devoid of "sentiments." To the contrary, operator interaction was rich in shared feelings, attitudes, and practices not only of doubtful bearing on getting the work out but often undeniably preventing production maximization. Nor can it be maintained that management, in applying its "sentiments of efficiency," was always ineffective. Perhaps solution to the human problem of industrial efficiency would best be expedited by abandoning altogether the use of contrasted caricatures handed down to us from a preindustrial social class structure. Instead of concerning ourselves with such blind-alley issues as who is "rational" and who is not, we might recognize with John Dewey that both intellectual and emotional activity are essentials of goal-directed behavior [8] and that the development of effective communication focusing on production goals is a matter of instituting interactional processes that engender ideas, sentiments, and plans for action held in common.

[7] William F. Whyte, "Semantics and Industrial Relations," *Human Organization*, VIII (Spring, 1949), 1–7.

[8] *Art as Experience* (New York: Minton, Balch & Co., 1934), p. 55.

Work Group Behavior and the Larger Organization

The individual's most immediate and meaningful experiences of work are obtained in the context of the work group and his work associates. The larger organization is experienced by indirection, but membership in the small group contributes directly to the shaping of attitudes and behavior toward the entire world of work. For this reason of potency, therefore, the contribution of the small group to the total organization has been a subject of substantial research by those interested in human relations in industry.

Conceptions of the Work Group

As Whyte observes, the individual is *not* a member of a single group within a larger structure.[1] Rather, he typically interacts in a variety of settings within the organization. It is the task of the researcher to identify those interaction patterns which are focused and concentrated so that it is reasonable to speak of a "group."

From *Research in Industrial Human Relations.* New York: Harper and Brothers, 1957, pp. 131–145. Reprinted with permission of the publisher.

A substantial portion of the material included is from a study by the author sponsored by the Bureau of Industrial Relations of the University of Michigan on the relationship of work group behavior to technological and organizational factors. Our major emphasis is on industrial work groups, although examples will be drawn from other work settings.

[1] William F. Whyte, "Small Groups in Large Organizations," in *Social Psychology at the Crossroads,* John Rohrer and Muzafer Sherif, eds. (New York: Harper, 1951), pp. 303–304.

If we follow all the members of the organization through their hours on the job, or find some "high" vantage point and observe the total of all interactions, we are likely to be impressed with this proliferation of memberships. Most apparent is membership, except for that unique individual, the president, in some *command group;* that is, the employee shares a common supervisor with a number of colleagues. Distinguishable from this group, but closely related, is a *functional* or *task group*—those employees who must collaborate in some fashion if the work task defined by the organization is to be accomplished. In fact, both of these groups are rather well defined by the larger organization, and the group typically retains those boundaries.

However, there are two other kinds of clusterings that tend to overlap and penetrate the organization in unexpected ways. They are not defined by the formal organization and are often included under the general term, informal organization. One has received much attention from researchers: the *friendship clique.* The other is less well studied, but equally important. That is the *interest group.* This is comprised of those employees who share a common economic interest and seek to gain some objective relating to the larger organization.

Memberships in these groups are not exclusive; often they will overlap considerably. However, the motivations of the members, and, more important, their behavior, are distinctive; and we have no reason to believe that the boundaries will be perfectly coincident.

The Command Group. Perhaps the most obvious kind of small group in the large organization is composed of the supervisor and his immediate subordinates. As Jacques observes, the entire organization is composed of interconnected *command groups*, the subordinates in one group being the superiors in their own command group, with the exception of the first level.[2] While we might expect that research would have emphasized this unit of the organization, if we exclude the manifold studies of leadership styles dealt with elsewhere in this volume, there are relatively few systematic explorations of the relationship between the leader and his subordinates as a group, as individuals, and among the subordinates themselves. Jacques' volume is a notable exception.[3] His examination of the command group has a strong psychiatric flavor. He stresses the leader's ambivalence: his *authority* over his subordinates and *dependence* upon them, his sense of isolation, the problem of integrating pair relationships (leader and individual subordinates) with cohesiveness among subordinates, and the mixed feelings of the subordinates as a group who find the leader both expendable and indispensable (one to be protected or exposed?).

The Friendship Clique. This has been conceived as the elementary building block of human organization. As Mayo writes, "Man's desire to be continuously associated with his fellows is a strong, if not the strongest human characteristic." [4]

At the workplace we find a multitude of friendship groups representing the diverse interests of the workers placed there by the organization. The boundaries of these clusterings appear to reflect the employees' off-the-job interests and associations or previous work experience. Age, ethnic background, outside activities, sex, marital status, and so on, comprise the mortar that binds the clique together.

The friendship group has emerged as the agency which welds the individual to the organization. Loyalty, even attachment, to the total organization with its impersonality, extended hierarchy, and social distance becomes ambiguous. However, attachment to the immediate and easily perceived face-to-face group is the predominant reality of organization experience. For the individual it provides a source of personal security in an impersonal environment.

Where cliques are largely nonexistent, as in the rapidly expanding aircraft plants of California, turnover can be enormous. The presumption is that stable social groups take time to crystallize; during the period of formation many potential members will leave voluntarily because they do not find an established unit with which they can affiliate. This in turn inhibits the formation of permanent groups; the process is self-defeating.

Thus Lombard and Mayo conclude that the naive administrator who seeks to break up these cliques because of the inefficiency and wasted motion of the purely social activities involved is actually doing a disservice to the organization.[5] In fact, they find that it takes skillful leadership to encourage their formation, at least in organizations undergoing rapid expansion. A recent well-received text [6] in the field of public administration comes out strongly on the side of encouraging on-the-job social life, concluding that production increased when social conversation was allowed. However, a study employing methods of precise interaction observation is unique in casting some doubts as to the positive correlation

---

[2] Elliot Jacques, *The Changing Culture of a Factory* (New York: Dryden Press, 1952), pp. 273–297.

[3] There are two other noteworthy recent exceptions. Argyris devotes a small volume to the relationship between a plant manager in a medium-sized factory and his immediate subordinates. (Chris Argyris, *Executive Leadership* [New York: Harper, 1954]). Two researchers at the Harvard Business School provide us with a very revealing study of the day-to-day changes in the relationship between a first-line supervisor and assembly-line girls during a period of technological changes —Harriet Ronken and Paul Lawrence, *Administering Changes* (Boston: Graduate School of Business Administration, Harvard University, 1952).

[4] Elton Mayo, *Social Problems of an Industrial Civilization* (Boston: Graduate School of Business Administration, Harvard University, 1945), p. 111.

[5] Elton Mayo and George F. Lombard, *Teamwork and Labor Turnover in the Aircraft Industry of Southern California* (Boston: Graduate School of Business Administration, Harvard University, 1940).

[6] Herbert Simon, Donald Smithburg, and Victor Thompson, *Public Administration* (New York: Knopf, 1950), pp. 113–114.

between social interaction and productivity.[7]

More serious criticism of the universal efficacy of friendship cliques, however, involves considerations of personality and work structure differences. A study of "rate busters" disclosed a significant majority who were indifferent to, if not hostile to, the social groupings they found on the job.[8]

A recent examination of British longshoremen finds that approximately half of the longshoremen on the docks studied have consciously avoided social entanglements of work group membership. Given an opportunity to join semipermanent gangs, they prefer random work assignments that leave them free to come and go at will, with no group responsibility.[9]

Formation of social groups also appears to be a function of the structure of the work situation itself. Argyris, in his Bank study, finds that incidence of informal social groupings among tellers is less than for bank employees who have less interaction with customers.[10] This conclusion would confirm a basic hypothesis of Chapple, that individuals seek some equilibrium in their rate and range of interaction.[11]

From this theoretical approach, we would expect that the whole range of group activities, not just social life, would be influenced by the interaction pattern fostered by the job. The previously cited study by the University of Liverpool researchers, for example, notes that dockworkers who were members of semi-permanent crews were rarely found among the informal leaders of the longshoremen or among the active participants in the union.[12] Moving in the other direction, Lipset concludes that because some jobs handicap workers in maintaining adequate off-the-job relations with other friends (e.g., unusual working hours as among printers, actors, and policemen), they tend to form more closely knit "fellow worker" groups, as evidenced by their record of high participation in local union activities.[13]

Similarly, George Strauss has observed an unusually high degree of membership participation in certain occupational groups involving relative isolation from fellow workers, like insurance salesmen, utility meter readers and substation operators.[14]

Such studies add to the trend toward considering the *need for social relations* as a variable worth studying in itself. It would be interesting to know, for example, whether industrial occupations in which there is high inter-worker dependence in the work process, such that almost constant interaction is required, show less social life than groups characterized by relatively independent operations.

The Task Group. Perhaps one of the most important aspects of small group behavior in large organizations is their relation to the work process itself. The formally designated task builds a group structure, just as do individual social needs and the organizational authority structure.

More specifically, the work process stimulates group controls of (1) work method, (2) output standards or productivity, and (3) relative compensation and prestige relationships.

1. IMPACT ON WORK METHOD. The experience of working in close proximity on a day-to-day basis induces methods that may depart from the organization's original conception of the job, or at least "fills in" the specific details of the operation not specified in the

---

[7] A. B. Horsfall and Conrad Arensberg, "Teamwork and Productivity in a Shoe Factory," *Human Organization*, VIII (Winter 1949), pp. 21 ff.

[8] These men tended to have a rural background emphasizing individualism. Orvis Collins and Donald Roy, "Restriction of Output and Social Cleavage in Industry," *Applied Anthropology*, V (Summer 1946), pp. 1–14.

[9] University of Liverpool, *The Dock Worker* (Liverpool: University Press of Liverpool, 1954), pp. 61 ff.

[10] Chris Argyris, *Organization of a Bank* (New Haven: Labor and Management Center, Yale University, 1954), p. 129.

[11] Eliot D. Chapple, "Applied Anthropology in Industry," in *Anthropology Today*, A. L. Kroeber, ed. (Chicago: University of Chicago Press, 1953), pp. 819–831. Many of the observations in this section are based on the theoretical work of Chapple.

[12] University of Liverpool, *op. cit.*, p. 72.

[13] Seymour M. Lipset, "The Political Process in Trade Unions: A Theoretical Statement," in *Freedom and Control in Modern Society*, Monroe Berger, Theodore Abel, and Charles Page, eds. (New York: Van Nostrand, 1954), pp. 101–102.

[14] Personal correspondence, Professor Strauss, University of Buffalo.

formal work plan. Thus, employees may exchange repetitive jobs, although such trading is illegal; one worker may do two jobs while a colleague rests; or, as Whyte [15] found, they may change the sequence of the operations to reduce tensions and provide short cuts. Roy observed similar "adjustments" in relations among tool room clerks, job sellers, and machinists where the objective was maximizing piece rate earnings.[16]

Some of these informal, or unplanned for, work methods may decrease worker output. For example, workers' machinations in Roy's machine shop tended to overstate make-ready time during job changes. However, other worker innovations, such as those described by Whyte, undoubtedly increase the total product. Gross found that radar teams, through communication circuits set up during off-the-job social periods, were compensating for deficiencies in the information provided by the formal organization.[17]

Similarly researchers have analyzed the initiative exhibited by a group of department store salesmen in evolving a new work pattern that solved a serious internal morale problem created by a new incentive system.[18]

However, the work structure can be designed so that elaborations of the informal group necessarily work in opposition to the major objectives of the organization. Recent studies of changes in the method of mining coal, conducted by the Tavistock Institute in Great Britain, illustrate such organization.[19] The change from jobs completed by small groups of miners in one shift to successive operations carried out by three shifts resulted in reduction of interaction and communication and a consequent decrease in the miners' recognition of their total responsibility for the operation.[20]

Thus the Tavistock studies suggest that the goal of the engineer in designing the technological organization is to provide the work group with a relatively autonomous task so that responsible *internal* leadership can develop. This kind of organizational structure is, in fact, the very essence of decentralization:

> A primary work organization of this type has the advantage of placing responsibility for the complete . . . task squarely on the shoulders of a single, small, face-to-face group which experiences the entire cycle of operations within the compass of its membership. For each participant the task has total significance and dynamic closure.[21]

The development of mutually convenient methods of conducting the work process can extend to the "job" of collective bargaining. We have ample evidence that union-management relationships at the work group level often depart radically from established practices and attitudes prevailing at higher levels, and may in fact contradict these other, more "formal" relationships.[22]

Aside from evolving methods which seem most convenient to work group members, the pattern of doing the job is fitted to the status system of the group. Those members with most prestige, if at all possible, receive the best jobs. Where possible, working location and equipment are similarly "assigned." And where these are not under group control, helping and trading can be adjusted to the status system. The exchange-of-favors system readily responds to the prestige hierarchy. Of course, the evaluation placed on jobs is itself a product of group interaction.

[15] William F. Whyte, "The Social Structure of the Restaurant," *The American Journal of Sociology*, LIV (January 1949), pp. 306–307.

[16] Donald Roy, "Quota Restriction and Goldbricking in a Machine Shop," *The American Journal of Sociology*, LVII (March 1952), pp. 427–442.

[17] Edward Gross, "Some Functional Consequences of Primary Controls in Formal Work Organizations," *American Sociological Review*, XVIII (August 1953), pp. 370–371.

[18] Nicholas Babchuck and William Goode, "Work Incentives in a Self-Determined Group," *American Sociological Review*, XVI (October 1951), p. 686.

[19] E. Trist and K. Bamforth, "Some Social and Psychological Consequences of the Longwall Method of Coal-Getting," *Human Relations*, IV, No. 1 (1951).

[20] The same problem can arise even though the employees are not separated into different time shifts. A study of a textile mill provides us with an example of the impact of worker-machine allocations. Cf. A. K. Rice, "Productivity and Social Organization in an Indian Weaving Shed," *Human Relations*, VI, No. 4 (1953).

[21] Trist and Bamforth, *op. cit.*, p. 6.

[22] Cf. Melville Dalton, "Unofficial Union-Management Relations," *American Sociological Review*, XV (October 1950), pp. 611–619.

The methods evolved within the group for task completion become firmly established. Where outside forces (e.g., technological change) threaten to induce changes, the ranks close and resistance is applied. In part, of course, this may be the natural reaction of the culprit fearing punishment for rule infractions. A more reasonable explanation of the informal group's resistance to change, however, is the intimate relationship between the task group as an entity and the work methods they have evolved. A threat to one is a real threat to the other.

2. IMPACT ON OUTPUT STANDARDS. Probably more attention has been given to this aspect of task group behavior than to any other. Starting with the work of Mathewson, and extending through the Western Electric studies, a long and distinguished line of studies indicate that work groups often formulate quite specific output standards and obtain close conformity from their members in *maintaining* these standards. Productivity itself is increasingly conceived of as a group phenomenon.

Several reasons have been advanced as to why output control occupies a place of such importance in the life of the group. Work standards are one of the most important aspects of the job, which can in some fashion be influenced by worker action. The energy expenditure required by the job is largely determined by the number of units required, rather than by the nature of the job itself. Presumably without group control management would be able to utilize individual differences, and competition for promotion and greater earnings, to obtain higher and higher standards. This would penalize particularly the slower worker and the older employee. It might, however, penalize all workers by cutting piece rates, where such exist, and/or reducing the number of employees required by the operation. "Run away" output might have internal ramifications. We have observed situations where group controls were weak, and younger, low-prestige employees exceeded the production and earnings records of their "betters." The results were calamitous for the status hierarchy of the department and ultimately for the effectiveness of the formal organization.

Output control is a basic objective of group action as well as an essential element in maintaining group stability. Not only the relationship of the members to one another, but the durability of the worker relationship to his job depends on the efficacy of this process. Again we need to note that the resultant is not always unfavorable to management. We have many instances on record where the group has sanctioned increasingly high productivity,[23] rejected fellow workers who could not maintain high output, and resisted threats to existing high quality standards.

Evidently a great deal of the interest in "informal group relations" is the result of this presumed relationship between output standards evolving within the group and actual worker productivity. Wilensky in an earlier chapter [of *Research in Industrial Human Relations*] reviews some of the efforts to find the magic formula to convert group norms from "low" to "high."

Some of the earliest research on productivity was based on the assumption that internal harmony in the work group would produce higher performance records. Increasingly researchers have become disillusioned with the relationship between social satisfaction and worker effort. Perhaps one of the most telling blows to the impetus to devote substantial energies to building work groups that are "sociometrically sound" is the provocative study by Goode and Fowler in a low morale plant. They found "the informal relationships which developed were such as to maintain pressures toward high production in the face of considerable *animosity* toward the owners and *among the workers themselves.*"[24] While their findings are severely limited by the somewhat unique environment they chose, it has become recognized that the relationship between friendship and output is a complex one.

More recently, Seashore finds in a study in a large "heavy equipment manufacturing company" that highly "cohesive" work groups are more likely to have output records that di-

[23] Cf. George Strauss, "Group Dynamics and Intergroup Relations," in William F. Whyte and others, *Money and Motivation* (New York: Harper, 1955), pp. 90–96.

[24] William Goode and Irving Fowler, "Incentive Factors in a Low Morale Plant," *American Sociological Review*, XIV (October 1949), p. 624; italics added by author.

verge *in either direction* from plant averages.[25] By implication, then, tightly knit work groups are almost as likely to have notably *poor* production records as outstandingly *good* ones.

The present author is inclined to believe that these inconsistencies in research results are due to an overemphasis on output as a part of informal group equilibrium. Control over output is also a major weapon in the arsenal of the group engaging in conflict with management, other work groups, and even the local union. We need to know more about the *total situation* facing a given work group, including these external factors, before predicting its work performance.

The evolution of the method of *group decision* for gaining acceptance for changes in production methods and output standards is recognition of the potency of group standards. The theory presumes that leadership methods that involve the entire work group in the change process have two major advantages:

(*a*) They can eliminate the major barrier of existing group standards which militate against any change, per se.

(*b*) More positively, they commit the individual to new efforts in the context of his group membership. In a sense, the individual "promises" his fellows to accomplish some change in his behavior. Valuing the opinions of his associates, he feels bound to maintain his agreement.

Ideally the "decision" itself becomes the new standard or norm of conduct for the task group. Similarly efforts to develop plant-wide incentive systems are premised on the assumption that output and effort are dependent on the relation of the work group to the total social system of the plant.[26]

3. IMPACT ON RELATIVE COMPENSATION AND PRESTIGE RELATIONSHIPS. The fact that jobs take on a significant social meaning can be seen in the importance attached to wage differentials within the group itself. For example, we have many instances on record when management assigned an equal value to each job and the group found significant distinguishing char-

acteristics. Jobs ranked by employees as *more important or desirable* are expected to have higher earnings than jobs ranked below. The established hierarchy is reinforced over time by the gradual perfection of the correlation between esteem accorded particular workers and prestige accorded to their jobs. The "more important" workers have moved to the "more important" jobs. (The importance attached to the job is not only a function of the earning capacity but also the quality of the surroundings, equipment, the tempo of the work required, etc.) Problems occur only when changes are introduced which violate the established hierarchy.

A persistent problem has been that jobs which the group evaluates as relatively undesirable may need to be compensated at a higher rate than the "desirable" jobs, in order to attract adequate personnel. However, this differential may be contrary to the status system of the work group. Similarly, jobs evaluated (by the group) as desirable may lack characteristics which would bring them a high rating under the organization's formal ranking plan. These contradictions between the group and the organization's ranking system become more important during periods of relative labor shortage, when new recruits are difficult to obtain and when the group undergoes aging.

While these several concepts of the "informal group" are not identical, and in some cases not even complementary in their basic dimensions, they do have one common feature. All stress equilibrium, the development of a system of interpersonal relations which stabilizes the work situation (among subordinates and between superior and subordinates), an interconnected series of friendship linkages, work flow relationships, output levels, and status-income relations. The objectives are the maintenance of individual and group stability by insuring a predictability of day-to-day events and effecting a *modus vivendi* as between individual on-the-job needs and the requirements of the formal organization.

As such, the *informal group* in any and all of its meanings is serving well-recognized and accepted human needs. Its existence and continued preservation are hardly matters for surprise. The building up of routines, of established methods of accomplishing tasks, of predictable social relationships, of group roles —these are all elements of structuring which

[25] Stanley Seashore, *Group Cohesiveness in the Industrial Work Group* (Ann Arbor: Institute for Social Research, University of Michigan, 1954), p. 98.
[26] Cf. William F. Whyte and others, *Money and Motivation, op. cit.,* p. 225.

social scientists have found typical of the human group. In fact, the elements define the group.

Particularly through the setting and maintenance of group standards, informal groups have protected their memberships from possible indiscretions that might reflect adversely on them all; also they have provided support for the individual, by acting as a buffer to outside organizations and by sustaining him through the provision of *known and acceptable* routines of behaving within the face-to-face work group.

Thus the informal group, as perceived in such studies, *reacts to* the initiations of other organizations, particularly management. Being defined in equilibrium terms, the reaction is always an attempt to *regain* the previous undisturbed state—to protect work methods, social relationships, and output levels incorporated in the norms of the group.

Concerted Interest as the Focus. Workers also band together into *interest groups.* These are formed not only to protect their members but also to exploit *opportunities* to improve their relative position. Improvements can take the form of "looser standards," a preferred seniority position, more overtime, more sympathetic supervision, correction of "inequities," better equipment, and countless other less tangible goals that make the job a better one and that often serve to substitute for the more traditional kinds of promotions and mobility.

Distribution of these benefits may be much influenced by pressures of united and determined informal groups. What management feels is "equitable," just as what the union determines is in the "members' interest," is determined to a large extent by attitudes expressed by those individuals who can support their demands by group reinforcements. Those work groups which for one reason or another are unable to exercise similar power in the market place of the plant are penalized. .

This is not the traditional concept of the informal group seeking conformity with established norms of conduct. These are much more "free enterprise" units, interacting in a struggle for maximization of utility. All are not equally aggressive in the struggle for self-improvement or equally well equipped with the wherewithal to do battle via the grievance procedure and the more direct pressure tactics on union and management. Some lack the spirit of combat, others the means, while only a restricted few are endowed with the characteristics associated with sustained "activity" and progress toward the goals they seek.

Much of what we say implies a degree of dual or even treble *disloyalty.* Other groups, management, the union, and fellow workers, are perceived as either barriers or sources of assistance. From the point of view of the interest group, it is not high identification or loyalty that counts, but rather the right tactics in using or ignoring these other aggregations.

Thus, management is neither "good" nor "bad," liked or disliked as such. In fact, this approach suggests that it may not always be fruitful to think in pro-management and pro-union terms. It may well be that a group which is satisfied with *itself*, with its ability to protect and improve its own interests, is more favorable to *both* union and management.[27]

The results for the larger plant may not be a system tending toward equilibrium at all. We might expect that certain combinations of pressure groups actually involve the organization in increasing instability—a trend toward disequilibrium. We have observed plants where the interaction of these groups involves increasingly greater discontent, turmoil, and nonadaptive behavior. That is, their behavior tends to reinforce the very problems it was designed to solve.

Similarly, the internal structure of these groups is much more responsive to changes in its external environment than is often implied in the concept of the informal work group as a relatively durable, impervious entity. Literally overnight, technical changes introduced by management can convert a cohesive task force into a disunited, apathetic "rabble," squabbling over internal differences. Similarly, we have observed a group of weakly-united employees become a force of some magnitude in the social system of the plant within a brief period, with no changes in personnel.

The existence of these *interest group* types suggests that greater attention should be given

[27] These areas . . . [are] further elaborated in the author's . . . study, *Technology and Work Group Behavior* (Ann Arbor: Bureau of Industrial Relations, University of Michigan, 1956).

to matching supervisory "types" with group "types." We have tended to think of effective supervision as being the product of a relationship between a good leader and his group, on the assumption that the group of subordinates was a constant. In fact, variations in the effectiveness of supervision may be as much due to inherent differences in the group itself as to the leadership practices exhibited by the supervisor.

The Internal Dynamics of the Work Group

We have concentrated primarily on the relationship of the small group to the larger organization, the functions served, the "compatibilities" and "incompatibilities." Therefore, we have failed to explore much of the research that stresses the intriguing inner processes of these groups, as semiautonomous organizations. This means neglecting the processes of self-selection and exclusion developed in the work of Moreno and his colleagues in the field of sociometry. We have also omitted the prolific findings of the "group dynamics school" with its emphasis on leadership patterns and role differentiation, factors contributing to cohesiveness, and the impact of the group itself on membership perceptions and attitudes. Bales and his associates at Harvard have probed deeply into the "ebb and flow" of the problem-solving process within the group. The sequential member roles have been analyzed effectively.

For our purposes it would seem appropriate at least to make specific reference to the work of George Homans. His work places substantial emphasis on the relationship of the internal life of the group to the outside environment (primarily the attitudes, organizational structure, and work method induced by management).[28]

[28] George Homans, *The Human Group* (New York: Harcourt Brace, 1950).

"Elaborations" of behavior and sentiment induced in the small group in turn modify the larger organization. While we believe an over-emphasis on the concept of *equilibrium* may be misleading, Homans' theorizing does provide a framework within which to relate the small group to the larger organization of which it is a part.

Conclusion

Clusterings of workers-on-the-job all have these characteristics: They stem from the uniqueness of individual personality, which refuses to combine into larger "wholes" without changing those entities. The sum of a group of individuals is something more than the total of the constituents; it is a new organization, because most of the members (there are significant exceptions as we have noted) obtain satisfaction in gaining acceptance as a part of the group, and the group itself wields an influence over its members. Put in another way, there are pressures toward *conformity* within the group. These pressures result in the establishment of accepted ways of living together. The way of life of the group includes a complex system of customs and rules, vested interests, and interaction patterns which govern the relationship of members of the group to one another and to the larger environment of which it is a part.

This observance of group-sanctioned behavior and attitudes "fills out" the rationally conceived organization. What is on paper an organization becomes a "living, breathing" social organism, with all the intricacies, emotions, and contradictions we associate with human relations. While no organization would long persist which did not provide its members with this opportunity for spontaneous "human relations," a major problem of the larger organization becomes one of successfully incorporating the small group.

Status and Status Hierarchies

BURLEIGH GARDNER AND DAVID G. MOORE

The idea of relative status, of who outranks whom, is a basic ingredient in our society. Furthermore, it is not a concept which can be readily eliminated or ignored, even though it seems counter to our basic tenet that "all men are equal." We see it in the home, where parents are the superiors of the children, and the older child is superior to or "ahead of" the younger. And the child looks forward to being an adult, the youngest wants to catch up with the eldest, etc. We see it in every organization; and in every community there are those who, by virtue of formal position, ability, birth, possessions, or luck, are looked on as being in some way above or superior to others. We hear it expressed in a myriad of phrases, such as "leading citizens," "no-accounts," "upper crust," "ordinary folks." All this tells us that even in America we have, not a system of pure equality, but one in which there are great differences in social status.

Now there are two kinds of status relations. One is that of the subordinate to his boss, or the enlisted man to his commanding officer. This status relationship involves not only a general difference in rank—the officer is always thought of as superior to his subordinates—but also the right to give orders. It is always connected with specific positions in organizations in which superiors give orders to subordinates. This relationship comprises the chain of command.

The other type of status relation does not involve the right to command. It merely expresses a concept of relative positions, of who outranks whom. For example, an upper-class executive is felt by the community to be somehow superior to the "po-white" fisherman; he will be deferred to in many ways, while the fisherman will be ignored; yet the executive, merely because of his high status, has no "right" to give the other orders.

Any organization chart is a diagram of positions occupied by individuals, and each person is identified by his position. Thus John Jones, a machinist, becomes a different person in the organization when he becomes John Jones, a foreman. Furthermore, these different positions fit into systems of ranks, or status hierarchies, in which one is seen as superior to another. These systems are most clearly seen in military organizations, where differences in rank are carefully spelled out so everyone can know who outranks whom.

The supervisory structure is, then, a status system in which it is accepted as a matter of course that each level has more status and prestige than the ones below it. In fact, the words used in discussing it show this status factor. We speak of superiors and subordinates, of higher and lower levels, of up and down, of above and below—all of which imply differences in rank in such a structure. The problem of status or prestige does not end with this simple supervisory hierarchy, however, but intrudes itself into all sorts of situations and in innumerable guises. In fact, the matters of relative status, of where each person fits in terms of it, of how each compares with others, present some of the most interesting and, to those involved, some of the most annoying and painful problems of people at work. Certainly, if no one was ever bothered by the status of himself or others, life would be much simpler for everyone.

As we have seen, the chain of command establishes the most clearly defined hierarchy, with the supervisor outranking the supervised. Now differences in rank extend beyond the command, or supervisory relationship, so that

From *Human Relations in Industry*. Homewood: Richard D. Irwin, 1955, pp. 103–116. Reprinted with permission of the publisher.

all foremen are considered superior to all workers just as all officers outrank all privates. Thus we have rank hierarchies based on ideas of relative position rather than on face-to-face relationships. And these types of status systems, which are very widespread both within industry and in society generally, have great influence on human behavior. In this chapter, we will examine some of the common types of status hierarchies and their significance in the work situation.

SHOP-OFFICE DISTINCTIONS. In the first place, we find the important status distinction between shop and office or "white-collar" jobs. Despite the talk about the "dignity of labor" and the pleasures of working with your hands, there is an almost universal feeling that the office jobs are in some sense "superior" to the shop jobs and that the person who runs a typewriter or adding machine has a higher status than the person who runs a drill press. This feeling was well expressed by a girl working on a shop job, who said:

> I'd really like to work in the office. Isn't it funny the way office people treat factory people? I don't see any difference between them myself, but the office people think they are so much better than the girls who work in the factory. Lots of them have the same education as the office girls, and we are just as refined as they are. They seem to think that factory girls are loud and rough, but there are just as many girls in the office who drink and smoke and are immoral as the girls in the shop. It just seems that having an office job makes them feel that they're better than we are. I've seen the difference in some people I know. One who came from a farm in Missouri went to school and got an office job. Well, she talks about her office job as much as she can and isn't near as friendly as she used to be. We don't have anything to do with each other any more.
>
> I've noticed it with other girls too. I'll meet them at church and they ask me where I work. I tell them. They ask if I work in factory or office. When I say factory, they say, "Oh," and then ask me if I don't get tired of it, and ask me if it's dirty. Then they take every chance to talk about their office jobs.
>
> My mother feels the same way as these

people do. She says that since I've worked in the factory I've gotten more boisterous. I talk in a louder voice, not as refined as I used to be. Well, you don't like to hear those things. You don't like to feel that something's happening to you.

In this interview, an important characteristic of the status system was expressed, that is, the fact that the person who occupies the higher status position tends to identify himself with the status of his position until it becomes a part of him which he carries into all his contacts with those of lesser status. Thus the girl who had obtained an office job began to draw apart from her former factory friends, and the factory girl was looked down upon by the office girls whom she met in church. And so the status of one's position is not something which is shed when he leaves his job; it is carried with him into all kinds of situations.

This interview also shows the general feeling of superiority which the higher-status group has toward the lower. Not only is their work felt to be of a higher order of importance or value, but they are superior beings. The office group tends to look down upon the shopworkers as inferiors in mind, manner, and morals. The shopworkers have grimy hands and poor taste, they say; they are loudmouthed and use coarse language; they are less educated, or at least less intellectual. Although these attitudes of office workers may seem to be extreme expressions of feelings of superiority, similar feelings are expressed by every high-status group toward their "inferiors." Executives have something of the same attitude toward foremen, foremen toward workers, the old-timers toward the newcomers, the skilled workers toward the semiskilled. In fact, we can safely say that everyone in a factory busies himself from time to time with looking down on someone, looking up to someone, or assuring himself that, in spite of what certain others think, he is just as good as they are. As the girl in the interview said, "We are just as good as they are," and in the next breath voiced her doubts.

STATUS AND WAGES. The rate of pay or earnings is, of course, another important source of status differences. This is quite in keeping with a business or factory as an economic enterprise in which everything is supposedly evaluated in terms of money. Thus the higher the pay, the higher the status of the job or the individual.

The ten-thousand-dollar-a-year man is far superior to the five-thousand-dollar man, or the dollar-forty-an-hour shopworker is superior to the eighty-five-cent man. In the same way, the job that pays a dollar-forty an hour is superior to the eighty-five-cent an hour job. ("Superior" in this sense does not always mean more desirable, since individual tastes in jobs vary considerably.) As a result, every work situation in which there is a gradation of wages has a status hierarchy revolving around these wages and one which is readily upset by any changes in the wage structure.

There is also a status system based upon the different kinds of jobs found in any work group. As a rule, the jobs requiring the most skill are at the top and those requiring the least are at the bottom, although other factors may enter in to disurb such a simple arrangement. For example, a job which receives a great deal of attention and recognition from the boss may become the superior job even though other jobs in the group require more skill. Sometimes, too, jobs acquire status because they are always held by long-service people who receive recognition because of their service.

SENIORITY AND STATUS. Seniority forms the basis for other status differences, with the old-timers feeling that they are somehow superior to the young people and newcomers. In most stable companies there is a feeling toward long-service people something like the attitude toward age which we find in our society generally. The youngsters are thought of as lacking in knowledge and understanding and are expected to give recognition and deference to their elders, while the very old have a place with certain rights and privileges because of their age. The special privileges of old-timers were demonstrated by the nurse in one factory. We quote from an observer's notes:

In a plant which had, before the war, found it necessary to employ only one nurse, the expansion due to the war brought the need for more nurses.

The original nurse had been with the company thirteen years. Then a male nurse was hired for the 4–12 shift. And when a 12–8 shift started, he was transferred to it. Two more nurses were hired, and since none of them wanted to work 4–12 all the time, it was agreed that they should alternate.

The nurse who had seniority took one turn at the afternoon shift and then refused to work it again. The doctor and the personnel manager agreed that she need not take her turn; and the other nurses, although they resented this evident favoritism, seemed to feel that it was done because she had been with the company so long.

ORGANIZATIONAL DIFFERENCES. There are also status differences among organizations, and in any plant there are usually certain organizations which are generally thought of as superior to others. The shop-office distinction accounts for some of this, as the strictly office organizations are usually superior to the shop organizations. As a result, a typist or file clerk with the shop department is usually thought to have a poorer," that is lower-status, job than the typist or file clerk in an accounting department. Also, organizations such as engineering or sales, where much of the work requires technical skills or special training, are usually of status superior to shop or accounting organizations. In all such cases the feeling of superiority does not remain merely the prerogative of the salesmen or engineers but carries over even to the most routine jobs in the organization. The office boy in the engineering department, for example, is likely to feel superior to the office boy in the accounting organization.

OCCUPATIONAL HIERARCHIES. We have seen how certain types of jobs carry differences of status. However, this extends often to very elaborate rankings in which there may be recognized differences between many jobs. Thus in many of the skilled trades, we find the hierarchy of apprentice, journeyman, master. In these, a man's position is based upon his progress through a clearly defined system of training and experience.

In addition, we see differences in rank between jobs based on the levels of skill required, such as the semiskilled versus skilled worker. Or the simpler machines are lower than the complicated machines. Or the job that requires long training outranks the one that requires little training. In general, all jobs in a plant can be placed on a scale which expresses the general beliefs as to where each fits in relation to the others.

As we have seen, many of the status systems are based on the characteristics inherent in the work organization. Supervisory rank, levels of skill, wage differences, etc., are largely defined within the organization. However, there are other types of status which are general to the society and are carried over into the work situation. In communities where the particular hierarchies do not already exist, they do not appear in the local industries.

MEN VERSUS WOMEN. In our society, women are traditionally defined as the "weaker sex," subordinate to the male. This traditional role of subordination and inferiority is carried over into the work situation. Women's jobs are thought of as simpler, requiring less skill, or in some way unsuitable for men. And attempts to place women in jobs habitually defined as men's work meet with considerable resistance from men. Also, the man who is placed alongside of women, doing the same work, feels that he is degraded.

NEGRO VERSUS WHITE. Here again we find status differences between the Negro and the white existing in our society. This is expressed in the most extreme form in the deep South, where the Negro is thought of as socially separate and inferior. There he is generally restricted to the lowest status and lowest paid jobs and is rarely permitted to occupy a supervisory position over whites. And while the system is less rigorous in the North, many of the same attitudes and restrictions still exist.

COMPLICATING FACTORS. These status systems are not nicely co-ordinated, however, so that the older person always gets more money, has the better job, or is higher in the supervisory structure. We see old-timers in some of the poorest jobs at the lowest pay. We see bright young executives who, with only short service, have climbed high in the supervisory ranks. We see office jobs paying less than shop jobs, or skilled workers earning more than their foremen. We see innumerable complicating factors, so that it seems impossible to present a simple picture of the status relationships between individuals within any plant or even in any one department.

We do find, however, that there is a feeling that these various status systems *should* be co-ordinated. This is most strongly expressed in the idea that superiors should earn more than their subordinates. Generally in the supervisory structure wages rise rapidly as you go up in the structure, and it is usually felt to be wrong for a foreman to get less pay than his subordinates. There is also some tendency for wages to increase with age, and a feeling that this should be so, especially when the rate of pay is not rigidly tied to the kind of job. Also, the more highly skilled jobs are often held by the long-service people who have worked themselves up. Interestingly enough, the status difference between office and shop is usually not recognized in pay, especially at the lower levels. Apparently the office jobs are sufficiently attractive, especially to girls, that they are preferred even if the wages are lower, so that in many organizations we find these "better" jobs being paid considerably less than the others.

"PLACING" PEOPLE. A matter of common interest and concern to everyone in the factory is the problem of "place" in the social organization. Everyone wants to know where other people "fit" in terms of the functional relations of the work and, what is to many even more important, in terms of the status systems. The newcomer is always faced by the questions, "Who are you?" and "Where do you fit?" In fact, one of the important aspects of getting acquainted on a new job is the process by which the newcomer finds out just where he belongs. He learns with whom he will work and what their relationship is to him and to each other; he learns who are is superiors in the line of authority, who can give him orders and who cannot, to whom he should defer and whom he can ignore. All this is the real function of much of the introduction and conversation which often takes place when a new worker comes into a group. For example, the foreman brings a new man over to Joe Blow on the dinkus assembly line, and the conversation goes like this:

FOREMAN: Joe, this is Jim Blank, who is going to work on this assembly. I wish you would show him how to do the job. (Telling Joe that Jim is new and inexperienced on the job.)

JOE: Howdy, Jim. You ever had any experience with dinkus assembly? (Trying to place Jim a little more accurately.)

JIM: No. I been on a drill press in the gadget department for a couple of years. (Letting Joe know that he is not entirely a greenhorn and has had experience on machines, as well as service with the company.)

JOE: You did? Why I worked over there when I first started eight years ago. Is old Jake, the foreman, still as 'sour-puss' as ever? (Telling Jim that he need not feel that two years of service amounts to much and that he knows about the gadget department also.)

JIM: Well, Jake's a pretty decent guy after all, even if he does act sour at times. I kinda hate to leave the department, but work was getting slack on the drill presses. (Showing a little annoyance at Joe's implied criticism of the gadget department, and also telling Joe that he had not left to get out of the place or because they did not want him.)

JOE: Yeah, I used to like Jake and hated to leave there myself. (Sensing Jim's irritation and trying to express a common attitude.)

Scenes such as this occur constantly; and in every one the individuals are consciously or unconsciously telling each other just where they fit and how they feel about it, and at the same time finding out about each other. When making introductions or when talking about newcomers, there is this same emphasis on "placing" people. Once the individual's place has been established, however, interest in him and gossip about him shifts to other topics.

SYMBOLS OF STATUS. Because of the importance of status, the individual himself is greatly concerned that he be placed properly, at least not in a position inferior to what he actually occupies. The private may be amused to be mistaken for a lieutenant, but the lieutenant who is mistaken for a private is really burned up. Undoubtedly, that is one of the important functions of military insignia. In industry people feel much the same way, with the result that almost every large plant has developed its own insignia, its own set of symbols by means of which everyone can be placed properly in the status system. In general, these symbols are not the simple and obvious types evolved by the Armed Forces but are much more subtle and indirect. The sort of clothes you wear, the desk you sit at, the position of your desk or workbench, the machine you operate, and many other things may indicate status. In fact, these things are often so indirect that the out-

sider is not aware that such a symbol system exists at all. Many executives, too, deny that there are such systems; but usually these denials are coupled with an assertion that, even if they do exist, they are wrong and should be abolished. Unfortunately for such a point of view, there is no way to stop people from trying to place one another or to keep them from being concerned about their own status.

Because of the importance of the distinction between shop and office, there is a strong tendency to differentiate between them in many ways, each of which becomes a symbol to indicate the position of the individual. While the nature of the work usually leads to a separation between office and shop groups, the separation itself becomes an important symbol of the difference in status. As a result, most office workers are upset and feel that they have lost status if they are moved from an office location to a shop location even though there is no change in the job. In most large plants where there is a separation of the office and shop organizations, there are usually separate washrooms for the office people; and any attempt to have the office people use the shop washrooms, or to bring shop people into the office washrooms, meets with strong resistance from the office people. To be forced to share lockers or washrooms with these "uncouth and inferior" people is a bitter pill to the office people. In such instances, all sorts of complaints are voiced about the crowded washrooms, about how untidy the shop people are, about how they threw paper towels or cigarettes on the floor or leave the washbasins grimy from their dirty hands, or about their bad manners and unrefined language. This whole attitude was well expressed in the behavior of a typist who had been transferred from an office location to the same work in a shop: rather than use the shop washrooms which were adjacent to her new location, she would walk across a building and up a flight of stairs to a washroom used by an office group.

In many companies there is a payroll distinction, too, between shop and office, the shopworkers being paid by the hour and the office by the week. Since both groups are actually paid every week, there is no obvious difference; yet the different payrolls assume the status differences of the two groups. And to move from the hourly to the weekly or salaried payroll is a step up in the world. In some cases this difference may be accentuated by having different time clocks or a different payday for each group, so that there remains no doubt as to where a person fits. Separate time clocks or paydays are, of course, usually thought of as devices to assist the payroll department in preparing the pay checks, or to spread the work load a bit; but it is surprising how often such devices get mixed up in the status system and become status symbols in themselves. And once they become status symbols, any attempt to change them meets with strong resistance from the people.

An almost universal characteristic of all types of status hierarchies is that certain prerogatives accompany high status; and as one ascends in the structure, he acquires certain rights and privileges which are denied to those below him. Some of these rights have to do with the symbols of status themselves. As one is promoted, he acquires the right to display the insignia of his new place. Others are much more tangible rewards, such as increased freedom from restraints, special rights, additional pay, and so on. For example, the following situation was observed in one small plant:

> As more machines were added to the departments, the girls who had the best records in attendance and production or showed aptitude for mechanics were made adjusters. This was considered a promotion, although there was no increase in pay. They had a small measure of authority in that they were responsible for seeing that the operators turned out perfect work and for adjusting the machines to make this possible. Since the adjusters operated the machines during the regular lunch period, they ate alone. There were no bells to ring to signify the beginning and end of their lunch period; so they took a few minutes extra. Although everyone knew about this, nothing was said, so the adjusters felt that they were a little above the ordinary workers.

These symbolic distinctions are well shown, too, in the shop-office division, with the office usually having definite privileges denied to the shop. For example, office workers frequently have a longer lunch hour than shop; they may be free to leave their desks to go to the washroom whenever they please, while the shop is limited to fixed rest pauses. Through the device of the weekly pay, the office workers may take time off or come in late without penalty, while the hourly paid shopworkers are usually paid only for the time they are actually on the job.

It is interesting that foremen are generally on the weekly payroll and so are grouped with the office people. It appears, then, that the ordinary factory is split into two groups, one of which is composed of the hourly paid shopworkers, the other of the weekly paid office workers and the entire superivsory staff. The nonsuperisvory office workers, furthermore, tend to think of themselves as akin to the supervisory and executive group rather than to the shopworkers.

Within the office group itself, there is usually a high development of status symbols. Almost anything in the work situation seems to have potentialities for becoming such a symbol, whether it be a desk, chair, telephone, location, arrangement of furniture, or whatnot. For example, a telephone directory usually becomes a sort of *Who's Who* which reflects status more than phone calls. Whether you have a telephone on your desk, or share one with the next desk, or have none at all may be a direct reflection of your status and is usually interpreted that way. In one large organization, desks were an important symbol: the lowest clerical workers worked at tables, the next level had single-pedestal desks with one bank of drawers, the superiors had larger, double-pedestal desks with two banks of drawers, and so on, up to the plant manager, who had a great big desk of fancy woods. In such a system, to give a man a promotion without the proper desk would have given rise to elaborate speculations as to whether he really rated the title or just what was wrong. It would be like promoting a lieutenant but telling him that he would have to still wear his lieutenant's bars, that he was not really a captain yet. The emphasis on these status symbols in one small factory was described by an office worker, as follows:

> This same vice-president has three assistant vice-presidents in his department besides his department manager. He gets them increasingly large bonuses each year. He can't give them all private offices, so he gathers them all into one special corner of the office

away from their secretaries, gives them each a desk *and* a table and more space for visitors. Their desks have leather desk pads with green blotters instead of the usual rubber mat, and, on the whole, he keeps them happy. But if one of them were to get a bronze wastebasket, they would each have to have one.

In the same way, offices for executives become important symbols of status. In most large organizations there are certain superior offices which, because of size or location, are preferred. Usually these better offices are occupied by the top-ranking men in the organization and reflect their status. Other offices may fit into the status pattern on the basis of their proximity to the "brass hats." Thus the office next to the president is superior to the one down the hall. Where offices occupy several floors of a tall building, the higher offices usually have the most status. The manager or president usually occupies the top floor, and the lesser officials are found somewhere below. In such cases, moving to a higher floor is getting up in the world in more ways than one. The importance of location as a status symbol affects the people who work for executives, too, so that their secretaries, stenographers, and even their office boys, feel very strongly the status significance of working on the top floor or in the office next to the president's suite. This was described by a girl in the personnel department of one organization, thus:

Then there is the social problem caused by the physical layout which comprises three floors. The executives' offices are on the tenth. (This is special!) Several departments, including accounting and payroll, are on the ninth. (This is O.K.) There is the eighth floor, with dictaphones, typing, filing. (This is Bargain Basement!) The girls on the eighth feel that the girls on the ninth and tenth look down on them. The secretaries on the tenth floor are supposed to be pretty high-hat. Girls on the ninth beg to be transferred "upstairs."

Among shopworkers, on the other hand, there is not quite so much emphasis upon status symbols. In general, a person's position in the shop is pretty clearly shown by the work he is doing. The man operating an automatic screw machine is obviously different from the sweeper or material handler, the machinist is superior to his helper, and anyone familiar with shopwork can place people easily in the general status system. This does not mean that shopworkers are not concerned about status, but merely that the work itself provides fairly obvious status insignia.

With office people, however, as pointed out, the symbols of status are often a major concern, and changes in them are sure to create disturbances. To account for such emphasis is difficult, but we may present two possible hypotheses. In the first place, the office and supervisory groups probably contain more people who want to improve their status. And these people naturally want to display evidence of any gains; they want people to know where they belong. At the same time, the nature of office work is such that all jobs look alike from a distance; people sitting at desks writing and shuffling papers may be either important executives or the most unimportant clerks. For that reason, it becomes important that the superior people acquire symbols to distinguish them from the rest. (And everyone gets upset if the new clerk gets the desk by the boss or one by the window.)

These status symbols are a constant source of conflict and anxiety. Each watches his equals lest they acquire symbols which he lacks; each longs to have the choice office or the large desk and schemes to get it; each judges the importance of his job by symbols which go with it. As a result, every change in arrangement, every movement of people or organizations, may upset the status systems and cause trouble.

AN EXAMPLE OF STATUS PROBLEMS. A situation involving status problems, changes, and disturbances in one small factory was described by a personnel officer, as follows:

Fred J., aged 45, was one of the most capable all round machinists in a tool industry of about 350 employees. A year and a half ago he was placed in charge of a night shift in the approximate capacity of superintendent. The night shift had just been started, and none of the day foremen who might have been eligible for the job seemed to want it.

The initial night force was small, but it grew rapidly to a total of 125 employees. The top management never made a clear announcement of Fred's position as super-intendent. He had the duties of a super-intendent except that one department oper-ated at night as an independent unit. No clear directive was given to the effect that Fred was in complete charge, although it was intended that this should be generally understood up to the point of his being responsible for all night activities except in the one independent department.

A great deal of antagonism having the appearance of jealousy immediately de-veloped among the foremen of the day shift. The day superintendent likewise seemed to resent the fact of there being another superintendent in the plant. He would often challenge Fred's right to deal with operational matters that extended through both shifts. In a showdown be-tween these two, Fred answered the chal-lenge by saying, "All right, let's go up to George's (the general manager's) office right now, and I'll apologize to you in his presence." The offer was declined.

Characteristic expressions of the day fore-man in referring to Fred would run some-what along the lines of "that fellow that's on nights. . . . I don't know what you'd call him. . . . He ain't a superintendent,

and I wouldn't even call him a foreman."

The management says that, had they clearly designated Fred as a superintendent, they would have had a blowup. They had to place him where they did because the job had to be done and there was no one else in the place who would take it and would have their confidence to the same extent.

Over a period of sixteen months Fred seems to have been winning his battle slowly. But the whole thing has been marked by a good deal of antagonism, fre-quent ignoring of notes left by Fred for the day supervision, and quite obvious buck-passing, such as the charging of scrap against the night shift when portions of it belonged unmistakably to the day shift.

In one instance Fred had one of his night operators mark each piece he turned out, a piece which was being produced by both shifts. In the inspector's reports on rejects, all the scrap was charged against the night shift. Fred examined the rejected pieces, found that his man's symbol was not on them, and demanded of the inspector, "How come?" The inspector explained: "The day superintendent told me to charge them that way."

Social Systems

GEORGE HOMANS

This chapter is a tough one, perhaps the tough-est in the book, but we had better know the worst at once. It tries to do two things at the same time. First, it tries to show how the kinds of generalization we shall be interested in are reached: how we go from simple descriptions

From *The Human Group*. New York: Harcourt, Brace and Co., 1950, pp. 25–40, 90–107, 108–113, 118–119. Copyright 1950 by Harcourt, Brace and World and reprinted with their permission.

of social events to uniformities in the behavior of a limited number of persons and groups and finally to generalizations that may apply to all groups. Second, it tries to define the words, or concepts, that will come into these highest generalizations. As we shall see, the two jobs mesh with one another and must be carried on together.

One of the big problems of sociology, as of all social science, is semantic: the problem of the relation between the words used and the observations made. The meanings of words are usually given by definitions, but the trouble with definitions, as one of the first great semanticists, Lord Bacon, pointed out, is that "the definitions themselves consist of words, and those words beget others: so that it is necessary to recur to individual instances, and those in due series and order."[1] Bacon meant that the end of the chain of words must be anchored in an act something like the one by which a mother teaches her child the meaning of the word *cow:* she points at the beast and says the word. Acts of this kind are not available to us. We are not in the open air watching a group in action, and we cannot learn the meaning of sociological concepts by having someone point to various items in the behavior of the group and, as he does so, name the concepts. But we can do the next best thing. We can take the descriptions of group behavior made by good observers, persons who, unlike ourselves, have been watching groups in the open air; we can point to certain things they saw and give these things names. The names are the concepts.

Our work presupposes the direct observation of human behavior. It does not for the most part deal with what men write in answer to a questionnaire or what they say when a research assistant has his foot in the door. It deals with what men say and do on the ordinary occasions of ordinary life. This kind of fact is surprisingly hard to collect; it demands an observer who is not himself so much a part of the situation that he cannot view it with a fresh eye, and one who does not, by the mere fact of his presence, change what would otherwise be said and done. Anthropologists who live with the tribes they study and who back up their lengthy questionings of native informants with firsthand observations of daily life collect this kind of material, and so do a few sociologists who study groups and communities in our own society. Our work relies on theirs. Some social scientists find this kind of material hard and unsatisfying to work with: it can seldom be converted into statistics and always leaves unanswered many interesting questions—and they shy away from it. Nevertheless it is the stuff of everyday existence, and we start with it here.

EVENTS IN THE SINGLE GROUP. We are going to begin with a description of everyday social events in a society not our own. The world is a stage, and one of its many scenes opens:

The room is low and rectangular. The left wall is filled by a door, closed, and a big stone fireplace, fitted for cooking. Chairs and benches are set around the fireplace. Against the back wall a table stands, and to the right of the table a colored picture hangs over a cabinet containing a small figure. The right wall is taken up by a dresser, full of kitchen gear and crockery, on one side of which is a door and on the other a staircase leading upstairs. Through a window over the table a yard, with a cart in it, is seen in dim light.

A woman opens the door, right, and comes into the room. She goes to the fireplace, rakes together the ashes on the hearth, some of them still alive, puts on new fuel, and rekindles the blaze. Then she fills a kettle with water and hangs it on a hook over the fire. When it boils, she makes tea; meanwhile she lays out dishes, cutlery, bread, and milk on the table, and gets ready to cook eggs.

A middle-aged man and two younger ones enter, exchange a few words with the woman, pull up chairs, sit down at the table, and begin to eat. The woman herself does not sit, but stands by, ready to bring up more food and drink if the men ask for them. When the men have eaten, the older one says to the younger ones, "Well, we'd better be off." They go out.

By this time a girl has joined the woman in the room, but not until the men have left do the two sit down for their meal. Before they have finished, crying is heard outside, right. The woman leaves and later returns carrying a young child in her arms. She fondles and comforts it, then feeds it in its turn.

She turns to the girl, who is already washing the dishes, with a remark about making butter. . . .[2]

We need not go on. This scene, or something much like it, has been enacted millions of times in the history of mankind, and it

---

[1] F. Bacon, *Novum Organum*, Bk. I, aphorism lix.

[2] Adapted from C. M. Arensberg and S. T. Kimball, *Family and Community in Ireland*, 35.

shows, of course, a farm family beginning a working day. It is not an American farm family, though families of this sort were common not so long ago in America and survive in some places still. It is a countryman's family in the southwest of Ireland. Farm families, differing from this one in some outward appearances, but perhaps not very different in essentials, have for centuries formed the foundations of society in Europe, the Near East, India, China, and much of the Americas. This social unit is characteristic of many of the countries that have the largest populations. Only in recent years and in a few places have we begun to see the appearance of a new kind of family. The old-fashioned farm family —if we may call it that—is still the commonest of human groups.

The scene is familiar. We begin and end with the familiar and are lucky to be able to do so, but the important point at the moment is not the familiarity of the scene. It is rather that a scene like this is part of the raw material of sociology: a description of a series of *events*, in each of which at one particular place and time a person did certain things, in certain physical surroundings, perhaps with certain implements and together with certain other persons. All science begins with process, the flux of things, the passing scene. Generalization must be true to events. We forget their vividness at our peril. And how refreshing they are! "Here," we can say, "is one kind of certainty. No matter how we interpret them, and no matter how far they fall short of telling the whole story, these things, at least these things, *happened*."

There can be little interpretation of, generalization from, single events. We can learn much—and it is good discipline, too—from trying merely to report, that is, from trying to describe human behavior in words altogether flat, simply descriptive, devoid of interpretation. In any strict sense, it cannot be done. Any noun implies some context; even a word like *table* implies something about the use of a physical object. But in the effort to leave out at least the higher levels of meaning, we can discover how much meaning we regularly put into our descriptions. Perhaps we shall see how easy it is to commit ourselves to an interpretation before we know what we are doing.

Our description of the farm family beginning the day is just such a flat description as a playwright might write in setting the opening scene of his play. The meaning unfolds only as the action of the play develops. Thus the older woman is not called the mother of the family, nor the man the father. "Mother" and "father" assume a certain scheme of social relationships, and from the single scene we cannot be sure that we are dealing with that kind of scheme. It is better to begin with distinctions like those between man and woman, youth and age. In the same way, the cabinet is not called a shrine. If we had called it that, we should have been assuming something that the single scene cannot tell us. Nevertheless, there are items in the description that might be remembered, should he run across them again, by anyone anxious to build up a picture of the relationships between the members of the family. For instance, the older man gives orders to the two younger ones or at least gives the signal to go out and begin the day's work. The woman likewise points out to the girl the job—making butter—that the two of them will do in the course of the day. Both women wait for the men to finish eating before they sit down themselves. The older woman comforts and plays with the baby. And so on. An observer builds up his picture of social relationships from repeated events like these.

CUSTOM. The next stage in the analysis of human behavior—and it always implies the first—is reached when we recognize simple recurrences in events, recurrences at different intervals. To go back to our farm family, we note that almost every day the men go out to work in the fields; that every year, at about the same season, they dig potatoes; that in this work the father directs the activities of the sons. The women do the chores around the house but do not work in the fields; so long as there is a youngster in the house, the mother feeds it, goes to it when it cries, comforts and protects it. And so on. The behavior of the members of a group is a symphony, a symphony that may have discords. There are different voices—as the wood winds are a voice in a symphony—each with its themes, which come in at different intervals, sometimes quietly, sometimes loudly, sometimes in the foreground, sometimes in the background. Often there is a conductor who is himself a voice, and there are recurrences in the group of voices, in the movement as a whole. Like lazy listeners, we who are at the symphony never hear all the voices and all their harmonies. We hear only the ones we are interested in hearing.

These recurrences in social behavior, when recognized as recurrences, are called customs. For the moment we are simply going to accept custom as a fact, giving notice at the same time that the fact raises an important question, which will be considered in a later chapter. We mention the question now only to show we are aware of it. Some students of society are inclined to take the recurrences in the behavior of a group for granted. They are interested in the details of particular customs, but not in custom itself as an aspect of group life. Other students go further, as Edmund Burke did years ago, and see custom as useful, even necessary. Men cannot plan for the future without relying on the massive regularities of expected behavior. Yet when everything intelligent has been said about the usefulness of custom, one more profound question remains: What makes custom customary? For the brute fact is that customs do change. In view of the constantly varied forces playing on society, it is amazing that anything can be recognized as persistent. The recurrences are miracles, not commonplaces; and miracles, if they happen often, are just the things we should study most closely. As soon as we do, we find that nothing is more defenseless than a custom, alone. Not single customs, but systems of custom, survive. Anthropologists used to talk about the "tyranny of custom" as if custom were a mold pressing social organization into a shape. This view is misleading. Custom is not something outside of, and apart from, social organization but is implicit in organization. These are large generalizations. We state them now, but only in a much later chapter shall we try to back them up. By that time we hope to have the tools to do the job.

The usual descriptions of groups consist of statements of custom, that is, recurrences in human behavior at different places or at different intervals. "The Irish countrymen live on isolated farms." . . . "The men of a Tikopia village commonly put out to sea together when they go fishing." The books and articles that are our sources, that we must work with, are full of such remarks. But we must never forget, having a lively sense of the shifting sands on which we build, that statements of custom, if they are worth anything, are founded on repeated observations of individual events in single scenes. With this in mind, let us return to the Irish farm family, and now study a description of the relationships between its members, particularly father, mother, and son. The description is a statement of custom: a summary of the recurrences in many single scenes like the one with which this chapter opened.

The growing child ordinarily sees his father as owner and principal worker of the farm. When the whole family group of father, mother, children, and whatever other relatives may be living with them, works in concert, as at the potato planting, the turf cutting, and the haymaking, it is the father who directs the group's activities, himself doing the heavy tasks. . . .

In his earliest childhood, of course, the mother looms larger in the child's consciousness than the father. The child's first duties, as soon as he can speak and walk, are to run on petty errands to neighbors and near-by "friends." Soon he is taking his father's meals to him in the fields or going on errands to the nearest shop. Until he is seven and has gone through First Communion, his place is in the house with the women, and his labor is of very little importance. After First Communion, at six or seven, he begins to be thrown more with his elder brothers, and comes to do small chores which bring him more and more into contact with his father and with the other men of the neighborhood . . . But not till he passes Confirmation and leaves school (generally at the same time) does he take on full men's work. Even then, as he becomes adult and takes on more and more of the heavy tasks of the farm work, he never escapes his father's direction, until his father dies or makes over the farm to him at his marriage . . .

It goes without saying that the father exercises his control over the whole activity of the "boy." It is by no means confined to their work together. Indeed, the father is the court of last resort, which dispenses punishment for deviations from the norm of conduct in all spheres. Within the bounds of custom and law he has full power to exercise discipline. Corporal punishment is not a thing of the past in Ireland, and, especially in the intermediate stages of the child's development, from seven to puberty, it gets full play.

It is during those years that the characteristic relationship between father and son is developed in rural communities. The son has suffered a remove from the previous almost exclusive control of its mother, in which an affective content of sympathy and indulgence was predominant, and is brought into contact for the first time with the father and older men. But the transfer is not completed. There is a hiatus in his development through the years of school when his participation in men's work and his relationship with his father has little chance of developing into an effective partnership. A real union of interests does not take place until after Confirmation and school-leaving, when for the first time his exclusive contacts and his entire day-to-day activity, particularly in farm work, will be with his father and the older men.

This fact colors greatly the relationship of father and son, as far as affective content goes. There is none of the close companionship and intimate sympathy which characterizes, at least ideally, the relationship in other groups. Where such exists, it is a matter for surprised comment to the small farmers. In its place there is developed, necessarily perhaps, a marked respect, expressing itself in the tabooing of many actions, such as smoking, drinking, and physical contact of any sort, which can be readily observed in any small farm family. Coupled with this is the lifelong subordination . . . which is never relaxed even in the one sphere in which farmer father and son can develop an intense community of interest—farm work. Nothing prevents the development of great mutual pride, the boy in his experienced and skillful mentor, tutor, and captain in work, and the man in a worthy and skillful successor and fellow workman, but on the other hand everything within the behavior developed in the relationship militates against the growth of close mutual sympathy. As a result, the antagonisms inherent in such a situation often break through very strongly when conflicts arise . . .

On the other hand, the relationship of mother and son has a very different content. Like that between father and son, it is the product of years of development. It is marked, too, by a similar retention of subordinate status on the part of the son. In farm work the boy is subject to the commands of his mother even when, fully adult, he has passed over exclusively to men's work. . . . But within the scope of such a subordination there is a quite different affective history. The relationship is the first and earliest into which a child enters. It is very close, intimate, and all-embracing for the first years of life; only gradually does the experience of the child expand to include brothers, sisters, and last, the older male members of the household.

Until seven, the child of either sex is the constant companion of its mother. If the family is numerous an elder child, usually a sister, may take over much of the mother's role, but the mother is always near-by. As the woman works in the house or fields, the child is kept by her side. In the house it usually sits in a crib by the fire or plays about on the floor, but always within sight and sound. It learns its speech from its mother, amid a flood of constant endearments, admonitions, and encouragements. The woman's work never separates her from the child. Custom imposes no restraints or interruptions in her solicitude. She looks after its comforts, gives it food, dresses it, etc. She constantly exercises restraints and controls over it, teaching it day by day in a thousand situations the elements of prudery, modesty and good conduct.

The controls she exercises are of a different kind from those of the father. She is both guide and companion. Her authority most often makes itself felt through praise, persuasion, and endearment. Only when a grave breach of discipline demands a restraining power greater than hers, or when an appeal to ultimate authority is needed, does the father begin to play his role. Especially in the years before puberty, the farm father enters the child's cognizance as a disciplinary force. The barriers of authority, respect, extra-household interests, and the imperatives of duty rather than of encouragement make it difficult for any intimacy to develop.

Even after Confirmation the child's relationship to his mother is not materially weakened. He becomes confirmed, it is true, in a masculine scorn for feminine interests and pursuits, but he can and must still look for protection to his mother against a too-arbitrary exercise of his father's power. In family disputes the mother takes a diplomatic, conciliatory role. From her intermediary position she can call upon the strongest ties between herself and her sons to restore rifts in parental authority and filial submission.

Throughout the years of the son's full activity in the farm economy under the father's leadership, the mother still remains the source of comfort and the preparer of food and is still infinitely solicitous of his welfare. It is only at marriage that the bond is broken . . . If the child must leave the farm for other walks of life, the closest possible relationship is still maintained. When one goes home, it is to see one's mother. There is always an attempt to carry on a correspondence. In exile, the bond lingers as a profound sentimental nostalgia.[3]

Before we go on to our main purpose, we must get some preliminaries out of the way. This passage describes a relationship between three persons, not the conventional triangle of a love story but the triangle that has father, mother, and son at its corners. The pattern of the relationship is clearly marked—which is a reason why we chose a description of an Irish family and not one of an American family. The latter is more familiar to us but its pattern is not so easily characterized. In the Irish family the relationship between mother and son is one of warm affection, the relationship between father and son is one of admiration mixed with respect. Moreover, these relationships are not peculiar to Ireland: it is interesting how often the pattern repeats itself in farm families, and indeed in other families, all over the world. Nor are these relationships inevitable. It is not simply "natural" that a son should love his mother, though we all like to think it is. He loves his mother be-

cause the repeated, thousand-times-repeated, events in which the two are brought together are of a certain kind. From earliest childhood she cares for him; but change her behavior and the emotion would change too. In like manner, the son's feeling for the father is colored by the father's control over him in the many-times-repeated events of farm work. Nor, to go a step further, are the two series of events —the events determining these mother-son and father-son relationships—isolated from the rest of the world. Instead they are related to the division of labor and assignment of authority in a going farm enterprise, surviving in an environment.

We shall not be misled by the use of the words "the child," "his mother," and "his father" in the singular. These are shorthand for "children," "mothers," and "fathers." An anthropologist would say that the passages quoted above tell us some of the customs of Irish countrymen, a statistician that they may perhaps express some kind of average in the behavior of a certain number of groups—Irish farm families—over a certain span of time. The statistician might find fault with the passages for not letting him know the relation between the "sample" and the "universe," that is, the relation between the number of groups directly observed and the larger number for whose behavior the average is supposed to hold good. He might also find fault with the passages for giving us no idea of the number of groups—there must be a few—whose behavior deviates in some degree from the average. He might say that the statements are by implication quantitative but that they do not let an outsider make any judgment of their quantitative reliability. His criticisms are good, and they can be answered only by raising new questions: How much more effort, in men, time, and money, would be needed to get the kind of data he wants? Given a limited supply of all three, how far would getting his kind of data interfere with getting a wider, though admittedly less reliable, coverage of group behavior? These are questions not of scientific morality but of strategy and, in the broad sense, economics: getting the most for one's money. They themselves beg for quantitative answers. And we might finally ask the different and more searching question: How far does the craving to get the kind of data a statistician considers reliable lead social scientists to take

---

[3] Reprinted by permission of the publishers from Conrad Maynadier Arensberg and Solon Toothaker Kimball, *Family and Community in Ireland*, Cambridge, Mass.: Harvard University Press, 1940, pp. 51–60.

up questions for which this kind of data can easily be secured instead of questions that are interesting for other reasons? To which the statistician might reply: If we are not getting what I want, are we getting anything on which we can found a science? We should keep these questions in mind, for much of the material we shall be working with is not of the kind the statistician wants.

DEFINITION OF CONCEPTS. Let us go back over our work so far. We began with a flat description of events within a single group; then we went on to a statement of the customs of an unspecified but limited number of groups: the families of Irish countrymen. The next step is a long one; in fact it will take up the rest of this book. We shall set up some hypotheses—and they will remain hypotheses because we shall only set them up, not prove them—that may sum up a few aspects of social behavior in an unlimited number of groups all over the world. There is no use saying now what these hypotheses are; we shall find out soon enough, and one move in particular we must make before we can formulate any hypotheses of high generalization, such as ours will be. We must define a few of the concepts that come into them. Though we cannot do so by pointing at objects and saying the concept, we can take the next best step. We can examine a passage like the one above, point out certain words in it, ask ourselves whether the aspects of social behavior to which the words refer have anything in common, and then, if they do, give a name to this common element. The name is the concept. We might have written a passage of our own for this purpose, but anyone can solve a problem if he sets it up himself. It is much more convincing to use someone else's passage, as we have done.

ACTIVITY. Let us look, then, at certain words and phrases in this passage, and first, perhaps, at words like these: *potato planting, turf cutting, haymaking, corporal punishment, smoking, drinking, gives food, dresses, looks after, plays, sits, walks, speaks, talks, First Communion, Confirmation.* In the passage we can pick out many more such words, and also some of greater generality, like *work* and *activity.* Let us agree that they have something in common, without committing ourselves on the question whether this something is im-

portant. They all refer to things that people do: work on the physical environment, with implements, and with other persons. If we want to be precise, we can say that all these words and phrases refer in the end to movements of the muscles of men, even though the importance of some of the movements, like talk and ceremonies, depends on their symbolic meaning. We shall speak of the characteristic they have in common as an *element* of social behavior, and we shall give it a name, as a mere ticket. It might be called *action*, if *action* had not been given a more general meaning, or *work*, if *work* did not have a special meaning in the physical sciences and may yet have an analogous one in sociology. Instead of either of these, we shall call it *activity*, and use it, in much the same way as it is used in everyday speech, as an analytical concept for the study of social groups.

We call activity an element, not implying that it is some ultimate, indivisible atom of behavior. It is no more than one of the classes into which we choose to divide something that might be divided in other, and less crude, ways. In fact we call it an element just because the vagueness of that word gives us room to move around in. Above all we must realize that activity is not a variable like temperature in physics: it cannot be given a single series of numerical values. Instead, a number of aspects of activity might be measured. We are sometimes able to measure the *output* or rate of production of certain kinds af activity, for instance, factory work, and sometimes the *efficiency* of activity, the relation to input to output. We might even be able to assign an index to the degree of *similarity* of one activity to another. And so on. These are true variables, at least in possibility, though we could not give them numerical values in every piece of research. In later chapters we shall have to make sure, when we speak of activity, which particular variable we have in mind.

INTERACTION. Going back now to the passage we are working with, let us look at expressions like these: the boy is *thrown with* his elder brothers; he comes more and more *into contact with* his father; he never *escapes from* his father's direction; he *participates* in the men's work; he is a *companion* of his mother; he goes to *see* his mother, and so on. The element that these phrases have in common is more or less mixed with other things, for in our language one word seldom states one clear idea. For instance, what does the word *see* mean in the phrase "going to see someone"? Yet there is a common element, and it seems to be some notion of sheer interaction between persons, apart from the particular activities in which they interact. When we refer to the fact that some unit of activity of one man follows, or, if we like the word better, is stimulated by some unit of activity of another, aside from any question of what these units may be, then we are referring to *interaction*. We shall speak of interaction as an element of social behavior and use it as an analytical concept in the chapters that follow.

We may find it hard to think consistently of interaction as separate from the other elements of behavior, but we shall have to do so in this book, and the fact is that in our everyday thinking we often keep it separate without realizing as much. When we say "Tom got in touch with Harry," or "Tom contacted Harry," or "Tom was an associate of Harry's," we are not talking about the particular words they said to one another or the particular activities they both took part in. Instead we are talking about the sheer fact of contact, of association. Perhaps the simplest example of interaction, though we should find it complex enough if we studied it carefully, is two men at opposite ends of a saw, sawing a log. When we say that the two are interacting, we are not referring to the fact that both are sawing: in our language, sawing is an *activity*, but to the fact that the push of one man on the saw is followed by the push of the other. In this example, the interaction does not involve words. More often interaction takes place through verbal or other symbolic communication. But when in the armed forces men talk about the chain of command, or in a business ask what officers report to what other ones, they are still talking about channels of communication—the chains of interaction—rather than the communications themselves or the activities that demand communications.

Just as several variables are included under the concept of activity, so several are included under interaction. We can study the *frequency* of interaction: the number of times a day or a year one man interacts with another or the members of a group interact with one another. We can measure the ratio between the amount of time one man is active, for instance, talking, and the *duration* of his interlocutor's activity. Or we can study the *order* of interaction: Who originates action? Where does a chain of interactions start and where does it go? If Tom makes a suggestion to Dick, does Dick pass it on to Harry? [4] Once again, we shall have to make sure from time to time that we are talking about one variable under interaction and not another. Our observations of this element can often be rather precise and definite, which gives them infinite charm for persons of a certain temperament.

When we called the first of our elements *activity*, we may have been using the obvious and appropriate word. But in calling the second element *interaction*, are we not needlessly using a strange word when a familiar one is on hand? Why not speak of *communication* rather than *interaction*? Our answer is: The word *communication* is neither general enough in one sense nor specific enough in another. When people think of communication, they think of communication in words, but here we are including under interaction both verbal and nonverbal communication. What is more, the word *communication* is used in several different ways in everyday speech. It may mean the content of the message, signal, or "communication" being transmitted, or the process of transmission itself, as when people speak of "methods of communication," or to the sheer fact, aside from content or process of transmission, that one person has communicated with another. Only to the last of these three do we give the name of interaction, and the unfamiliarity of the word may underline the fact that its meaning is specific. Nevertheless we shall, from time to time, when there is no risk of confusion, use the word *communication* in place of *interaction*, so that our language will not sound hopelessly foreign.

SENTIMENT. Now let us go back to our passage again and consider another set of words and phrases: *sentiments of affection, affective*

[4] For a systematic discussion of interaction as an element of social behavior, see E. D. Chapple, with the collaboration of C. M. Arensberg, *Measuring Human Relations* (Genetic Psychology Monographs, Vol. 22 (1940)).

content of sympathy and indulgence, intimate sympathy, respect, pride, antagonism, affective history, scorn, sentimental nostalgia. To these we shall arbitrarily add others, such as *hunger* and *thirst*, that might easily have come into the passage. What can we say these words have in common? Perhaps the most we can say, and it may not be very much, is that they all refer to internal states of the human body. Laymen and professional psychologists call these states by various names: drives, emotions, feelings, affective states, sentiments, attitudes. Here we shall call them all *sentiments*, largely because that word has been used in a less specialized sense than some of the others, and we shall speak of *sentiment* as an element of social behavior.

Notice the full range of things we propose to call sentiments. They run all the way from fear, hunger, and thirst, to such probably far more complicated psychological states as liking or disliking for individuals, approval or disapproval of their actions. We are lumping together under this word some psychological states that psychologists would certainly keep separate. Our employment of the concept *sentiment* can only be justified by what we do with it, so that at the moment all we can ask is indulgence for our failure in orthodoxy.

We must now consider a question that may not seem important but that has come up again and again, in one form or another, ever since the behaviorists first raised it. We can *see* activities and interactions. But if sentiments are internal states of the body, can we see them in the same way? It is true that a person may say he feels hungry or likes someone, and that in everyday life, if we are dealing with him, we take account of what he has to say about his own feelings. But scientists may be forgiven for believing that subjective judgments are treacherous things to work with. They are not reliable; we cannot tell whether two persons would reach the same judgment under the same circumstances, and reliability is the rock on which science is built. Some scientists even believe that they can reach important generalizations, in psychology and sociology, without paying any attention whatever to subjective judgments; and they would ask us whether there is anything we can point to as sentiment that has not already been included under activity and interaction. Can it be independently observed? Perhaps in some animals the

more violent sentiments can be so observed. In a dog or cat, pain, hunger, fear, and rage are marked by measurable changes in the body, particularly in the glands of internal secretion.[5] We assume that this is also true of human beings, but few of the necessary measurements can easily be made. For mild sentiments such as friendliness, and these are the ones we shall be working with most often here, we are not sure how far the bodily changes occur at all. The James-Lange theory that a sentiment and a set of visceral changes are one and the same thing cannot be driven too far. On an occasion that might conceivably have called for emotion, the undamaged human being reacts so as to cut down the amount of visceral change taking place. The body mobilizes for action, if that is appropriate, and reduces the merely emotional changes.

Science is perfectly ready to take leave of common sense, but only for a clear and present gain. Lacking more precise methods for observing sentiments, since the biological methods can only be used in special circumstances, have we anything to gain by giving up everyday practice? Have we not rather a good deal to lose? And what is everyday practice? In deciding what sentiments a person is feeling, we take notice of slight, evanescent tones of his voice, expressions of his face, movements of his hands, ways of carrying his body, and we take notice of these things as parts of a whole in which the context of any one sign is furnished by all the others. The signs may be slight in that the physical change from one whole to another is not great, but they are not slight so long as we have learned to discriminate between wholes and assign them different meanings. And that is what we do. From these wholes we infer the existence of internal states of the human body and call them anger, irritation, sympathy, respect, pride, and so forth. Above all, we infer the existence of sentiments from what men say about what they feel and from the echo that their words find in our own feelings. We can recognize in ourselves what they are talking about. All those who have probed the secrets of the human heart have known how misleading and ambiguous these indications can sometimes be, how a man can talk love and mean hate, or

[5] See W. B. Cannon, *Bodily Changes in Pain, Hunger, Fear, and Rage.*

mean both together, without being aware of what he is doing. Yet we act on our inferences, on our diagnoses of the sentiments of other people, and we do not always act ineffectively. In this book we are trying to learn how the elements of our everyday social experience are related to one another. Leaving out a part of that experience—and sentiment is a part—would be reasonable only if we had a better kind of observation to take its place. Some sciences have something better; ours does not yet.

We may end with a practical argument. This book is, in one of its intentions, an effort to bring out the generalizations implicit in modern field studies of human groups. If the men who made the studies felt that they could infer and give names to such things as sentiments of affection, respect, pride, and antagonism, we shall see what we can do with their inferences, remembering always that a more advanced theory than ours may have to wait for more precise and reliable observations. No theory can be more sophisticated than the facts with which it deals.

Under the element of *sentiment*, several different kinds of studies can and have been made. Perhaps the best-known ones are carried on by the public opinion pollsters and attitude scalers using questionnaires they get people to answer. Especially when they try to find out the *number* of persons that approve or disapprove of, like or dislike, a proposal for action or a candidate for public office, they are studying at least one variable under this element. Often they go further and try to discover not only how many persons approve or disapprove but the *conviction* with which they do so: whether they are sure they are right, feel somewhat less sure, or remain undecided. The pollsters may also try to find out the *intensity* of the sentiments concerned: a man may disapprove of something intellectually and yet not feel strongly about it. His emotions may not have been deeply aroused. . . .

The External System

The environment and its influences will be different for each group considered; . . . we note that the group is, at the moment we study it, persisting or surviving in its environment; and we infer, not unnaturally, that the behavior of the group must be such as to allow it to survive in the environment. Then we turn to the elements of group behavior: sentiment, activity, and interaction, and we say that the *external system* is the state of these elements and of their interrelations, so far as it constitutes a solution—not necessarily the only possible solution—of the problem: How shall the group survive in its environment? We call it external because it is conditioned by the environment; we call it a system because in it the elements of behavior are mutually dependent. The external system, plus another set of relations which we shall call the *internal system*, make up the total social system.

At the risk of anticipating some later steps in our argument, let us take everyone into our confidence on what we are trying to do. When we study a group, one of the first observations we can make is that the group is surviving in an environment, and therefore we say of the group, as of other organisms, that it is, for the moment at least, adapted to its environment. But this word *adaptation* is ambiguous. Does it mean that the characteristics of the group are determined by the environment? No, it does not, for the second observation we can make is that the characteristics of the group are determined by two classes of factors and not one only. These characteristics are determined by the environment, in greater or lesser degree according to the nature of the environment and of the group in question, and also by what we shall call for the time being the internal development of the group. But we are not yet at the end of our difficulties, for the third observation we can make is that the two classes of factors are not independent of one another. Full explanation of our meaning will take the rest of this book, but we can outline our argument now. Assuming that there is established between the members of a group any set of relations satisfying the condition that the group survives for a time in its particular environment, physical and social, we can show that on the foundation of these relations the group will develop new ones, that the latter will modify or even create the relations we assumed at the beginning, and that, finally, the behavior of the group, besides being determined by the environment, will itself change the environment.

In short, the relationship between group and environment is essentially a relationship of action and reaction; it is circular. But perhaps it is safer to say that it sounds circular when described in words and sentences. When we describe a phenomenon in ordinary language, we are bound to start with a particular statement, going on from there to a sequence of further statements, and if the phenomenon is complex and organic, the sequence has a way of coming back sooner or later to the statement with which we started. No doubt a series of simultaneous equations could describe the characteristics of the group more elegantly than words and sentences can, but we do not yet have the equations, and it may be that the equations cannot be set up before the verbal description has been made. If, then, we are limited to ordinary language, and if the tendency of ordinary language is to make the analysis of complex organic wholes sound circular, we propose in this book to relax, to fall in with this tendency of language rather than fight against it, and to analyze the relationship between group and environment as if it were a process having a beginning and an end, even though the point at which the process ends may be the point from which it started. Let us be candid and admit the method is clumsy, though it may be the best we have.

Our method has many analogies in the verbal description of physical processes. In describing a group, our problem is, for instance, a little like the problem of analyzing without the help of mathematics what happens to a set of interlinked springs when one of them is compressed. How shall a man describe in words what happens to a set of springs in a cushion or mattress when he sits on them? If he begins by sitting on any one spring and tries to trace from there the changes that take place in the rest of the springs, he will always find that the last spring in the series is linked back to the first and prevents the first from giving way under his weight as much as he thought it would. This, in fact, is the virtue of the set of springs.

Now let us use a more complicated analogy. We are all more or less familiar with the operation of the gasoline, or internal-combustion, engine. Let us ask ourselves how the operation of this engine was originally explained to us, or, better, how we should go about explaining it to someone else. We should, perhaps, begin by considering only one cylinder, instead of all the cylinders a real engine would have, and we should, just to get our exposition going, assume the cylinder and its contents to be in a certain state. We might, for instance, assume that the piston has reached the top of its stroke, and that the mixture of air and gasoline above the piston is hot and compressed. From then on, we should describe the operations of the engine as proceeding in sequence. A spark explodes the hot mixture; the explosion drives the piston downwards, and the moving piston transmits turning energy to the shaft. As the shaft turns, a system of cams opens valves in the cylinder head that admit a fresh mixture and allow the burnt gas to escape. The turning shaft also causes the piston to rise once more in the cylinder, compressing and heating the fresh mixture; and we are back where we started from, except that we have yet to account for the spark that set the whole process going. A generator is turned by the shaft, and this generator produces the electric current that explodes the mixture in the cylinder. And so the process goes on as long as the gasoline holds out.

The point we want to make is that although these operations in fact take place in a continuing cycle, we must nevertheless, language being what it is, describe them as if they took place in a sequence having a beginning and an end. Therefore we must assume a certain state of affairs at the beginning of our exposition, the existence of which we can account for only at the end. Thus we assume at the beginning the hot, compressed gas and the spark that ignites it, but we cannot account for the gas being in the cylinder, and being heated, compressed, and ignited, until we have reached the end of our explanation. At our convenience, we can choose any point in the cycle as the point from which our exposition starts, but, whatever point we choose, the problem of describing a cycle as a sequence of events still remains.

Now a group is obviously not an internal-combustion engine—our analogy is *only* an analogy—but we shall analyze the characteristics of the group as if we were dealing with some kind of ongoing circular process. No doubt this is not the only way in which the group could be analyzed, and no doubt, once we have finished making our analysis in this way, we shall be able to adopt a better way and throw away the old, just as one discards the scaffolding that has surrounded a house during construction. But having adopted this method of exposition, we encounter the same kind of difficulty we encountered with the gasoline engine. In describing the circular process in ordinary language, we are at liberty to begin at whatever point in the process we choose, but no matter what point that is, we must still assume at the beginning of our description the existence of certain conditions that we can account for only at the end. We choose to begin the analysis of the group with the external system, which we have defined as a set of relations among the members of the group that solves the problem: How shall the group survive in its environment? We do not say that the external system is the only possible solution to the problem. We do not say either that the group could do no worse or that it could do no better and still survive. We merely say that the external system is *one* solution of the survival problem. For us it is the equivalent of the assumption we made in describing the gasoline engine that the mixture was originally hot and compressed and that a spark was ready to explode it. Then, having assumed that some set of relations such as the external system must exist, we shall go on, as we did with the gasoline engine, and try to show why they do in fact exist or why the assumed relations are modified. The emphasis had better be on modification, for there is one great difference between describing the gasoline engine and describing the group. With the gasoline engine we show how the later events in the cycle create the very conditions we assumed in the beginning, whereas with the group we shall show that the later events in the cycle may modify the conditions we assumed in the beginning. We shall have to allow scope for emergent evolution.

Thus the external system first gives us a set of initial conditions from which our exposition can take its departure and then takes account of the fact that the adaptation of the group to its environment is partly determined by the nature of the environment, while leaving us free later to show how this adaptation is also in part determined by the internal development of the group.

To return from the general problem to the particular group we are studying at the moment, the first question we ask of the Bank Wiring group * is this: What does this group need to have in order to keep going in its particular environment? It needs motives (sentiments) on the part of its members, jobs (activities) for them to do, and some communication (interaction) between them. In other words, the members of the group must meet in some degree the plans of the Western Electric Company, and they must be adequately motivated to do so. We shall first take up each element of the external system separately and then in its mutual relations with the others. Until we have done this job we had better not try to define the external system any more rigorously. We must show, and not just say, what we mean.

SENTIMENT. The Bank Wiremen came to the Hawthorne Plant in the first instance with certain motives. The motives were generated by the circumstances of their lives outside the plant, but they were also part of their behavior within it. Some of the motives the men would have recognized: they were working for money, money to get food, to support a family, to buy and keep a car, to take a girl to the movies. These motives were the only ones the planners in the company took into account in devising the wage incentive scheme. Perhaps these were the only motives they thought they could successfully appeal to. At any rate, the men must have had many other reasons for working at Hawthorne that they

* The Bank Wiring group were employees of the Western Electric Company who were employed in connecting wires to banks of terminals used in telephone equipment. Some of these employees were placed in a seperate Observation Room where their behavior was intensively studied. This and other related investigations at the Hawthorne Plant of the Western Electric Company are reported in Fritz J. Roethlisberger and William J. Dickson, *Management and the Worker*, Cambridge, Mass.: Harvard University Press, 1939. Homans makes extensive use of the data reported about this group [Ed. note].

might not have admitted so easily: a feeling that a man was not a fully self-respecting citizen unless he had a job, a desire for the prestige outside the factory that comes from working up to a good job within it, the wish to belong to a company that was said to be a good place to work, and so on. These are all, by our definition, sentiments, and these were the motives for work that the men brought to the Bank Wiring Observation Room. Whatever other sentiments their association with their fellow workers might release in the men, these would still have had to be satisfied in some degree. Man does not live by bread alone, but he lives by bread at least. These sentiments were assets to the company in that they led to hard work; they were liabilities in that the company had to satisfy them. Sentiment as an element of co-operation always has this double aspect.

The sentiments we have been talking about are part of what is often called individual self-interest. Let us be clear as to what we mean by this famous phrase. In the first place, it may be that all motives are motives of self-interest in the sense that, given the situation in which he is placed, a man always tries to do as well as he can for himself. What he does may look to outsiders as if it were hurting rather than helping him; it may look impossibly altruistic rather than selfish, and yet modern psychology teaches us that, if we knew the full situation, both the social relationships and the psychological dynamics of the person concerned, we should find all his actions to be self-enhancing. But this is an aside; let us take up the question from another point of view. If we examine the motives we usually call individual self-interest, we shall find that they are, for the most part, neither individual nor selfish but that they are the product of group life and serve the ends of a whole group not just an individual. What we really mean by the celebrated phrase is that these motives are generated in a different group from the one we are concerned with at the moment. Thus from the point of view of the Bank Wiring Observation Room, the desire of a man to earn wages was individual self-interest, but from the point of view of his family it was altruism. Motives of self-interest in this sense are the ones that come into the external system. Sentiments, on the other hand, that are generated within the group we are concerned with at the moment include some of the ones

we call disinterested. Friendship between wiremen is an example. While sentiments of self-interest affected or influenced the behavior of the men in the room, they did not solely determine that behavior. If these sentiments had been alone decisive, output would perhaps have been higher. That both self-interest *and* something else are satisfied by group life is the truth that is hardest for the hard-boiled—and half-baked—person to see. As Mayo says, "If a number of individuals work together to achieve a common purpose, a harmony of interests will develop among them to which individual self-interest will be subordinated. This is a very different doctrine from the claim that individual self-interest is the solitary human motive." [6]

ACTIVITY. The activities of the group were in the first instance planned by the Western Electric Company engineers. Some of the men, with tools and fixtures, wired one kind of equipment; some of the men wired another. Some of the men soldered the connected wires into place on the terminals. Two men inspected the completed switches, both visually and with testing sets. A group chief supervised the whole. A trucker brought supplies into the room and took completed equipments out. Here were a number of different kinds of activity, ranging from manual work with tools through visual observation to activity that was largely verbal: supervision and direction. The activities were in theory different for different persons, and they were organized: each had a part in the production of a completed whole. Furthermore, the men were paid for their work in different amounts, according to a complicated system of group piecework. Note that the Western Electric organization tried to control more of the activities of the group than it was actually able to control. Nevertheless, it did to a very large extent settle what the men should do.

INTERACTION. In the same way, observing the behavior of the men, one could have mapped out a scheme of interaction among them, in abstraction from their sentiments and their activities, and one could have recognized that a part of the scheme was set by the company.

[6] E. Mayo, *The Political Problem of Industrial Civilization*, 21.

There were the necessary interactions between a solderman and the three wiremen he worked for, between an inspector and the wiremen and soldermen whose work he passed judgment on, between the group chief and all the men in the room. Then there were the almost inevitable interactions between the men who were thrown together by the physical geography of the room, especially between the wiremen and soldermen who worked together, some at the front, some in the middle, and some at the back of the room. Finally, the mere fact that all the men were together in a single room tended to increase interaction between each member of the group and every other.

PAIR RELATIONSHIPS. So far we have been doing with the description of the Bank Wiring Observation Room no more than we did . . . with the description of the Irish countryman's family. We have, to be sure, limited ourselves to that part of group behavior that is under the direct influence of the environment, but within this field what we have been doing is the same. We have been making a crude analysis, breaking the behavior of the men down into its elements of sentiment, activity, and interaction. We shall now take a new step in the application of our method, the first step in synthesis. What has been separated must be put together again. We shall study the relationships of mutual dependence among sentiment, activity, and interaction in the external system. More particularly, we shall study the relationships between pairs of elements, of which there are, logically, three: sentiment-activity, activity-interaction, and interaction-sentiment.

There is nothing complicated about the idea of mutual dependence. Just the same, we had better say what we mean by it, as it will come into our thinking over and over again. In physics, Boyle's law states that the volume of a gas in an enclosed space varies inversely with the pressure upon it. The greater the pressure, the smaller the volume of the gas. This statement, which is usually put in the form of an equation, expresses a relationship of mutual dependence, mutual because if either pressure or volume changes, the other variable will change too. If pressure is increased, volume will decrease. But if we choose to begin with volume instead of pressure, we say that if volume increases, pressure must decrease. This kind of relationship is most elegantly expressed in an equation, but in the field of sociology we should not pretend to use equations until we have data that are thoroughly quantitive. Instead we shall have to describe this kind of relationship in ordinary language, and here we are at once in trouble, because this is just the kind of relationship that ordinary language— at least any of the Western languages—is least well equipped to describe. Ordinary language, with its subjects and predicates, is geared to handling only one independent factor and one dependent factor at a time: someone is always doing something to somebody. Cause-and-effect thinking, rather than mutual-dependence thinking, is built into speech. Yet a situation that can accurately be described in cause-and-effect terms is just the kind that is encountered least often in sociology. Here the cause produces an effect, but the effect reacts upon the cause. In these circumstances, the very first effort to use ordinary language shows how crude a tool it is. Yet we shall do what we can with it, as we have nothing else. We may, for instance, say that an increase in the complexity of the scheme of activity in the external system will bring about an increase in the complexity of the scheme of interaction, but that the reverse is also true. The two are mutually dependent.

One other point should be made but not elaborated at this time. According to Boyle's law, the volume of a gas in an enclosed space varies inversely as the pressure put upon it only if the temperature is held constant during the process. If the temperature does vary, the relationship between volume and pressure will not have the simple form stated by the law. When we study the mutual dependence of two variables, we must somehow take account of the effect on these two of the other variables that enter the system. In the same way, when we make a statement about the mutual dependence of, for instance, interaction and activity, we must never forget that sentiment also comes into the system and may effect the relationships described. It is never enough to say that the relationship holds good "other things being equal." We must try to say what these other things are, and where they are "equal." This raises immense problems, which we shall not try to cope with at this time, if indeed we can ever cope with them adequately in social science.

MUTUAL DEPENDENCE OF SENTIMENT AND ACTIVITY. When we are thinking of the relationship of mutual dependence between sentiment and activity, we speak of sentiments as motives or drives. In the simplest form of the relationship, a motive gives rise to activity, and once the activity is successfully completed, the motive disappears. A man feels hungry; he gets something to eat and his hunger disappears. If his activity does not result in his getting something to eat, new sentiments, which we call frustration will be added to his original hunger, and we say that the activity was unrewarding or even positively punishing. He may then try a new one; if it ends in his getting something to eat, his hunger is allayed, and he will tend to repeat the activity the next time he feels hungry. We now say that the activity is rewarding, but do we mean anything more by this word that we saw the man eat the food and repeat the activity leading to it?

This is the relationship at its simplest. It is much more complicated when the motive is not something like hunger but something like a man's fear that he will be hungry in the future. Suppose that a man is afraid he will be hungry in the future if he does not now start plowing his field and doing other tasks in co-operation with other men that will lead in the end to loaves of bread on his table. The man's hunger is allayed when he gets food, but the fear does not necessarily disappear when the appropriate activities are carried out. Future hunger is still a threat. In these circumstances, *both motives and associated activities persist, both continuously recreated, but if either side of the relationship is changed, the other will be affected.* Returning to our example, we can say that, if for any reason the man is less afraid he will be hungry, he may not work so hard. And if, on the other hand, he finds some new set of activities that will yield more food than the old, he may become less fearful. The relationship between motive and activity is mutual.

This relationship seems to hold good whether the activity in question is obviously and directly useful or, like magic, takes the place of a useful activity that is unknown or impossible. In the absence of anything better to do, men must find even magic rewarding. The relationship also seems to hold good both for the sentiments we share with all men, such as fear, hunger, thirst, cold, and the like, and for the sentiments generated in a particular social situation, such as the need to be paid wages. Note how in the Bank Wiring Observation Room the company's wage incentive plan tried to establish a particularly close link between one sentiment (the desire for money) and one set of activities (production). That the plan did not altogether achieve its intended results does not mean that this link was unimportant. It means that other sentiments besides the need for money affected output. It is clear, for instance, that the sentiments of Green * . . . — "I'd like a job reading"—, sentiments that presumably were generated by his whole past history and experience in groups outside the plant, were among the forces making his output the lowest in the room. If the interviews with the workers had been reported more fully, we should know much more about the outside influences on the motives of the men.

We need not go further into the mutual dependence of sentiment and activity. After all, most of the science of psychology, and particularly that part called "learning theory," is devoted to studying it, and if we tried to compete with psychology our hopeless inadequacy in that field would be revealed even more clearly than it is already. All we can do is show how some of the problems studied by psychology fit into a general scheme for analyzing group behavior. Remember also that we are now considering only the sentiments that come into the external system. The sentiments of the internal system are rather different in kind, though their mutual dependence with activities is the same as that we have just described.

MUTUAL DEPENDENCE OF ACTIVITY AND INTERACTION. In the external system, the relationship of mutual dependence between activity and interaction links the division of labor with the scheme of communication in the group. In the Bank Wiring Observation Room, the total job of turning out completed equipments was divided into a series of separate activities: wiring, soldering, inspection, trucking, and, not least in importance, supervision. Each separate activity was assigned to a different individual or subgroup, and in many of the activities each unit of work—for instance, completing a single

* Green was one of the employees in the Bank Wiring Observation Room [Ed. note].

level of connections—took a certain length of time. But what has been broken up must be put together again. If finished equipments were to be turned out, interaction had to take place in a certain scheme between the men doing the different jobs.

Thus when a wireman had completed a level on one equipment he moved over to a second one, and that act was the signal for the solderman to begin soldering in place the connections of the first terminal. The wireman had interacted with the solderman: remember that by our definition interaction takes place when the action of one man sets off the action of another. And note that, in this instance, the wireman originated interaction with the solderman: he gave the signal to which the other responded. We can without danger call interaction communication provided we remember that communication is not necessarily verbal. There was no need for words to pass between wireman and solderman in order that communication between them should be effective. In the same way, the solderman's completion of his part of the task was the signal for the inspector to go to work, and if he discovered any defect, he would initiate interaction, almost necessarily verbal this time, with the workman responsible. Thus a continuous process of interaction brought together the separate activities that went into the completion of the product. Finally, if one of the company's regulations was too flagrantly violated, or the process of co-ordination failed at any point, the problem would come to the group chief's attention. Someone would bring the matter up to him, or he himself would initiate interaction to restore the established order.

Generalizing from the Bank Wiring Observation Room, we can say, then, that any division, among the members of a group, of the partial activities that go into the completion of some total activity implies a scheme of interaction among the persons concerned, and that *if the scheme of activities is changed, the scheme of interaction will, in general, change also, and vice versa.* The two are mutually dependent. Sometimes, and this is perhaps the more common situation, a man who is organizing a piece of work begins by dividing it up into separate activities, and then makes the scheme of interaction conform to his division. That is, he treats the scheme of activity as the independent or governing factor. Thus the

management of a plant may decide how an operation shall be divided among the workers and then devise an appropriate method of co-ordination. But this presupposes that an appropriate method of co-ordination can be put into effect, and the presupposition may be wrong. That is, the scheme of interaction may sometimes be the governing factor. Surely certain forms of the division of labor among the members of an industrial group were prohibitively expensive in the days before the conveyor belt was invented and made new schemes of interaction possible. In most circumstances, *both* factors are important.[7]

The division of labor makes the cost of work less in human effort or money. For this reason all societies have gone some distance in making their members specialists. From Adam Smith to Henry Taylor the uncriticized assumption was apt to be that the further the division was carried, the greater were the savings effected, that the further a job like shoemaking was broken down into its component specialties, and each assigned to a workman who did nothing else, the less would be the cost of making the shoe. Now we have begun to understand that the division of labor, like any other process, has its point of diminishing returns. Peter Drucker has shown how, in World War II and in some kinds of industrial work where conventional assembly lines could not be set up, the assigning of all the component specialties of any one job to one person or a group of persons, rather than to a number of separate individuals, turned out to be a cheaper way of manufacturing than any other.[8] Why the division of labor may reach a point of diminishing returns should be clear from our analysis. The division of labor is not something in itself; it always implies a scheme of interaction by which the different divided activities are co-ordinated. The indirect costs of setting up this scheme, including the costs that arise if supervision is inadequate, may offset the direct savings from specialization.

THE PYRAMID OF INTERACTION. What we said two paragraphs ago we must now take back in part. It is not universally true that as the

---

[7] In this and the following discussion, much reliance is placed on C. I. Barnard, *The Functions of the Executive*, ch. VIII.

[8] P. F. Drucker, "The Way to Industrial Peace," *Harper's Magazine*, Vol. 193 (Nov., 1946), 390.

scheme of activity changes the scheme of inter-action will change too. It is not true when the activity in question is supervision or leadership: the process by which departures from a given plan of co-operation are avoided or new plans introduced. In groups that differ greatly in the activities they carry on, the schemes of inter-action between leaders of different levels ·and their followers tend nevertheless to be strik-ingly similar. Let us see what this means by taking up the problem of the *span of control*, as organization experts call it: How many men can be supervised by a single leader? When the activities of a group are of such a kind that they can be co-ordinated largely through one-way interaction from the leader to the follow-ers, then the leader can supervise a rather large number of persons. An example is the con-ductor of a symphony orchestra, who may direct as many as a hundred men. But in gen-eral the interaction must be two-way: the leader gives orders, information, and exhorta-tion to his followers, but they must also supply him with information about themselves and the situation they face. In these circumstances the span of control becomes much smaller. It is significant how often a group of between eight and a dozen persons crops up under the super-vision of a single leader in organizations of many different kinds. The old-fashioned squad in the army is an example. And since the same kind of considerations govern the relations be-tween the leaders of the first level and their own leaders, and so on for higher and higher leaders in groups of larger and larger size, it is easy to see how the scheme of interaction, especially in big organizations, piles up into its characteristic pyramidical, or hierarchical, form. The leader-in-chief appears at the apex of the pyramid, working with a small group of lesser leaders; each lesser leader, level by level, works with his own small group of lead-ers of still lower rank, until finally at the broad base the rank and file are reached.

No matter what activities an organization carries on, this characteristic form of the inter-action scheme tends to appear; it appears in the Catholic Church as surely as it does in an industrial firm or an army. Therefore we must modify our earlier rule and say that *whatever changes occur in the scheme of activities of a group, the scheme of interaction between the leaders of various levels and their followers tends to keep the same general pyramidical*

form. Yet the modification is more apparent than real. If the conflict between the two rules distresses us, we can readily reconcile them. The pyramid scheme of interaction seems to make possible the supervision of the activities of a large number of persons, through two-way interaction between them and leaders of different levels. Whenever, therefore, this par-ticular activity, supervision, remains largely the same from organization to organization, then the scheme of interaction—the pyramid—through which supervision is exercised remains largely the same too. Our rule stated that if the scheme of activity changed, the scheme of interaction changed too. But the rule also implies that if the activity does not change—and the job of supervision is much the same from group to group—the interaction does not change either. The first rule holds after all, the second rule being merely one of its special cases.

The relation between the scheme of activities and the scheme of interaction in an organiza-tion is usually represented by the familiar organization chart, which shows the organiza-tion divided into departments and subdepart-ments, the various officers and subofficers oc-cupying boxes, connected by lines to show which persons are subordinate to what other ones. Every such chart is too neat; it tells what the channels of interaction ought to be but not always what they are. The pyramid-type chart is particularly misleading because it shows only the interaction between superiors and subordinates, the kind of interaction that we shall call, following Barnard, *scalar*.[9] It does not show the interaction that goes on between two or more persons at about the same level of the organization, for instance, between two department heads or, in the Bank Wiring Room, between a wireman and an inspector. This kind of interaction we shall call *lateral* interaction, though we must remem-ber there are borderline cases where the dis-tinction between scalar and lateral interaction disappears. The conventional organization chart represents the scalar but not the lateral interaction. If it were not for the unhappy association with predatory spiders, the facts would be much better represented by a web, the top leader at the center, spokes radiating

[9] C. I. Barnard, *Organization and Management*, 150.

from him, and concentric circles linking the spokes. Interaction takes place along the concentric circles as well as along the spokes. But even the web is too neat a picture.

It is a mistake to think of the pyramid—or the web—scheme of interaction as always created by conscious planning. It is so created in only a few instances, for example, the large formal organizations of modern Western society, and these, in their origins, modeled themselves on previously existing patterns. The pyramid occurs not only where it is planned, as in the Western Electric Company, but also where it is not planned, as in a street gang or primitive tribe. Sometimes the pyramid is imposed on a group, as supervision was imposed on the Bank Wiremen; sometimes, as we shall see, a group spontaneously creates its own pyramid. Sometimes a group, if it is to operate successfully on the environment, needs the pyramid; sometimes a group does not need the pyramid but creates it anyhow. In any event, the fact that a pyramid of interaction may be a practical necessity of effective operations on the environment is no guarantee that the pyramid will appear. As we mentioned earlier, the possiblility of coincidence between the practically necessary and the spontaneously produced is one of the fascinating discoveries that comes from the study of groups as of other organisms, but we shall never explain the existence of the pyramid of interaction or any other such item of group behavior by pointing out that it helps the group to survive in an environment. Even if we assume for the moment that it does help the group to survive, we shall sooner or later go on to examine in detail the mechanisms by which the item in question is produced. We shall study what the philosophers call efficient, rather than final, causes. But we are again running ahead of our argument. The immediate point is that the principles of organization are universal; they are not an invention of the Prussian general staff or of American big business.

The relationship between the scheme of activities and the scheme of interaction is the problem of *organization*, in the narrow sense of that word. When the leaders of military, industrial, and other concerns speak of organization, this is what they mean. For us the word has a much broader meaning, but the narrow one will do no harm so long as we know what it is. Since our concern is with the small group,

we had better not try to attain the higher reaches of organization theory, which apply only to large concerns. But one last point should be made. The complexity of organization does not end with the appearance of the hierarchy of leadership. In big concerns, several different hierarchies arise and intersect one another. The pyramid, from being two-dimensional, becomes three- and multi-dimensional, with several different chains of interaction between the followers and the upper leaders. In the jargon of the experts, a line-and-staff form of organization develops, and we shall have something to say about it in a later chapter, where the subject comes in naturally. For the moment we can summarize in the words of Eliot Chapple and Carleton Coon:

> The coordination needed in any complex technique is impossible without interaction. As we have seen, most complex techniques involve the activities of more than one person, and, in fact, where people practice a number of complex techniques, extensive interactions must take place to coordinate the work of manufacturing, to secure raw materials, and to exchange the goods produced. In other words, the growth of complexity in technical processes goes hand in hand with an increase in the amount of interaction and in the complexity of the interaction pattern.[10]

CONCLUSION. Logically, of course, a third relationship of mutual dependence exists: the mutual dependence of interaction and sentiment, but we shall choose to consider this a part of the internal system, to which we turn in the next chapter. The two aspects of group life that we call the external and the internal sysems are continuous with one another. The line between them can be drawn where we choose, arbitrarily, and we choose to draw it here. The only reason for drawing a line at all is to save words: we now can talk about the external system without repeating everything we have said in this chapter.

What goes into the external system is what we have shown goes in: the best definition is a process of pointing. If we must have a definition in words, we can say that the mutual dependence between the work done in a group

[10] E. D. Chapple and C. S. Coon, *Principles of Anthropology*, 250.

and the motives for work, between the division of labor and the scheme of interaction, so far as these relationships meet the condition that the group survives in an environment—this we shall regularly speak of as the external system. But remember that when we talk of a group's survival in an environment we always deceive ourselves to some degree. The group is not passive before the environment; it reacts. It even defines what its environment shall be. Its purposes make different aspects of the environment important. The relationship between group and environment is never a one-way matter. But we are weak creatures, and our tools of language and analysis are soft. We ought to say everything at once, yet in our desperation we find we have to start somewhere. We have chosen to begin with the environment and its influence on the group. We shall then show how the group, on the foundation of the relationships thus established, elaborates further tendencies of its own, which react so as to modify the adaptation to the environment. This again is not the truth, but a manner of speaking. Yet it is forced on us. What we need now is a willing and provisional suspension of disbelief. Until we have said everything, we shall have said nothing. We shall have to keep many balls in the air at the same time. Regard all our statements as partial truths until the last word and the last modification are in.

The Internal System

Long ago Arisotle wrote: "The city comes into existence in order that men may live; it persists that they may live well." [11] For Aristotle the city meant the small Greek city-state, such as Athens, which was much closer to the small group we are studying in this book than to the mass cities of modern times. At least the members of the governing class could have some direct contact with one another. For Aristotle the city was also the most familiar and important of organized human groups, and much that he says about it, including the remark just quoted, applies to all human groups. Elton Mayo used to make Aristotle's point in different language. He said that there is a tendency for any group of men to complicate

[11] *Politics*, I, 1, 1252b12.

the conditions of their life, to make the conditions more interesting, and that any circumstances interfering with the complication were felt emotionally as frustration. Chester Barnard's statement is still more elaborate.

> When the individual has become associated with a cooperative enterprise he has accepted a position of contact with others similarly associated. From this contact there must arise interactions between these persons individually, and these interactions are social. It may be, and often is, true that these interactions are not a purpose or object either of the cooperative systems or of the individuals participating in them. They nevertheless *cannot be avoided*. Hence, though not sought, such interactions are consequences of cooperation, and constitute one set of social factors involved in cooperation. These factors operate on the individuals affected; and, in conjunction with other factors, become incorporated in their mental and emotional characters. This is an effect which makes them significant. Hence, cooperation compels changes in the motives of individuals which otherwise would not take place. So far as these changes are in a direction favorable to the cooperative system they are resources to it. So far as they are in a direction unfavorable to cooperation, they are detriments to it or limitations of it. [12]

THE ELABORATION OF GROUP BEHAVIOR. Each of these men—Aristotle, Mayo, Barnard—is talking about the same phenomenon. When a number of persons have come together to form a group, their behavior never holds to its first pattern. Social life is never wholly utilitarian: it elaborates itself, complicates itself, beyond the demands of the original situation. The elaboration brings changes in the motives of individuals. This is the point that Barnard stressed especially; and the change in the attitudes of persons, brought about by their membership in groups, is perhaps the central topic of social psychology. But the elaboration also means changes in their activities and inter-

[12] Reprinted by permission of the publishers from Chester Irving Barnard, *The Functions of the Executive*, Cambridge, Mass.: Harvard University Press, 1938, p. 40. See also pp. 45, 52, 120, 286.

actions—changes, in fact, in the organization of the group as a whole.

This elaboration is the subject of the present chapter and the one following. In the last chapter we studied the *external system*—the behavior of a group so far as that behavior represents one possible answer to the question: How does the group survive in its particular environment? In the present chapter we shall begin the study of the *internal system*—the elaboration of group behavior that simultaneously arises out of the external system and reacts upon it. We call the system "internal" because it is not directly conditioned by the environment, and we speak of it as an "elaboration" because it includes forms of behavior not included under the heading of the external system. We shall not go far wrong if, for the moment, we think of the external system as group behavior that enables the group to survive in its environment and think of the internal system as group behavior that is an expression of the sentiments towards one another developed by the members of the group in the course of their life together.

In analyzing the internal system, we shall, as before, use the Bank Wiring Observation Room to illustrate our points, and we shall do so according to a definite plan. In the present chapter we shall take up the internal system as exemplified in the behavior of the group as a whole; in the next chapter we shall take it up as exemplified in the division of the group into cliques. In Chapter 3 we saw that the group was in some sense a unit and in some sense also a grouping of sub-units.

We shall again work with the three main elements of group behavior: activity, sentiment, and interaction, but in describing the internal system we shall find that these elements do not take quite the same form they do in the external system. Instead of the motives for getting a job, we shall have to deal with sentiments developed on the job, such as liking or disliking for other persons, approval or disapproval of the things other persons do. Instead of activities demanded by the job, we shall have to deal with activities spontaneously evolved that serve to express the attitudes of persons toward one another. And instead of interactions required for the co-ordination of practical activities, we shall have to deal with interaction elaborated socially—for fun, so to speak. We call the internal system a system, just as we called the external system one, because in it all three of the elements of social behavior are mutually dependent, and we shall, as before, take account of the mutual dependence by considering three pair relations: interaction-sentiment, sentiment-activity, and activity-interaction.

MUTUAL DEPENDENCE OF INTERACTION AND SENTIMENT. By the very circumstances in which they were placed, working together in the same room, the Bank Wiremen almost inevitably interacted with one another. They were, as we often say, thrown together. In our description of the external system, we did not go beyond statements like this, but the internal system takes up where the other leaves off. Interaction in the external system gives rise to sentiments that we treat as part of the internal system because they are not brought into the group by its members but released in the members by their life in the group. Specifically the Bank Wiremen, interacting with one another frequently, also became friendly. No doubt there were social isolates in the group, like Capek * and Mazmanian,* and no doubt the specially close friends were also members of the same clique, but it is all too easy in emphasizing the cliques and the anti-social individuals to lose sight of the wide-spread friendliness within the group as a whole. The relationship between association and friendliness is one of those commonly observed facts that we use all the time as a guide for action in practical affairs but seldom make an explicit hypothesis of sociology. We assume that if only we can "get people together," they will like one another and work together better. We also assume that the relationship between interaction and sentiment works in the other direction. If it is true that we often come to like the persons with whom we interact, it is also true that we are prepared to interact with persons we already like. That is, interaction and this particular kind of sentiment are mutually dependent.

Now let us try to make the hypothesis a little more explicit. We can begin by saying that *persons who interact frequently with one another tend to like one another.* But this does

* Members of the Bank Wiring group about whom sociometric data were reported by Roethlisberger and Dickson, *op. cit.* [Ed. note.]

not do justice to the quantitative and relative aspects of the relationship. Our words "like" and "dislike," "friendship" and "antagonism," are misleading. They make us think that there are only two values on the scale. We should think instead of a continuous gradation from hatred to love, with our usual words for the sentiments representing many different values on the scale. And even if we think in these terms, we are still in difficulties. When we say that Hasulak * liked Steinhardt * and disliked Mueller,* we may only mean that he liked Steinhardt more than he liked Mueller. If forced to choose between Mueller and some outsider as a companion, he might have found that he liked Mueller well enough. All our words for liking and disliking have relative and not absolute values. We cannot say how much Hasulak liked the men he knew, unless we have determined a zero point on the scale, a point, perhaps, where one man is indifferent, neither friendly nor hostile, to another. Setting up such a point and measuring the strength of sentiment with reference to it is not an easy task, as the social psychologists who study attitudes know, and we shall not undertake it here. Instead we shall allow for the quantitative aspect of sentiment and the other elements of social behavior by stating some of our hypotheses in differential form; for instance, by stating what small change will take place in the strength of sentiment if there is a small change in the frequency of interaction. Thus we can restate our original hypothesis as follows: *If the frequency of interaction between two or more persons increases, the degree of their liking for one another will increase, and vice versa.* This kind of hypothesis takes account of the fact that some sentiments form a scale without raising the question where the zero point on the scale lies. We should probably state all our later hypotheses in differential form, but we shall not in fact be tediously careful to do so.

But our hypothesis still does not take adequate account of the facts of group behavior. It does not take account of group elaboration or development. For instance, it is not hard to think of the original relationships among the Bank Wiremen being those of the

external system. The members of the group began by being thrown together in a certain room and working on certain jobs. But obviously the observed behavior of the Bank Wiremen went far beyond the original plan of work set up by the company. How shall we describe the process of growth and development? We can at least reformulate our hypothesis as follows: *If the interactions between the members of a group are frequent in the external system, sentiments of liking will grow up between them, and these sentiments will lead in turn to further interactions, over and above the interactions of the external system.* The interactions between Bank Wiremen were in fact more frequent than the setup of work required. It is not just that favorable sentiments increase as interaction increases, but that these sentiments then boost interaction still further. Our theory is that through processes like these a social system builds up or elaborates itself. But how far can the elaboration go? Clearly it cannot go on indefinitely; there must be forces bringing it to a halt; for one thing, the limitations of time will prevent the frequency of interaction from going beyond a certain level. But what is the level and what determines it? We raise these questions without being able to answer them.

A further complication can now be brought in. It was observed that the Bank Wiremen, after a time in the Observation Room, found themselves to some degree antagonistic toward the men remaining behind in the department, and that they expressed their antagonism in claims that the men in the department were in various small matters discriminating against them. In this instance, then, as in so many others, the liking of friends within a group carries with it some dislike of outsiders. The greater the inward solidarity, the greater the outward hostility. As before, this hypothesis is familiar. It is almost the principle of organization in some primitive tribes. A dictator may try to use it, believing that if he can cut down his subjects' interaction with, and inflame their distrust of, foreigners, he can maintain his own power and a primitive unity in his nation. Stated more precisely, the hypothesis is that *a decrease in the frequency of interaction between the members of a group and outsiders, accompanied by an increase in the strength of their negative sentiments toward outsiders, will increase the frequency of*

---

* Members of the Bank Wiring group about whom sociometric data were reported by Roethlisberger and Dickson, *op. cit.* [Ed. note.]

interaction and the strength of positive sentiments among the members of the group, and vice versa. This hypothesis is in turn a special case of a more general one, which we shall consider later and which may be stated as follows: *the nature of the relationships between the individuals A, B, C, . . . is always determined in part by the relationships between each one of them and other individuals M, N, O, . . .* In the present case, A, B, C, etc., are members of a particular group; M, N, O, etc., are outsiders, and we are considering, in the relationships between these persons, only the elements of interaction and sentiment. . . .

MUTUAL DEPENDENCE OF SENTIMENT AND ACTIVITY. In the Bank Wiring Observation Room group as a whole, we can see the mutual dependence of sentiment and activity most easily in the wide web of helping. There were few occasions when helping another man was required by the necessities of the work—indeed it was forbidden by the company; yet it took place just the same, and many of the men testified that helping and being helped made them feel better. Everyone took part in helping; it was not confined, as were some other activities, to soldering units. In fact it was one of the activities that united the whole group instead of dividing it into cliques, though there were some men, like Taylor, who were helped more than others. On the basis of the Bank Wiring Room, we can, therefore, state the hypothesis that *persons who feel sentiments of liking for one another will express those sentiments in activities over and above the activities of the external system, and these activities may further strengthen the sentiments of liking.* In the same way persons who dislike one another will express their disliking in activity, and the activity will increase the disliking. The circle may be vicious as well as beneficent. Stating the relationship

quantitatively, we can expect that any change in the sentiments of persons for one another will be followed by a change in the activities in which they express those sentiments. And the reverse will also be true: any change in the expressive activities—for instance, in the amount of help given—will be followed by a change in the sentiments of liking.

All sentiments seeks expression in action, and if the action is rewarding it will be repeated. The mechanism we are describing here is universal; it applies to the external system as much as it does to the internal. But in the external system the sentiments being expressed are those a person brings to the group from his life outside the group, whereas in the internal system the sentiments—favorable or unfavorable attitudes toward other members of the group—are generated or released in a person by his experience within the group. The activities in which the latter sentiments find expression may be of many kinds. In the Bank Wiring Room they took the form of mutual help. In other groups we shall see other ways of exchanging gifts and favors, and we shall see the appearance of new co-operative activities undertaken by the group as a whole.

MUTUAL DEPENDENCE OF ACTIVITY AND INTERACTION. The intimate relation between activity and interaction is obvious, here as in the external system. In fact it takes an uncomfortable effort of mind to separate them only to put them together again. In the Bank Wiring Room an activity like helping clearly implied interaction between the persons who helped one another and, moreover, an increase of interaction beyond what the wiring job demanded. The process is general. A great deal of social activity—dances, parties—is enjoyed less for the sake of the activity itself, which may be trivial, than for the possibilities of social interaction it affords.

Sociometrically Selected Work Teams
Increase Production

RAYMOND H. VAN ZELST

A great deal of the psychological literature has been devoted to the study of intra-group relations and their effect upon group morale and productivity. However, in spite of the research findings concerned with this interesting facet of social psychology a specific application of a well-known technique has been, perhaps, most grievously neglected. The technique referred to is, of course, the sociometric principles introduced by Moreno [1] which have been utilized so successfully by Jenkins [2] and by Jennings,[3] among others, in the study of leadership and interpersonal relations.

The purpose of sociometry is, perhaps, defined most aptly by Moreno [4] as, "A process of classification, which is calculated to bring individuals together who are capable of harmonious interpersonal relationships, and so create a social group which can function at the maximum efficiency and with a minimum of disruptive tendencies and processes."

The technique then in the light of the above statement would seem to be ideally suited for the structuring of work groups on the basis of the workers' choice of work partners.

In a previous study [5] the author tested the hypothesis that sociometrically arranged work teams would be significantly superior in both quantity and quality of output and also maintain a higher standard of group morale. Comparisons made during a three month experimental period showed the sociometric group to decidedly outperform the matched control group in job performance and also to report a greater degree of satisfaction with their job.

It is the purpose of this research to pursue further the findings of the above cited experiment in order to determine the genuineness of the observed differences and to explore the operational function of the application of "buddy-work-teams" in industry. Somewhat similar comparisons of performance were made throughout the 11 month duration of this construction project.

THE SUBJECTS AND THEIR OCCUPATIONS. The subjects used in this study were from building trades in the Chicago area. They comprised two work groups of carpenters and bricklayers composed originally of 38 and 36 members respectively. The workers had been together on the same job for an average of at least five months, and, so, were well acquainted with each other's personality and skill. The formulation of such opinions was facilitated by a considerable amount of fluctuation of work partner assignments previous to the experiment and, also, by the custom of members of the groups to meet with their specific group in an unfinished home to eat lunch and talk.

The workers were all union members and

From *Personnel Psychology*, Vol. 5, 1952, pp. 175–185. Reprinted with permission of the publisher and author. The footnotes have been adjusted for this printing.
[1] J. L. Moreno, *Who Shall Survive?* Washington, D.C.: Nervous and Mental Disease Publishing Company, 1937.
[2] J. G. Jenkins, *The Nominating Technique: Its Uses and Limitations.* Paper delivered Eastern Psychological Association annual meeting, Atlantic City: April, 1947.
[3] H. H. Jennings, *Leadership and Isolation.* New York: Longmans, Green, 1947.
[4] Moreno, op. cit., p. 11.

[5] Raymond H. Van Zelst, Validation of a Sociometric Regrouping. *J. Abnor. Soc. Psychol.* (to be published).

had a minimum of seven years experience in their trade. None of the subjects was employed in a supervisory capacity. The occupations in which they were engaged were of a highly skilled nature and came under a fixed wage standard rigidly maintained by both managements and union through mutual agreement. Their work was transitory in nature. The worker was seldom employed by the same company for longer than a six to nine month period.

The construction job upon which these groups were employed was a large housing project separated into two parts by a highway running through its center—one group working on each side of the thoroughfare. The homes were constructed in identical rows of eight—beginning on the highway and moving away.

METHODOLOGY. Prior to the beginning of the present experiment each worker was requested to nominate in order of preference three of his co-workers as his choice of work partner. The procedure used followed the three points of methodological significance as outlined by Young [6] for the restructuring of groups. "First, every individual is included as a center of affective response. Second, the choice of the subject is motivated by some wish or practical consideration. Third, the choice of the subject is always relative to some criterion."

The workers of the two groups were assembled on successive days prior to the beginning of the work day and were instructed as follows:

> You are now working with a partner who was not chosen by you, nor were you chosen by him. You are now given the opportunity to choose the persons with whom you would most like to work. You can choose any of the individuals in your own group. Write down your first choice; then your second and third choices, in order. Look around and make up your mind. Remember that one of the persons you choose now will probably be assigned as your work partner.

In the regrouping, workers were first arranged into mutual choice teams of two. Then,

in view of the occasional necessity for larger work teams for certain duties, compatible patterns for the fusion of two teams into a single group were worked out—also on the basis of co-worker choices. It was not deemed necessary in the opinion of the foremen and supervisor to go beyond this number since the jobs to be performed would not require larger groups. Twenty-two of the workers received their first choice as partners. Twenty-eight received their second and 16 their third. Eight of the workers were isolates.

In the formation of work teams isolates were paired until they could be successfully incorporated into a mutual choice group. Treatment of isolates and of newly-hired workers leading to their successful inclusion into the group will be discussed in detail in a forthcoming article. It was at no time necessary to cross skill lines and pair off a skilled worker with a comparatively unskilled partner in order to effect a mutually acceptable team. Perhaps skill level was one of the criteria used by the subjects in selecting their work partner.

Assignment of the newly formed teams was made two days after the collection of choices. The appointments were made by the foremen of the groups when they announced the work assignments of the day. This in no way violated previous procedures of work duty assignments. The structure put into effect was regarded as optimum by the author, supervisor and foremen.

In order to ensure the satisfactory alignment of workers into teams periodic checks of stability of choices were made. In all cases care was taken to leave undisturbed satisfactory worker groups. Instructions and methodology were identical with the above cited procedure save for a slight alteration of instructions to make them more amenable to the situation.

The checks as to stability of co-worker choices revealed only one noteworthy fluctuation which occurred in the groups assigned on the basis of third choice. In this group four incidences of voluntary change in co-worker partner choice and six changes for the incorporation of isolates and newly-hired individuals were made. The group structured on the basis of second choices had one voluntary alteration, while the first choice group had none. The former had two imposed alterations and the latter none. Such alterations as occurred voluntarily among the groups may be ac-

[6] P. T. Young, Motivation, Feeling and Emotion. In T. E. Andrews (ed.), *Methods of Psychology*. New York: John Wiley and Sons, 1948, p. 688.

counted for by the introduction of new choice possibilities in the form of the newly-hired employees, and by the possible reformulation of desirability opinions as to present work partner.

One-half of the changes made, both voluntary and imposed, occurred during the first two month period, while the remaining one-half was rather evenly distributed throughout the duration of the experiment. No disrupting incidences occurred during the course of the project.

THE CRITERIA. In order to assess the effectiveness of the sociometric procedures used, comparisons were made utilizing actual cost of construction indices, engineers' estimates of these costs (corrected for any wage or materials cost increase) made for the purpose of submitting a contractor's bid, and monthly-compiled turnover records.

Construction costs were made available from cost account records and were broken down into labor costs and materials costs, based upon a row of units basis (eight houses per row). The comparisons made were between the 11 month production record of the sociometric group and engineers' estimate of cost and with the groups' production record (nine months) prior to restructuring.

No actual monetary results will be reported here because of the company's desire for anonymity of identity and of cost figures. Instead the indices of labor cost and materials

cost used were arrived at by taking actual expenses in dollars and dividing through by a constant to arrive at the particular index used.

To determine if possible changes in the over-all skill level of the groups brought about by the turnover of employees and the hiring of new individuals might contaminate the criterion, several preliminary comparisons were made between pre-sociometric group output. In order to facilitate the proposed comparisons the 24 rows of units completed during the nine-month pre-experimental period were divided into six periods of four rows of units each to form a matrix. Critical ratios between labor costs and between materials costs were computed between the various cells. These results are shown in Table 1.

The number of employees leaving during the periods were as follows: 2, 4, 4, 6, 6, 7. The number of workers hired were 4, 6, 2, 4, 6, 6. The fact that a difference existed in the number of employees working from one period to the next is irrelevant since the criteria used is unaffected by the size of the work force. Table 1 shows none of the critical ratios to be significant.

The only factors which could conceivably have affected the productivity of these groups and so have contaminated the criteria used are changes in management practices, and there were none, changes in group level of skill, and changes in the weather. Since none of the critical ratios computed are significant it is reasonable to conclude that overall group pro-

Table 1. Critical Ratio Matrix Comparing Period Performance of Pre-experimental Group Productivity on Labor Costs (Lower Half of Matrix) and Materials Costs (Upper Half of Matrix)

LABOR COST PERIOD		I	II	III	IV	V	VI	MATERIALS COSTS PERIOD	
I. Mean	36.50		.72	1.06	.72	.72	.43	32.70	Mean I.
S.D.	.50							.44	S.D.
II. Mean	36.50	.00		.48	.00	.00	.00	33.00	Mean II.
S.D.	.50							.71	S.D.
III. Mean	36.80	.62	−.61		−.48	−.48	−.91	33.20	Mean III.
S.D.	.83							.44	S.D.
IV. Mean	36.70	.60	−.61	−.21		.00	.00	33.00	Mean IV.
S.D.	.44							.71	S.D.
V. Mean	37.00	1.16	1.12	.36	1.02		.00	33.00	Mean V.
S.D.	.71							.71	S.D.
VI. Mean	36.50	.00	.00	−.61	−.61	−1.41		33.00	Mean VI.
S.D.	.50							.00	S.D.

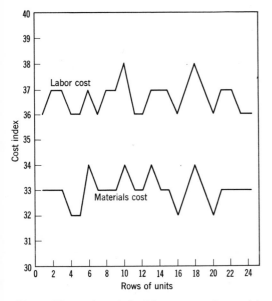

Fig. 1. Fluctuation of the labor costs and materials costs based on row of units (8 houses per row) during the pre-experimental period.

ductivity was unaffected by changes in the work force. Whether this result was produced by the restriction of individual output to group standards, to the tendency for deviations in ability of the newly-hired individuals to be counterbalanced and so cancelled, or to the possible increment of change being too slight to exert a difference, is not known. Such minor fluctuations as did occur are presented in Fig. 1. These fluctuations are probably due to weather changes—resulting in the switching from indoor to outdoor tasks, etc. However, this uncontrollable variable tends to be "averaged out" during the 20 month period of study.

The data, therefore, seem to support the conclusion that the productivity of these groups for the pre-sociometric period is a relatively stable and reliable criterion and that any changes in group level of productivity during the sociometric period can be explained on bases other than the introduction of new workers. That the engineers' estimate of costs is an accurate one is obvious since such an estimate must be precise to be used in competitive bidding for a contract.

RESULTS AND DISCUSSION. Analysis of the sociometric groups' productivity as compared with both engineers' costs estimates and pre-

experimental group productivity is presented in Table 2. Critical ratios of 27.75 on labor costs and 13.16 on materials costs between the restructured groups productivity and the pre-sociometric output criteria clearly indicate a definitely superior level of group output traceable only to the successful application of sociometric procedures and their effect in the work situation. Furthermore, Figs. 2 and 3 show that at no time during the experiment did actual costs even approximate previous costs. The continued decline in production costs is in all likelihood due to the success of improved techniques for the incorporation of isolates and of newly-hired workers into the work force. Also of interest is the significant drop in turnover between the two periods. Such a decrease probably indicates a greater sense of satisfaction on the part of the worker with his job and with the work situation.

Just what happened is best summed up by one of the men when he stated, "Seems as though everything flows a lot smoother. It makes you feel more comfortable working—and I don't waste any time bickering about who's going to do what and how. We just

Table 2. Comparative Criteria Performance Data of Groups and Engineers' Estimates of Anticipated Performance

VARIABLE	MEAN	S.D.	CRITICAL RATIO
1. Turnover			3.69
(a) before experimental period	3.11	1.03	
(b) during experimental period	.27	.23	
2. Labor Cost—per row of units			27.75
(a) engineers' estimate	37.20		
(b) before experimental period	36.66	.52	
(c) during experimental period	32.22	.67	
3. Material Costs—per row of units			13.16
(a) engineers' estimate	33.50		
(b) before experimental period	33.00	.57	
(c) during experimental period	31.00	.56	

seem to go ahead and do it. The work's a lot more interesting too when you've got your buddy working with you. You certainly like it a lot better anyway."

It must be noted, however, that the building trades with their "buddy-work-teams" are especially suited for a sociometric regrouping. The main drawback to a universal adoption of such techniques is the shifting of workers to different jobs while avoiding any change in job duties which would affect job performance, necessitate re-training the worker, etc. Among these building trades workers such a limitation was not a hindrance, for these workers do not operate according to assembly line procedures and so must be more or less equally adept at all phases of construction.

Further suppositions which must be met lie on management's side of the ledger. It is necessary that management have a democratic approach to the government of workers as well as recognizing the importance of group relations and manifesting an interest in worker preferences. Moreno's approach must allow social situations to define themselves and allow the participants in the situation to define the nature of their own needs and problems. An adequate handling of such procedures as used here should be based upon objective study and a recognition of the social stimuli impinging upon the worker, his attitudes and his

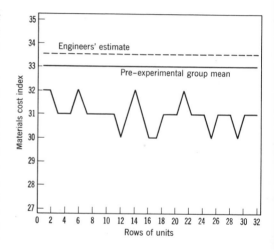

Fig. 3. Materials costs of sociometric group as compared with mean pre-experimental group and engineers' estimate of materials costs.

expectations. As Newcomb[7] declares, the nature of the group influence is in large part determined by the person to person relations within the group.

Sociometric methods, as is true of other methods, cannot be applied in a situation devoid of mutual trust and confidence. The methods of sociometry permit the worker to ventilate his needs and interests and allow him to his advantage to determine in part the social structure of the group in which he operates. Attitudes and values prevailing in the group are reflected by these measurements and the interpersonal relationships established are realistic and have meaning. The utilization of such data extends democracy into the work situation.

Looking back upon the results of both this study and its predecessor it would seem that a careful employment of "interpersonal relations" procedures increases the worker's sense of satisfaction and participation through an increase in his interest in and liking of his job, the removal of anxiety due to friction between work partners and the creation of a friendly, cooperative atmosphere.

The end result in this study has been a happier, more productive worker, who has given management a 5% savings in total production cost.

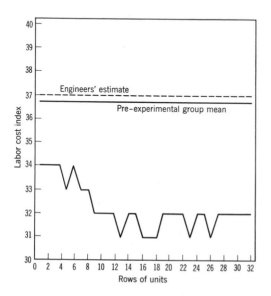

Fig. 2. Labor costs of sociometric group as compared with mean pre-experimental group and engineers' estimate of labor costs.

T. M. Newcomb, Studying Social Behavior. In T. E. Andrews (ed.), Methods of Psychology. New York: John Wiley and Sons, 1948, p. 372.

Effects of the Formal

Organization

on the Informal

PART THREE

UP UNTIL NOW we have considered the formal organization and the informal organization separately. In doing this we have been following a practice common in the field of organizations for some time. Certainly with a subject as complex as organizations there are distinct advantages, both for research and teaching purposes, in breaking the topic down into smaller, more manageable pieces. The danger in this practice is that we may lose sight of the fact that these are but parts of a larger concept and in doing so begin to consider each as a separate, self-contained subject. The unfortunate consequences of this conceptual division of the subject of organizations have already been noted.

This section is concerned with bringing these two major concepts of organization together. This is not easy, for the variables are not often the same in both the formal and the informal organization frameworks. Second, as has already been noted, the assumptions underlying each are in many ways different and not infrequently conflicting. Third, the relations that do exist are very complex. Decisions made as part of an analysis of the formal organization will have behavior consequences in the informal, which in turn may make modi-

fication of the formal organization desirable or even necessary. The events resulting from a single organizational decision, therefore, are multiple and frequently of a reciprocal nature.

To reduce this very involved area to manageable proportions, Part III will be developed within a number of very distinct restrictions. Principal among them is that here we shall consider things primarily from the point of view of the effects which decisions made in a formal organization context are likely to have on the informal organization. Some of the effects of the informal on the formal have been briefly noted in Part II. There are a considerable number of concepts which can be used to bridge the formal and the informal organizations. The need for brevity restricts us to considering only a few. It is hoped that these will serve as illustrations of how still other concepts can be used to link these two schools of thought.

In Part I it was noted that one of the things which plagued formal-organization theorists was that the behavior of organizational members frequently did not fit well into their model of an organization. As a result, when the behavior of a person in an organization was different from what was expected or de-sired, the formal-organization theorist was put in the position of assuming that people were either lazy, rebellious, or improperly trained. To correct this undesirable (from his point of view) behavior he had only a limited number of elements on which to draw. One was, of course, to use authority delegated through the organization to discipline the deviate organization members. Another was to presume that they were in ignorance of what was desired and therefore to train them. In Part II we saw that the issue was far more complex than this. Sometimes the actual be-havior deviated from that called for by the formal organization because the assumptions made about people and their behavior were erroneous or at least inadequate. At other times the formal-organization point of view poorly prepared a person to really understand the significance of the behavior he happened to observe. This is the case, for example, when people deviate from the methods prescribed by the formal organization in order to over-come problems, unanticipated by the formal-organization planner, that stand in the way of accomplishing organizational goals.

Ultimately it will be necessary for organiza-tion theorists to reconsider and restate the as-sumptions on which formal-organization the-ory rests and then to redevelop the whole model. The purpose of this part, however, is much more modest. Our task is to bring to-gether from both schools of thought elements which are either the same or closely related. This arrangement will permit the organization planner to trace the likely behavioral con-sequences of decisions made in the formal-organization context. He can then ask the question whether this is desired behavior. In this arrangement organization behavior no longer has to be viewed as a capricious, un-predictable element or as something only to be brought into organization planning through an intuitive insight. The planner's analysis will in many cases produce a different set of organizational arrangements than would likely result from just a consideration of the more traditional formal-organization arrangements. In fact, not only may a modification be made in the formal organization plan before any attempt is made to implement it, but the analysis may well cause a re-examination of the basic objectives toward which the organ-ization is directed. It can lead to the point where the behavioral aspects of organization are brought in, not as something to be con-trolled and bent to the will of the formal organization planner, but instead as basic fac-tors to be incorporated in the overall planning of the final organization.

A Formal-Informal Organization Nexus

Many points can be examined in an attempt to join or bring closer together the two ap-proaches to organization. Space, however, re-stricts us to consider but one. For this we choose an element which looms very large in our thinking of both the formal and the in-formal organization; namely, the position or job. Several aspects of a job can be handled by both schools of analysis. We shall consider three.

Job Content. One of the functions of the formal organization is to identify individual jobs or positions and to specify the duties and responsibilities which go with them. As we have noted, the traditional formal organization planner, when developing a definition for a particular job or a position, employed a variety of concepts, among them specialization of labor and the various ways in which tasks can be grouped in order to best suit the tech-nology used and the products made. In an at-tempt to make organizations more efficient through the use of such concepts there has been a tendency to carry job specialization to a fairly high degree. As specialization of labor is carried further, jobs are defined in greater detail and become more restricted in their content. From studies in organizational be-havior we have come to appreciate the very great importance of work itself as a source of satisfaction. Consequently, the more we re-strict the content of a job the more difficult it becomes for a person to realize any high level of personal satisfaction from doing his work (Walker and Guest, Trist and Bamforth, Worthy). The content of a job can be defined or explained in many different ways. We shall primarily consider three.

REPETITIVENESS. One thing we might note about jobs is the number of elements they contain. Some jobs have a great many elements, meaning that in order to complete one work cycle a large number of steps or operations have to be completed. Therefore, during a day there are not many work cycles completed. Other jobs, particularly specialized jobs in our mass production industries, have relatively few elements; consequently each work cycle is completed rather quickly, permitting a great many work cycles to be completed during a day. Needless to say, repetitiveness makes jobs dull and monotonous, and therefore socially less attractive.

CONTROL OVER SEQUENCE. Some people, for example clerks in some offices, may have assigned to them a variety of duties which they may take up in whatever order they choose as long as the work assigned to them is completed within some reasonable time limit. They can, therefore, decide the order in which work elements will be handled and they can also decide when. In contrast to this are jobs in which a person may not deviate from a prescribed sequence, and further, in which they may not even have control of the times at which they must begin and finish each job element. Again the assembly line is a convenient illustration for this last condition, for here workers must usually do things in a very closely prescribed manner with the beginning and completing of a work cycle controlled by the rate at which the assembly line moves.

CONTROL OVER METHOD. In some lines of work a person is given an end result to be accomplished and then left pretty much on his own to devise the ways or methods by which this end result is to actually be achieved. Nevertheless, as jobs have become more specialized and as efforts have been made to make the execution of jobs more efficient, there has been an increasing tendency for not only the end result to be specified but also the methods which are to be used. As a result we find, especially in our mass production industries, many positions or jobs in which a person is told exactly how to perform the most minute motions involved in the task assigned him.

Other dimensions can be used to define the content of a job, but these three are among the most useful and can easily be identified in almost any work assignment. Two of them deal with different aspects of decision making on the part of a person filling a position. At first it would seem that there was a strong

relation between the amount of decision making left in the hands of a job occupant and the degree of satisfaction he received from his work, and further, that this satisfaction would be reflected in increased productivity. Unfortunately these relations do not always hold, and although there can be a fairly close relation between the amount of decision making exercised by a job holder and the level of personal satisfaction he receives from his work, there is not the same close relation between these two elements and productivity. The reasons for this are many. Some have to do with the fact that productivity is a factor which entails many elements other than the richness of decision making left in the hands of a job holder. It also is partially allied with the fact that giving one person increased decision-making prerogatives usually entails some decrease in the decision making which can be left to another party. Hence, when workers are given increased decision-making prerogatives relevant to the conduct of their work, it means for this to be real and significant that their superiors must thereby reduce to some degree, and certainly change, the nature of decision making they can perform. Needless to say, the reverse also holds.[1]

Job content, then, is one place where formal- and informal-organization considerations can profitably be applied at the same time. The advantages of increased specialization and routinization of work are well known from the formal-organization point of view. Up to a point increased specialization or reduced job content will produce great increases in efficiency. The question before us is, at what point does further specialization or reduced job content produce disadvantages which are great enough to prohibit them being carried further? This is not an easy question, for it is both a technical question open to objective analysis and also a value question which has as its base the issue of what satisfaction people should be expected to get from their work, an issue which has a subjective answer.

Job Relations. When a job is defined in an organization, it is established in relation to a host of other positions. Sometimes the relations between it and other positions are vague and

[1] See, for example, Nancy C. Morse and Everett Reimer, "The Experimental Change of a Major Organization Variable," *Journal of Abnormal and Social Psychology,* Vol. 52, 1956, pp. 120–129.

not very strong, while in other situations the reverse is true. To complicate the matter further there are a variety of different relations which may exist. Let us consider only two.

INTERDEPENDENCY. By interdependency we mean the degree to which a person filling a position sees his success in his job as being dependent on others. Quite obviously there are some jobs in which people would have very little likelihood of seeing any strong interdependencies between themselves and others. In other positions, however, such interdependencies do exist and are very strong. A number of elements influence the degree to which people see themselves as interdependent—many of them controllable by management. One of the aims which the organization planner might have in mind is to create an organization where these interdependencies are heightened.

Perceiving interdependencies is one thing—providing conditions in which they can be satisfied is another. The formal organization may aid, frustrate, or ignore these necessary conditions. When people see a high degree of interdependency, they may go to great lengths to provide unofficially arrangements that are necessary to their work. Let us consider a situation where a man can perform his job only if someone in a preceding work position has completed his. If the earlier work has not been done, he may have to do extra work or may not be able to work at all. If he is paid on an incentive plan this can mean a definite loss in pay. Perceiving this interdependency, a person in the following position may go to considerable lengths to make personal contact with the individual doing the work preceding him in order to obtain through friendship, favor, or perhaps even bribery the assurance that these earlier activities will be performed properly (Trist and Bamforth).

SOCIAL DISTANCE. We have already noted in Part I that specialization of labor can be carried out along several dimensions. Two of particular importance are the horizontal, that is, differentiation of work on the same level; and the vertical, that is, differentiation of hierarchial work into superior and subordinate positions. Both these divisions can have a tendency of increasing social distance. Certainly the references to the gulf of understanding which often separates superiors and subordinates are so numerous as not to need repetition here. Perhaps not quite as easily recognized is the fact that as jobs become more different, even on the same level, the interests of people become further apart. As the work of people becomes separated further, the important concerns are different, and consequently people have a much more difficult time in communicating and understanding each other's points of view and interests. When differences of knowledge, interest, and responsibility increase the social separation between people, they decrease the potential satisfaction that can be obtained from the work situation (Worthy).

Job Interrelations. The formal organization not only sets up specifications, which a person must satisfy, of duties and responsibilities; it also establishes conditions that have a profound influence on the interrelations between positions and hence on the interactions between people. We will consider two: namely, interactions that are permitted and interactions that are required (Kipnis).

PERMITTED INTERACTIONS. Some people have jobs which are of such a nature that they have a great deal of freedom of movement and consequently can, if they choose, come in contact with many individuals. Expediters and office boys are of this type. On the other hand, other people have jobs which make it exceedingly difficult for them to have much interaction with others, such as long-distance truck drivers or night watchmen. These are extreme situations, of course, and there are many gradations between them. They point out, however, that there may be wide variations in the opportunities people will have to associate voluntarily with others on the job. Obviously opportunity is not the only factor that will encourage one person to seek out another or to hold the other in high regard. It is one element, however, and if other conditions are proper, such as perceived interdependency or status desirability, we would expect to see such interactions take place. We are, in short, concerned here not with the interactions the external system requires but those it will permit because barriers of one sort or another have not been erected.

REQUIRED INTERACTIONS. On the other hand, a formal organization may clearly spell interactions that must take place between people as they carry out their assigned duties. The waitress must interact with the customer, and the receptionist must interact with the caller. One very definite control of interaction established by the formal organization is the work flows, which are established to carry out many types of work in an organization.

WORK FLOW. A work flow is a relatively simple concept, being the sequence of steps or operations, usually contained in a variety of positions, through which something passes in order to accomplish a particular end. For example, one work flow would be the traditional assembly line. Here the item being made passes from one work position to another, where different parts are added or adjustments made, until finally the completed product has been assembled. There are, however, many other types. For example, there is the work flow which begins with a customer in a restaurant giving an order to the waitress, which is taken by the waitress into the kitchen area where it may pass through several other hands, finally resulting in an assembled dinner which comes to the waitress who in turn brings it to the customer. There are numerous such flows in any organization. Many, although by no means all, are established as part of the formal organization. A point which is of interest to us here is that, as a person filling a position in a work flow receives work from the preceding position and then passes it on to the following position, he usually, although not always, is brought into contact with the people who fill these positions. Here is a situation which would seem to fit nicely into the Homans scheme, and we would be quickly tempted to hypothesize that the people who are brought into interaction because of a work flow would therefore develop positive sentiments, that is, feelings of liking toward each other. This is an understandable first interpretation, and it may well be what actually happens, but as Homans warns, and a study of the restaurant industry clearly dramatizes, the very opposite may be the case (Whyte). To understand this, we have to take into account two other factors.

The first of these is that the occupants of various positions in a work flow may view each other not as equal but as different in ways which become quite important. One very definite distinction that may exist is the distinction of status. In Whyte's study of the restaurant industry it was noted that serious difficulties developed when the occupants of two positions interacting in a work flow had different status. A second factor, that of initiation of work must also be taken into account.

INITIATION OF WORK. On investigating an interaction between people we find that there are actually a variety of dimensions to consider. Time is one; some interactions are long, some are short. Another dimension of considerable importance is that sometimes the interactions between party A and party B result in having B do something, and we say that the interaction was one in which A initiated work for B. Such a situation, of course, is seen many times each day. The foreman talks to the worker and in doing so gives him an order about some work he should perform, which the worker then proceeds to do; or the teacher gives the student an assignment, which the student then executes. These familiar examples, do not seem to be particularly distinctive, except when we note how apparently minor variations can change this from an accepted, apparently satisfactory, arrangement to an unsatisfactory one. It is important to note that in the illustrations given a person of higher status, who along with this status had a legitimate authority, was initiating work for a person in a lower status position. If the reverse exists, and a person in a lower status position initiates work for one in a higher, then different results can be expected (Whyte).

The Use of the Homans Model to Analyze Formal-Informal Organization Relations. To make explicit what is by now doubtless obvious, we have been reviewing how the planner of the formal organization as he specifies the major elements of the formal organization is also specifying a considerable portion of the external system in the Homans model. In specifying duties or methods of a job he is identifying the activities a person will do. In structuring positions he is influencing the way people will view their jobs and the jobs of others. He specifies interrelations between jobs and hence he designates interactions between people who hold the jobs. Once we have plugged these elements of the formal organization into the social system we are able to use the Homans model to analyze the social consequences of these decisions. Further, elements which are not part of the formal organization, such as prejudice, can be brought into the analysis. The technical analysis of the traditional formal organization planner, concerned with matters of technology (that is, requirements of manufacturing methods, engineering requirements of the product) and economics (that is, minimum cost, maximum capital return) can now be linked with social analysis. The broad or total view of organizations adopted in this text needs such an inclusive method of sociotechnical analysis.

A Reconsideration of Interaction and Sentiment. In previous discussions (Part II) of interactions and sentiments certain elements have been left somewhat up in the air. It had been observed that it would be erroneous to presume that interactions would necessarily promote positive sentiments. In fact, a number of studies, Whyte's among them, clearly show that strong negative sentiments can develop. This apparent paradox is resolved if we shift our thinking a little bit and define the relation more accurately, as, in fact, Homans does, by stating that interactions will apparently increase the strength of the sentiments people have toward each other. The point to note is that this increase may be in either a positive or a negative direction. The direction would seem to be determined by the sentiments which people bring with them into a particular situation, such as sentiments about status.

Implications of Classical Organization Assumptions for the Informal Organization

In the beginning of this part it was noted that some of the assumptions underlying formal-organization theory would doubtless be substantially modified in the future. This is hardly the time to attempt a thorough examination of them. It is, however, important to note one or two, in order to expand the picture of what we have been developing, for up until now we have been considering rather elementary and, of necessity, highly simplified situations and relations. Such simplicity, although useful for purposes of explanation, does not properly convey the complexity of the situation that exists in organizations.

Obtaining coordination between jobs or for that matter between work groups, departments, and divisions of a company which are interdependent, as was noted in Part I, is one of the most difficult and challenging issues in the study of organizations. The question of how to achieve a level of coordination at which people do their jobs well and uncalled for or unanticipated difficulties are adequately handled is probably the most difficult to answer in this field of study.

A basic assumption of the classical school is that coordination comes from the central authority in the organization structure. The organization is viewed as an instrument in which authority from a central source is brought to bear on the individual organization members to assure that they will perform their work in a proper way. If there is a deviation from orders, it is the function of the next higher level of supervision, through corrective orders and/or discipline, to bring the behavior back into line. From such a point of view it can be understood that an organization can be thought of as an instrument through which the executives at the top bring pressure to bear on those at the lower level to perform work as specified by the higher authority. Needless to say, not all organizations operate in this way, but it is not too difficult to understand how some can and have key executives who feel that this is the proper fashion in which to operate. When this does happen, many things about an organization change (Argyris). Information about a man's performance can well be routed first to the higher authority, who will then go to him demanding correction of something he for the first time finds is wrong or undesirable. The relation between line and staff personnel, for example, can change quite drastically if the staff personnel start to be used as channels through which the top executives gather information about and apply pressure on lower levels of management. The pressure applied can have a variety of effects on the informal organization. If it is fairly uniform and applied to all, it may increase group cohesion. On the other hand, if the pressure contains a threat of a penalty or punishment which may fall on one person but not on others, many disruptive forces may arise within the group as its members try to avoid the punishment. An illustration would be finding a stolen article in a tent that sleeps six boys at a summer camp. The implication is that one is the guilty party and must be punished, and we may well find the boys accusing each other and attempting to throw the guilt on someone other than themselves. As a result, whatever group cohesion existed before may be partially or totally destroyed. With cohesion reduced and perhaps replaced by hostile competition, cooperation and coordination are greatly reduced.

Another aspect of this assumption of the necessity of centralized use of authority to promote coordination is that superiors will have to spend a considerable portion of their time directly overseeing the work of their subordinates. From this it follows that the superior should not have too many subordinates and should also spell out in some detail what is expected from his subordinates. These considerations bring us, of course, back to the topics of centralization and decentralization, which we previously considered. In this section we turn to some further matters, particularly, what decentralization can mean for the behavior of subordinates and some of the structural relations that limit the degree of decentralization possible (Worthy).

Summary

In this introduction attention has been given to finding ways in which elements of the formal and the informal organization can be brought closer together in order to understand better the reciprocal effects which exist. Ideally, this search would lead to a line of analysis that could begin from one point of view and be extended through to the other. Such an arrangement is certainly necessary if we are ever to develop a complete and integrated concept of organizations. Although this is necessary and obviously very desirable, such an objective is still some considerable way off. There are a number of points at which research and theory will permit us to bridge the two major schools of thought. In this introduction only a few were chosen. Primarily we have given attention to the job, work relations, and the work unit. Even with these concepts the material chosen is more illustrative than exhaustive. It is hoped, however, that what has been examined will point first to the possibility of linking the different concepts of organization and second, to showing some of the ways in which it can be done. It is hoped that as the reader comes into contact with other studies or theories he will ask

the question, "In what way will this knowledge permit the construction of a more inclusive concept of organizations?"

An Overview of Parts I, II, and III

The first three parts of this book are intended to provide an overall picture of organization. They form the foundation on which the later sections are developed. Although they are separately developed along more or less traditional lines, repeated statements have been made to remind the reader that they are only part of a whole. It may be well then to briefly show one way the material covered can be brought together into a fairly well-connected set of relations.

The basic model we are using is presented in Fig. 6. This figure in essence merely combines the submodels covered in earlier sections. It shows the formal organization as being influenced by three basic classes of exogenous factors—the objectives of the organization; the technology and resources available; and the general economic, political, and social conditions which face the organization. The first two, (1) objectives, (2) technology and resources, influence the division of labor which in turn influences both the job activities and job relations. At the same time, the division of labor increases the, need for coordination. This increased need for coordination again influences matters relating to job activity and job relations. The conditions facing the organization are one class of influences on the leadership style, which is dictated, in one way or another, by the top management. This in turn influences other job activities and job relations. The end result of everything so far has been a particular set of job activities and job relations. These in turn produce a set of products or services for which the organization was originally intended. The organization also produces a set of satisfactions, both material and psychological, for the organizational members. This product, however, can be considered only tenuously connected to our formal organization concepts, and to understand it we must in turn incorporate some thinking about the informal organization.

The job relations and job activities set up by the formal organization mold important elements in the external system, one part of

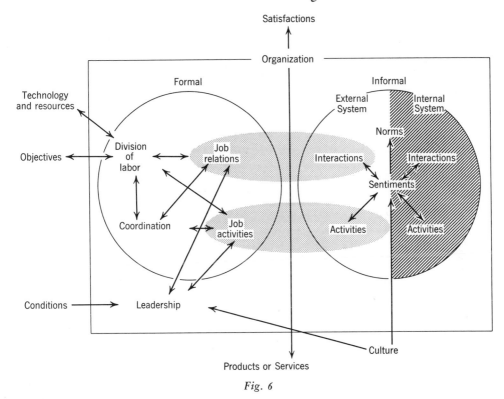

Fig. 6

the total social system in which people in groups find themselves. In particular, job relations and job activities influence the interaction and the activities in the external system which in turn will have a profound impact on the sentiments that people develop in a particular organizational setting. All their sentiments, however, are not developed here. Some are brought with them into the organization from their home life, their previous experiences; in short, from what we might call their culture. The sentiments that exist will profoundly influence the interactions and activities which people develop as part of the internal system, that is, the sets of activities and relations which spring from the conditions in which people find themselves. This is one way of viewing the relations. The important thing to note, however, is that most of these are reversible or, to put it another way, the relations are reciprocal. Hence, the interactions and activities which develop in the internal system will again influence the sentiments which people have. They may take the form of, for example, norms about work, which again may influence the way in which people carry out the activities or perform the interactions specified in

the external system. Needless to say, as soon as these matters are influenced, the informal organization is affecting the way jobs are performed or the job relationships which exist and at this point the informal organization has its profound impact on how real the formal organization may actually become.

This impact of the informal organization on the formal can be traced back through the remaining relations in the model. For example, because some of the job activities are not being carried out as specified, members of management may change their leadership style and, as a result, engage in much closer supervision, imposing authority and external discipline.

Another reverse relation, which has already been discussed, may occur when management becomes aware of the fact that a specified job activity is causing difficulties, perhaps as a result of excessive specialization, and may seek a new way of dividing work in which the degree of specialization is reduced.

The other reverse relations indicated in the figure are in many cases discussed in the readings covered. Rather than trace them through at length we leave this as an exercise for the reader.

The Man on the Assembly Line

CHARLES R. WALKER AND ROBERT H. GUEST

There are a lot of good things about my job. The pay is good. I've got seniority. The working conditions are pretty good for my type of work. But that's not the whole story. . . . You can't beat the machine. They have you clocked to a fraction of a second. My job is engineered, and the jigs and fixtures are all set out according to specifications. The foreman is an all right guy, but he gets pushed, so he pushes us. The guy on the line has no one to push. You can't fight that iron horse.

> Worker on an assembly line, interviewed by the authors

Machines alone do not give us mass production. Mass production is achieved by both machines *and* men. And while we have gone a long way toward perfecting our mechanical operations, we have not successfully written into our equation whatever complex factors represent man, the human element.

> Henry Ford II, in a talk before the American Society of Mechanical Engineers, shortly after he was made President of the Ford Motor Company.

The principal social and psychological problems connected with mass production and human nature have been stated many times and in many different forms. Their importance in an age of advancing technology is hardly in dispute. The question has become rather: What shall we do about them?

Here are a few of the common problems. Since individuals react very differently to in-

dustrial occupations, what are the personality characteristics of those who adjust quickly to—and appear to thrive on—mechanically paced and repetitive jobs? What, on the other hand, are the personality characteristics of those who suffer mentally and physically on such jobs—and who therefore tend to perform them badly? Can the adjustment problem, in other words, be solved by selection? Or is the modern work environment simply *wrong* for the normal human being?

Or to take an engineering and management approach: In the present state of the mechanical arts, what part of a worker's skill and power can the engineer build into a machine? What must he leave out? Precisely how and to what extent in the most mechanized sectors of our economy does the human equation still affect quantity and quality?

Or again, granted that the principles of mass production such as breakdown of jobs into their simplest constituent parts are sound and vital to efficient manufacture, have we yet found how to combine these principles with equally well authenticated principles of human behavior?

Or taking still another approach, if a man spends a third of his life in direct contact with a mass-production environment, why should we not consider important (to him and to society) the hours of living time he spends inside the factory—as important and valuable, for example, as the product he produces which is consumed outside the factory? We talk of a high standard of living, but frequently we mean a high standard of consumption. Man consumes in his leisure, yet fulfills himself not only in his leisure but in his work. Is our mass-production work environment making such fulfillment more difficult?

A short way to sum up these and a great

From *Harvard Business Review*, Vol. 38, No. 3, May–June 1952, pp. 71–83. Reprinted with permission of the publisher.

many more questions is: To what degree can —or should—men be "adjusted" to the new environment of machines, and to what degree is it possible to adjust or rebuild that environment to fit the needs and personalities of men?

Need for Systematic Study. Despite the tremendous contribution of mass-production methods to the productiveness of the economic system under which we live, and notwithstanding the fact that editors, philosophers, and propagandists have long speculated and written about the beneficent or injurious effects of highly mechanized jobs on human behavior, there has been singularly little systematic effort to discover "whatever complex factors represent man, the human element" in the mass-production method as such. The relatively small number of studies which have been made of assembly-line and other types of repetitive work have been mostly laboratory experiments, not explorations of experience in actual industrial plants.

A notable exception is the series of monographs which for some 25 years have been published from time to time under the auspices of the British Medical Council on the effects of mechanization and the repetitive job on productivity and *mental* fatigue. Even these, however, have only touched occasionally on the subject of assembly lines, and have never at all—to the best of our knowledge—dealt specifically with that advanced sector of a mass-production economy, the final assembly line of a plant making a large, complex product like automobiles.

SURVEY OF AUTOMOBILE ASSEMBLY PLANT. For these reasons the authors undertook two years ago an exploratory survey of a modern automobile assembly plant.[1] This is intended as the first of a series of studies designed to define more clearly the several "human equations" involved in assembly work, to prepare and sharpen tools of research, and to look for proximate and empirical answers to the more acute practical problems posed for men and management.

In this article- we shall emphasize how an

[1] The full details of this survey are being published in book form, *The Man on the Assembly Line*, by the Harvard University Press (June 1952).

assembly line looks and feels to the men who work on it, rather than its importance to the engineers who designed it, the executives who manage it, or the public who buys its product.

In order to preserve the anonymity of those who freely supplied information—managers, workers, and union leaders—the plant in question has been called Plant X. Over a period of months 180 workers were interviewed in their homes about all phases of their life on "the line." These workers constituted a substantial —and representative—sample of the total number of productive workers in the plant.

Nearly 90% of the men working at Plant X came from jobs where the pace of work was not machine-governed in a strict sense, and from jobs over 72% of which were not repetitive. In short, the area from which they were recruited had few mass-production factories. One might say, then, that these men were like the majority of workers who in the past 30 years have made the transition from occupations characteristic of the first industrial revolution to work environments characteristic of a mass-production era. Their attitudes should be all the more revealing.

Most people, in thinking about an assembly line and the workers on it, focus only on the effect of the line on what a man does hour by hour, even minute by minute, with his mind and his muscles. Any serious study of the human effects of the mass-production method, however, must extend its field of vision. For the method not only impinges directly on a man's immediate or intrinsic job but molds much of the character of the in-plant society of which he is a part, including both his relations with his fellow workers and his relations with management. Accordingly we shall discuss the impact of the mass-production method not only directly but indirectly on human nature.

DEFINITION OF MASS-PRODUCTION METHOD. But what is the "mass-production method?" We must have a definition if our discussion and our findings are to be understandable.

Although the methods of mass production or, more accurately and specifically for our purposes, the methods of *progressive manufacture* have been defined and discussed in different ways by different writers, it is agreed by nearly everyone that these methods derive from at least two fundamental and related ideas: (1) standardization and (2) interchangeability of parts.

Given these basic ideas, plus the accurate machining methods which make them applicable to manufacture, Ford was able to work out and apply the three following additional "principles" of progressive manufacture: (3) the orderly progression of the product through the shop in a series of planned operations arranged so that the right part always arrives at the right place at the right time; (4) the mechanical delivery of these parts and of the product as it is assembled to and from the operators; and (5) a breakdown of operations into their simple constituent motions.[2]

Let us look now at how these principles translate themselves into job characteristics from the standpoint not of the engineer but of the man on the assembly line. In the first place, most automobile assembly jobs are *mechanically paced* (especially those on the main line). In the second place, since the engineer has broken the jobs down into simple and separate elements and assigned only a few to each man, they are clearly *repetitive*. Among other characteristics of most jobs are these: they have a low skill requirement, permit work on only a fraction of the product, severely limit social interaction, and predetermine for nearly every worker any use he may make of tools and methods.

Taken together, automobile assembly-line jobs exemplify all these characteristics, but not every job exemplifies all of them. Put another way, in spite of many common characteristics, automobile assembly jobs are far from being equal—either as to the quantity or quality of job content or as to the satisfaction or dissatisfaction which workers derive from them. They differ both in the number of the several assembly-line characteristics they exemplify and in the degree of impact of any one characteristic. An understanding of this point must mark the beginning of any serious inquiry into the relation of human behavior to assembly-line work.

Attitude toward Jobs. But that is enough of making distinctions. Now let the men on the

[2] This is a rephrased and slightly more explicit statement of the three principles of mass production as set down in "Mass Production" by Henry Ford in the *Encyclopaedia Britannica*, Fourteenth Edition, Vol. 15, pp. 38–39.

assembly line tell us themselves about their jobs, and tell us also what they like and what they do not like about them. Here are six jobs by way of illustration: two on the main moving line, one off the main line but on a moving conveyer, one off the main line and not on a moving conveyer, one repair job on the line, and one utility job on the line. These six will illustrate at least the principal differences in human impact of mass-production assembly-line jobs. (It should be remembered, however, that these six are not representative of the distribution of jobs in the whole plant, where one-half the jobs are on the *main moving assembly line*. Specifically the distribution of jobs in our sample was as follows: main assembly line, 86; subassembly on moving belt, 28; subassembly not on moving belt, 38; repairmen, 14; utility men, 11; and other, 3.)

ON THE MAIN MOVING LINE. Here is the way the assembler of the baffle windbreaker in the trim department describes his job:

> As the body shell moves along the line, I start putting on a baffle windbreaker (two fenders fit on it) by putting in four screws. Then I put nine clips at the bottom which hold the chrome molding strip to the body. On another type of car there is a piece of rubber which fits on the hood latch on the side and keeps the hood from rattling. I drill the holes in the rubber and metal and fit two screws in. Also I put four clips on the rubber in the rear fender. On another type of body, I put the clips on the bottom molding, and in the trunk space I put two bolts which hold the spare tire clamp. I repeat these things all the time on the same types of car.

How does this man's job measure up in terms of some of the characteristics we have mentioned, particularly pace and repetitiveness?

To begin with, the job is on the main line and the worker rides along on the conveyer, completing his cycle of operations in less than two minutes while the conveyer is moving over a distance of about 30 feet. He then walks to his starting point and begins over again. In short, his pace is directly determined by the moving belt. On the other hand, he is sometimes able to work back up the line and so secure a breather for himself.

The job is clearly repetitive, but there is

some element of variety since between five and ten operations are required to complete the job cycle. There are also different models to be worked on. Comparing the repetitiveness of this job with that of other assembly jobs, it is somewhere in the middle range—far less repetitive than a single-operation job and far more repetitive than the job of a repairman.

Similarly, in the matter of skill it is in the middle as assembly-line jobs go. Because of the number of parts handled, learning time is slightly longer than that for many assembly jobs. The worker reported that it took him a month to do the job properly. As for the expenditure of physical energy, it is a light job.

ALSO ON THE MAIN MOVING LINE. Or consider the job of the worker who installs toe plates and who performs operations typical of short-cycle, on-the-main-line jobs:

> I put in the two different toe plates. They cover the holes where the brake and clutch pedals are. I am inside the car and have to be down on the seat to do my work. On one kind of car I put in the shift lever while another man puts in the toe plates.

While doing his job this man rides along in the car and must complete the job before he is carried too far. After finishing his work cycle he returns to his station, climbs into another car, and begins another installation. Thus his pace is strictly governed by the moving line. This particular worker told the interviewer that he did not mind the pace.

Such a job which demands but two operations in a two-minute cycle is highly repetitive. Only slight variety is introduced when the man installs a shift lever instead of a toe plate on certain cars.

The job demands very little skill and has a learning period of just two days. Although the worker gets in and out of cars 20 or 30 times an hour, his expenditure of physical energy on the actual assembly operation is slight.

OFF THE MAIN LINE BUT ON A MOVING CONVEYER. The job of a seat-spring builder is typical of those off the main line but on a moving belt:

> I work on a small conveyer which goes around in a circle. We call it a merry-go-round. I make up zig-zag springs for front seats. Every couple of feet on the conveyer

there is a form for the pieces that make up the seat springs. As that form goes by me, I clip several pieces together, using a clip gun. I then put the pieces back on the form, and it goes on around to where the other men clip more pieces together. By the time the form has gone around the whole line, the pieces are ready to be set in a frame, where they are made into a complete seat spring. That's further down the main seat cushion line. The only operation I do is work the clip gun. It takes just a couple of seconds to shoot six or eight clips onto the spring, and I do it as I walk a few steps. Then I start right over again.

This job is clearly paced by a moving conveyer quite as much as if it were on the main line. A comment by the worker regarding his previous job emphasized the point: "I liked the piecework system on my old job. If I wanted to stop for a few minutes, I could. You can't do that here."

As for variety, there is none. The job is highly repetitive, consisting of one set of operations repeated every few seconds on a part which is standard for all models.

The skill requirement is minimum. This worker gave two days at his learning time, with a few days more "in order to do it like I do it now."

As for physical energy, the job would probably be rated as light since the worker guides an automatic hand gun. But there is considerable fatigue because the worker performs the operation standing up.

The worker's over-all estimate of the job is typical. As to what he liked about the job, he mentioned good pay, steady work, and good working hours—in that order of priority. As to what he disliked, he said that he could not set his own pace, that he did not have interesting work, and that his job was physically tiring.

OFF THE MAIN LINE BUT NOT ON A MOVING CONVEYER. We turn to a blower-defroster assembler who works off the main line and not on a moving belt:

> I work at a bench on blower defrosters. The blowers come in two parts. I take one part and attach the blower motor to it. I then connect the fan to the motor shaft. Then I take the other half of the air pipe and put two parts together with fourteen

screws. I test the motor to see if it works, and if it does, I put in a fifteenth screw which grounds it to the pipe. The materials are brought to me and put in a pile by a stock chaser. After I finish, I put each assembled blower on one of six shelves.

Here is an example of a job where pace is only indirectly determined by the main line. The worker must keep his shelves stocked with a supply of blower defrosters, but he has some choice of pace in doing so. He may work fast and "build up a bank," then slow down and take a breather. Or he may choose to work quite steadily. The demands of the stock-chaser who brings him materials and takes away the finished assembly are the determinants of his work pace, rather than the moving conveyer.

There is not much variety since there are only three operations. However, a slight variation is introduced through differences in models. The worker called his job completely repetitive but said he did not mind it.

His job operations require a minimum of skill: "I learned it in a couple of hours, though it took me about a week to get up speed." He does not move around, and the materials he handles are light, so very little physical energy is demanded.

Summing up his job, this worker gave good bosses, good pay, and good working conditions as his first three reasons for liking the job. He mentioned only one thing he disliked: "I cannot do different things."

REPAIRMAN. Here is a job description by a repairman in the car-conditioning section of the chassis department:

I work in a pit underneath the final line. The cars move along over the pit. On the previous assembly operations, the inspectors for the under parts of the car have indicated where parts were missing or damaged or not properly attached. There are any number of things which can be wrong, and they are usually different for each car. Sometimes we have a run of the same thing which we have to work on until they get at the bug earlier in assembly operations. The shock absorbers may be bad, gas line in wrong, brake lines or spring attachments off. I fix whatever I see checked by the inspector. The others in the pit do the same thing. I just work down the line until I get it cleared up. Sometimes

I have to work down a long way on one thing. Other times it's just a simple problem on a number of different things.

This worker is on the main line, but his pace is not strictly governed by the moving conveyer. "We don't feel the pressure of the line since we don't have to do just one thing in a given area and length of time."

The variety the job offers is derived from the nature of the work. "There are any number of things which can be wrong, and they are usually different for each car. . . . There is something different all the time."

As for skill, the job as repairman requires manual skill and mechanical experience. A garage repairman's job would be a good preparation. (The man whose job description is given here had, in fact, worked as a repairman in a garage before coming to Plant X.)

The job varies between light and medium-heavy work, with the expenditure of physical energy called for changing appreciably from job to job and from day to day.

The worker's personal satisfaction with his job was clear. He gave as three reasons for liking the job: "I can set my own pace, I have good working conditions, and I have steady work." He also commented favorably on being able to "use my brains," "do different things," and "choose how the job is to be done."

UTILITY MAN. A utility man in the chassis department describes his job as follows:

I work on the whole length of that part of the chassis line beginning with motor drop up to where the wheels are mounted. My job is to fill in wherever I am needed. A man might be absent or away from the job or may need help on the job.

We start where the motor is lowered onto the frame (motor mount). The clutch assembly is installed and hooked up. Then the exhaust system is attached and the bolts tightened. The clutch assembly bolts and the motor mount bolts are also tightened. In the next area on the line the brake chambers are filled and bled.

Off to the side, the subassembly men put the steering column together. The steering post and the Pittman arm assembly are put in. Further down the line, men put in air cleaners and inject hydraulic fluid for the transmission.

Next, the brakes are tested and the clutch linkage hooked up. The bumper brackets are put on; a serial number is attached next; and then the bumper brackets are tightened up. Finally, the chassis is sprayed, mounted on wheels, and moved on toward body drop. All in all, about 28 men work on these jobs, each man with his own special operation. I go on each of these jobs, depending on where I am needed most. It is different each day. Some of the jobs are hard to learn, so when I take over one on which I haven't had much experience, it's hard to keep up. I have been learning how to do the work ever since I've been in the plant. I can never learn everything because new changes are always being made.

The pace of this utility man's work, since it is on the main line, is as strictly governed as that of any assembly worker. In certain ways he may feel the pressure more acutely than some of those for whom he substitutes, since he has less practice on any single job than its regular holder.

To compensate him, however, there is plenty of variety, for, as he points out, he shifts about among 28 different jobs. Notice how in describing his many tasks this utility man gives a very clear account of the whole segment of assembly operations in the chassis department.

Notice, too, the character of a utility man's skill. It is the sum of many little skills of many repetitive jobs. The learning time is six months to a year. The worker said: "Sometimes I walk up and down checking the line. I ask questions of the different men. I rarely stay on the same job more than a couple of days." That his job is not easy is suggested by an additional comment:

Some days you feel like learning, other days you don't. On jobs that take time to learn, you get disgusted because it's hard to keep up. A utility man, when on a job, has more trouble keeping up than the regular man.

This man mentioned good pay, steady work, and good bosses as the three main reasons for liking his job, in that order. Other items bearing on the immediate job which he liked were "having interesting work, having to use my brains, doing many different things," as in the case of the repairman, and also "talking with others." He had only one complaint about the job: that it was "physically tiring."

SUMMARY OF ATTITUDES TOWARD JOBS. In all of this classification of the automobile assembly workers' jobs, we have clearly been concerned not with an engineering analysis but with factors which have an effect on satisfaction or dissatisfaction with the immediate job. Mechanical pace, repetitiveness, minimum skill requirement, and the other factors were all found reflected in attitudes and feelings.

These examples underline some of the commonest facts and feelings which are part of the daily experience of the productive worker in an assembly plant. To recall a few:

1. Contrary to popular belief, all jobs on an assembly line are not alike, either in skill, variety, learning time, or the degree of satisfaction or dissatisfaction which they offer the average wage earner.

2. There are definite ways on certain jobs to get a break or a breather, such as "working back up the line," or "bank building."

3. There is a general, though not a unanimous, desire to move from highly paced jobs to jobs which are less highly paced, and "off the line."

4. It is evident from the statements of the six workers—which for illustrative purposes we have selected from 180—that other factors such as good pay, a good foreman, and a secure job must be considered in appraising the total index of a worker's satisfaction or dissatisfaction.

Major Reactions of Workers. Looking over the range of factors connected with their immediate jobs by all the men interviewed, we see that the two which were given greatest prominence were (1) mechanical pacing and (2) repetitiveness.

TO MECHANICAL PACING. We asked no direct attitude questions on the first and central characteristic of any automobile assembly plant— the moving conveyer—but nearly every worker expressed his opinions about it when describing his job, when talking about the company, or at some other point in the interview. These free-association comments on pace as governed by the moving conveyer showed that: (1) A large majority of the workers regarded the moving line or belt as an undesirable feature of the job. (2) A small minority expressed themselves as enjoying the excitement of the moving line.

Following are typical comments of workers who were highly critical of the line:

> The bad thing about assembly lines is that the line keeps moving. If you have a little trouble with a job, you can't take the time to do it right.

> On the line you're geared to the line. You don't dare stop. If you get behind, you have a hard time catching up.

> The line speed is too great. More men wouldn't help much. They'd just expect more work out of an individual. There's an awful lot of tension.

> I don't like rushing all the time. . . . I don't mind doing a good day's work, but I don't like to run through it.

> The work isn't hard; it's the never-ending pace. . . . The guys yell "hurrah" whenever the line breaks down. . . . You can hear it all over the plant.

In contrast, a minority liked the challenge and excitement of keeping up with the line:

> I do my job well. I get some satisfaction from keeping up with a rapid-fire job. On days when the cars come off slowly, I sometimes get bored.

> I get satisfaction from doing my job right and keeping up with the line.

> It makes you feel good . . . when the line is going like hell and you step in and catch up with it.

TO REPETITIVENESS. Turning now to the job characteristic, repetitiveness, our findings are that: (1) A majority of the workers were critical of the repetitive character of their jobs. (2) A minority preferred the repetitive character of their work or were indifferent to it. (3) A large number of workers compared on-the-line jobs unfavorably with off-the-line jobs, because off-the-line jobs offered more variety.

We found we were able to correlate the number of operations a man performed (which can serve as a rough measure of repetitiveness) with expressions of interest or lack of interest in his job. The number of operations performed on any given job was determined not by direct questioning but by analysis of the job descriptions. The workers, however, were asked directly: "Would you say your job was very interesting, fairly interesting, not at all interesting?" The correlation with number of operations was as follows:

OPERATIONS PERFORMED	VERY OR FAIRLY INTERESTING	NOT VERY OR NOT AT ALL INTERESTING
1	19	38
2–5	28	36
5 or more	41	18

In the column of workers giving a positive rating to "interest," the number of workers increases as the number of operations increases. In other words, there is a tendency for interest in work to vary directly with the number of operations performed.

Following are typical comments of those men who were critical of the repetitive nature of their jobs:

> I dislike repetition. One of the main things wrong with this job is that there is no figuring for yourself, no chance to use your brain. It's a grind doing the same thing over and over. There is no skill necessary.

> I'd rather work for a small company any day. They're interested in doing good work, and they are willing to allot enough time for it. The assembly line is no place to work, I can tell you. There is nothing more discouraging than having a barrel beside you with 10,000 bolts in it and using them all up. Then you get a barrel with another 10,000 bolts, and you know every one of those 10,000 bolts has to be picked up and put in exactly the same place as the last 10,000 bolts.

> I'd like to do different things on this job. I get bored. It's the same thing all the time. Cars always coming down the line endlessly every time I look up.

> I would like to perform different operations, but I do the same thing all the time. I always know what I'm going to do when I come in. There's nothing to look forward to like there was on my old job.

The monotony is what I don't like. It's pretty noisy, but you get used to that. I'd never get used to the monotony. I dislike the plant for this reason.

It's not a matter of pace. It's the monotony. It's not good for you to get so bored. I do the same thing day after day; just an everlasting grind.

The job gets so sickening—day in and day out plugging in ignition wires. I get through with one motor, turn around, and there's another motor staring me in the face.

A minority of workers who declared that they were indifferent to or preferred doing the same thing over and over again commented as follows:

I keep doing the same thing all the time, but it doesn't make any difference to me.

Repeating the same thing you can catch up and keep ahead of yourself. I like the routine. You can get in the swing of it.

We do the same thing all the time, but I don't mind it really.

I like doing the same thing all the time. I'd rather stay right where I am. When I come in in the morning, I like to know exactly what I'll be doing.

I like to repeat the same thing, and every car is different anyway. So my job is interesting enough.

Explanation of why this minority group either preferred or was indifferent to the factor of repetitiveness in contrast to the majority of workers in our sample would appear to lie in the pattern of their individual personalities. An investigation of the psychological characteristics of men who react this way is clearly suggested. We sought but found no other unique characteristics in the group as regards education, age, or any of the other categories of information we used.

Effect of Human Equation. In the introductory paragraphs of this article we reviewed some of the typical questions on which it was hoped research into the human equation of assembly-line work might throw light, including some of special interest to both the production manager and the engineer: What part of a worker's skill and power can the engineer build into a machine? What must he leave out? Precisely how and to what extent in the most mechanized sectors of our economy does the human equation still affect quantity and quality?

INFLUENCE OF WORKERS ON QUALITY. So far as assembly lines go, there is still a widespread belief on the part of *outsiders* that the machine has completely taken over and that on mechanized conveyer-line jobs the individual has no influence on quality. There is also a belief widely held by *insiders* (employers and production managers) that, even though the quality of individual performance on a mechanized job may still be important for the final product, the average worker no longer cares or gets satisfaction from doing a good job.

In Plant X, both beliefs were shown to be unfounded.

As many as 79 men in the sample of 180 felt that it was difficult to sustain the kind of quality performance which was expected of them or which they themselves wanted to sustain. To most of the 79, *this was a discouraging and negative feature of the job.*

About half the workers felt it was possible to do the kind of quality job expected of them. Few of these workers, however, had jobs which were strictly line-paced. Rather they included mostly repairmen, utility men, workers on off-line jobs, or men on the line who had longer time cycles or greater freedom to move up and down the line. Typical comments among this group were:

No time limit is set on my job, so I can do it right. I get satisfaction out of really fixing a job. I can usually get this, but sometimes the company doesn't want the cars fixed as well as I'd like to.

I get satisfaction and quality because I have time to complete my job right.

I never let a car go by with my number on it unless it is done right. Maybe some of the men on the line don't get quality.

You can take time to get quality. It's not like on the line when you have to rush so much. And I get satisfaction. It makes me feel good when I put out a good day's work and get no kickbacks.

The effects of poor-quality work on job satisfaction were reflected in many of the comments of men on conveyer-paced jobs:

The cars come too fast for quality. It's quantity instead of quality. I'm doing the best I can, but could do a neater job slower.

On an assembly line you just do it once; if it's wrong, you have no time to fix it. I get no satisfaction from my work. All I do is think about all the things that went through wrong that should have been fixed. My old job was nothing like this.

I try to do quality work, but I'm too rushed. This keeps me from getting pleasure from the work. They say "haste makes waste," and they're getting plenty of both.

I'd rather do less work and do it right. How can you get quality when they don't give you time? The "quality" signs they have mean nothing.

These comments tend to show that the characteristics or components of the assembly man's immediate job do have a significant bearing upon the quality of the product, and that mass production restricts rather than eliminates the "human factor" as a determinant of quality for any given part or for the total product. Most workers were conscious of this fact. For a substantial number, inability to put out quality was a source of irritation while putting out quality was a source of job satisfaction.

Constructive Measures by Management. Are there any measures that management can take to modify on-the-job conditions of work in the interest of greater efficiency and of increased satisfaction for the individual operator?

One answer to this question may be sought in the elements of satisfaction or of compensation which some workers already found in their jobs. To begin with, it should be remembered that there was a minority of workers who preferred or were indifferent to repetitiveness and mechanical pacing. Presumably by improved methods of recruiting and selection this minority could be increased. Then there were a number of men who found their immediate jobs on and off the line satisfying—actually all the repairmen and utility men interviewed with one exception. The only measures needed here are protective—to make sure that the content of these jobs is not diluted.

This still leaves the majority of the production workers. Here the clue to constructive action lies in the fact that many of them reacted favorably to particular features of their jobs:

1. Social interaction breaking the monotony.
2. Enough operations on their particular jobs to give variety.
3. Opportunity to work back up the line and get a breather.
4. Opportunity to build up a bank and get a breather.
5. Opportunity to alternate one set of operations with another set of a substantially different character.
6. Opportunity to alternate jobs with other workers within the same section.
7. A long time cycle encompassing a larger number of operations than usual and of a more interesting character.

A practical directive for management would appear to be exploration of the possibility of extending these and other desirable features, so that more assembly men could share in them. The degree of that extension would necessarily vary with the special circumstances—physical and organizational—of individual plants, and with the ingenuity of management; but there would be few plants where something could not be done in this direction.

Detailed discussion of such measures is beyond the scope of this article, but the tenor of our thinking may be indicated by reference to two of the seven features to which Plant X workers reacted favorably.

JOB ROTATION. Take Number 6—alternation of jobs between workers, a technique often called "rotation." At Plant X we were struck with the unusually high degree of job satisfaction expressed by the members of one work group under a particular foreman. With the permission and encouragement of their foreman, the men were working under a system of job rotation. It was to this system that the members of the group ascribed their relatively high job satisfaction. And to the same system the section foreman owed in part a smoothly running and efficient work unit. Top plant management is now encouraging a more widespread application of this practice.

In connection with any system of job rotation the question immediately comes to mind: Since it requires some effort to learn several jobs instead of one, will not the worker—unless he is exceptional—object? Many managers seem to find it difficult to get workers to change jobs frequently.

The best answer to this question about worker resistance is the pragmatic one. In certain sectors on the line at Plant X rotation *is* working. Moreover, in other industries and on other types of assembly lines the practice of rotation is steadily gaining ground. For most people learning to do something new is hard work, and it is only undertaken when an adequate reward is held out. For a considerable number of assembly-line workers the rewards of variety and of possessing a repertory of skills will be sufficient.

Of course, some resistance to an experiment in rotation is to be expected. The key to the situation lies, we suggest, in the word "experiment." Where rotation has been successfully installed on other types of assembly lines, it has usually been started as an experiment, with management guaranteeing to the work group or to any single individual a return to stationary assignments if desired—and rarely have the workers wished to return.

Another question is: Will the work be done as well or as fast under job rotation? The answer for the Plant X section which practices it is an affirmative. For other work groups in other industries with which the authors are familiar, the answer has also been "yes." Of course there are work situations where job rotation appears either altogether impractical or less efficient. But always the real test is in the over-all and long-term performance of the group. Gains in quality and a drop in turnover or absenteeism may balance some decrease in output, if it occurs.

JOB ENLARGEMENT. Or consider Number 7—a long-time cycle encompassing a larger number of operations than usual and of a more interesting character, sometimes called "job enlargement." Here is a concept and a practice that has proved successful in decreasing monotony without impairing efficiency in certain sectors of other industries. We here suggest that it be introduced experimentally into automobile assembly work.

Job enlargement is simply the recombining of two or more separate jobs into one. Certain plant managers in other industries have been finding that a law of diminishing returns applies to the subdivision of jobs and that a recombination of certain fractured parts has increased efficiency. This points toward a lengthening of time cycles. Job enlargement in the sense in which we suggest it does not mean turning automobile assembly back into the hands of master mechanics with one worker assigned to the assembly of one car. It does mean paying greater attention to psychological and social variables in the determination of time cycles and, by the same token, paying more attention to the *content* of individual jobs.

To one unfamiliar with assembly-line work experience, the difference between a job with five operations and a job with ten, or between a job taking two minutes to perform and a job taking four minutes, might seem a matter far too trivial to concern anyone. Our data have shown that this is not true. Management has a vital interest in such matters; the proper assignment of time cycles throughout an assembly plant will make an important difference in the efficiency of the plant. As for the worker, one of the most striking findings of this study is the psychological importance of even minute changes in his immediate job experience.

At the risk of oversimplification, the point may be summarized this way: Other things being equal, the difference between a satisfied and a dissatisfied worker may rest on whether he has a ten-opration or a five-operation job.

Relationship among Workers. Another place to look for possibilities of improvement is in the area of indirect influences—the impact of mass-production methods on the plant's social structure. Ever since the early studies of Elton Mayo, it has been widely accepted that the character of the "work group" frequently exercises a decisive influence on a worker's efficiency—not to mention on his satisfaction on the job. How did the technology of the automobile assembly line affect the grouping of men at Plant X?

Most workers are located along the "main line" according to the particular manpower requirements of each segment of the assembly process. Each operator works in a limited area completing his own operations independently of others as the car is carried by the conveyer down the line. A particular individual may talk with the men immediately around him, but these men cannot be said to comprise a bona fide work group in the usual sense of the term. Take as an illustration the polishing line. Figure 1 shows in diagrammatic form an actual interaction pattern of a left-front-door polisher, Worker E.

The ten men from A to J comprise a work group of which Worker E is a part, and he has some social contact with all the other nine. His really close contacts, however, are only with C, D, F and G. Note that these four workers comprise a group—*but only from E's point of view.* As to the social relationship pattern of G, his immediate group would consist of E, F, H and I; it would not include C and D, who were clearly members of E's group. Further variations occur, for example, when a line makes a bend or loop and brings men in dif-

ferent sections closer together. Thus each man, because of the nature of conveyer operations, has a slightly different circle of associates from that of the man next to him. So it goes along the entire stretch of a line, a line well over two miles long.

In our interviews these men exhibited little of what the sociologist would call "in-group awareness." Rarely, for example, did they talk about "our team" or "our group" or "the men in our outfit." Instead, the following remark was typical: "I've been here over a year, and I hardly know the first names of the men in the section where I work."

In sharp contrast, however, to the majority of line workers, a minority—principally off-line operators—worked on bona fide teams or crews; that is, they were members of a close working group, were functionally interdepend-

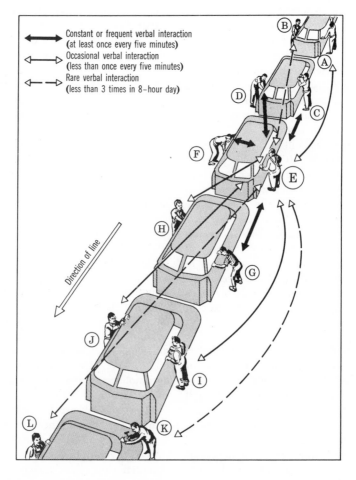

Fig. 1. *Social interaction pattern of typical main assembly line worker—polisher in the paint department.*

ent, and frequently assisted their fellows or exchanged operations with them. On charting the interaction pattern of such groups it was found that the frequency of conversational exchange was high and constant for nearly all members of the group. Of greater significance, the group exhibited a marked *esprit-de-corps* not found among the bulk of line operators.

It is clear that the present technology of an automobile assembly line limits social interaction and does not lend itself to the arrangement of men in bona fide teams or crews. It is suggested, however, that in the design of *new* plants, and at periods of retooling or of layout revisions, an effort be made to maximize the opportunities for social interaction and for team relationships.

Relations with Management. Still another area of social relationships—that of worker to supervisor—is crucial to an intelligent understanding of social organization.

The formal organizational structure of the various production departments in Plant X was similar to that found in many plants. In interviews with workers we came to know the quality of relationship between workers and supervisors.

FOREMEN. Qualitative comments by the men about their foremen suggested a relatively informal and friendly relationship on the part of the majority. The average foreman had from 15 to 25 men under him, and talking between worker and foreman was generally frequent, friendly, and informal. The sort of remarks one hears about any good foreman were also heard here, as for example: "Our foreman is a real good guy. We're lucky. If he got into trouble, the whole department would back him right up."

There were criticisms of foremen, but usually these were not directed at the individual. Rather they were aimed at the "line" and the role the foreman had to play with reference to the line. As one man said: "After all, the foreman has to be a pusher, and nobody likes to be pushed. He's got to hold his job. If he doesn't push, somebody else will get his job."

Often men exonerated foremen for "pushing" since they recognized that the compulsion of line production was not the fault of the foremen. One man put it this way: "I guess you'd say the foreman gets along with the men. But they don't need a foreman. *The line is the foreman.* You have to keep up with the line."

HIGHER SUPERVISORS. An interesting finding which came out of the study was the relationship, or lack of it, between workers and management above the foreman level. The 180 men in our sample were asked to indicate contacts with supervisors in their department at the general foreman and department-head levels. Only 59 reported that they talked with their general foreman as often as once a week; 15 put it at on to three times a month; and 88 said less than once a month. Contact between workers and upper departmental supervisors was even less, with 70% saying they spoke with their department heads less than once a month. (Departments ranged in size from 200 to 400.)

It is significant in this connection that in a steel fabricating plant which we recently studied the workers talked far more frequently with supervisors above the foreman level. There the nature of the process and the high degree of worker skills made for a closer relationship. It was an everyday experience to find a superintendent in charge of 400 men talking with an individual worker or group of workers. He did this because the technical and skilled judgment of the individual worker was important in the production process.

On the automobile assembly line, on the other hand, because of the high degree of mechanization and fractional assembly there appears to be less need for supervisors to discuss production matters with individual workers. Management relies on the judgment of the engineer, not the worker. Thus the basic factor which determines the rate and quality of worker-supervisor interaction is the technology of mass production.

Impact on Wage Structure. Not the least important secondary effect of the mass-production method has been its impact on the wage structure. A leveling of workers' skills has inevitably resulted in a narrowing of differentials between wage grades, in contrast to industries where the latest mass-production methods have not been applied. For example, in the steel fabricating plant which we investigated—a seamless tube mill—the differential between the rates of the lowest and of the highest paid workers was over a dollar an hour.

At Plant X, however, the differential between the lowest paid and the highest paid was around 10 cents for the major categories of production workers, and over half the workers in the production departments received exactly the same hourly wage.

It is obvious that changes in skill levels and in wage categories affect what the wage administrator calls the "system of job progression." Before the application of mass-production methods most industries had many well-defined steps in their ladders of promotion. Mass-production methods, while often raising the general level of wages and bringing other benefits, have knocked out a good many rungs in these promotion ladders. To turn again to the steel mill for contrast: there were as many as seven or eight steps from laborer to roller, each one associated with progressively higher wages, skills, and prestige.

This system of promotion, with its connotations of growth, incentive, and progress, has been weakened or virtually eliminated on the assembly line. Almost any assembly worker can—and some do—say: "There are hundreds of jobs like mine, not much better, not much worse. The differences are so slight—or seem so slight to management—that I am interchangeable." Consequently, to escape a resulting sense of anonymity as much, perhaps, as to escape monotony, the average worker at Plant X does not aspire to climb into another slightly better production job, but rather into a utility man's job or a repairman's job or out of production altogether, where he can be recognized, and where also he can recognize himself, as an individual.

Most of the benefits of the mass-production method are obvious and have often been celebrated. If we are to continue to enjoy them and to expand and refine the method, we should understand more fully its impact on the traditional organization of industry. Surely the problems as well as the promises of mass production are worthy of study.

Conclusion. It is obviously impossible in a single article to do more than sketch some of the problem areas in the broad field of relations between mass production and human nature. Concerning the direct impact of the method on the individual we made a few empirical suggestions and tried to point out at least one direction in which management might seek practical solutions.

But what can be said about the *indirect* impact of mass production on human nature through the character of work groups, the wage structure, and the promotion system? In a negative sense, at least, all these phenomena appear to be related: At Plant X they tended to increase the workers' sense of anonymity within the production enterprise of which they were functional parts. In fact, one way to express the net result of these several influences might be to say that little sense of membership in a common work community existed. (Our evidence showed that to some extent membership in the union gave the worker the feeling of personal identity and "belonging" which neither the shop nor relations with management supplied.)

It seems to us significant that the average worker appeared to be oppressed by this sense of anonymity *in spite of the fact that he declared himself well satisfied with his rate of pay and the security of his job.* The answer to this problem in the most general terms would appear to be a program designed to re-create the sense *and also* the reality of a bona fide work community. And for such a program to be successful we believe that both union and management would have to agree on the measures to be taken.

A comment by a man on the line will suggest the nature of the problem more clearly than many paragraphs of exposition:

> There is a different feeling in this plant. It's much bigger than people around here have ever seen. It's just like the kid who goes up to a grown-up man and starts talking to him. There doesn't seem to be a friendly feeling. At the plant I used to work in there was a different feeling. Everyone spoke to everyone else. . . . Nobody goes to other departments in this plant. The understanding could be better—happier and much easier. Here a man is just so much horsepower.

Perhaps the human needs in Plant X are merely an expression in more explicit terms of the needs of our industrial civilization. The problem of reintegrating the several faculties of man into a significant unity presents itself in many fields—in industry, science, and government, to name but three—in an age of over-specialization.

It is striking that throughout the survey of Plant X both union and management agreed with the authors that the more basic problems to be explored were not those connected with a particular plant, industry, or corporation. Rather they were problems related to technological and organizational trends common to modern industry. Both agreed that modern American civilization as we know it rests upon mass-production principles quite as much as upon the natural resources of the United States. The attitude of both, therefore, was a simple and heartening one: *Since these problems exist, let us get all the facts we can. In time we shall be able to solve them.*

As Saint-Exupéry, the French aviator and author wrote:

> The Machine is not an end. . . . It is a tool . . . like the plough.

If we believe that it degrades Man, it is possibly because we lack the perspective for judging the end results of transformations as rapid as those to which we have been subjected. What are two hundred years in the history of the Machine when compared with two hundred thousand years in the history of Man? We have scarcely established ourselves in this country of mines and of central electricity. It is as if we had hardly begun to live in the new house that we have not yet finished building. Everything has changed so rapidly around us: human relations, conditions of work, customs. . . . Every step in our progress has driven us a little further from our acquired habits, and we are in truth pioneers who have not yet established the foundations of our new country.[3]

[3] Antoine de Saint-Exupéry, *Terre des Hommes* (Paris, Gallimard, 1939), p. 58.

Selections from Social and Psychological Consquences of the Longwall Method of Coal-Getting

E. L. TRIST AND K. W. BAMFORTH

Mechanization and the Problem of Intermediate Organization. With the advent of coal-cutters and mechanical conveyors, the degree of technological complexity of the coal-getting task was raised to a different level. Mechanisation made possible the working of a single long face in place of a series of short faces. In thin seams short faces increase costs, since a large number of "gates" (see Fig. 1) have to be "ripped" up several feet above the height of the seam to create haulage and trav-

From *Human Relations*, Vol. 4, No. 1, 1951, pp. 6–38. Reprinted with permission of the publisher, Tavistock Publications Ltd., and the authors.

elling facilities. In British coal, seams less than 4 ft. in thickness are common, so that there was a tendency to make full use of the possibility of working optimally long rather than optimally short faces. For this reason, and for others also, discussion of which is beyond present scope, the longwall method came into being. Applicable to thick as well as to thin seams, it became the general method of coal-getting in the British industry, enabling the average type of pit, which may contain three or four seams of different thickness, to work its entire coal economically, and to develop its layout and organize its production in terms of a single, self-consistent plan. In America, where

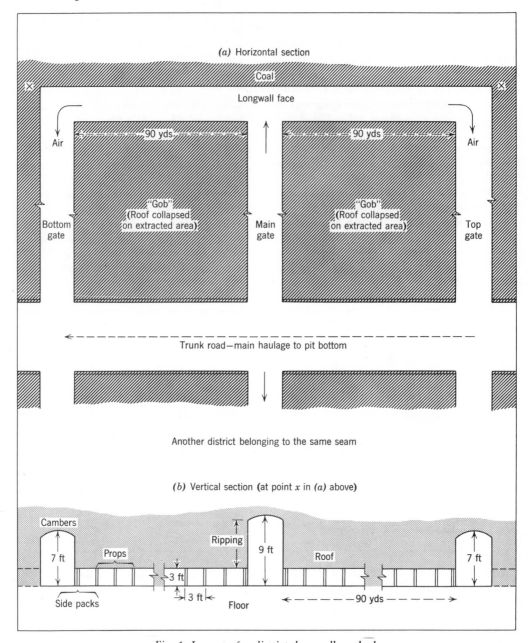

Fig. 1. Layout of a district, longwall method.

thick seams are the rule, mechanization has developed in terms of shorter faces and room-and-pillar techniques.

The associated characteristics of mechanized complexity, and of largeness as regards the scale of the primary production unit, created a situation in which it was impossible for the method to develop as a technological system without bringing into existence a work rela-tionship structure radically different from that associated with hand-got procedures. The artisan type of pair, composed of the skilled man and his mate, assisted by one or more labourers, was out of keeping as a model for the type of work group required. Need arose for a unit more of the size and differentiated complexity of a small factory department. A structure of intermediate social magnitude began therefore to emerge. The basic pattern round which the work relationships of the longwall production unit were organized became the cycle group of 40–50 men, their shot-firer and shift "deputies," who were responsible to the pit management for the working as a whole. Only in relation to this total cycle group could various smaller sub-groups secure function and acquire social form.

This centring of the new system on a differentiated structure of intermediate social magnitude disturbed the simple balance that had existed between the very small and very large traditional groups, and impaired the quality of responsible autonomy. The psychological and sociological problems posed by the technological needs of the longwall system were those with respect to which experience in the industry was least, and towards which its traditions were antithetical. The consequences of this conflict between the demands of the new situation and the resources available from past experience will be taken up in the light of the detailed account, which will now be presented, of the longwall system itself.

Features and Difficulties of the Longwall Production Unit as a Whole [1]

The Scale and Spatio-Temporal Structure of the Three-Shift Cycle. In the longwall method, a direct advance is made into the coal on a continuous front; faces of 180–200 yds. being typical, though longer faces are not uncommon. The work is broken down into a standard

[1] The procedure followed both in the text and in Figs. 1 and 2 and Table 1 has been to build up a model of the system in terms of the experience of a group of faces similarly run and well known at first hand. What follows is therefore an account of one version of the system, though the version is a common one. Faces exist that are twice as long as that given. In thick seams these may require 40–50 fillers alone (even more), apart altogether from other personnel. In thin seams with high gates more than twice the number of rippers given may be employed, 8 or more on the main gate and some 6–4 on the side gates respectively. On shorter faces there may be only one borer and at least one gummer. Under some conditions packing and drawing-off are separated from belt-

series of component operations that follow each other in rigid succession over three shifts of seven and a half hours each, so that a total coal-getting cycle may be completed once in each twenty-four hours of the working week. The shift spread of the 40 workmen needed on an average face is: 10 each to the first ("cutting") and second ("ripping") shifts; 20 to the third ("filling") shift. The amount of coal scheduled for extraction varies under different conditions but is commonly in the neighbourhood of 200 tons per cycle. A medium-size pit with three seams would have 12–15 longwall faces in operation simultaneously.

These faces are laid out in districts as shown in Fig. 1. Since the longwall method is specially applicable to thin seams, Fig. 1 has been set up in terms of a 3-ft. working. The face, extending 90 yds. on either side of the main gate is within average limits for a seam of this thickness. The height of the face area—that of the 3-ft. seam itself—may be contrasted with the 9 ft. and 7 ft, to which the main and side gates have been ripped and built up as permanent structures with cambers and side-packs. By regulation, props must be placed every 3 ft., and the line of props shown in Fig. 1*b* is that placed immediately against a coal-face waiting to be filled off. The area marked "Gob" (to use a term common in mining vernacular) indicates the expanse from which the coal has already been extracted. On this area the roof is left to collapse. Only the tunnels made by the main and side gates, which

work, and loading-point personnel are included as face workers. There are differences in nomenclature in different areas, e.g. "dinters" for "rippers." Variations arise partly from differences in natural conditions (thickness of seam, hardness of coal, type of roof and floor, etc.), partly from preferences in the matter of lay-out, and partly from the amount and character of the equipment available or judged necessary. Though conveyor serviced, quite a long face may be hand-got if the coal is soft; alternatively, two cutting units may be employed if its is hard and the face exceptionally long. Belts are of several varieties ("floor," "plate," "top," etc.). Where the seam is thick enough to eliminate ripping an approximation may be made to a two-shift system. Productivity varies widely in accordance with these differences, as does smoothness of functioning and the degree of stress experienced. Nevertheless, all are versions of one method. The basic pattern is the same.

are used for ventilation and for haulage and travelling, are kept open. These tunnels may sometimes extend for distances of 2 miles, and even more, before the coal face itself is reached from the trunk road leading from the pit bottom.

In each coal-getting cycle the advance made into the coal is equal to the depth of the undercut. A cut of 6 ft. represents typical practice in a thin seam with a good roof. All equipment has to be moved forward as each cycle contributes to the advance. The detail in the face area is represented in Fig. 2, where the coal is shown cut and waiting for the shot-firer, whose task is the last to be performed before the fillers come on. The combined width of the lanes marked "New Creeping Track" and "New Conveyor Track" equals the depth of 6 ft., from which the coal has been removed by the fillers on the last shift of the previous cycle. As part of the preparation work of the current cycle (before the fillers can come on again), the conveyor has to be moved from its previous position in the "old Conveyor Track" to its present position, shown in Fig. 2, in the "New Conveyor Track," against the face. At the same time the two lines of props on either side of the "Old Creeping Track" are withdrawn (allowing the roof to sag or collapse) and thrown over beside the conveyor for the fillers to use in propping up their roof as they get into the next 6 ft. of coal. The term "creeping track" refers to the single, propped, 3-ft. lane, adjacent to that occupied by the conveyor but on the side away from the coal. It allows free passage up and down the face, and is called a creeping track since in thin seams the low roof makes it necessary for all locomotion to take the form of "creeping," i.e. crawling on the hands and knees.

The mass-production character of the longwall operation necessitates a large-scale, mobile layout of the type described. But the spatio-temporal structure imposed by the long face and the shift sequence makes a difficult habitat when considered as a theatre in which effective communication and good working relationships must be maintained between 40 men, their shot-firer and shift deputies. On the one hand, the group is spread over 200 yds. in a tunnel 2 yds. wide and 1 yd. high, cross-cut only by the main and side gates; on the other, it is spread over 24 hours and divided up in three successive shifts. The production engi-

neer might write a simple equation: 200 tons equals 40 men over 200 yds. over 24 hours. But there are no solutions of equivalent simplicity to the psychological and social difficulties raised. For psychological and social difficulties of a new order appear when the scale of a task transcends the limits of simple spatio-temporal structure. By this is meant conditions under which those concerned can complete a job in one place at one time, i.e., the situation of the face-to-face, or singular group.

Once a job is too big for a singular group, a multiple group comes into existence, composed of a number of sub-groups of the singular type. In these differentiated organizations of intermediate social magnitude, problems of inter-group relationships are superimposed on, and inter-act with, the intra-group tensions of the primary components. In the longwall production unit, the scale of the task introduces the contradiction of spatio-temporal disintegration as a condition of multiple group integration.

The Differentiation and Interdependence of Tasks. Occupational roles express the relationship between a production process and the social organization of the group. In one direction, they are related to tasks, which are related to each other; in the other, to people, who are also related to each other. At workman level, there are seven of these roles in the longwall system—borer, cutter, gummer, belt-breaker, belt-builder, ripper, and filler—which are linked to the component tasks of the production process. In Table 1 the functions of these seven categories in the interrelated technological and social structures are described in detail in a comprehensive table. For analytical purposes, however, it is necessary to treat separately these two different aspects of occupational roles; and, in this section, consideration will be given to the interdependence of component tasks in the production process, and to occupational roles so far as they are related to this. These tasks fall into four groups, concerned with (1) the preparation of the coal-face for shot-firing, (2) shifting the conveyor, (3) ripping and building up the main and side gates, and (4) moving the shot coal on to the conveyor.

The face preparation tasks are all performed on the first shift. They include boring holes for the shot-firer, with pneumatic or electrically operated drills, near the roof of the seam

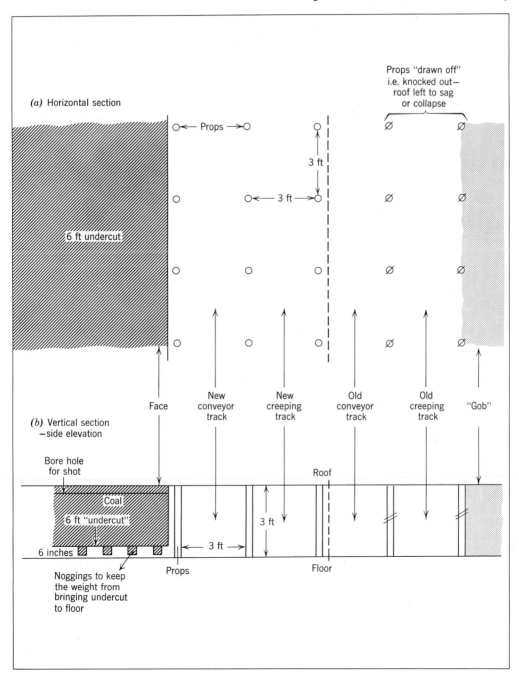

Fig. 2. Coal face as set for filling shift.

through to the depth of the undercut, at short distances (within each filler's "length") along the entire expanse of face; driving the coalcutter so that the blade or "jib" makes an even undercut into the coal some six inches from the floor to whatever depth has been assigned, again along the entire expanse of face; taking out the six inches of coal (called the "gummings") left in the undercut, so that the main weight of coal can drop and break freely when the shots are fired; placing supporting "noggings" underneath it so that this weight does

Table 1. Occupational Structure in the Longwall System

SHIFT SEQUENCE	OCCUPATIONAL ROLES	NO. OF MEN	METHODS OF PAYMENT	GROUP ORGANIZATION	TASKS	SKILLS	STATUS DIFFERENCES AND RANKING
First (usually called "cutting" shift). Either night, 8 P.M.–3.30 A.M., or afternoon, 12 noon–7.30 P.M. (borers start an hour earlier). Though alternating between night and afternoon, personnel on the cutting shift are never on days.	Borer	2	Per hole	Interdependent pair on same note.	Boring holes for shot-firer in each stint to depth of undercut.	Management of electric or pneumatic drills, placing of holes, judgment of roof, hardness of coal, etc.	4.5, equal in pair.
	Cutter	2	Per yard	Interdependent pair on same note, front man and back man.	Operating coal-cutter to achieve even cut at assigned depth the entire length of the face; knocking out (front man), re-setting (back man) props as cutter passes. Back man inserts noggings.	Requires rather more "engineering" skill than other coal-face tasks. Mining skills in keeping cut even under changing conditions, watching roof control.	1, front man senior and responsible for cut; back man assists; cutting is the key preparation task.
	Gummer	4	Day wage	Loose group attached to cutters, through front man without supervisory authority.	Cleaning out undercut, so that clear space for coal to drop and level floor for filler. The coal between undercut and floor is called "the gummings."	Unskilled, heavy manual task, which unless conscientiously done creates difficulties for filler, for when gummings left in, the shot simply blows out and coal is left solid.	7, equal in group; some chance of promotion to cutter eventually.

Belt-breaker	2	Per yard	Interdependent pair on same note.	Shifting belt-engine and tension-end into face clear of rippers; breaking up conveyor in old track, placing plates, etc., ready new track, drawing off props in old creeping track; packing as required.	Belt-breaking is a relatively simple engineering task; engine shifting is awkward and heavy; drawing off and packing involve responsibility for roof control and require solid underground experience.	4.5, equal in pair.
Belt-builder	2	Per yard	Interdependent pair on same note.	Reassembling conveyor in new track; positioning belt-engine and tension-end in line with this; testing running of reassembled conveyor; placing chocks; packing as required.	As with breaking, the level of engineering skill is relatively simple; inconvenience caused to fillers if belt out of position. The roof control responsibilities demand solid underground experience.	4.5, equal in pair.
Ripper	8	Cubic measure	Cohesive functionally inter-related group on same note.	To "rip" "dirt" out of main and side gates to assigned heights; place cambers and build up roof into a solid, safe and durable structure; pack up the sides. The ripping team carries out all operations necessary to their task, doing their own boring. The task is . . . seen through by the group [during] . . . one shift.	This work requires the highest degree of building skill among coal face tasks. Some very heavy labour is entailed. Since the work is relatively permanent there is much pride of craft. On the ripper depends the safety of all gates and main ways.	2, the status of the "main ripper" is next to that of the front man on the cutter, but he is not separately paid. The group usually contains all degrees of experience and is egalitarian.

Second (usually called the "ripping" shift). Either night or afternoon alternating with cutting shift. Rippers may start rather later than builders. None of these personnel go on day shift proper.

(Continued)

Table 1. Continued

SHIFT SEQUENCE	OCCUPA- TIONAL ROLES	NO. OF MEN	METHODS OF PAYMENT	GROUP ORGANIZATION	TASKS	SKILLS	STATUS DIFFERENCES AND RANKING
Third (usually called "filling" shift). Either day, 6 A.M.–1.30 P.M., or after-noon, 2 P.M.–9.30 P.M. Never night.	Filler	20	Weight—tonnage on con-veyors.	Aggregate of individuals with equal "stints"; all on same note; frac-tionated re-lationships and much isolation.	The length of the "stint" is determined by the depth of the cut and the thickness of the seam. Using hand or air pick and shovel, the filler "throws" the "shot" coal on to the conveyor until he has cleared his length, i.e. "filled off." He props up every 2 ft. 6 in. as he works in.	The filler remains in one work place while condi-tions change. Considerable underground experience is required to cope with bad conditions. Each man is responsible for his own section of roof. Bad work on other shifts makes the task harder. It is heavy in any case and varies in dif-ferent parts of the wall.	4.5, equal through-out the group; "corner" men are envied, reputation of being good or bad workman is important.
3 shifts	7 roles	40 men	5 methods	4 types	The common background of "underground" skill is more important than the task differences.		Differences in status and weekly earn-ings are small, apart from the case of the gum-mers.

not cause it to sag down to the floor while the "cut" is standing during the next shift. These tasks are performed in the order given. Three of the seven work roles are associated with their execution, two men being fully occupied boring the holes, a further two in managing the coal-cutter, and four in clearing out the undercut.

The success of the shots fired at the end of the second shift to make the coal finally ready for the filler depends on the efficiency with which each of these interdependent preparation tasks has been carried out. Bad execution of any one of them diminishes, and may even cancel out, the effect of the shots, with consequent havoc in the lengths of the particular fillers where such breakdowns have occurred. Holes bored too low leave a quantity of coal, difficult to extract, clinging to the roof after the shots have been fired. If the roof is sticky, this gives rise to "sticky tops." Holes not bored through to the full depth of the undercut create the condition of "hard backs," the shots having no effect on this part of the coal. The coal-cutter only too frequently has a tendency to leave the floor and "get up into the coal," producing an uneven cut. This means less working height for the filler, and also less wages, since his tonnage is reduced. When the "gummings" are left in, the shot is wasted; the coal has nowhere to drop and the powder blows out of the hole (usually up the "cutting break" in the roof) so that the mass to be extracted is left solid. Failure to insert noggings, which leads to the cut sagging down, also renders useless the services of the shot-firer.

The group of operations concerned with the conveyor involves—since forward movement is blocked by props which must be left standing—breaking up the sections of belt in the old conveyor track and building them up in the new. Each of these tasks requires two men: the belt-breakers and belt-builders. The dismantling part is done on the first shift in the wake of the cutting operation. The reasons include the necessity of shifting belt-engines and tension-ends out of the gate areas (where they are positioned when the conveyor is working) in order to allow the ripping operation to proceed. The reassembly of the conveyor is the only task performed in the face area during the second shift. Unless the conveyor is properly jointed, set close to the new face, and accurately sighted in a straight line, a further crop of difficulties arise, and frequent stoppages may interfere with filling. The most modern types of belt, e.g., floor belts, avoid the labour of breaking up and reassembling plates. Belt-engines and tension-ends are cumbersome equipment, but they must nevertheless be shifted every day. Similarly, the last two lines of props have to be taken down and thrown forward.

The third group of tasks comprises those that entail ripping up the roof of the main and side gates to the depth of the undercut, and building them up with a stable roof and firmly packed sides so that haulage- and air-ways can advance with the face. Unless this work is expertly done, the danger of roof falls is acute, with the likelihood both of men and equipment being blocked in the face. This work is carried out by a team of 7–8 rippers.

Only when all these operations have been completed, can the shots be fired and the fillers come on. For the filling operation, the entire face is divided up into equal lengths—except that the corner positions are somewhat shorter in view of difficulties created by the proximity of belt-engines and tension-ends. In a 3-ft. seam, lengths would be 8–10 yds., and some 20 fillers would be required, 10 in each half-face of 90–100 yds. Each filler is required to extract the entire coal from his length, going back to the depth of the 6 ft. undercut. When he has thrown his last load on to the conveyor he has "filled off," i.e., finished his "length" or "stint." As he progresses into his coal, he has the additional task of propping up his roof every 3 ft. As well as a hand-pick and shovel, his tool kit includes an air pick, used for dealing with some of the difficulties created by bad preparation, or in any case when his coal is hard.

At a later point there will be a discussion of the differential distribution of bad conditions among the lengths of a face. Here it may be noted that the face is not "filled off" until each and every length has been cleared, and that until this has been done, the new cycle cannot begin. Disorganization on the filling shift disorganizes the subsequent shifts, and its own disorganization is often produced by the bad preparation left by these teams. Every time the cycle is stopped, some 200 tons of coal are lost.

So close is the task interdependence that the system becomes vulnerable from its need for one hundred per cent performance at each step. The most sensitive interaction is between the face-preparation activities and filling, but it is in relation to this that social organization is weakest. This point will be taken up in later sections.

The Segmented Quality of the Social Organization. With respect to the way in which the work roles have been institutionalized as regards the persons and groups concerned, a basic segregation of the various categories of workers from each other follows from the fact that it has been the traditional practice for a face-worker to be trained in only one of the seven roles, and to spend all or most of his underground life in this one occupation. This basic segregation of roles is intensified by the five different methods of payment described in Table 1, and by the exaggeration of status differences, despite the common background of "underground skill" and the equivalence of earnings (apart from the rather lower rate received by the gummers).

It is still further reinforced by the segregation of shifts. As will be seen from the shift time-tables, the three shifts never meet. Moreover, the two preparation groups alternate on the so-called "back shifts" while the fillers alternate on "days" and "afternoons," so that a far-reaching community, as well as work, split is effected between the fillers and the others. The "back shift" men are either going to or coming from work in the evening, so that they are cut off from normal community activities during the week. Even at week-ends they are down the pit either on Saturday afternoon or Sunday evening.

As regards the primary work groups in which those performing the various roles participate, there are four radically different patterns: the series of interdependent pairs—borers, belt-builders, and belt-breakers; the extended pair organization of the cutters and gummers; the self-sufficient group of eight rippers; and the aggregate of twenty fillers spread out over the 200-yd. face. The uneven social quality of these different types of primary groups will be discussed . . . [later], both with respect to intra- and inter-group relations. This unevenness, taken together with the role and shift segregation, works against the social integration of the cycle group as a whole. Yet, in view of the close interdependence of tasks, the social integration of the total work group is a first essential of the system.

It is submitted that the non-existence of the cycle group as a social whole in face of the interdependence of the component tasks is one of the major contradictions present in the longwall method. The social organization is a simple reflection of the "job breakdown." Because this latter is reintegrated into a technological whole by the task sequence it does not follow that the differentiated role-groups concerned are also and thereby reintegrated into a social whole. Differentiation gives rise to the need for social as well as technological integration. No attempt seems to have been made in the longwall method to achieve any living social integration of the primary and shift groups into which the cycle aggregate has been differentiated. This, of course, is a common omission in mass-production systems. . . .

Four Types of Group Defence

Informal Organization. The functional isolation of the filler within his own group, which leaves him "officially" alone with his "coals," is met by an attempt to develop informal, small-group organization in which private arrangements to help each other out are made among neighbours, in twos, threes, or fours. But these solely interpersonal arrangements are undependable and open to manipulation for anti-social and competitive as well as for mutually protective ends. A number of isolates is left over. The total face group is incapable, except defensively, of acting as a socially responsible whole, since not even private allegiances are owed outside the small informal groups. These in turn are without responsible autonomy; the absence of institutionalized mutual obligation means that there are no statutory group tasks, and each individual can be held ultimately responsible only for clearing his own length. Internal "rows" the more easily break up the informal "coalitions," whose morale tends to be of the clique type.

Examples were, however, given to the writers of stable groups who stuck to each other and worked well over long periods. One informant said of these: "Here things are more like the old times in the pit." Groups of this kind were envied and also criticized for being "too close." They appeared sometimes to be held together by a natural leader, and at others to be made up of individuals of generally good personality. Most informants were agreed that there was a tendency for the extremes to sort themselves out; there were "good" and "bad" faces as well as "good" and "bad" cliques within a particular face aggregate. But all this happened as it might. There was no support from the system.

Isolates, it appears, are either individualists —who "won't even share timber"—or men with bad reputations, with whom others refuse to work. Amongst these are the unconscientious—who "won't help out at the end of a shift" and who are frequently absent—and the helpless—who "cannot learn to look after themselves under bad conditions." Others, whose stamina is deficient (whether through age, illness, or neurosis) and whose lengths are often uncleared in consequence, are dropped from the informal groups.

Only to a very limited extent, therefore, does his informal group organization meet the filler's need for a secure role in a primary group within his own shift. In view of the extent of his dependence on the performance of those in the other two shifts, his need for this foundation is greater than that of any of the other occupational groups, while the resources available to him are fewer.

Reactive Individualism. His small group failing, the filler is thrown on to himself and against others. The second defence against isolation is the development of a reactive individualism, in which a reserve of personal secrecy is apt to be maintained. Among his own shift mates there is competitive intrigue for the better places—middle positions are avoided; from these "it is a long way to creep" —and for jobs in workings where conditions are good there is a scramble.

On some faces described to the writers, fear of victimization was rife, particularly in the form of being sent to work in a "bad place"; the deputy being more easily turned into a persecutor in view of the guilt arising from the intrigue and deception which the men practised both against him and against each other. Against the deputy, advantage is taken of the scope afforded in the underground situation for petty deception over such matters as time of leaving the pit, or the "measure that is sent up" (amount of coal filled on to the conveyor). With the deputy, however, men are also prepared to enter into alliance against each other, often for very good reasons—to stop mates from going absent and by so doing throwing more work on to the others.

As regards outside groups, practices of bribing members of the other shifts in the hope of getting a "good deal" in one's own length were mentioned by several informants. Tobacco is taken to the cutter; gummers are stood a pint on Sunday. These practices are to be regarded as symptoms of a state of affairs rather than as widespread in themselves.

The effect of this defensive individualism is to reduce the sense of secure identification in the larger pit collectivity, which was the second principle on which the older equilibrium was based.

Nowhere is the mistrust that shift mates have of each other more in evidence than in controversies over bye-work "slipping off the note." On what is referred to as the "big note" is entered all the contract and bye-work done during the week by the shift aggregate. This note is issued to one man called "the number man" since he is identified by his check-number. In no sense is this individual a representative appointed by his mates. Only rarely is he an informal leader. Customarily he is a "corner man," whose length adjoins the main gate, i.e., the man most conveniently within reach of the deputy. When asked about bye-work he does not always know what has been done at the far ends of the face and he is under no obligation to stop his own work to find out. But though a number of men will grouse about their pay being short, mentioning this or that item as having "slipped off the note," very few ever bother to check up. There are men who have worked on a face for three or four years and never once seen their own big note. Yet these are among the more ready to accuse the corner man or the deputy. The corner man is suspected at least of never forgetting to make the most of his own assignments. To the deputy is ascribed the intention of keeping the costs of his district down. Conspiracy between the two is often alleged. Only when a major rumpus occurs are such suspicions put to the test, but showdowns of this kind are avoided as apt to peter out in squabbles proving nothing.

The competition, intrigue, unwillingness to put allegations to the test and the reserve of personal secrecy, are parts of one pattern. Whatever their personal wishes, men feel under pressure to be out for themselves, since the social structure in which they work denies them membership in any group that can legitimize interdependence. In this respect reactive individualism makes a basic interpretation of the social structure of the filling shift and is the only form of authorized behaviour.

Mutual Scapegoating. Fillers almost never see those who work on the "back shifts," and this absence of contact gives full scope for mutual and irresponsible scapegoating. When there is a crisis, and the filling shift is unable to fill off, the "buck" is passed to the other shifts—or vice versa if disorganization has occurred elsewhere. It is frequently also passed to the deputy, who is blamed for not finding substitutes, and to repair men, brought in, but too old to stand the pace.

For these to pass the buck back to the fillers is fruitless. As they do not exist as a responsible whole, they, as a group, are not there to take the blame, and the individual filler can always exempt himself. Since bad conditions and bad work interact so closely, it is usually difficult to pin blame specifically. Mutual scapegoating is a self-perpetuating system, in which nothing is resolved and no one feels guilty. For all concerned to remain in collusion with such a system is a defence which allows each to make his "anonymous contribution" to the "group mentality," [2] which sabotages both the goal of cycle productivity and the needs of the individual for a membership in a satisfying work-group. So far as this pattern obtains, all strike at each other in a mock war in which no one is hurt yet all suffer.

This defence can also be seen as a "backhanded" attempt to recover the supportive unity lost through reactive individualism in a way that is consistent with it. For all to be "in the bad" together is at least a way of being together. If one's contribution to a group is to help carry the badness of others, the group's contribution to oneself is to allow one to leave some of one's own badness in the group by being granted, for example, the privilege of withdrawal so that one's absence is sanctioned

on a fair share of occasions. This "formula" provides a workable scheme since the tacit agreement is only too plausibly maintained that the badness both of the group and of the individual are exclusively effects of the system which the group is compelled to operate without having power to change, i.e., these effects are regarded as "induced" rather than also as "own" forces. The group and the individual can therefore deny and get rid of their own badness by ascribing it to the system. The good of the group becomes its power to preserve the good of individual members by limiting the degree of their exposure to the bad system. The alternative would be constructive limitation of its real deficiencies so that it might be operated with more productive results and a higher degree of mutual satisfaction.

Not that the system is felt as entirely bad since it is the means by which a living is earned. Moreover, under present conditions this living is a good one, both in terms of wages and of community status. But the benefits which these "goods" bring are not realized in the work activities of the group. They lie outside the work system, which is tolerated as a means to external ends rather than accepted also as an end in itself, worthy of wholehearted pursuit in virtue of the internal satisfactions it affords. When these different aspects of the matter are put together the expectation emerges of a balance being struck which would allow things to tick over, though with a degree of social illness costly alike to productivity and to personal well-being. This expectation accords with reality.

Self-Compensatory Absenteeism. Withdrawal is the fourth form of defence, complementing mutual scapegoating, and absenteeism is to be regarded as a recognized social technique within this pattern. For example, one filler, returning from his week's holiday with pay, complained that the first two shifts had "knocked it all out of him." The gummings had been left in. His coal was solid. He had had the air-pick on all day. "I've tried cursing 'em but it's no use, and pleading with 'em but it's no use. I'll take a day off for this."

When conditions on a face deteriorate, especially in ways that are predictable, absenteeism among fillers sometimes piles up to a point where the remainder have to stay down an

[2] W. R. Bion, "Experiences in Groups, III," *Human Relations,* Vol. II, No. 1, January, 1949, pp. 13–22.

extra two or three hours in order to clear the face. Should this situation repeat itself for more than a day or two, those coming on shift often meet at the pit-head baths before presenting themselves for work. If less than a certain number arrive, all go home.

Absenteeism of this self-compensatory type, though carried out as an act of aggrieved defiance against a system, felt in these circumstances as persecutory is an attempt on the part of the individual to prolong his work life at the coal-face. For without the respite of occasional absences, he feels that he would soon become unable to carry on. In view of the accentuated differences both in wages and in status between face workers and repair, haulage, or surface personnel, the goal of remaining at the coal-face for as long as possible would appear to operate as a powerful motivational force in determining the behaviour of the ordinary face-worker. . . .

Conclusions

The fact that the desperate economic incentives of the between-war period no longer operate means a greater intolerance of unsatisfying or difficult working conditions, or systems of organization, among miners, even though they may not always be clear as to the exact nature of the resentment or hostility which they often appear to feel. The persistence of socially ineffective structures at the coal-face is likely to be a major factor in preventing a rise of morale, in discouraging recruitment, and in increasing labour turnover.

The innovations in social organization of face-work groups, which have begun to appear, and the success of some of these developments, suggest that the organizational changes brought about by nationalization provide a not inappropriate opportunity for the experimental working through of problems of the types which have been indicated. It can certainly be said with some confidence that within the industry there exist the necessary resources and creativity to allow widespread constructive developments to take place.

As regards the longwall system, the first need is for systematic study and evaluation of the changes so far tried.[3] It seems to the present writers, however, that a qualitative change will have to be effected in the general character of the method, so that a social as well as a technological whole can come into existence. Only if this is achieved can the relationships of the cycle work-group be successfully integrated and a new social balance be created.

The immediate problems are to develop formal small-group organization on the filling shift and to work out an acceptable solution to the authority questions in the cutting team. But it is difficult to see how these problems can be solved effectively without restoring responsible autonomy to primary groups throughout the system and ensuring that each of these groups has a satisfying sub-whole as its work task, and some scope for flexibility in work-pace. Only if this is done will the stress of the deputy's role be reduced and his task of maintaining the cycle receive spontaneous support from the primary work groups.

It is likely that any attempts in this direction would require to take advantage of the recent trend of training face-workers for more than one role, so that interchangeability of tasks would be possible within work teams. Moreover, the problem of shift segregation will not be overcome until the situation is altered in which one large group is permanently organised round the day shift and the others round the back shifts. Some interchange between roles in preparation and filling tasks would seem worth consideration. Once preparation workers and fillers could experience each other's situations, mutual understanding and tolerance would be likely to increase.

It is to be borne in mind that developments in room-and-pillar methods appear to be stressing the value of the strongly-knit primary work-group and that the most recent advances in mechanization, such as power loaders or strippers, both require work teams of this kind.

[3] One of the most interesting of these is "An Experiment in Continuous Longwall Mining at Bolsover Colliery," W. V. Sheppard, The Institution of Mining Engineers, Annual General Meeting, Jan. 1951.

Interaction between Members of Bomber Crews
as a Determinant of Sociometric Choice

DOROTHY MCBRIDE KIPNIS

Several investigators of neighborhood groups have concluded that sheer physical proximity between the dwelling-units of two persons will affect the likelihood that a friendship will develop between them.[1] For example, Festinger, Schachter, and Back studied social relationships among residents of a student housing project. They found that friendships were most common between next-door neighbors, less common between people whose houses were separated by another house, and so on, until there were very few friendships between people living more than four or five houses apart.

From *Human Relations*, Vol. 10, No. 3, August, 1957, pp. 263–270. Reprinted with permission of the publisher, Tavistock Publications Ltd., and the author.

This research was supported in part by the United States Air Force under Contract No. AF(038)–25726, monitored by Air Force Personnel and Training Research Center.

Permission is granted for reproduction, translation, publication, use, and disposal in whole and in part by or for the United States Government. The author is particularly indebted to Dr. Fred E. Fiedler and Mr. Walter A. Cleven for their assistance during the entire study. She also wishes to acknowledge with thanks the help of Dr. R. L. French and Dr. T. B. Roby of the Crew Research Laboratory for making available the necessary data for this study.
[1] See T. Caplow and R. Forman, "Neighbourhood Interaction in a Homogeneous Community," *Amer. Sociol. Rev.*, Vol. XV, pp. 357–66, 1950; L. Festinger, S. Schachter, and Kurt Back, *Social Pressures in Informal Groups*, New York: Harper and Brothers, 1950; and R. K. Merton, "The Social Psychology of Housing," in Wayne Dennis (ed.), *Current Trends in Social Psychology*, Pittsburgh: Univer. of Pittsburgh Press, 1948.

In this housing development, much of the social life of the community revolved around a central court in each block. Residents tended to be social isolates if their houses faced away from this central court. Even such factors as the location of mailboxes and outside staircases affected the development of friendships in an adjoining project consisting of apartment buildings.

Festinger *et al.* conceptualize their results in terms of two variables: "physical distance" and "functional distance." The first of these is distance in yards or some other physical measure, while functional distance is measured in terms of use of the same facilities or overlapping of customary routes in the performance of regular activities. When either physical or functional distance is small, a large number of accidental meetings or "passive contacts" occur, and some of these develop into closer relationships.

This interpretation has implications for the development of personal relationships in formally organized groups. An organizational structure ordinarily necessitates contacts between some members of the group and restricts interaction between others. The interpersonal preferences of members of organized groups might then be more a function of their positions or status in the group than of any more personal attributes. The methodological implications for studies relating personality attributes and sociometric choice, as well as for the interpretation of preferences of members of organized groups, are obvious.

The present investigation is concerned with the prediction of sociometric choices of members of B-29 bomber crews. The amount of interaction possible or necessary between any two members of the crew during flight, and to some extent before and after flight, is dictated by crew position. Each crew member has a designated physical location in the plane, and many members of the crew are sufficiently separated that only inter-phone communication is possible. Each crew member also has specified jobs to perform, some of which require interaction with certain other members of the crew. If differential amount of contact plays the same role in the development of friendships between members of working teams as in the formation of neighbourhood groups, sociometric choices should follow the channels of interaction dictated by the crew organization. We hypothesize, therefore, that sociometric preferences of crew members can be predicted (a) from their physical location in the plane and (b) from their job responsibilities or functions.

more choices than lower-ranking enlisted men.[2] In addition, the crew consists of five officers and six enlisted men, and both officers and enlisted men may tend to restrict their choices to their own groups. To control both of these effects, we restricted comparisons to cases in which two or more men of fairly equal status differed in amount of interaction with a third crew member. If two officers differed in amount of interaction required with a specified enlisted man, we predicted that the officer with the greater amount of interaction would show more liking for the enlisted man than the officer who had less interaction. Similarly, if one enlisted man was frequently required to work with a certain officer while another was not, we predicted that the enlisted man who worked with the officer would show more liking for him.

Procedure

SUBJECTS. The subjects (Ss) were members of B-29 crews in training at Randolph Air Force Base. Sociometric preferences of members of four training classes were obtained. Each class consisted of 17 or 18 crews of 11 men each. As some crew members were absent at the testing session, the total number of subjects tested was 705; 320 officers and 385 airmen.

INDICES OF SOCIOMETRIC PREFERENCE. Preference scores were derived from responses to a short questionnaire. This questionnaire, the *Position Description Form*, consists of sociometric questions developed by the Crew Research Laboratory, AFPTRC, and is administered routinely to crews in training (4). Ss were asked to check once or twice, according to the certainty of their choice, the crew members they would prefer in each of the following criterion situations: (a) arranging a crew party, (b) helping to load special cargo, (c) going to town for the evening, (d) returning from behind enemy lines, and (e) as a companion at a lonely outpost.

As responses to the five items were highly correlated, all scores were based on the sum of choices on all five questions.

Differences in prestige strongly affect sociometric preferences in B-29 crews. Officers with high prestige receive on the average many

Results

Estimates of differential amounts of interaction were made on the basis of (a) physical distance between positions occupied by crew members during flight and (b) functional distance resulting from interaction made necessary by job responsibilities, both in ground-training and during flight. The basis for each prediction, specific procedures, and results will be given for each hypothesis in turn.

Physical Distance as a Determinant of Sociometric Preferences. The B-29 is divided into three main compartments, and each crew member is assigned a position in one of the three compartments which he occupies during most of the flight. Informal interaction is thus largely confined within compartments. Even within the same compartment, equipment and physical obstructions may prevent interaction between persons who are quite near each other.

Two predictions were made on the basis of physical positions. Both involve the navigator (an officer) and the radio operator (an enlisted man). These two crew members occupy the same section of the forward compartment of the plane, and both are somewhat isolated from other crew members. Therefore, we predicted (a) that radio operators would show more liking for navigators than would other

[2] Fiedler, F. E. Unpublished research.

enlisted men and (*b*) that navigators would show more liking for radio operators than would other officers.

THE RADIO OPERATOR-NAVIGATOR RELATIONSHIP. Radio operators' preferences for their navigators were compared with preferences expressed by each of four other enlisted men. These four men were the central fire control gunner and the right, left, and tail gunners. The four gunners all occupy positions in rear compartments of the plane, and have relatively little opportunity for interaction with the navigator.

Each airman's preference for the navigator was categorized according to whether the

Table 1 shows the average preferences for the navigator expressed by radio operators, and by each of the four gunners. In each case, radio operators show more liking for the navigator than the other airman, and each of the differences is significant beyond the .05 level.[4] Navigators are then more likely to be preferred by radio operators than by other airmen, as was expected.

THE NAVIGATOR-RADIO OPERATOR RELATIONSHIP. We also predicted that navigators would show stronger preferences for radio operators than would other officers. Three other officers have rank and prestige similar to the navigator, but are assigned to locations that allow less com-

Table 1. Comparison of Radio Operators' and Control Airmen's References for Their Crew Navigators

CREW POSITION OF CONTROL AIRMAN	AVERAGE PREFERENCE FOR NAVIGATOR	AVERAGE RADIO OPERATOR'S PREFERENCE FOR NAVIGATOR	DIFFERENCE	*t*	N *
Central fire control gunner	.77	1.14	.36	2.23 *	44
Left gunner	.63	1.10	.48	2.97 **	40
Right gunner	.79	1.14	.36	2.02 *	42
Tail gunner	.73	1.10	.37	2.25 *	41

* .05 > *p*, one-tail test.
** .01 > *p*, one-tail test.

* *t*'s are computed for correlated data because airmen's preferences are correlated within crews. Consequently, N varies slightly because of missing data for the control airman.

navigator was his most preferred officer, was intermediate, or was his least preferred officer. The navigator was considered most preferred whenever he received the maximum number of choices given by the airman to an officer, and least preferred whenever he received the minimum number of choices given to an officer.[3] All other preferences were classified as intermediate. Weights of 0 (least preferred), 1, and 2 (most preferred) were assigned to the three categories.

[3] Choices given to one officer, the aircraft commander, were here disregarded as he has greater prestige than the other four officers. Airmen who chose all four other officers an equal number of times were eliminated from the sample.

munication with the radio operator. One (the radar observer) sits in a rear compartment with the gunners, while two others (the pilot and the bombardier) sit in the forward compartment but are separated from the radio operator by bulkheads. These three officers' preferences for the radio operator were compared with navigators' preferences for the same radio operators.

The number of times each officer chose the radio operator was converted into a percentage based on his total number of choices of the five lower-ranking airmen. This procedure controls variation between officers in the strength of their preferences for officers over

[4] All probabilities are given for one tail only.

Table 2. Comparison of Navigators' and Control Officers' Preferences for Radio Operators

CREW POSITION OF CONTROL OFFICER	AVERAGE PERCENTAGE OF CHOICES GIVEN TO RADIO OPERATORS *	AVERAGE PERCENTAGE OF NAVIGATORS' CHOICES GIVEN TO RADIO OPERATORS	DIFFERENCE	t	N
Radar observer	18.1	28.1	10.0	2.53 **	48
Pilot	19.1	26.9	7.8	2.59 **	53
Bombardier	17.0	24.0	7.0	2.40 *	52

* $.05 > p$, one-tail test.

** $.01 > p$, one-tail test.

* The percentage computed = 100 (number of choices to the radio operator)/Total number of choices to the radio operator, central fire control gunner, and right, left, and tail gunners.

enlisted men, and also weights data from officers who showed strong preferences for one or two men even though they gave no choices at all to the rest. Specifically, then, the hypothesis is that the navigator will give a greater proportion of his choices of enlisted men to the radio operator than will the other three officers.

Table 2 shows the average percentages of choices given to radio operators by navigators, and by each of the other officers. In all three comparisons, the navigator gives a greater share of his choices to the radio operator, and the difference between the navigator and the other officer is significant beyond the .05 level. Thus, navigators and radio operators each show more liking for the other than do other crew members of their respective statuses.

Functional Distance as a Determinant of Sociometric Preferences. Some of the men in the B-29 crew have regular duties requiring them to interact with specific other members of the crew. We also expected contacts of this kind to increase the likelihood that friendships would develop between the men concerned.

THE CENTRAL FIRE CONTROL GUNNER-BOMBARD-IER RELATIONSHIP. The central fire control gunner and bombardier furnish one instance where we might expect this process to take place. The central fire control gunner is the senior gunner of the crew, while the bombardier is the officer in charge of the gunners. The central fire control gunner's duties entail both inter-phone contacts with the bombardier dur-

ing flight and interaction with the bombardier on the ground before and after flight. The other gunners and the radio operator have less occasion to interact with the bombardier. Consequently, we should expect the central fire control gunner to show more liking for the bombardier than the other gunners and the radio operator.

This prediction was tested by the same procedure used to test the prediction concerning radio operators' preferences for navigators. Each airman's preference for the bombardier was categorized according to whether the bombardier was his most preferred officer, was intermediate, or was least preferred. Weights of 0 (least preferred), 1, and 2 (most preferred) were again assigned to the three categories.

Table 3 shows central fire control gunners' and other airmen's average preferences for the bombardier. In all but one case, central fire control gunners' preferences are significantly greater than those of the other airmen. It will also be noted that the airman who likes the bombardier least is the radio operator, who has almost no direct work contacts with the bombardier. The results at both extremes in amount of interaction are then consistent with the hypothesis.

THE AIRCRAFT COMMANDER-PILOT RELATION-SHIP. A second case in which functional distance should affect sociometric preferences involves two officers, the aircraft commander and the pilot. The aircraft commander is ac-

Table 3. Comparison of Central Fire Control Gunners' and Control Airmen's Preferences for their Crew Bombardiers

CREW POSITION OF CONTROL AIRMAN	AVERAGE PREFERENCE FOR BOMBARDIER	AVERAGE CENTRAL FIRE CONTROL GUNNER'S PREFERENCE FOR BOMBARDIER	DIFFERENCE	t	N
Radio operator	.68	1.30	.62	3.77 **	44
Right gunner	1.00	1.27	.27	1.67	44
Left gunner	1.02	1.27	.25	1.72 *	45
Tail gunner	1.00	1.25	.25	1.81 *	44

* $.05 > p$, one-tail test.
** $.01 > p$, one-tail test.

tually the senior pilot of the plane, while the pilot is the co-pilot. These two men work together closely during the flight and, in addition, attend ground school classes together. None of the three other officers—the navigator, the radar observer, and the bombardier—works so closely or continuously with the pilot as does the aircraft commander. Pilots should then be better liked by aircraft commanders than by the other officers.

Pilots, on the average, receive 8.41 choices from their crew commanders. These same pilots receive an average of 7.46 choices from the navigators in their crews. The difference is significant at the .02 level ($t = 2.27$, N = 61).

Bombardiers' and radar observers' preferences could not be compared with those of aircraft commanders because it was found that officers differed significantly in the total number of choices that they gave to other officers, disregarding direction. Both aircraft commanders and navigators made more choices than the other three officers. As this difference makes a comparison between aircraft commanders' preferences with those of an officer giving fewer choices ambiguous, other comparisons were not made.

The fact that the aircraft commander and navigator make most choices is consistent with our general hypothesis in that these two officers are the most central officers in the crew in terms of their functions as crew members. The aircraft commander's role involves contact with all other officers, since he is held responsible for crew performance, while the navigator exchanges information both with

the bombardier and with the radar observer as well as with the aircraft commander and pilot. Thus, the two men who are required to interact to a considerable extent with all other officers also tend to show stronger preferences for them.

THE OFFICER-CENTRAL FIRE CONTROL GUNNER RELATIONSHIP. From the general hypothesis that proximity and interaction are determinants of sociometric preferences, we should expect a man who is required to work with one other crew member, but not at all with a second, to show a stronger preference for the man with whom he works. We have not tested this hypothesis directly because of the difficulty in controlling prestige in the present situation. However, a comparison between the choices of men who are required to work with both individuals and the choices of men who are required to work with only one of them will also serve to estimate prestige effects. If differences in preferences are a function of differences in prestige, men who work with both others should also show differences in the strengths of their preferences for them, while if the difference can be correctly considered to be a result of interaction, men who work with both others should prefer them equally.

One instance where this comparison can be made involves the extent to which officers, as compared with enlisted men, prefer the central fire control gunner over other airmen. Officers ordinarily have more contact with the central fire control gunner than they do with other lower-ranking airmen because of his supervisory responsibilities. Other enlisted men, on the other hand, have as much contact with each other as with the central fire control gunner. Therefore, we might expect officers to prefer the central fire control gunner over other enlisted men to a greater extent than enlisted men themselves will prefer him over other members of their own group.

This proves to be the case. The central fire control gunner receives, on the average, 5.7 more choices from officers than the second most popular airman with officers, the tail gunner.[5] This difference is highly significant ($t = 5.79$, $N = 45$, $.01 > p$). The central fire control gunner and tail gunner are also the two most popular airmen with enlisted men. However, in this case, the difference between the two airmen in number of choices received is .2, which is not significant ($t = .13$, $N = 47$). Thus, the central fire control gunner's greater popularity occurs only with the group that has little contact with the other airmen.

mines only which other individuals a specific person meets, or whether proximity continues to exert influence even beyond the stage of initial acquaintanceship. In the present study, it is apparent that the latter is the case. The crews consisted of only 11 men who had worked together frequently before the sociometric data were gathered, so that all of the men knew all other members of their crew fairly well. Even within this small group, crew members were better liked by others who had worked with or near them most frequently. Thus, the data suggest a process such that as two men interact with each other more and more, they begin to seem more likeable to each other. The content of interaction, and the conditions under which it will have such an effect, need further specification. However, exploration of the types and consequences of interaction might be a highly fruitful means of increasing our understanding of interpersonal preferences.

Discussion

The results of the present study indicate that physical and functional proximity are factors to be considered in evaluating the interpersonal preferences of members of organized groups. The hypothesis that proximity is a determinant of interpersonal preferences appears to apply as well in B-29 crews as in the previous studies of housing developments.

In addition to testing this hypothesis in a different context, the present study also extends the interpretation of results in one major respect. The investigations of housing projects do not make it clear whether proximity deter-

Summary and Conclusions

The study tested the general hypothesis that sociometric preferences of members of bomber crews are a function of the formal organization of the crew. The crew organization is such that a specific physical position in the plane and specialized job responsibilities are assigned to each man. Both physical positions and job responsibilities enhance or restrict the opportunities for interaction among crew members. We hypothesized that crew members would be best liked by others who had greatest opportunity for interaction with them.

The results support the conclusion that interpersonal preferences of crew members are affected by the crew organization, and that greater amounts of contact (resulting from organizational requirements) facilitate the development of stronger preferences.

---

[5] One enlisted man, the flight engineer, was omitted as he usually has both higher rank and greater prestige than the other enlisted men. Only crews for which data were available for all officers or enlisted men were included in the analysis.

Work Flow and Status

WILLIAM F. WHYTE

In discussing the kitchen as a status system, we have only incidentally taken account of the fact that the kitchen is part of a communication and supply system, which operates to get the food from the range onto the customer's table. Looking at it this way will bring to light other problems.

Where the restaurant is small and the kitchen is on the same floor as the dining room, waitresses are in direct contact with cooks. This does not eliminate friction, but at least everybody is in a position to know what everybody else is doing, and the problems of communication and coordination are relatively simple.

When the restaurant is large, there are more people whose activities must be coordinated, and when the restaurant operates on several floors, the coordination must be accomplished through people who are not generally in face-to-face contact with each other. These factors add tremendously to the difficulty of achieving smooth coordination.

The cooks feel that they work under pressure—and under a pressure whose origins they cannot see or anticipate.

As one of them said,

It's mostly the uncertainty of the job that gets me down, I think. I mean, you never know how much work you're going to have to do. You never know in advance if you're going to have to make more. I think that's what a lot of 'em don't like around here. That uncertainty is hard on your nerves.

For a cook, the ideal situation is one in which she always has a sufficient supply of

From *Human Relations in the Restaurant Industry*, copyright 1948 by McGraw-Hill Book Co., pp. 47–60. Reprinted with permission of the publisher.

food prepared ahead so that she is never asked for something she does not have on hand. As one of them said, "You have to keep ahead or you get all excited and upset."

Life would be simpler for the cook if she were free to prepare just as much food as she wanted to, but the large and efficiently operated restaurant plans production on the basis of very careful estimates of the volume of business to be expected. Low food costs depend in part upon minimizing waste or leftover food. This means that production must be scheduled so as to run only a little ahead of customer demand. The cook therefore works within a narrow margin of error. She can't get far ahead, and that means that on extra-busy days she is certain sometimes to lose her lead or even to drop behind.

When the cook drops behind, all the pressures from customer to waitress to service pantry to runner descend upon her, for no one between her and the customer can do his job unless she produces the goods. From this point of view, timing and coordination are key problems of the organization. Proper timing and good coordination must be achieved in human relations or else efficiency is dissipated in personal frictions.

While these statements apply to every step in the process of production and service, let us look here at the first steps—the relations of cooks to kitchen runners to the service pantry.

When the restaurant operates on different floors, the relations must be carried on in part through mechanical means of communication. There are three common channels of this nature, and all have their drawbacks. Use of a public address system adds considerably to the noise of the kitchen and service pantries. The teleautogragh (in which orders written on the machine on one floor are automatically recorded on the kitchen machine) is quiet but sometimes unintelligible. Orders written in a hurry and in abbreviated form are sometimes misinterpreted so that sliced ham arrives when sliced toms (tomatoes) were ordered. Besides, neither of those channels operates easily for two-way communication. It is difficult to carry on a conversation over the public address system, and, while kitchen runners can write their replies to orders on the teleautograph, this hardly makes for full and free expression. The telephone provides two-way communication, but most kitchens are so noisy that it is difficult to hear phone conversations. And then in some restaurants there is only one telephone circuit for the whole house, so that when kitchen and pantry runners are using it, no one else can put in a call.

The problems that come up with such communication systems can best be illustrated by looking at a particular restaurant, Chandler's, where teleautograph and phone were used.

A kitchen supervisor was in charge of Chandler's kitchen, and pantry supervisors were in charge of each pantry, under her general supervision. There was also an assistant supervisor working in the kitchen.

The supplying function was carried on in the kitchen by two or three runners (depending upon the employment situation) and by a runner on each of the service-pantry floors. Food was sent up by automatic elevator.

The kitchen runners were supposed to pick up their orders from storage bins, iceboxes, or direct from the cooks. When the order was in preparation, the cook or salad girl was supposed to say how long it would be before it was ready, and the runner would relay this information by teleautograph to the service pantries. When the cooking or salad making had not been begun, the runner had no authority to tell the cook to hurry the order. Before each meal, the cook was given an open order (a minimum and maximum amount) on each item by the kitchen supervisor. She worked steadily until she had produced the minimum, and, from then on, she gauged her production according to the demands that came to her from the runner. That is, if the item was going out fast, she would keep producing as fast as she could until she had produced the maximum. Beyond this point she could not go without authorization from her supervisor. Ideally, the supervisor and cook would confer before the maximum had been

reached in order to see whether it was necessary to set a new figure, but this did not always happen.

While the runner could not order the cook to go beyond her maximum, his demands did directly influence her behavior up to that point. He originated action for her.

That was at the base of his troubles. Among kitchen employees, as we have seen, the cooks have the highest status. In Chandler's, runners had a low status, just above potwashers and sweepers. The jobs were filled by inexperienced employees, women or men who, if they performed well, were advanced to something of higher status. Their wages were considerably lower than the cooks', and the cooks also had a great advantage in seniority. In this particular case, the age difference was important too. The runners were a young man, a teen-aged boy, and a young girl, while the cooks were middle-aged women.

The runners would have been in a more secure position if they had been in close touch with a supervisor, but here the communication was sporadic and ineffective. The supervisor was inclined to let the runners fend for themselves.

When the runners put pressure on them, the cooks were inclined to react so as to put the runners in their place. For example, we observed incidents like this one. One runner (Ruth) asked another to get some salmon salad from the salad girl. The second runner found that the salad girl had no more on hand.

"They want me to get some more of that salmon salad," he said. "Could you make it, please?"

"Who told you that?" she asked.

"Ruth did."

"You can tell Ruth that I don't take no orders from her. I have a boss, and I don't take no orders from nobody else. You can just tell her that."

Now it may have been that the salad girl had made her maximum and could not go on without authorization from her supervisor, but the runner had no way of knowing that this was the case. He put his request to her politely, and she could have responded in kind by saying she was sorry that she could not make more without consulting the supervisor. Instead she responded aggressively, as if she felt a need to make it clear that no mere runner was going to originate action for her.

Even when they complied with the runner's requests, the cooks sometimes behaved so as to make it appear as if it were really they who originated the action. They always liked to make it clear that they had authority over the foods after they had been prepared, and that they could determine what should be done with them. While this was a general reaction, the salad girl was most explicit in such cases.

A runner went to look for some boiled eggs. The salad girl was not present at the moment, so he could not ask her, but after he had got the eggs from the icebox, he saw that she was back at her station. He showed her the pan of eggs, asking, "What about that?"

> "I don't like that," she said belligerently. "You have no business taking them eggs out of the icebox without asking."
>
> "Well, I'm asking you now."
>
> "I have to know how much there is. That's why I want you to tell me. . . . Go on, you might as well take them now that you have them."
>
> On other occasions when he asked her for salad, she would say, "Why don't you people look in the icebox once in a while?"

In such a case, whatever the runner did was wrong. The salad girl's behavior was irrational, of course, but it did serve a function for her. Behaving in this way, she was able to originate action for the runner instead of being in the inferior position of responding to his actions.

The runners also had difficulty in getting information out of the cooks. When there was a demand from the service pantries, and the food could not be sent up immediately, the runners were always supposed to give an estimate as to when they could furnish the item. This information they were expected to get from the cooks. The cooks sometimes flatly refused to give a time and were generally reluctant to make an estimate. When they did give a time, they nearly always ran considerably beyond it.

Incidentally, time seems to be used as a weapon in the restaurant. It is well known that customers feel and complain that they wait for a table or for service far longer than they actually do. Waitresses, as we observed them, estimated their waiting time on orders as much as 50 to 100 per cent more than the actual

time. While they were not conscious of what they were doing, they could express impatience with the service-pantry girls more eloquently by saying, "I've been waiting 20 minutes for that order," than by giving the time as 10 minutes. In the front of the house, time is used to put pressure on people. In the back of the house, the cooks try to use time to take pressure off themselves. They say that an item will be done "right away," which does not tell when it will be done but announces that they have the situation well in hand and that nobody should bother them about it. Giving a short time tends to have the same effect. It reassures the runner, who reassures the service pantries. When the time runs out, the pantry runners begin again to demand action, but it may take a few minutes before the pressure gets back to the cooks, and by that time the item may really be ready for delivery. Furthermore, the cook's refusal to give a time turns the pressure back on runners and other parts of the house—a result that she is not able to accomplish in any other way.

In the case of some of the inexperienced cooks, it may be that they simply did not know how to estimate cooking time, but that would hardly explain the persistent failure of all the cooks to cooperate with the runners in this matter.

The management was quite aware of this problem but had no real solution to offer. One of the pantry supervisors instructed a kitchen runner in this way:

> ". . . You have to give us a time on everything that is going to be delayed. That is the only way we can keep things going upstairs. On our blackboards we list all our foods and how long it will take to get them, and most of the time we have to list them 'indefinite.' That shouldn't be. We should always have a definite time, so the waitress can tell the guest how long he will have to wait for his order. We can't tell the guest we're out of a certain food item on the menu and that we don't know how long it will take to replace it. They'll ask what kind of a restaurant we're running."
>
> The runner thought that over and then went on to question the supervisor. "But sometimes we can't get that information from the cooks. . . . They won't tell us, or maybe they don't know."

"Then you should always ask the food-production manager. She'll tell you, or she'll get the cook to tell you."

"But the cooks would think we had squealed."

"No, they wouldn't. And if they did, all right, it's the only way they'll ever learn. They've got to learn that, because we must always have a time on all delayed foods."

"Yes, but surely we couldn't tell on them if they refused to give the information."

"Yes, you could. You have to. They'll have to learn it somehow."

The efficiency of this system depended upon building up a cooperative relationship between cooks and runners. For runners to try to get action by appealing to the boss to put pressure on the cooks is hardly the way to build up such a relationship. It is clear that, considering their low status in relation to the cooks, runners are not in a position to take the lead in smoothing out human-relations difficulties.

Some of the runner's problems arise out of failure to achieve efficient coordination and communication between floors. For example, on one occasion one of the upstairs floors put in a rush order for a pan of rice. With some difficulty, the kitchen runner was able to fill the order. Then, 15 minutes later, the pan came back to the kitchen again, still almost full, but apparently no more was needed for the meal. The cooks gathered around the elevator to give vent to their feelings. This proved, they said, that the rice had not been needed after all. Those people upstairs just didn't know what they were doing. After the meal was over, the kitchen runner went up to check with the pantry runner. The pantry man explained, "I ran out of creole, and there wasn't going to be any more, so I had no use for any more rice."

This was a perfectly reasonable explanation, but it did not reach the cooks. As a rule, the cooks had little idea of what was going on upstairs. Sometimes there would be an urgent call for some food item along toward the end of the meal-time, and it would be supplied only after a considerable delay. By the time it reached the service pantries, there would no longer be a demand for it, and the supply would shortly be sent back. This would always upset the cooks. They would then stand around and vow that next time they would

not take it seriously when the upstairs people were clamoring for action.

"In the service pantries," one of the cooks said, "they just don't care how much they ask for. That guy, Joe [pantry runner], just hoards the stuff up there. He can't always be out of it like he claims. He just hoards it."

A kitchen runner made this comment:

Joe will order something and right away he'll order it again. He just keeps calling for more. Once or twice I went upstairs, and I saw he had plenty of stuff up there. He just hoards it up there, and he has to send a lot of stuff downstairs. He wastes a lot of stuff. After I caught on to the way he works, I just made it a rule when he called for stuff and the first floor was calling for stuff at the same time, I divided it between them.

On the other hand, when Joe was rushed and found that he was not getting quick action on his orders, his tendency was to make his orders larger, repeat the orders before any supply had come up, and mark all his orders *rush*. When this did not bring results, he would call the kitchen on the phone. If all else failed, he would sometimes run down into the kitchen himself to see if he could snatch what he needed.

This kind of behavior built up confusion and resentment in the kitchen. When orders were repeated, the kitchen runners could not tell whether additional supply was needed or whether the pantry runners were just getting impatient. When everything was marked rush, there was no way of telling how badly anybody needed anything. But most serious of all was the reaction when the pantry runner invaded the kitchen.

One of them told us of such an incident:

One of the cooks got mad at me the other day. I went down there to get this item, and boy, did she get mad at me for coming down there. But I got to do *something*! The waitresses and the pantry girls keep on yelling at me to get it for them. Well, I finally got it, or somehow it got sent upstairs. Boy, she was sure mad at me, though.

Apparently the cooks resented the presence of any upstairs supply man in the kitchen, but they were particularly incensed against Joe, the runner they all suspected of hoarding food.

One of them made this comment:

> That guy would try to come down in the kitchen and tell us what to do. But not me. No sir. He came down here one day and tried to tell me what to do. He said to me, "We're going to be very busy today." I just looked at him. "Yeah?" I said, "who are you? Go on upstairs. Go on. Mind your own business." Can you beat that! "We're going to be very busy today!" He never came down and told *me* anything again. "Who are you?" I asked him. That's all I had to say to him.

Here the runner's remark did not have any effect upon the work of the cook, but the implication was that he was in a superior position, and she reacted strongly against him for that reason. None of the cooks enjoy having the kitchen runners originate action for them, but, since it occurs regularly, they make some adjustment to it. They are not accustomed to any sort of relationship with the pantry runners, so when they come down to add to the pressure and confusion of the kitchen, the cooks feel free to slap them down.

It was not only the pantry runners who invaded the kitchen. The pantry supervisors spent a good deal of time and energy running up and down. When an upstairs supervisor comes after supplies, the kitchen reaction is the same as that to the pantry runners—except that the supervisor cannot be slapped down. Instead, the employees gripe to each other. As one kitchen runner said,

> I wish she would quit that. I wonder what she thinks she's doing, running down here and picking up things we're waiting for. Now like just a minute ago, did you see that? She went off with peaches and plums, and we'd never have known about it if I hadn't seen her. Now couldn't she have just stepped over here and told us? . . . She sure gets mad a lot, doesn't she? She's always griping. I mean, she's probably a nice person, but she's hard to get along with at work—she sure is!

There were other pantry supervisors whose presence in the kitchen did not cause such a disturbance. The workers would say that so-and-so was really all right. Nevertheless, whenever a pantry supervisor dashed into the kitchen to look for supplies, it was a sign to everybody that something was wrong—that somebody was worried—and thus it added to the tension in the atmosphere and disturbed the human relations of the regular supply system—such as they were.

In this situation, the kitchen runner was the man in the middle. One of the service-pantry girls we interviewed put it this way:

> Oh, we certainly are busy up here. We don't stop even for a moment. I think this is the busiest place around here. It's bad when we can't get those foods, though. We get delayed by those supply people downstairs all the time. I could shoot those runners. We can be just as busy up here—but down there it's always slow motion. It seems like they just don't care at all. They always take all the time in the world.

On the other hand, the cooks blamed the inefficiency of the runners for many of their troubles. They felt that the runners were constantly sending up duplicate orders just through failure to consult each other on the progress of their work. Actually, according to our observation, this happened very rarely, but whenever a runner was caught in the act, this was taken as proof that duplication was common practice. The failure of the runners to coordinate their work efficiently did annoy the cooks in another way, as they were sometimes asked for the same order within a few seconds by two different runners. However, while this added to the nervous tension, it did not directly affect the flow of supplies.

Such were the problems of supply in one restaurant where we were able to give them close attention. However, as it stands, this account is likely to give a false impression. The reader may picture the restaurant as a series of armed camps, each one in constant battle with its neighbor. He may also get the impression that food reaches customers only intermittently and after long delays. . . .

To us it seemed that the restaurant was doing a remarkable job of production and service, and yet, in view of the frictions we observed, it is only natural to ask whether it would not be possible to organize the human relations so as to make for better teamwork and greater efficiency.

According to one point of view, no basic improvement is possible because "you can't change human nature." . . .

But is it all just personalities and personal inefficiency? What has been the situation in other restaurants of this type (operating on several floors) and in other periods of time?

Unfortunately we have no studies for other time periods, but we do have the testimony of several supervisors who have had previous experience in restaurants facing similar problems, and who have shown themselves, in the course of our study, to be shrewd observers of behavior in their own organizations. Their story is that the friction and incoordination we observed were not simply a war-time phenomenon. While increased business and inexperienced help made the problem much more acute, the friction came at the same places in the organization—between the same categories of people—that it used to. The job of the kitchen runner, apparently, has always been a "hot spot" in such an organization.

This, then, is not primarily a personality problem. It is a problem in human relations. When the organization operates so as to stimulate conflict between people holding certain positions within it, then we can expect trouble.

Selections from The Impact of Budgets on People

CHRIS ARGYRIS

What This Study Tries to Do. The purpose of the study is to examine problems and to raise questions concerning the possible human relations effects budgets have upon supervisors. Because of the nature of the problem this study cannot present final solutions to problems, nor answer questions in any definitive way. It can merely define a wider aspect of the budget problem and suggest possible solutions. Each controller must light up these approaches with his own experience. In short, this study, the first of its kind attempted by the Foundation, is primarily exploratory.

Because of the indefinable limits of the human problems in this area, the research team decided to focus its attention on how the

From *The Impact of Budgets on People*, prepared for the Financial Executives Research Foundation, formerly, Controllers Institute Research Foundation. Copyright 1952 by Controllers Institute Research Foundation. Reprinted with permission of the publisher.

supervisors feel about budgets and how the finance people feel about the same budgets. The group sought answers to questions such as these.

1. How do the finance people see their job?

2. What problems do the finance people see in relation to factory people? What problems don't they perceive?

3. Similarly, how do the factory supervisors see their job?

4. What problems do factory supervisors perceive in relation to the finance people and/or budgets? What problems don't they perceive?

5. What similarities and differences exist between factory people and finance people with regard to values, attitudes, and feelings toward budgets?

It should be pointed out that due to the exploratory nature of the study no recommendations could be made to the managements of the plants studied, which could then be observed in action, checked, and analyzed by the research team. Therefore, it is extremely difficult to present many recommendations based solely upon these findings. There is, however, a growing body of practical suggestions developed in other research work which is relevant to some of the problems unearthed by this report. In our recommendations we have drawn upon these suggestions because they are relevant and, we hope, useful to the controller.

How the Research Task Was Accomplished. The problem of human factors in the use of budgets is an extremely difficult one. Not only is the subject of budgets per se complicated, but, to make matters more difficult, budgets are so closely interrelated with the other parts and functions of organization that it would be an immense task to study carefully and thoroughly the problem as a whole.

The process of preparing manufacturing cost budgets is much the same in all four companies. In all cases the process starts with a meeting of the controller, the assistant controller and a top management group to determine over-all financial goals for the company in the forthcoming year. The controller's staff then translates the financial goals into the detailed cost breakdowns required for departmental budgets. This preliminary budget is sent to all superintendents who are asked to scrutinize the budget carefully and report any alterations they wish made.

Once the superintendents have their budget modifications clearly in mind, a meeting is held with the controller and his staff. Both parties come to the meeting "armed to the teeth" with ammunition to back their demands. After the disagreements are resolved, all parties sign the new budget proposal. The superintendents return to their offices, awaiting the new budget and the expected drive to "put it over."

Some Limitations of the Study. Any study whose approach is purely exploratory must be conducted within the limits of fairly well-defined boundaries. These are some of the more important limitations imposed upon this study by its exploratory nature:

1. None of the plants studied has a supervisory incentive system as a part of its budget system. This seems a serious limitation and points to the need for further research.

2. The report does not include any material

concerning the effects budgets have upon the workers in the plant. Casual interviews with workers suggested that they are definitely affected. How much they are affected, and through what channels, is not clear. This problem also deserves further study.

3. Budgets constitute only one of the evaluation processes management uses. As is commonly known, most evaluation processes tend to have "two strikes against them" simply because they tend to set goals for, and make evaluations of, the supervisors. As such, budgets do not escape the usual complaints. Moreover, it appears that many complaints are focused upon the budget because the budget is one of the few evaluation processes that is always in writing, and therefore concrete. Thus, some of the supervisors tend to use it as a "whipping post" in order to release their feelings about many other, and at times totally unrelated, problems.

What Budget People Think Is the Use of Budgets. To the budget people, budgets have an extremely important function in the organization as the "eyes and the ears of the plant." They provide the answers to most questions and the budget people see themselves as the "answer men" of the organization. Consider the following examples:

> First let me say that budgets are the watchdog of this company. What do I mean by that? Two things: First, if we have profit, there's no problem; Second, if we are losing money, what can we do about improvement—any kind of improvement?

> We guard the fields. The budget department has to constantly strive to improve the goods and make the plant better. There is always room to make things better.

There is, therefore, an important emphasis made on budget people constantly finding things that are "sour," looking for weaknesses and, in general, looking for things that are wrong, not right.

Another emphasis is equally important. All the budget people interviewed insisted that the errors found and the weaknesses uncovered should immediately be sent to top management.

> If I see an inconsistency, I'll go to top management and report it. No, I never go

to the supervisor in charge. It is our job to report any inconsistencies to the top management.

Once the information is in top management's hands, it is up to it to take action. In other words, budget results are primarily top management control instruments.

Coupled with the task of finding weaknesses and reporting them to top management is a third emphasis on doing the reporting soon. Budget results can be effective only when they are "hot off the griddle." Whatever pressure budgets may generate to "motivate" a factory man to better his record would be lost if action was not taken immediately.

> It's our philosophy that we've got to get these figures to top management when they're hot. They're no good when the job is cold. As it is now, with our records, top management can get the factory supervisors together and do something right away.

A fourth emphasis is on using the budget as a means for putting pressure on operating supervisors.

> As soon as we examine the budget results and see a fellow is slipping, we immediately call the factory manager and point out, "Look Joe, you're behind on the budget. What do you expect to do about it?"
> True, he may be batting his brains out already on the problem but our phone call adds a little more pressure—er—well, you know, we let them know we're interested.

Finally, budget people believe that budgets present a goal, a challenge to factory people. They think that without budgets factory people would have nothing "to shoot for"—would lack the help of a great motivating instrument. For example:

> Production budgets set the goals. The budgets, yes, the budgets, set a challenge for those fellows (factory). It's something for them to shoot for. They need something to shoot for. All of us need a goal.

In summary, budget personnel see budgets as performing at least the following important functions:

1. They are a means to make things better. There is always room for improvement. Inconsistencies, errors, weaknesses are constantly being discovered, examined, and reported to top management.

2. Properly used, they are a means of instituting improvements quickly. Budgets are of most value when their results are in the hands of top management as soon as possible.

3. They are a means of putting pressure on factory supervisors.

4. They provide a goal, a motivating force for the factory people.

What Budget People Think Are the Differences between Their Outlook and That of Factory Supervisors. If the budget people see any important differences between the outlook of operating people and themselves, such information should be of value in ascertaining how "basic" are the causes of misunderstanding between the budget and production parts of the organization.

The results indicate that budget people see some very basic differences. For example:

> I would say that factory people have a different outlook on life. They tend to be more liberal toward others.
> The financial people, on the other hand, look at life more coldly. To them, it's all figures. The only thing they look at is what amount of money is involved. It's the total figure that counts.

> The factory supervisors' outlook on things is different. They emphasize today. Yes, they're looking at only the short run. We have to look at things in the long run. We have to see the whole unit. They worry about their individual departments.

> I think you'd almost say there are personality differences between factory and finance. We (finance) tend to approach everything with figures. We have to. We've been retained that way. Factory people approach it without worrying about costs.

> Yes, there are differences. We (finance) have been trained to see things as they are —to study them logically and systematically. We've been trained to look at a problem and say, "Well, this is it, one two, three, bang, that's it."

The differences described above may be clues for understanding the human problems that arise. For example, if the factory supervisors are, in fact, only interested in the short run and if the budget staff does not see the short run as being crucial, then trouble will arise. Similarly, if the budget staff has a basically different outlook on problems from the factory supervisors, this difference will tend to increase disagreements.

What Budget People Think Are Their Problems with Factory Supervisors. The budget people were asked to describe what they felt was the most difficult problem they faced in their relationships with factory supervisors. The majority of the replies fell into a very consistent pattern. The most pressing problem was "selling" budgets to factory supervisors. The budget people believed that the task was almost insurmountable. It was interesting to see that the three most often stated reasons for this problem with factory supervisors were (*a*) lack of education on the part of factory supervisors, (*b*) lack of interest, and (*c*) misunderstanding and/or mistrust of budgets.

What Budget People Think Are Some of the Solutions to These Problems. Most of the solutions suggested by budget people seem to revolve around educating, or training, factory people in the appreciation and use of budgets.

These are some of the suggestions.

1. Supervisors should be taught the use and need for budgets in the company and specifically in their departments.

2. If possible, budgets should be explained so the supervisor would know exactly how and why budgets are constructed the way they are. (Most finance people were quick to caution against overwhelming the factory man with minute details of financial "buzz words." They all pointed out that the explanations should be kept as simple as possible.)

3. Closely connected with the above is the budget staffs' desire that factory people have more acquaintance with, and therefore respect for, the everyday problems of the finance staff in administering budgets.

4. Interestingly enough, most of the top controllers believed that the problems of administering the budget would not be alleviated until finance people, as well as factory people, changed. They felt that the budget people should be given a thorough course in self-understanding and in understanding and getting along with others—in other words, a course in human relations.

These, then, are the human problems involved in the administration of budgets and what can be done about them, as seen by the budget people.

What Factory Supervisors Think Is the Use of Budgets. Just how important are budgets and budget departments to factory supervisors? Each factory supervisor was asked to name the department which affected him the most and then the second most important. Fifty-seven percent considered production control as number one and forty-five percent chose the budget department as number one. Of the fifty-seven percent who picked the production control department as number one, all but one supervisor chose the budget department as the second most important department.

It seems relatively safe, therefore, to say that budgets wield an important influence in the production supervisor's world. Here . . . [is a] typical comment:

> Well, if you want to study a department that has its clutches everywhere, go into the budget department. That's all over this plant.

In general, the supervisors close to the employees hardly ever used budgets. In fact, they suggested that the best way to cause trouble was to mention a budget directly or indirectly to the employees. The supervisors higher up in the line of authority did use them. Of course, their usage varied, but in general the budgets were used. We shall see subsequently that the amount of use by upper-level supervisors was closely related to the way they handled their subordinates.

USE BY FRONT-LINE SUPERVISORS. In all the plants studied the research team obtained a definite impression that budgets were "taboo" with the employees who did the work. The writers could not help but sense an informal, but highly effective group norm of "no one speaks of or uses budgets seriously." This is, of course, merely an impression. No interviews were conducted with the employees to test the impression. Some idea of the validity of this observation may be obtained if one examines parts of the statements made below by the supervisors close to the people. These statements should also give the reader a vivid picture of the feelings and the human problems faced by these supervisors.

You can't use budgets with the people. Just can't do anything like that. People have to be handled carefully and in our plant, carefully doesn't mean with budgets. Besides, I don't think my people are lazy.

No, can't do it because some people see budgets as a target against a man. I'll have to admit that we cannot display the budget in front of our people. You have to be careful, you know. The first thing you know you'll have a grievance against you. We don't ask a man to look at a budget. Oh well, what we might do is put it under his nose so he can't help but see it. I should say, if we show the budget to any worker, it's only one out of every six.

No, no, I couldn't ever use a budget in front of my people. I just wouldn't dare. And, mind you, I don't think my top management would want us to. We wouldn't get any production out if we did.

Budgets, therefore, are far from being "cold pictures" of past production to the people. Rather they are symbols of something which may arouse fear, resentment, hostility, and aggression on the part of the employees toward the company and which may lead to decreased production.

The supervisor is, therefore, forced to refrain from mentioning budgets. He tries to accomplish what top management desires in distributing budget results, by translating these results into informal shop language and thereby calling these results to the attention of the employees. If he is not able to do this, he doesn't mention budgets at all.

The price for mentioning budgets is high. The supervisor who uses them explicitly is faced with a resentful work group which may express this resentment in many different ways, all of which lead to trouble for the supervisor.

It is not difficult, therefore, to see why a supervisor does not dare use budgets as some budget people want him to.

USE BY TOP-FACTORY SUPERVISORS. We have seen that front-line supervisors are not able to use budgets freely with their employees. Top-factory supervisors, on the other hand, seem to use budgets quite frequently and strongly on the supervisors below them.

Clearly, the closer one is to the employees, the less one can use budgets to increase production or arouse interest in production. If such is the case, one begins to wonder about the supervisor who is in the position of receiving all the pressure from above, but cannot pass on the pressure to the people below him. Does all this pressure stay with the supervisor?

What Factory Supervisors Think Are Budget Problems. Although there may be some differences among levels of supervision in the use of budgets, all the supervisors, regardless of their rank, were pretty much agreed concerning the limitations of budgets. Some of the limitations mentioned were:

BUDGET REPORTS ONLY INCLUDE RESULTS, NOT REASONS. Perhaps one of the greatest criticisms of budgets was the fact that they never included the reasons why they were not achieved by a certain supervisor. There was considerable feeling about this problem. Supervisors disliked intensely the fact that their departments would look "sick" on the budget while the reasons for the "sickness" were never published along with the results.

Budgets never show the reasons why they have not been met. They never take into account all variables that affect production.

The budget might contain the finance man's explanation: e.g., "The reason 'why' this budget has not been met is excess labor costs, or too much waste of time getting the job ready to be produced, etc.," but such reasons were not the real explanations as seen by the supervisors. They wanted the budget to state why they had excess labor costs, or why it took too long to get the job ready.

In other words, the supervisor's why was never included. Only the why of the budget man was included.

The following supervisor sheds additional light on the subject. It is interesting to note that he realizes why the budgets are not broken down further. But it is perhaps more interesting to note that even though he understands why budgets give only the total picture, he still feels quite strongly about them. Such data cannot help but lead one ot wonder if a knowledge about budgets will really alleviate the feelings about them.

As I see it, budgets are for top management. Top management is only interested in the total picture. They just want to see the results. They're just interested in knowing if the goal has been met.

The deviations, the headaches are all ironed out for them at the end of the budget. But, you can bet your boots, they are not ironed out for me. They remain, to remind me of the many things that can go wrong in my department. It's like this: I'm in the forest. I see hundreds of different trees (problems) that go to make it up. Top management is up in the air looking down on the forest. They see a mass of green. Now the budget measures that mass of green, but they don't tell the top management anything about the different trees that make up the green. You might put it this way—my job is to worry about the feelings that go to make up these figures. Finance peoples' job is to worry about the figures without the emotions.

EMPHASIS ON HISTORY. Another closely allied problem is that budgets emphasize past performance. Budgets are historical documents. As such, they are used primarily to project some predictions about the future based on the past.

Factory supervisors, on the other hand, place little emphasis on the past and hardly ever have time to think of the future. Their emphasis is on the present day-to-day situation.

RIGIDITY OF BUDGETS. In addition to the emphasis on the past, supervisors felt there was an equally negative emphasis on rigidity of standards. Once established, budget people seemed to dislike changing standards. Most budget people, the factory supervisors stated, were inflexible.

This rigidity of the finance people, as seen by the factory supervisors, leads to some important feelings on the part of the latter. For example:

I'd say one of the biggest problems is that budgets are set up on past performance. Once they come up with a figure, they hate

to leave it. Two years ago, my budget on errors was 100, now it's 150, but our production has increased a lot more.

Somehow the budget people freeze the figures in their minds and they just don't want to change.

BUDGETS APPLY PRESSURE FOR AN EVER-CHANGING GOAL. One of the more important criticisms the factory people had was the feeling that the people who set the budgets were never satisfied. For example:

If I meet this budget, those guys up there will only raise it.

Or,

You can't let them know that you made the budget without too much trouble. If you do they'll up it as sure as hell.

These were typical remarks made by most of the factory supervisors. (In no case did the top-factory supervisor consider this to be a criticism.) It was quite obvious that the factory supervisors wondered when, if ever, the optimum level would be reached. For example:

They make a budget and then constantly increase it. There's too much of that constant raising and raising that thing. Pretty soon the boys catch on and figure out it's the same old stuff. So they don't respond.

THE IMPLICATION THAT BUDGETS MOTIVATE SUPERVISORS TO DO A BETTER JOB. As we have seen earlier, the finance people perceive budgets as goal-setters for factory supervisors. They feel that the supervisors are "kept on the ball" because of budgets. Some finance people suggest that factory supervisors would be "lost" without budgets. On the other hand, factory supervisors resent quite strongly being thought of as people who would lose their motivation if it were not for budgets.

Some of them agreed that budgets had a function of helping them accomplish their work, but few if any saw budgets as the creator of their motivation. To accept budgets as motivators is to imply that supervisors do not have adequate interest in their jobs. This is seen as an insult to a man's integrity and the factory supervisors resent it strongly. For example:

I don't care much for budgets. I can use them, but I don't need them. My job is to get out the production, and I do the best I know how. What do I need budgets for? Now budgets can't help me in that.

Budget! Well, I know this is the way the other fellows feel about it. They don't want to be bothered with them. We do our job, and we do the best job we can. That's it. No matter what comes out, we know we've done our best.

BUDGETS ARE NOT REALISTIC. Another important criticism made by factory supervisors was that some budgets were purposely kept high so that they were almost impossible to meet. The supervisors definitely and sincerely resent this practice. They resent it primarily for two reasons.

Such a practice places a supervisor in a situation where he can never succeed. One supervisor expressed this when he said:

There's not much sense in setting a budget that's too high. What good is it? If a man doesn't meet it, he's going to say, "to hell with it." It's going to get him to think they're never satisfied. If you ever want to discourage a guy, just give him a budget you know he can't meet.

Such a practice implies that the company does not believe the supervisor's own desire to do a good job is sufficient to meet reasonable budgets. The unrealistic budget is used to spur supervisors on, but it does not work and is resented.

What Factory Supervisors Think Are the Differences between Their Outlook and That of the Budget People. [Earlier] . . . some differences in outlook between financial people and factory people as seen by the financial people were described. What are the differences in outlook as seen by the factory supervisors?

The first four basic differences as seen by the factory supervisors have already been discussed. They were:

1. Finance people are primarily interested in the past and the future. They don't think of the present.

2. Finance people tend to be too rigid once they have set up their figures.

3. Finance people see only the total picture.

They never see the many problems that go to make up the total picture. They worry only about end results.

4. Finance people tend to see life only as a set of figures. They take the emotions out of life and deal only with the cold figures.

Some other differences have not been previously mentioned:

1. Finance people cannot see the other person's point of view. They know almost nothing about the problems a supervisor is faced with daily.

2. Finance people have a language of their own. It is completely different from the language of the shop.

3. The final difference is more in the area of attitudes. It was best expressed by one supervisor who said:

A big problem with budget people, and all finance people for that matter, is that basically they are—well—let's see—yes—sarcastic.

I think that they think they're the whole show. If you're asking for our opinions, we think they have an over-exalted opinion of their position.

What Factory Supervisors Think Are Solutions to Some of These Problems

1. By far the most frequent and most stressed recommendation made by factory supervisors was that the finance people should learn to see the other person's point of view. The supervisors recommended that the finance people be given a "taste" of factory problems. Some typical comments were:

They are not fully acquainted with our everyday production problems. They don't realize our troubles and our difficulties. The best thing to do is to bring them down and see our problems.

I'd tell you what I'd teach them: to know my job. See the problems I have. Bring them down here and see what really goes on.

2. The financial people should undergo some training to learn that budgets are not final. They are merely opinions. One supervisor stated:

Yes, I could recommend a good thing. I wish they could have their thinking about budgets changed. They are too rigid. Budgets are statements of opinions not facts.

That's their big trouble. They think budgets are facts.

3. The financial people should change their belief that the employee is lazy and wants to do as little work as possible. For example:

I'd like to see them change their attitude that employees are out to get them (budget people) and do as little work as they can get away with.

4. Closely related to recommendation (3) above is one that recurred often: finance people should change their belief that the best way to raise production is through pressure.

5. Financial people should be taught that they are not superior to factory supervisors. Some typical comments:

I'd deflate their ego—I'd give them something to take them down a peg.

I'd like to teach them not to think their budgets are too important.

The Problem of Pressure. One of the most common of the factory supervisors' attitudes about budgets was that budgets were used as a pressure device to increase production efficiency. Many cases were cited to support this point. Finance people also admitted that budgets helped "keep people on the ball" by raising their goals and increasing their motivation. The problem of the effects of pressure applied through budgets seems to be the core of the budget problem.

THE CAUSES OF PRESSURE. Employees and front-line supervisors believe that the cause for pressure from the top is due to top management's belief that most employees are basically or inherently lazy. Employees and front-line supervisors also feel that top management believes that employees do not have enough motivation of their own to do the best possible job.

The interviews with top management officials revealed that the employees' beliefs were not totally unfounded, as a few quotations from some of the top management (both line and finance) make clear:

I'll tell you my honest opinion. Five per cent of the people work, ten per cent of the people think they work. And the other eighty-five per cent would rather die than work.

I think there is a need for more pressure. People need to be needled a bit. I think man is inherently lazy and if we could only increase the pressure, I think the budget system would be more effective.

Such feelings, even if they are never overtly expressed toward employees, filter through to the employees in very subtle ways. Budgets represent one of the more subtle ways. Once the employees sense these feelings exist in top management, they may become very resentful.

THE EFFECTS OF PRESSURE. How do people react to pressure? In three of the plants studied factory supervisors felt they were working under pressure and that the budget was the principal instrument of pressure. Management exerts pressure on the work force in many ways, of which budgets is but one. Budgets, being concrete, seem to serve as a medium through which the total effects of management pressure are best expressed. As such they become an excellent point of focus for studying the effect of pressure on people in a working organization.

THE CREATION OF GROUPS. An increase in tension, resentment, suspicion, fear and mistrust may not be the only result of ever stronger management pressures transmitted to supervisors, and in turn, to employees. We know, from psychological research, that people can stand a certain amount of pressure. After this point is passed, it becomes intolerable to an individual. We also know that one method people have to reduce the effect of the pressure (assuming that the employees cannot reduce the pressure itself) is to join groups. These groups then help absorb much of the pressure and the individual is personally relieved.

The process of individuals joining groups to relieve themselves of pressure is not an easy one. It does not occur overnight. The development of a group on such a basis seems to have the following general stages of growth.

First, the individuals "feel" the pressure. They are not certain, but they sense an increase in pressure.

Second, they begin to see definite evidences

of the pressure. They not only feel it, they can point to it.

Since they feel this pressure is on them personally, they begin to experience tension and general uneasiness.

Next, the people usually "feel out" their fellow workers to see if they sense the pressure.

Finding out that others have noted the pressure, the people begin to feel more at ease. It helps to be able to say, "I'm not the only one."

Finally, they realize that they can acquire emotional support from each other by becoming a group. Furthermore, they can "blow their top" about this pressure in front of their group. Gradually therefore, the individuals become a group because in becoming a goup they are able to satisfy these needs:

1. A need to reduce the pressure on each individual.

2. A need to get rid of tension.

3. A need to feel more secure by belonging to a group which can counteract the pressure.

In short, a new, cohesive group has developed to combat management pressure. In a sense, the people have learned that they can be happier if they combine against this management pressure.

Suppose now that top management, aware of the tensions which have been generated and the groups which have been formed, seeks to reduce the pressure. The emphasis on budgets is relaxed. Perhaps even the standards are "loosened." Does this then destroy the group? After all, its primary reason for existence was to combat the pressure. Now, the pressure is gone. The group should eventually disintegrate.

The answer seems to be that the groups continue to exist!

The evidence for this is not as conclusive as it should be. Therefore, the following explanation should be considered primarily in the realm of inference and conjecture rather than scientific fact.

These factors seem to operate to keep the group in existence:

1. There is a "time lag" between the moment management announced the new policy and the time the workers put it into effect.

2. The individuals have made a new and satisfactory adjustment with each other. They have helped to satisfy each other's needs. They are, as the social scientist would say, "in equilibrium" with each other. Any attempt to destroy this balance will tend to be resisted even if the attempt represents an elimination of a "bad" or unhealthy set of conditions. People have created a stable pattern of life and they will resist a change in this pattern.

3. The individuals fear pressure will come again in the future. Because of this feeling, they will tend to create unreal conditions or to exaggerate existing conditions so that they can rationalize to themselves that pressure still exists and, therefore, the need for the group also exists.

PRESSURE ON FRONT-LINE SUPERVISORS. But what about the foreman? Strong pressures converge upon him. How does he protect himself from these pressures?

He cannot join a group against management, as his work force does. For one reason, he probably has at least partially identified himself with management. For another reason, he may be trying to advance in the hierarchy. Naturally, he would not help his chances for advancement if he joined a group against management.

The evidence of the previous chapter seems to indicate that the line supervisor cannot pass all the pressure he receives to his employees. Time and time again the factory supervisors stated that passing the pressure down would only create conflict and trouble which would lead to a decrease in production.

The question arises, where does the pressure go? How do the supervisors relieve themselves of at least some of the pressure? There is evidence to suggest at least three ways in which pressure is handled by the supervisors:

1. Interdepartmental strife. The foremen release some of the pressure by continuously trying to blame fellow foremen for the troubles that exist. "They are," as one foreman expressed it, "trying to throw the dead cat in each other's backyard."

In three plants observed, much time was spent by certain factory supervisors in trying to lay the blame for errors and problems on some other department.

2. Staff versus factory strife. The foremen released much of the pressure by blaming the budget people, production control people and salesmen for their problems. The data already presented concerning factory supervisors' at-

titudes towards budget people substantiate this point.

3. "Internalizing" pressure. Many supervisors who do not express their feelings about the pressure have in reality "internalized" it and, in a sense, made it a part of themselves. Such damming up of pressure seemed to be expressed in the following ways:

(*a*) Supervisor *A* is quiet, relatively non-emotional, seldom expresses his negative feelings to anyone, but at the same time he works excessively. Supervisor *A* can be found working at his desk long after the others have gone home. As one supervisor expressed it, "That guy works himself to death."

(*b*) Supervisor *B* is nervous, always running around "checking up" on all his employees. He usually talks fast, gives one the impression that he is "selling" himself and his job when interviewed. He is forever picking up the phone, barking commands and requesting prompt action.

Both of these types (or a combination of these types) are expressions of much tension and pent up emotions that have been internalized. People working under such conditions finally are forced to "take it easy," or they find themselves with ulcers or a nervous breakdown.

But that is not the end of the problem. Constant tension leads to frustration. A frustrated person no longer operates as effectively as he was accustomed. He finds that he tends to forget things he used to remember. Work that he used to do with pleasure, he now delegates to someone else. He is no longer able to make decisions as fast as he did months ago. Now he finds he has to take a walk or get a cup of coffee—anything to get "away from it all."

SUCCESS FOR BUDGET SUPERVISORS MEANS FAILURE FOR FACTORY SUPERVISORS. Students of human relations agree that most people want to feel successful. We observe people constantly defining social and psychological goals, struggling to meet them, and as they are met, feeling successful.

Finance and factory supervisors are no exception. The typical finance supervisor does his work as best he can. He hopes and expects just praise of this work from his superior. Most of his success comes, therefore, from his superior's evaluation. It is the "boss" who will

eventually say "well done," or commend a promotion. In other words, a finance supervisor measures his success on his job, to a substantial degree, by the reactions of his superior.

The situation is the same for the factory supervisor. He also desires success. Like the finance supervisor, much of his success also derives from the comments and behavior the "boss" exhibits. In short, the factory supervisor is also oriented toward the top for an evaluation of how well he is doing his job.

What is the task of a good and successful finance supervisor? The reader will recall that the finance people perceive their task as being the watchdog of the company. They are always trying to improve the situation in the plant. As one finance supervisor said, "Always, there is room to make it better." And finally, the reader will recall the statement that, "The budget man has made an excellent contribution to this plant. He's found a lot of things that were sour. You might say a good budget man . . . lets top management know if anything is wrong."

In other words, their success derives from finding errors, weaknesses, and faults that exist in the plant. But, when they discover these errors, weaknesses, and faults, they also single out a "guilty party" and implicitly, at least, accuse him of failure. This is true because in finding weaknesses, errors or faults in a certain department, one is at the same time telling the factory supervisors that "things aren't going along as well as they could be." This, naturally, gives many factory supervisors a feeling of failure.

To be sure, such an occurrence will not make every supervisor feel he has failed. Some supervisors do not worry much about their job. Therefore, we find that the supervisor who really feels the failure is the one who is highly interested in doing a good job.

REPORTING SHORTCOMINGS OF THE FOREMAN. The way in which these shortcomings are reported is also important:

Assume that finance man *A* discovers an error in foreman *B*'s department. How is this error reported? Does the finance man go directly to the factory foreman? In the plants studied the answer, usually, is "no."

The finance man cannot take the "shortest" route between the foreman and himself. For one reason, it may be a violation of policy for a staff man to go directly to a line man. But, more important (from a human point of view), the staff man derives his success when his boss knows he is finding errors. Therefore, his boss would never know how good a job finance man *A* is doing unless it came to his attention. In short, perhaps because of organizational regulations but basically because much success in industry is derived from above, the finance person usually takes his findings to his own boss, who in turn gives it to his, and so on up the line and across and down into the factory line structure.

Taking the long way around has at least one more positive value for finance people. The middle and top management finance people also derive some success in being able to go to the plant manager and point to some newly discovered weaknesses in the factory. Therefore, not only one man obtains feelings of success, but all interested people up the entire finance structure obtain some feeling of satisfaction.

But, how about the factory people? The answer seems evident. They experience a certain sense of "being caught with their pants down."

Finally, to add insult to injury, the entire incident is made permanent and exhibited to the plant officials by being placed in some budget report which is to be, or has been, circulated through many top channels.

EFFECTS OF FAILURE ON PEOPLE. One might ask: What effects does this kind of failure have upon an individual? If they were insignificant, obviously we would not be concerned. Such is not the case. Feelings of failure can have devastating effects upon an individual, his work and his relationships with others.

Lippitt and Bradford, reporting on some ingenious scientific experiments conducted on the subject of success and failure, state that people who fail tend to:

1. Lose interest in their work.
2. Lower their standards of achievement.
3. Lose confidence in themselves.
4. Give up quickly.
5. Fear any new task and refuse to try new methods or accept new jobs.
6. Expect failure.
7. Escape from failure by daydreaming.
8. Increase their difficulty in working with others.

9. Develop a tendency to blame others, to be over-critical of others' work and to develop troubles with other employees.

On the other hand, people who succeed tend to:

1. Raise their goals.
2. Gain greater interest in the activity in which they are engaged.
3. Gain greater confidence in their ability in the activity.
4. Increase their persistence to future goals.
5. Increase their ability to cooperate and work.
6. Increase their ability to adapt readily to new situations.
7. Increase their emotional control.

In summary, we should point out that finance people aren't inherently "out to get them" as factory people in the plants described them. Rather, they are placed in a social organization where the only way in which they can receive success is to place someone else in failure.

THE WALL BETWEEN FINANCE AND FACTORY PEOPLE. At least two more very interesting conditions are related to this peculiar position which the finance people hold:

First, since the budget people are always looking for weaknesses, errors, and faults, they begin to develop a philosophy of life in which their symbol for success is, not only the error discovered, but the very thought of the discovery of a possible new error. "Weaknesses," "discovery of errors made by others"—which are symbols of failure for others—are symbols of success for the budget people.

The realization and admission by budget people of the peculiar position in which they are placed, leads to the second interesting condition. The budget people tend to become defensive about their work. They don't like placing people in failure, but they have to. Being aware of this difficulty and the negative feelings it may create, they tend to become defensive about queries concerning "their books" or their methods. One has the feeling that, at times, they use their technical "know-how" and language to confuse the factory people. This confusion of the factory people serves, of course, as a defense for the budget man. As one man suggested, "After all, if they don't know anything about budgets, how can they criticize them?" In short, the ignorance of the factory people concerning budgets may become a wall behind which the finance people may work unmolested. It is interesting to note that one of the major causes of insecurity among factory supervisors concerning budgets (i.e., "we can't understand them") is one of the primary factors of security for the budget people.

THE PROBLEM OF DEPARTMENT-CENTER SUPERVISORS. We have already shown that supervisors are partially evaluated by budget records. The factory supervisor, who desires to be known as being an efficient, effective supervisor, must make certain that his daily, weekly, monthly, and quarterly results compare favorably with the predicted results defined by the budgets. In short, a factory supervisor will feel successful, other things being equal, when he "meets his budget."

The phrase "meets his budget" is crucial.

Such a philosophy overlooks an extremely important point, perhaps described by the statement, "An organization is something different from the sum of the individual parts." The difference of the whole from the sum of the parts lies in the fact that the parts of an organization exist in certain relationships with each other. It is these relationships which create the difference.

WHAT MAKES AN ORGANIZATION. Parts, alone, do not make a whole organization. One cannot conceive of "adding" parts of an organization any more than adding together the hundreds of pieces that make up a watch in order to make the watch run. The crucial problem is to place the parts in correct relationship to each other.

Without laboring the point it seems clear that important relationships between departments are disregarded by an overemphasis on the individual departments. If everyone made certain his own department was functioning correctly, but at the same time, did not pay attention to the functioning of his department in relation to others, then trouble would still arise.

CONTROLLING CONFLICTS AMONG DEPARTMENTS. It might be suggested that the control of the relationships between departments rests with the plant manager, or some higher authority. From his high position, he is best able to control the conflict between departments. The crux of the matter is that this is all the leader

can do, i.e., control conflict. He is unable to eliminate it since the causes for the conflict are not within his reach. Since the top leader controls this conflict, the supervisors increasingly look to the leader to "break up a fight" or settle a dispute. This forces the supervisors to become increasingly dependent upon the leader. Furthermore, the more successful the top leader is, the less the supervisors need to worry about cooperation. They soon learn that the leader will solve any inter-departmental problems.

An example will illustrate the point.

In one of the plants studied a mistake was made on a customer order. The customer sent the material back to the plant. The error was corrected and the material sent back to the customer.

The cost of making the correction was nearly three thousand dollars. The error, especially since it was so large, had to be entered in the budget records. Some department had to be charged with the error. The problem was, who should be charged with the error?

For two months, supervisors of the departments most likely to be blamed waged a continuous campaign to prove their innocence. Each supervisor blamed the others. No one wanted the error on his record. The supervisors actually spent hundreds of man-hours arguing and debating among themselves. Emotions were aroused, people began calling each other names. Finally, two of the supervisors refused to talk to each other. Conflict reigned among the supervisors.

But, the supervisors were not the only persons in conflict. The division manager was also in conflict. He had to make the decision. To charge any supervisor with such an error would certainly invite hostility from that supervisor. This hostility might have further effects in the future. The division manager did not want to risk a weakening of his relationship, especially with a supervisor. But, he had to make a decision.

A meeting was held with the interested supervisors. The problem was discussed until just about everybody and everything that could be blamed, were blamed for the error. The division manager finally "gave in." He decided to place the error under "general factory loss." No department would be affected. The plant, as a whole, would carry the stigma. The division manager expressed his thoughts behind his decision to the research worker as follows:

> Take that big three thousand dollar error. We have to charge it up to someone. One man blames sales, another someone else. Everyone refuses to admit it might be their own fault. They each blame someone else.
>
> Well, I don't know. Perhaps, I thought it might be best to put the whole thing under general factory loss. Or else, they'd be hurt.

Note that the supervisors are willing to have the plant as a whole take the blame. But, they resist any attempts to place the blame on their individual departments.

In summary, budgets and budgeting tend to make the supervisor think of his, and essentially only his, department. Budget records, as administered, foster a narrow viewpoint on the part of the user. The budget records serve as a constant reminder that the important aspect to consider is one's own department and not one's own plant. As a result, supervisors become department centered rather than plant centered.[1]

BUDGETS AS A MEDIUM FOR PERSONALITY EX-PRESSION. The final problem to be discussed became evident only after a series of interviews with different controllers and top factory officials. Then it became obvious that the way people expressed their interest in budgets, and the way in which they described and used them, were directly related to the pattern of leadership they used in their daily industrial life.

For example, if a rather domineering, aggressive, "go-getting" top executive was interviewed, his presentation of the problem would also be made in a domineering, aggressive, "go-getting" manner. Therefore, although it is accurate to state that budgets are composed of "cold, nonhuman symbols" (i.e., figures), it is equally valid to state that once human beings use these "nonhuman figures," they project onto these figures all the emotions and feelings at their command.

Because budgets become a medium of per-

sonality and leadership expression, and since people's personalities and leadership patterns are different, this research study found a number of methods with which top factory executives used budgets. A few of these methods are illustrated by the following comments made by top factory supervisors:

> I go to the office and check that budget every day. I can then see how we're meeting the budget. If it's O.K., I don't say anything. But, if it's no good, then I come back here (smiles) and give the boys a little . . . Well, you know. I needle them a bit. I give them the old . . . hm . . . well . . . you know what . . . the old needle.

> I make it a policy to have close contact, human contact, with all the people in my department.

> If I see we're not hitting the budget, I go out and tell them I have $40,000 on the order.
> Well, they don't know what that $40,000 means. They think it's a lot of money so they get to work.

> Human factor, that's important. If you treat a human being like a human being, you can use them better and get more out of them.

> You know, it's a funny thing. If I want my people to read the budget, I don't shove it under their nose. I just lay it on my desk and leave it alone. They'll pick it up without a doubt.

It is hoped that the above descriptions are adequate to convey the point that budgets furnish a means of expression. They serve to permit the user's pattern of leadership to blossom forth.

Summary

This exploratory research has led to the tentative conclusion that budgets and budgeting can be related to at least four important human relations problems:

First, budget pressure tends to unite the employees against management, and tends to place the factory supervisor under tension. This tension may lead to inefficiency, ag-

[1] One method to remedy this problem is to attempt to have the staff person report directly to the factory. For an interesting statement of this case see: Douglas MacGregor, "The Role of the Human Relations Consultant," *Journal for the Study of Social Issues*, Vol. IV, Summer 1948.

gression, and perhaps a complete breakdown on the part of the supervisor.

Second, the finance staff can obtain feelings of success only by finding fault with factory people. These feelings of failure among factory supervisors lead to many human relations problems.

Third, the use of budgets as "needlers" by top management tends to make the factory supervisors see only the problems of their own department. The supervisors are not concerned with the other people's problems. They are not "plant-centered" in outlook.

Finally, supervisors use budgets as a way of expressing their own pattern of leadership. When these patterns result in people getting hurt, the budget, in itself a neutral thing, often gets blamed.

In the preceding pages we have discussed our observations and findings in an extremely complex field—the impact of budgets upon people. Because problems are so complex and our research so obviously exploratory, we undertake the task of suggesting lines of action with considerable humility.

Organizational Structure and Employe Morale

JAMES C. WORTHY

INTRODUCTION. This discussion will review some of the findings of the research conducted by Sears, Roebuck and Co. in the field of employe attitudes and morale. This research is an integral part of our company's personnel program; its primary purpose is to assist executives in their efforts to maintain sound and mutually satisfactory employe relationships. Such relationships are conceived by our management not only as a positive good in themselves but as an essential condition for the continued economic success of the enterprise.

We have had 12 years of experience in the formal study of employe morale. During that period our surveys have covered over 100,000 employes, working in several hundred different company units both in Sears, Roebuck proper and in a number of other organizations as well. Types of employes covered include sales and clerical personnel, manual and

From *American Sociological Review*, Vol. 15, April 1950, pp. 169–179. Reprinted with permission of the author and the publisher, American Sociological Association. This paper was read at the annual meeting of the American Sociological Society held in New York, Dec. 28–30, 1949.

professional workers, supervisory employes, and executives. The size of units surveyed has ranged from fewer than 25 employes to more than 10,000. Many different types of units have been surveyed, including retail stores, mail order plants, factories, warehouses, and offices. The geographical distribution of employes covered would correspond rather well with the geographical distribution of the U.S. population. By the same token, the communities in which units surveyed have been located cover practically the full range of sociological and cultural categories to be found in this country, except the small town and the rural.

METHODS OF STUDY. Time does not permit any detailed account of our survey methods; however, some brief explanation is necessary if only to indicate the extent to which confidence can be reposed in our findings.

Our original surveys were based solely on questionnaires, which were answered anonymously by employes. The questions covered a great variety of subjects—practically every subject, in fact, which we thought likely to have any influence on employe attitudes. In other words, the questionnaires had the simple, straightforward purpose of finding out how well employes liked their jobs, what their attitudes were toward supervision and management, and what factors in their employment situation might be contributing to dissatisfaction or poor working relationships. We assumed that when we had learned these things we would be able to take specific action to correct specific problems and thus restore peace and harmony where any lack thereof was found to exist.

We did find certain things that were susceptible of direct management action, but we also found many things that were difficult to take hold of. It soon became apparent that we were dealing with an infinitely complex system of influences and relationships, and not with a simple system of logical cause and effect. We began to question the adequacy of questionnaires and found, as we analyzed thousands of employe responses, that we could not even be sure we were asking the right questions or asking them in the right way.

Finally, there were real difficulties in attempting to analyze the significance of questionnaire responses. What was a "good" score on a certain point? Was a 65% "favorable" response to a question about employe discount policy equivalent to a 65% "favorable" response to a question about wage rates? Beyond certain relatively superficial points, there was often great uncertainty as to just what the tabulation of responses meant and what, if anything, could or should be done about it.

We have handled this problem by developing quite a different type of questionnaire and by supplementing it with other techniques (notably interviewing). Instead of covering a great many specific points, the questionnaire we now use seeks only to determine the general "feeling tone" of employes with respect to six key aspects of their working environment: (1) the company in general, (2) the local organization, (3) the local management, (4) immediate supervision, (5) fellow employes, and (6) job and working conditions. Ten items are included under each of these headings on which employes can express varying degrees of satisfaction or dissatisfaction. In scoring, we are not concerned with responses to each particular item in the questionnaire, but rather with the *general tendency* of responses in each of the six areas. In this respect, the questionnaire is patterned after the familiar "interest" or "personality" schedules used in psychological testing. As with such schedules, our questionnaire results can be expressed in "profiles." Furthermore, we have enough "cases" (i.e., units surveyed) to be able to translate raw scores into percentiles, thus greatly facilitating the process of interpretation and comparative analysis. As our survey people gain more experience in relating different types of profiles to concrete situations, they are developing real skill in using questionnaire results as a diagnostic tool.

The function of the questionnaire is not, however, to secure detailed information, but rather to "take the temperature" of an organization and its various subdivisions, to determine whether the general level of morale is high or low, and to point out areas of stress and strain which may be tending to undermine cooperative working relationships. In other words, by means of the questionnaire, we are able to locate problem departments and to identify the general nature of employe dissatisfactions. Only within broad limits, however, does the questionnaire tell *why* morale may be low. The real task of determining the "why" falls to a team of carefully trained interviewers. Because the questionnaire has already indicated the general nature and location of problems, the interviewing team is able to concentrate its time and energies on those departments and employe groups most requiring attention.

Surveys are conducted by members of the company's regional personnel staffs, with technical direction and coordination from the national personnel office in Chicago. (Administrative control of survey activities is strictly a regional responsibility.) People conducting the surveys receive special training in nondirective interviewing and in certain aspects of sociological and anthropological theory which we have found to contribute meaningfully to understanding the problems of organizations. In large part, they are trained by the case method, not only through studying reports dealing with "classic" situations (of which by this time we have a fair variety) but also through participating directly in survey work under the tutelage of experienced survey personnel.

In this connection, it should be noted that the entire survey program makes extensive use of clinical methods, not only for training younger practitioners, but for analyzing the significance of survey results and for working out necessary corrective measures with the executives responsible for the operating units involved. The participation of line executives, with their intimate and long-standing knowledge of their own organizations, in these "clinical sessions" has contributed greatly to both the pragmatic value of the survey program and the growth of knowledge and understanding on the part of survey personnel. Valuable as our extensive statistical data has been and is, most of the insights and hypotheses which the program has produced have been an outgrowth of this clinical approach.

Thus, the scope of our survey program has broadened significantly since its inception 12 years ago. We have found that there is more to good morale than high wages and pleasant working conditions (although these are of unquestioned importance). We have learned that effective leadership involves more than "winning friends and influencing people" (although social skill is an essential ingredient of executive capacity). It has gradually become clear that to understand what might be taking place within any particular working group we must have some knowledge of a variety of factors both internal and external to the group itself, and that, above all, we must have some dynamic conception of the manner in which these factors relate themselves one to the other and to the total situation of which each is an influencing and influenced part.

The scope of the surveys has thus been broadened to include the functioning of the organization as a whole and the entire pattern of technical processes and formal and informal relationships which comprise it. To the extent permitted by practical operating considerations, community and regional factors are likewise taken into account. In recognition of this broader scope, our surveys are no longer known as "*morale* surveys" but as "*organization* surveys." Determining the level of morale has ceased to be an end in itself and is now useful chiefly as a means of diagnosing the problems of an organization. Above all, our survey teams seek to deal not merely with the superficial manifestations of problems, but with the basic influences which have created the problems.

Surveys are concerned not merely with discovering the nature and origin of difficulties; their primary purpose is problem-solving. To this end, the survey team attempts to give the local manager a more complete picture of his organization and the way it is functioning, and to help him understand the various factors operative in his particular situation and their effects, not only on the attitudes and behavior of his people, but on the efficiency with which his organization is functioning. With this clearer picture of his organization, the manager is in a better position to take constructive action directed at the root of his problem rather than its superficial symptoms. However, the long-range objective of the survey program is not so much to correct immediate situations as to assist in developing the kind of organizations that can solve their own problems. A survey has failed in this essential purpose unless it leaves the particular store, plant, or department stronger and more self-reliant than it was before.

Our survey program is thus primarily an administrative device: its chief function is to assist local executives in doing a better job of handling the problems of their organizations. However, the surveys have also provided highly useful information about certain fundamental problems of human relations. One of the responsibilities of the research and planning staff of the national personnel office is the constant analysis and evaluation of survey data and the development of working hypotheses based on these data. Time will not permit any general review of our findings to date, but I would like to indicate some of the general directions of our current thinking.

A PROBLEM OF INTEGRATION. One line of thought on which we are working is the possibility of developing a typology of the malfunctioning of organization which can be useful in studying social groups as the typologies used by psychiatrists are useful in studying the malfunctioning of personality. This possibility was first suggested by the frequency with which the questionnaire "profiles" tended to form themselves into patterns with which we began to grow familiar. Our interviewing, likewise, attested that certain types of problems tended to occur in fairly well organized syndromes. For instance, we have found that certain kinds of difficulties typically follow changes in key management staff. We can usually predict not only what difficulties are likely to occur but the exact sequence in which they are likely to appear.

A typology of the malfunctioning of organization would be useful not only for scientific purposes but for administrative purposes as well, for with it could be developed a symptomatology by which problem situations could be diagnosed and acted upon more rapidly and more accurately. As already pointed out, our survey program is primarily an administrative device. Useful as it has been for this purpose, it has certain unwieldy features because sometimes it has to go a rather long way around to reach a fairly simple conclusion. For administrative purposes, we would be far better off if we had a group of people (preferably our administrators themselves) skilled at recognizing and diagnosing symptoms and dealing with the problem thus defined according to whatever therapy had been found useful for that particular type of difficulty.

It would be even more useful to be able to predict with reasonable accuracy the probable consequences of a given event or a given set of circumstances and to set in motion early a series of moves designed to minimize any adverse possibilities. We are able to do precisely this on a number of counts (for instance, cases of key executive changes) and our success here encourages us in our efforts to broaden the area in which we can predict with confidence.

As to our survey program as a whole, we are, as things stand now, somewhat in the position the medical profession would be in if the physician had to give a basic metabolism to determine whether a patient had a cold in the head. To continue the analogy, if we had a workable symptomatology (no matter how tentative), we could recognize the head cold and treat it accordingly. On the other hand, if the symptoms in the case indicated a more dangerous or more complicated disability, we could always apply our equivalent of the basic metabolism or such other procedure as the circumstances might require.

Any typology of malfunctioning must relate, of course, to the underlying dynamic system and not merely to the symptoms. All of our research testifies to the frequency with which the identical symptom can arise from entirely different factors. In one context, complaints over wages can be a danger signal; in another, merely an indication of the normal desire of everyone to be making a little bit more than he is. Sometimes, complaints over wages can really be complaints over wages; at other times, they can be merely a convenient target against which to direct verbalizations of resentment that arise out of situations that have little to do with wages. Because of the unreliability of symptoms taken in isolation we have found it more and more useful to think in terms of syndromes. The fact that our questionnaire is so constructed as to yield results in the form of profiles has greatly aided this purpose.

The psychiatrists have found the concept of *integration* a useful one around which to organize their ideas about personality and its disorders. We think a similar concept, related to group phenomena, could form the basis of a useful typology of the malfunctioning of organization. Certainly, the degree of integration (internal and external) of any organization relates very directly to the underlying dynamic factors in operation. One type of failure of integration leads to one type of difficulty which is different from that likely to arise from another type of failure of integration. Moreover, the methods for dealing with the two sets of circumstances are likely to differ, although often many of the superficial symptoms may be identical.

The scope of this paper does not permit a systematic exposition of the concept of integration. One of its aspects, however, is suggested by consideration of the problem of size of the organizational unit. Our researches demonstrate that mere size is unquestionably one of the most important factors in determining the quality of employe relationships: the smaller the unit the higher the morale, and vice versa. It is clear that the closer contact between executives and rank and file prevailing in smaller organizations tends to result in friendlier, easier relationships. To employes in such units the "big boss" is not some remote, little-known, semi-mythical personage but an actual, flesh and blood individual to be liked or disliked on a basis of personal acquaintance.

In broader terms, the smaller organization represents a simpler social system than does the larger unit. There are fewer people, fewer levels in the organizational hierarchy, and a less minute subdivision of labor. It is easier for the employe to adapt himself to such a simpler system and to win a place in it. His work becomes more meaningful, both to him and to his associates, because he and they can readily see its relation and importance to other functions and to the organization as a whole. The organization operates primarily through the face-to-face relationships of its members and only secondarily through impersonal, institutionalized relationships. The closer relations between the individual employe and the top executive in such a situation are only one aspect—but an important one—of the relatively simple and better-integrated social system of the smaller organization.

The importance of both external and internal integration is emphasized by other findings of our surveys. One of the most suggestive of these is that morale tends to be substantially lower in the large, industrialized metropolitan centers and higher in the smaller and less complex communities. For closely related reasons, morale tends to be lower in the Eastern sections of the country and higher in the West and South. Likewise, the simpler the industrial base of the community and the more homogeneous its population, the higher the level of employe morale.

These factors obviously relate, by various means, to the social characteristics of employe groups, and these social characteristics have an important bearing on the problem of integration. In certain cities of the south, a high percentage of employes grew up in small towns or in the country. Often their first job, after migrating to the "big city," is with our company. A great many of these young people have had religious upbringing which, together with parental admonitions, emphasizes the rightness of hard work for its own sake and the moral obligation of the employe to give his employer a full day's work for a fair day's pay.

Employes of units in large metropolitan centers, particularly those located in the East, are likely to have somewhat different social characteristics. Instead of coming from smaller towns and rural communities, most of them are likely to have originated within the metropolitan area itself. Likewise, many of them are likely to be the children or grandchildren of foreign-born stock whose personalities have been strongly molded by the special circumstances and influences of growing up within ethnic communities. The marked tendency toward lower morale among employes drawn from such groups seems, in part at least, to reflect the high degree of social disorganization characteristic of the great metropolitan agglomerations.

An important element of this disorganization is the tendency for sharp cleavages to develop between different groups comprising the community, and one of the most significant of these cleavages is that between workers and management. Where the rank and file members of an organization have been drawn largely from working class homes in which factory employment has been the chief means of family support for two or three generations, their patterns of thinking and systems of value will be those of the urban working class. One characteristic of their way of life, growing out of their family and neighborhood experiences and traditions, is often a latent or overt distrust of the employer and a strong tendency to identify their security and well-being with their fellow-workers and not with the employer. The management of an organization employing large numbers of people with this type of background is thus likely to involve complications seldom encountered in what is sometimes described as the "less mature" regions of the country.

The problem, however, is by no means an insuperable one. No better testimony is needed than the survey showings of many of our own company units. Despite the fact that in some locations employes may be drawn from backgrounds representing all that is worst in social disorganization, morale in many such units is unusually high. A thoroughgoing urban working class background on the part of the rank and file is significant chiefly because it tends to create attitudes and values which do not correspond fully with those usually characteristic of management and executive groups, and because this difference in outlook frequently leads to *mutual* misunderstanding and lack of confidence. Under these circumstances, not only are management's action and motives frequently misinterpreted by the rank and file, but management itself is often at a loss as to ways and means by which it can effectively mobilize the interest and cooperation of employes in achieving the aims of the enterprise.

This gap can be bridged—and our surveys

provide striking proof of that fact—by *skillful and understanding leadership operating in an organizational structure which facilitates rather than inhibits effective integration.* Both leadership and structure are of crucial importance. The structural aspect, however, has received relatively less attention. Moreover, there are a number of curious and significant interrelations between type of structure and character of leadership that will bear close investigation.

ORGANIZATIONAL STRUCTURE. The results of our research suggest that over-complexity of organizational structure is one of the most important and fundamental causes of poor management-employe relationships in our modern economic system, and that until this problem is faced and corrected no substantial improvement in those relationships is likely to be possible.

In viewing many business enterprises, one cannot but be impressed by the number of different departments and sub-departments into which they are divided, and the extent to which the activities of both individuals and groups have been highly specialized. In a very large number of cases, employes perform only elementary, routine functions because jobs have been broken down "scientifically" into their most elementary components. The resulting specialization undoubtedly has certain advantages, such as requiring less skilled people, shorter training time, etc. In many cases, however, the process has been carried to such extremes that jobs have little inherent interest or challenge; operations have been reduced to the simplest possible repetitive level and the worker makes nothing he can identify as a product of his own skill.

One has the feeling of division of labor having gone wild, far beyond any degree necessary for efficient production. Peter F. Drucker, in a penetrating analysis, has pointed out that over-specialization is not an inevitable consequence of mass production and that, "The traditional assembly line is simply a piece of poor engineering judged by the standards of human relations, as well as those of productive efficiency and output." [1]

The evidence of the studies conducted in our own company strongly support this conclusion, for we have found that where jobs are broken down too finely we are more likely to have both low output and low morale. Conversely, the most sustained efforts are exerted by those groups of employes who perform the more complete sets of tasks (e.g., salesmen, supervisors, master mechanics, etc.), and these likewise exhibit the highest levels of morale and esprit de corps.

The sharp trend toward over-specialization in our economy has not been limited, of course, to individual jobs. Just as particular activities have been broken down into their simplest possible components and each component assigned to a different person, so many *operations* (often after having been highly "simplified") have been separated out of the broader complex of activities of which they are a part and set up as specialized and semi-independent organizational entities. While over-specialization of individual jobs is serious enough, this over-specialization of the functions of entire departments and sub-departments has even more far-reaching consequences.

For one thing, it brings together in one place large numbers of employes on the same job level (and that level is likely to be fairly low where there has been any considerable over-specialization of individual jobs). This is another way of saying that the size of the administrative unit has been greatly expanded. Let us suppose an organization which performs three essential functions, A, B, and C. Let us suppose further that the volume of output requires three units of each function. Under these circumstances the organization could be set up in either of two ways:

1. It could be set up in three divisions, each function (A, B, and C) being represented in each division and each division, therefore, being a relatively independent administrative entity.

2. On the other hand, the organization could be set up in three *functional* divisions, one division having all three A units, another all three B units, and the third all three C units. In this case, none of the three divisions has any independence; each can operate only in closest coordination with the other two. Under the first alternative, there are really three administrative units; under the second only one, and that, by definition, three times as large.

[1] Peter F. Drucker, "The Way to Industrial Peace," *Harper's Magazine*, November, 1946.

This second type of arrangement is typical of much modern organization practice, both in industry and government. It is assumed that this separation and specialization of activities will permit better supervision, make possible smoother scheduling, and generally improve efficiency. There may be a certain spurious efficiency in this kind of organization but it is likely to have many off-setting liabilities.

One of the most serious of these liabilities is the fact that it so greatly expands the size of the administrative unit. Much of industry's present vast scale of operation is required not so much by economic or technical factors as by an unhappy and unnecessary principle of organization. The experience of many companies, of which my own is one, demonstrates that it is entirely possible to have many of the economic and technical advantages of large size without sacrificing too many of the essential human advantages of small size.

A further liability of over-functionalization is the fact that, from the standpoint of the individual employe, it tends to destroy the meaning of the job. He and those around him are working at highly specialized tasks which have meaning to management because they are a necessary part of a total process. But the worker cannot see that total process; he sees only the small and uninteresting part to which he and his fellows are assigned. In a real sense, the job loses its meaning for the worker—the meaning, that is, in all terms except the pay envelope.

Thus a very large number of employes in American industry today have been deprived of the sense of performing interesting, significant work. In consequence, they have little feeling of responsibility for the tasks to which they are assigned. Management in its efforts to maintain production in face of the resulting apathy is likely to resort to increasing supervisory pressure, but this procedure only creates more resistance on the part of employes. Sometimes the resistance is only passive, in the sense that employes fail to respond to the pressure or find means of avoiding it. Under certain circumstances, however, it can take more active form and lead to the creation of resistance groups in which employes band together (commonly through union organization) to exert a corresponding pressure against supervision and management.

Over-functionalization thus requires close and constant supervision at the work level to maintain production. Furthermore, the supervisors themselves must be closely supervised and controlled to assure the necessary degree of coordination between the many different units into which the organization has been subdivided. In a simpler type of organization structure, coordination can usually be achieved on a fairly informal basis because there are fewer artificial barriers in the form of departmental separations and lines of authority.

Where the work of the organization is broken down into so many functional divisions, however, cooperation can no longer be achieved spontaneously. After all, each functional unit was set up as a distinct entity in order that it might achieve a more efficient system. Each unit, therefore, tends to operate primarily in terms of its own systems rather than in terms of the needs of the other departments with which it must cooperate. Each unit becomes jealous of its own prerogatives and finds ways to protect itself against the pressure or encroachments of others. Conflict develops on the employe as well as the supervisory level, thus forcing an extra load on higher levels of management who must be constantly reconciling differences.

In order to achieve the necessary degree of coordination and cooperation between administratively separated functions, management is thus forced not only to build up an elaborate hierarchy of many supervisory levels, but to institute a wide variety of formal controls. Unfortunately, these controls are themselves often a source of conflict, because the individual supervisor or manager is under strong compulsion to operate in such a manner as to make a good showing in terms of the particular set of controls to which he is subject, and often he can do so only at the expense of impairing the service he is expected to render to other departments. This conflict is particularly acute when two closely related functions report up two different administrative lines and operate under two different systems of standards and controls.

The management of organizations which have been over-functionalized to the extent characteristic of much of modern business imposes a severe burden on the top administrative staff. Functions and activities have been so subdivided and specialized that no individual unit can operate except in closest coordination with others, and the system is often so complex that this coordination cannot take place spontaneously. If it is to occur at all, it must occur on the basis of specific administrative action from the top, which requires the development of a specialized staff to assist the top administrator.

This growth of staff complicates the situation still further, because an evitable consequence is the elaboration of formal controls of various kinds to permit the staff to perform the functions and exercise the responsibilities which have been delegated to it or which it gradually assumes in an effort to strengthen its own position or extend its own authority. The result is a gradual undermining of the line organization for the benefit of the staff, an impairment of flexibility and adaptability, and a weakening of the effectiveness of the entire organization.

An objective appraisal suggests that to too large an extent work processes have been analyzed from a strictly "rational" or mechanical point of view with too little attention to the human factors involved. As a result, functions have been separated out of their context and set up as semi-independent activities. Necessary collaboration and cooperation between the units thus artificially separated becomes possible only through an elaborate system of controls and a complicated administrative hierarchy. Under these circumstances, management necessarily becomes strongly centralized, despite the frequently expressed concern of business leaders over the need for greater delegation of authority and responsibility. Too often, this is simply impossible because the nature of the organization structure makes effective decentralization impossible. For much the same reason, such organizations often require from their top administrators a high degree of driving pressure to hold the system together and make it operate with a reasonable degree of efficiency.

Where this is the case, executives and supervisors down the line quite understandably tend to pattern their own methods after those of their superiors. In many cases the copying may be done unskillfully and in such a way as to exaggerate the worst features of the pressure methods. As a result, supervisory methods at the middle and lower levels of over-functionalized organizations are often crude and inept.

Furthermore, the degree of pressure often required from the top is likely to create an atmosphere of anxiety and apprehension within the executive and supervisory group. This atmosphere tends to amplify the severity of pressure as it moves downward in the organization, so that even a moderate amount of pressure at the top is often greatly magnified by the time it reaches the lower levels. Attitudes of mind characterized by fear and apprehension are not particularly conducive to real skill in managing and leading subordinates. Above all, poor supervisory techniques at the lower levels of an organization generally reflect the experience and type of supervision to which the supervisors themselves have been subjected over the years and which they have come to accept as normal and expected behavior.

The significant point in all this, however, is that the over-complex, over-functionalized organization structure is likely to require the driver type of leader; the over-use of pressure as a tool of supervision is thus related primarily to the character of the structure and only secondarily to the character of the individual at the head of it. (On the other hand, it is recognized that the personality of the top man may have a great deal to do with the kind of organization structure he sets up. This entire problem of the reciprocal relationships between structure and personality should be studied carefully.)

SYSTEMS COMPARED. The most striking feature of the over-elaborate type of organization structure is its lack of integration, a deficiency which can be only partially and very unsatisfactorily overcome by driving pressure from the top. Our studies suggest that this type of structure is not only bad human relations but equally unsound from a standpoint of productive efficiency. Our studies also suggest that alternative systems of organization are conceivable and eminently practical.

For one thing, we seriously question the necessity for much of our present high degree of over-specialization and over-functionalization. The so-called "scientific management movement" which has given such impetus in this direction is based to a considerable extent on an extremely inadequate conception of human motivation and social organization. It has tended to approach the problems of management from an almost purely mechanistic point of view and has tried to organize human efforts in much the same way an engineer might design a machine. Much of our present over-specialization is based on this type of thinking.

However, the experience of a number of companies indicates that individual jobs and departmental functions need not be broken down to this degree in order to achieve productive efficiency. Quite the contrary; their experience has been that both efficiency and morale are best served by keeping specialization to a minimum. The experience of these companies likewise indicates that organization structures and administrative hierarchies can be vastly simplified, thus making possible a far higher degree of decentralization of authority and responsibility.

In the course of our survey work we have had an opportunity to study a fairly wide variety of organization structures. We have been struck by the sharp contrasts between otherwise comparable units which differ mainly in the complexity of their organizational structure and in the degree to which authority and responsibility are effectively decentralized to those farther down the line. A review of some of these contrasts may be instructive.

In the more elaborate and complex organizations, the individual supervisor or executive is subject to constant control and direction and has little opportunity to develop the qualities of initiative and self-reliance. In systems characterized by extensive management decentralization, primary reliance is placed on the personal initiative and capacity of the people in the organization. There is usually a conspicuous lack of detailed supervision and of formal controls, and executives and supervisors (and to a large extent rank and file employes) enjoy considerable freedom in the way they accomplish their jobs.

They are judged primarily by their results, not on the details of the way they get those results. This concentration on end-results rather than on system and controls, together with management's alertness to recognize and reward good results, develops initiative and self-reliance and generates a far more powerful driving force than could ever be imposed from the top down. This pattern of administration not only gets today's job done better but permits the individual to grow and develop in a way that is impossible in more centralized systems. Furthermore, it contributes strongly to morale because employes work in an at-mosphere of relative freedom from oppressive supervision and have a sense of individual importance and personal responsibility which other types of arrangements often deny them.

A number of highly successful organizations have not only paid little heed but have gone directly counter to one of the favorite tenets of modern management theory, the so-called "span of control," which holds that the number of subordinate executives or supervisors reporting to a single individual should be severely limited to enable that individual to exercise the detailed direction and control which is generally considered necessary. On the contrary, these organizations often deliberately give each key executive so many subordinates that it is impossible for him to exercise too close supervision over their activities.

In this type of organization structure, the individual executive is thrown largely on his own to sink or swim on the basis of his own ability and capacity. He cannot rely to more than a limited extent on those above him, and these superiors, by the same token, cannot too severely restrict, through detailed supervision and control, their subordinates' growth and development.

Not all individuals can function effectively in this type of set-up. It requires a very large measure of self-confidence and personal capacity. The system tends to weed out those who lack these qualities in adequate degree. Those who are able to adapt to this type of organization, however, are likely to be not only better executives but also the type of people who can build and maintain teamwork and cooperation and a high level of employe morale, not so much because they consciously attempt to do so but because these results are a natural by-product of their ways of operating and a reflection of their own personalities.

On the other hand, in organizations characterized by many levels of supervision and elaborate systems of controls, the individual not only has little opportunity to develop the capacities of self-reliance and initiative but the system frequently weeds out those who do. Furthermore, those who survive in this type of organization are often likely, by virtue of the very qualities which enabled them to survive, to have personalities and ways of operating which do not make for greatest skill in building employe teamwork and cooperation.

An organization with few layers of supervision and a minimum of formal controls places a premium on ability to stimulate and lead. The driver type of executive, who functions through maintaining constant pressure and whose chief sanction is fear cannot operate as effectively in such an organization. In the more simple types of organization structures, where management has been effectively decentralized, an executive accomplishes results and moves to higher levels of responsibility chiefly to the extent that he is able to secure the willing, enthusiastic support of his colleagues and subordinates; he does not have the "tools" (with which a more centralized system would to some extent provide him) to accomplish the result in any other manner. The outcome is not only a higher level of accomplishment but, at the same time, a more satisfying type of supervision and a higher level of employe morale.

CONCLUSION. Our studies have shown that employe morale and operating efficiency are closely related to the degree the organization is integrated. Integration is not necessarily achieved, however, when the organization meets the requirements of machine-logic. As a matter of fact, what may appear to be logical from a purely technical standpoint may run directly counter to the personal and social demands of employees. We have seen a number of organizations which have a logical technology, division of labor, and hierarchy of control but which are badly disorganized from the standpoint of the actual working relationships of the people involved. Such organizations are well-integrated only on paper. In actual fact, they are irritating and frustrating from the standpoint of employes and inefficient, troublesome, and costly from the standpoint of management.

Our research indicates that two trends in particular are making effective integration difficult and contributing to the progressive deterioration of management-employe relations. One is the trend toward increasing size of the administrative unit; the other, the trend toward increasing complexity of organizational structure. Both trends appear logical in terms of widely held theories of business organization, but in both cases improvements in mechanical efficiency are at some point over-balanced by losses in the willingness and ability of employes to cooperate in the system. Moreover, the larger, more complex organizations are likely to become unadaptive and rigid, and to find it difficult to meet the requirements of economic and social change.

Intelligent planning on the part of management in setting up the formal structure of organizations can do much to improve the quality of human relations in industry. Flatter, less complex structures, with a maximum of administrative decentralization, tend to create a potential for improved attitudes, more effective supervision, and greater individual responsibility and initiative among employes. Moreover, arrangements of this type encourage the development of individual self-expression and creativity which are so necessary to the personal satisfaction of employes and which are an essential ingredient of the democratic way of life.

PART FOUR

Organizational

Adaptation

PART FOUR

THUS FAR we have been largely concerned with organizations as economies. That is, we have been for the most part looking at an organization as an arrangement of people, resources, ideas, duties, and other elements that produce and distribute efficiently, or at least in a satisfactory manner, things which those with an interest in an organization want. Hence, we have frequently come across statements which say, "An organization exists because people working together in an organized systematic way can produce more, better, or different things than they can produce working individually." In short, up to now organizations have been viewed as instruments to provide productivity or efficiency. Although this emphasis on organizations as economies is valid, it would be a mistake to consider them only in this light. Intentionally or not, organizations thus far have been looked upon as static. There is no provision for the organization to change as goals or conditions change. Yet this is an exceedingly important aspect of organizations and deserves attention. Hence, we must now consider organizations both as economies and as adaptive systems (Selznick). Before getting into the discussion of organizational adaptation, which is the purpose of this part, let us first consider the issue of organization variability.

One characteristic that makes the study of organizations both interesting and frustrating is their uniqueness. No two organizations are exactly alike. True, there are types or styles which may identify common features of large numbers of organizations, but even those of the same general type or style will have many differences that separate them from each other. The knowledge of what these differences are is interesting and to some degree useful. The number of variations is so great, however, that a detailed knowledge of many organizations would not be particularly valuable. The likelihood of ever meeting another organization exactly like those which are known in detail is extremely remote. Nevertheless, the study of variation among organizations can be very valuable if we give attention to the reasons for the variations. Equally important, the knowledge of these factors will identify the things which, when they change, bring about, or should bring about, a change in the organization. The study of organization variation and adaptation is only in its beginning stages. This section will be directed to: the need for organizational change, some of the factors which

276

make change necessary, and some of the ways in which change or adaptation takes place in an organization.

The Need for Organizational Change

In Part I the point was made that an organization is the result of a great many elements, the principal classes of these being:

1. The objectives of the organization, which will have a profound influence on the structure, size, and methods of operation.

2. At the same time the conditions facing the organization, the economy, the political situation, marketing factor, the technology available both to it and to competing or allied organizations, and many other factors of a similar nature will have an important impact on the nature of the organization.

3. The resources which the organization can draw on, in the form of people, ideas, material, capital, will in turn have a significant influence.

Our view then is that there are many factors, external or within an organization, which mold an organization. In discussing an organization as an economy, we are considering the question of what arrangements of elements best suits these sets of external and internal factors. When considering an organization as an adaptive system, we are interested in how well and in what way it adjusts to a change in any one of these factors. Let us consider these two points a little further.

Variations in Organizations

There is sometimes a tendency to presume that firms in the same type of business, of approximately the same size, would have the same form of organization. This is an understandable but unfortunately incorrect assumption. If the point of view held in this part is correct, a difference in any one of the major factors influencing an organization would also require a different organization to develop, and even though organizations or business firms may share many common factors, it is seldom that all of them are identical. Let us consider as an illustration two firms which make the same products, operate in the same city, and have essentially the same machinery,

resources, and size; in short, which have or face many similar organization-forming factors. The difference between them is that the owners of one firm desire to produce a limited number of different styles and forms of their product, stressing long production runs and high-quality products, and the other firm places an emphasis on maximizing immediate profits by rapidly changing the style of the product to suit the immediate market demands. In short, the basic difference between the two firms is their policies relevant to their products and their market relations which reflect some fundamental differences in objectives. Such a situation is analyzed by Chowdhry and Pal, and they show how these differences in policy are reflected in a number of organizational differences. Needless to say, if one firm were to change its policies, say from long production runs to meeting current market demands, its organization would also have to change.

An organization may change its objectives in a variety of ways. The established top executives may see changed conditions or new opportunities which cause them to redefine organizational goals. On the other hand, the top leadership of the organization may be changed in some way, with new members influencing the basic directions to be taken (Selznick).

The next consideration is, what happens when environmental conditions change drastically enough to require a major modification in the organization. Lawrence gives us an excellent description of how one firm, in response to environmental changes, planned and carried out a fundamental reorganization, shifting from a centralized to a decentralized style of organization.

Variations among organizations can occur for a variety of other reasons. Some are in response to pressures, actual or anticipated from the environment, whereas others are in response to internal forces. For example, staff departments, such as the personnel department, according to the normative view covered earlier should assume a neutral, supportive role, offering advice and assistance to the line, but never giving orders or directions. Actual experience shows a number of situations where decisions are made by the staff for the line to follow. A variety of factors have been identified as promoting such a situation revealing the complexity of factors which mold an actual organization (Myers and Turnbull).

Organizational Innovation

Thus far we have been considering organizational adjustment, that is, the response of the organization to various factors. The next step is to consider the situation where the organization is in some way involved with the change in factors to which it must in turn respond. For example, when an organization grows, it must make many adjustments to its increased size. As an organization increases in size the execution of the managerial function by the executive hierarchy discussed in Part I becomes more complex and difficult and hence we would expect a larger managerial hierarchy to be necessary. This is not, however, a simple, direct relation. With some types of organizational growth the increase in the executive hierarchy is relatively slight so that ratio between the number of executive personnel to the size of the organization decreases, whereas for other types of organizational growth the opposite is true (Anderson and Warkov).

Growth is not the only type of change which the organization both initiates and responds to. An organization is based, among other things, on a technology. In fact there are usually several technologies

One class of technologies is involved with carrying out the company's basic objectives. For example, a business firm dedicated to manufacturing automobiles draws on a number of technologies: industrial engineering, which lays out the assembly line; mechanical engineering, which designs motors; chemical engineering, which provides fuels; and on and on.

In addition to this, there is a technology involved in carrying out the managerial function, which guides, coordinates, and plans work on accomplishing the basic goals of the organization. In this sense, accounting is a technology used in the execution of the managerial function. The technologies involved in manufacturing have had some spectacular developments which have laid the underpinnings for much of our economic development. The technologies involved with the managerial function have progressed far less rapidly. To a considerable extent the conceptual development has been much slower, and until recently the

execution of the managerial function has rested on a hand labor technology. Accounting systems, for example, may be fairly sophisticated, but in the past they were largely executed by people using paper and pencil or perhaps simple mechanical machines like typewriters and hand calculators. The execution of the managerial function received a tremendous boost with the development of electronic data processing equipment which enables us to mechanize many related technologies: accounting, quality control, etc. In fact this equipment provides the opportunity for the development of technologies which were unthought of, perhaps impossible, when work in the managerial function had to be carried out exclusively by hand labor.

When new technologies, and particularly mechanized technologies, are introduced into an organization, they create new and different problems of their own, which frequently do not have solutions to be found in our traditional patterns of practice. In manufacturing, for example, we are usually dealing with flow patterns requiring considerable coordination, conditions which may not be amply served by our more conventional thoughts of that organization (Jasinski). When we mechanize some managerial activities, we may eliminate much hand labor work and program some of the managerial decisions. Unfortunately, we frequently neglect or are incapable of anticipating the requirements, for example, in the executive hierarchy, necessary to adapt to and utilize these new devices and opportunities fully (Weber).

Adaptation to Provide for Organizational Needs

In order to carry out its purposes and to survive, an organization must continually have inputs of various resources. At times the acquisition of resources is a fairly simple procedure. In other situations, however, the acquisition of resources and maintaining them at a level which will satisfy organizational needs becomes a problem of considerable magnitude. For example, one of the key resources needed by an organization is personnel. Yet, acquiring the type of personnel needed to fit or carry out organizational objectives can be a very difficult task, so much so that we may see within an organization several fundamental changes in order to provide for this necessary resource. The first and most expected is the development of a unit within the organization to be primarily concerned with the acquisition of new personnel, that is, a personnel function. For the personnel function to succeed, however, it is often necessary that the organization itself be such that it will attract the type of people desired. Hence, there is the problem of developing an organizational image which is attractive enough to lure prospective personnel to it. To do this, the actual operation and structure of the organization may have to change considerably (Smigel).

We have chosen as our illustration the resource of personnel, but it is not too difficult to consider the same factors as relevant to the acquisition of many other resources. To acquire capital many business firms have established separate organizational components and have worked hard to create a proper image. Not only that, but firms will provide certain internal operations or facilities, such as an accounting system, or for that matter a research function to assure the providers of the capital that their money is being invested in a desirable company. Although less obvious, somewhat the same thing would seem to be applicable to the acquisitions of most other resources.

Much of what we have said suggests that there is a close parallel between organizational change and the executive hierarchy. Defining their terms somewhat differently, investigators who have studied this issue specifically have found a direct relation between innovation in an organization and the proportion of what in accounting terms would be called non-productive employees, which are usually the executives and the members of the firm who work in clerical or professional occupations (Harbison).

Summary

In this introduction we have looked at an organization with two thoughts in mind. First, what are the classes of events which influence the shape and form and nature of an organization, and how do they do this; and second, what changes in these factors will bring about changes in the organization, and above all, how does this come about? We have, therefore, looked at an organization, first to examine the external factors which impinge on it and mold it, and second, internally, to examine the adjustments which are made to these factors. Toward the end we have considered what is involved in supplying the needs and requirements of the organization itself in the long-term pull or as it sets new directions in compliance with requirements of its environment or its policy formulators.

An organization has been discussed both as an economy, largely from a static point of view, and as an adaptive organism, which must adjust continually to a wide variety of factors, some of them external to the organization, some of them internal. At times the process of adjusting to one set of external conditions requires that a sequence of internal adjustments be made within the organization. To carry it further, we note that within an organization today, particularly the larger ones, there are specialized units which are particularly directed to this activity of, in one way or another, facilitating the adaptation of the organization. We note marketing research functions, engineering and research, and organizational planning, to name but a few.

Foundations of the Theory of Organization

PHILIP SELZNICK

Trades unions, governments, business corporations, political parties, and the like are formal structures in the sense that they represent rationally ordered instruments for the achievement of stated goals. "Organization," we are told, "is the arrangement of personnel for facilitating the accomplishment of some agreed purpose through the allocation of functions and responsibilities." [1] Or, defined more generally, formal organization is "a system of consciously coordinated activities or forces of two or more persons." [2] Viewed in this light, formal organization is the structural expression of rational action. The mobilization of technical and managerial skills requires a pattern of coordination, a systematic ordering of positions and duties which defines a chain of command and makes possible the administrative integration of specialized functions. In this context *delegation* is the primordial organizational act, a precarious venture which requires the continuous elaboration of formal mechanisms of coordination and control. The security of all participants, and of the system as a whole, generates a persistent pressure for the institutionalization of relationships, which are thus removed from the uncertainties of individual fealty or sentiment. Moreover, it is necessary for the relations within the structure to be determined in such a way that individuals will be interchangeable and the organization will thus be free of dependence upon personal qualities.[3] In this way, the formal structure becomes subject to calculable manipulation, an instrument of rational action.

But as we inspect these formal structures we begin to see that they never succeed in conquering the non-rational dimension of organizational behavior. The latter remain at once indispensable to the continued existence of the system of coordination and at the same time the source of friction, dilemma, doubt, and ruin. This fundamental paradox arises from the fact that rational action systems are inescapably imbedded in an institutional matrix, in two significant senses: (1) the action system —or the formal structure of delegation and control which is its organizational expression— is itself only an aspect of a concrete social structure made up of individuals who may interact as *wholes*, not simply in terms of their formal roles within the system; (2) the formal system, and the social structure within which it finds concrete existence, are alike subject to the pressure of an institutional environment to which some over-all adjustment must be made. The formal administrative design can never adequately or fully reflect the concrete organization to which it refers, for the obvious reason that no abstract plan or pattern can—or may, if it is to be useful—exhaustively describe an empirical totality. At the same time, that which is not included in the abstract design (as reflected, for example, in a staff-and-line organization chart) is vitally relevant to the maintenance and development of the formal system itself.

From *American Sociological Review*, Vol. 13, Feb. 1948, pp. 25–35. Reprinted with permission of the author and the publisher, American Sociological Association.
[1] John M. Gaus, "A Theory of Organization in Public Administration," in *The Frontiers of Public Administration* (Chicago: University of Chicago Press, 1936), p. 66.
[2] Chester I. Barnard, *The Functions of the Executive* (Cambridge: Harvard University Press, 1938), p. 73.

[3] Cf. Talcott Parsons' generalization (after Max Weber) of the "law of the increasing rationality of action systems," in *The Structure of Social Action* (New York: McGraw-Hill, 1937), p. 752.

Organization may be viewed from two standpoints which are analytically distinct but which are empirically united in a context of reciprocal consequences. On the one hand, any concrete organizational system is an *economy;* at the same time, it is an *adaptive social structure.* Considered as an economy, organization is a system of relationships which define the availability of scarce resources and which may be manipulated in terms of efficiency and effectiveness. It is the economic aspect of organization which commands the attention of management technicians and, for the most part, students of public as well as private administration.[4] Such problems as the span of executive control, the role of staff or auxiliary agencies, the relation of headquarters to field offices, and the relative merits of single or multiple executive boards are typical concerns of the science of administration. The coordinative scalar, and functional principles, as elements of the theory of organization, are products of the attempt to explicate the most general features of organization as a "technical problem" or, in our terms, as an economy.

Organization as an economy is, however, necessarily conditioned by the organic states of the concrete structure, outside of the systematics of delegation and control. This becomes especially evident as the attention of leadership is directed toward such problems as the legitimacy of authority and the dynamics of persuasion. It is recognized implicitly in action and explicitly in the work of a number of students that the possibility of manipulating the system of coordination depends on the extent to which that system is operating within an environment of effective inducement to individual participants and of conditions in which the stability of authority is assured. This is in a sense the fundamental thesis of Barnard's remarkable study, *The Functions of the Executive.* It is also the underlying hypothesis which makes it possible for Urwick to suggest that "proper" or formal channels in fact function

to "confirm and record" decisions arrived at by more personal means.[5] We meet it again in the concept of administration as a process of education, in which the winning of consent and support is conceived to be a basic function of leadership.[6] In short, it is recognized that control and consent cannot be divorced even within formally authoritarian structures.

The indivisibility of control and consent makes it necessary to view formal organizations as *cooperative* systems, widening the frame of reference of those concerned with the manipulation of organizational resources. At the point of action, of executive decision, the economic aspect of organization provides inadequate tools for control over the concrete structure. This idea may be readily grasped if attention is directed to the role of the individual within the organizational economy. From the standpoint of organization as a formal system, persons are viewed functionally, in respect to their *roles*, as participants in assigned segments of the cooperative system. But in fact individuals have a propensity to resist depersonalization, to spill over the boundaries of their segmentary roles, to participate as *wholes*. The formal systems (at an extreme, the disposition of "rifles" at a military perimeter) cannot take account of the deviations thus introduced, and consequently break down as instruments of control when relied upon alone. The whole individual raises new problems for the organization, partly because of the needs of his own personality, partly because he brings with him a set of established habits as well, perhaps, as commitments to special groups outside of the organization.

Unfortunately for the adequacy of formal systems of coordination, the needs of individuals do not permit a single-minded attention to the stated goals of the system within which they have been assigned. The hazard inherent in the act of delegation derives essentially from this fact. Delegation is an organizational act, having to do with formal assignments of functions and powers. Theoretically, these assign-

---

[4] See Luther Gulick and Lydall Urwick (editors), *Papers on the Science of Administration* (New York: Institute of Public Administration, Columbia University, 1937); Lydall Urwick, *The Elements of Administration* (New York, Harper, 1943); James D. Mooney and Alan C. Reiley, *The Principles of Organization* (New York: Harper, 1939); H. S. Dennison, *Organization Engineering* (New York: McGraw-Hill, 1931).

[5] Urwick, *The Elements of Administration, op. cit.*, p. 47.

[6] See Gaus, *op. cit.* Studies of the problem of morale are instances of the same orientation, having received considerable impetus in recent years from the work of the Harvard Business School group.

ments are made to roles or official positions, not to individuals as such. In fact, however, delegation necessarily involves concrete individuals who have interests and goals which do not always coincide with the goals of the formal system. As a consequence, individual personalities may offer resistance to the demands made upon them by the official conditions of delegation. These resistances are not accounted for within the categories of coordination and delegation, so that when they occur they must be considered as unpredictable and accidental. Observations of this type of situation within formal structures are sufficiently commonplace. A familiar example is that of delegation to a subordinate who is also required to train his own replacement. The subordinate may resist this demand in order to maintain unique access to the "mysteries" of the job, and thus insure his indispensability to the organization.

In large organizations, deviations from the formal system tend to become institutionalized, so that "unwritten laws" and informal associations are established. Institutionalization removes such deviations from the realm of personality differences, transforming them into a persistent structural aspect of formal organizations.[7] These institutionalized rules and modes of informal cooperation are normally attempts by participants in the formal organization to control the group relations which form the environment of organizational decisions. The informal patterns (such as cliques) arise spontaneously, are based on personal relationships, and are usually directed to the control of some specific situation. They may be generated anywhere within a hierarchy, often with deleterious consequences for the formal goals of the organization, but they may also function to widen the available resources of executive control and thus contribute to rather than hinder the achievement of the stated objectives of the organization. The deviations tend to force a shift away from the purely formal system as

the effective determinant of behavior to (1) a condition in which informal patterns buttress the formal, as through the manipulation of sentiment within the organization in favor of established authority; or (2) a condition wherein the informal controls effect a consistent modification of formal goals, as in the case of some bureaucratic patterns.[8] This trend will eventually result in the formalization of erstwhile informal activities, with the cycle of deviation and transformation beginning again on a new level.

The relevance of informal structures to organizational analysis underlines the significance of conceiving of formal organizations as cooperative systems. When the totality of interacting groups and individuals becomes the object of inquiry, the latter is not restricted by formal, legal, or procedural dimensions. The *state of the system* emerges as a significant point of analysis, as when an internal situation charged with conflict qualifies and informs actions ostensibly determined by formal relations and objectives. A proper understanding of the organizational process must make it possible to interpret changes in the formal system —new appointments or rules or reorganizations —in their relation to the informal and unavowed ties of friendship, class loyalty, power cliques, or external commitment. This is what it means "to know the score."

The fact that the involvement of individuals as whole personalities tends to limit the adequacy of formal systems of coordination does not mean that organizational characteristics are those of individuals. The organic, emergent character of the formal organization considered as a cooperative system must be recognized. This means that the *organization* reaches decisions, takes action, and makes adjustments. Such a view raises the question of the relation between organizations and persons. The significance of theoretical emphasis upon the cooperative *system* as such is derived from the insight that certain actions and consequences are enjoined independently of the personality of the individuals involved. Thus, if reference is made to the "organization-paradox"—the tension created by the inhibitory consequences

[7] The creation of informal structures within various types of organizations has received explicit recognition in recent years. See F. J. Roethlisberger and W. J. Dickson, *Management and the Worker* (Cambridge: Harvard University Press, 1941), p. 524; also Barnard, *op. cit.*, c. ix; and Wilbert E. Moore, *Industrial Relations and the Social Order* (New York: Macmillan, 1946), chap. xv.

[8] For an analysis of the latter in these terms, see Philip Selznick, "An Approach to a Theory of Bureaucracy," *American Sociological Review*, Vol. VIII, No. 1 (February, 1943).

of certain types of informal structures within organizations—this does not mean that individuals themselves are in quandaries. It is the nature of the interacting consequences of divergent interests within the organization which creates the condition, a result which may obtain independently of the consciousness or the qualities of the individual participants. Similarly, it seems useful to insist that there are qualities and needs of leader*ship*, having to do with position and role, which are persistent despite variations in the character or personality of individual leaders themselves.

Rational action systems are characteristic of both individuals and organizations. The conscious attempt to mobilize available internal resources (e.g., self-discipline) for the achievement of a stated goal—referred to here as an economy or a formal system—is one aspect of individual psychology. But the personality considered as a dynamic system of interacting wishes, compulsions, and restraints defines a system which is at once essential and yet potentially deleterious to what may be thought of as the "economy of learning" or to individual rational action. At the same time, the individual personality is an adaptive structure, and this, too, requires a broader frame of reference for analysis than the categories of rationality. On a different level, although analogously, we have pointed to the need to consider organizations as cooperative systems and adaptive structures in order to explain the context of and deviations from the formal systems of delegation and coordination.

To recognize the sociological relevance of formal structures is not, however, to have constructed a theory of organization. It is important to set the framework of analysis, and much is accomplished along this line when, for example, the nature of authority in formal organizations is reinterpreted to emphasize the factors of cohesion and persuasion as against legal or coercive sources.[9] This redefinition is logically the same as that which introduced the conception of the self as social. The latter helps make possible, but does not of itself fulfill, the requirements for a dynamic theory of personality. In the same way, the definition of authority as conditioned by sociological factors

of sentiment and cohesion—or more generally the definition of formal organizations as cooperative systems—only sets the stage, as an initial requirement, for the formulation of a theory of organization.

Structural-Functional Analysis. Cooperative systems are constituted of individuals interacting as wholes in relation to a formal system of coordination. The concrete structure is therefore a resultant of the reciprocal influences of the formal and informal aspects of organization. Furthermore, this structure is itself a totality, an adaptive "organism" reacting to influences upon it from an external environment. These considerations help to define the objects of inquiry; but to progress to a system of predicates *about* these objects it is necessary to set forth an analytical method which seems to be fruitful and significant. The method must have a relevance to empirical materials, which is to say, it must be more specific in its reference than discussions of the logic or methodology of social science.

The organon which may be suggested as peculiarly helpful in the analysis of adaptive structures has been referred to as "structural-functional analysis." [10] This method may be characterized in a sentence: *Structural-functional analysis relates contemporary and variable behavior to a presumptively stable system of needs and mechanisms.* This means that a given empirical system is deemed to have basic needs, essentially related to self-maintenance; the system develops repetitive means of self-defense; and day-to-day activity is interpreted in terms of the function served by that activity for the maintenance and defense of the system. Put this generally, the approach is applicable on any level in which the determinate "states" of empirically isolable systems undergo self-impelled and repetitive transformations when impinged upon by external conditions. This self-impulsion suggests the relevance of the term "dynamic," which is often used in referring to physiological, psychological, or social

[9] Robert Michels, "Authority," *Encyclopedia of the Social Sciences* (New York: Macmillan, 1931), pp. 319ff.; also Barnard, *op. cit.*, c. xii.

[10] For a presentation of this approach having a more general reference than the study of formal organizations, see Talcott Parsons, "The Present Position and Prospects of Systematic Theory in Sociology," in Georges Gurvitch and Wilbert E. Moore (ed.), *Twentieth Century Sociology* (New York: The philosophical Library, 1945).

systems to which this type of analysis has been applied.[11]

It is a postulate of the structural-functional approach that the basic need of all empirical systems is the maintenance of the integrity and continuity of the system itself. Of course, such a postulate is primarily useful in directing attention to a set of "derived imperatives" or needs which are sufficiently concrete to characterize the system at hand.[12] It is perhaps rash to attempt a catalogue of these imperatives for formal organizations, but some suggestive formulation is needed in the interests of setting forth the type of analysis under discussion. In formal organizations, the "maintenance of the system" as a generic need may be specified in terms of the following imperatives:

1. THE SECURITY OF THE ORGANIZATION AS A WHOLE IN RELATION TO SOCIAL FORCES IN ITS ENVIRONMENT. This imperative requires continuous attention to the possibilities of encroachment and to the forestalling of threatened aggressions or deleterious (though perhaps unintended) consequences from the actions of others.

2. THE STABILITY OF THE LINES OF AUTHORITY AND COMMUNICATION. One of the persistent reference-points of administrative decision is the weighing of consequences for the continued capacity of leadership to control and to have access to the personnel or ranks.

---

[11] "Structure" refers to both the relationships within the system (formal plus informal patterns in organization) and the set of needs and modes of satisfaction which characterize the given type of empirical system. As the utilization of this type of analysis proceeds, the concept of "need" will require further clarification. In particular, the imputation of a "stable set of needs" to organizational systems must not function as a new instinct theory. At the same time, we cannot avoid using these inductions as to generic needs, for they help us to stake out our area of inquiry. The author is indebted to Robert K. Merton who has, in correspondence, raised some important objections to the use of the term "need" in this context. [12] For "derived imperative" see Bronislaw Malinowski, *The Dynamics of Culture Change* (New Haven: Yale University Press, 1945), pp. 44ff. For the use of "need" in place of "motive" see the same author's *A Scientific Theory of Culture* (Chapel Hill: University of North Carolina Press, 1944), pp. 89–90.

3. THE STABILITY OF INFORMAL RELATIONS WITHIN THE ORGANIZATION. Ties of sentiment and self-interest are evolved as unacknowledged but effective mechanisms of adjustment of individuals and sub-groups to the conditions of life within the organization. These ties represent a cementing of relationships which sustains the formal authority in day-to-day operations and widens opportunities for effective communication.[13] Consequently, attempts to "upset" the informal structure, either frontally or as an indirect consequence of formal reorganization, will normally be met with considerable resistance.

4. THE CONTINUITY OF POLICY AND OF THE SOURCES OF ITS DETERMINATION. For each level within the organization, and for the organization as a whole, it is necessary that there be a sense that action taken in the light of a given policy will not be placed in continuous jeopardy. Arbitrary or unpredictable changes in policy undermine the significance of (and therefore the attention to) day-to-day action by injecting a note of capriciousness. At the same time, the organization will seek stable roots (or firm statutory authority or popular mandate) so that a sense of the permanency and legitimacy of its acts will be achieved.

5. A HOMOGENEITY OF OUTLOOK WITH RESPECT TO THE MEANING AND ROLE OF THE ORGANIZATION. The minimization of disaffection requires a unity derived from a common understanding of what the character of the organization is meant to be. When this homogeneity breaks down, as in situations of internal conflict over basic issues, the continued existence of the organization is endangered. On the other hand, one of the signs of "healthy" organization is the ability to effectively orient new members and readily slough off those who cannot be adapted to the established outlook.

This catalogue of needs cannot be thought of as final, but it approximates the stable system generally characteristic of formal organizations. These imperatives are derived, in the sense that they represent the conditions for survival or self-maintenance of cooperative systems of organized action. An inspection of these needs suggests that organizational survival

---

[13] They may also *destroy* those relationships, as noted above, but the need remains, generating one of the persistent dilemmas of leadership.

is intimately connected with the struggle for relative prestige, both for the organization and for elements and individuals within it. It may therefore be useful to refer to a *prestige-survival motif* in organizational behavior as a short-hand way of relating behavior to needs, especially when the exact nature of the needs remains in doubt. However, it must be emphasized that prestige-survival in organizations does not derive simply from like motives in individuals. Loyalty and self-sacrifice may be individual expressions of organizational or group egotism and self-consciousness.

The concept of organizational need directs analysis to the *internal relevance* of organizational behavior. This is especially pertinent with respect to discretionary action undertaken by agents manifestly in pursuit of formal goals. The question then becomes one of relating the specific act of discretion to some presumptively stable organizational need. In other words, it is not simply action plainly oriented internally (such as in-service training) but also action presumably oriented externally which must be inspected for its relevance to internal conditions. This is of prime importance for the understanding of bureaucratic behavior, for it is of the essence of the latter that action formally undertaken for substantive goals be weighed and transformed in terms of its consequences for the position of the officialdom.

Formal organizations as cooperative systems on the one hand, and individual personalities on the other, involve structural-functional homologies, a point which may help to clarify the nature of this type of analysis. If we say that the individual has a stable set of needs, most generally the need for maintaining and defending the integrity of his personality or ego; that there are recognizable certain repetitive mechanisms which are utilized by the ego in its defense (rationalization, projection, regression, etc.); and that overt and variable behavior may be interpreted in terms of its relation to these needs and mechanisms—on the basis of this logic we may discern the typical pattern of structural-functional analysis as set forth above. In this sense, it is possible to speak of a "Freudian model" for organizational analysis. This does not mean that the substantive insights of individual psychology may be applied to organizations, as in vulgar extrapolations from the individual ego to whole nations or (by a no less vulgar inversion) from

strikes to frustrated workers. It is the *logic*, the *type* of analysis which is pertinent.

This homology is also instructive in relation to the applicability of generalizations to concrete cases. The dynamic theory of personality states a set of possible predicates about the ego and its mechanisms of defense, which inform us concerning the propensities of individual personalities under certain general circumstances. But these predicates provide only tools for the analysis of particular individuals, and each concrete case must be examined to tell which operate and in what degree. They are not primarily organs of prediction. In the same way, the predicates within the theory of organization will provide tools for the analysis of particular cases. Each organization, like each personality, represents a resultant of complex forces, an empirical entity which no single relation or no simple formula can explain. The problem of analysis becomes that of selecting among the possible predicates set forth in the theory of organization those which illuminate our understanding of the materials at hand.

The setting of structural-functional analysis as applied to organizations requires some qualification, however. Let us entertain the suggestion that the interesting problem in social science is not so much why men act the way they do as why men in certain circumstances *must* act the way they do. This emphasis upon constraint, if accepted, releases us from an ubiquitous attention to behavior in general, and especially from any undue fixation upon statistics. On the other hand, it has what would seem to be the salutary consequence of focusing inquiry upon certain necessary relationships of the type "if . . . then," for example: If the cultural level of the rank and file members of a formally democratic organization is below that necessary for participation in the formulation of policy, then there will be pressure upon the leaders to use the tools of demagogy.

Is such a statement universal in its applicability? Surely not in the sense that one can predict without remainder the nature of all or even most political groups in a democracy. Concrete behavior is a resultant, a complex vector, shaped by the operation of a number of such general constraints. But there is a test of general applicability: it is that of noting whether the relation made explicit must be *taken into account* in action. This criterion represents an empirical test of the significance of social science generalizations. If a theory is significant it will state a relation which will either (1) be taken into account as an element of achieving control; or (2) be ignored only at the risk of losing control and will evidence itself in a ramification of objective or unintended consequences.[14] It is a corollary of this principle of significance that investigation must search out the underlying factors in organizational action, which requires a kind of intensive analysis of the same order as psychoanalytic probing.

A frame of reference which invites attention to the constraints upon behavior will tend to highlight tensions and dilemmas, the characteristic paradoxes generated in the course of action. The dilemma may be said to be the handmaiden of structural-functional analysis, for it introduces the concept of *commitment* or *involvement* as fundamental to organizational analysis. A dilemma in human behavior is represented by an inescapable commitment which cannot be reconciled with the needs of the organism or the social system. There are many spurious dilemmas which have to do with verbal contradictions, but inherent dilemmas to which we refer are of a more profound sort, for they reflect the basic nature of the empirical system in question. An economic order committed to profit as its sustaining incentive may, in Marxist terms, sow the seed of its own destruction. Again, the anguish of man, torn between finitude and pride, is not a matter of arbitrary and replaceable assumptions but is a reflection of the psychological needs of the human organism, and is concretized in his commitment to the institutions which command his life; he is in the world and of it, inescapably involved in its goals and demands; at the same time, the needs of the spirit are compelling, proposing modes of salvation which have continuously disquieting consequences for worldly involvements. In still another context, the need of the human organism for affection and response necessitates a commitment to elements of the culture which can provide them; but the rule of the super-ego is uncertain since it cannot be completely reconciled with the need for libidinal satisfactions.

Applying this principle to organizations we may note that there is a general source of tension observable in the split between "the motion and the act." Plans and programs reflect the freedom of technical or ideal choice, but organized action cannot escape involvement, a commitment to personnel or institutions or procedures which effectively qualifies the initial plan. *Der Mensch denkt, Gott lenkt.* In organized action, this ultimate wisdom finds a temporal meaning in the recalcitrance of the tools of action. We are inescapably committed to the mediation of human structures which are at once indispensable to our goals and at the same time stand between them and ourselves. The selection of agents generates immediately a bifurcation of interest, expressed in new centers of need and power, placing effective constraints upon the arena of action, and resulting in tensions which are never completely resolved. This is part of what it means to say that there is a "logic" of action which impels us forward from one undesired position to another. Commitment to dynamic, self-activating tools is of the nature of organized action; at the same time, the need for continuity of authority, policy, and character are pressing, and require an unceasing effort to master the instruments generated in the course of action. This generic tension is specified within the terms of each cooperative system. But for all we find a persistent relationship between *need* and *commitment* in which the latter not only qualifies the former but unites with it to produce a continuous state of tension. In this way, the notion of constraint (as reflected in tension or paradox) at once widens and more closely specifies the frame of reference for organizational analysis.

For Malinowski, the core of functionalism was contained in the view that a cultural fact must be analyzed in its setting. Moreover, he apparently conceived of his method as pertinent to the analysis of all aspects of cultural systems. But there is a more specific problem, one involving a principle of selection which serves to guide inquiry along significant

[14] See R. M. MacIver's discussion of the "dynamic assessment" which "brings the external world selectively into the subjective realm, conferring on it subjective significance for the ends of action." *Social Causation* (Boston: Ginn, 1942), chaps, 11, 12. The analysis of this assessment within the context of organized action yields the implicit knowledge which guides the choice among alternatives. See also Robert K. Merton, "The Unanticipated Consequences of Purposive Social Action," *American Sociological Review*, I, 6 (December, 1936).

lines. Freud conceived of the human organism as an adaptive structure, but he was not concerned with all human needs, nor with all phases of adaptation. For his system, he selected those needs whose expression is blocked in some way, so that such terms as repression, inhibition, and frustration became crucial. All conduct may be thought of as derived from need, and all adjustment represents the reduction of need. But not all needs are relevant to the systematics of dynamic psychology; and it is not adjustment as such but reaction to frustration which generates the characteristic modes of defensive behavior.

Organizational analysis, too, must find its selective principle; otherwise the indiscriminate attempts to relate activity functionally to needs will produce little in the way of significant theory. Such a principle might read as follows: *Our frame of reference is to select out those needs which cannot be fulfilled within approved avenues of expression and thus must have recourse to such adaptive mechanisms as ideology and to the manipulation of formal processes and structures in terms of informal goals.* This formulation has many difficulties, and is not presented as conclusive, but it suggests the kind of principle which is likely to separate the quick and the dead, the meaningful and the trite, in the study of cooperative systems in organized action.[15]

The frame of reference outlined here for the theory of organization may now be identified as involving the following major ideas: (1) the concept of organizations as cooperative systems, adaptive social structures, made up of interacting individuals, sub-groups, and informal plus formal relationships; (2) structural-functional analysis, which relates variable aspects of organization (such as goals) to stable needs and self-defensive mechanisms; (3) the concept of recalcitrance as a quality of the tools of social action, involving a break in the continuum of adjustment and defining an environment of constraint, commitment, and tension. This frame of reference is suggested as providing a specifiable *area of relations* within which predicates in the theory of organization

will be sought, and at the same time setting forth principles of selection and relevance in our approach to the data of organization.

It will be noted that we have set forth this frame of reference within the over-all context of social action. The significance of events may be defined by their place and operational role in a means-end scheme. If functional analysis searches out the elements important for the maintenance of a given structure, and that structure is one of the materials to be manipulated in action, then that which is functional in respect to the structure is also functional in respect to the action system. This provides a ground for the significance of functionally derived theories. At the same time, relevance to control in action is the empirical test of their applicability or truth.

Cooptation as a Mechanism of Adjustment. The frame of reference stated above is in fact an amalgam of definition, resolution, and substantive theory. There is an element of *definition* in conceiving of formal organizations as cooperative systems, though of course the interaction of informal and formal patterns is a question of fact; in a sense, we are *resolving* to employ structural-functional analysis on the assumption that it will be fruitful to do so, though here, too, the specification of needs or derived imperatives is a matter for empirical inquiry; and our predication of recalcitrance as a quality of the tools of action is itself a *substantive theory*, perhaps fundamental to a general understanding of the nature of social action.

A theory of organization requires more than a general frame of reference, though the latter is indispensable to inform the approach of inquiry to any given set of materials. What is necessary is the construction of generalizations concerning transformations within and among cooperative systems. These generalizations represent, from the standpoint of particular cases, possible predicates which are relevant to the materials as we know them in general, but which are not necessarily controlling in all circumstances. A theory of transformations in organization would specify those states of the system which resulted typically in predictable, or at least understandable, changes in such aspects of organization as goals, leadership, doctrine, efficiency, effective-

---

[15] This is not meant to deprecate the study of organizations as *economies* or formal systems. The latter represent an independent level, abstracted from organizational structures as cooperative or adaptive systems ("organisms").

ness, and size. These empirical generalizations would be systematized as they were related to the stable needs of the cooperative system.

Changes in the characteristics of organizations may occur as a result of many different conditions, not always or necessarily related to the processes of organization as such. But the theory of organization must be selective, so that explanations of transformations will be sought within its own assumptions or frame of reference. Consider the question of size. Organizations may expand for many reasons—the availability of markets, legislative delegations, the swing of opinion—which may be accidental from the point of view of the organizational process. To explore changes in size (as of, say, a trades union) as related to changes in non-organizational conditions may be necessitated by the historical events to be described, but it will not of itself advance the frontiers of the theory of organization. However, if "the innate propensity of an organizations to expand" is asserted as a function of "the inherent instability of incentives" [16] then transformations have been stated within the terms of the theory of organization itself. It is likely that in many cases the generalization in question may represent only a minor aspect of the empirical changes, but these organizational relations must be made explicit if the theory is to receive development.

In a frame of reference which specifies needs and anticipates the formulation of a set of self-defensive responses or mechanisms, the latter appear to constitute one kind of empirical generalization or "possible predicate" within the general theory. The needs of organizations (whatever investigation may determine them to be) are posited as attributes of all organizations, but the responses to disequilibrium will be varied. The mechanisms used by the system in fulfillment of its needs will be repetitive and thus may be described as a specifiable set of assertions within the theory of organization, but any given organization may or may not have recourse to the characteristic modes of response. Certainly no given organization will employ all of the possible mechanisms which are theoretically available. When Barnard speaks of an "innate propensity of organization to expand" he is in fact formulating one of the general mechanisms,

[16] Barnard, *op. cit.*, pp. 158-9.

namely, expansion, which is a characteristic mode of response available to an organization under pressure from within. These responses necessarily involve a transformation (in this case, size) of some structural aspect of the organization.

Other examples of the self-defensive mechanisms available to organizations may derive primarily from the response of these organizations to the institutional environments in which they live. The tendency to construct ideologies, reflecting the need to come to terms with major social forces, is one such mechanism. Less well understood as a mechanism of organizational adjustment is what we may term *cooptation*. Some statement of the meaning of this concept may aid in clarifying the foregoing analysis.

Cooptation is the process of absorbing new elements into the leadership or policy-determining structure of an organization as a means of averting threats to its stability or existence. This is a defensive mechanism, formulated as one of a number of possible predicates available for the interpretation of organizational behavior. Cooptation tells us something about the process by which an institutional environment impinges itself upon an organization and effects changes in its leadership and policy. Formal authority may resort to cooptation under the following general conditions:

1. When there exists a hiatus between consent and control, so that the ligitimacy of the formal authority is called into question. The "indivisibility" of consent and control refers, of course, to an optimum situation. Where control lacks an adequate measure of consent, it may revert to coercive measures or attempt somehow to win the consent of the governed. One means of winning consent is to coopt elements into the leadership or organization, usually elements which in some way reflect the sentiment, or possess the confidence of the relevant public or mass. As a result, it is expected that the new elements will lend respectability or legitimacy to the organs of control and thus reestablish the stability of formal authority. This process is widely used, and in many different contexts. It is met in colonial countries, where the organs of alien control reaffirm their legitimacy by coopting native leaders into the colonial administration. We find it in the phenomenon of "crisis-patriotism" wherein normally disfranchised groups

are temporarily given representation in the councils of government in order to win their solidarity in a time of national stress. Cooptation is presently being considered by the United States Army in its study of proposals to give enlisted personnel representation in the court-martial machinery—a clearly adaptive response to stresses made explicit during the war, the lack of confidence in the administration of army justice. The "unity" parties of totalitarian states are another form of cooptation; company unions or some employee representation plans in industry are still another. In each of these cases, the response of formal authority (private or public, in a large organization or a small one) is an attempt to correct a state of imbalance by *formal* measures. It will be noted, moreover, that what is shared is the *responsibility* for power rather than power itself. These conditions define what we shall refer to as *formal cooptation.*

2. Cooptation may be a response to the pressure of specific centers of power. This is not necessarily a matter of legitimacy or of a general and diffuse lack of confidence. These may be well established; and yet organized forces which are able to threaten the formal authority may effectively shape its structure and policy. The organization in respect to its institutional environment—or the leadership in respect to its ranks—must take these forces into account. As a consequence, the outside elements may be brought into the leadership or policy-determining structure, may be given a place as a recognition of and concession to the resources they can independently command. The representation of interests through administrative constituencies is a typical example of this process. Or, within an organization, individuals upon whom the group is dependent for funds or other resources may insist upon and receive a share in the determination of policy. This form of cooptation is typically expressed in informal terms, for the problem is not one of responding to a state of imbalance with respect to the "people as a whole" but rather one of meeting the pressure of specific individuals or interest-groups which are in a position to enforce demands. The latter are interested in the substance of power and not its forms. Moreover, an open acknowledgement of capitulation to specific interests may itself undermine the sense of legitimacy of the formal authority within the community.

Consequently, there is a positive pressure to refrain from explicit recognition of the relationship established. This form of the cooptative mechanism, having to do with the sharing of power as a response to specific pressures, may be termed *informal cooptation.*

Cooptation reflects a state of tension between formal authority and social power. The former is embodied in a particular structure and leadership, but the latter has to do with subjective and objective factors which control the loyalties and potential manipulability of the community. Where the formal authority is an expression of social power, its stability is assured. On the other hand, when it becomes divorced from the sources of social power its continued existence is threatened. This threat may arise from the sheer alienation of sentiment or from the fact that other leaderships have control over the sources of social power. Where a formal authority has been accustomed to the assumption that its constituents respond to it as individuals, there may be a rude awakening when organization of those constituents on a non-governmental basis creates nuclei of power which are able effectively to demand a sharing of power.[17]

The significance of cooptation for organizational analysis is not simply that there is a change in or a broadening of leadership, and that this is an adaptive response, but also that *this change is consequential for the character and role of the organization.* Co-

[17] It is perhaps useful to restrict the concept of cooptation to formal organizations, but in fact it probably reflects a process characteristic of all group leaderships. This has received some recognition in the analysis of class structure, wherein the ruling class is interpreted as protecting its own stability by absorbing new elements. Thus Michels made the point that "an aristocracy cannot maintain an enduring stability by sealing itself off hermetically." See Robert Michels, *Umschichtungen in den herrschenden Klassen nach dem Kriege* (Stuttgart: Kohlhammer, 1934), p. 39; also Gaetano Mosca, *The Ruling Class* (New York: McGraw-Hill, 1939), pp. 413ff. The alliance or amalgamation of classes in the face of a common threat may be reflected in formal and informal cooptative responses among formal organizations sensitive to class pressures. In a forthcoming volume, *TVA and the Grass Roots*, the author has made extensive use of the concept of cooptation in analyzing some aspects of the organizational behavior of a government agency.

optation involves commitment, so that the groups to which adaptation has been made constrain the field of choice available to the organization or leadership in question. The character of the coopted elements will necessarily shape (inhibit or broaden) the modes of action available to the leadership which has won adaptation and security at the price of commitment. The concept of cooptation thus implicitly sets forth the major points of the frame of reference outlined above: it is an adaptive response of a cooperative system to a stable need, generating transformations which reflect constraints enforced by the recalcitrant tools of action.

Production Planning and Organizational Morale

KAMLA CHOWDHRY AND A. K. PAL

This is a study of the interaction of production planning and management practices, and the effect of these on the morale of the supervisory staff of two Indian cotton textile mills. The two mills are located in a large city, where the main industry is textiles. Both mills are operating in a common social and economic climate, subject to the same type of market fluctuations and to a similar pattern of labor-management relations. In both mills, like the rest of the industry, the top executive control is with the managing agent who acquires the right of control through the Managing Agency Agreement.[1]

From *Human Organization*, Vol. 15, No. 4, pp. 11–16. Reprinted with permission of the publisher, Society for Applied Anthropology.

Dr. Kamla Chowdhry is Director, Human Relations Division, Ahmedabad Textile Industry's Research Association: Dr. A. K. Pal is on the staff of the Human Relations Division, Ahmedabad Textile Industry's Research Association, Ahmedabad, India.

The authors are grateful to Professor Charles A. Myers, Director of Industrial Relations Section, M.I.T., for help in planning the study and discussing the results at various stages. The research was financed in part by funds made available by the Inter-University Study of Labor Problems in Economic Development.

[1] The Managing Agency Agreement allows the transfer of Managing Agency rights to the sons and other members of the joint family. The Managing Agents are generally not salaried people but by contract in the Managing Agency Agreement receive a commission which may be a percentage of profits or gross sales. The Managing Agent and his family are generally the major shareholders in the company.

The markets to which the goods of these mills go are similar. There are frequent fluctuations in the market due to cotton prices, changes in government policy, consumer demand, etc. A significant difference between the two mills is the policy of the management in meeting these fluctuations in the market. In Mill A the manufacturing program is frequently altered to manufacture types of cloth that the market demands at the moment and that would yield the highest profits at that time. This is the prevalent pattern in the industry. In Mill B, the manufacturing program is relatively stable. There have been no changes for years in the counts spun, and even in the cloth manufactured not many significant changes have been introduced. The mill has emphasized and established a reputation for quality, and their manufactured goods have a steady market demand. Probably only half a dozen of the 65 mills in the city follow this practice.

The object of this study is to examine the implications of the above basic differences in the policy of management on the functioning of the organization. More specifically, we sought (1) to determine in what way this policy is reflected in the organizational structure and in the management practices prevailing in the two mills, and (2) to examine the effect of the prevailing organizational structure and management practices on the satisfaction of members and the efficiency of each organization.

Research Procedure. Both mills are composite units, with spinning, weaving, dyeing, bleaching and finishing operations. This study was restricted to the spinning and weaving sections only, which comprise the major part of the textile mills. The organization and functioning of these two departments were studied with the help of top management and supervisory staffs. The research staff visited the mills almost daily over a period of three months and observed the activities going on, the interactions and relationships of people, and conducted interviews on certain aspects of organization and management practices. Fixed question-free answer interviews were held with the managing agents, production managers, and twenty-four departmental heads, assistants and supervisors. Mill A and Mill B are compared in terms of formal organizational structure, delegation of responsibility and authority, communication and consultation practices, and the satisfaction and stability of members working in the organization.

Organizational Structure. The formal organizational structures of Mill A and Mill B are given in Fig. 1. The hierarchical levels and their designation in industry are as follows: managing agent, production manager, departmental head, assistant, supervisor, jobber and worker.

MILL A. In Mill A the top executive is the managing agent, and he is in overall charge of the production and the sales of the organization. The next level in the formal structure consists of the production manager, who is the technical adviser to the agent. The third level in the organization is composed of departmental heads, who, however, report directly to the agent. The agent also has direct contact with the departmental heads, but he sometimes passes instructions through the production manager. The departmental heads discuss their problems and difficulties with the production manager, but in a more informal way in the hope that he will be able to present their case to the agent more effectively.

The departmental head reports to the agent once or twice daily in the latter's office. The agent tells them of the changes he wishes to introduce in the manufacturing program, and they in turn inform the agent about efficiency, balance of production, shortage of material and spare parts, labor difficulties, etc.

No clear procedure is followed by the assistant and supervisors about reporting. They

report to the departmental head, but they are also asked to report directly sometimes to the production manager or to the agent. The supervisors report to the assistant or departmental head depending on whoever is available, or with whom they have better relations.

It is also clear from Fig. 1, that there are more senior personnel working on the day shift than on the night shift and that the night shift is mainly in charge of junior personnel. Thus, there are two assistants on the day shift in the Spinning Department against one on the night shift. Similarly, in the Weaving Department there are three assistants on the day shift but none on the night shift. This makes the organizational structure very unbalanced in the two shifts. The weaving master says, concerning the senior personnel in the day shift:

> It is rather unfortunate that all my assistants are placed on the day shift. It is absolutely necessary to have at least one assistant (of loomshed) on the night shift. I am trying to persuade the agent to transfer X or Y to the night shift.

On the other hand, the spinning master desires to place senior staff on the day shift:

> I prefer to keep the assistants on the day shift—otherwise I would not be able to cope with the work. We do all the settings on the day shift. The night shift people only run the machines.

Another feature of the organization of Mill A is that supervisors and sometimes assistants, are transferred from one shift to another, without a corresponding change in the personnel of the rest of the department. According to factory rules, jobbers and workers change systematically every month from day to night shift. But the assistants and supervisors who are not covered by the factory regulations do not change their shift regularly; they move, but on an *ad hoc* basis, depending on other considerations. This results in the continuity of work relationships being frequently disrupted, in a certain amount of confusion as to who is to report to whom, and in problems of relationships that arise when there is no clear and stable structure of reporting and getting work done.

One loomshed supervisor says:

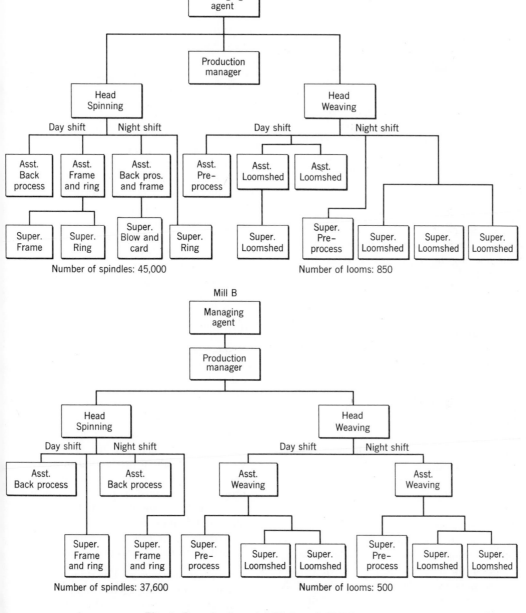

Fig. 1. *Organization of Mill* A *and Mill* B.

I don't like this system. I mean no system. I don't know who is my boss, so I have developed a system of working independently.

Another supervisor says:

I like to be with the same group of workers all the time. I like to change shifts with them. You have got to know your workers to get along well with them. But here you don't know where you will be tomorrow.

MILL B. In Mill B, also, the managing agent is the top executive who has overall charge of production and sales of the organization. The next level is the production manager. He is the technical adviser to the agent and also co-ordinates the manufacturing program of the different departments. The departmental heads mainly report to the production manager. There are no changes in the manufacture of counts in spinning, but if changes in the sorts woven are to be introduced, the sales manager sends direct information to the weaving master or the assistant concerned.

The departmental heads report to the production manager during the latter's round in the department. The departmental heads do not have a daily direct contact with the agent in his office concerning current production problems, as was the case in Mill A. The assistants report to the departmental heads and are not generally called directly by the production manager or the agent for information. The supervisors generally report to the assistants, but sometimes to the departmental head directly.

In Mill B the organizational structures of both day and night shifts are similar. There is the same number of staff in both the shifts and there is an equal distribution of senior staff on the day and night shifts, so that the night shift is not delegated to junior staff as in Mill A. Also, there is a systematic regular change of shift for the assistants and supervisors, with the changeover of shifts for workers and jobbers. The same assistants and supervisors work with the same group of jobbers and workers so that there is stability of relationships from the assistant to the worker level. Work relationships in terms of reporting, making inquiries, etc. with the persons concerned are clear and the channels well established.

As mentioned earlier, there are frequent changes in the manufacturing program of Mill A which necessitate frequent technical changes in the department. Most of these technical changes are made on the day shift resulting in more senior staff on the day shift. Mill B which has a more stable manufacturing program does not have to concentrate its senior staff in the day shift and can consequently afford to distribute its senior staff in the two shifts and have a more balanced structure in each shift.

Management Practices. The problems of introducing manufacturing changes do not only affect the formal organizational structure of the mill, but they also influence management practices of delegation of authority, of communication and of consultation.

MILL A. Thus, in Mill A, the managing agent has to give frequent directives for change of counts and sorts. Targets have to be fulfilled and deadlines of delivery dates have to be met since the manufacturing is geared to fluctuating demand in the market. Working under these pressures the agent is constantly checking up on efficiency, production and quality of product. All this tends to result in centralized decision-making and in close and detailed supervision of the departments.

In order that top management can supervise each stage closely, there is a tendency to short-circuit in giving instructions, or in making inquiries about production, quality, adequate flow of material, etc. The agent or the production manager gets directly in touch with the assistants and supervisors for either giving instructions or receiving information.

The resultant pressures on middle and lower management can be seen from some of their remarks quoted below:

> SPINNING MASTER: I am leaving the mill soon. I am satisfied with the salary, but I cannot stand the agent's production policy of many changes. These changes are too much to cope with.

> SPINNING SUPERVISOR: The agent and the production manager call me almost every day to inquire about production and balance of production . . . the constant change of program is responsible for low efficiency. . . . The agent should listen to the technicians and draw up a plan of production according to the existing machines and not according to the whims of the market.

> SPINNING SUPERVISOR: The thing that worries me most is the agent's policy of constant change of materials. Most of my time and energy is spent trying to keep balance of production. . . . The agent often sends for me to inquire about production targets, shortages and flow of materials. . . .

Almost every member in the Spinning Department expresses his dissatisfaction concerning the frequent changes of manufacturing program and the resultant problems—efficiency, balance of production, and feelings of anxiety and tension. Top management has direct contact with almost every member in the department in order to supervise and inquire about production. The members in the Weaving Department feel the same way about the changes and the frequency of changes introduced in the sorts manufactured as the members in the Spinning Department.

For example, the weaving master says:

> The agent's policy is very short-sighted, since his guiding factor is always immediate profit. This policy is reflected in the constant change of sorts. At present all the sorts which were running a month ago have completely disappeared. Such a quick changeover is not economical and it puts the staff into great difficulty. It is almost impossible to retain a high level of production under such conditions and then the blame is put on the technical staff!

The assistants and supervisors especially connected with the loomshed mention the agent's concern about production and quality of production and how they are frequently called into his office to explain the high damages.

> LOOMSHED SUPERVISOR: The agent wants both high efficiency and good quality. I have been called several times to explain high damage. . . . For example, recently a new and a heavy sort was introduced and there was high damage and low efficiency. The agent was very upset and annoyed with everybody, from the weaving master to the workers. I was called to explain the bad working and was fired . . . but no discharge notice was served. It is going too far if the supervisors are held responsible when a bad sort is introduced and there is so much damage.

When new "sorts" (types of cloth) are introduced which the technical staff believes will not yield good efficiency or good quality, then top management feels the need for close supervision to see the working performance of the new sort, and to induce the technical staff to fulfill the targets for production and quality. This type of situation makes it necessary for the agent to maintain close and detailed supervision of the departments. The assistants and supervisors all have to report to him directly, especially when a difficult sort is being run.

THE ASSISTANT WEAVING MASTER: I meet the agent and the production manager. They ask me about the working of the department and I prepare a special report for the agent which I submit every Monday. . . . I am always pressed for better and higher production.

THE SENIOR LOOMSHED SUPERVISOR: The agent controls the department himself. I am given instructions by him about new sorts, change in loom speeds, discipline in the loomshed, etc.

LOOMSHED SUPERVISOR: My duty is to follow the instructions of the agent. . . . He has called me several times to explain about high damages. . . .

These quotations illustrate reactions to centralized decision-making, by-passing in communication, and dissatisfaction and frustration among the staff. The end is a climate of resentment against management and management goals.

An example which indicates the extent to which some members of the management staff in Mill A have lost their sense of identification with management and management goals is given below. It refers to a situation where the agent tried to consult the staff about the advisability of buying a new machine. One of the staff members said:

> After the talk by the representative of the company manufacturing machine X was over, the agent asked, "Do you or do you not advise me to buy this machine?" All the members said, "We agree that you should buy the machine." . . . It is his money, let him spend it the way he likes.

MILL B. Let us see the picture in Mill B where the manufacturing program is relatively stable. Some interview comments illustrate the difference.

SPINNING MASTER: The management of this mill is very good and the general atmosphere of working is pleasant. There is no interference from the top in the working of my department. . . . I report to the agent and to the production manager. . . . During the entire period of my work here so far, nobody has asked for the efficiency of the department, but always about quality.

. . . I would like to give quality material, so that consumers can say that Mill B has the best spinning.

WEAVING MASTER: The agent and the production manager consult me on technical matters. . . . I am in charge of the department, and the management does not interfere in my work. (All departmental problems concerning damages, spare parts, etc., are solved within the department. No supervisor or assistant mentions that he is called by the office to explain about efficiency, balance of production or high damage rate. Almost everybody mentions that this is a good mill to work in, the management is good, and that there is no pressure about production or efficiency. The impression is that the working of the departments is smooth and there is a high degree of satisfaction of members with management and management practices.)

The change of sorts in Mill B has been commented on by two persons:

PRODUCTION MANAGER: The sales manager makes his demands and the production departments have to give way to his requirements. The difficulties of the production departments are not considered. . . .

WEAVING MASTER: If rationalization is to be introduced the mill will have to standardize the type of cloth to be manufactured. Markets should be stabilized by the mills. There is no sense in manufacturing 30 and 32 yards and 40 and 42 in the same sorts. The unnecessary changeover in the department for such differences increases the cost of production.

Even in Mill B there are some protests about the change of sorts demanded by the sales manager, but there is not that feeling of pressure, strain and anxiety in the departments as found in Mill A.

There is also considerable identification with management's goals and a sense of pride in most members about this mill. The satisfaction of members is reflected in their long service in the same mill. Most members have worked in Mill B for from 10 to 25 years, whereas in Mill A, there has been considerable turnover in the senior staff. Within one year, since the completion of the field study, 8 out of 17 of the management staff have left in Mill A.

Conclusions. In terms of the research questions raised earlier, it is clear that the manufacturing policies of management in Mill A and Mill B influence the organizational structure and the management practices of each case. Thus, in Mill A the picture is one of frequent changes in the manufacturing program, frequent technical and personnel changes in departments, centralized control and decision making, "by-passing" in communication, dissatisfaction of members, resentment against management, especially among the senior staff, and a sense of insecurity and instability among members. In Mill B, the picture is one of a relatively stable manufacturing program, smoothly functioning departments, stable work groups, relative decentralization in control and decision-making, stable communication channels similar to the formal structure, satisfaction with management, and a sense of security and stability in the organization.

There are two further implications of the study that we should like specifically to emphasize:

1. There is an interrelation of management policies and management practices, an interrelation that perhaps stems from an inherent interdependence of these factors. Perhaps the clusters of factors found in Mill A and Mill B are a result of a basic approach, an attitude, a point of view, a frame of mind, and this is reflected in the totality of behavior, whether in policies or practices that a particular management follows. In other words, management involves a certain philosophy, and not merely certain techniques of management.

2. An organizational structure which is based only on the technical needs of the situation can defeat the very purposes of the organization. To function efficiently, management must take into account the social as well as the technical demands of the situation. The organization of Mill A has developed around the technical needs demanded of a manufacturing program of frequent changes. The senior staff has been kept on the day shift to make the necessary technical adjustments. The working of the night shift has consequently been delegated to junior supervisors. In such a system efficiency and quality are affected. There are complaints about the lack of sufficient back-

stuff and of poor quality, somebody gets blamed in the process, relationships become strained, and there is a constant reshuffling of staff, transferring of personnel from one shift to another to maintain an equilibrium for collaboration and efficient working. These *ad hoc* transfers of supervisors from one shift to another also result in a sense of instability and insecurity. The management does not seem to be aware of this consequence of its production policy. Unless management becomes aware of these reactions to its policy and undertakes to compensate for the continual upheaval, the possible advantages resulting from its policy cannot be realized.

In contrast, the organization of Mill B has also developed around its technical needs, but the technical needs in this case are related to a stable manufacturing program. There are not many technical changes that have to be introduced, the senior staff is equally distributed, and it is consequently possible for management to have a systematic transfer of shifts. All this has resulted in a system promoting stable relationships and close human association at work.

Similar conclusions have been emphasized in a study of 12 industrial organizations sponsored by UNESCO.[2] It mentioned that one of the

[2] Jerome F. Scott and R. P. Lynton, *The Community Factor in Modern Technology*, UNESCO, Paris, 1952, 169.

features peculiar to efficient institutions was found to be:

> . . . intimate human association at work. Physical conditions are so arranged that small numbers of people work closely together and can easily communicate with each other. . . . Without the security that comes from the feeling of belonging to a group, the individual is liable to become unadaptable, resentful and socially ill.

Therefore, in planning an organization's structure, not only have the technical demands to be taken into account, but the social system that underlies a particular technology and work process must also be considered. In an organization where frequent changes in production schedules are contemplated, it is all the more necessary for the organizational structure and the operating practices of management to be such that they can fluctuate with the strains and stresses inherent in a situation of constant changes. A greater degree of attention and emphasis must be paid to problems of organization and organizational practices in such cases. However, it is possible for management to provide a flexible structure and to follow policies which lessen rather than increase the strains and tensions inherent in an organization where constant change is part of the routine.

Plans for Changing Organizational Behavior

PAUL LAWRENCE

. . . [W]e have been looking at the traditional behavior patterns in the Food World organization. By many standards this was a

From *The Changing of Organizational Behavior Patterns*, pp. 45–68. Boston. Copyright 1958 by the Division of Research, Harvard Business School. Reprinted with permission of the publisher.

picture of a successful organization. It was growing,. it was making money, and to some extent it was providing satisfaction to its employees at all levels. But we also saw certain potential trouble spots in this organization. In this chapter our focus will be more on these trouble spots, and more particularly on the way these problems were diagnosed by a group of five executives who, in 1953 and 1954, were making an intensive review of the organization and its competitive environment, and working out plans for introducing some sweeping organizational changes.

In 1953 these five men had various top management assignments, but to simplify matters we shall refer to them by the titles they assumed after the 1955 reorganization; namely, vice president of sales, merchandising manager, store operations manager, personnel manager, and a fifth who had left the company by 1955. This small group of five executives had worked closely with one another for many years. They had found as they worked with one another that they tended to have a common view of the organization's problems, as well as common aspirations for its future. The senior man in the group and its leader in these planning functions was the vice president of sales. While these were not the only men involved, they were the prime movers in assessing the organization, in developing plans, in getting these plans approved by others, and in implementing them. The description of these events that follows will be presented in a fairly logical sequence in order to keep the matters clarified, but the reader should remember that these men did not work out these ideas in this particular sequence or in such a systematic fashion. For example, the vice president of sales recalled that he had originally got the idea for the central part of the plan in 1938. Other parts of the plan also had a long history of thought behind them. In 1955 these men had still not formalized on paper all the aspects of their plan, even though it was well formulated in their minds.

Management Appraisal—1954

Industry Trends. In order to gain perspective on the strengths and weaknesses of their own organization, these executives were doing a great deal of thinking about the trends of the entire supermarket industry and what this meant for the company's future competition. In addition to their general knowledge of the industry, these men made visits to some of the leading but noncompeting firms in the industry to learn of their appraisal of the industry's future and of their long-range organizational plans. Out of this review grew several conclusions. They concluded that, while the industry

would continue to expand, the explosive growth of the large supermarkets which had come largely at the expense of the small grocery stores was beginning to run its course. While they expected to continue changing their marketing methods, they did not foresee in the near future any revolution in methods comparable to the changes of the past two decades. They predicted that the most crucial competition of the future would be with other modern supermarkets and more particularly those run by strong, local independents.

> Our toughest competition is from local independents. Chains don't bother us too much, but when a fellow is right there on the spot and can battle with local conditions, he's got an edge on us if we can't move quickly enough. What we've got to do is to be sure that we're always in a good competitive position relative to the other people in this business. We think the important thing in doing this for the next few years is to be a little more flexible and a little more aggressive in our stores, and in order to do that, we have to have a clean-cut organization behind those stores. We want the advantages of the independent in being able to take quick, appropriate action on the local scene combined with the advantages of big business—merchandising specialists, high-volume purchasing, area-wide advertising, well-known names, and that sort of thing.

They saw the local independent as having a potential advantage in being able to tailor his store to any unique merchandise needs of his customer, to build his own employee team, and to watch personally over expense control. They believed that the final advantage would go to the company that could successfully build an organization that would combine the advantages of both size and flexibility. This size-up of the competitive future of the industry was critical to all the subsequent organizational planning. By reaching the conclusions they did, these executives were in effect gambling that the competitive edge of the future in the indusrty would go to the company that put its emphasis on building a well-coordinated organization that was, in addition, highly adaptive at the local store level. This meant not putting emphasis on other possibilities—radical new designs for stores, radical new food-handling methods, building a high-powered promotional system, or even building a more tightly regimented organization. This policy decision to emphasize the building of a strong decentralized organization was based on, not only the review of the competitive picture, but also the appraisal these executives made of the internal problems the company was having in achieving its potential effectiveness.

Internal Organizational Problems. As these executives looked around them in their own organization, they saw several major problem areas. Their diagnosis of these problem areas grew out of a special study of the organization that the group carried out on their own initiative in 1953. At that time this group decided that they were out of touch with what was going on in the stores and, more particularly, with how the district management was supervising the stores. They set up a series of questions that they wanted to have answered concerning district supervision. They then undertook to spend at least one day visiting stores with each of the district managers and assistant district managers to observe what went on. The informal report of this survey as well as direct quotations from these executives will be used to describe their final analysis of the organization's major problems.

One of the chief problems these men saw in the organization resulted from what they characterized as "one man leadership." One of them said:

Our business has grown to the point where the stimulation that has been provided for the organization by the top people in this business, and in the past this has been mostly by [the president], just isn't felt much any more down at the bottom of the organization. We're getting too big for that style of management to carry the whole load.

Another one stated:

Back in the old days [the president] used to go into a store and radiate a lot of enthusiasm. He would cheer everybody up and make them excited about the organization and give them about a dozen ideas and then walk out. The people would try out those ideas, but, when nobody expressed any continued interest in them, they would slide back to their old habits.

This last quotation hints at another major organizational problem seen by these executives. They were concerned with the inconsistency of leadership from the top. They attributed this not only to a lack of consistent follow-up on programs that were initiated by top management, but also to the fact that there was, in effect, a split command at the top. The stores were receiving directions both from the store operations hierarchy and from the merchandising hierarchy. The latter group not only did the buying and pricing, but also, through its strong ties to the assistant district managers, got into the handling and displaying of merchandise in the stores.

The pattern has been that merchandising people from the home office go out to the store and give the store people instructions on how to display their merchandise and how to price it and how to set up their racks, etc. In the past this has been done in such a way that it undercuts the district manager and the local manager. He doesn't always know what instructions are whose and who has been told to do what.

The vice president of sales stated:

As you know [the former vice president of merchandising] really went in big for a lot of flashy promotions. I simply don't agree with that whole approach. As far as I'm concerned, I think we should be in a position to compete over the long pull on sound merchandising policy. I believe in stressing the fundamentals of good merchandising, and not jumping around from one promotion stunt to another.

On another occasion he said:

It has been very difficult to get things done with the split command between store operations and merchandising. There were counter orders, conflicting orders, and a lack of consistent direction. We were following a zig-zag course. The men were getting one thing one day and another the next. The people in the field soon caught on and got by by directing themselves to the things the top was interested in for the moment.

A third major organizational problem seen by these men was overcentralization and a related lack of responsible decision-making at the middle and lower levels of supervision. As one man put it:

> The byword of the day has been, "If you have a problem, call somebody at headquarters and they will fix it up." Our top managers have been excellent fire fighters, but there has been very little organized planning. Our thinking at the supervisory levels has simply atrophied.

These men saw little evidence of supervision at the district or store level taking the initiative in finding ways of improving their stores. They saw instead an almost complete dependence on the thinking and ideas of top management.

> There is too much reliance on general office thinking and decisions. Supervisors have been stymied by general office pressure. They take "no" for an answer too readily and do not fight for their beliefs. Supervisors are fighting fires, not solving basic problems in line with an organized program.

These comments were made on the basis of observing these men in action even though the group also concluded:

> As a group, the company's district management are fine men, sincere, hard-working, interested in their own growth and that of the company.

Another closely related concern was with what these executives saw as a communication gap between top management and the store personnel. They were worried about the slippage between what top management wanted and what actually happened in the stores. One of them stated:

> We don't kid ourselves that what we at headquarters want to see happen in the stores and what actually does happen out there, are the same thing. Top management has not been keeping themselves very well informed about what the real problems are in the stores.

They saw the communications as being pretty much one way and felt that as a result top management was apt to be unrealistic in its planning and the lower level supervisors felt left out of things.

The people in the stores got to feeling that they had no representatives at headquarters who would really go to bat for them.

To summarize these problem areas, this group of executives were worried about organizational problems at every level of management. At the top they were concerned with too much one-man leadership, a lack of consistent leadership, and too much emergency "fire-fighting" instead of steady effort toward planned objectives. At the district management and store management level they saw a lack of creative thinking and initiative, a lack of a two-way communication link between the top and the bottom, and too much of a "fire-fighting" approach to store supervision. Given this appraisal of their problems, the group of executives proceeded to lay out their ideas for reorganization, in terms both of general objectives and of specific action steps.

Reorganization Plans in Management Terms

General Objectives. The executives, in expressing their objectives for the reorganization, used such terms as "decentralization" and "systematic management procedures." While different executives used different terms, they all seemed to have a basic agreement on what they wanted. The researcher heard such statements as:

> We're very interested in setting up a straightforward organizational basis in this company. I believe we need to have a certain amount of structure and some sense of objectives and goals in order to get good results. We're going to operate by giving a man responsibility to go ahead and do his job.

> There are two important aspects of our plans. One, we need a few key people who must be able to think through problems, and must be able to direct groups toward their solution; and two, we must have a decentralization of thought, action, and authority. The purpose of this whole thing, this whole program, is to bring our action as close as possible to the arena of battle.

The vice president of sales summed it up:

I'm in favor of setting a systematic administrative framework whereby we're running our business with something other than a one-man approach.

These executives had some quite specific plans on how they wanted to go about reaching these general objectives.

Top Management Structural Change. The first specific step in the plans of these executives was to make certain structural and personnel changes in top management that would enable these men to proceed to make changes further down the line. This step involved combining the jobs of vice president of operations and vice president of merchandising into the single job of vice president of sales. This move gave the group the singleness of top command that they felt was necessary to avoid the inconsistencies of leadership of the past. The former vice president of merchandising was transferred to quite a different post in the business. The former store operations manager left the company and was replaced by one of the group of five key executives, and the newly created job of merchandising manager was filled by another from the group. These moves at the top level put the key executives who initiated the reorganization plan in a position to exercise the formal authority to implement the plan. These top management moves had required careful planning and considerable time and effort, but our story will not include a detailed analysis of them. Figure 1 is an organization chart indicating these moves and other shifts in supervision.

Store Manager Plan. These executives believed that the most important part of their reorganization plan was the development of a new position in the organization, the store manager. They believed that if they could de-

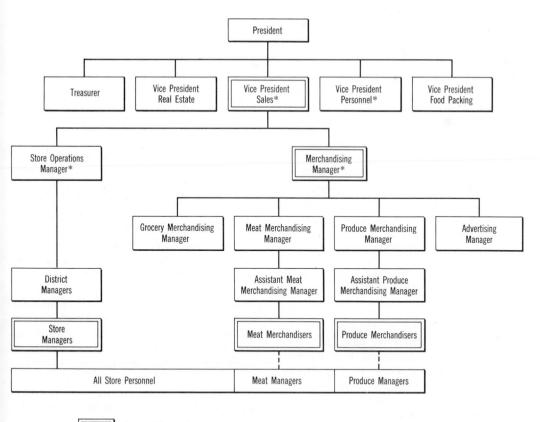

Fig. 1. *Partial organization chart, 1955.*

velop the right kind of over-all manager in each one of their larger supermarkets, they could go a long way toward achieving their general objectives. The most important thing they wanted from the store manager was to provide the store with unified administrative leadership. They wanted the store managers to build up a spirit of unity among all the store employees and a store-wide approach to problems that was lacking in the three-headed leadership of the existing stores.

> I think the number one thing we want from [the store manager] is capable administrative leadership. We need a man in the store who can provide dynamic and stimulating leadership. If we've got a good man, it can make an awful lot of difference in our business. You see we operate on a margin of only $1\frac{1}{2}\%$ profit on our sales. Our payroll runs to about ten times our profit margin. If we have good administrative leadership, it allows us to get all the more productivity in our stores and it's going to make a tremendous difference in our ability to compete.

They were secondly interested in store managers as a way of improving communications between the stores and the general office.

> We want our store managers to provide a better link between our stores and our district and top management. He can be the one who receives the general directions that come down from the top and interpret them intelligently for the local situation. He can also be the one to keep the top informed about what the problems are in the store. We particularly need that second point.

A third objective was to provide through the store manager for better local merchandising methods.

> We want him to provide some judgment as to good merchandising methods that are sort of tailor-made for the local needs. In every one of our stores we sell basically about the same merchandise but there are some variations between different stores and different neighborhoods. We think that variation, while it isn't much in terms of volume, is very important in terms of running a good store. We want to have specialties in our stores that appeal to the local

people. That small difference can be very important in terms of customer appeal.

Finally, they were convinced that there was a need for an over-all supervisor in the store who would have the time and ability to do some advance planning and systematically work toward planned objectives. They wanted a store manager who would also generate ideas and take a great deal more initiative in the conduct of the entire business.

> I want to see businessmen running my stores. I want a store manager to come into my office and say: "My store is going to hell. I've made a study of the town. I think we should build a store over here. Traffic count is high; competition just built on the other side of town. It's a good solid, middle-class neighborhood. Just our type. I recommend you build." I haven't got people in this business talking that way yet, but that's what I want.

In summary, they saw the new store managers as the key to combining the advantages of a chain operation with the advantages of the strong independent.

Middle Management Changes. Closely related to the idea of introducing a strong store manager were certain changes in the supervisory link between the home office and the stores. The principal feature of the plan at this level was to shift the assistant district managers from the line function of directly supervising the perishable departments in each store to the staff job of acting as merchandisers. Where these men had been reporting to the district managers, they were now to report to their respective merchandising managers (formerly called buyers). The objective of this change was to build a single unified chain of command from the store operations manager through the district managers directly to the new store managers, while still providing the perishable departments with some staff merchandising help through the new merchandisers.

The new store operations manager stated his objective of how he would like to see the merchandisers work with the new store managers in the following terms:

> I want the merchandiser to be a technical adviser to the store manager on the perish-

able departments. This can be a two-way deal because the store manager is the merchandiser's agent for following up on the merchandiser's ideas in the store.

New Control Procedures. As an additional part of this plan, these executives were introducing a number of new control procedures in the company. The principal one of these was a new procedure for budgeting sales volume and payroll in each of the stores. Prior to the start of each three-month period, each district manager was expected to work out with his store managers or department managers a target for sales volume and payroll. In turn, the store operations manager worked out his own targets for each one of these stores. These two sets of targets, which were independently developed, were then reconciled by a discussion between the store operations manager and his district managers. Once these targets were agreed upon, they could then be used to compare against the actual operating results which were reported to the stores by four-week and again by three-month periods.

The store operations manager stated the objectives of this program in these terms:

> Our whole objective in putting in this new budget system was so that the men on the road and the fellows in the stores would not feel that these targets had been imposed on them. What we're trying to achieve here is to have a realistic budget that everyone has participated in arriving at so that the fellows will feel that they've got an attainable target to shoot at.

As another part of the budgetary procedure, the new merchandising manager worked out sales targets by product classification (grocery, meat, and produce) with his different managers. The executives did not worry about completely reconciling these figures with those prepared by the stores. As the new store operations manager put it:

> My figures may or may not be the same as the merchandising manager submits, but these are the figures I use with my men and if he wants to submit a different figure to management, I told him that's his business. This doesn't seem to be causing any trouble, however, because the figures I come up with and the figures he comes up with and uses

have been turning out to be very close to each other.

As an additional part of their new control procedure, these executives were introducing a more systematic way of evaluating the field personnel. They looked to the new budgeting procedures for considerable help in making better evaluations of their personnel, but they also were adopting more systematic forms for the periodic review of the performance of each of the men in the organization. The store operations manager commented on his reasons for this program:

> Of course, you'll see this form we're using here is nothing new or startling. It's a pretty standard setup. What we're really interested in is getting our people out in the stores to think more about the fact that their performance is being judged by their immediate superiors in the store and the district managers. We, in turn, want to rely more on these reports from these field supervisors in making our selections for advancement. We hope this will tend to minimize any feeling that these promotions are based on luck or the chance opinion of somebody at headquarters.

A third aspect of the new control procedures was a program to write up more complete and accurate job descriptions for all the jobs in the organization. The executives felt that the discussions that would have to precede reaching an agreement on job descriptions would help the people in the organization to clarify in their own minds just what was expected of them. They thought that the resulting descriptions would also be useful in the training of personnel that were new in the organization or moving to new assignments. They wanted the descriptions to arise out of meetings that would be held at different levels to get greater agreement on the content and nature of the different jobs.

A fourth program the executives introduced to secure better control procedures was a new system for ordering merchandise in the stores. The procedure centered around a mathematical formula that had been developed to use the previous week's sales for each item in the store as the basis for determining the next week's order for that item. This system was designed to keep the store's inventory at a minimum, while still providing safeguards that the store would not run out of any item. As a part of this same program, a new procedure was developed for allocating space on the store display shelves for the many items carried.

New Communication Procedures. As a final part of their plan for reorganizing the company, these executives developed some new routine communication procedures, designed, not only to help the organization conduct its normal day-to-day business, but also to help implement the changes that have been outlined above.

Every other week all the district managers were called to a meeting at headquarters that consisted of two parts. The first part was a session with the merchandising manager and some of his key people to discuss future merchandising plans. The second part of this meeting was conducted by the store operations manager to discuss with his district manager group some of their current problems. On alternate weeks it was planned to call all the store managers into a meeting at headquarters to have a discussion on their common problems with the store operations manager. The new mechandising manager also conducted weekly meetings at headquarters with each of his major merchandising groups.

Not all these meetings were new to the organization but in every case the purpose of the meetings had changed. Where formerly these meetings had provided a place for instructions to be handed out to field people, the new plan involved using these meetings more as a place to provide two-way communication. They were therefore organized as discussion meetings with opportunity provided for field people to raise their problems with headquarters people and to participate in making decisions and plans.

In addition to this schedule of meetings these executives were planning on keeping in touch with their field organization more systematically on an individual basis. For instance, the store operations manager scheduled three days of every week to travel with his district managers as they made their supervisory tours of their stores. The other top people also scheduled a considerable number of days to travel with the district managers to keep in touch with store operations.

Summary. The organization of Food World in the mid-50's was one that had evolved through the years essentially on a trial-and-error basis. It was an organization which had grown as a result of the thousands of day-to-day pressures on the business to conduct itself in a healthy and competitive way. The last chapter demonstrated that the organization that had evolved through the years had many inherent strengths. In 1954 the company had good stores and good central warehousing equipment, but its primary assets were still its people. These people were, by and large, loyal to the organization, hard-working, and highly skilled in the diverse operations of buying, transporting, displaying, advertising, accounting, and housekeeping that were the essential functions of their business. They were also highly skilled at perpetuating their own organizational arrangements for doing work. By this we mean that they were good at indoctrinating new members of the organization into the customary codes and practices of the organization. We saw a quick glimpse of grocery clerks indoctrinating new clerks in the codes of the organization, and the researcher saw the same process going on at all levels of the organization. So the company had an organization that knew its business and knew how to perpetuate itself.

Onto this scene came a small group of key executives who felt dissatisfied with the existing organization even while recognizing many of its strengths. Fundamentally they felt that what was making the company competitive in the mid fifties would not be good enough to make them competitive in the mid sixties. What they believed the company needed to lead in their industry was not something that you could buy like a new warehouse or a new group of larger stores—not that these items were not also in the thinking of these executives as essential ingredients. But they felt that the most critical ingredient that the company needed was a new and different internal system for getting work done. They believed that they needed a new kind of organizational system for coordinating the work of the people toward achieving the organizational purposes.

The thing that makes these plans particularly significant for study was the fact that they were the product of a deliberate and conscious effort to draw up a model for an optimum organization. It would be false to give the impression that top management's plans were a highly detailed blueprint, but they were certainly a great deal more systematic than "a seat of the pants" hunch. The men who had evolved these plans had accumulated many years of experience in the industry and the company. They had held many discussions among themselves as to what were the strengths and weaknesses of their own company. They had made systematic studies of what was going on in their own organization. They had gone on trips to leading competitors throughout the country to observe their organizational methods and to discuss their ideas with the chief executives of these companies. So it is accurate to say that their plans constituted a deliberate long-range planning of organizational behavior. This kind of planning effort was a new experience for Food World. While such long-range planning of organizational behavior is, of course, not unique in business generally, it is probably less common than is usually thought.

The reader at this point might have a number of doubts and questions about the reorganization plans as worked out by the top management of Food World. Was management's thinking too utopian? Were they seeking a magic cure-all? This management group did not think of their plan as fool-proof or fixed. The president commented:

No organization plan is static. It will always be necessary for us to make changes to improve the plan. I know of no perfect organizational plan.

The reader may also have noticed some ways in which the company's plan was not completely consistent. For example, the objective of decentralizing some of the decision-making might well find itself working at cross purposes with another aspect of the plan, namely, the grocery ordering system which, in effect, would diminish the amount of judgment that store people would use in ordering their merchandise. The management was aware of these inconsistencies and even had a phrase for them, "retailing doubletalk." They felt that these inconsistencies were an inevitable part of achieving the objectives they desired.

The reader might also be wondering if the plans were not much too comprehensive and ambitious to be implemented at one time. The Food World management did not naively think that all the changes that they had in mind could be introduced at one time or even over a fairly short time period. They had in mind a time schedule that involved introducing these changes over a fairly long period of time. The changes have been described in this chapter in terms of being one plan because they were one plan in conception, but not in the sense of being installed at one point of time. The details of management's timetable are not important here but, suffice it to say, that a very few experimental store managers had been trained and installed in 1954, the new budget system was started in early 1954, most of the formal organizational changes were made in January 1955, and during 1955 the program of introducing store managers was speeded up as were the introduction of the other new control and communication procedures. One key executive commented in 1955:

The whole store manager program is like a weak new sapling. It will take years of constant care and attention to get it to grow into a strong, self-sufficient tree.

So as of late 1954 the executives concerned had built a systematic model in their minds of how they wanted the organizational system to operate in the future. They had gained the approval of their executive colleagues. They were starting to take the initial formal steps to implement the plans that are outlined above.

Thus far we have looked at these plans exclusively in management's terms. Now, before proceeding, we need to sharpen the focus of our study and restate management's objectives in concrete terms that would allow an outside researcher to measure whether or not the objectives were achieved. We also shall restate the reorganizational plans in terms of our concept of the organization as a social system, in order to make our findings more useful for understanding other organizations.

Reorganization Plans in Researcher's Terms

The top management executives, in their roles as leaders of the Food World social system, wished to change some of the critical behavior patterns of the system. They were motivated ot do this as a result of their observation of anticipated external pressures on the system and as a result of their perception of certain malfunctioning in the system itself that threatened its health and survival. They wanted their plans to have a significant effect on behavior throughout the entire organization. The researcher, however, could not hope to observe and measure all the effects of the reorganization. He chose, therefore, to concentrate his observations on two strategically critical positions; the store manager and the district manager. This choice was made on the assumption that the men in these positions would have to make the most changes in their behavior, and the desired results further down the line would be dependent upon their making these changes. We shall therefore be focusing our intensive study on the behavior of the people in these two strategic positions.

Members of top management stated their ideas about the desired behavior changes in terms of "decentralization" and "clear-cut administrative framework." They were not completely happy with these terms because they knew that they were subject to differing definitions, but regardless of the words they had a pretty clear idea of what they wanted. For our research purposes, however, we need to define these desired behavioral changes in more concrete and measurable terms. To do this we shall take the two key positions, the store manager and the district manager, and see in what specific ways management desired them to change their behavior. In other words, what were management's new requirements for the roles of these positions?

New Required Role—Store Manager. Earlier in this chapter we saw some general statements of top management concerning its objectives for the new role of the store manager. These statements specified the model of the new role requirements that we must now translate into terms of concrete behavior. For convenience and clarity we shall subdivide the role requirements into the three elements of behavior—the kind of *activities* the store manager was to engage in, the kind of *interaction* he was to have with others, and the kind of *sentiments* he was to hold.

ACTIVITIES. Management expected the new store manager to spend considerable time in all departments of the store observing what was going on (in contrast to doing physical work). It expected him to analyze past performance and work out future plans and objectives.

INTERACTIONS. Management expected the new store manager to interact down the line primarily with his three department heads (in contrast to working directly with clerks). These interactions were to be two-way, problem-solving conversations in which the subordinate participated in choosing departmental objectives and merchandising methods, and in making personnel decisions. It expected the store manager to initiate interactions with the staff merchandisers to seek their technical assistance in the perishable department but not to let themselves or their department managers be dominated by these merchandisers. As regards his superior, the district manager, he was expected not only to receive and interpret instructions from above but also to pass on ideas and problems.

SENTIMENTS. Management expected the store manager to conceive of himself as a businessman concerned with the over-all well-being of his store for the future as well as the present. He was to be loyal to the organization but feel more self-sufficient rather than dependent on his superiors. He was to have an enthusiasm for the possibilities of the store that would be reflected in his subordinates' attitudes. He was to think of himself as a leader and developer of his subordinates rather than as a dominator of them.

In considering the required role described above, we need to remember that the organization plans called for recruiting most of the new store managers from positions as grocery managers or other departmental managers in stores. From what we saw . . . [earlier] it is evident that the new store manager role requirements are by no means the same thing as the existing pattern of activities, interactions, and sentiments practiced by departmental managers. In fact, it might be predicted that these changes are so great that they could not be successfully made without the intelligent and active support of his immediate supervisor, the district manager.

New Required Role—District Manager. We saw . . . [earlier] that the district managers had traditionally been a strong link between top management and the store organization. They were traditionally giving their store personnel frequent and detailed supervision on the way top management wanted the work of the stores conducted. These were the men who were accustomed to making hundreds of detailed decisions about how the stores were to operate. They were giving instructions on how they wanted merchandise displayed, how they wanted work schedules handled, how they wanted the store plant maintained, and the hundreds of other detailed items involved in good store operation. We have seen that the whole system worked so that the store people had been trained to be loyal and hard-working order takers, and, so far as they were concerned, these orders were emanating from the district manager who to them had always been their personal "big boss," who would have the dominant voice in determining their own personal future with the organization. Under the new organizational plan, these district managers were being asked to change drastically their traditional role. Top management's new role requirements for the district managers are spelled out below in terms of concrete behavior.

ACTIVITIES. The district manager was still expected to spend most of his time going from store to store in his territory observing and talking with his subordinates. He was, however, expected to spend more time looking over the perishable departments because of his loss of the assistant district managers. He was also expected to spend more time on planning functions and less on "fire fighting" current problems.

INTERACTIONS. The district managers were expected to provide opportunities for their subordinate store managers to assume more decision-making functions. They would have to converse with their fledgling store managers so that these men would assume greater responsibilities and discharge them adequately. This meant that in their interactions with their subordinates they were expected to make a fundamental change toward adopting a more problem-solving, two-way type of communication. They would have to strike a relatively even balance between the amount of time they spent talking to their subordinates and the time their subordinates spent doing the talking to them. It was expected that the district managers

would still be in frequent contact with the staff merchandisers (their former assistant district managers), but instead of the traditional boss-subordinate pattern it was to be a relationship of a line-staff nature with the district manager calling on the merchandiser for advice and staff assistance and, in turn, teaching the store manager to use this staff assistance intelligently. The district manager was also to be expected to adopt different interaction practices with his superiors in the organization. This was most apparent in the way the plan called for conducting different types of headquarters meetings with the district manager group. These meetings were no longer to be primarily briefings where the district managers were told what top management orders they were to carry out, but rather they were now expected to do a more systematic job of keeping top management informed on the problems arising in the field and on the suggestions for improvement that were coming from the field. What is more, they were expected to participate more in making the plans and decisions that affected operations.

SENTIMENTS. Like the store managers, the district managers were expected to conceive of themselves as more independent, self-sufficient businessmen who were concerned with the long-range well-being of their districts. They were even to think of their role as superiors, as being more that of teachers and developers of the capacities of their store managers.

These new role requirements were in considerable contrast to the customary ways of thinking and behaving that prevailed among these men. The district managers were, then, expected to change their role in the organization drastically—to change their behavior in every one of their key relationships, up, down, and sideways, that made up their daily work existence. These changes were strategically critical to the success of the entire reorganization plans since they were an essential prerequisite to changing the daily working practices of the people in the store. . . .

Management Change Methods. The top management of Food World adopted a number of specific methods to clarify the new role requirements for store managers and district managers. The executives worked out new job definitions with the people concerned, gave speeches on what they expected of the new setup, wrote up various descriptions of what they wanted in the company's house organ, and redrew the company's official organization chart. They knew, however, that these customary steps to establish the new required roles had to be supplemented by other change methods—new work procedures and new incentives.

The new control procedures that required sales and expense goals to be agreed on at the store manager and district manager level were designed to foster the required interaction pattern. The same was true of the new procedure for having these supervisors participate in the systematic evaluation of their employees. Likewise the new type of management meetings were designed to give these supervisors a chance to practice filling the required roles.

Finally top executives gave their supervisors some explicit and implied incentives for behaving in terms of the new roles. They offered store departmental managers the incentive of a higher status title, "store manager," and increased pay for demonstrating that they could adequately meet the role requirements for store manager. With the district manager they implied that the larger, more desirable districts or even higher management jobs would go to those who could meet the new role requirements, while there was an implicit threat that failure to meet the requirements could result in demotion.

Line and Staff in Industrial Relations

CHARLES A. MYERS AND JOHN G. TURNBULL

The industrial relations function in American management has developed rapidly over the past 20 years as unionization, labor shortages, and growing management recognition of the importance of the human factor in industry have combined to raise its stature and position in the company organization.

The "proper" organizational role of the industrial relations director or personnel officer has been the subject of much discussion. Probably the most widely held view is that it is a staff function. This means giving advice, assistance, and counsel to the line organization in the formulation of industrial relations policies and in the handling of industrial relations

From *Harvard Business Review*, Vol. 34, No. 4, July–August 1956, pp. 113–124. Reprinted with permission of the publisher.

Authors' note. We wish to acknowledge the help of Maynard N. Touissoint, Graduate Assistant in the Industrial Relations Section, Massachusetts Institute of Technology, who helped with some of the interviews on which the findings presented in this article are based.

problems, but not taking from the line the responsibility for making decisions affecting people. This responsibility is held to be one which the line officers, as *managers,* cannot effectively delegate if they are to do their jobs.

How close is this "ideal" concept of the industrial relations function to actual practice in American industry?

Examination Called for

We start with the fact that the industrial relations officer performs a variety of functions which are not uniform among companies or even within the same company.[1] But we do not know whether this is simply the result of haphazard organization or whether it indicates that no basic organizational principles can be applied to the industrial relations function. We

[1] See John T. Dunlop and Charles A. Myers, "The Industrial Relations Function in Management," *Personnel,* March 1955, p. 3.

do not even know how much the decision-making process varies with the type of problem under consideration, or what difference there is, if any, between the location of *formal* authority to make a decision (usually the line) and the place where the decision is *effectively* made.

Obviously there is real need for a more systematic examination of what the industrial relations director or personnel officer actually does in a number of problem and policy areas. With more knowledge and understanding, individual companies can better organize their own industrial relations activities. The aim of this article is to provide such an approach, with particular emphasis on these questions:

1. How does the industrial relations director view his own role in the organization?

2. How are personnel policies formulated, and who initiates and approves changes?

3. How are the personnel administration functions—hiring, promotion, layoff, discipline, training, safety, and so on—handled?

4. Who negotiates with the union, interprets the contract, and handles grievances?

5. What problems does the industrial relations director see as a consequence of his organizational role and activities in the company?

Survey of Experience. To get the answers we conducted a small but intensive research project:

Interviews were held with industrial relations officers in 34 firms with which the Industrial Relations Section at the Massachusetts Institute of Technology had previous contacts. These officers were interested in re-examining with us the organizational role of industrial relations in their firms.

The 34 companies in the sample consisted of 24 manufacturing firms in 10 different industries, 2 food distribution chains, 2 department stores, 5 banks and insurance companies, and 1 engineering and construction firm. They ranged in size from 500 employees to nearly 30,000; 25 had collective bargaining agreements with unions; and 29 had multiplant operations.

Since most of these firms were in the Boston area, 8 companies in the middle Atlantic states and in the Midwest were checked to guard against the chance of geographical bias. Common patterns of experience began to emerge early in the interviews, and our belief is that a much larger sample with wider geographical distribution would not have materially affected our conclusions.

In each case, personal interviews averaging two hours in length were held with the principal industrial relations officer or officers (who were associated, in several cases, with different branches of the company). A schedule of questions was used, but free and detailed responses were encouraged.

Apparent Contradiction. One of the most striking results of the interviews was the contradiction between belief and practice. Not one industrial relations director, when asked to define his organizational role, answered, "I operate primarily in a line capacity" (except, of course, with respect to his own department). Rather, the typical response was that he operated in a staff capacity or, at most, in some combination of staff and line capacity. But when he went on to describe how he handled particular personnel or labor relations functions, it was clear that in a number of situations *he made the effective decisions.* He may not have had the formal authority to do so, but he "called the shots." To illustrate:

In one rather extreme instance, the industrial relations director, who called himself a staff man, also said he made decisions on most promotions, could overrule the foreman on disciplinary action without getting higher approval for his action, disciplined foremen for failing to follow established personnel policies, had rather complete discretion in negotiating the terms of a new contract with the union, was sole interpreter of the union agreement for management, and handled all grievances after the first step!

How can such contradictions be explained? We suspect that the answer is that the term "staff" has become so customarily associated with the "proper" functioning of an industrial relations department that most practitioners simply give what they consider the expected or acceptable response to the question of their status. In any event, it is clear that we must go far beyond any generalized examination of the industrial relations function in management.

5 Types of Administration

In order to understand the variations that are found in practice, it is helpful to visualize a spectrum or a theoretically possible range of methods of administering the industrial relations function:

TYPE 1. The line handles a personnel function completely, as for example when a foreman recruits, selects, places, and inducts workers for his own department, in the absence of a formal industrial relations department. Or the plant manager negotiates the collective bargaining agreement, and various levels of the line organization administer it.

TYPE 2. The line delegates to an industrial relations unit the responsibility for providing advice only. For example, the industrial relations department may counsel a foreman on the best methods of recruiting and selecting his work force, or on request it may give advice on negotiating a collective bargaining agreement or settling a grievance.

TYPE 3. The line formally delegates to an industrial relations department the responsibility for providing advice *and* service, with the line retaining and utilizing *continuing* decision-making and review authority. Thus, the industrial relations officer recruits and screens candidates for employment, but the final decision to accept or reject any candidate always rests with the foreman in whose department he would work. In the labor relations sphere, the staff specialist may assist the line in preparing for and in negotiating the collective agreement, and he may recommend to the line methods for settling grievances at the second or third step.

TYPE 4. The line formally delegates to an industrial relations department the responsibility for making final decisions in particular functional areas, subject only to *periodic* review of the effectiveness of the delegation or subject to the right of the affected line official to appeal to higher authority. Thus, the personnel officer may recruit and actually select all employees, with the foreman or supervisor having no authority to accept or reject any individual candidates, except possibly having the right of appeal. Or the labor relations specialist may be given broad, effective decision-making power

to negotiate agreements with unions and in settling grievances. (This method can also be used when an industrial relations consultant or attorney from outside the company is hired to negotiate the union agreement or settle the grievance.)

TYPE 5. The industrial relations department gets by default (or may even usurp) the decision-making authority in a given functional area.

Type 5 and even Type 4 go beyond what commonly has been considered good organizational practice. The type corresponding to the staff role recommended in much of the literature on industrial relations is Type 3.[2]

Companies Classified. In our studies we did not encounter any Type 1 cases, because the firms interviewed were large enough to have personnel or labor relations departments. We also found no Type 2 cases; these are probably rare because must industrial relations departments provide important services for the line organization and go beyond the "advice only" stage. Type 5 cases were difficult to detect in the interviews, but we suspect that a strong personality in the industrial relations position often succeeds in getting control of decision-making authority without formal or explicit delegation, or that authority may "gravitate" to him because of his special skill—in the settlement of grievances, for example.

All except one of the nonunionized companies were of Type 3. That is, the majority of their industrial relations functions (primarily personnel administration, since they were not unionized) were handled by the line. However, in each case there may have been some specific exceptions. Thus, in discipline and discharge, safety, management development programs, and wage and salary administration, the effective decision-making power often rested in the personnel officer. The one other nonunion company could be classified as Type 4 in the majority of its personnel functions.

Most of the unionized companies also fell into the Type 3 category in both their personnel administration and labor relations activities. But again there were exceptions in the per-

[2] Type 3 has been spelled out in detail by Robert Saltonstall in "Who's Who in Personnel Administration," *Harvard Business Review*, July–August 1955, p. 75.

sonnel functions, as noted above, and in specific labor relations practices. For instance, it was not uncommon for the labor relations personnel to make effective decisions on contract interpretation and on grievance settlements. Routine problems in particular were handled in this manner, while decisions on critical issues more frequently required line approval.

A few of the unionized companies were basically Type 4 in their labor relations activities. In at least five cases, this department had extensive authority in the negotiation of the collective bargaining agreement, in its interpretation, and in the settlement of grievances. There may even have been a trace of the Type 5 pattern in some of these instances.

12 Specific Functions

With these general conclusions in mind, let us turn now to a more detailed examination of the specific tasks or functions that confront the industrial relations department. How are they handled in the companies interviewed? What do industrial relations and personnel managers have to say about them?

Industrial Relations Policy. Except where the collective bargaining agreement is involved and the union initiates changes, suggestions for introducing or altering industrial relations policies most commonly originate in the industrial relations department. According to one man:

> We're paid to be experts in this field. Our main task is to keep ahead of current developments; we'd be in a mess if we didn't. The last thing in the world I want is for one of our line people to come back from a convention and ask, "How come we don't have this or that policy?"

Regardless of the source from which policy suggestions arise, in all the companies we looked at the industrial relations unit is charged with the responsibility of investigating the suggestion, working up a concrete proposal if the idea has merit, and otherwise processing the proposal. However, consultation with people in the line organization is frequent, and in some firms policy committees consider proposed changes.

If the proposal is minor in nature, the industrial relations unit frequently will be given specific authority to approve. Any major proposal customarily requires final approval by a vice president, president, executive committee, or board of directors. But, except for the critical cases, this final approval is of the rubber-stamp variety in a number of companies; the staff executive makes the effective decision. Thus, one industrial relations director noted:

> Over the years I've built up a fair amount of experience in this business; moreover, over the years top management has learned to trust my judgment. So I guess in most cases top management does rubber stamp most of my proposals. They've come to accept my advice. This doesn't mean I've never made any mistakes. Far from it. But it illustrates the case.

Hiring and Promotion. In the majority of cases we studied, line officers effectively decide who is to be hired, promoted, transferred, laid off, and retired. The staff provides advice and service—service in the way of recruiting, interviewing, testing, and keeping records.

Here again, however, the staff may exert considerable influence if not formal decision-making authority. For instance, it may be consulted on a promotion case, where its competence in psychological testing may be utilized. (This is frequently true for all promotions to and at managerial levels.) Indeed, in many companies the staff executive's expertise is so respected that the line will hesitate to recommend a promotion unless the personnel people concur. Hence the staff has an effective influence which may be tantamount to making the decision. As one personnel manager noted:

> In a really critical case, if I disagreed with the line on a promotion, I'd take the battle up higher. Otherwise, I'd make my feelings known, and if they were disregarded, I'd let the line have its way. But I have been right in enough critical cases so that the line hesitates if I do not concur.

One or two other variations can be noted. In tight labor markets the personnel people effectively do the actual hiring; the foreman customarily has the right to discharge a man before the end of his probationary period, but he more or less accepts all candidates sent to him. In the hiring of salaried and managerial employees, by contrast, there is a tendency to give the department head (or equivalent line officer) much more discretion; he has the privilege of looking over eligible candidates before any decision is made.

In the hiring of college graduate trainees, the personnel department often has full authority. The reason for this is interesting. As one personnel spokesman noted:

> We know the needs from our replacement tables. But if we let the line department heads look over and interview prospective candidates, we would have a big battle as to who was going to get whom. This way we hire the college boys and ration them out.

Discipline and Discharge. Here again, basic authority is usually held by the line, with the staff providing a policy framework and consultative assistance. But the personnel staff has much more actual decision-making authority here than in hiring, promotion, and transfer. In a majority of cases the actual *approval* of the personnel department has to be secured before a discharge can be effected; in some cases the personnel staff may even be able to overrule lower line decisions. There are several reasons for this:

1. Management feels that discharge is a severe penalty and should not be exacted unless a clear case can be shown. The personnel staff can provide the means for investigating the validity of the discharge.

2. There is a need for uniformity in the application of discipline and of discharge penalties. Supervisors and middle management men could be trained to do this, but in many firms it appears more easily accomplished by a specialized staff unit.

Conflicts may still be resolved by appeal to higher line authority, but many cases are really decided by the industrial relations officer. In a majority of companies, however, the line *administers* the penalty; the personnel people are not the "axe men." As one director put it:

> We are not the whipping boys. This is something best done by the supervisor. In the old days our office had a bad name; we were supposed to have a closet full of whips; and if you ever got called up here, you would quake in your boots. But all that is changed now.

An interesting sidelight to the discipline problem existed in two companies where authority to discipline and discharge had recently been restored to the line. One personnel manager commented:

> You hear that the supervisor feels he ought to have disciplinary authority in order to control his department. In our company this right was recently returned to them. And you should have heard the howls. They felt we weren't earning our money. Discipline is a dirty business. And they were only too happy to let us do it, as had been done for the past 30 years.

Employee Training. The common practice is for the line to make the final decision as to whether an employee training program would or would not be used, with the personnel staff customarily "training the trainers" and helping to decide course content and teaching procedures when programs were introduced. Although the line had the final authority to accept or reject a training course, most personnel men indicated they gave a lot of time and effort to "selling" the line men on training. In a small number of multiplant companies with sizable central training staffs, there was a greater tendency for the staff group to make effective decisions, particularly with respect to training programs at the branch level.

2. *Management Development.* As for training at higher levels, the interviews revealed that the industrial relations director frequently makes decisions as to whether or not to establish a supervisory training or management development program. When a program is set up, he often decides on its content, presentation, and general administration. These decisions occasionally lead to a broadening of the staff's implicit authority.

We found a number of cases where lower and middle management officers (and new college trainees) were aware that the industrial relations officer had an important voice in management development and therefore in promotion. Hence "advice" given by the staff man to the line manager became an "order," since it would not be wise for the latter to cross a person with some degree of control over his future. One personnel director indicated that this had become a serious problem with respect to college trainees who came to him for job training assignments:

It's a standing custom among the trainees who see me to ask each other, "Did you get the $100 look this morning? Or only the $10 look?" And it's more than a joking matter.

Safety Programs. While the day-to-day enforcement of safety is the responsibility of the first-line supervisor, the staff has considerable authority over line supervisors in matters of plant safety policies, procedures, and equipment (in contrast to accident prevention programs of an educational nature, where they remain in a staff capacity). This practice appears to rest in part on a practical legal consideration: safety requirements and workmen's compensation demand close adherence to a set of legal regulations. Hence rigorous control is necessary. While it is preferable to work through the line wherever possible, there may be cases in which time or other circumstances do not permit it.

Wages and Salaries. In compensation matters personnel staffs operate in two basically different ways. After a formal wage and salary program has been introduced (a line decision in the companies that we examined), personnel tends to have rather complete authority in its administration. This includes the power to decide, for example, on the job evaluation system to be used, the specific rate structure, and procedures for moving within and between grades. In some instances, even where there were job evaluation and salary administration committees which included representatives of the line organization, the personnel director, or his deputy, frequently dominated these committees through his special knowledge and skill.

All this is a perfect illustration of how "expert knowledge" breeds decision-making authority. As one personnel man explained:

Our policy is to keep the rate structure in line. So we make wage surveys periodically. We are the ones who get and interpret the information. And our suggestions are in effect decisions. Why? Because we have the knowledge. Line management could go out and make its own survey. But this is unthinkable, unless we should go off the deep end.

By contrast, in the assignment of individual pay rates the line tends to maintain a higher degree of control. Where discretion is involved in initially assigning a rate to a man and in changing his rate (as in increases within rate ranges), the immediate supervisor plays the key decision-making role. In a minority of companies the personnel department has to be advised of any changes, and in a still smaller number of cases its approval has to be secured. The purpose of requiring approval is precautionary; it is not held wise to permit a rate increase if all the individual's personnel records, located centrally, indicate otherwise.

The Control Function. In a majority of cases, the personnel department is responsible for policing" personnel policies—especially when trouble occurs, as when a complaint or grievance is brought to the attention of the personnel staff. Our respondents stressed that *how* the staff executive talks to the line is as important as *what* he says. An informal approach is generally preferred. For example, the staff man might go to the foreman charged with violating company policy and say:

Joe, I'm sure you know company policy on this matter. But we've had some complaints, and I thought I'd kick it around with you.

Personnel men feel that it is better to work directly with the violator" at the first step rather than to go to his superior. But if the violations continue, "we go to his superior and lower the boom," one personnel director added.

In a small number of cases the personnel officer initially takes a stronger attitude toward the erring line supervisor:

I bring the fellow in and say, "These are the rules. Get on the ball or there is no place in the organization for you!

If I find the line not making adequate checks, I raise hell with them.

Does this "control" function create difficulties for the personnel staff in its relation with the line organization? The majority view is that it does, but that this is inherent in the situation and that it can be minimized appreciably by "not trying to appear as if we were running the show, but speaking softly and cooperatively." It is clear, however, that this entire area is one in which personnel people do not feel comfortable. Enforcement of personnel policies is not likely to win anyone first prize in a popularity contest.

Labor Negotiations. The majority of industrial or labor relations directors in our study are involved in the contract negotiation process either as principal or alternate spokesmen.

Where they are principals, their ultimate authority tends to be limited, since basic questions, such as union security or the amount of a wage increase, are almost without exception decided by top line management. But within these specified limits, the labor relations specialist may be given considerable discretion in negotiating the details of the collective bargaining agreement.

In addition, the specialist may have a good deal of authority by virtue of his power to advise top management, prior to negotiations, regarding "what it will take to settle." Because of his expert knowledge, he may, in effect, make the decision on the probable settlement; the line executives may hesitate to overrule his judgment—especially if he has been proved right in the past.

In a small number of cases examined, the labor relations specialist exercised what approximated "unlimited authority" in negotiating the agreement. In one company, the labor relations director excluded all line personnel, except the president, from the negotiations and, moreover, did not report to them at any stage of the negotiation on what was transpiring or on how matters were developing. It was his belief that such reporting would "foul up the situation."

Why do some companies use this approach? Apparently some line managers, especially those with backgrounds in merchandising, engineering, and research, feel that labor relations is a distasteful, strange, and tough business which is best shifted to specialists. More frequently, however, line managers in manufacturing firms accept labor relations as part of their operating responsibilities.

Interpreting the Agreement. The common practice is for the industrial or labor relations department to interpret the agreement on a decision-making rather than a purely advisory basis. Even when the line management takes the lead in negotiating the agreement, the responsibility for interpretation is frequently placed on the staff man who has participated in the bargaining process and whose expertise

has assisted the line in the details of contract phraseology and meaning. More than this, managements feel the need for uniform interpretation of the agreement throughout the company, and uniformity is best achieved by delegating the responsibility to a specialist.

This is especially true in the routine cases where the supervisors and middle managers seek guidance on the application of a particular clause in the agreement. The specialist's view becomes decisive. None of the executives interviewed reported any difficulties with the line organization in centralizing the responsibility for contract interpretation in the hands of the specialist. Apparently the line accepts this is a perfectly logical delegation in a specialized area affecting the whole organization.

Processing Grievances. In a majority of cases the line processes grievances through the first and second steps. Customarily, the advice of the labor relations unit is sought, and in a number of instances the advice becomes an order. "Sell, then tell" was the way several industrial relations directors characterized their approach.

Why should the labor relations specialist have any authority to "tell"? The chain of reasoning appears to be as follows:

> In most unionized companies, enough grievance cases have arisen so that there is a body of precedent on almost every issue that arises. The labor relations department, as interpreter of the agreement, has a record of these precedents. It can indicate, therefore, what equity and consistency would call for in any case. It can also indicate whether a case, if processed to arbitration, would be likely to be won or lost. Therefore, expert knowledge permits it to make effective decisions.

In a majority of companies, the labor relations director is listed at the third stage in the grievance procedure. Can he negotiate a settlement? Yes. Can he do it on his own authority? Commonly, no. In the majority of cases, clearance with higher line authority is required. But such clearance is frequently only nominal. According to one staff man:

> I called the president and told him if I settled this way, we'd probably avoid a strike, which I knew from our competitive position he was anxious to do. He told me,

"Is that your view? Go ahead and settle. That's what we hired you for."

In a minority of cases the labor relations director feels free to settle even without recourse to higher authority.

Contract Enforcement. While the collective bargaining agreement tends to be enforced by its very institutional setting (the union pressing grievances if it is not), there are still some problems analogous to those involved in enforcing personnel policies. And they tend to be resolved in the same way: informal discussion with the "violator" followed, where necessary, by discussions with his superior. A tougher attitude is likely to be taken, however, probably because of pressure from the union. When labor relations personnel were asked, "What would you do about a supervisor who persistently violated the spirit of the agreement?" a frequent response was, "We'd get rid of him." And while the line would do the actual "ridding," the labor relations officer would have an important voice in the process.

5 Sets of Influences

What accounts for the many variations in the authority and responsibility of the industrial relations director? Our study indicates that five sets of influences are at work.

Unionism. This is probably the most important single factor shaping the role of the industrial relations function in management. Where a strong labor organization exists, and where its decision-making processes are also centralized, a similar pattern develops in the management organization. A central, specialized labor relations unit is needed. The specialization becomes so technical that it appears more difficult to "teach" the line than it does for the specialists to handle the problems themselves. Hence, there is a natural drift, if not always a specific delegation of authority, toward decision-making responsibility in the labor relations functions.

The following section from one of the interviews illustrates the importance of union pressure on the location of the responsibility for labor relations.

INTERVIEWER: Are you listed in any stage of the grievance procedure?

RESPONDENT: Yes, at the third stage.

INTERVIEWER: Can you settle the grievance yourself, or do you have to secure approval up the line for your decision?

RESPONDENT: I have complete power to settle. I call the shots. I do not consult higher authority unless it is a higher authority issue. Then I would solicit their thinking.

INTERVIEWER: Suppose you had a foreman who was in the wrong on a grievance, and the case came to you. Would you let it go to arbitration, let the arbitrator lose face to save the foreman's face?

RESPONDENT: No, we'd let the foreman hang.

INTERVIEWER: Why?

RESPONDENT: We've got a hell of a militant union breathing down our necks. We can't afford to get the organization into trouble merely to save an individual.

Size and Organization. We found some tendency for the industrial relations department to exercise line responsibility in more of its functions when the size of the company increased and as multiplant operation became more common. The need for company-wide uniformity of policy and practice is the main factor here, and apparently it is best achieved through centralized responsibility. But the larger firm is also likely to be confronted with the more centralized union, and it is difficult to evaluate the relative importance of these two influences. In fact, in several of the smaller firms in our sample the industrial relations director was most conspicuously operating in a decision-making rather than advisory or service capacity toward the line organization.

Expert Knowledge. When the industrial relations officer makes effective decisions in the functional areas outlined above, he does so frequently because the line executives have become increasingly dependent on his expert knowledge and informed judgment. It would seem that the longer the industrial relations man has served the organization and the more often his advice or suggestions to line managers have proved to be right, the stronger has become his position in their eyes, and the less they are inclined to "go their own way." What happens is that when a few individualists get "burned" by ignoring the industrial relations director's advice, the die is cast. His advice thereafter becomes the effective decision. Frequently, also, formal delegation of authority to him will be increased.

Strong Personalities. The drift of decision-making authority, in fact if not in precise organizational delegation, to the industrial relations department has been accelerated by the presence of strong personalities. Some of the men interviewed turned out to be close to the staff type idealized in the literature; they operate through patient advice and persuasion, and consider themselves successful if they can increase the skill and responsibility of the line officers in handling problems in personnel and labor relations. But other industrial relations men obviously enjoy more authority, and the force of their personality is such that authority "gravitates" to them.

The collective personality of top line management also is important, as noted earlier. In collective bargaining, negotiating agreements, and settling grievances, the staff executives tend to have more authority in merchandising, engineering, and research-oriented firms than in the average manufacturing firms.

Effective Ideas. Professional journals, books, and education are influential in shaping the role of the industrial relations director in some companies. For example, the personnel department in one company was moving from a line to a staff role because the new director had been a student in the advanced management course of an authority who convincingly expounded the staff principle in personnel administration. In another case, a personnel textbook with the same point of view had been instrumental in shaping the manner in which the industrial relations department functioned.

In contrast with the foregoing factors, geographic and economic differences do not appear to account for many differences in the industrial relations director's authority (although perhaps our sample was too small to support a generalization on this point). Type of industry and product also do not seem to be important influences in the firms we studied (this would not necessarily be true of industries in which multi-employer bargaining has emerged).

Organizational Size and Functional Complexity:

A Study of Administration in Hospitals

THEODORE R. ANDERSON AND SEYMOUR WARKOV

One of the important problems in any organization is the coordination of the various activities which occur within it. This coordination function is normally performed by the administrative component of the organization. The relative size of this component is an important dependent variable in much organization theory. In particular, the coordination of activities is alleged to become relatively more difficult (requiring a more than proportionately greater expenditure of time or energy or both) with an increased number of personnel and with a greater variety of role activities or tasks.

For example, Durkheim asserted that growing density of population in a society results in increasingly complex forms of organization.[1] Similarly, both Spencer and Simmel propose that an increase of size necessitates more complex forms of communication.[2] It is commonly claimed that, in addition to its effect on organizational complexity, growth also brings

about a disproportionate increase in the size of the administrative component.[3] Finally, more and more complex tasks may require that the coordination of an organization's differentiated components be accomplished by an increasingly larger administration.[4]

Despite the apparently widespread interest in the concomitants of organizational size and complexity, few systematic researches have been undertaken to test the basic hypotheses. There are not many comparative studies of several large-scale organizations, presumably because of the expense of gathering data on such organizations. The tendency in research has been, instead, to focus attention upon one or at most a very few organizations. These studies present illustrative material and, at times, suggestive conclusions, but they do not represent tests of the hypotheses or conclusions.

Terrien and Mills provide one of the two systematic empirical studies in this general area. They make the Parkinsonian proposal that "the relationship between the size of the administrative component and the total size of its containing organization is such that the

From *American Sociological Review*, Vol. 26, Feb. 1961, pp. 23–28. Reprinted with permission of the authors and the publisher, American Sociological Association.

[1] Emile Durkheim, *On the Social Division of Labor in Society,* translated by George Simpson, New York: Macmillan, 1933, Part 2.

[2] Herbert Spencer, *Principles of Sociology*, New York: Appleton, 1898, Vol. I, pp. 525–528; Georg Simmel, "The Number of Members as Determining the Sociological Form of the Group," translated by A. W. Small, *American Journal of Sociology*, 8 (1902–1903), pp. 1–46.

[3] For a general discussion of this and other points relating to organizational size, and a review of the literature, see Theodore Caplow, "Organizational Size," *Administrative Science Quarterly*, I (March, 1957), pp. 484–505.

[4] See, e.g., Max Weber, *The Theory of Social and Economic Organization*, translated by A. M. Henderson and T. Parsons, New York: Oxford University Press, 1947, pp. 324–337.

larger the size of the containing organization, the greater will be the proportion given over to its administrative component."[5] Data on school districts of California support this hypothesis in that the administrative component contained a higher mean percentage of the total staff in large than in small school districts. Bendix, in the other systematic study, presents evidence pointing in the opposite direction. Using data drawn from German industrial experience between 1907 and 1933, he shows that the percentage of administrative salary workers (of all employees) declines with increasing size of establishment for concerns with at least six employees. On the other hand, the per cent of salaried technicians increases with growing size.[6] This paper presents further data bearing upon these contrasting hypotheses and upon the hypothesis relating organizational complexity to the relative size of the administrative component.

DATA AND METHOD. Relevant data were secured for Veterans Administration hospitals in the United States for the year 1956. These data were derived from reports on the number of hospital personnel in various structural categories which are published monthly by the Central Office of the Veterans Administration.[7] Only hospitals discharging at least 40 tuberculous patients were included in the sample.[8] In 1956, there were 51 such hospitals; two were eliminated for technical reasons.[9]

Thus 49 Veterans Administration hospitals, each with a substantial number of tuberculous patients, make up the final sample.

The dependent variable, the relative size of the administrative component, was measured by the per cent of all employees classified in the category, "General Hospital Administration." This component includes the Manager's Office, the Registrar's Office, and the Fiscal, Personnel, and Supply units.[10] The first independent variable, organizational size, was measured by the Annual Average Daily Patient Load (hereafter called ADPL) and was estimated for 1956 from the three months of February, May, and October. An alternative measure of organizational size is the total hospital labor force—that is, the denominator of the dependent variable. For the two groups of hospitals studied here (see below) these two measures of size are essentially equivalent. The correlations between these measures within each group of hospitals being .966 and .977, only one measure of size, namely, ADPL, was utilized in the main analysis.

The second independent variable, organizational complexity, was inferred from structural characteristics of the hospitals in the sample, which were divided into two distinct groups. Nineteen were classified as Tuberculosis Hospitals by the Veterans Administration. The percentages of the ADPL in these hospitals with pulmonary tuberculosis ranged from a low of 44 to a high of 100, with a median of 91.5 per cent. The other 30 hospitals were classified as General Medicine and Surgery Hospitals (hereafter called GM&S). A wide range of diseases are regularly treated in these hospitals, including internal diseases and psychiatric illness as well as tuberculosis. The percentages of the ADPL with pulmonary tuberculosis in this second group ranged from a low of three to a high of 41, with a median of 16.5 per cent. It is assumed in this paper that the TB hospitals are less complex organizationally than are the GM&S hospitals in that fewer types of diseases are treated on a regular basis.

The concept of organizational complexity poses serious methodological and measurement

[5] F. C. Terrien and D. C. Mills, "The Effect of Changing Size Upon the Internal Structure of an Organization," *American Sociological Review*, 20 (February, 1955), p. 11.

[6] Reinhard Bendix, *Work and Authority in Industry*, New York: Wiley, 1956, p. 222, Table 7.

[7] *Supplement, VA Statistical Summary*, Washington, D.C.: Central Office, Veterans Administration, January to December, 1956.

[8] These were originally assembled for the purpose of studying medically unsanctioned withdrawal from hospitals on the part of tuberculosis patients. See Seymour Warkov, *Irregular Discharge from Veterans Administration Tuberculosis Hospitals: A Problem of Organizational Effectiveness*, Ph.D. thesis, Yale University, 1959. The analysis reported in this paper, however, is not based upon this study.

[9] One hospital was eliminated because in fact it comprised two separate hospitals; the second because its administrative personnel were combined with those of another hospital in the statistical summary.

[10] The Annual estimate for this component is based on the table reporting full-time equivalent hospital personnel employed in VA hospitals, *Supplement, VA Statistical Summary*, June, 1956.

problems. Udy's recent attempt to clarify the concept and to measure the degree of complexity suggests that it comprises three elements: the number of tasks performed, the maximum number of specialized operations ever performed at the same time, and the existence or non-existence of combined effort.[11] Using these criteria, it is reasonable to consider the GM&S hospitals as more complex because, not only are all tasks performed in the TB hospitals also carried out in the GM&S hospitals, but many other services that are regularly rendered in the GM&S hospitals are not provided in the TB hospitals. Of course, these two groups of hospitals also differ in many ways other than in complexity. For this reason, conclusions about complexity should be interpreted with caution.

It is important to note that the design used here permits the influence of size to be studied independently of the influence of complexity. All of the TB hospitals have about the same complexity. Furthermore, all of the GM&S hospitals have at least approximately the same degree of complexity, although some variation probably exists among them. Thus, within each category, complexity is sufficiently constant so that any relationship between size and proportion of personnel in administration is not substantially influenced by complexity. Other hospitals were excluded from the analysis because their inclusion would tend to confound the effects of complexity and size. The size of the sample used here is sufficient to demonstrate statistically the impact of the data upon the hypotheses; it is believed that the avoidance of a confounding effect is more important for the purpose at hand than an increase in sample size.

RESULTS. The emperical results may be presented as replies to a series of questions. First, is there a relationship between type of hospital and organizational size? The data indicate that the GM&S hospitals are significantly and substantially larger than are the TB hospitals. In 1956, the mean ADPL (or size) of the GM&S hospitals was 770 and only 335 for the TB hospitals.

Second, do GM&S and TB hospitals differ

[11] Stanley H. Udy, Jr., "The Structure of Authority in Non-Industrial Production Organizations," *American Journal of Sociology*, 64 (May, 1959), pp. 582–584.

with respect to the proportion of personnel in administration? The fact that about 12.5 per cent of the employees were in administration in both types of hospitals is clearly inconsistent with previous research findings and speculations. According to existing theory, larger, more complex hospitals have a higher proportion of staff in administration. The interpretation of this contrary finding is deferred for the moment.

Third, is there a relationship between hospital size and percentage of personnel in administration? Since the GM&S hospitals were so much larger than the TB hospitals it seemed unreasonable to treat them as a single homogeneous group. Hence, this question was asked of each hospital type.

The TB hospitals were divided into three categories, with roughly one-third of them in each. The mean per cent of employees in administration within each category is shown by the following figures:

	SIZE: UNDER 250	250– 400	ABOVE 400
No. of hospitals	5	8	6
Mean per cent	15.6	12.0	10.7

It is clear that the larger the hospital the *smaller* the per cent of all personnel in administration. An analysis of variance of these data indicates significance beyond the .01 level. Further, Eta^2 is .577, indicating that 58 per cent of the variance in percentage of employees in administration can be accounted for by variations in size. Thus size is a powerful explanatory variable, although in a direction opposite to that expected.

That this result is not a peculiarity of TB hospitals is indicated by the results for the GM&S hospitals. Here, different size categories were used so as to place, as in the former case, approximately one-third of the hospitals in each, with the following results:

	SIZE: UNDER 600	600– 900	ABOVE 900
No. of hospitals	12	9	9
Mean per cent	14.0	12.0	11.0

Again, the larger the hospital the *smaller* the per cent of all personnel in administration.

These results are also significant beyond the .01 level, and Eta^2 is .556, almost identical to the figure for the TB hospitals. This divergent finding, then, has some degree of generality, applying at least to two quite different types of Federal hospitals.[12]

Fourth, is the relationship between size of hospital and proportion of personnel in administration linear? The fact that within each type of hospital Eta^2 proved to be significantly greater than r^2 provides a negative answer. A scatter diagram of these data (not presented here) suggests that the slope of the regression line becomes more horizontal as size increases. It is possible that the slope might actually become positive with sufficiently large hospitals, but this is only a speculation, in view of the limitations of the present data.

Finally, if size is controlled or held constant, do the hospital types differ in per cent of employees in administration? This is in fact the case, but the hospital types differ so much in size that all of the observations cannot be brought to bear upon the question (especially because the size regressions are not linear). In particular, only one size category (between 300 and 600) included an appreciable number of each type of hospital. Furthermore, within this reasonably narrow range, the GM&S and TB hospitals had roughly the same size distribution. In this range, the 11 TB hospitals averaged only 11.1 per cent of personnel in administration; the corresponding figure is 14 per cent for the 12 GM&S hospitals. This difference is significant at the .01 level. Thus, the earlier finding of no overall difference in the average per cent of employees in administration appears to be entirely a function of the size differential between the two types of hospital. In general, if GM&S hospitals may be considered to be more complex than TB hospital, then these data tend to confirm the hypothesis that organizational complexity and the relative size of the administrative component are positively related, as expected. However, the data refute, at least for these organizations, the hypothesis that organizational size and relative size of the administrative component are positively related; indeed they suggest perhaps the counter hypothesis.

DISCUSSION. On the surface, at least, the findings reported in this paper are in direct contradiction to those reported by Terrien and Mills. Moreover, these results are substantially at variance with what is apparently the common conception (among sociologists and others) of the relationship between organizational size and the relative size of the administrative component. There appear to be, in general, two ways to resolve these discrepancies. First, either or both sets of data may be inadequate in some way to test the hypothesis under discussion. Second, these two sets of data may not, in fact, be directly comparable. In the latter case, it should be possible to develop theoretical statements consistent with both sets of findings.

Both sets of data are derived from relatively straightforward enumeration procedures conducted by state and federal agencies. For fiscal and other reasons the accuracy of these data is important within the agencies concerned. There is no reason to suspect that either set of basic data is in substantial error, certainly not to the degree necessary to eliminate the conclusion in contradiction to the earlier study.

Another possible explanation of this finding is that the administrative component was incorrectly identified or categorized in at least one of the two studies. There is no doubt that some administrative activities are performed by personnel who are not so classified. However, there is no reason to believe that the proportion of such personnel is substantially greater (or lesser) in large than in small organizations, which have a specialized, designated administrative component. Accordingly, it is reasonable to conclude that both the findings of Terrien and Mills and of the present investigation accurately reflect organizational processes which are (therefore) not directly comparable. If so, an explanation is called for which renders these findings mutually consistent.

The following propositions are offered as one possible resolution of the apparent discrepancy between the two sets of findings. The propositions are based upon the fact that some of the school districts studied by Terrien and Mills include more than one school and

_____

[12] It is important to emphasize the fact that an inverse relationship is not an artifact of the measure of size used here. Identical results were obtained using the labor force measure of size.

upon the assumption that the larger school districts incorporate more schools than do the smaller districts. In contrast, each of the organizations in the present study has a single location. Thus:

1. The relative size of the administrative component *decreases* as the number of persons performing identical tasks in the same place increases.[13]

2. The relative size of the administrative component *increases* as the number of places at which work is performed increases.

3. The relative size of the administrative component *increases* as the number of tasks performed at the same place increases (or as roles become increasingly specialized and differentiated).

If these propositions are correct, then Terrien and Mills' findings may be interpreted as confirming the second proposition and *not* as nullifying the first proposition. Our findings, on the other hand, support the first and third propositions but do not bear upon the second one. Given this interpretation, the relative size of the administrative component in a single school should decline as school size increases, provided that the organizational complexity of the schools is held constant. In practice, it might prove difficult to devise an effective measure of organizational complexity within schools. These propositions are presented tentatively, of course, pending further investiga-

[13] This proposition appears to be consistent with commonplace observations. For example, as any teacher knows, administering a test in the same room to four times more students than usual does not require four times as many proctors. An alternative possibility is that the inverse relationship holds up to a point, and then becomes positive, thus producing an overall U-shape. Our data suggest that the curve flattens out eventually, but do not suggest the existence of an upturn.

tion of these and other types of organizations.

At least one alternative means of rectifying the two sets of findings is available. The school districts and hospitals may differ in the extent to which they are subject to centralized authority. Where the central authority is powerful, special constraints may inhibit the emergence of the relationship between size and administration that would otherwise occur. In particular, some special bureaucratic constraint may operate within government hospitals which inhibits the "free" growth of the administrative component.

It is also important to recognize that these propositions, even if confirmed empirically, are not necessarily sufficient to explain all structural and temporal variations in the relative size of the administrative component. Specifically, the inclusion of a proposition concerning the routinization of roles would undoubtedly improve the general explanation of variations in the relative size of the administrative component. Routinization is not discussed in this paper because the apparent contradiction between the two sets of findings could be resolved without taking it into account.

On the other hand, these propositions appear to explain adequately the apparent overall increase in the relative importance of administrative activities within organizations during the past several decades (as evidenced by the rapid rise in the per cent employed in clerical occupations, for instance). It is often suggested that this increase in administration is a function of the sheer growth in organizational size. If our propositions are correct, however, the explanatory variable is organizational complexity rather than organizational size. Clearly, more systematic studies are required before any such conclusions can be considered to be substantially confirmed.

Adapting Organization to New Technology

FRANK J. JASINSKI

Getting a new machine or production process to live up to advance expectations is often a hard job. Few are the companies that have not had frustrating experiences at one time or another in achieving the improvements that were *supposed* to come from a new line of automatic presses, or a more modern extrusion process, or a promising change in the conveyer system.

Invariably the question comes up: What went wrong? Sometimes, of course, the trouble is simply that the estimates in cost savings or productivity increases were too optimistic. Sometimes the engineering is faulty. Sometimes the loss of a key supervisor, a strike, or a change in some other part of the plant is to blame. And sometimes the new technology is too hard on workers and supervisors, or threatens them in some way so that they resist it.

We are all familiar with such troubles. They are cited again and again. But there is another common type of difficulty—one that is rarely cited. It is a peculiarly *management* problem in that it both begins and ends with management, and no group *but* management can deal with it effectively.

Let me state this problem first in an abstract way; later we can go into detail and illustration. The idea is this: *a change in production or technology affects organizational relationships.* For example, a supervisor may find himself working with other supervisors and groups with whom he has had little contact before, or he may find himself reporting to different people, or different people reporting to him. *When management overlooks these social changes, it generally fails to realize the full potential of a change in technology,* however

From *Harvard Business Review*, Vol. 37, No. 1, Jan.–Feb. 1959, pp. 79–86. Reprinted with permission of the publisher.

well thought out the innovation was from an engineering standpoint. The potential may then be achieved only after a difficult and costly period of readjustment. The duration of the readjustment period and the degree of technological potential finally attained depend, for the most part, upon management's awareness of the relationship between technology and organization and upon its ability to keep one in harmony with the other through changing times.

Management has established and maintains staffs of engineers who devote considerable time and effort to evaluating new plant sites, designing processes, and making meticulous plant layouts. In contrast, it makes only a nominal, if any, corresponding study of the organizational requirements of a new technological process. Rather, it usually tries to extend the existing organizational structure to the new process. And here is where much of the difficulty lies.

The Outmoded Vertical. Traditional business organization runs on a vertical line, relying almost solely on superior-subordinate relationships. Orders and instructions go down the line; reports and requests go up the line. But technology, including both integrated data processing and integrated machine production, has developed on what might be called a horizontal plane; that is, the machine cuts across superior-subordinate relationships, affecting the jobs of people in different areas, departments, and work groups. Superimposing a strictly vertical organization structure on a technology which emphasizes horizontal and diagonal relationships can and does cause obvious difficulties.

Typical of the kinds of relationships required by modern technology is the progressive fabricating and assembly line. Here the need to make the right decision or take the necessary action at the right time at the right place is immediate. Managers, in order to solve an immediate problem, have to deal horizontally with their peers and diagonally with people at different levels who are neither superiors nor subordinates. To follow established, formal routes would be too time-consuming, too costly, and too disruptive.

Necessary as these horizontal and diagonal relations may be to smooth functioning of the technology, or work flow, they are seldom defined or charted formally. Nonetheless, wherever or whenever modern technology does operate effectively, these relations exist, if only on a nonformal basis. In other words, certain individuals have developed their own techniques to work satisfactorily outside of (or in place of) the formal framework. They have usually done so after a period of trial and error and emerge as outstanding performers because they can deal effectively with equals, nonsubordinates, and nonsuperiors—undefined relationships which nevertheless are essential to the technology.

Certainly it is management's job not only to recognize these new kinds of relationships but also to take steps to enable them to function definitely and smoothly. A few managers have recognized the discrepancy between organization and technology, and have taken steps to integrate the two. They have achieved such integration in a variety of ways, which essentially may be classified as:

1. Changing the technology to conform with the existing organizational structure.

2. Changing the organization so as to define and formalize the relationships required by the technology.

3. Maintaining both the existing organization and the existing technology but introducing mechanisms to reduce or minimize the discrepancies between the two.

In appraising these steps we will want to look at the kinds of problems which arise when technology and organization are not integrated, and at specific examples of what can be and has been done to recognize and alleviate the basic causes of these problems.

Horizontal Relations. Let us start out by considering a technology which dramatizes the horizontal nature of the work flow—the automobile assembly line. I shall present the kinds

of problems which can arise and the nonformal adjustments some members of management have made, as revealed by the Technology Project at Yale University.[1]

PRESSURE FOR SHORT CUTS. The automobile assembly line winds its way, almost uninterruptedly, for several miles through the plant. The conveyer carries each automobile "without a stop" through five departments, past the areas of 10 general foremen, through the sections of 50 or 60 foremen, and past the work stations of thousands of workers.

When the "body" starts out, it is a flat sheet of metal comprising the car floor; at the end of the conveyer the car, now complete, is driven off into the test area. In between there are innumerable feeder lines or tributaries which bring parts to the main conveyer to be attached to the gradually evolving body. The entire plant and the efforts of all the employees are geared to the task of getting the right part to the right place at the right time.

There is, therefore, considerable interdependence both among production workers and between the production and nonproduction groups. The holes for a particular bit of chromium trim are drilled before the body is prepared for painting; the trim is attached a mile or so down the line. The piece of trim has to be on hand, brought there by a materials handler. And the tools of both driller and "attacher" have to operate at top efficiency—the responsibility of the maintenance man.

In other words, the foreman, to be effective, has to synchronize and coordinate the efforts of many individuals to achieve his production goals. He has to supervise the work of his direct subordinates; he has to make sure that parts are readily and continuously available; he has to ensure peak performance of all equipment in his area; he has to keep "tabs" on quality; and he has to track down and attempt to

[1] For previous findings, see Charles R. Walker and Robert H. Guest, *The Man on the Assembly Line* (Cambridge, Harvard University Press, 1952); Charles R. Walker, Robert H. Guest, and Arthur N. Turner, *The Foreman on the Assembly Line* (Cambridge, Harvard University Press, 1956); also Walker and Guest, "The Man on the Assembly Line," *Harvard Business Review,* May–June 1952, p. 71; and Arthur N. Turner, "Management and the Assembly Line," *Harvard Business Review,* September–October 1955, p. 40.

correct defective work done in previous sections which may be hampering his operators' work.

Yet, despite the importance of all these relations to smooth work flow, the organization does not define them formally. In fact, the formal relations are such that additional difficulties are introduced. For example:

> Although the workers report to the foreman and he, in turn, to the general foreman, others who are essential to the work flow do not. The materials handler reports up a separate and distinct vertical plane. So do the maintenance man and the inspector.

> Again, although production defects are within the line production organization, they may be caused by a foreman who reports to a different general foreman and sometimes even to a different superintendent.

Theoretically, the foreman can report any deficiency in services from supporting groups to his general foreman. This procedure is formally and clearly defined. Time on the assembly line, however, is crucial; cars pass a given work station at the rate of one every 1.5 minutes. Unless an error is corrected immediately, the consequences can be far-reaching. The foreman cannot afford to spend time hunting down the general foreman; he has to attend to the matters immediately and directly. To do so he has to deal with other foremen (on the horizontal plane) and also with materials handlers, maintenance men, inspectors, and other foremen's workers (on the diagonal plane).

READJUSTMENTS REQUIRED. In view of the importance of horizontal and diagonal relations to assembly-line technology, the whole concept of superior-subordinate relations is out of place—at least, in much of the plant during much of the time. The formal boxes and directional arrows on the organization chart cannot set the tone for everyday activities. Unless this is recognized, problems can arise.[2] As one perceptive foreman commented: "When you deal with someone from another department, you have to show a smile."

Unfortunately, the Technology Project has

[2] Frank J. Jasinski, "Foreman Relationships Outside the Work Group," *Personnel*, September 1956, pp. 130–136.

revealed that many supervisors, accustomed to behaving according to the usual vertical channels, have not learned to relate effectively on a horizontal plane:

> In case I get stuff coming into my department that is wrong I usually let my general foreman know . . . and he goes over and gets it straightened out. I couldn't do that myself because, after all, I'm just another foreman.

> Actually, the job I'm doing now is that of a general foreman because I'm checking on these six foremen all the time. I've got the responsibility of letting them know that they're slipping up in one job or another, but I haven't got the authority to *tell* them to button up. Lots of times I have to go to my general foreman.

This lack of patterning and clarity in horizonal relationships frequently creates clashes between foremen. One worker provided this dramatic illustration:

> The foremen go around sticking files into one another's heads in front of the men. Just today we thought we were going to see a fist fight between our foreman and another one. They were screaming like washerwomen at one another. Fine example— they hate one another.

Hardly the way to get a job done! Yet these difficulties do not derive from personality clashes. Repeated reports of similar incidents throughout this particular plant strongly indicate a basic shortcoming on the part of the organization to adjust to the incoming technology.

Interestingly enough, there are a number of foremen who *have* been able to establish and maintain satisfactory nonformal relations with other foremen and with staff and service groups. This means spending much time with persons other than their immediate subordinates. Indeed, contrary to the traditional emphasis on the importance of the vertical foreman-worker relationships, the demands of technology are such that good foremen actually have to interact *most* of the time in horizontal and diagonal relations. As a matter of fact, the foremen judged most effective by their superiors are the very ones who spend the least amount of time with their own workers.

At the time of our study, management was not aware of the relations required by the work flow—or, at least, it had not done much to formalize those relations. In fact, the individual foremen making the necessary adjustments sometimes had to do so in violation of official policy.

KEY TO SUCCESS. Horizontal and diagonal relationships, such as those described, exist in virtually all business and industrial organizations.[3] A classic example involves a group of drill line operators in a factory who, even in the face of vigorous management disapproval, resisted the formal logics of an incentive system and continued to devise nonformal methods and relations for getting the work done.

There is no dearth of evidence to indicate that, whether or not the firm operates under the pressing immediacy of an automobile assembly line, the degree of production success depends in good measure upon the mutual adjustment or harmonious integration of the organizational structure and the technology. Where this integration is faulty, those individuals who are able to utilize satisfactorily the nonformal relations required are the successful ones. Where management has recognized the need for integration and has taken steps to achieve it, the efforts of individuals are made that much easier and more effective.

Having considered the kinds of conflict which can arise between the technology and the organization, let us now turn to examples of how some managers have effected a more satisfactory integration. As stated earlier, these methods are: changing the technology, changing the organization, and (less radically) introducing mechanisms to reduce discrepancies between organization and technology.

Changing the Technology. Ordinarily, managers consider technology to be inviolate. And frequently it is. After all, in making steel, for example, the metal has certain physical properties which require a certain timing and sequence of operations whether it is made in an American, Russian, or Indian mill. As a result, there are not many dramatic examples

available of managers' making changes in the technology to adapt it to the existing organizational structure. The illustrations that are available, however, should serve to make the point. For instance, though it is not generally thought of in these terms, the shift from process to product layout in industry is a fairly widespread technique for effecting just such a change. Most of the integrated machine-processing units would fall into this category.

ONE-MAN SUPERVISION. Formerly, under the process layout, the manufactured item would go from the rough turning or lathe department to the mill and drill department, to the heat treat department, back to the grinding department, and so on until it finally went to the assembly department—with a different foreman in charge of each department. That is why there are so many meetings in such industrial organizations trying to pin down responsibility for schedule delays and errors in manufacturing.

It is true that, where volume warrants such a change, reorganizing the technology into a product layout brings about considerable savings in materials handling. This is usually the reason given for such a change. The product is no longer shunted between departments but goes uninterruptedly down a single line.

Yet the product layout conforms to the traditional organizational structure, and a number of managers have utilized it for that reason. With the product layout, one man, whether a foreman or superintendent, is responsible for the entire product. He has control over rough turning, mill and drill, heat treat, grinding, and even assembly. The operators who perform these diverse operations all report to him —in an established, clearly defined superior-subordinate relationship. Integration between organization and technology is thus achieved.

This kind of integration is possible only when the product can be made by the number of employees reporting to a specific foreman. When more workers are required, and two, three, or even more foremen are involved, closely knit integration becomes difficult.

As automatic equipment takes over more and more operations and as the actual number of employees is reduced, the number of products which can be manufactured in a product layout supervised by one foreman will increase. However, most industrial products, for one

---

[3] See William F. Whyte, *Money and Motivation* (New York, Harper & Brothers, 1955), pp. 53–66, and "Economic Incentives and Human Relations," *Harvard Business Review*, March–April 1952, p. 73.

reason or another, still do not lend themselves to "one-foreman product layout" integration. In such instances, managers need to rely on one of the other methods to be discussed here.

Changing the Organization. The impact of recent technological innovations has forced many managers to take a second look at their organization, particularly with the advent of modern data-processing equipment. This equipment requires information in a certain form. Where managers have used it as more than simply a change in "hardware," the equipment has triggered sweeping revisions of data-processing departments. To prepare information efficiently for the processing equipment, managers have completely reorganized traditional departments. In this connection there are the telling, though perhaps exaggerated, stories of companies that revised their organizations in anticipation of delivery of data-processing equipment only to realize such great savings through the reorganization process itself that they canceled their orders for the equipment.

SUCCESSFUL SOLUTIONS. Charles R. Walker in his book, *Toward the Automatic Factory,*[4] describes one instance of conflict between the new technology and the existing formal organization and how that conflict was finally resolved:

> A $40 million installation of a semiautomatic seamless tube mill failed to meet engineers' production estimates for nearly three years. There were a number of variables that were responsible for this delay, and most of them could be termed human factors.
>
> Among these variables was the fact that the amount of production was pretty much regulated by the automatic machinery. An important variable in the level of production was "downtime"—the length of time it took to make a repair or a mill changeover for a different size of product. As with most industrial organizations, those interruptions of production involved "nonproduction" personnel: crane operators, maintenance men, and repairmen. Most of

[4] New Haven, Yale University Press, 1957, pp. 126–142; see also Walker's "Life in the Automatic Factory," *Harvard Business Review,* January–February 1958, p. 111.

these nonproduction men did not report to line management directly; they reported vertically along separate lines of authority. Further, while the men on the mill crew were paid for what they produced by an incentive plan, the crane operators and maintenance men were paid on day rates.

> In other words, though the technology required the mill crew, the crane operators, and the maintenance men to work as a cohesive unit, management through its formal organization and its incentive plan treated them as separate entities, even to the extent of paying them differently. Productivity suffered as a result.
>
> It was not until the workers convinced management (and the union, as a matter of fact) that the incentive plan should be extended to cover the entire work group— as required by the technology of the semiautomatic steel mill—that productivity increased. Following this and other changes, production not only met the engineers' original estimates of capacity but far exceeded them.
>
> Had management recognized the new organizational structure required and made the necessary adjustments at the outset, then much of the three-year period of costly adjustment might have been avoided.

Undoubtedly, other managers have had similar experiences as one of the consequences of rapid technological innovation. Some may have recognized the nature of the problem and acted to alleviate it. Others may have simply let it ride. It is quite possible for a plant to function for quite some time with a conflict between its organization and the technology —but at less than optimal efficiency. It is also possible for such a plant to benefit from integration even after a lengthy period of such conflict.

A case in point is A. K. Rice's now famous Indian weaving-shed study:

> Organization and technology had been firmly established for a long time. As in the steel mill, the weaving technology required a high degree of coordination between the weavers and a variety of service people—especially during a change of cloth, a break in the yarn, and the loading and unloading of the loom. But the representatives from the servicing units who worked with

a particular weaver varied considerably from one group activity to the next. The groups lacked uniformity and continuity over time. There was confusion as to who reported to whom and who had authority over whom. This, and the lack of group continuity, resulted in inefficiencies as well as high damage in production.

Then changes in the organization were introduced so that it would conform more closely with the technological requirements. For example, small work groups were created, with internal leadership, which existed as a unit over time and so were better able to cope with technological requirements satisfactorily. As a result, efficiency jumped 10% and damage dropped 7%.[5]

TEMPORARY MEASURES. Obviously, the dramatic and thorough revisions described above are not always feasible or practical in modern business and industry. But managers frequently have made smaller organizational changes that border on being mechanisms. They can be of a temporary or quasi-official nature, or permanently incorporated.

Such temporary measures include coordinators or project heads who provide an organizational short circuit for the duration of a crash program. Best known, perhaps, are the temporary realignments during World War II in invasion task forces. Just prior to and during the invasion one man headed all participating service units. Following the successful completion of the invasion, the task force regrouped into separate and independent units reporting along individual service lines.

In industry, similar groups or teams are temporarily formed to carry out a specified purpose. Many engineering research departments function on a project team basis permanently. Another kind of quasi-official organizational change is the use of an expediter, who, unlike the coordinator or project head, has no direct authority over the individuals with whom he relates.

Still another kind of organizational measure, widely used to cope with horizontal relations, is the meeting. This form enables representatives from the several departments to raise, discuss, and resolve problems requiring the joint efforts of two or more department heads attending the meeting. Here again, the traditional and time-consuming formal channel is bypassed. Usually interdepartmental or interdivisional meetings are held at a top-management level; their usefulness or necessity at lower levels has yet to be fully explored by many organizations.

Other managers have found it expedient to include functions which have been traditionally staff responsibilities under production personnel control. For instance, in an aircraft engine company on the East coast, management transferred its "tool trouble" groups from the master mechanic's department to production and created a new job classification (with quality control functions) under each production foreman.

In fact, considerable attention is currently being given by several large corporations to the question of how many of the service functions can be handed over to the foreman. This is an attempt, it would seem, to fall back on the well-established vertical, superior-subordinate relationships and thus avoid the nebulous and consequently difficult line-staff relationships. The limitations described previously in discussing the product-layout plan, however, would apply equally in this instance. The product must be one that requires no more individuals—machine operators and the transferred service personnel—than a foreman can adequately supervise or manage.

Introducing Mechanisms. Still other managers faced with a discrepancy between technology and organizational structure have attempted to solve the dilemma by changing neither technology nor organization but by introducing new mechanisms. In this case, we are not concerned with minor organizational moves such as have been described in the preceding section, but with procedures or routines.

A dramatic example taken from the restaurant industry of the introduction of a mechanism is provided by William F. Whyte.[6] The

---

[5] "Productivity and Social Organization in an Indian Weaving Shed," Human Relations, November 1953, p. 297; see also a subsequent report, "The Experimental Reorganization of Non-Automatic Weaving in an Indian Mill," *Human Relations,* August 1955, p. 199.

[6] *Human Relations in the Restaurant Industry* (New York, McGraw-Hill Book Company, Inc., 1948), Chapter 6.

problem confronting him was a simple but vexing one:

> Viewing the situation *in formal organizational terms,* the waitresses reported vertically to the hostess; the counterman reported along another vertical line of "command" to the kitchen supervisor. Although not explicit, there was some indication that the countermen considered themselves at a higher organizational level than the waitresses. But *technologically* the work flow was from the customer to the waitress to the counterman. This ran against the formal organization. Not only was the relationship between waitress and counterman formally undefined; it also went diagonally, from a lower to a higher level.

In the cases cited by Whyte, a few individuals were able to adjust to this nonformal relationship, but they emerged as exceptions to the usual conflict pattern. Unfortunately, management did not recognize and take advantage of this adjustment and formalize these effective nonformal relationships in order to extend them to others in the organization.

Recognizing the conflict, Whyte introduced a mechanism to reduce it:

> As an experiment, one waitress wrote out her orders and placed them on a spindle. Her orders were always ready before those of other waitresses who had called theirs in at the same time. If she was not ready for a hot food order, the counterman would voluntarily place it in the warmer for her. Furthermore, he took a liking to her and made a bet with the bartender that she, like himself, was of Polish extraction—which she was not.[7]

Thus, an uncomplicated mechanism reduced the conflict between the technological work flow and the organizational setup without changing either.

OTHER ILLUSTRATIONS. The use of paper work as a mechanism to reduce possible conflict in formally undefined relationships is a commonplace in industry. Requests from production foremen, for example, go regularly to personnel, engineering, accounting, and other staff and service groups. Such requests cut across

[7] *Human Relations in the Restaurant Industry* (New York, McGraw-Hill Book Company, Inc., 1948), p. 69.

the formal organization both horizontally and diagonally. Conversely, reports may also cut across the organization through the "copy to . . ." technique while going up the line vertically.

Very often, the amount and type of paper work (copies of requests and reports) do not correspond to actual need. Many are destined to end up in the "circular file" simply because the paper work routes do not follow the lines required by the technology. (Machine accountants, aware of this discrepancy and pressed for tabulating time, occasionally run a check on the use made of various reports; they purposely delay circulation of a report for a few days or a week to see how many people will actually call for it. Thus they have been able, unofficially, to eliminate a number of outdated reports.)

The automobile assembly line provides additional illustrations of mechanisms employed by management to meet technologically required horizontal and diagonal relations:

> An operator who hangs doors is in direct contact with the operator who puts them in proper sequence on the overhead conveyer. In the event of a misscheduled door, the line operator has a "squawk" box through which he can call for a substitute door. Here we have a horizontal relationship between two hourly operators, one in production and one in material control.
>
> The worker who loads the overhead conveyer is guided in turn in his door scheduling by the "telautograph," which transmits information from an earlier point on the line from another hourly operator in the material control department. This operator notes the sequence of models and body types of cars passing his station on the line. The information is transmitted simultaneously to various schedulers in the plant who have to synchronize their operations with this sequence.
>
> In the event of a mechanical or tool breakdown, time is especially important. When a line worker cannot perform his operation because of such a breakdown, he immediately signals for help through a whistle system: he uses one signal for a mechanical breakdown, another for an electrical one. The appropriate repairman (who is stationed nearby) comes over to repair the de-

fect with a minimum of delay. For a worker to stop the line until he finds his foreman to report the breakdown in the traditional vertical plane would be absurd.

Several managements have adopted programs to facilitate nonformal relations. These range from company-wide social affairs, such as picnics, banquets, or sports teams, to a systematic rotation program whereby individuals at supervisory and middle-management levels transfer periodically from one department to another. Ostensibly, the purpose of such a program is to "broaden" the experience of the individual; actually the more important by-product is that it establishes friendships horizontally and diagonally, and thus encourages and facilitates nonformal relations required by the work flow.

Although many of these and other mechanisms can be effective and may, indeed, be the only means to reduce a discrepancy between technology and organization, it still is worthwhile to make broader and more basic changes in either the technology or the organization.

Conclusion. Frequently, the traditional, formally defined vertical relations in business and industrial organization prove inadequate to cope with modern technology. New technologies require new organizational setups, and it is being found increasingly that industrial processes require horizontal and diagonal relations which are not patterned or clearly defined.

Such lack of clarity can impair the production process. The work flow can create difficulty where the vertical lines are strongly emphasized and where the flow violates those lines —as was the case in the restaurant example cited. But when the formal organization is permissive, nonformal relations in the horizontal and diagonal planes arise to cope with the technological process. We saw that the more successful assembly-line foremen learned to relate with other foremen and their workers. But these relationships were not usually recognized formally; they existed on an individual and nonformal basis.

Management can work toward an integration between technology and organization in several ways: (1) by changing the technology, (2) by changing the organization, and (3) by introducing mechanisms. All these methods have been used effectively to some degree, but the difficulty occurs in that management's attempts toward integration generally lack a systematic and purposeful approach. They may just happen over time, arise as temporary expedients, or emerge as a solution to a crisis situation. Many managers have yet to explore the deeper relation between technology and the organization.

The advent of electronic data processing and integrated machine processing has forced some managers to reorganize departments to meet technological needs. Many such revisions, however, are limited to a small portion of the organization, to the areas of greatest immediate pressure. Cannot more be done? The case studies cited, as well as the successful partial steps taken by businessmen and industrialists thus far, indicate a need for a systematic analysis of technology and organization. This analysis might include the following steps:

1. Examine the work flow of the technology to determine what relations are required.

2. Identify the points where the formal organization meets these requirements and where it does not.

3. Discover what nonformal relationships exist at present to meet the technologically required relations which are not encompassed by the formal organization.

4. Determine what formalization does exist to cope with relations falling beyond the traditional vertical planes.

5. Decide which of the nonformal relations might be profitably formalized.

6. Provide measures to facilitate the nonformal relations which are still required but which may best remain nonformal.

It will not be possible to formalize through new mechanisms or through technology and organization changes all of the nonformal relations required by the work flow. It should be possible, however, to remove or reduce the *major* points of variance between the technology and the organization. It makes sense for a company that has been farsighted enough to bring in a new technology to be equally farsighted in recognizing that established organizational patterns will not usually serve with the same effectiveness as they once did. If the new technology is to live up to production expectations, then management must see to it that organization relationships are carefully restudied and wisely redirected.

Selections from Change in Managerial Manpower

with Mechanization of Data-processing

C. EDWARD WEBER

INTRODUCTION. Technological development, it has been argued, requires the firm to increase its use of managerial manpower in comparison to total manpower.[1] Technological development may therefore result in the bureauc-

From *The Journal of Business*, Vol. 32, No. 2, April 1959, pp. 151–163. Copyright 1959 by The University of Chicago Press. Reprinted with permission of the publisher, University of Chicago Press.

[The author is] . . . indebted to Frederick H. Harbison and Bela Gold. The period of research was covered by a grant from the Industrial Relations Section, Princeton University.

[1] The direct relation between technology and the relative use of managerial manpower was suggested by Reinhard Bendix, *Work and Authority in Industry: Ideologies of Management in the Course of Industrialization* (New York: John Wiley & Sons, 1956), pp. 119–20, and Frederick Harbison, "Entrepreneurial Organization as a Factor in Economic Development," *Quarterly Journal of Economics*, LXX, No. 3 (August, 1956), 368–71, and "Steel Management on Two Continents," *Industrial Relations Quarterly Review*, X, No. 2 (March, 1955), 119–20. The author submitted that the firm's relative need for managerial resources may be associated with any innovation, whether the innovation is in products and processes or in marketing, distribution, or organization (see "Managerial Growth and Development: A Tentative Explanation of the Increasing Use of Managerial Manpower in Comparison to Total Manpower" [unpublished Ph.D. dissertation, Princeton University, 1957]). For an alternative view see Seymour Melman, *Dynamic Factors in Industrial Productivity* (Oxford: Basil Blackwell, 1956), pp. 91–92. An amusing explanation is presented in an article, "Parkinson's Law," *Economist*, November 19, 1955, pp. 635–37.

ratization of enterprise.[2] Relatively more managerial manpower is required, perhaps, because of the nature of the operations under the new technology and as a consequence of the opportunities resulting from the change to the new technology.

The cases studied indicate that the process of mechanizing data-processing requires initially considerably more managerial manpower than will finally be required to maintain the mechanized process. However, availability of trained personnel and possibly unused capacity of extremely efficient data-processing equipment may result in continuing changes in methodology as well as expansion of special reports and operations analysis.

Managerial manpower is defined as those persons who, as members of the entrepreneurial organization, are primarily involved in planning and innovation, co-ordination, administration and control, and routine supervision of the enterprise.[3] Operationally, manage-

[2] This, of course, depends upon whether the relative size of management may be considered to be an aspect of bureaucratization (see Bendix, *op. cit.*, pp. 211–16).

[3] Harbison, "Entrepreneurial Organization as a Factor in Economic Development," *op. cit.*, pp. 364–79. Harbison also includes the management of risk and uncertainty bearing as one of the activities of the entrepreneurial organization, but this activity is excluded in the above definition because of the difficulty of defining operationally persons who are involved in risk and uncertainty bearing. Harbison defines the entrepreneurial functions as those of an organization rather than as those of an individual. Managerial manpower is considered to be those persons who participate in one or more of the functions as members of the "organization."

rial manpower is defined to include employees exempt from the minimum-wage and over-time-pay provisions of the Fair Labor Standards Act because of their executive, administrative, or professional status.[4] Employees classified as executive, administrative, and professional are approximately those persons in the line organization from supervisors to the chief executive officers and those persons in the staff organization with equivalent status. Executive employees supervise the work of others; administrative employees perform work that is directly related to management policy or general business operations of the firm or the firm's customers; and professional employees perform original and creative work and have specialized academic training.

The purpose of the paper is to examine the manpower changes which accompanied a particular technological change—the mechanization of data-processing. . . .

A COSTING OPERATION IN A BASIC STEEL COMPANY. The processing of cost information was mechanized between 1952 and 1957 in one of the works of a basic steel company. The costing operation involved assigning production and labor costs to commodities and profit centers. The posting, computing, and transcribing were done manually for the most part prior to 1952, while this work was done in conjunction with tabulating equipment and a medium-sized, general-purpose computer by June, 1957. The manpower changes which paralleled the mechanization of costing operations presented an interesting situation (see Table 1). Clerical employment decreased in number and as a proportion of total employment, and supervisory employment remained constant in number but increased as a proportion of total employment.

Extensive changes in clerical activity accompanied the technical change in data-processing. In the accounting operation a number of activities were eliminated. Typing of cost reports was no longer necessary, since their duplica-

[4] For the definition of who is an executive, administrative, or professional employee see *Regulations, Part 541* (Washington, D.C.: Wage and Hour and Public Contracts Division, U.S. Department of Labor, 1950), pp. 2–3, and *Explanatory Bulletin, Regulations, Part 541* (Washington, D.C.: Wage and Hour and Public Contracts Division, U.S. Department of Labor, 1954), pp. 1–21.

tion was obtained from the tabulation process. Posting, totaling balancing, and transcribing were also done in the tabulating and computing system, and the corresponding manual operations were eliminated. Finally, the physical carrying of "working sheets" among cost clerks was eliminated, since the balancing and posting operations were performed on tabulating and electronic equipment instead of by clerks.

On the other hand, the posting of cost data on machine cards was added to the accounting operation under the new technology. The additional activity involved determining the account to which the individual charge or sum of charges should be allocated, selecting the machine card prepunched for that account, and writing the charge on the machine card in pencil. Other activities which were added to the accounting operation were increases in the volume of data processed for foreman incentives and in the number of special reports. The compiling of data for special reports and foreman incentives was not directly associated with the new technology, but their manpower requirements could not be isolated from the manpower required for the new method of costing. The gain in clerical activity, however, was apparently not sufficient to offset the loss in such activity, since the clerical personnel in the accounting operation declined from 39 to 22 persons (see Table 1).

Computing and tabulating operations were given additional activities, but there was no change in the number of personnel related to these operations (see Table 1). The tabulating and computing department key-punched the penciled information into the machine cards and operated the tabulating and computing equipment which posted, totaled, and balanced the information. The rise in productivity was given as the explanation for the constant number of personnel, even though the activity of the department increased. During the period being studied, there were machine improvements, increased know-how in their operation, and increased know-how in the scheduling of manpower. Accordingly, there might have been an increase in clerical personnel in tabulating and computing if machine and administrative productivity had not increased during the mechanization of costing.

The number of supervisors did not change in accounting, although the number of clerical personnel declined (see Table 1). The constant number of supervisors was attributed to the efforts to establish the new methods and to the relationship between the assistant supervisor and the administrative personnel. The person interviewed said that approximately half the supervisor's efforts were directed toward modifying or streamlining the manual operations which were being integrated into the mechanized process. Some of the supervisor's work,

The increase in administrative personnel occurred in the accounting operations (see Table 1). Before the mechanization of costing, the accounting operations had one administrative employee, a cost analyst. This position was replaced by that of section supervisor, and the number was increased to four. The new position combined the duties of the cost analyst with other duties. The cost analyst had pre-

Table 1. *Distribution of Employment Associated with the Utilization of a Medium, General-Purpose Computer and Tabulating Equipment in a Costing Operation at a Steel Works, 1952 and 1957*

	OPERATION OF COMPUTING AND TABULATING EQUIPMENT		ACCOUNTING OPERATION		TOTAL	
	No. Employed	Employment as Per Cent of Operation	No. Employed	Employment as Per Cent of Operation	No. Employed	Employment as Per Cent of Operation
Clerical and semi-technical:						
1952	22	91.7	39	90.7	61	91.0
1957	22	91.7	22	75.9	44	83.0
Total managerial:						
1952	2	8.3	4	9.3	6	9.0
1957	2	8.3	7	24.1	9	17.0
Administrative:						
1952	—	—	1	2.3	1	1.5
1957	—	—	4	13.8	4	7.5
Supervisory:						
1952	2	8.3	3	7.0	5	7.5
1957	2	8.3	3	10.3	5	9.4
Total employment:						
1952	24	100.0 *	43	100.0 *	67	100.0 *
1957	24	100.0 *	29	100.0 *	53	100.0 *

* The components may not add up to the total because of rounding of percentage figures.

consequently, was said to have been shifted to the assistant supervisor. The major duties of the assistant supervisor were formally transferred to a new position, section supervisor, which primarily involved administrative work. In practice, however, the assistant supervisor retained these duties—assigning, supervising, and reviewing clerical work. Either one of two explanations seemed plausible. The administrative work of the new position may have been more time-consuming than originally anticipated, or the company may have been unwilling to displace the assistant supervisor.

pared and edited a monthly letter on the cost experience of various profit centers. As mentioned above, the section supervisors formally took over the supervision of the clerical accounting operations; but, in practice, the assistant supervisor appeared to have retained the function. The additional activities which appeared to be associated with the expansion of administrative personnel were twofold. The section supervisors were said to analyze and interpret costing data for line supervisors and advise them on handling accounting items. The section supervisors were also given the responsibility for compiling special reports which interpreted cost data.

The additional administrative personnel, consequently, were associated with the extension of cost analysis. The person interviewed believed that the mechanization of costing made possible the more elaborate reporting of information which was necessary for the most extensive analysis. The more extensive analysis, however, was attributed to the effort to gain greater operating efficiency by evaluating and comparing costs continually. Essentially, there was a change in the orientation of accounting from keeping books on cost results to analyzing the results. The more elaborate reporting of information required complex and specialized accounting procedures for each cost area, and the more complex and specialized accounting procedures along with the more extensive analysis apparently required a concomitant increase in the number and specialization of administrative personnel.

Between 1952 and 1957 the use of manpower for establishing the costing system and procedures varied from one to five. Three persons were being utilized at the close of the period under review to continue the development of tabulating and electronic procedures for costing.[5] The difference in the number utilized for establishing systems and procedures

at the manufacturing company and at the steel company may be explained by the breadth of operations involved. The informational systems included in the analysis of the manufacturing company were payroll, inventory, sales, fixed assets accounting, and production control, while only cost accounting was included in the analysis of the steel company.

In sum, the *decrease* in clerical and semitechnical personnel was attributed to a change in the manpower required to process data with the new methods from that required to process data with the old methods, but the *increase* in managerial personnel was not attributed to such a change. The absence of a decline and the increase in managerial personnel were attributed to the efforts to modify manual clerical operations, to the extension of cost analysis, and, perhaps, to a lag in reducing supervisory personnel. The relative and numerical rise in managerial personnel would have been greater if all the manpower concerned with establishing and developing the costing system and procedures had been included. Both the efforts to revise manual operations and the efforts to develop and initiate new techniques were part of the process of changing to the new methods, and the efforts to extend cost analysis were believed to be part of the process of changing the cost-price relationship. One may surmise, accordingly, that the relative growth of managerial personnel was primarily associated with the process of changing to the new techniques and with management's over-all efforts to modify company operations.

[5] Two of the three were managerial personnel and were not included in Table 1, since they were not employed in the costing operations at the steelworks. The third was a semitechnical employee, and he was included in Table 1 under computing and tabulating operations. The relative growth of managerial personnel would have been greater, therefore, if all the manpower concerned with establishing the costing system and procedures had been included.

The Impact of Recruitment on the Organization
of the Large Law Firm

ERWIN O. SMIGEL

Competition for the services of a "special kind" of lawyer has forced the large law firms [1] to modify their structure in order to compete more effectively with each other and with other agencies seeking similar legal talent. This paper analyzes (1) some of the personnel requirements for the legal staff of the large law firm, (2) the changes in environment which influence recruitment mechanisms and processes, and (3) the way these factors have resulted in adaptive organizational change. It thus provides examples of some aspects of structural alteration in an organization—an area where illustrations are sorely needed. [2] In addition, the study provides information concerning side effects of planned organizational change.

It is hoped that the following discussion carries meaning beyond the understanding of some structural changes in law firms. The functioning and perhaps the survival of social systems in general depend on their personnel. This, in turn, as in the law office, is contingent on how well a system is organized to recruit and maintain its supply of manpower. The recruitment mechanism is not a separate or distinct department or organ of a social system. Any feature of a social system, for example, conditions of job security or an organization's reputation for fair dealing, may enhance or depress its attractiveness to the prospective member and from this point of view may be considered an aspect of the recruitment system or mechanism. Any part of an organization, then, may be important to the recruitment process.

Alterations in the environment, in the available labor market, say, or in the competitive situation, or changes in the functions of an organization requiring personal qualities or skills or both which are different from those the system currently recruits, may result in

From *American Sociological Review*, Vol. 25, Feb. 1960, pp. 56–66. Reprinted with permission of the author and the publisher, American Sociological Association.

Revision of a paper read at the annual meeting of the American Sociological Society, August, 1958. The research was supported by a grant from the Graduate School at Indiana University and by a Fellowship in Law and the Behavioral Sciences at the University of Chicago Law School. This paper deals with a small portion of a larger study of the Wall Street lawyer and the organization of large law firms. . . . [The author is] indebted to Albert K. Cohen for his numerous suggestions.
[1] Only law firms with 50 or more lawyers were considered large. Eighteen of the 21 law firms with 50 or more lawyers in New York City are included in this study. The largest firm had 125 lawyers connected with it. Three firms located outside New York were also studied in order to test the importance of location on the organization of law offices.

[2] For an excellent historical analysis of the effect of recruitment, see Sigmund Diamond, "From Organization to Society: Virginia in the Seventeenth Century," *American Journal of Sociology*, 53, March, 1958, pp. 457–475.

changes in a social system. Since so much depends upon the nature of personnel, both the failure of a system to recruit individuals capable of carrying on its activities and the difficulty or insecurity in obtaining such personnel are serious sources of strain to which the system may be highly sensitive. Organizational changes are often made to reduce such strain. Of course, adaptive changes of this kind occur not only in law firms but in other social units.

METHOD. The data for this paper were obtained from a number of sources, among them semistructured interviews, averaging two hours, with 188 lawyers from 21 different large law firms. Placement officers of the law schools at Chicago, Columbia, Harvard, Yale, and New York Universities were also interviewed and, where possible, their office records were examined. In addition, some senior law students from these schools were asked about their job preferences. A simple thematic content analysis was undertaken of job announcements sent to Harvard Law School. Finally, an analysis was made of the background characteristics of all the partners (468) of 20 large law firms in New York City.[3]

PERSONNEL REQUIREMENTS. The large law offices and especially the giants of Wall Street have, as one associate put it, ". . . an inflated idea of what they want. They're looking for well rounded men who are law review."[4] Actually they want more than that. They want men who also have pleasing personalities, are from the "right" schools with the "right" social backgrounds, have a "cleancut" appearance, and are endowed with tremendous stamina. A former dean of a law school states:

> To get a job they [students] should be long enough on family connections, long enough on ability or long enough on personality, or a combination of these. Something called acceptability is made up of the sum of its parts. If a man has any one of these things, he could get a job—if he has two of them,

he can have a choice of jobs—if he has three, he could go anywhere. . . .

The large law firms prefer the man with all three attributes: lineage, ability, and personality. What they want, what they need, and what they get are related, but are not necessarily the same thing. The large law firms recruit manpower in order to do their job, provide continuity to the firms, and keep existing performance up to the clients' expectations and to the lawyers' own high standards. It is not essential for the operation of a firm that all of their lawyers have all three attributes. This is so if only because the firms have developed a hierarchical system of practice which allows the best and most experienced lawyers to supervise those less able and less experienced. The firms' actual needs, in fact, include lawyers who can and are willing to do routine work. The firms' recruitment policies, moreover, are generally geared to what is wanted and not to what is absolutely needed. The senior men are accustomed to dealing with able and energetic people and would be impatient with others. In addition, seeing themselves as an elite and viewing their work as highly important, they want to perpetuate this image. Thus there is keen competition for the preferred lawyer—the personable man from one of the select eastern law schools, who graduated with honors from an Ivy League college, and was at the top of his law school class. That high academic attainment in law school is important in recruitment is noted in a Harvard Law School report which states that many firms request "as a qualification that a man have 'B or better' grades."[5] Confirmation of this point is found in the breakdown of the job activities since graduation of the Yale Law School graduating classes for 1955, 1956, and 1957, which reveal that 53 per cent of the Yale men the large law firms in New York City employed came from the top quarter of their

---

[3] Data for this analysis were derived from the 1957 issue of the *Martindale-Hubbell Law Directory*, Rahway, N.J.: Quinn and Boden, 1957, Vol. II.

[4] Law review or law journal men are law students who run the legal journals and who usually are at the top academically of their class.

[5] *Harvard Law School Placement Information* (a leaflet published at Harvard), September, 1956, p. 3. Walter S. Carter is credited, "as far back as 1860," with initiating the recruiting system adopted by the larger law firms. It was his practice to pick the best students from the law schools and take them into his office. See Otto E. Koegel, *Walter S. Carter, Collector of Young Masters*, New York: Round Table Press, 1955, pp. x, 3, 8.

classes, and that 27 per cent were from the first decile.

The large firms want and obtain men from the elite eastern law schools. Seventy-four per cent of the sample graduated from Harvard, Yale, and Columbia law schools. A survey of the 468 partners listed in the *Martindale-Hub-bel Law Directory* of 1957 from 20 large New York City firms shows that 71 per cent of them were graduates of Harvard, Yale, and Columbia. This figure is of special importance since almost all men who become partners (employers) in large law offices begin their careers as associates (employees) fresh from law school. Significantly, also, 32 per cent of these men are listed, or belong to families who are listed, in the Social Register.

CHANGES IN THE ENVIRONMENT. While the large firms obtain some of the men they want, each firm wants a greater proportion of these men.[6] The increasing competition for these elitists initially stems from the increasing amount of practice going to this kind of firm. This expansion of legal work is generally attributed to the continuing growth of big business and to the multiplication of laws affecting commerce.[7] Riesman also suggests that "it takes more people to do the same amount of work and that ever higher standards of conspicuous production go into the definition of the standard of work—Parkinson's law, in other words." [8] Personal observation suggests that while Wall Street lawyers work very hard today, they probably do not work as hard (as indicated by historical sources) as their predecessors did in the past—another reason why

more lawyers are needed to do the job now.[9]

The growing number of large law firms throughout the country is perhaps of more importance. One author, by examining the legal directories published up to 1900, found that most firms were very small (by current standards) during the nineteenth century.[10] Today, in addition to the 21 large offices in New York City, there are seventeen large law firms operating in other sections of the country; in 1949 only five of the seventeen could have boasted of 50 or more lawyers. These firms along with most of the other large legal organizations have grown in size. Available figures for the population of lawyers for fifteen of these large firms located outside of New York indicate that in 1959 about 347 more lawyers were connected with these organizations than in 1949. This increase discloses only a portion of the call for lawyers, for during the 1949–1959 decade some lawyers left the firms and other law school graduates had to be found to replace them. These firms look for the same kind of lawyers as do the more numerous Wall Street firms. Forty-one per cent of the lawyers from one large California law office graduated from Harvard and Yale law schools. Generally, however, (and this is particularly true of Texas firms though not of the largest Massachusetts firm) large offices outside of New York are more willing to hire lawyers from schools other than the eastern elite institutions.

The turnover in the New York firms is sizable, often more than ten men a year for the larger offices. This occurs in part because of the departure of misfits and malcontents and in part because a number of Wall Street firms have recently adopted an "up-or-out" policy:

[6] It is not possible in this paper to present extensive evidence indicating the increased demand for the preferred lawyer. Much of the material for this assertion is to be found in the detailed interviews upon which a good portion of this study is based. To supplement these interviews and the available literature, in an effort to further assure accuracy, copies of the manuscript were sent to lawyers (including some managing partners and associate deans of law schools) involved with large law firms. They were asked to comment on the verity of the data. None took exception to the above statement.

[7] See, e.g., J. D. Wright, "The Lawyer's Role in Modern Industry," *Western Reserve Law Review,* 9 (September, 1958), pp. 425–426.

[8] Letter from David Riesman, September 8, 1958.

[9] Henry W. Taft in *A Century and A Half At the New York Bar* (New York: privately printed, 1938, p. 40) quotes Mr. Strong, a member of a firm which eventually became the large Wall Street firm of Cadwalader, Wickersham, and Taft, and who in 1824 wrote: "During the whole winter I have been confined in the office from about 8 in the morning till about 10 at night and at work as busily as a man in harvest." See also David Riesman, "Law and Sociology: Recruitment, Training and Collagueship," *Stanford Law Review,* 9 (July, 1957), p. 666.

[10] Edwin C. Austin, "Some Comments on Large Law Firms," *The Practical Lawyer,* 3 (April, 1957), p. 9.

if a firm decides that an associate is not going to be made a partner, he is informed of the decision so that he may either look for another job or accept one found for him by the firm. This policy, plus the insistent demands made by the firm's corporate [11] clients for lawyers to work in their organizations, creates a constant call for preferred lawyers. Thus the usual demand for such lawyers is increased by the departure of more associates from the law firms. In addition, there is initial recruiting competition for the preferred lawyer by government agencies, the courts, corporations, and universities.

Competition is complicated by the proportional reduction in admissions to the Bar in the United States. The rate of admission in 1930 was 81 per million population, in 1958 only 57.[12] It is further complicated by the large law firms' preference for men from the Ivy League eastern schools and the fact that these institutions have had no significant rise in the number of registrants,[13] and by the firms' reluctance to hire women [14] and lawyers from other "minority" groups. This reluctance is breaking down, probably because of changes in the general atmosphere concerning minority groups—and because of increasing competition. The large firms also seek men from the midwest, though not in any great numbers; but the graduates from the midwestern schools

seem not to have the same predilection as do students from eastern elite schools to join large law firms.

While most large law firms are now employing Jewish lawyers as associates, they probably limit the number of Jews they will accept. Judge Proskauer, a senior partner in a major "Jewish" firm, in 1949, wrote:

> . . . It did not take me many days to discover that the doors of most New York law offices in 1899 were closed with rare exceptions, to a young Jewish lawyer. Fifty years have elapsed since then and I am happy to record that there has been a distinct improvement in the situation; though it still remains true that generally the Jewish student must qualify twice for such employment.[15]

This continuing, though impressively modified restriction against Jewish lawyers, cuts down the number of potential recruits who meet at least the high academic requirements demanded by the large firms. That this seems to be the case is reenforced by the estimates of law school officials who indicate that the proportions of Jewish students attending Ivy League law schools has increased. Their estimates are borne out in some measure by a B'nai B'rith report of a 54 per cent increase in Jewish enrollments in Ivy League colleges between 1946 and 1955; [16] such undergraduate training is a prelude perhaps to matriculation in Ivy League law schools. In addition, the number of Jews at the top of their graduating classes is large. At Yale Law School, for example, it was estimated by contributors to the *Law Journal* that 63 per cent of the members of the journal for 1955–1956 and 1956–1957 were Jewish. By eliminating some Jews from consideration the firms cut down their potential supply of academically superior individuals.

WHAT LAW SCHOOL GRADUATES WANT. What the large law firms want has been described; what they can obtain depends not only on the available supply and competitive conditions

---

[11] Wright finds that private industry employed 15,063 full-time practicing lawyers in 1954, 3,789 more than they did in 1950. *Op cit.,* p. 427.

[12] Ross L. Malone, "Lawyers—Supply and Demand," *Trusts and Estates,* 98 (March, 1959), p. 186.

[13] Comparison of the combined law school registration of Harvard, Yale, and Columbia for 1948 and 1958 indicates a gain of only 151 students, an increase of five per cent. However, the 1958 registrants represent a *decrease* of 550 students from the year 1947. These figures are based on data compiled by John G. Hervey; see "Law School Registration, 1949," *Journal of Legal Education,* 2 (Winter, 1949), pp. 218, 220–221, and "Law School Registration, 1958," *Journal of Legal Education,* 11 (2, 1958), pp. 259, 263, 266.

[14] Women lawyers are not discussed in this paper. There are only eighteen in New York City who list themselves as working in large New York Law firms in a directory of women lawyers. Dorothy Thomas, editor, *Women Lawyers in the United States,* New York: Scarecrow Press, 1957.

[15] Joseph M. Proskauer, *A Segment of My Times,* New York: Farrar, Straus and Young, 1950, p. 30.

[16] Robert Shosteck, *The Jewish College Student,* Washington, D.C.: B'nai B'rith Vocational Service, 1957, p. 37.

but on the relationships between what the firms have to offer and what the potential recruits themselves want. The law school senior thinks about where he wants to go, what he wants to do, and how he wants to practice.

Location of the job is often mentioned as a consideration, the West being frequently cited as a preference. The evidence indicates, however, that if the fledgling lawyer believes that opportunity lies in New York City and the East instead of San Francisco and the West, he will go East. Harvard Law School records, for example, show that of the 105 Harvard men hired by the large law firms in New York City for a selected three-year period, 21 stated that they had hoped to obtain positions outside of New York City.

Many law seniors have no particular preferences as to fields of the law. These undecided constituted the largest number in the 1957 graduating class at Harvard.[17] While the rest of the class did indicate preferences, the desired fields of work named by most seniors often differ from later choices. This was true for members of the sample. Again, the larger opportunity rather than a specific branch of the law seems to be the more important element influencing job choice. As the market becomes more competitive, however, the neophyte can become more selective, and therefore the ability of the firm to offer the location and specialty the potential recruit prefers becomes correspondingly more important.

Perhaps of greater significance to the young lawyer is the setting in which he chooses to practice. A major decision the job seeker from the eastern elite schools must make is whether or not to practice in a large law firm. Many students, of course, especially from the eastern schools, desire to practice in large law firms. This is evidenced by the many uninvited but welcome applicants for jobs in large law firms each year. It is understandable that these offices should draw a considerable number of men, for they offer prestige, good starting salaries, and a potentially high future income; they also handle the largest and probably the most interesting corporate matters and are at the

center of the business community's power structure. But many other students have clearly decided against the large firm for such reasons as the following: "I don't want to get lost in those law factories." "They make you specialize too soon." "I don't care for that kind of impersonal practice; I want to help people with their problems." "The work is too routine." "You're not your own boss." "You don't get enough responsibility." "The work is too hard." "You have to wait too long to become a partner—you can move up faster in a small firm." "I want to have some time with my family." "You don't see clients or learn how to get them."

Many lawyers who finally enter the large law firms hold attitudes about the firms shared by those who do not enter them. These reluctant lawyers look for an organization where they will not feel as lost, will not have to specialize as quickly, and where they will do more responsible and interesting work. In addition to this desire to modify the negative aspects of work in the large law firm, some men, explain their choice of a particular organization by citing available postgraduate education, a chance to get ahead quickly, the opportunity to deal with "big matters," work with interesting people, or several of these reasons.

Law students, however, often base their job choices according to placement officers and the evidence obtained from interviews with seniors and individuals in the sample, on personal bias, half truths, myths, fads, and other factors not normally considered important in making such decisions. The recruiter must take these factors into account in a tight job market.

The most frequently heard "reputational myth" involves the notion that one or two firms work much harder and much longer than other large firms. There are legends about the kinds of clients of a firm; there is the rumor that certain offices will not hire female or Jewish lawyers. Often a firm is given a "short-term halo" based on the report of a returning alumnus. The decision to join a certain firm sometimes depends upon how a man "feels" about the organization. Thus one associate reporting on a position he had refused: "While they offered me a job, I didn't feel they wanted me"; and a student respondent speaking of a partner who had just interviewed him: "He's the nicest fellow I've ever met."

[17] *Harvard Law School Placement Information, op. cit.*, p. 2. Examination of other information bulletins reveals some variation in the order of preference.

To the anxious recruit the hiring partner represents a symbol of things to come.

IMAGE-MAKING MACHINERY. It is to these wishes and notions that law firms must cater and that, when appropriate, they try to manipulate or change. In a competitive market, with its scarcity of preferred men, students can be selective. Under these circumstances, the firms first sell the idea of practicing in the large organizations to the reluctant or ambivalent recruit. (The Harvard Law School Association of New York City holds a smoker each Christmas holiday for Harvard Law School job hunters to which they invite speakers who present the case for employment in large law firms, small firms, and corporations.) The firms then try to sell themselves individually, hoping that these devices will maximize their chances to attract the preferred type of men.

To change, maintain, or create attractive images, and to assure or reassure the recruit, the firms send notices to the placement offices of the law schools in which they plead innocent to certain detrimental charges and claim desirable attributes. This is part of their "image-making machinery." In order to determine the content of these notices, announcements sent to Harvard Law School were analyzed. Examples from these bulletins illustrate the main themes: Most of them are designed to bolster a desire to defeat a fear.

One fear law students have about the large firm is that they will be forced to specialize before they know what they really wish to do. Some firms belittle this anxiety by assuring that they are ". . . not as rigidly departmentalized as some very large offices," or by reporting that "In so far as possible, law clerks are given an opportunity to work on problems in those fields in which they are most interested and are not required to select a specialty or confine their work to one field." Hand in hand with qualms about early specialization is the anxiety about not receiving "proper training." Attempts are made to allay both of these fears. One announcement reads:

> Men coming with the firm directly out of law school are not assigned to a department of the office until they have been with the firm for one or two years. During this period conscious effort is made to see that these men have the opportunity to work

with as many different partners in as many different fields of the law as possible. Emphasis is placed on broad general experience. This will include not only research work and preparation of memoranda of law but also drafting legal papers, participation in conferences and with clients, attendance at court hearings, several weeks' experience in the managing clerks' department and generally a month with the New York legal aid society.

Some firms announce that they do not use the pool system (through which a lawyer can be assigned to do anything for anybody), hoping that this statement will help to blunt the senior's fear that he will "get lost" in the large organization. To assure him of his independence, one firm declares: "It is the purpose of our training to bring a man to the point where he can work independently as quickly as he is able to." To assure recruits of security, firms announce that they do not place men from the outside over old associates; or that they receive requests from corporations for lawyers, so that if individuals are not admitted to partnerships their future nevertheless is assured.

These promotional notices to the law schools make a difference, but their effect is limited. In addition to announcing opportunities, they may weaken the resolve of some men against the large law firm and strengthen favorable predisposition of others. Mainly they make claims for their firms and assist in creating an image. Over a period of time, however, such promotional activities can have only limited influence. For if the claims are not implemented by commitments which correspond to the reality of the organizational experience, disappointed personnel and a seriously damaged public image spread by disaffected personnel are the result. In the long run, then, the credibility of the firms' claims depends to a great extent on their readiness to back up their statements by corresponding changes in organizational structure and functioning.

ORGANIZATIONAL ADAPTATION. Competition for lawyers among the large law firms in New York City is limited in two major ways: the firms will not pirate an employee from another law office; and they maintain a gentlemen's agreement to pay the same beginning salary, commonly called the "going rate." [18] However, although these agreements limit salary competition somewhat, they intensify competition in other respects. Most of these firms are old and conservative and proud of both these attributes, and therefore impose upon themselves further limits as to what they will do to attract legal talent. Nonetheless, it is necessary for immediate and long-run survival to recruit "proper" legal talent. To do this, changes in the organization of the law firms have been made to meet the demands of the recruit. This has occurred despite the fact that there is resistance to such change, especially on the part of the older, more conservative partners. These men, who often seem to think of themselves as akin to small-town general practitioners, do not like the notion of a segmented, departmentalized, hierarchical organization, regarding it as something not quite professional. They also resent the time reorganization may take away from the practice of the law and make changes only when they persistently believe that they must. When changes do take place they do not happen quickly. [19]

Law firms no longer believe that they can afford to wait until the candidate comes to them: more and more, firms are sending lawyers to visit the major schools to look over the crop for the next year. Harvard, for example, was visited in 1955–1956 by representatives of 185 law firms and corporations, and in 1956–1957 by 194 prospective employers. This practice, and the tradition of law offices of seeing anyone who wants a job, have led to the formalization of the role of "hiring partner," who is generally one of the most attractive and personable of the partners. Creation of this position is an early attempt by a firm to put its best foot forward. The hiring partner is needed not only to attract graduates but to save the valuable time of other partners. While visiting the various law schools, the hiring partner weeds out the poorer prospects and invites the better ones to visit the firm in New York. The hiring partner is also more able than his colleagues to evaluate the candidates since he sees a good percentage of all applicants. In addition to the men invited to visit firms, each year between the Thanksgiving and Christmas holidays there is a mass migration of other young lawyers to Wall Street.

Some firms—in self defense but also to maintain good will and a good reputation at the law schools and with the legal profession, while at the same time continuing their work and recruitment—have set up elaborate systems to take care of the estimated 300 to 400 candidates seen during the year. One large firm developed the following system:

[18] A small number of cases have been reported in which these agreements were not strictly adhered to.

The going rate in 1958 was 6,500 dollars for a beginning lawyer; it was 4,000 dollars in 1953. Thus, while the major firms agree on salary, they must take into consideration competition from other sources. The firms do compete, however, by raising psychic, as well as other kinds of relatively intangible, "income."

Another indication of increased competition is found in the reports that some firms are beginning to "wine and dine" prospective employees, using recruiting techniques of big business. This is not only an index of competition; it also irritates many lawyers who must resort to this procedure, even though in only a limited way, for they feel it is not "professional."

Competition for the preferred lawyer is further pointed up by the willingness of law firms to hire some seniors, although they are scheduled to go into the armed forces before they can practice, in order to insure the firm of their services after they are discharged.

[19] Cf. Emily P. Dodge, "Evolution of a City Law Office, Part 1: Office Organization," *Wisconsin Law Review*, 2 (March, 1955), p. 182.

Any lawyer who applies for a position is interviewed, no one being turned away. Ten to twelve associates are designated as interviewers. The receptionist tries to spread the work around. Each associate rates the candidate as a "one," "two," or "three." If rated "one," the candidate is sent to a partner who sits on the hiring committee. If rated "two," the applicant may be "all right" but the associate does not think him acceptable; but he is also sent to a partner—though generally he is given less time. A "three" rating means that the applicant is rejected; even rejected candidates, however, are sent to a partner, though not necessarily one who is a member of the hiring committee. The partner spends five minutes with a "three" and then sends him on his way—but he tries to leave the applicant with a favorable impression of the firm. If the partner disagrees with the associate, he refers the candidate to a member of the hiring committee, where each man rated as "one" is sent immediately. At least three people on the hiring committee see this highly rated applicant. If the candidate passes this test, then the hiring partners have him see other partners.

Not all firms have such an elaborate procedure. One law office assigns fourteen partners to duty, three different ones each day, who do the screening. This procedure reflects the view that better public relations are maintained if partners do the initial interviewing rather than associates. If one of these partners passes favorably on an applicant, he is sent to two or more partners. Eventually he is interviewed by the hiring partner, who sees all candidates and compares them, a process which requires valuable time; but this expenditure is thought to be necessary and well worthwhile.

Another device of the large law firms to further selective recruitment is to invite second-year law students to clerk with them during the summer. Most firms do not really need these "summer boarders" as workers, but their value is threefold: the boarders get to know the firm; they provide the firm with a preview of their ability—if they are good and are liked, they are offered jobs when they graduate; in any event, they return to the law schools and report what they have seen. Spending some time being pleasant to the summer boarders and at times designating partners to look after them during their temporary stay, these clerks, it is hoped, will help to paint a favorable picture of the firms.

When a firm makes a major revision in its organization because of recruitment, it does so to meet the similar demands of a number of candidates. Generally such a change is further justified because it also satisfies other internal requirements. In some instances the alterations are made primarily to satisfy other demands and secondarily as a recruitment device.

One request most applicants make of law firms is that they provide opportunities for training. This request is closely related to the seniors' fear that they will be forced into quick specialization. Candidates are told that they will be provided diversity in their work, and the firms try to do this. Usually this plan is frustrated by the fact that an associate who has

been successful in one kind of work becomes known as "good" or "expert" in that particular area of law; more of his colleagues then send him work in his now acclaimed "specialty," so that soon he becomes an expert in fact. Thus, it is costly for the firm to change his functions, and partners who have been relieved of this particular job and hence save time and energy, are reluctant to take it on again. Consequently, the associate remains in his special area and does not get the broad training he desires. More and more firms, however, finding themselves committed to training their new men (because it is a good recruiting device, to be sure, but also because many partners think that it helps to make better lawyers and therefore benefits the firm), are beginning to formalize further their educational programs. In a sense these firms are becoming postgraduate vocational schools.

One of the largest law partnerships is ahead of the others in this respect. The hiring partner in this office, who had devised the educational program, found that it was attracting candidates and was becoming known in law schools and throughout the "street." This formalized program, designed to provide for varied experience, is described by its sponsor as follows:

We have a rotating system. An associate has to spend a portion of three years in three different departments. I keep a chart of where they've been and how long they stay and when they've been in a department long enough I move them. We found that unless you have regular notices that the man is changing departments you don't move the man properly. If you do it without the records and without the formality, you find that a man is never free and the people involved in the problem have forgotten about rotating.

This firm decided that this program had to be installed if they were going to give good training. Despite this, it still meets with individual resistance. A partner will say "I just get a man trained and you take him away from me." Some of the partners said that we aren't running a school. They feel, however, that eventually they will get good lawyers. The associates like it and that's one reason why I get such good results in hiring. We do a lot of things for our associates. We even send them to special courses, like tax courses.

As they debate the merits of large firms, recruits often complain that "you don't get ahead fast enough—it takes forever to make partner." Some firms assign the title "Junior Partner" to their senior associates, perhaps creating the illusion that the associates are moving up faster than they actually are—and this illusion may aid the firm in its recruitment efforts. Many firms have initiated rules and other changes to reassure ambitious recruits. For example, candidates fear competition from relatives of partners, and members of a firm may fear the possibility of taking a colleague's unqualified son into the firm as a partner. Hence the increasing adoptions of a rule against nepotism.

Anxiety about being lost in the giant firm is often mentioned by both the applicant and the young associate. The pool system, although it functions formally as a training device, adds to that concern. In addition, many associates do not feel that this plan for work assignment is "professional." Because of the disapproval of the assignment of bright young lawyers to more or less mechanical jobs, some firms are doing away with the pool system.

The "up-or-out rule" is designed to provide that lawyers who are not going to be made partners leave the firm and so insure a constant flow of new talent into the organization. This rule also has the side effect of counteracting the complaint that "you never know how you're doing," it requires that eventually (usually within a ten-year period) associates be informed that they are not going to be partners. Thus the rule guarantees a steady turnover in the law firms. One consequence is that some offices function as employment centers in order to give security to their associates, to demonstrate their own view that it is not "professional" (or at least not "nice") to fire a lawyer, and to provide their corporate clients with good legal and executive talent. Generally the managing partner solicits jobs and suggests associates from his firm to fill them. Some offices cultivate this function more than others and can provide excellent job opportunities for their future alumni. While not every man can become a partner, very few leave the firm without a good position—some-

times one paying a higher salary than the missed partnership itself. The firms which best provide employment outlets win the reputation for "taking care of their men."

AN ADDITIONAL TYPE OF ADJUSTMENT. During World War II many large firms began to accept Jewish lawyers as associates at an accelerated rate. These Jews were usually in the top of their classes in the Ivy League colleges and law schools, and the firms, initially at any rate, hired them partly because competition made it difficult always to secure the lawyers they preferred. Probably it will become more of a problem, however, for law firms to continue to recruit Jewish lawyers if they do not promote some of them to partnerships. This is especially the case at the present time, since some of these lawyers are approaching completion of the approximately ten-year maturation period during which partnerships are decided. The American Jewish Congress survey of lawyers' employment experience reported in 1954 that there already existed some reluctance on the part of Jews to apply for certain jobs: "Over one-third [35 per cent] of the Jewish respondents [from the 1951 graduating class of Chicago, Columbia, Harvard and Yale law schools] reported that they refrained from making application to certain law firms and business houses because of a belief that these firms used discriminatory employment practices. . . ." [20] More recently one respondent declared that "the reason we don't have more Jews [in the firm] is that too many of them feel that they won't become partners and leave. Some won't even take a job with the firm."

Jewish lawyers appointed as partners provide models of success for Jewish candidates, demonstrating that it is possible for them to become partners. Certain New York offices have already promoted some of their Jewish associates to partnerships. (A few firms in the past have included Jewish partners, but usually these were "German" Jews whose families had been in this country for generations, and many of them have had important business connec-

[20] American Jewish Congress, Commission on Law and Social Action, *A Survey of the Employment Experiences of Law School Graduates of Chicago, Columbia, Harvard, and Yale Universities,* New York: mimeographed, 1954, p. 2.

tions.) Most respondents believe that the other firms will soon follow this example. This change in policy not only represents new unofficial rules but may alter the social complexion and perhaps the "family" and clublike atmosphere of the law office. Nonetheless, even "white shoe" firms[21] are now recruiting Jewish lawyers, and these firms also will find, if they wish to hire the bright Jewish law review editor, that it is good recruitment policy to provide models of success.

SIDE EFFECTS RESULTING FROM ORGANIZATIONAL CHANGE. Changes designed to aid recruitment affect the organization beyond the desired goal, and each alteration produces side effects. Formalization of the position of hiring or assignment partner, for example, means that the lawyers occupying this position assume new managerial duties and are compelled to curtail their practice of the law. The development of these managerial posts also signifies that the younger partners who usually fill them must be given enough authority to carry out their roles. This necessity results in a slight shift in the power relations within the firms.

In some instances, what began as a small alteration has snowballed into something of major importance. Many firms, as noted above, now promise the recruit job security—either within the firm or elsewhere. It was not too difficult to fulfill this promise until some law offices instituted the "up-or-out rule"; but then the increased placement needs required a great deal of work. It is important that the firms satisfy both their corporate clients and their associates, since their activities in these areas are closely tied in with their ability to recruit and to place more men. The relatively minor task of finding jobs for some of their associates with corporate clients has grown to large proportions; one firm estimates that it has as many as 800 alumni.

Similarly, the promise made by law offices to provide advanced training for their recruits has led some firms to formalize their educational procedures. Among the side effects of

this change is the development of additional managerial and tutorial duties and the loss of some measure of freedom by partners, for it is now difficult for them to keep men they have personally trained and whom they like.

Other side effects have been noted. Tasks which were meant to be temporary or minor tend to become fixed—for example, running employment bureaus, recruiting at law schools, taking in summer boarders. Almost all such changes call for new rules and further integration on the part of the law firms.

SUMMARY AND DISCUSSION. The recruitment standards of the large law firm are high, and they are hard to meet because competition for preferred men is strong and increasing. Therefore, law school graduates who fulfill the high standards can be more discriminating than formerly in their choice of jobs. The law offices try to satisfy some of the demands of the preferred graduates in a number of different ways, and not all firms have adopted all methods.

The development of "image-making machinery," however, is an adaptation made by all of the large firms. Most offices also have formalized the role of "hiring partner." Other changes include provisions for training, speedier advancement into the rank of junior or limited partner, "up-or-out" rules, regulations against nepotism, and reduction of discrimination against the employment of Jews and women.

These alterations are designed partly to help the firms meet the manpower problems, and the adaptations constitute changes in the recruitman mechanism. This mechanism includes any aspect of the structure or functioning of the system that affects the intake and loss of personnel. Therefore, changes in the mechanism refer not only to the recruitment process in the narrow and commonly understood sense but also to alterations in the firm which affect its attracting and holding power. These alterations can take place in any port of an organization, for in reality the whole system is part of the recruitment mechanism.

Organizational changes to meet the demands of growing competition for preferred lawyers often produce unanticipated consequences, mainly in the direction of increased bureaucratization. This tendency is indicated by the

[21] Firms, like the schools themselves, are sometimes called "white shoe" when they are composed in large part of lawyers from Ivy League schools with Social Register backgrounds.

development of formal rules and formal strat-ification and the formalization of training duties.[22]

Some changes and side effects of planned change lead to new strains and dilemmas. Con-cerning the function of the law firm: "Are we a law firm or a school?" On the employ-ment of women and Jews: "What will our clients think?" "What will it do to our little family?" In satisfying short-term needs as against possible long-term benefits: "If we in-augurate an 'up-or-out' policy we will be los-ing men who know their job and are valuable to the firm." On the use of corporation tech-niques of recruitment: "Is it professional?"—There are other problems, but the most in-teresting development has come about because the best students and young associates wish to be treated in what they consider to be a more professional manner—they want more independence and responsibility—and the firms needing these young lawyers set up systems of rules to protect them from the severity of im-personal organization. The young associate re-ceives short-run protection; the firm in the long-run becomes more bureaucratic. The law firms soon may be facing another and perhaps more important problem growing out of the need for further bureaucratic procedure at the possible cost of a less professional staff.

[22] While these features are not in themselves equivalent to bureaucracy they are among its de-fining characteristics. The relationship of bureauc-racy to the legal profession will be given fuller treatment in another publication.

Manpower and Innovation: Some Pointers for Management

FREDERICK HARBISON

Over the past 50 years, the percentage of man-agers, staff specialists, scientists, engineers, and other highly skilled workers in relation to total employment in industry has been steadily in-creasing, while the proportion of production workers has equally steadily declined. Latest available figures from the Bureau of Labor Sta-tistics show that, since the end of World War II, this trend has accelerated. Between 1947 and 1957, for example, while there was only about a 1 per cent increase in the numbers of produc-tion workers, the employment of non-produc-tion workers rose by some 55 per cent. From 1955 to 1957, there was actually a decrease in the absolute numbers of production workers, as compared with a 10 per cent increase in the employment of non-production workers. In fact, 90 per cent of the increase in manufactur-ing employment during the years 1947–1957 was accounted for by non-production workers.

Just why there has been this tremendous in-crease in the employment of executive, staff, professional, and technical personnel is a mat-ter of considerable dispute. Some writers on the subject, for example, have pointed to it as proof of the inexorable workings of "Parkin-son's Law," according to which, as is well known, administrators are bound to multiply, irrespective of the actual need for their serv-ices. Others have taken the view that the pro-liferation of reports now required by govern-ment agencies has been mainly responsible. Automation, the increased investment in re-search and development, the quickened pace of process and product innovations, company reorganizations, new administrative practices,

From *Personnel*, Vol. 36, No. 6, Nov.–Dec. 1959, pp. 8–15. Reprinted with permission of the pub-lisher, American Management Association.

and the high tax rates on profits have also been suggested as possible explanations.

The Industrial Relations Section at Princeton University recently undertook a study designed to clarify this question. Since a full account of the study's findings has been published in a special report,* I shall not attempt to review them in detail here. Rather, I propose to focus on the inferences which we of the Industrial Relations Section have drawn from the data we obtained.

Major Conclusions of the Study

To place the subject in its proper perspective, a brief account of the design of the study may, however, be in order. We began by obtaining employment statistics for the years 1947 and 1955 from 50 enterprises in a wide range of manufacturing and non-manufacturing industries. Some of the companies included were selected because it was expected that they would have experienced pronounced changes in the composition of their workforces; others were chosen because it seemed likely that their employment experience would show little change. Some were chosen mainly to provide coverage of significant industry groups. Though it cannot be claimed that the sample was statistically representative of U. S. industry as a whole, as it turned out, the experience of the participating companies appeared to correspond fairly well with what we know of national trends.

The statistics obtained were then used as a frame of reference for interviews with representatives of 47 of the 50 companies studied. In these interviews, we mainly sought to determine the factors accounting for changes, or the absence of changes, in each firm's occupational structure.

Here it may be said that we encountered considerable difficulty in obtaining the data we were seeking. Very few of the participating companies had personnel records that were sufficiently accurate to show the precise changes that had taken place in their occupational structure. Furthermore, few company

* S. E. Hill and F. Harbison, *Manpower and Innovation in American Industry*. Princeton University, Industrial Relations Section, Princeton, N.J., 1959.

representatives were able to recall what events had been associated with the changes their statistics revealed. In fact, many of the companies were not even aware that any changes had taken place, until they prepared the statistics we had requested. Nevertheless, the data we were able to obtain pointed to the following conclusions:

1. THE INCREASE IN HIGHLY TRAINED PERSONNEL AS A PERCENTAGE OF TOTAL EMPLOYMENT IN THE COMPANIES STUDIED WAS PRIMARILY THE RESULT OF INNOVATION. Under this term we include technological innovation—the introduction of new products or processes—and organizational innovation—the creation of new administrative units and new systems of management. Both these types of innovation had required increases in executive, administrative, and professional personnel in the companies studied. Technological innovation had also changed the composition of employment by decreasing the employment of production workers.

The automation of either production processes or office procedures provided especially striking examples of the relationship between innovation and employment composition. Automation, our data showed, usually resulted in the greater use of highly trained specialists, at the same time making it possible to effect substantial savings in manual or clerical work forces. In other words, automation nearly always led to the substitution of both high-talent manpower and capital for unskilled and semi-skilled personnel.

2. IN GENERAL, THE RATE OF INNOVATION APPEARED TO GOVERN THE RATE OF INCREASE IN THE USE OF SKILLED PERSONNEL OF ALL KINDS. The companies showing the greatest increases in non-production workers as a proportion of their total employment were invariably those which had made the most spectacular or far-reaching changes in products, processes, and organization.

3. COMPANIES THAT HAD THEMSELVES DEVELOPED NEW PRODUCTS OR DESIGNED NEW PROCESSES OR SYSTEMS OF ADMINISTRATION SHOWED A MUCH SHARPER INCREASE IN THE EMPLOYMENT OF HIGH-TALENT MANPOWER THAN FIRMS THAT RELIED PRIMARILY ON OUTSIDE CONSULTANTS OR EQUIPMENT SUPPLIERS. For example, the computer manufacturer studied required vastly

more high-talent manpower than companies that merely used computers. Our evidence indicates, in other words, that the companies that originate new processes, products, or administrative methods invariably use a greater proportion of high-talent manpower than those that merely adopt the innovations that others have developed.

4. THE DEVELOPMENT OF INNOVATIONS APPEARS TO HAVE AFFECTED THE OCCUPATIONAL STRUCTURE OF ENTIRE INDUSTRIES. Between 1947 and 1955, the ratio of non-production workers increased sharply in the aircraft, electronics, chemical, ordnance, and petroleum companies studied—all of them industries that had developed innovations for their own use, or for use by others. On the other hand, the proportion of highly skilled personnel increased less rapidly in the textile, apparel, lumber, railroad, and utility industries, which adopted, for the most part, innovations developed by others.

5. INNOVATION TENDS TO SPAWN MORE INNOVATION. Our data indicated that product and process innovation by one company in an industry was a spur to innovation among its competitors. The growth of research and development was one example of this tendency.

6. NO EVIDENCE WAS FOUND TO SUPPORT THE "PARKINSON'S LAW" HYPOTHESIS. Bureaucratic expansion, more popularly known as "empire building," may have been at work in some of the companies studied, particularly during periods of high prosperity and high profits. Nevertheless, the study indicated that, in comparison with other factors, it played only a very minor part in the increase in the proportion of non-production employees in company workforces.

7. INCREASING COMPANY SIZE AND THE ALLEGED INCREASE IN THE NUMBER OF REPORTS REQUIRED BY GOVERNMENT AGENCIES, WERE ALSO FOUND TO BE ERRONEOUS EXPLANATIONS FOR SHIFTS IN OCCUPATIONAL STRUCTURE. Among the companies studied, those that grew in size but did not innovate tended to employ a constant or declining percentage of their workforces in executive, professional, and related occupations. The reports required by government agencies were mentioned as a source of change in employment structure only by public utilities and railroads—in other words, the only

companies subject to direct government regulation. Companies in other industries said that most of the information required by government agencies was also necessary for the effective management of their affairs.

Hence, we concluded, the shift to greater use of high-talent manpower in the companies studied was associated primarily with dynamism and progress rather than with bureaucratic expansion or unwarranted increases in overhead costs. Although we were not able to measure the impact of the greater use of such personnel on total payroll costs, our interviews showed that innovation, and the increases in employment of skilled personnel which it required, resulted in higher overhead costs which bore fruit either in a decrease in total costs or an improvement in the quality of the products or services supplied.

What inferences may be drawn from these findings? Assuming that the rate of discovery and innovation in industry will be no less rapid over the next 20 years than it has been during the past decade (surely, not an implausible assumption), there are some implications well worth considering by every forward-looking management.

Some Implications for Management

1. MOST COMPANIES HAVE NEGLECTED TO ESTIMATE ACCURATELY THEIR FUTURE MANPOWER REQUIREMENTS. The majority of the companies we studied had made no serious attempt to estimate the occupational composition of their future labor forces. Moreover, the few that had made estimates of this kind had based them on the quite erroneous assumption that their present occupational composition would remain unchanged, which is tantamount to assuming that there will be no major innovations in the future. In 1955, for example, one company had made a five-year forecast of its manpower requirements. But by 1957, the number of managerial and professional employees the company estimated it would be employing in 1960 had already been exceeded. Here, obviously, no attempt had been made to study past changes in the company's occupational structure as a possible guide to future needs. And though many of the companies we studied were making detailed plans for the introduction of new processes, new products, and even

new systems of administration, in no case did we find any serious attempt to translate these plans into terms of the human resources needed to carry them out.

2. THE GREATER UTILIZATION OF PROFESSIONAL AND MANAGERIAL MANPOWER RESULTS IN AN INCREASE IN FIXED AND OVERHEAD COSTS. Almost all the companies we studied were concerned with the problem of mounting overhead expenses. In some, the total payments to salaried workers were already greater than the total wage bill for hourly rated or piece workers. In a few cases, the total compensation of managers and professional personnel was nearly equal to that of production personnel.

The trend here is clear. Total payments to wage earners are decreasing, whereas total payments to salaried workers are increasing, and in most companies the sharpest increases in total labor costs are undoubtedly those represented by managerial and professional personnel. The increase in the employment of professional, managerial, and other salaried employee groups in manufacturing between 1947 and 1957 caused total salaries to rise from one-fourth of manufacturing labor costs in 1947 to about one-third in 1957. During the 1949 and 1954 recessions, wage costs decreased more rapidly than salary costs.

3. UNIONS WILL DECLINE IN MEMBERSHIP. It is now fairly evident that the proportion of union members in American industry is likely to fall as the proportion of manual production workers drops. Unions in the United States have not as yet demonstrated much capacity for organizing technical, professional, and managerial personnel, and progress has been notably slow even in the organization of clerical personnel. Radical changes in the psychological orientation of white-collar employees as well as in the approach of unions toward them are needed to alter this situation. Only through the somewhat unlikely development of extremely inept management coinciding with unusually adept union strategy can we expect any substantial growth of union membership among white-collar workers to take place.

4. COMPETITION FOR PERSONNEL IN THE LABOR MARKET IS UNDERGOING A FUNDAMENTAL CHANGE. Companies are experiencing little or no difficulty in hiring manual and the less-skilled clerical workers. Indeed, many are more concerned about having to release such workers than with recruiting them. At the same time they are facing stiffer competition in hiring engineers, and even sharper competition in finding creative research scientists and engineers. Interfirm competition for managers and top administrative staff is also increasing. In the future, therefore, competitive relationships between firms in the labor market will be less related to general wage agreements with unions of manual workers and more dependent on the prices that persons of high training and talent are able to command for their services.

5. THE CHANGING COMPOSITION OF EMPLOYMENT WILL FORCE MANY COMPANIES TO REVISE THOROUGHLY OR DISCARD ALTOGETHER SOME LONG-STANDING NOTIONS OF WAGE AND SALARY ADMINISTRATION. In the future, it will become more important to base compensation on the capacities of individuals rather than upon categorical job descriptions. In many cases, professional personnel in non-supervisory positions may have to be given higher pay than managers. In fact, the entire hierarchical relationship between positions in an enterprise may have to be completely overhauled as old skills become obsolete and new ones rise in strategic importance.

Some companies are already faced with the necessity of paying a bright young mathematician fresh out of graduate school the same salary they now pay a manager with 15 to 20 years' service. As one company executive remarked to us: "What use is our salary administration program in ascertaining what we should pay for the best electronics engineer in the country?" In short, when competition in the labor market is for "brains" rather than for "hands," an entirely new approach to thinking about wage and salary administration may well be required.

6. EVEN MORE IMPORTANT THAN THE LARGER NUMBERS OF HIGHER-TALENT PEOPLE IN INDUSTRY IS THE PROBLEM OF THEIR EFFECTIVE UTILIZATION. It is more difficult in many cases to develop the industrial climate conducive to making highly talented people more creative than it is to provide incentives for making manual workers more productive. In dealing with high-talent manpower, entirely different concepts of the organization of work, of incentives, and of "human relations" between mana-

gers and the managed are necessary. This means that personnel policies will need to be thoroughly reexamined in the years ahead.

Much of the past effort in personnel administration has been directed toward treating the common man—the wage earner and the clerical employee—fairly and equally. Seniority systems have been created to eliminate favoritism and discrimination; job evaluation has been used to provide equal pay for equal work. In working out such problems as general wage increases, call-in pay, overtime, compensation for work on Saturdays and Sundays, vacations, pensions, supplementary unemployment benefits, sickness benefits, and related matters, the aim of the administrator has always been to establish rules for insuring equal and non-discriminatory treatment of the various categories of manual and clerical labor—in other words, to achieve conformity and consistency.

The Uncommon Man

But the skills and concepts that have worked well enough in dealing with the common man are not always those most appropriate for handling high-talent manpower. The engineer of today, the scientist, the professional person, is the *uncommon man*, the atypical being, the brainy guy, or the egg-head with queer but nonetheless valuable ideas. In dealing with employees of this type, the important thing is to know how to detect the differences rather than the similarities between people.

Objective discrimination and differential treatment are the vital skills required for the selection and effective use of high-talent manpower. Unfortunately, it is far more difficult for a manager to deal with people differently than it is for him to treat them uniformly, because to most people differential treatment means unfair discrimination. A simple illustration of this fact is the conventional retirement policy which requires that all employees cease work at a certain age. In its application to high-talent manpower, this policy needs revision.

7. THE FUTURE PRESAGES PROFOUND CHANGES IN THE TOP COMMAND POSTS OF INDUSTRY. It should be almost blindingly obvious to most companies that the greater employment of brainpower in industry will demand smarter and much more thoroughly and broadly trained top executives. It will not be possible for a top manager to learn by experience alone the things he must know to direct the affairs of tomorrow's enterprises. Even today, large companies are too complicated to be understood by the too-narrowly educated pragmatist. The top executive must be able to coordinate the activities, inspire the enthusiasm, and command the respect of highly educated technical specialists in virtually every branch of the business. He must make decisions on the basis of judgments of subordinates which often are in conflict. As a generalist, he must have appreciation for as well as some means of appraising the work of many specialists. He must even possess the skill to teach the specialist at times to think like a generalist. And tomorrow the task will be far more demanding than it is today.

There is now a widespread recognition among executives that automated production lines, computers, and resort to high-priced management consultants may eliminate the work of droves of manual and clerical workers. But such advances always exact their price.

The Price to Be Paid

Part of the price to be paid is, of course, the expenditure for new equipment or the installation of new systems. Even more important, but less readily visible, is the cost of more highly trained specialists, more mathematical brains, more research scientists, more sophisticated managers to organize their efforts, and more executive specialists whose advice must be sought in making more difficult decisions based upon vastly more information. Already, as some writers have pointed out, a new "technology of information" stemming from the new techniques of electronic data processing and the application of statistical and mathematical methods to decision-making problems is beginning to take hold in American business. As one executive interviewed observed, "The manager of tomorrow must be almost as fluent in the language of mathematics as he is in English." This is probably true, but by the same token, he must be far more than a mathematician!

8. ALL ALONG THE LINE, GREATER EMPHASIS NEEDS TO BE PLACED ON FORWARD MANPOWER PLANNING. Possibly the most important implication for company policy-makers suggested by this study is the need for companies to appraise their future development not merely with reference to markets, processes, and financial resources but also in terms of the human resources that will be required. Of all economic resources, high-talent manpower takes longest to develop and hence demands the most careful consideration in planning for the future. Yet, the criteria governing the recruitment of college graduates as well as most professional and executive training programs within industry fail to reflect any realistic projection of the manpower requirements of tomorrow.

For the most part, companies are still preoccupied with their immediate requirements and with short-run development projects. When it comes to long-range manpower planning, few organizations really know where they are or whither they are tending. Consequently, they are baffled by the question of what to do about manpower development and confused about how to go about it in this century of rapid and unprecedented change.

The challenge—and the question for the future—is simply this: Can the development of high-level manpower and the building of high-level management in industry keep pace with the spectacular and ever-accelerating development of science?

Individual Adjustments

to the Formal and

Informal Organizations

P A R T　　　F I V E

COLLECTIVITIES, BE THEY small groups or larger, more complex types, have until now received almost all our attention. This, as explained in the beginning of the book, is by design. We have considered the adjustments the formal organization makes to accommodate the informal organization and also the reverse adjustments. In addition, the adjustment an organization makes to its environment has also been considered. With all this, the individual and the adjustments he must make have received but scant attention.

Not only have the individual's adjustments not been examined, but the material presented thus far might actually leave an unintentionally erroneous impression. We can get the picture that the individual fits comfortably into the informal organization; that the only frictions he may have are the same as those of the informal organization, namely with the larger or formal organization. Such an impression is understandable, but it is neither intended nor correct.

It is really more accurate and useful, particularly in analyzing positions above the work level, to view the individual as being in some middle position between the formal and the informal organization (see Fig. 7). In such a

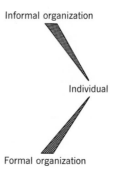

Informal organization

Individual

Formal organization

Fig. 7

position the individual is placed under pressures and subject to attractions from both quarters which at times are compatible, many times are divergent, and other times are in conflict. Subject to such an array of forces, the individual's position is frequently not particularly comfortable. This section, then, is primarily concerned with examining the individual in this middle area, analyzing some of the myriad of factors impinging on him and noting some of the ways in which he adjusts to these conditions.

Individual Orientations

Earlier in this text we have several times touched on the topic of organizational loyalty. It is now time to consider it more directly.

Most of us have met people whom we recognize as being loyal to the organization they are in. To them the success and welfare of the organization are matters of considerable importance. If the organization has a problem, it is a matter about which they are concerned. They are the opposite of people who, although not necessarily antagonistic toward the organization they are in, are at least apathetic about it. If they are attracted to any organization or group, it is different from the one they are in. A convenient way to designate these two types of orientation is to call those loyal to the organization they are in "locals" and those orientated toward some outside group "cosmopolitans" (Gouldner, 1957).

We are interested in a person's orientation because it helps us understand and predict his behavior in an organization. Formal organization policies, rules, and opportunities will probably have more influence for the local than for the cosmopolitan. It helps us understand, for instance, why a research worker in a company with a strong dedication to his branch of science may not be too interested in being promoted to a manager's position. It also helps us understand why executives in the company may find the scientist's refusal of the promotion so baffling.

Individual Response to Norms, Rules, and Reward Systems

A person entering an organization with some intention of "fitting himself in" in order to hold a position or advance within the organization will be faced with a large number of "ground rules" with which he will have to comply. However, before he can live up to them he must first learn what they are. The rules established by the formal organization may not present too much difficulty, for they are written out and publicized. But the unofficial organization rules, which tell a man what to wear on the job in order to comply with the wishes of top executives, how to handle customers' complaints, or what sort of practices with suppliers are acceptable, and a host of other exceedingly important guides for individual behavior, present a more subtle problem. Learning these is in many ways similar to learning the norms of the informal organization. In some ways, however, it is more difficult. Norms will frequently be brought to a person's attention rather promptly through a variety of pressures from the informal organization; razzing, petty harassment, etc. No one may take the time, however, to bring to the attention of the newcomer the unofficial organization rules established by higher executives, leaving the individual to learn them as quickly as he can before he gets into trouble. The processes of learning these important things depends to no small degree on the individual's acuteness and sophistication (Breed).

For the person ambitious to rise in an organization, who wants to know what he has to do to show himself worthy of advancement, sometimes acute observation is not sufficient to tell him what he has to know. He may not learn until after he has acted that a particular behavior is approved or disapproved. An interesting example would be the individual who learns through trial and error that in order to gain his superior's approval, therefore, presumably his support for advancement, that he must not exhibit too much originality, that he must instead be willing to execute faithfully and completely the orders, instructions, and wishes of his boss. He learns this in part through either the censure or the praise given by his boss. He may be reprimanded when he fails to live up completely to the boss's suggestion and may also find that his own suggestions are met with either silence, rejection, or sarcasm.

To put this a little more abstractly, his superior and the organization can reward him in a positive way through praise, wage increase, or promotions, or in a negative fashion through chastisement, reprimand, or withholding of pay increases and promotions. In short, the individual learns from this reward pattern what he is expected to do within the organization.

The idea of a reward system to train members of an organization in what is desirable behavior is, like many organizational concepts, a slippery topic. Although it appears to be a simple idea which should be easy to apply, the fact is that it often produces totally unexpected and perhaps undesired results.

Let us look at the training sometimes given

children. A three-year-old child after having done something wrong is told by its mother that it will be punished by its father when he gets home from work. When the father gets home, he carries out the mother's wishes and physically educates him to the difference between right and wrong. Or does he? If this were to happen several times, it is quite possible that the thing the child learns is not be around when his father gets home, because if he is, he stands a good chance of getting a spanking. The child learned something—but not what was intended.

In an organization things are far more complex than this simple illustration. The larger, more varied set of rewards in an organization may train people to become interested in parts of the organization at the expense of effectively accomplishing the organizational goals (Merton). At other times, the reward system may so heighten the motivation for individual accomplishment that cooperation and, hence, coordination is weakened or destroyed (Blau, 1954).

A topic related to reward systems can be introduced by the question of, "rewards for what?" In a broad sense, people are rewarded for behavior which is organizationally desirable. There are many ways of defining desirable behavior. From a formal-organizational point of view one would be behavior which complies with organizational rules. In a formal organization, rules are one of the principal instruments to specify what is desirable, or for that matter, undesirable. They represent standing decisions, known throughout the organization, which can be used to guide behavior in any applicable situation. In doing this they save much managerial time in not requiring each manager to make the new decision each time a repetitive type of problem comes up. Further, it guarantees that different people, facing similar problems, will behave in the same way.

It would be a mistake, however, to assume that the advantages of rules will be clear to everyone or that the only functions they will serve are those intended by the formal organization plan. A rule placed in the social setting between a superior and subordinate can affect the relation in a number of ways, or to put it more accurately can be made to serve a variety of functions in molding the resultant superior-subordinate relation. Further use of the rule

to serve these functions is in the hands of the parties most directly involved, the superior and the subordinates (Gouldner, 1954).

In summary, then, we can envision an individual faced with a wide array of norms and rules which will influence and guide his behavior. His reaction to them will depend, among other things, on how well he has learned what they are and the different degrees of importance they have for him. The importance to him will in turn be partially dependent on the views he has as to what is important, which he brings with him into the organization, and on the things he has learned while in the organization. The issue facing the individual is that the guides for his behavior and the rewards open to him come from two principal sources—the formal and the informal organizations. The dilemma before him is how to cope with these two classes of pressures.

Filling Positions in the Management Hierarchy

Adjustments and Dilemmas of the Individual in the Organization. We have reached the point where we will consider what the individual can or does do when faced with the different and conflicting, or at least divergent, demands on him from the informal and formal organizations. What happens, for example, to the supervisor who recognizes that he is a member of the formal organization hierarchy and yet must obtain the support, cooperation, and some degree of acceptance of a work group the norms of which he knows to be in conflict with the rules and standards of the company? He has several possibilities open to him. He could, at all times, insist on enforcing the rules and norms of the organization. Or, he could permit the violation of certain company rules in order not to require the members of the group to violate group norms. An example of this would be the foreman who permits workers to shift jobs in accordance with their norm of helpfulness even though there is a formal company rule prohibiting such practice. This strategic leniency, or slippage, has certain consequences both on the performance of the organization and on the performance of the group, and particularly on the influence of the supervisor (Blau, 1956). Strangely enough, the results of such slippage are not always detrimental to the interests of the formal organization. They may actually at times facilitate accomplishment of organizational objectives. For example, if the illicit job switching mentioned earlier actually permits a reduction in the monotony of the work, the result well may be either an increase in production or a decrease in turn-over or perhaps even both. At the same time such slippage may enhance the prestige and the power of the supervisor relevant to his subordinate, thereby making him actually more effective than he would have been if he had firmly adhered to the rules. Of course, there is the possibility, under other circumstances, of such slippage working to the disadvantage of the formal organization.

This conflict between the formal and informal rules exists not only in a hierarchical sense but well may exist in horizontal fashion, for example, when a man has to live according to certain rules and at the same time conform to norms of his peers. The formal organization may issue rules stating he must behave in a specified manner on certain matters, but the informal exchange of favors and norms of helpfulness may put strong pressure on him to bend or ignore these formal rules.[1] An example might be a nurse in the factory dispensary who should not administer certain common medicines except to patients who meet certain conditions, but who may willingly give extra supplies of aspirins and other simple medicines when requested by fellow workers even though there is no apparent immediate need.

Adjustment Problems Stemming from the Formal Organization. It would be incorrect to assume that the only problems for the individual arise from the differences or strains between the formal and informal organizations. A number of very serious problems arise from conditions created by the formal organization.

One such set of problems are the classic and chronic difficulties between line and staff mangers. It may be well to review and bring together a number of things mentioned earlier in various places in this book about line and staff. The classic definition of staff is that it is

a position which assists and advises the line, that it has no authority of command, but only an authority of knowledge or ideas. Unfortunately, only a relatively few staff positions in large organizations accurately fit this definition.[2] Some of the ways in which actual staffs differ from this normative definition and also some of the reasons why they differ have been examined in earlier sections.

In spite of the fact that we can readily find many instances in which actual staffs differ from the classical definition and differ with a great deal of functional utility, the classical definition is widely known and accepted. The fact that it is, is one of the sources of difficulty. The line manager who believes, and perhaps has been told by his superiors, that staff is advisory and not in a position to have any direct control over him, will be understandably confused and resentful to find that staff can and does influence him in many ways, some acts of the staff having the effect of orders (even if disguised by some more polite term), and usually with the active, or at least understood, support of higher authorities.

Another source of difficulties lies in the perceptions of line and staff personnel of the organization they are in. It is frequently held that the staff man, with his specialized training is, in many cases, more accurately described as a cosmopolitan and the line executive as a local. Even if the position of the staff man were accurately and adequately defined, these underlying differences as to what is important would raise serious difficulties.

Looking at the staff man we see him in a position which can be described briefly as follows. His training and professional values tell him there are ways things should be done. These are not always congruent with the way the formal organization says things should be

---

[1] For an interesting discussion of this and related points see Ralph M. Turner, "The Navy Disbursing Officer as a Bureaucrat," *American Sociological Review*, Vol. 12, 1947, pp. 342–348.

[2] We could argue that the definition is right and the departments which deviate from it are wrong and should be brought back into line. This line of thinking was followed in the literature for a long while. Cf. Sampson, *The Staff Role in Management.* New York: Harper, 1955. Several recent papers have from both theoretical and empirical analysis concluded that the theory will have to be drastically revised to explain actual organizations adequately. Cf. Golombiewski, "Toward the New Organization Theories: Some Notes on 'Staff'," *Midwest Journal of Political Science*, Vol. V (Aug. 1961), pp. 237–259.

done, and both may be at variance with the way things are actually done in the organization (Dalton).

No managerial position in the organization has been studied more intensively than that of the foreman, or to use more general terms, the first line supervisor. This position on the border between the managerial hierarchy and the working part of the organization contains all the organizational mechanisms discussed in this section, with a number of them more dramatically brought forth than in any other position. It is here that the difficulties arising from the different assumptions behind the formal and informal organizations' concepts are most dramatically illustrated. It is the occupant of this position who, because he is in the position least capable of doing anything about these differences, feels the greatest strain. He is in a position where a number of different parties, his superiors, his peers, and his subordinates, are in effect all defining his job for him. They do this in part by preparing formal job descriptions, rules, and union contracts and agreements, but largely by forming sets of expectations of how he will act in his position. How well the first line supervisor, or for that matter, any manager succeeds depends in part on two things: how well he perceives these different sets of expectations, and the degree of congruency between or among them. Higher management obviously does not con-

trol all these expectations. Its own planning of the organization, however, will be vastly improved if it takes into account the expectations' existence and that they will have a profound influence on actual organizational behavior (Jasinski).

This section deals with a very fundamental problem, namely, how the individual responds when placed in a position between a formal and an informal organization, both of which are to some degree important to him. His behavior is not only influenced by both but also important to both. Further, both are in a position to reward or punish him in response to the adequacy of his behavior. In some way, however, the individual adjusts to these different forces and arrives at some degree of equilibrium and stability. Unfortunately, such a condition is frequently disturbed. One way for this to occur is for the individual to be advanced within the formal hierarchy, a change which opens a vast array of new conditions, opportunities and rewards.

We shall conclude this text, then, at the point on which we might have begun; examining the behavior and adjustment of the individual. Our interest here, however, has been in behavior as response to a complex environment. We could have not analyzed this without first achieving some understanding of both the nature and the complexity of this environment.

Cosmopolitans and Locals

ALVIN W. GOULDNER

Sociologists have long since documented the empirical utility of role theory. It may be, however, that concepts stagnate when small theoretical investments yield large imperical dividends. The very currency of role concepts may invite complacency concerning their theoretical clarity.

Although the larger theory of social roles could doubtless profit from serious recasting and systematic reappraisal,[1] this is not the place for so ambitious an undertaking. All that

From *Administrative Science Quarterly*, Vol. 2, No. 3, Dec. 1957, pp. 282–292. Reprinted with permission of the publisher, Graduate School of Business and Public Administration, Cornell University.

The author wishes to thank the Social Science Research Council and the Research Board of the University of Illinois for funds which made possible completion of the analysis of the data. During the course of the research Helen P. Gouldner, Esther R. Newcomb, Henry Bobotek, and Ruth Landman assisted in various parts of the work. Carol Tucker guided the factor analysis through the Illiac. Raymond Cattell, Percy Tannenbaum, and George Suci were generous in allowing consultation with them in connection with the factor analyses. Particular thanks are due Robert K. Merton and Paul F. Lazarsfeld for a painstaking reading of a first draft and for numerous cogent suggestions. Needless to say, responsibility for all errors is entirely the author's.

[1] Such an overhauling seems well begun in the recent volume by S. F. Nadel, *Theory of Social Structure* (Glencoe, Ill., 1957). Efforts moving in a similar direction may also be found in Marion J. Levy, Jr., *The Structure of Society* (Princeton, 1952), pp. 157–166, and in Robert K. Merton, *Social Theory and Social Structure* (Glencoe, 1957), pp. 368–380, 415–420.

will be essayed here are some limited questions relating to role analysis. In particular, an attempt will be made to develop certain distinctions between what will be termed "manifest" and "latent" identities and roles.

Since role theory already encompasses a welter of concepts,[2] the introduction of new concepts requires firm justification. Concepts commend themselves to social scientists only as tools with which to resolve problematic situations. Unless this criterion is insisted upon, there inevitably eventuates a sterile formalism and a needless proliferation of neologisms. We must therefore justify the proposed distinction between manifest and latent roles by indicating the theoretic context from which it emerged and by showing its use in various studies.

Theoretical Considerations. A social role is commonly defined as a set of expectations oriented toward people who occupy a certain "position" in a social system or group. It is a rare discussion of social role that does not at some point make reference to the "position" occupied by a group member. Despite its frequent use, however, the notion of a social "position" is obscure and not likely to provide cleancut directives for social research. Often, it is used as little more than a geometrical metaphor with little value for guiding the empirical studies of behavioral scientists.

It seems that what is meant by a "position"

[2] The variety of these role concepts is well displayed in Erving Goffman, *The Presentation of Self in Everyday Life* (Edinburgh, 1956), and is discussed with great cogency in Joseph R. Gusfield, General Education as a Career, *Journal of General Education*, 10 (Jan. 1957), 37–48.

is the social identity which has been assigned to a person by members of his group. That is, group members may be regarded as acting in the following manner: (1) They observe or impute to a person certain characteristics; they observe certain aspects of his behavior or appearance which they employ as clues to enable themselves to answer the question "Who is he?" (2) These observed or imputed characteristics are then related to and interpreted in terms of a set of culturally prescribed *categories* which have been learned during the course of socialization. Conversely, the culturally learned categories focus attention upon certain aspects of the individual's behavior and appearance. (3) In this manner the individual is "pigeonholed"; that is, he is held to be a certain "type" of person, a teacher, Negro, boy, man, or woman. The process by which the individual is classified by others in his group, in terms of the culturally prescribed categories, can be called the assignment of a "social identity." The types or categories to which he has been assigned *are* his social identities. (4) When this assignment of identity is consensually or otherwise validated in the group, people then "ask themselves" what they know about such a type; they mobilize their beliefs concerning it. Corresponding to different social identities are differing sets of expectations, differing configurations of rights and obligations. In these terms, then, a social role is a shared set of expectations directed toward people who are assigned a given social identity.

Obviously the people in any one group have a variety of social identities. In a classroom, for example, there are those identified as "students," but these same people are also identified as men, women, young, mature, and so on. In the classroom situation, it is primarily their identity as students that others in the group regard as central and properly salient. It is also the expectations congruent with this salient identity that are most appropriately activated and have the fullest claim to application. But while the expectations congruent with the student identity are most institutionally relevant and legitimately mobilizable, it is clear that in various ways certain of the other identities do "intrude" and affect the group's behavior in sociologically interesting ways. For example, there is usually something happening between the students that is influenced by their sexual identities.

It is necessary to distinguish, then, between those social identities of group members which are consensually regarded as relevant to them in a given setting and those which group members define as being irrelevant, inappropriate to consider, or illegitimate to take into account. The former can be called the *manifest* social identities, the latter, the *latent* social identities. Let us be clear that "social identities," manifest or latent, are not synonymous with the concept of social status. Social identities have to do with the way in which an individual is in fact *perceived* and classified by others in terms of a system of culturally standardized categories. Social statuses, however, refer to the complex of culturally standardized categories to which individuals in a group may be assigned; they are sometimes also defined as the hierarchical "position" of the individual in relation to others, as well as the culturally prescribed expectations directed toward those in this position.[3]

---

[3] The terminological disparities with respect to the definition of "status" barely fall short of being appalling. Among the varying definitions which may be found are the following: (1) "a position in the social aggregate identified with a pattern of prestige symbols . . ." D. Martindale and E. D. Monachesi, *Elements of Sociology* (New York, 1951), p. 540; (2) the "successful realization of claims to prestige . . . the distribution of prestige in a society . . ." H. Gerth and C. W. Mills, *Character and Social Structure* (New York, 1953), p. 307; (3) "a measure of the worth or the importance of the role," R. Freedman, A. H. Hawley, W. S. Landecker, and H. M. Miner, eds., *Principles of Sociology* (New York, 1952), p. 148; (4) "the rank position with respect chiefly to income, prestige, and power—one or all of these," G. Knupfer in R. O'Brien, C. C. Shrag, and W. T. Martin, *Readings in General Sociology* (New York, 1951), p. 274; (5) "a collection of rights and obligations . . ." R. Linton, *The Study of Man* (New York, 1945), p. 113; (6) a "complex of mutual rights, obligations, and functions as defined by the pertinent ideal patterns," T. Parsons, *Essays in Sociological Theory Pure and Applied* (Glencoe, Ill., 1949), p. 42; (7) "a position in the general institutional system, recognized and supported by the entire society . . ." K. Davis, *Human Society* (New York, 1949), p. 87. One could go on. That these varying definitions are not necessarily contradictory is small consolation and certainly no guarantee that they all refer to the same things. Nowhere do these definitions become more opaque than when—as they fre-

Expectations which are associated with the manifest social identities can be termed the manifest social *roles*, while expectations oriented toward the latent identities can be called the latent social roles. Just as others can be oriented toward an individual's latent identities, so, too, can the individual himself be oriented to his own latent identities. This is, of course, to be expected in the light of Mead's role theory, which stresses that an individual's self-conception is a function of the judgments and orientations which significant others have toward him.

At the present time, little systematic attention is given to the functioning of either latent identities or roles. It is too easy to focus on the more evident manifest identities and roles in a group. As a result, even in a world on which Freudian theory has made its impact, many sociologists give little indication of the fact that the people they study in offices, factories, schools, or hospitals are also males and females. The sociologist's assumption often seems to be that the latent identities and roles are as irrelevant as the people whom they are studying conventionally pretend. The fact seems to be, however, that these do affect group behavior.

This is, of course, obvious from the most commonplace of questions. For example: Are the career chances of industrial workers affected by their ethnic identity? Are "old-timers" in a group more or less friendly toward each other than with those of less tenure? Do college professors take note of and behave somewhat differently toward members of the college football team who are taking their courses? Do Unitarian ministers sometimes refer to their "Jewish" parishioners?

While it is obvious that individuals in a group have a variety of social identities, and not merely one, we need conceptual tools that firmly distinguish between different types of social identities and facilitate analysis of the varying ways in which they influence group behavior. While it is obvious that a group member may have many social identities, it needs to be stressed that not all of them are regarded as equally relevant or legitimately activated in that group. This is precisely the point to which the concepts of latent identities and roles direct attention.

This implies that when group members orient themselves to the latent identities of others in their group, they are involved in a relationship with them which is not culturally *prescribed* by the group norms governing their manifest roles. It implies, also, that they are utilizing reference persons or groups which are not culturally prescribed for those in their roles. Thus the concepts of latent identities and roles focus research on those patterns of social interaction, and lines of orientation, which are not prescribed by the group under study. It would also seem clear that latent identities and roles are important because they exert pressure upon the manifest roles, often impairing conformity with their requirements and endemically threatening the equilibrium of the manifest role system. In contrast, the concept of manifest roles focuses on the manner in which group norms yield *prescribed* similarities in the behavior and beliefs of those performing the same role.

The role of "elders" in a gerontocratic society, with the deference and respect due them by their juniors, is in these terms a manifest role. For, in this case, the rights and obligations of elders are culturally prescribed. Here to be an "elder" is a societally relevant identity. Note, however, that even in the American factory elders may also receive some special consideration and similar if not equal deference from their juniors. Here, however, the role of the elder is a latent one, being based upon an assignment of identity which is not regarded as fully legitimate or as clearly relevant in the factory, even if fully acknowledged in the larger society.

This distinction between manifest and latent roles directs us to search out and specify the latent identities, and the expectations corresponding to them, which crosscut and underlie those which are culturally prescribed in the group under study. The concept of latent roles suggests that people playing *different* manifest roles may be performing *similar* latent roles and, conversely, that those performing the *same* manifest role may be playing *different*

---

quently do—they refer to a status as a "position" in something. The ready familiarity of the word position seems to induce paralysis of the analytic nerve. Needless to say such terminological confusion begets efforts at neologistic clarification which may then only further becloud the field. We can only hope that this has not happened here.

latent roles. The concept of latent role may then aid in accounting for some of the differences (in behavior or belief) among those in the same manifest role or for some of the similarities among those having different manifest roles. Neither the similarities nor the differences mentioned above need be due to the intrusion of "personality" factors or other individual attributes. They may derive from the nature of the latent roles, that is, from the responses to the latent identities of group members, which yield culturally unprescribed yet structured interactions and orientations with others.

The problem that will be explored in the following analysis is whether there are latent identities and roles of general significance for the study of the modern complex organization. That is, can we discern latent identities and roles which are common to a number of different complex organizations? In this connection, we will explore the possibility that, as distinguished from and in addition to their manifest identities, members of formal organizations may have two latent social identities, here called "cosmopolitan" and "local." [4] Development of these concepts may enable organizational analysis to proceed without focusing solely on the relatively visible, culturally differentiated, manifest organizational identities and roles, but without confining analysis to an undifferentiated blob of "bureaucrats." There are of course other latent identities which are of organizational significance, and, in . . . [a second article] we shall consider a more complex structure of latent identities.

[4] These terms are taken from Robert K. Merton, "Patterns of Influence, Local and Cosmopolitan Influentials," in Merton, op. cit. Merton's terms are used with respect to types of roles within communities rather than in connection with formal organizations, as they are here. Moreover, Merton's focus is on the conjunction between influence and cosmopolitans-locals, whereas our analysis applies cosmopolitan and local orientations to role players apart from considerations of their influence. Note, also, the similarity between my own discussion of "latent" identities and roles and that of R. Linton, in T. N. Newcomb and E. L. Hartley, eds., Readings in Sociology (New York, 1947), p. 368.

Concerning Cosmopolitans and Locals

A number of prior researches have identified certain role-playing patterns which appear convergent with each other and which, further, seem to be commonly based upon those latent identities which will be called "cosmopolitans."

In a study of a factory,[5] "The General Gypsum Company," I noted a type of company executive which I called the "expert." Experts tend to be staff men who never seem to win the complete confidence of the company's highest authorities and are kept removed from the highest reaches of power. Much like staff men in other companies, these experts can advise but cannot command. They are expected to "sell" management on their plans, but cannot order them put into effect. It is widely recognized that these experts are not given the "real promotions." The expert is under pressure to forego the active pursuit of his specialty if he wishes to ascend in the company hierarchy. Among the reasons for the experts' subordination may be the fact that they are less frequently identified as "company men" than others in the executive group. The "company man," a pervasive category for the informal classification of industrial personnel, is one who is regarded as having totally committed his career aspirations to his employing company and as having indicated that he wishes to remain with it indefinitely. In effect, then, company personnel were using a criterion of "loyalty to the company" in assigning social identities to members of their organization. A company man is one who is identified as "loyal."

Experts are less likely to be identified in this manner in part because their relatively complex, seemingly mysterious skills, derived from long formal training, lead them to make a more basic commitment to their job than to the organization in which they work. Furthermore, because of their intensive technical training, experts have greater opportunities for horizontal job mobility and can fill jobs in

[5] Alvin W. Gouldner, Patterns of Industrial Bureaucracy (Glencoe, Ill., 1954). It may be worth mentioning that the research published here represents an effort at deliberate continuity and development of some of the conceptions that emerged in the Patterns volume.

many different organizations. As E. C. Hughes would say, they are more likely to be "itinerants." Consequently, experts are less likely to be committed to their employing organization than to their specialty.

The expert's skills are continually being refined and developed by professional peers outside of his employing organization. Moreover, his continued standing as a competent professional often cannot be validated by members of his own organization, since they are not knowledgeable enough about it. For these reasons, the expert is more likely than others to esteem the good opinion of professional peers elsewhere; he is disposed to seek recognition and acceptance from "outsiders." We can say that he is more likely to be oriented to a reference group composed of others not a part of his employing organization, that is, an "outer reference group."

Leonard Reissman's study of the role conceptions of government bureaucrats provides another case in point.[6] Among these is the "functional bureaucrat" who is found to be oriented toward groups outside of his employing bureaucracy and is especially concerned with securing recognition from his professional peers elsewhere. If he is an economist, for example, he wants other economists to think well of him, whether or not they are his organizational associates. The functional bureaucrats are also more likely to associate with their professional peers than with their bureaucratic colleagues. They are less likely than other types of bureaucrats to have sentiments of loyalty to their employing bureaucracy. Finally, more than other bureaucrats their satisfaction with their job depends upon the degree to which their work conforms with professional standards, and they seem to be more deeply committed to their professional skills. In short, Reissman's "functional bureaucrat" is much the same as our "expert," insofar as both tend to manifest lesser organizational loyalty, deeper job commitment, and an outer reference group orientation, as compared with their colleagues.

A third study, by Vernon J. Bentz,[7] of a city college faculty, again indicates the interrelationship of these variables and suggests their relevance in another organizational setting. Bentz divided the college faculty into two groups, those who publish much and those publishing little or nothing. Publication as such is not of course theoretically interesting, but it becomes so if taken as an index of something else. The difficulty is that it is an ambiguous index. Within limits, it seems reasonable to treat it as an index of the degree of commitment to professional skills. However, "high" publication might also indicate a desire to communicate with other, like professionals in different organizations. The high publisher must also take cognizance of the publications which others elsewhere are producing. Thus high publication may also be an index of an outer reference group orientation. High publishers also tend to deemphasize the importance which their own college department had to them and to express the feeling that it had comparatively little control over them. This might be taken to imply a lower degree of commitment or loyalty to that particular group.

Although Bentz's research findings are less direct than the others examined, they do seem to point in the same direction, indicating similarities between the high publisher, the functional bureaucrat, and the expert. They were also particularly useful to my own later study of a college by suggesting indices for some of the significant variables.

These three cases suggested the importance of three variables for analyzing latent identities in organizations: (1) loyalty to the employing organization, (2) commitment to specialized or professional skills, and (3) reference group orientations. Considerations of space do not permit this to be developed here, but each of these studies also found role-playing patterns polar to those discussed. This led us to hypothesize that *two* latent organizational identities could be found. These were:

1. COSMOPOLITANS: those low on loyalty to the employing organization, high on commitment to specialized role skills, and likely to use an outer reference group orientation.

2. LOCALS: those high on loyalty to the employing organization, low on commitment to specialized role skills, and likely to use an inner reference group orientation.

[6] Leonard Reissman, A Study of Role Conceptions in Bureaucracy, *Social Forces*, 27 (1949), 305–310.
[7] Vernon J. Bentz, "A Study of Leadership in a Liberal Arts College" (Columbus, O.: Ohio State University, 1950; mimeo.).

Cosmopolitans and locals are regarded as *latent* identities because they involve criteria which are not fully institutionalized as bases for classifying people in the modern organization, though they are in fact often used as such. For example, "loyalty" usually tends to be taken for granted and is, under normal circumstances, a latent social identity in a rational bureaucracy. For example, it may be preferred, but it is not usually prescribed, that one should be a "company man." While loyalty criteria do become activated at irregular intervals, as, for example, at occasional "testimonial dinners" or during outbursts of organizational conflict and crisis, other criteria for identifying personnel are routinely regarded as more fully legitimate and relevant. For example, skill and competence or training and experience are usually the publicly utilized standards in terms of which performances are judged and performers identified.

While organizations are in fact concerned with the loyalty of their personnel, as indicated by the ritual awarding of gold watches for lengthy years of "faithful service," the dominant organizational orientation toward rationality imposes a ban of pathos on the use of loyalty criteria. Organizational concern with the skill and competence of its personnel exerts pressure against evaluating them in terms of loyalty. Indeed, one of the major dilemmas of the modern organization is the tension between promotions based on skill versus promotions based on seniority, the latter often being an informal index of loyalty. Despite the devotion to rational criteria in the modern organization, however, considerations of loyalty can never be entirely excluded and loyalty criteria frequently serve as a basis for assigning latent identities. In some measure, loyalty to the organization often implies the other two criteria, (1) a willingness to limit or relinquish the commitment to a specialized professional task and (2) a dominant career orientation to the employing organization as a reference group. This linking of organizational criteria is only barely understood by the group members. Thus cosmopolitans and locals are also latent identities because the *conjunction* of criteria involved is not normatively prescribed by the organization.

Each of the other two criteria involved may, however, become an independent basis for assigning organizational identities. For example, in the modern organization people tend to be distinguished in terms of their commitment to their work as well as to their employing organization. A distinction is commonly made between the "cynics" and "clock watchers" or those who are just "doing time," on the one hand, and those who "believe in" or are "fired up" by their task.[8] This distinction is based on the common, if not entirely documented, assumption that the latter are likely to be superior role performers.

It is, however, relatively difficult to know how a person feels about his job; it is easier, and is therefore frequently regarded as more important, to know how he *does* it. Performance rather than belief more commonly becomes the formal criterion for assigning organizational identity. Nonetheless, belief is never totally neglected or discarded but tends, instead, to become a basis on which more latent identities are assigned.

While the significance of reference group orientation varies from one type of organization to another, it remains a commonplace if somewhat subtle criterion for assigning latent identities. In colleges, groups distinguish between "insiders" and "outsiders," sometimes using such informal indices as whether or not individuals orient themselves to certain "schools of thought" or people, share familiarity with a prestigious literature, or utilize certain styles of research. In trade unions, different identities may be assigned to those who orient themselves to political movements or to professional peers in other types of organizations and to those who are primarily oriented to the more limited goals of the union—the "union men." Such identities are not fully institutionalized or legitimated, although they may obliquely impinge on promotions, election to office, and evaluation of performance.

[8] For a broader discussion of this problem, see Howard S. Becker and Blanche Geer, "The Fate of Idealism in Medical School" (unpublished paper, available from authors at Community Studies, Inc., Kansas City, Mo.).

Social Control in the Newsroom:
A Functional Analysis

WARREN BREED

Top leaders in formal organizations are makers of policy, but they must also secure and maintain conformity to that policy at lower levels. The situation of the newspaper publisher is a case in point. As owner or representative of ownership, he has the nominal right to set the paper's policy and see that staff activities are coordinated so that the policy is enforced. In actuality the problem of control is less simple, as the literature of "human relations" and informal group studies and of the professions [1] suggests.

Ideally, there would be no problem of either "control" or "policy" on the newspaper in a full democracy. The only controls would be the nature of the event and the reporter's effective ability to describe it. In practice, we find the publisher does set news policy, and this policy is usually followed by members of his staff. Conformity is *not* automatic, however, for three reasons: (1) the existence of ethical journalistic norms; (2) the fact that staff subordinates (reporters, etc.) tend to have more "liberal" attitudes (and therefore perceptions) than the publisher and could invoke the norms

to justify anti-policy writing; and (3) the ethical taboo preventing the publisher from commanding subordinates to follow policy. How policy comes to be maintained, and where it is bypassed, is the subject of this paper.

Several definitions are required at this point. As to personnel, "newsmen" can be divided into two main categories. "Executives" include the publisher and his editors. "Staffers" are reporters, rewrite men, copy readers, etc. In between there may be occasional city editors or wire editors who occupy an interstitial status. "Policy" may be defined as the more or less consistent orientation shown by a paper, not only in its editorial but in its news columns and headlines as well, concerning selected issues and events. "Slanting" almost never means prevarication. Rather, it involves omission, differential selection and preferential placement, such as "featuring" a pro-policy item, "burying" an anti-policy story in an inside page, etc. "Professional norms" are of two types: technical norms deal with the operations of efficient news gathering, writing, and editing; ethical norms embrace the newsman's obligation to his readers and to his craft and include such ideals as responsibility, impartiality, accuracy, fair play, and objectivity.[2]

Every newspaper has a policy, admitted or

From *Social Forces*, Vol. 33, May 1955, pp. 326–335. Reprinted with permission of the author and the publisher, University of North Carolina Press. Copyright 1955, University of North Carolina Press.

[1] See, for instance, F. J. Roethlisberger and William J. Dickson, *Management and the Worker* (Cambridge: Harvard University Press, 1947); and Logan Wilson, *The Academic Man* (New York: Oxford University Press, 1942).

[2] The best-known formal code is The Canons of Journalism, of the American Society of Newspaper Editors. See Wilbur Schramm (ed.), *Mass Communications* (Urbana: University of Illinois Press, 1949), pp. 236–38.

not.[3] One paper's policy may be pro-Republican, cool to labor, antagonistic to the school board, etc. The principal areas of policy are politics, business, and labor; much of it stems from considerations of class. Policy is manifested in "slanting." Just what determines any publisher's policy is a large question and will not be discussed here. Certainly, however, the publisher has much say (often in veto form) in both long-term and immediate policy decisions (which party to support, whether to feature or bury a story of imminent labor trouble, how much free space to give "news" of advertisers' doings, etc.). Finally, policy is covert, due to the existence of ethical norms of journalism; policy often contravenes these norms. No executive is willing to risk embarrassment by being accused of open commands to slant a news story.

While policy is set by the executives, it is clear that they cannot personally gather and write the news by themselves. They must delegate these tasks to staffers, and at this point the attitudes or interests of staffers may—and often do—conflict with those of the executives.[4] Of 72 staffers interviewed, 42 showed that they held more liberal views than those contained in their publisher's policy; 27 held similar views, and only 3 were more conservative. Similarly, only 17 of 61 staffers said they were Republicans.[5] The discrepancy is more acute when age (and therefore years of newspaper experience) is held constant. Of the 46 staffers under 35 years of age, 34 showed more liberal orientations; older men had apparently "mellowed." It should be noted that data as to intensity of attitudes are lacking. Some staffers may disagree with policy so mildly that they conform and feel no strain. The present essay is pertinent only insofar as dissident newsmen are forced to make decisions from time to time about their relationship to policy.[6]

We will now examine more closely the workings of the newspaper staff. The central question will be: How is policy maintained, despite the fact that it often contravenes journalistic norms, that staffers often personally disagree with it, and that executives cannot legitimately command that it be followed? The frame of reference will be that of functional analysis, as embodied in Merton's paradigm.[7]

The present data come from the writer's newspaper experience and from intensive interviews with some 120 newsmen, mostly in the northeastern quarter of the country. The sample was not random and no claim is made for representativeness, but on the other hand no paper was selected or omitted purposely and in no case did a newsman refuse the request that he be interviewed. The newspapers where chosen to fit a "middle-sized" group,

---

[3] It is extremely difficult to measure the extent of objectivity or bias. One recent attempt is reported in Nathan B. Blumberg, *One-Party Press?* (Lincoln: University of Nebraska Press, 1954), which gives a news count for 35 papers' performance in the 1952 election campaign. He concluded that 18 of the papers showed "no evidence of partiality," 11 showed "no conclusive evidence of partiality," and 6 showed partiality. His interpretations, however, are open to argument. A different interpretation could conclude that while about 16 showed little or no partiality, the rest did. It should be noted, too, that there are different areas of policy depending on local conditions. The chief difference occurs in the deep South, where frequently there is no "Republican" problem and no "union" problem over which the staff can be divided. Color becomes the focus of policy.

[4] This condition, pointed out in a lecture by Paul F. Lazarsfeld, formed the starting point for the present study.

[5] Similar findings were made about Washington correspondents in Leo C. Rosten, *The Washington Correspondents* (New York: Harcourt, Brace,

1937). Less ideological conflict was found in two other studies: Francis V. Prugger, "Social Composition and Training of the Milwaukee Journal News Staff," *Journalism Quarterly*, 18 (Sept. 1941), pp. 231–44, and Charles E. Swanson, The Mid-City Daily (Ph.D. dissertation, State University of Iowa, 1948). Possible reasons for the gap is that both papers studied were perhaps above average in objectivity; executives were included with staffers in computations; and some staffers were doubtless included who did not handle policy news.

[6] It is not being argued that "liberalism" and objectivity are synonymous. A liberal paper (e.g., *PM*) can be biased too, but it is clear that few liberal papers exist among the many conservative ones. It should also be stressed that much news is not concerned with policy and is therefore probably unbiased.

[7] Robert K. Merton, *Social Theory and Social Structure* (Glencoe: Free Press, 1949), esp. pp. 49–61. Merton's elements will not be explicitly referred to but his principal requirements are discussed at various points.

defined as those with 10,000 to 100,000 daily circulation. Interviews average well over an hour in duration.[8]

There is an "action" element inherent in the present subject—the practical democratic need for "a free and responsible press" to inform citizens about current issues. Much of the criticism of the press stems from the slanting induced by the bias of the publisher's policy.[9] This criticism is often directed at flagrant cases such as the Hearst press, the *Chicago Tribune* and New York tabloids, but also applies, in lesser degree, to the more conventional press. The description of mechanisms of policy maintenance may suggest why this criticism is often fruitless, at least in the short-run sense.

How the Staffer Learns Policy

The first mechanism promoting conformity is the "socialization" of the staffer with regard to the norms of his job. When the new reporter starts work he is not told what policy is. Nor is he ever told. This may appear strange, but interview after interview confirmed the condition. The standard remark was "Never, in my —— years on this paper, have I ever been told how to slant a story." No paper in the survey had a "training" program for its new men; some issue a "style" book, but this deals with literary style, not policy. Further, newsmen are busy and have little time for recruit training. Yet all but the newest staffers know what policy is.[10] On

being asked, they say they learn it "by osmosis." Sociologically, this means they become socialized and "learn the ropes" like a neophyte in any subculture. Basically, the learning of policy is a process by which the recruit discovers and internalizes the rights and obligations of his status and its norms and values. He learns to anticipate what is expected of him so as to win rewards and avoid punishments. Policy is an important element of the newsroom norms, and he learns it in much the following way.

The staffer reads his own paper every day; some papers *require* this. It is simple to diagnose the paper's characteristics. Unless the staffer is naive or unusually independent, he tends to fashion his own stories after others he sees in the paper. This is particularly true of the newcomer. The news columns and editorials are a guide to the local norms. Thus a southern reporter notes that Republicans are treated in a "different" way in his paper's news columns than Democrats. The news about whites and Negroes is also of a distinct sort. Should he then write about one of these groups, his story will tend to reflect what he has come to define as standard procedure.

Certain editorial actions taken by editors and older staffers also serve as controlling guides. "If things are blue-penciled consistently," one reporter said, "you learn he [the editor] has a prejudice in that regard."[11] Similarly an executive may occasionally reprimand a staffer for policy violation. From our evidence, the reprimand is frequently oblique, due to the covert nature of policy, but learning occurs nevertheless. One staffer learned much through a series of incidents:

> I heard [a union] was going out on strike, so I kept on it; then the boss said something about it, and well—I took the hint and we had less coverage of the strike forming. It was easier that way. We lost the story, but what can you do?

> We used a yarn on a firm that was coming to town, and I got dragged out of bed for that. The boss is interested in this industrial stuff—we have to clear it all through

[8] The data are taken from Warren Breed, The Newspaperman, News and Society (Ph.D. dissertation, Columbia University, 1952). Indebtedness is expressed to William L. Kolb and Robert C. Stone, who read the present manuscript and provided valuable criticisms and suggestions.

[9] For a summary description of this criticism, see Commission on the Freedom of the Press, *A Free and Responsible Press* (Chicago: University of Chicago Press, 1947), chap. 4.

[10] While the concept of policy is crucial to this analysis, it is not to be assumed that newsmen discuss it fully. Some do not even use the word in discussing how their paper is run. To this extent, policy is a latent phenomenon; either the staffer has no reason to contemplate policy or he chooses to avoid so doing. It may be that one strength of policy is that it has become no more manifest to the staffers who follow it.

[11] Note that such executives' actions as blue-penciling play not only the manifest function of preparing the story for publication but also the latent one of steering the future action of the staffer.

him. He's an official in the Chamber. So . . . after a few times, it's irritating, so I get fed up. I try to figure out what will work best. I learn to try and guess what the boss will want.

In fairness it should be noted that this particular publisher was one of the most dictatorial encountered in the study. The pattern of control through reprimand, however, was found consistently. Another staffer wrote, on his own initiative, a series about discrimination against Jews at hotel resorts.

> It was the old "Gentlemen's Agreement" stuff, documented locally. The boss called me in . . . didn't like the stuff . . . the series never appeared. You start to get the idea. . . .

Note that the boss does not "command"; the direction is more subtle. Also, it seems that most policy indications from executives are negative. They veto by a nod of the head, as if to say, "Please don't rock the boat." Exceptions occur in the "campaign" story, which will be discussed later. It is also to be noted that punishment is implied if policy is not followed.

Staffers also obtain guidance from their knowledge of the characteristics, interests, and affiliations of their executives. This knowledge can be gained in several ways. One is gossip. A reporter said:

> Do we gossip about the editors? Several of us used to meet—somewhere off the beaten path—over a beer—and talk for an hour. We'd rake 'em over the coals.

Another point of contact with executives is the news conference (which on middle-sized papers is seldom *called* a news conference), wherein the staffer outlines his findings and executives discuss how to shape the story. The typical conference consists of two persons, the reporter and the city editor, and can amount to no more than a few words. (Reporter: "One hurt in auto accident uptown." City editor: "Okay, keep it short.") If policy is at stake, the conference may involve several executives and require hours of consideration. From such meetings, the staffer can gain insight through what is said and what is not said by executives. It is important to say here that policy is not stated explicitly in the news

conference nor elsewhere, with few exceptions. The news conference actually deals mostly with journalistic matters, such as reliability of information, newsworthiness, possible "angles," and other news tactics.

Three other channels for learning about executives are house organs (printed for the staff by syndicates and larger papers), observing the executive as he meets various leaders and hearing him voice an opinion. One staffer could not help but gain an enduring impression of his publisher's attitudes in this incident:

> I can remember [him] saying on election night [1948], when it looked like we had a Democratic majority in both houses, "My God, this means we'll have a labor government." (Q: How did he say it?) He had a real note of alarm in his voice; you couldn't miss the point that he'd prefer the Republicans.

It will be noted that in speaking of "how" the staffer learns policy, there are indications also as to "why" he follows it.

Reasons for Conforming to Policy

There is no one factor which creates conformity-mindedness, unless we resort to a summary term such as "institutionalized statuses" or "structural roles." Particular factors must be sought in particular cases. The staffer must be seen in terms of his status and aspirations, the structure of the newsroom organization and of the larger society. He also must be viewed with reference to the operations he performs through his workday, and their consequences for him. The following six reasons appear to stay the potentially intransigent staffer from acts of deviance—often, if not always.[12]

---

[12] Two cautions are in order here. First, it will be recalled that we are discussing not all news, but only policy news. Secondly, we are discussing only staffers who are potential non-conformers. Some agree with policy; some have no views on policy matters; others do not write policy stories. Furthermore, there are strong forces in American society which cause many individuals to choose harmonious adjustment (conformity) in any situation, regardless of the imperatives. See Erich Fromm, *Escape From Freedom* (New York:

1. *Institutional Authority and Sanctions.* The publisher ordinarily owns the paper and from a purely business standpoint has the right to expect obedience of his employees. He has the power to fire or demote for transgressions. This power, however, is diminished markedly in actuality by three facts. First, the newspaper is not conceived as a purely business enterprise, due to the protection of the First Amendment and a tradition of professional public service. Secondly, firing is a rare phenomenon on newspapers. For example, one editor said he had fired two men in 12 years; another could recall four firings in his 15 years on that paper. Thirdly, there are severance pay clauses in contracts with the American Newspaper Guild (CIO). The only effective causes for firing are excessive drunkenness, sexual dalliance, etc. Most newspaper unemployment apparently comes from occasional economy drives on large papers and from total suspensions of publication. Likewise, only one case of demotion was found in the survey. It is true, however, that staffers still fear punishment; the myth has the errant star reporter taken off murders and put on obituaries—"the Chinese torture chamber" of the newsroom. Fear of sanctions, rather than their invocation, is a reason for conformity, but not as potent a one as would seem at first glance.

Editors, for their part, can simply ignore stories which might create deviant actions, and when this is impossible, can assign the story to a "safe" staffer. In the infrequent case that an anti-policy story reaches the city desk, the story is changed; extraneous reasons, such as the pressure of time and space, are given for the change.[13] Finally, the editor may contribute to the durability of policy by insulating the publisher from policy discussions. He may reason that the publisher would be embarrassed to hear of conflict over policy and the resulting bias, and spare him the resulting uneasiness; thus the policy remains not only covert but undiscussed and therefore unchanged.[14]

2. *Feelings of Obligation and Esteem for Superiors.* The staffer may feel obliged to the paper for having hired him. Respect, admiration and gratitude may be felt for certain editors who have perhaps schooled him, "stood up for him," or supplied favors of a more paternalistic sort. Older staffers who have served as models for newcomers or who have otherwise given aid and comfort are due return courtesies. Such obligations and warm personal sentiments toward superiors play a strategic role in the pull to conformity.

3. *Mobility Aspirations.* In response to a question about ambition, all the younger staffers showed wishes for status achievement. There was agreement that bucking policy constituted a serious bar to this goal. In practice, several respondents noted that a good tactic toward advancement was to get "big" stories on Page One; this automatically means no tampering with policy. Further, some staffers see newspapering as a "stepping stone" job to more lucrative work: public relations, advertising, free-lancing, etc. The reputation for troublemaking would inhibit such climbing.

A word is in order here about chances for upward mobility. Of 51 newsmen aged 35 or more, 32 were executives. Of 50 younger men, 6 had reached executive posts and others were on their way up with such jobs as wire editors, political reporters, etc. All but five of these young men were college graduates, as against just half of their elders. Thus there is no evidence of a "break in the skill hierarchy" among newsmen.

4. *Absence of Conflicting Group Allegiance.* The largest formal organization of staffers is the American Newspaper Guild. The Guild, much as it might wish to, has not interfered with internal matters such as policy. It has

---

Farrar and Rinehart, 1941), and David Riesman, *The Lonely Crowd* (New Haven: Yale, 1950).
[13] Excellent illustration of this tactic is given in the novel by an experienced newspaperwoman: Margaret Long, *Affair of the Heart* (New York: Random House, 1953), chap. 10. This chapter describes the framing of a Negro for murder in a middle-sized southern city, and the attempt of a reporter to tell the story objectively.

[14] The insulation of one individual or group from another is a good example of social (as distinguished from psychological) mechanisms to reduce the likelihood of conflict. Most of the factors inducing conformity could likewise be viewed as social mechanisms. See Talcott Parsons and Edward A. Shils, "Values, Motives and Systems of Action," in Parsons and Shils (eds.), *Toward a General Theory of Action* (Cambridge: Harvard University Press, 1951), pp. 223–30.

stressed business unionism and political interests external to the newsroom. As for informal groups, there is no evidence available that a group of staffers has ever "ganged up" on policy.

5. *The Pleasant Nature of the Activity.* IN-GROUPNESS IN THE NEWSROOM. The staffer has a low formal status vis-à-vis executives, but he is not treated as a "worker." Rather, he is a co-worker with executives; the entire staff cooperates congenially on a job they all like and respect: getting the news. The newsroom is a friendly, first-namish place. Staffers discuss stories with editors on a give-and-take basis. Top executives with their own offices sometimes come out and sit in on newsroom discussions.[15]

REQUIRED OPERATIONS ARE INTERESTING. Newsmen like their work. Few voiced complaints when given the opportunity to gripe during interviews. The operations required—witnessing, interviewing, briefly mulling the meanings of events, checking facts, writing—are not onerous.

NON-FINANCIAL PERQUISITES. These are numerous: the variety of experience, eye-witnessing significant and interesting events, being the first to know, getting "the inside dope" denied laymen, meeting and sometimes befriending notables and celebrities (who are well-advised to treat newsmen with deference). Newsmen are close to big decisions without having to make them; they touch power without being responsible for its use. From talking with newsmen and reading their books, one gets the impression that they are

proud of being newsmen.[16] There are tendencies to exclusiveness within news ranks, and intimations that such near out-groups as radio newsmen are entertainers, not real newsmen. Finally, there is the satisfaction of being a member of a live-wire organization dealing with important matters. The newspaper is an "institution" in the community. People talk about it and quote it; its big trucks whiz through town; its columns carry the tidings from big and faraway places, with pictures.

Thus, despite his relatively low pay, the staffer feels, for all these reasons, an integral part of a going concern. His job morale is high. Many newsmen could qualify for jobs paying more money in advertising and public relations, but they remain with the newspaper.

6. *News Becomes a Value.* Newsmen define their job as producing a certain quantity of what is called "news" every 24 hours. This is to be produced *even though nothing much has happened.* News is a continuous challenge, and meeting this challenge is the newsman's job. He is rewarded for fulfilling this, his manifest function. A consequence of this focus on news as a central value is the shelving of a strong interest in objectivity at the point of policy conflict. Instead of mobilizing their efforts to establish objectivity over policy as the criterion for performance, their energies are channeled into getting more news. The demands of competition (in cities where there are two or more papers) and speed enhance this focus. Newsmen do talk about ethics, objectivity, and the relative worth of various papers, but not when there is news to get. News comes first, and there is always news to get.[17] They are not rewarded for analyzing

---

[15] Further indication that the staffer-executive relationship is harmonious came from answers to the question, "Why do you think newspapermen are thought to be cynical?" Staffers regularly said that newsmen are cynical because they get close enough to stark reality to see the ills of their society, and the imperfections of its leaders and officials. Only two, of 40 staffers, took the occasion to criticize their executives and the enforcement of policy. This displacement, or lack of strong feelings against executives, can be interpreted to bolster the hypothesis of staff solidarity. (It further suggests that newsmen tend to analyze their society in terms of personalities, rather than institutions comprising a social and cultural system.)

[16] There is a sizeable myth among newsmen about the attractiveness of their calling. For example, the story: "Girl: 'My, you newspapermen must have a fascinating life. You meet such interesting people.' Reporter: 'Yes, and most of them are newspapermen.'" For a further discussion, see Breed, *op. cit.,* chap. 17.

[17] This is a variant of the process of "displacement of goals," newsmen turning to "getting news" rather than to seeking data which will enlighten and inform their readers. The dysfunction is implied in the nation's need not for more news but for better news—quality rather than quantity. See Merton, *op. cit.,* "Bureaucratic Structure and Personality," pp. 154–5.

the social structure, but for getting news. It would seem that this instrumental orientation diminishes their moral potential. A further consequence of this pattern is that the harmony between staffers and executives is cemented by their common interest in news. Any potential conflict between the two groups, such as slowdowns occurring among informal work groups in industry, would be dissipated to the extent that news is a positive value. The newsroom solidarity is thus reinforced.

The six factors promote policy conformity. To state more exactly how policy is maintained would be difficult in view of the many variables contained in the system. The process may be somewhat better understood, however, with the introduction of one further concept—the reference group.[18] The staffer, especially the new staffer, identifies himself through the existence of these six factors with the executives and veteran staffers. Although not yet one of them, he shares their norms, and thus his performance comes to resemble theirs. He conforms to the norms of policy rather than to whatever personal beliefs he brought to the job, or to ethical ideals. All six of these factors function to encourage reference group formation. Where the allegiance is directed toward legitimate authority, that authority has only to maintain the equilibrium within limits by the prudent distribution of rewards and punishments. The reference group itself, which has as its "magnet" element the elite of executives and old staffers, is unable to change policy to a marked degree because first, it is the group charged with carrying out policy, and second, because the policy maker, the publisher, is often insulated on the delicate issue of policy.

In its own way, each of the six factors con-

tributes to the formation of reference group behavior. There is almost no firing, hence a steady expectation of continued employment. Subordinates tend to esteem their bosses, so a convenient model group is present. Mobility aspirations (when held within limits) are an obvious promoter of inter-status bonds as is the absence of conflicting group loyalties with their potential harvest of cross pressures. The newsroom atmosphere is charged with the related factors of in-groupness and pleasing nature of the work. Finally, the agreement among newsmen that their job is to fasten upon the news, seeing it as a value in itself, forges a bond across status lines.

As to the six factors, five appear to be relatively constant, occurring on all papers studied. The varying factor is the second: obligation and esteem held by staffers for executive and older staffers. On some papers, this obligation-esteem entity was found to be larger than on others. Where it was large, the paper appeared to have two characteristics pertinent to this discussion. First, it did a good conventional job of news-getting and news-publishing, and second, it had little difficulty over policy. With staffers drawn toward both the membership and the reference groups, organization was efficient. Most papers are like this. On the few smaller papers where executives and older staffers are not respected, morale is spotty; staffers withhold enthusiasm from their stories, they cover their beats perfunctorily, they wish for a job on a better paper, and they are apathetic and sometimes hostile to policy. Thus the obligation-esteem factor seems to be the active variable in determining not only policy conformity, but morale and good news performance as well.

Situations Permitting Deviation

Thus far it would seem that the staffer enjoys little "freedom of the press." To show that this is an oversimplification, and more important, to suggest a kind of test for our hypothesis about the strength of policy, let us ask: "What happens when a staffer *does* submit an anti-policy story?" We know that this happens infrequently, but what follows in these cases?

The process of learning policy crystallizes into a process of social control, in which devia-

[18] Whether group members acknowledge it or not, "if a person's attitudes are influenced by a set of norms which he assumes that he shares with other individuals, those individuals constitute for him a reference group." Theodore M. Newcomb, *Social Psychology* (New York: Dryden, 1950), p. 225. Williams states that reference group formation may segment large organizations; in the present case, the reverse is true, the loyalty of subordinates going to their "friendly" superiors and to the discharge of technical norms such as getting news. See Robin M. Williams, *American Society* (New York: Knopf, 1951), p. 476.

tions are punished (usually gently) by reprimand, cutting one's story, the withholding of friendly comment by an executive, etc. For example, it is punishment for a staffer when the city editor waves a piece of his copy at him and says, "Joe, don't *do* that when you're writing about the mayor." In an actual case, a staffer acting as wire editor was demoted when he neglected to feature a story about a "sacred cow" politician on his paper. What can be concluded is that when an executive sees a clearly anti-policy item, he blue-pencils it, and this constitutes a lesson for the staffer. Rarely does the staffer persist in violating policy; no such case appeared in all the interviews. Indeed, the best-known cases of firing for policy reasons—Ted O. Thackrey and Leo Huberman—occurred on liberal New York City dailies, and Thackrey was an editor, not a staffer.

Now and then cases arise in which a staffer finds his anti-policy stories printed. There seems to be no consistent explanation for this, except to introduce two more specific subjects dealing first, with the staffer's career line, and second, with particular empirical conditions associated with the career line. We can distinguish three stages through which the staffer progresses. First, there is the cub stage, the first few months or years in which the new man learns techniques and policy. He writes short, non-policy stories, such as minor accidents, meeting activity, the weather, etc. The second, or "wiring-in" stage, sees the staffer continuing to assimilate the newsroom values and to cement informal relationships. Finally there is the "star" or "veteran" stage, in which the staffer typically defines himself as a full, responsible member of the group, sees its goals as his, and can be counted on to handle policy sympathetically.[19]

To further specify the conformity-deviation problem, it must be understood that newspapering is a relatively complex activity. The newsman is responsible for a range of skills and judgments which are matched only in the professional and entrepeneurial fields. Oversimplifications about policy rigidity can be avoided if we ask, "*Under what conditions can the staffer defy or by-pass policy?*" We have already seen that staffers are free to argue news decisions with executives in brief "news conferences," but the arguments generally revolve around points of "newsiness," rather than policy as such.[20] Five factors appear significant in the area of the reporter's power to by-pass policy.

1. The norms of policy are not always entirely clear, just as many norms are vague and unstructured. Policy is covert by nature and has large scope. The paper may be Republican, but standing only lukewarm for Republican Candidate A who may be too "liberal" or no friend of the publisher. Policy, if worked out explicitly, would have to include motivations, reasons, alternatives, historical developments, and other complicating material. Thus a twilight zone permitting a range of deviation appears.[21]

2. Executives may be ignorant of particular facts, and staffers who do the leg (and telephone) work to gather news can use their superior knowledge to subvert policy. On grounds of both personal belief and professional codes, the staffer has the option of selection at many points. He can decide whom to interview and whom to ignore, what questions to ask, which quotations to note, and on writing the story which items to feature (with an eye toward the headline), which to bury, and in general what tone to give the several possible elements of the story.

3. In addition to the "squeeze" tactic exploiting executives' ignorance of minute facts, the "plant" may be employed. Although a paper's policy may proscribe a certain issue from becoming featured, a staffer, on getting a good story about that issue may "plant" it in another paper or wire service through a

---

[19] Does the new staffer, fresh from the ideals of college, really "change his attitudes"? It would seem that attitudes about socio-economic affairs need not be fixed, but are capable of shifting with the situation. There are arguments for and against any opinion; in the atmosphere of the newsroom the arguments "for" policy decisions are made to sound adequate, especially as these are evoked by the significant others in the system.

[20] The fullest treatment of editor-reporter conferences appears in Swanson, *op. cit.*
[21] Related to the fact that policy is vague is the more general postulate that executives seek to avoid formal issues and the possibly damaging disputes arising therefrom. See Chester I. Barnard, *Functions of the Executive* (Cambridge: Harvard University Press, 1947).

friendly staffer and submit it to his own editor, pleading the story is now too big to ignore.

4. It is possible to classify news into four types on the basis of source of origination. These are: the policy or campaign story, the assigned story, the beat story, and the story initiated by the staffer. The staffer's autonomy is larger with the latter than the former types. With the campaign story (build new hospital, throw rascals out, etc.), the staffer is working directly under executives and has little leeway. An assigned story is handed out by the city editor and thus will rarely hit policy head on, although the staffer has some leverage of selection. When we come to the beat story, however, it is clear that the function of the reporter changes. No editor comes between him and his beat (police department, city hall, etc.), thus the reporter gains the "editor" function. It is he who, to a marked degree, can select which stories to pursue, which to ignore. Several cases developed in interviews of beat men who smothered stories they knew would provide fuel for policy—policy they personally disliked or thought injurious to the professional code. The cooperation of would-be competing reporters is essential, of course. The fourth type of story is simply one which the staffer originates, independent of assignment or beat. All respondents, executives and staffers, averred that any employee was free to initiate stories. But equally regularly, they acknowledged that the opportunity was not often assumed. Staffers were already overloaded with beats, assignments, and routine coverage, and besides, rewards for initiated stories were meager or non-existent unless the initiated story confirmed policy. Yet this area promises much, should staffers pursue their advantage. The outstanding case in the present study concerned a well-educated, enthusiastic reporter on a conventional daily just north of the Mason-Dixon line. Entirely on his own, he consistently initiated stories about Negroes and Negro-white relations, "making" policy where only void had existed. He worked overtime to document and polish the stories; his boss said he didn't agree with the idea but insisted on the reporter's right to publish them.

5. Staffers with "star" status can transgress policy more easily than cubs. This differential privilege of status was encountered on several papers. An example would be Walter Winchell during the Roosevelt administration, who regularly praised the president while the policy of his boss, Mr. Hearst, was strongly critical of the regime. A *New York Times* staffer said he doubted that any copy reader on the paper would dare change a word of the copy of Meyer Berger, the star feature writer.

These five factors indicate that given certain conditions, the controls making for policy conformity can be bypassed. These conditions exist not only within the newsroom and the news situation but within the staffer as well; they will be exploited only if the staffer's attitudes permit. There are some limitations, then, on the strength of the publisher's policy.

Before summarizing, three additional requirements of Merton's functional paradigm must be met. These are statements of the consequences of the pattern, of available alternative modes of behavior, and a validation of the analysis.

Consequences of the Pattern

To the extent that policy is maintained, the paper keeps publishing smoothly as seen both from the newsroom and from the outside, which is no mean feat if we visualize the country with no press at all. This is the most general consequence. There are several special consequences. For the society as a whole, the existing system of power relationships is maintained. Policy usually protects property and class interests, and thus the strata and groups holding these interests are better able to retain them. For the larger community, much news is printed objectively, allowing for opinions to form openly, but policy news may be slanted or buried so that some important information is denied the citizenry. (This is the dysfunction widely scored by critics.) For the individual readers, the same is true. For the executives, their favorable statuses are maintained, with perhaps occasional touches of guilt over policy. For newsmen, the consequences are the same as for executives. For more independent, critical staffers, there can be several modes of adaptation. At the extremes, the pure conformist can deny the conflict, the confirmed deviate can quit the newspaper business. Otherwise, the adaptations seem to run in this way: (1) Keep on the job but blunt the sharp corners of policy where possible ("If I wasn't here the next guy would let *all* that crap go through . . ."); (2) Attempt to repress the conflict amorally and anti-intellectually ("What the hell, it's only a job; take your pay and forget it . . ."); (3) Attempt to compensate, by "taking it out" in other contexts: drinking, writing "the truth" for liberal publications, working with action programs, the Guild and otherwise. All of these adjustments were found in the study. As has been suggested, one of the main compensations for all staffers is simply to find justification in adhering to "good news practice."

Possible Alternatives and Change

A functional analysis, designed to locate sources of persistence of a pattern, can also indicate points of strain at which a structural change may occur. For example, the popular recipe for eliminating bias at one time was to diminish advertisers' power over the news. This theory having proved unfruitful, critics more recently have fastened upon the publisher as the point at which change must be initiated. Our analysis suggests that this is a valid approach, but one requiring that leverage in turn be applied on the publisher from various sources. Perhaps the most significant of these are professional codes. Yet we have seen the weakness of these codes when policy decisions are made. Further leverage is contained in such sources as the professional direction being taken by some journalism schools, in the Guild, and in sincere criticism.

Finally, newspaper readers possess potential power over press performance. Seen as a client of the press, the reader should be entitled to not only an interesting newspaper, but one which furnishes significant news objectively presented. This is the basic problem of democracy: to what extent should the individual be treated as a member of a mass, and to what extent fashioned (through educative measures) as an active participant in public decisions? Readership studies show that readers prefer "interesting" news and "features" over penetrating analyses. It can be concluded that the citizen has not been sufficiently motivated by society (and its press) to demand and apply the information he needs, and to discriminate

between worthwhile and spurious information, for the fulfillment of the citizen's role. These other forces—professional codes, journalism schools, the Guild, critics and readers—could result in changing newspaper performance. It still remains, however, for the publisher to be changed first. He can be located at the apex of a T, the crucial point of decision making. Newsroom and professional forces form the base of the T, outside forces from community and society are the arms. It is for the publisher to decide which forces to propitiate.

Suggestions for Validation

The Merton paradigm requires a statement concerning validation of the analysis. Checks could be forthcoming both from social science researchers and from newsmen. If the latter, the newsman should explicitly state the basis for his discussion, especially as regards the types of papers, executives, and staffers he knows. A crucial case for detailed description would be the situation in which staffers actively defied authority on policy matters. Another important test would be a comparative description of two papers contrasted by their situation as regards the six factors promoting conformity, with particular reference to the variable of obligation and esteem held toward superiors, and the factors permitting deviation. In any event, the present exploratory study may serve as a point of departure.

A second type of validation may be suggested. This would focus on the utility of the paradigm itself. Previous studies have been based on functional theory but before the development of the paradigm.[22] Studies of diverse social systems also lend themselves to functional analysis, and such comparative research could function not only to build systematic theory but to test and suggest modifications of the paradigm. Situations characterized by conflict and competion for scarce goals seem particularly well suited to functional analysis. Several points made in the present essay might have been overlooked without the paradigm.[23]

[22] References are cited in Merton, *Social Theory and Social Structure, op. cit.*, and also in the works of Talcott Parsons.
[23] That the paradigm might serve best as a checklist or "insurance," or as a theoretical guide to

Summary

The problem, which was suggested by the age-old charges of bias against the press, focussed around the manner in which the publisher's policy came to be followed, despite three empirical conditions: (1) policy sometimes contravenes journalistic norms; (2) staffers often personally disagree with it; and (3) executives cannot legitimately command that policy be followed. Interview and other data were used to explain policy maintenance. It is important to recall that the discussion is based primarily on study of papers of "middle" circulation range, and does not consider either non-policy stories or the original policy decision made by the publishers.

The mechanisms for learning policy on the part of the new staffer were given, together with suggestions as to the nature of social controls. Six factors, apparently the major variables producing policy maintenance, were de-

___

fledgling scholars, is shown by the excellence of an article published before the paradigm—and quite similar to the present article in dealing with problems of policy maintenance in a formal organization: Edward A. Shils and Morris Janowitz, "Cohesion and Disintegration in the Wehrmacht in World War II," *Public Opinion Quarterly*, 12 (Summer 1948), pp. 280–315.

scribed. The most significant of these variables, obligation and esteem for superiors, was deemed not only the most important, but the most fluctuating variable from paper to paper. Its existence and its importance for conformity led to the sub-hypothesis that reference group behavior was playing a part in the pattern. To show, however, that policy is not iron-clad, five conditions were suggested in which staffers may by-pass policy.

Thus we conclude that the publisher's policy, when established in a given subject area, is usually followed, and that a description of the dynamic socio-cultural situation of the newsroom will suggest explanations for this conformity. The newsman's source of rewards is located not among the readers, who are manifestly his clients, but among his colleagues and superiors. Instead of adhering to societal and professional ideals, he re-defines his values to the more pragmatic level of the newsroom group. He thereby gains not only status rewards, but also acceptance in a solidary group engaged in interesting, varied, and sometimes important work. Thus the cultural patterns of the newsroom produce results insufficient for wider democratic needs. Any important change toward a more "free and responsible press" must stem from various possible pressures on the publisher, who epitomizes the policy making and coordinating role.

Bureaucratic Structure and Personality

ROBERT K. MERTON

A formal, rationally organized social structure involves clearly defined patterns of activity in which, ideally, every series of actions is func-

___

From *Social Forces*, Vol. 18, 1940, pp. 560–568. Reprinted with permission of the author and the publisher, University of North Carolina Press. Copyright 1940, University of North Carolina Press.

tionally related to the purposes of the organization.[1] In such an organization there is integrated a series of offices, of hierarchized statuses, in which inhere a number of obliga-

___

[1] For a development of the concept of "rational organization," see Karl Mannheim, *Mensch und Gesellschaft im Zeitalter des Umbaus* (Leiden: A. W. Sijthoff, 1935), esp. pp. 28 ff.

tions and privileges closely defined by limited and specific rules. Each of these offices contains an area of imputed competence and responsibility. Authority, the power of control which derives from an acknowledged status, inheres in the office and not in the particular person who performs the official role. Official action ordinarily occurs within the framework of preexisting rules of the organization. The system of prescribed relations between the various offices involves a considerable degree of formality and clearly defined social distance between the occupants of these positions. Formality is manifested by means of a more or less complicated social ritual which symbolizes and supports the "pecking order" of the various offices. Such formality, which is integrated with the distribution of authority within the system, serves to minimize friction by largely restricting (official) contact to modes which are previously defined by the rules of the organization. Ready calculability of others' behavior and a stable set of mutual expectations is thus built up. Moreover, formality facilitates the interaction of the occupants of offices despite their (possibly hostile) private attitudes toward one another. In this way, the subordinate is protected from the arbitrary action of his superior, since the actions of both are constrained by a mutually recognized set of rules. Specific procedural devices foster objectivity and restrain the "quick passage of impulse into action." [2]

The ideal type of such formal organization is bureaucracy and, in many respects, the classical analysis of bureaucracy is that by Max Weber.[3] As Weber indicates, bureaucracy involves a clear-cut division of integrated activities which are regarded as duties inherent in the office. A system of differentiated controls and sanctions are stated in the regula-

tions. The assignment of roles occurs on the basis of technical qualifications which are ascertained through formalized, impersonal procedures (e.g. examinations). Within the structure of hierarchically arranged authority, the activities of "trained and salaried experts" are governed by general, abstract, clearly defined rules which preclude the necessity for the issuance of specific instructions for each specific case. The generality of the rules requires the constant use of *categorization*, whereby individual problems and cases are classified on the basis of designated criteria and are treated accordingly. The pure type of bureaucratic official is appointed, either by a superior or through the exercise of impersonal competition; he is not elected. A measure of flexibility in the bureaucracy is attained by electing higher functionaries who presumably express the will of the electorate (e.g. a body of citizens or a board of directors). The election of higher officials is designed to affect the purposes of the organization, but the technical procedures for attaining these ends are performed by a continuous bureaucratic personnel.[4]

The bulk of bureaucratic offices involve the expectation of life-long tenure, in the absence of disturbing factors which may decrease the size of the organization. Bureaucracy maximizes vocational security.[5] The function of security of tenure, pensions, incremental salaries and regularized procedures for promotion is to ensure the devoted performance of official duties, without regard for extraneous pressures.[6] The chief merit of bureaucracy is its technical efficiency, with a premium placed on precision, speed, expert control, continuity, discretion, and optimal returns on input. The structure is one which approaches the com-

---

[2] H. D. Laswell, *Politics* (New York: McGraw-Hill, 1936), pp. 120–21.

[3] Max Weber, *Wirtschaft und Gesellschaft* (Tübingen: J. C. B. Mohr, 1922), Pt. III, chap. 6, pp. 650–678. For a brief summary of Weber's discussion, see Talcott Parsons, *The Structure of Social Action* (New York: McGraw-Hill, 1937), esp. pp. 506 ff. For a description, which is not a caricature, of the bureaucrat as a personality type, see C. Rabany, "Les types sociaux: le fonctionnaire," *Revue générale d'administration,* LXXXVIII (1907), 5–28.

[4] Karl Mannheim, *Ideology and Utopia* (New York: Harcourt, Brace, 1936), pp. 18n., 105 ff. See also Ramsay Muir, *Peers and Bureaucrats* (London: Constable, 1910), pp. 12–13.

[5] E. G. Cahen-Salvador suggests that the personnel of bureaucracies is largely constituted of those who value security above all else. See his "La situation matérielle et morale des fonctionnaires," *Revue politique et parlementaire* (1926), p. 319.

[6] H. J. Laski, "Bureaucracy," *Encyclopedia of the Social Sciences.* This article is written primarily from the standpoint of the political scientist rather than that of the sociologist.

plete elimination of personalized relationships and of nonrational considerations (hostility, anxiety, affectual involvements, etc.).

Bureaucratization is accompanied by the centralization of means of production, as in modern capitalistic enterprise, or as in the case of the post-feudal army, complete separation from the means of destruction. Even the bureaucratically organized scientific laboratory is characterized by the separation of the scientist from his technical equipment.

Bureaucracy is administration which almost completely avoids public discussion of its techniques, although there may occur public discussion of its policies.[7] This "bureaucratic secrecy" is held to be necessary in order to keep valuable information from economic competitors or from foreign and potentially hostile political groups.

In these bold outlines, the positive attainments and functions of bureaucratic organization are emphasized and the internal stresses and strains of such structures are almost wholly neglected. The community at large, however, evidently emphasizes the imperfections of bureaucracy, as is suggested by the fact that the "horrid hybrid," bureaucrat, has become a *Schimpfwort*. The transition to a study of the negative aspects of bureaucracy is afforded by the application of Veblen's concept of "trained incapacity," Dewey's notion of "occupational psychosis" or Warnotte's view of "professional deformation." Trained incapacity refers to that state of affairs in which one's abilities function as inadequacies or blind spots. Actions based upon training and skills which have been successfully applied in the past may result in inappropriate responses *under changed conditions*. An inadequate flexibility in the application of skills will, in a changing milieu, result in more or less serious maladjustments.[8] Thus, to adopt a barnyard illustration used in this connection by Burke, chickens may be readily conditioned to interpret the sound of a bell as a signal for food. The same bell may now be used to summon the "trained chickens" to their doom as they are assembled to suffer decapitation. In general, one adopts measures in keeping with his past training and, under new conditions which are not recognized as *significantly* different, the very soundness of this training may lead to the adoption of the wrong procedures. Again, in Burke's almost echolalic phrase, "people may be unfitted by being fit in an unfit fitness"; their training may become an incapacity.

Dewey's concept of occupational psychosis rests upon much the same observations. As a result of their day to day routines, people develop special preferences, antipathies, discriminations and emphases.[9] (The term psychosis is used by Dewey to denote a "pronounced character of the mind.") These psychoses develop through demands put upon the individual by the particular organization of his occupational role.

The concepts of both Veblen and Dewey refer to a fundamental ambivalence. Any action can be considered in terms of what it attains or what it fails to attain. "A way of seeing is also a way of not seeing—a focus upon object A involves a neglect of object B."[10] In his discussion, Weber is almost exclusively concerned with what the bureaucratic structure attains: precision, reliability, efficiency. This same structure may be examined from another perspective provided by the ambivalence. What are the limitations of the organization designed to attain these goals?

For reasons which we have already noted, the bureaucratic structure exerts a constant pressure upon the official to be "methodical, prudent, disciplined." If the bureaucracy is to operate successfully, it must attain a high degree of reliability of behavior, an unusual degree of conformity with prescribed patterns of action. Hence, the fundamental importance of discipline which may be as highly developed in a religious or economic bureaucracy as in the army. Discipline can be effective only if the ideal patterns are buttressed by strong sentiments which entail devotion to one's duties, a keen sense of the limitation of one's authority and competence, and methodical performance of routine activities. The ef-

[7] Weber, *op. cit.*, p. 671.

[8] For a stimulating discussion and application of these concepts, see Kenneth Burke, *Permanence and Change* (New York: New Republic, 1935), pp. 50 ff.; Daniel Warnotte, "Bureaucratie et Fonctionnarisme," *Revue de l'Institut de Sociologie*, XVII (1937), 245.

[9] *Ibid.*, pp. 58–59.

[10] *Ibid.*, p. 70.

ficacy of social structure depends ultimately upon infusing group participants with appropriate attitudes and sentiments. As we shall see, there are definite arrangements in the bureaucracy for inculcating and reinforcing these sentiments.

At the moment, it suffices to observe that in order to ensure discipline (the necessary reliability of response), these sentiments are often more intense than is technically necessary. There is a margin of safety, so to speak, in the pressure exerted by these sentiments upon the bureaucrat to conform to his patterned obligations, in much the same sense that added allowances (precautionary over-estimations) are made by the engineer in designing the supports for a bridge. But this very emphasis leads to a transference of the sentiments from the *aims* of the organization onto the particular details of behavior required by the rules. Adherence to the rules, originally conceived as a means, becomes transformed into an end-in-itself; there occurs the familiar process of *displacement of goals* whereby "an instrumental value becomes a terminal value." [11]

Discipline, readily interpreted as conformance with regulations, whatever the situation, is seen not as a measure designed for specific purposes but becomes an immediate value in the life-organization of the bureaucrat. This emphasis, resulting from the displacement of the original goals, develops into rigidities and an inability to adjust readily. Formalism, even ritualism, ensues with an unchallenged insistence upon punctilious adherence to formalized procedures.[12] This may be exaggerated to the point where primary concern with conformity to the rules interferes with the achievement of the purposes of the organization, in which case we have the familiar phenomenon of the technicism or red tape of the official. An extreme product of this process of displacement of goals is the bureaucratic virtuoso, who never forgets a single rule binding his action and hence is unable to assist many of his clients.[13] A case in point, where strict recognition of the limits of authority and literal adherence to rules produced this result, is the pathetic plight of Bernt Balchen, Admiral Byrd's pilot in the flight over the South Pole.

According to a ruling of the department of labor Bernt Balchen . . . cannot receive his citizenship papers. Balchen, a native of Norway, declared his intention in 1927. It is held that he has failed to meet the condition of five years' continuous residence in the United States. The Byrd antarctic voyage took him out of the country, although he was on a ship flying the American flag, was an invaluable member of an American expedition, and in a region to which there is an American claim because of the exploration and occupation of it by Americans, this region being Little America.

The bureau of naturalization explains that it cannot proceed on the assumption that Little America is American soil. That would be *trespass on international questions* where it has no sanction. So far as the bureau is concerned, Balchen was out of the country

---

[11] This process has often been observed in various connections. Wundt's *heterogony of ends* is a case in point; Max Weber's *Paradoxie der Folgen* is another. See also MacIver's observations on the transformation of civilization into culture and Lasswell's remark that "the human animal distinguishes himself by his infinite capacity for making ends of his means." See R. K. Merton, "The Unanticipated Consequences of Purposive Social Action," *American Sociological Review*, I (1936), 894–904. In terms of the psychological mechanisms involved, this process has been analyzed most fully by Gordon W. Allport, in his discussion of what he calls "the functional autonomy of motives." Allport emends the earlier formulations of Woodworth, Tolman, and William Stern, and arrives at a statement of the process from the standpoint of individual motivation. He does not consider those phases of the social structure which conduce toward the "transformation of motives." The formulation adopted in this paper is thus complementary to Allport's analysis; the one stressing the psychological mechanisms involved, the other considering the constraints of the social structure. The convergence of psychology and sociology toward this central concept suggests that it may well constitute one of the conceptual bridges between the two disciplines. See Gordon W. Allport, *Personality* (New York: Henry Holt & Co., 1937), Chap. 7.

[12] See E. C. Hughes, "Institutional Office and the Person," *American Journal of Sociology*, XLIII (1937), 404–413; R. K. Merton, "Social Structure and Anomie," *American Sociological Review*, III (1938), 672–682; E. T. Hiller, "Social Structure in Relation to the Person," *Social Forces*, XVI (1937), 34–44.

[13] Mannheim, *Ideology and Utopia*, p. 106.

and *technically* has not complied with the law of naturalization.[14]

Such inadequacies in orientation which involve trained incapacity clearly derive from structural sources. The process may be briefly recapitulated. (1) An effective bureaucracy demands reliability of response and strict devotion to regulations. (2) Such devotion to the rules leads to their transformation into absolutes; they are no longer conceived as relative to a given set of purposes. (3) This interferes with ready adaptation under special conditions not clearly envisaged by those who drew up the general rules. (4) Thus, the very elements which conduce toward efficiency in general produce inefficiency in specific instances. Full realization of the inadequacy is seldom attained by members of the group who have not divorced themselves from the "meanings" which the rules have for them. These rules in time become symbolic in cast, rather than strictly utilitarian.

Thus far, we have treated the ingrained sentiments making for rigorous discipline simply as data, as given. However, definite features of the bureaucratic structure may be seen to conduce to these sentiments. The bureaucrat's official life is planned for him in terms of a graded career, through the organizational devices of promotion by seniority, pensions, incremental salaries, etc., all of which are designed to provide incentives for disciplined action and conformity to the official regulations.[15] The official is tacitly expected to and largely does adapt his thoughts, feelings, and actions to the prospect of this career. But *these very devices* which increase the probability of conformance also lead to an over-concern with strict adherence to regulations which induces timidity, conservatism, and technicism. Displacement of sentiments from goals onto means is fostered by the tremendous symbolic significance of the means (rules).

Another feature of the bureaucratic structure tends to produce much the same result.

Functionaries have the sense of a common destiny for all those who work together. They share the same interests, especially since there is relatively little competition insofar as promotion is in terms of seniority. In-group aggression is thus minimized and this arrangement is therefore conceived to be positively functional for the bureaucracy. However, the esprit de corps and informal social organization which typically develops in such situations often leads the personnel to defend their entrenched interests rather than to assist their clientele and elected higher officials. As President Lowell reports, if the bureaucrats believe that their status is not adequately recognized by an incoming elected official, detailed information will be withheld from him, leading him to errors for which he is held responsible. Or, if he seeks to dominate fully, and thus violates the sentiment of self-integrity of the bureaucrats, he may have documents brought to him in such numbers that he cannot manage to sign them all, let alone read them.[16] This illustrates the defensive informal organization which tends to arise whenever there is an apparent threat to the integrity of the group.[17]

It would be much too facile and partly erroneous to attribute such resistance by bureaucrats simply to vested interests. Vested interests oppose any new order which either eliminates or at least makes uncertain their differential advantage deriving from the current arrangements. This is undoubtedly involved in part in bureaucratic resistance to change but another process is perhaps more significant. As we have seen, bureaucratic officials affectively identify themselves with their way of life. They have a pride of craft which leads them to resist change in established routines; at least, those changes which are felt to be imposed by persons outside the inner circle of coworkers. This nonlogical pride of craft is a familiar pattern found even, to judge from Sutherland's *Professional Thief*, among pickpockets who, despite the risk, delight in

---

[14] Quoted from the *Chicago Tribune* (June 24, 1931, p. 10) by Thurman Arnold, *The Symbols of Government* (New Haven: Yale University Press, 1935), pp. 201–2. (My italics.)

[15] Mannheim, *Mensch und Gesellschaft*, pp. 32–33. Mannheim stresses the importance of the "Lebensplan" and the "Amtskarriere." See the comments by Hughes, *op. cit.*, 413.

[16] A. L. Lowell, *The Government of England* (New York, 1908), I, 189 ff.

[17] For an instructive description of the development of such a defensive organization in a group of workers, see F. J. Roethlisberger and W. J. Dickson, *Management and the Worker* (Boston: Harvard School of Business Administration, 1934).

mastering the prestige-bearing feat of "beating a left breech" (picking the left front trousers pocket).

In a stimulating paper, Hughes has applied the concepts of "secular" and "sacred" to various types of division of labor; "the sacredness" of caste and *Stände* prerogatives contrasts sharply with the increasing secularism of occupational differentiation in our mobile society.[18] However, as our discussion suggests, there may ensue, in particular vocations and in particular types of organization, the *process of sanctification* (viewed as the counterpart of the process of secularization). This is to say that through sentiment-formation, emotional dependence upon bureaucratic symbols and status, and affective involvement in spheres of competence and authority, there develop prerogatives involving attitudes of moral legitimacy which are established as values in their own right, and are no longer viewed as merely technical means for expediting administration. One may note a tendency for certain bureaucratic norms, originally introduced for technical reasons, to become rigidified and sacred, although, as Durkheim would say, they are *laïque en apparence*.[19] Durkheim has touched on this general process in his description of the attitudes and values which persist in the organic solidarity of a highly differentiated society.

Another feature of the bureaucratic structure, the stress on depersonalization of relationships, also plays its part in the bureaucrat's trained incapacity. The personality pattern of the bureaucrat is nucleated about this norm of impersonality. Both this and the categorizing tendency, which develops from the dominant role of general, abstract rules, tend to produce conflict in the bureaucrat's contacts with the public or clientele. Since functionaries minimize personal relations and resort to categorization, the peculiarities of individual cases are often ignored. But the client who, quite understandably, is convinced of the "special features" of *his* own problem often objects to such categorical treatment. Stereotyped behavior is not adapted to the exigencies of individual problems. The impersonal treatment of affairs which are at times of great personal significance to the client gives rise to the charge of "arrogance" and "haughtiness" of the bureaucrat. Thus, at the Greenwich Employment Exchange, the unemployed worker who is securing his insurance payment resents what he deems to be "the impersonality and, at times, the apparent abruptness and even harshness of his treatment by the clerks. . . . Some men complain of the superior attitude which the clerks have."[20]

Still another source of conflict with the

---

[18] E. C. Hughes, "Personality Types and the Division of Labor," *American Journal of Sociology*, XXXIII (1928), 754–768. Much the same distinction is drawn by Leopold von Wiese and Howard Becker, *Systematic Sociology* (New York: John Wiley & Sons, 1932), pp. 222–25 *et passim*.

[19] Hughes recognizes one phase of this process of sanctification when he writes that professional training "carries with it as a by-product assimilation of the candidate to a set of professional attitudes and controls, *a professional conscience and solidarity. The profession claims and aims to become a moral unit.*" Hughes, *op. cit.*, p. 762 (italics inserted). In this same connection, Sumner's concept of *pathos*, as the halo of sentiment which protects a social value from criticism, is particularly relevant, inasmuch as it affords a clue to the mechanisms involved in the process of sanctification. See his *Folkways* (Boston: Ginn & Co., 1906), pp. 180–181.

[20] " 'They treat you like a lump of dirt they do. I see a navvy reach across the counter and shake one of them by the collar the other day. The rest of us felt like cheering. Of course he lost his benefit over it. . . . But the clerk deserved it for his sassy way.' " (E. W. Bakke, *The Unemployed Man*, New York: Dutton, 1934, pp. 79–80). Note that the domineering attitude was *imputed* by the unemployed client who is in a state of tension due to his loss of status and self-esteem in a society where the ideology is still current that an "able man" can always find a job. That the imputation of arrogance stems largely from the client's state of mind is seen from Bakke's own observation that "the clerks were rushed, and had no time for pleasantries, but there was little sign of harshness or a superiority feeling in their treatment of the men." Insofar as there is an objective basis for the imputation of arrogant behavior to bureaucrats, it may possibly be explained by the following juxtaposed statements. "Auch der moderne, sei es öffentliche, sei es private, Beamte erstrebt immer und geniesst meist den Beherrschten gegenüber eine spezifisch gehobene, 'ständische' soziale Schätzung." (Weber, *op. cit.*, 652.) "In persons in whom the craving for prestige is uppermost, hostility usually takes the form of a desire to humiliate others." (K. Horney, *The Neurotic Personality of Our Time*, New York: Norton, 1937, pp. 178–79.)

public derives from the bureaucratic structure. The bureaucrat, in part irrespective of his position within the hierarchy, acts as a representative of the power and prestige of the entire structure. In his official role he is vested with definite authority. This often leads to an actual or apparent domineering attitude, which may only be exaggerated by a discrepancy between his position within the hierarchy and his position with reference to the public.[21] Protest and recourse to other officials on the part of the client are often ineffective or largely precluded by the previously mentioned esprit de corps which joins the officials into a more or less solidary in-group. This source of conflict *may* be minimized in private enterprise since the client can register an effective protest by transferring his trade to another organization within the competitive system. But with the monopolistic nature of the public organization, no such alternative is possible. Moreover, in this case, tension is increased because of a discrepancy between ideology and fact: the governmental personnel are held to be "servants of the people," but in fact they are usually superordinate, and release of tension can seldom be afforded by turning to other agencies for the necessary service.[22] This tension is in part attributable to the confusion of status of bureaucrat and client; the client may consider himself socially superior to the official who is at the moment dominant.[23]

Thus, with respect to the relations between officials and clientele, one structural source of conflict is the pressure for formal and impersonal treatment when individual, personalized consideration is desired by the client. The conflict may be viewed, then, as deriving from the introduction of inappropriate attitudes and relationships. Conflict within the bureaucratic structure arises from the converse situation, namely, when personalized relationships are substituted for the structurally required impersonal relationships. This type of conflict may be characterized as follows.

The bureaucracy, as we have seen, is organized as a secondary, formal group. The normal responses involved in this organized network of social expectations are supported by affective attitudes of members of the group. Since the group is oriented toward secondary norms of impersonality, any failure to conform to these norms will arouse antagonism from those who have identified themselves with the legitimacy of these rules. Hence, the substitution of personal for impersonal treatment within the structure is met with widespread disapproval and is characterized by such epithets as graft, favoritism, nepotism, apple-polishing, etc. These epithets are clearly manifestations of injured sentiments.[24] The function of such "automatic resentment" can be clearly seen in terms of the requirements of bureaucratic structure.

---

[21] In this connection, note the relevance of Koffka's comments on certain features of the pecking-order of birds. "If one compares the behavior of the bird at the top of the pecking list, the despot, with that of one very far down, the second or third from the last, then one finds the latter much more cruel to the few others over whom he lords it than the former in his treatment of all members. As soon as one removes from the group all members above the penultimate, his behavior becomes milder and may even become very friendly. . . . It is not difficult to find analogies to this in human societies, and therefore one side of such behavior must be primarily the effects of the social groupings, and not of individual characteristics." K. Koffka, *Principles of Gestalt Psychology* (New York: Harcourt, Brace, 1935), pp. 668-9.

[22] At this point the political machine often becomes functionally significant. As Steffens and others have shown, highly personalized relations and the abrogation of formal rules (red tape) by the machine often satisfy the needs of individual "clients" more fully than the formalized mechanism of governmental bureaucracy.

[23] As one of the unemployed men remarked about the clerks at the Greenwich Employment Exchange: " 'And the bloody blokes wouldn't have their jobs if it wasn't for us men out of a job either. That's what gets me about their holding their noses up.' " Bakke, *op. cit.*, p. 80.

[24] The diagnostic significance of such linguistic indices as epithets has scarcely been explored by the sociologists. Sumner properly observes that epithets produce "summary criticisms" and definitions of social situations. Dollard also notes that "epithets frequently define the central issues in a society," and Sapir has rightly emphasized the importance of context of situations in appraising the significance of epithets. Of equal relevance is Linton's observation that "in case histories the way in which the community felt about a particular episode is, if anything, more important to our study than the actual behavior. . . ." A sociological study of "vocabularies of encomium and opprobrium" should lead to valuable findings.

Bureaucracy is a secondary group mechanism designed to carry on certain activities which cannot be satisfactorily performed on the basis of primary group criteria.[25] Hence behavior which runs counter to these formalized norms becomes the object of emotionalized disapproval. This constitutes a functionally significant defence set up against tendencies which jeopardize the performance of socially necessary activities. To be sure, these reactions are not rationally determined practices explicitly designed for the fulfilment of this function. Rather, viewed in terms of the individual's interpretation of the situation, such resentment is simply an immediate response opposing the "dishonesty" of those who violate the rules of the game. However, this subjective frame of reference notwithstanding, these reactions serve the function of maintaining the essential structural elements of bureaucracy by reaffirming the necessity for formalized, secondary relations and by helping to prevent the disintegration of the bureaucratic structure which would occur should these be supplanted by personalized relations. This type of conflict may be generically described as the intrusion of primary group attitudes when secondary group attitudes are institutionally demanded, just as the bureaucrat-client conflict often derives from interaction on impersonal terms when personal treatment is individually demanded.[26]

The trend toward increasing bureaucratization in Western society, which Weber had long since foreseen, is not the sole reason for sociologists to turn their attention to this field. Empirical studies of the interaction of bureaucracy and personality should especially increase our understanding of social structure. A large number of specific questions invite our attention. To what extent are particular personality types selected and modified by the various bureaucracies (private enterprise, public service, the quasi-legal political machine, religious orders)? Inasmuch as ascendancy and submission are held to be traits of personality, despite their variability in different stimulus-situations, do bureaucracies select personalities of particularly submissive or ascendant tendencies? And since various studies have shown that these traits can be modified, does participation in bureaucratic office tend to increase ascendant tendencies? Do various systems of recruitment (e.g. patronage, open competition involving specialized knowledge or "general mental capacity," practical experience) select different personality types? Does promotion through seniority lessen competitive anxieties and enchance administrative efficiency? A detailed examination of mechanisms for imbuing the bureaucratic codes with affect would be instructive both sociologically and psychologically. Does the general anonymity of civil service decisions tend to restrict the area of prestige-symbols to a narrowly defined inner circle? Is there a tendency for differential association to be especially marked among bureaucrats?

The range of theoretically significant and practically important questions would seem to be limited only by the accessibility of the concrete data. Studies of religious, educational, military, economic, and political bureaucracies dealing with the interdependence of social organization and personality formation should constitute an avenue for fruitful research. On that avenue, the functional analysis of concrete structures may yet build a Solomon's House for sociologists.

---

[25] Cf. Ellsworth Faris, *The Nature of Human Nature* (New York: McGraw-Hill, 1937), pp. 41 ff.

[26] Community disapproval of many forms of behavior may be analyzed in terms of one or the other of these patterns of substitution of culturally inappropriate types of relationship. Thus, prostitution constitutes a type-case where coitus, a form of intimacy which is institutionally defined as symbolic of the most "sacred" primary group relationship, is placed within a contractual context, symbolized by the exchange of that most impersonal of all symbols, money. See Kingsley Davis, "The Sociology of Prostitution," *American Sociological Review*, II (1937), 744–55.

Co-operation and Competition in a Bureaucracy

PETER M. BLAU

This paper discusses performance and variations in competitiveness among twelve interviewers in two small sections of a public employment agency.[1] The duties of the interviewers in both sections were essentially alike. They received requests for workers over the phone. The order forms on which job openings were described were filed in a common pool in each section. Most of the official's time was spent interviewing applicants for jobs. After ascertaining the client's qualifications, the interviewer searched the sectional files for suitable vacancies. If an acceptable job was found, he referred the client to it and later phoned the employer to determine whether the client had been hired.

The statistics which show how many interviews and how many placements each person in the section did are passed around to all interviewers. Of course, you look at them and see how you compare with others. This creates a competitive spirit,

said one of the interviewers, voicing the sentiments of most of his fellows. In a period of job shortages, competition took the form of trying to utilize job openings before anybody else did. Interviewers were so anxious to make

From *American Journal of Sociology*, Vol. 59, May 1954, pp. 530–535. Reprinted with permission of the publisher, The University of Chicago Press. Copyright 1954, The University of Chicago Press.
[1] These data are part of a study on interpersonal relations in two government agencies conducted under a fellowship of the Social Science Research Council, which is hereby gratefully acknowledged. The entire study is soon to be published under the title "The Dynamics of Bureaucracy."

There were seven interviewers in Section A and five in Section B. Seven of the twelve were women.

placements that they even resorted to illicit methods. Said one:

> When you take an order, instead of putting it in the box, you leave it on your desk. There was so much hiding of orders under the blotter that we used to ask, "Do you have anything under your rug?" when we looked for an order. You might leave an order you took on the desk, or you might leave it on the desk after you made no referral. . . . Or, you might take an order only partially; you write the firm's name, and a few things; the others you remember. And you leave it on the pad [of order blanks]. You keep on doing this, and all these orders are not in the box.
>
> You can do some wrong filling out. For instance, for a rather low-salary job, you fill out "experience required." Nobody can make a placement on that except you, because you, alone, know that experience isn't required. Or, if there are several openings [on one order], you put the order into "referrals" [file category for *filled* job openings] after you make one placement. You're supposed to put it into "referrals" but stand it up, so that the others can see it. If you don't, you have a better chance of making the next placement than somebody else. And time and again you see four, five openings on one order filled by the same person. [In one case on file eight out of nine openings on one order had been filled by the same interviewer.]

The major opportunity for competitive monopolization of job openings occurred when they were received from employers. Since illicit practices were concealed from the observer, the extent of competition could not be determined through questioning or direct

381

observation [2] but was betrayed by the record of official transactions. The extent to which an interviewer filled the vacancies he had re-

[2] This is clearly indicated by the comment of one of a group of special interviewers, who were expected to use the job openings of the regular interviewers but usually had great difficulty in doing so: "Oh, they hide everything from us. We got more orders when you [the observer] sat in the middle of that section than ever before. We laughed about it. Interviewers would hand us orders asking whether we could use them—when you were looking. That had never happened before."

ceived over the phone with his own clients in excess of chance expectations furnishes an index of competitiveness. (Col. 4 in Table 1 shows this index; Col. 1–3 present the data on which it is based.)

STRUCTURAL CONDITIONS AND COMPETITIVENESS. The members of Section A were more competitive than those of Section B. The last two columns in Table 1 also show that the interviewer's competitiveness was related to his productivity in Section A (Pearsonian $r = +.92$), but this was not the case in Section B ($r = -.20$). In other words, hoarding of jobs

Table 1. Competitiveness and Producitvity in Section A and in Section B

	OPENINGS RECEIVED * (1)	REFERRALS MADE BY RECIPIENT (2)	RATIO OF REFERRALS TO OPENINGS (3)	COMPETI- TIVENESS † (4)	PRO- DUCTIVITY ‡ (5)	NUMBER OF PLACEMENTS (6)
Section A:						
Adams	34	19	0.56	3.9	0.70	100
Ahman	62	27	0.44	3.1	0.49	70
Ajax	40	28	0.70	4.9	0.97	139
Akers	71	32	0.45	3.2	0.71	101
Ambros	69	18	0.26	1.8	0.45	65
Atzenberg	106	43	0.41	2.9	0.61	87
Auble	10	3	0.30	2.1	0.39	56 §
Section B						
Babcock	16	7	0.44	2.2	0.53	46
Beers	58	19	0.33	1.6	0.71	62
Bing	51	15	0.29	1.5	0.75	65
Borden	17	7	0.41	2.1	0.55	48 §
Bush	43	19	0.42	2.1	0.97	84
Section A	392	170	0.43	3.0	0.59	590
Section B	185	67	0.36	1.8	0.67	289

* The great differences between interviewers in this column show that some were much more successful than others in inducing employers, or telephone operators, to channel requests for workers to them personally. This form of rivalry does not involve competitive interaction.

† Competitiveness index (col. 4): The proportion of job openings received to which the recipient made a referral (col. 3) times the number of members of the section. (This represents the observed divided by the expected frequency of referrals made by the recipient of a job opening.) Base period: First half of April, 1949.

‡ Productivity index (col. 5): The number of placements made (col. 6) divided by the number of job openings available, that is, the number of openings in the section per interviewer. Base period: April, 1949.

§ The number of placements was adjusted for the two interviewers absent for more than five days during April. Since the sectional numbers of placements were not revised, the values in col. 6 add up to more than the two totals shown.

was an effective way to improve an interviewer's placement record only in one of these two groups.

The members of Section B were more co-operative: they discouraged competitive practices by making them ineffective. When they learned about interesting vacancies, they often told one another, but an interviewer who manifested competitive tendencies was excluded from the network of reciprocal information and lost the respect of his co-workers. Any advantage of hoarding jobs was, at least, neutralized by such lack of co-operation, as is indicated by the absence of a relation between competitiveness and productivity in this group. Since competitive practices made an interviewer unpopular and failed to raise his productivity, they were infrequent.

These officials themselves attributed the greater competitiveness in Section A to the ambitiousness of several members: "There is usually one individual who starts it, who becomes a pace-setter. Once it has started, it is too late." The others, so interviewers claimed, have to follow suit. However, the most competitive member of Section A in recounting her reactions when production records were first introduced made it clear that this explanation of competition on the basis of personality characteristics is inadequate:

> When they introduced statistics, I realized how fast I worked. I even wanted to drop lower. I didn't mind working fast as long as it didn't show, but when it showed up like that on the record, I wanted to work less. But you know what happened? Some of the others started to compete with each other and produced more than I did. Then I thought to myself, "Since I can do it, it's silly to let them get ahead of me." I'm only human. So I worked as fast as before.

When statistical records made the superior performance of this interviewer public knowledge, she decided to work less, possibly in response to pressures the others had brought to bear upon her. While complaining about her unfair standards, however, the other members of the section also improved their own performance. Consequently, this interviewer, just like the others, felt constrained by colleagues to compete for an outstanding record. One or two members of Section B, on the other hand, were also accused of competitive tendencies, but their colleagues successfully discouraged their expression in monopolistic practices. It is in this sense that the competitive practices of one group and the co-operative practices of the other were social factors, calling for explanation in sociological rather than psychological terms, as Durkheim has long since emphasized.[3]

Differential conditions affected the development of these two groups. First, the supervisor in Section A relied heavily on performance records in evaluating interviewers: "And here, in the production figures, is the answer to the question: How good are you? Here you see exactly how good the work you did was." Interviewers often mentioned the pressure thus exerted: "[Especially] around rating time, you get this competition. You don't care whether the best person gets the pob, but you try to make the placement yourself." In contrast, the new supervisor in Section B surprised his subordinates by rating them more leniently than they had expected, and not primarily on the basis of production records. Consequently, as one interviewer reported, "we became less anxious about statistics; another experience like that, and we might forget all about placement credit."

Second, a common professional orientation existed only in Section B. While the members of Section A had been assigned, and had received their training, at different times, the majority of those in Section B received their training together after World War II, at a times when intensive counseling had been stressed, since many returning veterans needed occupational advice. One official said of this period:

> When I first came here, in May, 1946, we had a very nice bunch. It was like an all-day consultation; we discussed placements with each other all day long. At that time, the veterans came back, and there was a lot of emphasis on counseling. Nobody asked you how many placements you made, then. The emphasis was on quality, and we consulted with each other all day.

[3] Emile Durkheim, *The Rules of Sociological Method* (Chicago: University of Chicago Press, 1938), pp. 110 and *passim*.

In this situation, the group developed a common professional code, which discouraged speedy placement as constituting defective employment service. In effect, this orientation transformed competitive practices from illegitimate means for desirable ends into illegitimate means for worthless ends. If such practices did occur, they were vigorously opposed on moral grounds as violating the interest of clients. Nevertheless, as will be shown presently, competition could not have been effectively curbed if the supervisor's evaluation practice had engendered acute anxiety over productivity. However, the existence of this code would have made it difficult for the supervisor to judge performance mainly by productivity, since doing so would have stamped him as ignorant of the essentials of good employment service.

No opportunity for the development of a *common* professional code had existed in Section A. Since competitiveness prevailed in this group, the individual whose personal professional standards made him reluctant to compete either became the deviant whose productivity suffered or modified his standards and entered the race with the others.

<u>Third</u>, most members of Section A had been appointed to temporary civil service positions during World War II. They were on probation pending permanent appointments when production records were originally introduced and even afterward remained subject to lay-offs due to reductions in staff. Their insecurity led them to strive to impress superiors with outstanding performance. In contrast, all but one of the members of Section B were veterans, whose employment could not be terminated except for cause. As one envious colleague put it, "They felt that nothing could happen to them, because they were veterans, and had super-seniority."

Differences in these three conditions—security of employment, opportunity for the development of a common professional orientation, and the evaluation practice of the supervisor—gave rise to two dissimilar social structures. Productivity was highly valued in Section A and became associated with the individual's standing in the group, while striving for sheer productivity was disparaged in Section B. Thus, whereas the most productive and most competitive member of Section A was considered the best interviewer by her co-workers and was most popular with them,[4] the most productive member of Section B was least respected and least popular. As a result of these structural differences, co-operative norms prevailed only in Section B.

The interviewers in *both* sections disliked working in a competitive atmosphere. A member of Section A said: "If I see that an interviewer keeps orders on her desk, I take them and put them in the box. . . . Of course, you don't make friends that way." Since the majority in this section, including its most popular members, were highly competitive, to antagonize them was to threaten one's own standing in the group. This deterred interviewers from discouraging competitive practices. Antagonizing a deviant, however, does not endanger one's status. Consequently, since a striver was unpopular in Section B, its members could use sanctions freely to combat competitive practices and enforce co-operative norms.

SOCIAL COHESION AND PRODUCTIVITY. Table 1 shows that the group most concerned with productivity was less productive than the other group. Fifty-nine per cent of the job openings received in Section A were filled, in contrast to 67 per cent in Section B. (The 8 per cent difference is significant on the .01 level.) Another implicit paradox is that competitiveness and productivity were directly related for individuals in Section A but inversely related for the two groups.[5]

Anxious concern with productivity induced interviewers in Section A to concentrate blindly upon it at the expense of other considerations. In their eagerness to make many placements they often ignored their relationships with others as well as official rules. Competitiveness in this group weakened social co-

---

[4] She was most often mentioned by members of her own section in answer to the questions, respectively, "Who are the best interviewers?" and "Who are your friends in the office?"

[5] For another example of such disparity between individual and corresponding group data see the discussion of promotion opportunities and attitudes toward promotion in Samuel A. Stouffer *et al.*, *The American Soldier* (Princeton: Princeton University Press, 1949), I, 250–54. Kendall and Lazarsfeld discuss the methodological significance of such findings in Robert K. Merton and Paul F. Lazarsfeld (eds.), *Continuities in Social Research* (Glencoe, Ill.: Free Press, 1950), pp. 193–95.

hesion, while co-operativeness in Section B strengthened it. This difference is further shown by the fact that usually none of the members of Section A spent their rest periods together, whereas all but one of those of Section B, a newcomer when this study was being made, did. Social cohesion enhanced operating efficiency by facilitating co-operation and by reducing status anxiety.

Although the members of both groups had occasion to assist one another, greater effort was required to elicit such co-operation in Section A. The social interaction that occurred in the office during the twenty-four busiest hours of one week was recorded and classified as official and private contacts, that is, those directly concerned with a specific job or client, and all others. The frequency of an interviewer's official contacts with colleagues was related to his productivity in Section A (rank correlation $= +.98$) but not in Section B (rank correlation $= +.08$). This suggests that only interviewers who kept, as one put it, "hopping around all the time" to retrieve job orders that others kept on their desks were able to make many placements in the competitive section. In the cohesive group, on the other hand, the co-operation needed for making placements occurred as a matter of course, and not only in response to special requests. This effort was not required for high productivity.

To maximize his placements, the interviewer in Section A hoarded jobs and simultaneously tried to prevent others from doing so, thereby antagonizing his co-workers, whose co-operation he needed if he was to do well. The members of this section therefore attempted to conciliate colleagues whom their competitive practices had alienated. Often, shortly after having interfered with her operations, an interviewer paid another a compliment about her work or her apparel. The most competitive interviewer was in the habit of taking time out to joke with her co-workers and was proud of making more placements than anybody else, "nevertheless." Actually, this compensating friendliness, which made her popular despite her competitiveness, helped her to be productive.

In Section A, interviewers had to make special efforts at conciliation in order to make placements, but this was not necessary in Section B. At least, this impression is corroborated by the finding that frequency of private contacts with others was also related to productivity in Section A (rank correlation $= +.84$) but not in Section B (rank correlation $= +.13$). The members of the cohesive group, whose operating practices did not put colleagues at a disadvantage, did not have to devote time and energy to solicit and encourage co-operation, since it was not extended reluctantly. Their spontaneous co-operation improved operating efficiency.

Social cohesion also lessened the status anxiety generated by the evaluation system. Such anxiety is most acute in the individual who does not feel integrated in his work group and therefore seeks to derive social recognition from excelling at his task and from approval of superiors. Friendly relations with co-workers made the standing of the individual in the cohesive group independent of his productivity, particularly since fast work was disparaged as a sign of superficial service. The consequent reduction of anxiety in the antiproductivity-oriented group actually raised its productivity.

Fluctuations in productivity illustrate the dysfunction of status anxiety. Section B had not always operated more efficiently than Section A. Its productivity had been lower during the two months preceding the last rating but had abruptly increased then, while that of Section A had declined, as Table 2 shows.

The two groups found themselves in different situations before and after they were rated. The members of Section A were familiar with the rating standards of their supervisor, for she had rated them in previous years. Their anxiety led them to work especially hard immediately before the annual rating. The members of Section B, on the other hand, had never before been rated by their new supervisor. They were also concerned about their record but could not calm their anxiety by concentrating upon certain tasks, because they did not know what the supervisor would stress; the explanation he gave to his subordinates was too vague and adhered too strictly to official procedures to help them to foresee his actual practices. This unfocused anxiety was particularly detrimental to efficient performance. Later, when the interviewers found out that they were not rated primarily on the basis of statistical records, their anxiety largely subsided and their productivity increased. In contrast, the experience of the members of Section A, whose rating was strongly influenced by their production records, intensified their status anxiety, but, when the rating was over, anxiety was no longer channeled into exceptionally hard work, with the result that their productivity declined below that of Section B.

Social cohesion is no guaranty against anxiety in a bureaucracy. Civil service status is too important to officials for them to remain immune to the threat of losing it. But when no such threat is felt, social cohesion reduces anxiety by divesting productivity of its significance as a symbol of status in the work group. Diminished anxiety as well as smoother cooperation then enable those in the cohesive group to perform their tasks more efficiently than the others.

In the absence of social cohesion, competitive striving for an outstanding performance record became a substitute means for relieving status anxiety in Section A. This psychological function of competition is illustrated by the following incident: The interviewers in this section became very irritable, and one of them even became physically ill, when a temporary supervisor, who tried to prevent competitive practices, interfered with their method of allaying anxiety. Status anxiety reduced operating efficiency. Even in the cohesive group, productivity was low when the unknown rating standards of a new supervisor produced

Table 2. Productivity before and after Rating

	SECTION A		SECTION B	
December, 1948	0.64	(619)*	0.56	(317)
January, 1949	0.70	(941)	0.56	(472)
February, 1949 (rating)	0.56	(1,342)	0.60	(477)
March, 1949	0.59	(1,335)	0.71	(448)
April, 1949	0.59	(1,001)	0.67	(433)

* Numbers in parentheses are the numbers of job openings available on which the productivity index—the proportion of these openings that were filled—is based.

acute and diffuse anxiety. Otherwise, however, the cohesive group was more productive, because social cohesion relieved status anxiety by making the individual's standing in the group independent of his productivity. The very competitive striving that undermined the group's cohesiveness also served to lessen the individual's status anxiety in a noncohesive situation. The hypothesis that the cohesiveness of the group and the competitiveness of the individual in the less cohesive group both reduce status anxiety explains the paradox that the *less competitive group* as well as the *more competitive individual* in the competitive group each was particularly productive.

About the Functions of Bureaucratic Rules

ALVIN W. GOULDNER

In seeking to account for the development of bureaucracy we have, so far, conformed to the time-honored canons of the working de-

From *Patterns of Industrial Bureaucracy*. Glencoe: Free Press, 1954, pp. 157–180. Reprinted with permission of the publisher.

tective; that is, we have sought to demonstrate first, the "motives," and then the "opportunity." In considering the first, it has been suggested that the "motives" comprise an effort to solve the problem of worker "apathy"; in examining the "opportunity," attention has been given to the recalcitrance of the human material, and to the question of whether the "victim" is cussedly resistant or quietly acquiescent.

By analogy, we are not so much interested in the "crime" as in the career of the criminal, and this, of course, is shaped by more than his motives or opportunities. It depends also on what *happens* in the course of such a career. Whether the criminal escapes or is caught is no petty detail; whether he satisfies his motives or frustrates them influences the development of his career.

Similarly, we were interested in the "career" of bureaucratic patterns. Wherever bureaucratic patterns are found to be relatively entrenched, it must be assumed that their "career" has resulted in a net balance of gains greater than that of the losses, though it would be foolhardy to assume that there had been *no* losses at all. Above all, this means that the *consequences* which are brought about by bureaucratic methods of administration must be examined if their *survival* is to be understood. Here the problem is not one of motives or opportunities, or intentions and powers; it is rather a question of the practical results which sustain bureaucratic patterns once initiated. In fine, the questions are: What gains were secured by bureaucratic procedures; what problems were actually mitigated; what tensions were eased by their use?

A final *caveat:* Attention will be focused here on only one aspect of bureaucracy, the bureaucratic rules. The discussion will be confined to the functions of these rules, and no analysis will be made of the functions of other characteristic features of bureaucratic organization, such as a highly specialized division of labor. In addition to expedient considerations, this decision derived from the fact that bureaucratic rules are central to Max Weber's theory of bureaucracy. If organizations (like organisms) operate in terms of a "safety margin" factor, developing their tension-reducing mechanisms beyond the point required for routine operations, then it may well be that hypotheses about the functions of bureaucratic rules will yield hypotheses of broader generality, which are applicable to other bureaucratic characteristics.

THE PROBLEM OF "CLOSE SUPERVISION." The problem may be opened by reviewing a point touched upon before: If a supervisor viewed a worker as unmotivated, as unwilling to "do a job," how did the supervisor respond; how did he attempt to solve this problem? He usually attempted to handle this by directing the worker more closely, by watching him carefully, and explicitly outlining his work obligations. As one foreman said: "If I catch a man goofing off, I tell him in an a,b,c, way exactly what he has to do, and I watch him like a hawk 'til he's done it." This was precisely what Peele did when he first entered the plant as manager and found that the workers were resisting him.[1]

At first glance this might appear to be a stable solution; it might seem as if "close supervision" would allow the supervisor to bring the problem under control. Actually, however, there were commanding reasons why supervisors could not rest content to supervise their workers closely and to remind them endlessly of what had to be done. One motive was fairly obvious: The supervisor could not watch all of his men all of the time. As a surface fore-

[1] Students of industrial behavior will at once note that we have been led back to the lair of a hoary problem whose origins, however indeterminate, have a certifiable antiquity. John Stuart Mill, for example, had long since observed the connections between "close supervision" and the managerial estimate of workers' motivation to work: "The moral qualities of the laborers are fully as important to the efficiency and worth of their labor as the intellectual . . . it is well worthy of meditation, how much of the aggregate of their labor depends upon their trustworthiness. All the labor now expended in watching that they fulfill their engagement, or in verifying that they have fulfilled it, is so much withdrawn from the real business of production to be devoted to a subsidiary function rendered needful not by the necessity of things but by the dishonesty of men. Nor are the greatest precautions more than very imperfectly efficacious, where, as is now almost invariably the case with hired laborers, *the slightest relaxation of vigilance is an opportunity eagerly seized for eluding performance of their contract.*" (Our emphasis— A. W. G.) Longmans, Green and Co., Ltd., London, 1926 edition, pp. 110–111. More recently, the problem of "close supervision" has been given careful attention at the University of Michigan. One of the most theoretically sophisticated accounts of this work is to be found in Daniel Katz and Robert Kahn, "Human Organization and Worker Motivation," in *Industrial Productivity*, edited by L. Reed Tripp, Industrial Relations Research Association, Madison, Wisconsin, 1951, pp. 146–171.

man remarked, "As soon as I turn my back on some of these guys, they slip me the knife."

There is, though, one basis on which the supervisor could feel confident that workers would do their jobs even when he was *not* around; that is, if the supervisors believed that workers themselves wanted to do what was expected of them. As John Stuart Mill remarked in this connection, "Nor are the greatest *outward* precautions comparable in efficacy to the monitor *within*." [2] Indeed, it may be suspected that this was *one* of the factors alerting management to the problem of the worker's motivation; for a motivated worker made the job of supervision earlier.

There is, however, another consideration that made "close supervision" a dangerous solution to the problem of the unmotivated worker. Specifically, workers viewed close supervision as a kind of "strictness" and punishment. In consequence, the more a supervisor watched his subordinates, the more hostile they became to him. Workers shared standardized conceptions of what a "good" or legitimate foreman should be like, and almost universally, these insisted that the good foreman was one who "doesn't look over your shoulder." From the workers' standpoint a "driving" foreman was "bad," and they would retaliate by withholding work effort. As a hopper worker asserted:

> If the foreman doesn't work well with us, we don't give him as good work as we can . . . I just don't care, I let things slide.

In other words, close supervision enmeshed management in a vicious cycle: the supervisor perceived the worker as unmotivated; he then carefully watched and directed him; this aroused the worker's ire and accentuated his apathy, and now the supervisor was back where he began. Close supervision did not solve his problem. In fact, it might make the worker's performance, in the super's absence, even less reliable than it had been.

Must it be supposed, however, that "close supervision" *invariably* corrodes the relationship between the worker and his superior? Does it do so under any and all conditions? What is there *about* close supervision which

disturbs relations between workers and supers? To consider the last question first: Notice that close supervision entails an intensification of face-to-face direction of the worker. In such a context, it becomes very *evident* exactly "who is boss." This, in turn, suggests one of the distinctive conditions which underpin the strains induced by close supervision; for ours is a culture in which great stress is placed upon the equality of persons, and in such a cultural context *visible* differences in power and privilege readily become sources of tension, particularly so if status differences do not correspond with traditionally prized attributes such as skill, experience, or seniority.

Close supervision violated norms of equality internalized by workers, and they responded by complaining that the supervisor was "just trying to *show* who is boss." Workers' devotion to this norm was indicated also by their preference for supervisors who did not act as if they were "better than anyone else"; they insisted that supervisors, or for that matter other workers, should not behave like "big shots." In other words, they were hostile to those who put forth claims of personal superiority.[3]

Again, workers expressed the feeling that close supervision violated their culturally prescribed expectations of equality by saying that such a supervisor was "trying to make a *slave* out of us."

Supervisors, as well as workers, were frequently oriented to the same egalitarian norms. For example, the production manager for the entire Company expressed these sentiments in the following way:

> "Here's the real secret to successful human relations: The real key lies in treating your employees like human beings. *I'm no better than any one of the plant workers.* Oh,

---

[2] Mill, *ibid.* [*sic*], p. 111. This statement was deleted from the third (1852) edition. (Our emphasis—A. W. G.)

[3] That this is a culturally induced sentiment, as significant in a military as in an industrial setting, may be inferred from the warning addressed to U. S. Army officers during the last war: ". . . do not make the mistake of thinking of yourself as a superior individual . . . ," officers were cautioned in "Military Courtesy and Discipline," W. D. Man. FM 21-50, June 15, 1942, quoted in S. A. Stouffer, E. A. Suchman, Leland C. DeVinney, Shirley A. Star, and Robin M. Williams, Jr., *The American Soldier*, Vol. 1, Princeton University Press, Princeton, N. J., 1949, p. 387.

maybe I can afford a little better car, or a home in Penmore.[4] I can send my kids for a music lesson while they can't. *But these things don't make me any better than them.*"

To the extent that a supervisor was oriented to norms of equality, the continual exercise of direct face-to-face supervision might be expected to create tensions for him. As one board plant foreman confided: "Sometimes I wonder who the hell am I to tell these guys what to do."

THE EXPLICATIONAL FUNCTIONS OF BUREAUCRATIC RULES. In this context, some of the functions performed by bureaucratic rules can perhaps be more readily discerned. First, it can be noted that the rules comprise a functional equivalent for direct, personally given orders. Like direct orders, rules specify the obligations of the worker, enjoining him to do particular things in definite ways. Usually, however, rules are given, or are believed to be given, more deliberation than orders, and thus the statement of obligations they explicate can be taken to be definitive. Since the rules are also more carefully expressed, the obligations they impose may be less ambiguous than a hastily worded personal command.[5] Looked at in this light, rules are a form of communication to those who are seen as desirous of evading responsibilities, of avoiding commitments, and of withholding proper and full performance of obligations. Comprising in one facet an explicit body of obligations, the rules serve to draw a worker's *attention* to managerial expectations and to dissolve the residues of diffuseness which may allow the

worker to "hedge." Thus, on the one hand, the rules explicate the worker's task while on the other, they shape and specify his relationships to his superior. Stated in the language of the political scientist, the rules serve to narrow the subordinate's "area of discretion." The subordinates now have fewer options concerning what they *may* or *may not* do, and the area of "privilege" is crowded out by the growing area of "obligation."

It might be asked, why were work obligations comparatively diffuse in the mine, but much more explicit on the surface? An illustration previously used was the situation in which a group of workers were standing around, waiting for the mine head to assign them. He stepped out of his office and said, "One of you, clean out the rock crusher."

How was a *specific* individual chosen for this "dirty" job? This was the question asked a worker who had been through the situation. "It's simple," he replied. "We all just turn around and *look* at the newest guy in the group and he goes and does it." In other words, there existed an *informal* norm among miners to the effect that *new* workers got the dirty jobs; it was a norm to which the men were so sensitive that a mere "look" could bring the expected results. The informal group among miners spontaneously and with solidarity acted to enforce its norms. The informal group and its norms, then, constituted a functional equivalent for bureaucratic rules to the degree, at least, that it served to allocate concrete work responsibilities and to specify individual duties. It would appear, therefore, that the explication of obligations provided by bureaucratic rules is particularly necessary where there is no other instrumentality, specifically an effective informal group, which does this.[6]

---

[4] A middle class suburb in the area.

[5] Mill also saw the function of rules as a definitive statement of explicit obligations. He insisted that the successful conduct of a business required two things, "fidelity and zeal." Fidelity, easier to obtain than zeal, could be partly ensured when "work admits of being reduced to a *definite set of rules;* the violation of which conscience cannot easily blind itself, and on which responsibility may be enforced by the loss of employment." Nevertheless, he conceded, many things needed for business success cannot be reduced to "distinct and positive obligations." Finally, in this connection, he adds "the universal neglect by domestic servants of their employer's interest, wherever these are not protected by some fixed rule, is a matter of common remark . . ." *Ibid.,* p. 139.

[6] This situation is in seeming contrast to one described by William Foote Whyte in his perceptive, *Human Relations in the Restaurant Industry,* McGraw-Hill Book Co., New York, 1948. Whyte recounts an incident in which a supervisor gave an order to two women, without specifying which one was to carry it out. Whyte remarks, "For effective action, orders and directions must be definite and clear as to what must be done, *how* and *when* it is to be done, and *who is to do it.*" (*Ibid.,* p. 261.) Our own formulations are not necessarily in contradiction to Whyte's practical strictures. From our viewpoint, however, Whyte's conclusions should be limited to situations in which informal co-

THE SCREENING FUNCTIONS OF RULES. A second, less obvious, function of bureaucratic rules can be observed if we notice that, in part, they provide a substitute for the personal repetition of orders by a supervisor. Once an obligation was incorporated into a rule, the worker could not excuse himself by claiming that the supervisor had failed to tell him to do a specific thing. To take one example: The worker who operated a machine without using the safety guard could not "pass the buck" by saying that the supervisor neglected to mention this when he gave him a task. Since there existed a standing rule that "safety guards should always be used," the supervisor need not warn the worker of this every time he instructed him to use a machine.

Once standing rules have been installed, there are fewer things that a supervisor has to direct a worker to do; thus the frequency and duration of worker-foreman interaction in their *official* capacities is somewhat lessened. Morever, even if the super does intervene in his capacity as a superior, he need not appear to be doing so on his own account; he is not so apt to be seen as "throwing his weight around." He can say, as one foreman said about the no-absenteeism rule: "I can't help laying them off if they're absent. *It's not my idea.* I've got to go along with the rules *like everyone else.* What *I* want has nothing to do with it." In other words, the rules provide the foreman with an impersonal crutch for his authority, screening the superiority of his power which might otherwise violate the norm of equality. Instead, equality presumably prevails because, "like everyone else," he, too, is bound by the rules which the plant manager has sanctioned.

Differences in power which are not justifiable in terms of the group's norms, or which violate them, seem to establish a situation requiring the utilization of impersonal control techniques. Impersonal and general rules serve in part to obscure the existence of power disparities which are not legitimate in terms of the group's norms.[7] The screening function of the rules would seem, therefore, to work in two directions at once. First, it impersonally bolsters a supervisor's claim to authority without compelling him to employ an embarrassing and debatable legitimation in terms of his personal superiority. Conversely, it permits *workers* to accept managerial claims to deference without committing them to a merely personal submission to the supervisor that would betray their self-image as "any man's equal."

THE "REMOTE CONTROL" FUNCTION OF RULES. It would be a mistake, however, to continue assuming that management instituted rules only when it perceived workers as unmotivated. For top management was often as much concerned with the low motivation of those in the lower echelons of its own ranks, i.e., middle management, as it was with workers'.

[7] William F. Whyte has made an observation in his restaurant studies which, if reconceptualized, in effect constitutes an interesting example of this pattern. Whyte points out that tension arises between the waitresses and the pantry help who fill their orders, under several conditions: when the waitresses are *younger* than the pantry people—even though both groups are women; or when those in the pantry are *men.* It would seem that these tensions emerge because *traditional* criteria of authority in our society are being violated. That is, younger people are initiating action for older people, while our cultural prescriptions prefer that power be vested in older folk. Again, women are initiating action for men, while the culture prescribes that men should wield the power. In an acute analysis, Whyte makes the following interpretation of the "insignificant-looking spindle" on which the waitresses place their orders, and from which the pantry people take them. "Wherever the people on the receiving end of the orders are related to the order givers as males vs. females, or older vs. younger, then it is important for the pantry help to have some *impersonal* barrier to block the pressure from themselves." (*Ibid.,* p. 75.) In other words, instead of having the waitresses orally inform the pantry help of what they want, the waitresses can now write it out and place their order on the spindle. The pantry personnel can pick the order off the spindle without coming into direct interaction with the waitresses and without seeming to take orders from those culturally prescribed as inferiors. The spindle thus masks the existence of a relationship which violates internalized cultural prescriptions.

hesion among workers has deteriorated so that they are unable to apply pressure to get the work done themselves, or if they are *unwilling* to do so. Our earlier point, about the tensions generated by close supervision, leads us to suspect that Whyte's prescriptions of detailed orders signify the presence of a motivational problem which may only be further exacerbated by the remedy he proposes.

This was quite evident in Peele's feeling that foreman and supervisors were "shirking." It was also a pattern that was more generally evident. Thus, for example, if all supervisors could be "counted on" to enforce safety regulations there would have been no need for the main office to employ a "safety engineer" to check upon safety conditions in the local plants.[8]

The problem of handling the "enemy within" was sometimes more difficult than that of coping with those in the "out-group." For at least on the factory level, in-group and out-group could stand face to face and might sniff watchfully at each other, and could place their confidence for a while in "close supervision." But what could the safety engineer, for example, do to control some twenty-five plants? How could he control the supervision of safety work throughout the entire Company by means of "close supervision" alone? (Notice that the safety engineer's problem was only an extreme case of a common problem; it was not qualitatively different from that experienced by many of the plant's middle managers).

In some way the safety engineer had to utilize a "spot check" system. That is, he made occasional visits to a plant, spending a little while there, and then moved on to another factory. If, however, each plant was to operate on a unique basis, each having its own distinctive techniques for handling safety, it would be difficult for the safety engineer to make his *own* judgment about plant conditions. He would be forced to place greater reliance on local management, which was precisely what he wanted to avoid. Insofar as he had established certain general rules applying to all plants, he could go to each one and "see for himself." He could "tell at a glance" whether the rules concerning machine guards or debris on the floor were being followed. In part, then, the existence of general rules was a necessary adjunct to a "spot check" system; they facilitated "control from a distance" by those in the higher and more remote reaches of the organization.[9]

There was another aspect of the rules which was also helpful to control from a distance. This was their *public* character. Because the rules were publicly known, an "enemy" could be used to control an "ally." For example, when the safety engineer inspected a plant he was not averse to speaking to workers whom he himself characterized as "troublemakers." The safety engineer told of a plant tour which he had made while in the company of a "troublemaker." This worker showed the engineer that there was a pile of debris in front of the blacksmith's bench, and took him to another spot and showed him how a machine had had its guard removed. He could only do this because the rules were public knowledge, and like everyone else, the "troublemaker" knew what they were. On the basis of these observations the safety engineer could then apply pressure to the supervisors. In sum, the *public* character of the rules enabled deviance to be detected by the *out-group*. This enlarged the information channels open to the heads of the in-group, in turn enabling them to keep their own junior officers in line.

These considerations lead us to expect that bureaucratic rules flourish, other things being equal, when the senior officers of a group are impressed with the recalcitrance of those to whom they have delegated a measure of com-

---

[8] Safety rules are discussed more fully in Chapter X [of *Patterns of Industrial Bureaucracy*].

[9] Some further implications of this, in the context of labor relations problems, may be seen from the comments of Frederick H. Harbison and Robert Dubin about the General Motors Company: "A rigid grievance procedure has made it easier for the corporation to control the decisions and actions of management's rank and file. Thousands of plant managers, department superintendents and foremen have been dealing with union representatives on a day-to-day basis. Many of them have been inexperienced in labor relations, and some were bound to make mistakes. *The existence of a system of rules has made it easier to top company officials to locate quickly those spots where local management has been 'off base.'*" (Our emphasis—A. W. G.) *Patterns of Union-Management Relations*, Science Research Associates, Chicago, 1947, pp. 83–84. The remote control function of bureaucratic measures has also been noted by Franz Neumann and Julian Franklin. For example, Franklin writes: "Rigid hierarchy and a precisely articulated framework of offices and functions make it possible for discretionary policy to be set at *one point* outside the bureaucracy and then to be administered automatically at all levels of the hierarchy." "The Democratic Approach to Bureaucracy," *Readings in Culture, Personality and Society*, Columbia College, N. Y., n. d., p. 3.

mand. In other words, bureaucratic patterns are particularly useful to the degree that distrust and suspicion concerning role performance has become diffuse and directed to members of the "in-group," as well as to those on the outside; and when, as the Old Testament puts it, "A man's enemies are the men of his own house."

THE PUNISHMENT LEGITIMATING FUNCTIONS OF RULES. Faced with subordinates who were only reluctantly performing their roles, or at least, who were seen in this way, management was experiencing a status-threatening and hence aggression-provoking situation. The supervisor wanted to eliminate these threats when they arose and to prevent their recurrence. These were the supervisor's needs which emerged from his relations with workers when the latter began to behave apathetically ("goldbricking") or disobediently ("talking back"). On another level, the personality plane, the supervisor was beginning to "burn up" and was getting set to "blow his top." He was, in brief, accumulating a cargo of aggression with which he had to do something.

Why didn't the supervisor express his aggression and "tell the worker off"? Why didn't he *punish* the worker, thereby killing two birds with one stone; namely, unburdening himself of hostile feelings and compelling the worker to conform to his expectations? After all, punishment, or the infliction of "pain, failure, or ego-degradation" [10] upon the worker might help to bolster the supervisor's threatened status and salve his wounded ego.

There was one important drawback. Among surface workers in particular, and for the Company as a whole, supervisors were expressly forbidden, formally, to express aggression. As seen when contrasting miners with the more bureaucratized surface workers, the overt expression of aggression was taboo among the latter. Moreover the Company "labor relations manual" asserted that "A *friendly* attitude toward . . . all employees will provide the basis for sound Company-employee relations in each plant." The manual also insisted that one of the characteristics of every good employee was an "ability to *control emotion*."

[10] Norman F. Maier, *Frustration*, McGraw-Hill Book Co., 1949, p. 194.

In the face of these proscriptions, it was difficult to express aggression openly.

In our society, moreover, it is not permissible to inflict a punishment under any and all conditions. There seems to be a deep-grooved inscription in our culture which asserts that punishment is permissible only on the condition that the offender could know *in advance* that certain of his behaviors are forbidden.[11] This is one of the sentiments which underlies the rejection of *ex post facto* laws in our legal structure. If it has become a formally announced legal principle that "ignorance of the law is no excuse," this has, in part, been necessary because traditional folkways informally insist that ignorance of the law constitutes an extenuating circumstance.

Within the plant, orientation to this traditional norm was expressed in several ways. First, the frequent claim that so-and-so was a good foreman because he gave his workers a "second chance," a factor in the "indulgency pattern," implied that such a foreman did *not* take the first opportunity that presented itself to inflict a punishment. Instead he used this first deviaion as an occasion to *warn* the worker that future infractions would meet with punishment.

That punishments which were not preceded by warnings were only doubtfully legitimate, in the eyes of plant personnel, can be inferred from the introduction of the formal warning notice. One of the functions of the *worker's signature* on the warning notice was to forestall a claim that he had not been warned and could not, therefore, be punished. Day, the old personnel manager, complained precisely of this point after he had been demoted, saying, "Why didn't Peele tell me about it long before now, instead of just replacing me?"

Bureaucratic rules, then, serve to legitimate the utilization of punishments. They do so be-

[11] Here, again, there is evidence suggesting that we are dealing with a culturally induced sentiment rather than one peculiar to this factory or to industrial phenomena alone. On the basis of their wartime studies of the U. S. Armed Forces, the authors of *The American Soldier* suggest that punishment is more likely to be effective if "the men are given specific *advance* warning about the consequences of an occurrence of the offense, since *most men consider fair warning as a condition for fair punishment*." *Ibid.*, p. 425. (Our emphasis—A. W. G.)

cause the rules constitute statements in advance of expectations. As such, they comprise explicit or implicit *warnings* concerning the kind of behavior which will provoke punishment.

In actuality, the establishment of a rule explicating an obligation is frequently accompanied by a specific statement of the punishment, i.e., another rule specifying the punishment which will result if the first rule is violated. Two things, rather than one, have thus been clarified: (1) what is expected of the man and (2) what will happen to him if he does *not* fulfill these expectations. For example, the no-absenteeism rule did not merely state that the worker must not be absent without cause; it also specifically provided that he was to be layed off a like number of days for those which he took.

In brief, when rules explicate obligations, they are producing consequences recognized and intended by most participants in the situation. When rules explicate a punishment, however, they are legitimating the use of punishments, a consequence sometimes not at the center of the group's intention or awareness. The relationship between the explicational and the punishment functions of rules is like the relation between the locomotive and the trains which it pulls. Attention can all too readily be diverted to the noisy, smoking locomotive in the vanguard, while the attached trains carrying the pay load are easily neglected.

An example of the punishment function of the rules occurred in the dehydrating section of the mill: There were a number of large vats, used to heat and dehydrate the gypsum into powder, which occasionally needed to be cleaned out. A rule specified that the man who went down into one of these vats must wear a harness with a rope leading up to the top; there was also supposed to be someone at the top holding onto the rope and watching the man inside. These precautions stemmed from the fear that a man at the bottom of a vat could be killed by fumes or smothered by a cave-in of the "cake" covering the inside of the vat.

One day a main office executive passed through the plant on an inspection tour and noticed a rope leading down into a vat. He looked over the side and saw a worker cleaning it out, but there was no one around at the top watching the man and guarding the rope. Immediately the executive looked for the man's foreman, who was not to be seen. After a search, however, he discovered the foreman doing exactly the same thing, cleaning out a vat without having someone watch him. The executive then "raised hell" with the foreman and took it to higher plant authorities.

In short, the first thing the executive did when he discovered the infraction of vat-cleaning rules, was to look for someone to punish and blame. Instead of calling the man up from the vat, he left him down there. Instead of doing something to forestall an accident, the manifest function of this rule, he exploited the situation as an opportunity to inflict a punishment.

The rules thus channel aggression, providing permissible avenues for its expression and legitimating the utilization of punishments. To the extent that possible objects of punishment and aggression are members of the "in-group," as suggested in our discussion of the "remote control" function of rules, it becomes all the more necessary to legitimate meticulously the use of these control measures. For, by and large, aggression and punishments directed toward in-group members are not preferred patterns of behavior in our culture and require especially unambiguous justification. Bureaucratic rules are thereby particularly functional in a context in which reliance upon the in-group has been shaken. . . .

THE APATHY-PRESERVING FUNCTION OF BUREAUCRATIC RULES. Nor is this the last of paradoxes. For though bureaucratic rules were fostered by situations involving worker apathy, or its semblance, the rules actually contributed to the preservation of work apathy. Just as the rules facilitated punishment, so, too, did they define the behavior which could permit punishment to be *escaped*. . . . The rules served as a specification of a *minimum* level of acceptable performance. It was therefore possible for the worker to *remain* apathetic, for he now knew just how *little* he could do and still remain secure.

For example, after Peele had ruled that workers could not "punch in early" and accumulate a little overtime in that way, one mill worker said acidly.

Well, if that's the way he wants it, that's the way he wants it. But I'll be damned if I put in any overtime when things get rough and they'd like us to.

Said another worker:

O.K. I'll punch in just so, and I'll punch out on the nose. But you know you can lead a horse to water and you can lead him away, but it's awful hard to tell just how much water he drinks while he's at it.

This, of course, is the stuff of which "bureaucratic sabotage" is made. "Bureaucratic sabotage" is deliberate apathy fused with resentment, in which, by the very act of conforming to the letter of the rule, its intention is "conscientiously" violated. The worker's feeling and attitudes toward his work were thus essentially left untouched by the bureaucratic rules. The worker could, as it were, take any attitude toward his work that he wished, so long as he conformed to the rules. The rules did little to modify *attitudes* toward work, but were significant primarily as guidelines for *behavior*. In the last analysis, it would seem that proliferation of bureaucratic rules signify that management has, in effect if not intention, surrendered in the battle for the worker's motivation. In his study of *Social Organization*, Charles Horton Cooley came to much the same conclusion:

Underlying all formalism, indeed, is the fact that it is psychically cheap; it substitutes the outer for the inner as more tangible, more capable of being held before the mind *without fresh expense of thought and feeling*.[12]

And again:

. . . the merely formal institution does not enlist and discipline the soul of the individual, but takes him by the outside, his soul being left to torpor or to irreverent and riotous activity.[13]

Thus bureaucratic rules may be functional for subordinates, as well as for superiors; they permit "activity" without "participation"; they enable an employee to work without being emotionally committed to it.

[12] C. H. Cooley, *Social Organization*, Chas. Scribner's Sons, 1919, p. 349. (Our emphasis—A. W. G.)
[13] *Ibid.*, p. 343.

This function of bureaucratic rules is of peculiar importance since it suggests one of the inherent sources of bureaucratic rules' instability; for the rules do not seem to *resolve* the very problem, worker apathy, from which they most directly spring. Insofar as formal rules merely "wall in," rather than resolve, worker apathy, it may be expected that other mechanisms more competent to muster motivations will challenge and compete with them.[14]

BUREAUCRATIC RULES AND CLOSE SUPERVISION. What does this mean in terms of the problem of "close supervision"? It implies that bureaucratic rules do not eliminate the need for "close supervision" but, instead, primarily function to reduce the tensions created by it. Insofar as close supervision springs from management's perception of workers as failing to perform their role-obligations and as being unmotivated, the institution of rules in no way suffices to resolve this problem. The rules do not recharge the worker's motivation, but merely enable him to know what management's exectations are and to give them minimal conformance. Thus the tensions originally spurring supervisors to use "close supervision" remain untouched.

It is, instead, the secondary problems created by close supervision that are somewhat mitigated by bureaucratic rules: With the rules,

[14] It may well be that this is one of the organic contradictions of bureaucratic organization that make it susceptible to infiltration and displacement by "charismatic" elements, which involves loyalty to leadership based on belief in the leader's unusual *personal* qualities. Weber vaguely explained the vulnerability of bureaucracy as a breakdown of its efficiency in the face of new problems and accumulating tensions. He did little to analyze the specific nature of these tensions and tended to focus on their origins in the environment, neglecting their inner-organizational sources. We are suggesting, in effect, that bureaucratic authority is supplanted by charismatic when it is no longer possible to bypass the question of motivation. Charismatic leadership, it has been widely noted, has an ability to arouse new enthusiasms and to ignite irrational sources of motivation inaccessible to the bureaucrat. Indeed, some observers have insisted that this is one of the distinctive characteristics of modern totalitarianism. Thus George Orwell, in his *1984*, brings this novel to its climax when his hero is being tortured not merely to confess, nor to conform—but to *believe*.

the supervisor is now enabled to show that he is not using close supervision on his own behalf, but is merely transmitting demands that apply equally to all (the screening function); the supervisor is now more able to use a "spot-check" system to control workers with whom he cannot have frequent interaction (the remote control function); he now has a clear-cut basis for deciding, and demonstrating to his superiors if need be, that workers are delinquent in their role-performances (the explicational function); he now has firm grounds for punishing a worker if he finds him withholding obligation-performance (the punishment-legitimating function); or he can relax the rules, thereby rewarding workers, if they do perform their role obligations as he wants them to (the leeway function). In general, then, the rules reduce certain role tensions.

To repeat: These various functions of the rules largely serve to mitigate tensions *derivative* of "close supervision," rather than to remove all the major tensions which *create* it. Indeed, the rules now make close supervision feasible. The rules thus actually perpetuate one of the very things, i.e., close supervision, that bring them into being. The dynamics of the situation are of this sort:

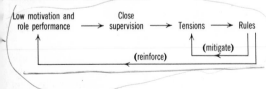

One may well wonder how bureaucratic rules could be perpetuated and sustained, if they actually removed the tensions leading to close supervision, rather than mitigating the tensions stemming from it. For if this happened low motivation would be raised to a satisfactory level; there would then be less need for close supervision; hence fewer tensions would be generated by it, and, in consequence, there would be less need for these tensions to be reduced by bureaucratic rules. To put it more sharply, bureaucratic rules seem to be sustained not only because they mitigate some tensions, but, also, because they *preserve* and allow other *tensions* to persist. If bureaucratic rules are a "defense mechanism," they not only defend the organization from certain tensions (those coming from close supervision),

but they also *defend other tensions* as well (those conducing to close supervision).[15]

It should not be supposed, however, that all the consequences of bureaucratic rules are equally reinforcing to low motivation and thereby to close supervision. Obviously, the apathy-preserving function of the rules does this most directly. It may be taken as "given," however, that punishments are more likely to impair motivation, and thus encourage close supervision, than rewards,[16] other things being equal. It therefore seems warranted to conclude that the punishment function is more apt to reinforce low motivation, and with it close supervision, than is the leeway function.

[15] This seems to have some bearing on certain more *general* problems involved in the functional analysis of organizations, which can be elucidated by comparing our approach with that employed by Philip Selznick. (See Selznick, "Foundations of the Theory of Organization," *American Sociological Review*, Feb., 1948, pp. 25–35). Selznick emphasizes the utility of concepts describing organization defensive mechanisms. He suggests that organizations develop recurrent defensive mechanisms, in a manner analogous to the human personality. These mechanisms, he holds, reduce tensions to the organization from threats which impinge upon it from its environment. Selznick illustrates this with the concept of "cooptation": Thus when the leadership body of a group loses the consent of a segment of the group over which it claims authority, a tension is established. One of the defensive mechanisms which may then become operative to reduce this tension, according to Selznick, is the "cooptation" of a prominent member of the dissenting segment onto the leadership body. This "formal" cooptation may extract increased consent from the sub-group, thereby reducing the tension experienced by those claiming authority. For example, an imperial colonial administrative body may coopt a tribal chief to the imperial administrative organ. Now, in what sense has the tension been reduced? One thing seems clear at least: The conditions which originally motivated the tribesmen to withdraw consent may in no way have been altered by the cooptation. Actually, the cooptation may safeguard the tensions which the tribesmen are experiencing and which led them to withhold consent. By inhibiting verbalization of their grievances, by directing attention and energies away from them, the cooptation of the tribal leader may allow these tensions to remain concealed and to continue to fester. In other words, defense mechanisms may actually defend the circumstances which produce the tension itself.

[16] Cf., N. R. F. Maier, *ibid.*

Hence we should expect that the more a specific administrative pattern is organized around the punishment functions of rules, the more it will impair motivation and reinforce the need for close supervision.

The discussion of management's perception of both workers and middle management, and the analysis of close supervision, suggest that the extreme elaboration of bureaucratic rules is prompted by an abiding distrust of people and of their intentions. Quite commonly, such rules serve those whose ambitions do not generate the ready and full consent of others; they diminish reliance upon and withhold commitments to persons who are viewed as recalcitrant and untrustworthy. In the extreme case, they seem to comprise an effort to *do without people altogether*. This could not be stated with greater frankness than in the words of Alfred Krupp, the munitions manufacturer:

> What I shall attempt to bring about is that *nothing shall be dependent upon the life or existence* of any particular person; that nothing of any importance shall happen or be caused to happen without the foreknowledge and approval of the management; that

the past and the determinate future of the establishment can be learned in the files of the management *without asking a question of any mortal*.[17]

If the several assessments made in various parts of this chapter are assembled into a complete diagnosis, it appears that bureaucratic rules proliferate when a social organization is riven by the following tensions: (1) Managerial distrust and suspicion become pervasive and are directed, not only toward workers, but also toward members of the managerial in-group as well. (2) Disturbances in the informal system which result in the withholding of consent from the formally constituted authorities; the informal group is either unwilling or unable to allocate work responsibilities and gives no support to management's production expectations. (3) Finally, the appearance of status distinctions of dubious legitimacy, in an egalitarian culture context, which strain the formal authority relationships.

[17] Quoted in Frederick J. Nussbaum, *A History of the Economic Institutions of Modern Europe*, F. S. Crofts and Co., New York, 1933, p. 379. (Our emphasis—A. W. G.)

Strategic Leniency and Authority

PETER M. BLAU

A psychological explanation of the failure to enforce strict discipline among subordinates might attribute it to poor leadership. Some supervisors are overly lenient. it could be held, because inborn or acquired personality traits prevent them from asserting their authority over others and maintaining effective leadership. Note that this explanation assumes as a matter of course that the bureaucratic superior who appears lenient merely indulges his subordinates and is less effective than the disciplinarian in discharging his supervisory responsibilities. Empirical evidence, however, indicates that the very opposite is the case.

A study of twenty-four clerical sections in an insurance company analyzed the relationship between method of supervision and productive efficiency.[1] In closely supervised sections, whose heads gave clerks detailed instructions and frequently checked up on them, productivity was usually lower than in sections where employees were given more freedom to do the work in their own way. Moreover, supervisors who were primarily concerned with maintaining a high level of production, interestingly enough, were less successful in meeting this goal than those supervisors who were more interested in the welfare of their subordinates than in sheer production; in the latter case,

productivity was generally higher. Finally, groups who worked under more authoritarian supervisors were, on the whole, less productive than those supervised in a relatively democratic fashion. Other studies have also found that disciplinarian supervisors are less effective than more liberal ones.[2]

Such findings are often misinterpreted as signifying that democratic ways are superior to authoritarian ones. But this is a rather loose use of the term "democratic," the exact meaning of which is worth preserving. Since "democracy" denotes rule from below (literally, "people's rule") and not from above, one person's supervision of others can, by definition, not be democratic. This is not the place for a discussion of the relation between democracy and bureaucracy; the final chapter is reserved for this purpose. But here it should be noted that tolerant supervisory practices, in contrast to disciplinarian ones, are neither democratic nor an indication that controlling power over subordinates has been surrendered. On the contrary, leniency in supervision is a potent strategy, consciously or unconsciously employed, for establishing authority over subordinates, and this is why the liberal supervisor is particularly effective.

Let us clarify the concept of authority. First, it refers to a relationship between persons and not to an attribute of one individual. Second, authority involves exercise of social control which rests on the *willing* compliance of subordinates with certain directives of the superior. He need not coerce or persuade sub-

From *Bureaucracy in Modern Society*. New York: Random House, 1956, pp. 70–79. Copyright 1956 by Random House. Reprinted with permission of the publisher.

[1] Daniel Katz, Nathan MacCoby, and Nancy C. Morse, *Productivity, Supervision and Morale in an Office Situation*. Ann Arbor: Institute for Social Research, University of Michigan, 1950, especially pp. 17, 21, 29.

[2] See for instance, F. J. Roethlisberger and William J. Dickson, *Management and the Worker*. Cambridge: Harvard University Press, 1946, pp. 452–53.

ordinates in order to influence them, because they have accepted as legitimate the principle that some of their actions should be governed by his decisions. Third, authority is an observable pattern of interaction and not an official definition of a social relationship. If a mutinous crew refuses to obey the captain's orders, he does not in fact have authority over his men. Whatever the superior's official rights to command obedience and the subordinates' official duties to obey him, his authority over them extends only to conduct that they voluntarily permit to be governed by his directives. Actual authority, consequently, is not granted by the formal organizational chart, but must be established in the course of social interaction, although the official bureaucratic structure, as we shall see presently, facilitates its establishment.

What are some of the practices of a lenient foreman or supervisor? Above all, he allows subordinates to violate minor rules, to smoke or talk, for example, despite the fact that it is prohibited by management. This permissiveness often increases his power over them by furnishing him with legitimate sanctions that he can use as he sees fit. If an action of his subordinates displease him, the supervisor can punish them by commanding: "Cut out the smoking! Can't you read the sign?" Had he always enforced the rule, this penalty would not have been available to him. Indeed, so crude a use of sanctions is rarely necessary. The mere knowledge that the rule exists and, possibly, that it is enforced elsewhere, instills a sense of obligation to liberal superiors and induces subordinates more readily to comply with their requests.

Whereas the disciplinarian supervisor generally asserts his official prerogatives, the lenient and relaxed one does not. The latter attempts to take the wishes of his subordinates into account in arranging their work schedule, although he has the right to assign their work at his own discretion. Sometimes he goes to special trouble to accommodate a subordinate. Instead of issuing curt commands, he usually explains the reasons for his directives. He calls his subordinates by their first names and encourages their use of his first name (especially in democratically minded American organizations). When one of his subordinates gets into difficulties with management, he is apt to speak up for him and to defend him. These different actions have two things in common: the superior is not required to do them, and his subordinates greatly welcome his doing them. Such conduct therefore creates social obligations. To repay the supervisor for past favors, and not to risk the cessation of similar favors in the future, subordinates voluntarily comply with many of his requests, including some they are not officially required to obey. By refraining from exercising his power of control whenever it is legitimate to do so, the bureaucratic superior establishes effective authority over subordinates, which enables him to control them much more effectively than otherwise would be possible.

Complementary role expectations arise in the course of interaction between superior and subordinates and become crystallized in the course of interaction among subordinates. As the superior permits subordinates to violate some rules and to make certain decisions themselves, and as they grow accustomed to conform with many of his directives, they learn to expect to exercise discretion in some areas and to follow supervisory directives in others, and he learns to expect this pattern of conduct from them. The members of the work group, by watching one another at work and talking among themselves about the manner in which they perform their duties, develop social consensus about these role expectations and thereby reinforce them. The newcomer to the group, who must be taught "how things are done around here" as distinguished from "what's in the book," provides an opportunity for further affirming this consensus by making it explicit.

The resulting common role expectations are often so fully internalized that employees are hardly aware of being governed by them. The members of one department might find it natural for their supervisor to interrupt their work and tell them to start on a new task. The members of another department in the same organization might consider such a supervisory order as gross interference with their work, since they had become accustomed to using their discretion about the sequence of their tasks, yet readily comply with other directives of the supervision. These role expectations of independence from the supervisor in some areas and unquestioning obedience in others define the limits of his authority over subordinates.

POWER OF SANCTION. The preceding comments apply to informal leadership as well as to bureaucratic authority. The informal leader, like the prudent bureaucratic superior, establishes his authority over his followers by creating social obligations.[3] Once a relationship of authority exists, both bureaucratic superior and informal leader can afford to word their orders as mere suggestions, because even these are readily followed by the rest of the group. Neither of them usually needs sanctions to command obedience, though sanctions are available to both of them in case they wish to use special inducements, since praise or blame of the person in the superordinate position itself exerts a powerful influence.

Nevertheless, there is a fundamental distinction between informal leadership and bureaucratic authority. Informal leadership freely emerges among a group of peers. It is initially the result of personality differences that have become socially magnified. Some members of the group excel in activities that are highly valued by all, whether these are street fighting or solving complex problems; these few will be more respected, and their opinions will carry greater weight. The person in the extreme position, if he also finds ways to obligate the others to him, is expected to be the group's leader.

Bureaucratic authority, on the other hand, prevents the group itself from conferring the position of leadership upon the member of their choice. The voluntary obedience of subordinates must converge upon the individual officially placed in the position of supervisor, irrespective of his personal characteristics. The bureaucratic mechanism that makes this state of affairs a predictable occurrence is the superior's power to impose sanctions, typically in the form of periodic ratings of the performance of his subordinates, which influence their chances of advancement and of keeping their jobs.

The dependency of bureaucratic subordinates upon their immediate superior produced by his rating power engenders frustrations and anxieties for adults. It forces employees to worry about their supervisor's reaction at every step they take. An effective way to weaken or avoid such feelings is to identify with the bureaucratic system of normative standards and objectives. By making this system a part of their own thinking, employees transform conformity with its principles from submission to the superior's demands into voluntary action. Guided by internalized standards, they are less likely to experience external restraints in performing their duties. Moreover, once the hierarchical division of responsibility has been accepted as a basic principle of the organization, it becomes less threatening to a person's self-esteem to obey the supervisor's directives, since he is known to be duty-bound to issue them, just as it is not degrading to obey the traffic directions of a policeman. Dependence on the superior's rating encourages the adoption of a bureaucratic orientation, for the disadvantages of dependence can thereby be evaded.

It is of crucial importance that this process of identification with bureaucratic standards does not occur in isolation but in a social situation. All members of the work group find themselves in the same position of dependence on their supervisor. (In fact, all members of the bureaucratic organization are, in varying degrees, dependent on their immediate superiors.) Together, they can obtain concessions from the supervisor, because he is anxious to obligate them by granting some of their demands. In exchange, they feel constrained to comply with many of his directives. Typically, a strict definition is given to the limits of this effective authority. Subordinates can often be heard to remark: "That's the supervisor's responsibility. He gets paid for making those decisions." This does not mean that operating employees shirk responsibilities, as indicated by their willingness to shoulder those they define as their own. But the social agreement among the members of the work group that making certain decisions and issuing certain directives is the duty of the supervisor, not merely his privilege, serves to emphasize that following them does not constitute submission to his arbitrary will but conformity with commonly accepted operating principles. In such a situation, which prevails in some organizations though by no means in all, subordinates do not experience the supervisor's exercise of authority over them as domination; neither are they necessarily envious of his responsibilities, since

[3] For a clear illustration of this point in a street corner gang, see William F. Whyte, *Street Corner Society*. Chicago: University of Chicago Press, 1943, pp. 257–262.

they frequently consider their own more challenging than his.

The effective establishment of authority obviates the need for sanctions in daily operations. If a supervisor commands the voluntary obedience of subordinates, he need not induce them to obey him by promising them rewards or threatening them with punishment. In fact, the use of sanctions undermines authority. A supervisor who is in the habit of invoking sanctions to back his orders—"You won't get a good rating unless you do this!"—shows that he does not expect unqualified compliance. As subordinates learn that he does not expect it, they will no longer feel obligated unconditionally to accept his directives. Moreover, employees resent being continually reminded of their dependence on the supervisor by his promises and threats, and such resentment makes them less inclined to carry out his orders.

This is the dilemma of bureaucratic authority: it rests on the power of sanction but is weakened by frequent resort to sanctions in operations. A basic difference, however, should be noted between the periodic rating of the performance of subordinates, which can be called a *diffuse sanction*, and *specific sanctions* recurrently employed to enforce particular commands. Since all employees know that their immediate superior is officially required to evaluate their operations at periodic intervals, this evaluation is neither a sign that he does not expect unqualified compliance with his directives nor a reason for annoyance with him. This diffuse sanction, imposed only annually or every few months, though creating the dependence of subordinates upon their supervisor, does so without constantly endangering their willingness to be guided by his requests, as the habitual use of specific sanctions (including promises of good ratings and threats of poor ones) would.

While the mere fact that the supervisor administers ratings is not resented by his subordinates, low ratings might well antagonize some of them. But bureaucratic mechanisms exist that enable the supervisor to shift the blame for negative sanctions. For example, statistical records of performance, which are kept in many white-collar offices as well as factories, furnish the supervisor with objective evidence with which he can justify low ratings by showing the recipients that the poor quality of their work left him no other choice. Instead of blaming the supervisor for giving them a poor rating, these employees are forced to blame themselves or to attribute the rating to the "statistics," which are often accused, rightly or wrongly, of failing to measure the qualitative aspects of performance.*

His intermediate position in the hierarchy provides the supervisor with another justification mechanism. He can place the responsibility for giving low ratings or instituting unpopular requirements on his superiors, to whom he is accountable. Oftentimes a supervisor or foreman will tell his subordinates that he does not like certain standards any better than they do but "those brass-hats in the front office" insist on them. In most organizations, one or a few superintendents or assistant managers (or deans) become the scapegoats who are blamed for all negative sanctions and unpopular requirements. Since the attitudes of employees toward these administrators in removed positions is much less relevant for effective operations than their attitudes toward their immediate superior, the displacement of aggression from him to them is in the interest of the organization. Clients or customers can also serve as scapegoats of aggression—the supervisor can blame their demands for instituting procedures that inconvenience employees. And if he joins subordinates in ridiculing clients or customers, a frequent practice in service occupations, the supervisor further reduces antagonism against himself by standing united with the employees against outsiders.

Periodic ratings, then, increase the dependency of the members of a bureaucracy on their superiors but at the same time allow them to escape from disturbing feelings of dependency by internalizing the principles that govern operations. Although the responsibilities the supervisor is required to discharge occasionally arouse the animosity of some subordinates, various mechanisms divert such antagonism from the supervisor to other objects. These two elements of the bureaucratic structure conspire to provide a fertile soil for the establishment of supervisory authority. Together, they permit supervisors to obligate subordinates willingly to follow directives.

Various circumstances, however, can prevent

---

* Of course, quantitative records also facilitate the supervisor's task of evaluating operations.

such favorable conditions in the bureaucratic organization. The disciplinarian supervisor may antagonize subordinates, through recurrent use of sanctions and in other ways, and thereby undermine his effective authority over them as well as their motivation to put effort into their work. The lenient supervisor may be so reluctant to displease subordinates that he refrains from evaluating their performance in accordance with rigorous standards, giving all of them high ratings. This practice invalidates the incentive system, which enhances the interest of employees in accomplishing specified results in their operations. The manipulative supervisor may employ devious techniques to conceal from subordinates his attempts to impose his arbitrary will upon them, for example, by frequent and unwarranted utilization of scapegoats. While manipulative techniques have a fair chance of being successful in temporary pair relationships, as between customer and salesman, their chances of success in relatively permanent relationships within a group are very slim. For sooner or later, some member is apt to see through them, and he is not likely to keep this a secret. Once they are discovered, manipulative techniques have a boomerang effect. Employees who realize that their superior tries to manipulate them are prone to suspect all of his statements and generally to resist his efforts to influence their performance.

These and other disruptive tendencies can be observed in hierarchical organizations, but methods of supervision that encourage operating efficiency are also evident. In the absence of a much larger body of information about bureaucracies than we now possess, it is impossible to know which of these opposite conditions is more frequent. Nevertheless, the fact that authority is sometimes effectively exercised without domineering subordinates or lowering their morale, rare as this may be, demonstrates that such a state of affairs is actually possible and not merely a utopian ideal type.

Conflicts between Staff and Line Managerial Officers

MELVILLE DALTON

In its concentration on union-management relations, industrial sociology has tended to neglect the study of processes inside the ranks of industrial management. Obviously the doors to this research area are more closely guarded than the entry to industrial processes through the avenue of production workers, but an industrial sociology worthy of the name must sooner or later extend its inquiries to include the activities of all industrial personnel.

The present paper is the result of an attempt to study processes among industrial managers. It is specifically a report on the functioning interaction between the two major vertical groupings of industrial management: (1) the *staff* organization, the functions of which are research and advisory; and (2) the *line* organization, which has exclusive authority over production processes.

Industrial staff organizations are relatively new. Their appearance is a response to many complex interrelated forces, such as economic competition, scientific advance, industrial expansion, growth of the labor movement, and so on. During the last four or five decades these rapid changes and resulting unstable conditions have caused top industrial officials more

From *American Sociological Review*, Vol. 15, June 1950, pp. 342–351. Reprinted with permission of the author and the publisher, American Sociological Association.

and more to call in "specialists" to aid them toward the goal of greater production and efficiency. These specialists are of many kinds including chemists, statisticians, public and industrial relations officers, personnel officers, accountants, and a great variety of engineers, such as mechanical, draughting, electrical, chemical, fuel, lubricating, and industrial engineers. In industry these individuals are usually known as "staff people." Their functions, again, for the most part are to increase and apply their specialized knowledge in problem areas, and to advise those officers who make up the "line" organization and have authority [1] over production processes.

This theoretically satisfying industrial structure of specialized experts advising busy administrators has in a number of significant cases failed to function as expected. The assumptions that (*a*) the staff specialists would be reasonably content to function without a measure of formal authority [2] over production, and that (*b*) their suggestions regarding improvement of processes and techniques for control over personnel and production would be welcomed by line officers and be applied, require closer examination. In practice there is often much conflict between industrial staff and line organizations and in varying degrees the members of these organizations oppose each other.[3]

The aim of this paper is, therefore, to present

and analyze data dealing with staff-line tensions.

Data were drawn from three industrial plants [4] in which the writer had been either a participating member of one or both of the groups or was intimate with reliable informants among the officers who were.

Approached sociologically, relations among members of management in the plants could be viewed as a general conflict system caused and perpetuated chiefly by (1) power struggles in the organization stemming in the main from competition among departments to maintain low operating costs; (2) drives by numerous members to increase their status in the hierarchy; (3) conflict between union and management; and (4) the staff-line friction which is the subject of this paper.[5] This milieu of tensions was not only unaccounted for by the blue-print organizations of the plants, but was often contradictory to, and even destructive of, the organizations' formal aims. All members of management, especially in the middle and lower ranks,[6] were caught up in this conflict system. Even though they might wish to escape, the obligation of at least appearing to

---

[1] *Inside* their particular staff organization, staff officers also may have authority over their subordinates, but not over production personnel.

[2] To the extent that staff officers influence line policy they do, of course, have a certain *informal* authority.

[3] Some social scientists have noted the possibility of staff-line friction, and industrial executives themselves have expressed strong feelings on the matter. See Burleigh B. Gardner, *Human Relations in Industry* (Chicago: Richard D. Irwin, Inc., 1945) and H. E. Dimock, *The Executive in Action* (New York: Harper & Brothers, 1945). Dimock believes that we are too "staff-minded" and that we should become more "executive-minded" (p. 241). A high line officer in a large corporation denounced staff organizations to the writer on the ground of their "costing more than they're worth," and that "They stir up too much trouble and are too theoretical." He felt that their function (excepting that of accountants, chemists, and "a few mechanical engineers") could be better carried out by replacing them with "highly-select front-line foremen [the

lowest placed line officers] who are really the backbone of management, and pay them ten or twelve thousand dollars a year."

[4] These plants were in related industries and ranged in size from 4,500 to 20,000 employees, with the managerial groups numbering from 200 to nearly 1,000. Details concerning the plants and their location are confidential. Methodological details concerning an intensive study embracing staff-line relations and several other areas of behavior in one of the plants are given in the writer's unpublished doctoral thesis, "A Study of Informal Organization Among the Managers of an Industrial Plant," (Department of Sociology, University of Chicago, 1949).

[5] Because these conflict areas were interrelated and continually shifting and reorganizing, discussion of any one of them separately—as in the case of staff-line relations—will, of course, be unrealistic to some extent.

[6] From bottom to top, the line hierarchy consisted of the following strata of officers: (1) first-line foremen, who were directly in charge of production workmen; (2) general foremen; (3) departmental superintendents; (4) divisional superintendents; (5) assistant plant manager; (6) plant manager. In the preceding strata there were often "assistants," such as "assistant general foreman," "assistant superintendent," etc., in which case the

carry out formal functions compelled individuals to take sides in order to protect themselves against the aggressions of others. And the intensity of the conflict was aggravated by the fact that it was formally unacceptable and had to be hidden.

For analytical convenience, staff-line friction may be examined apart from the reciprocal effects of the general conflict system. Regarded in this way, the data indicated that three conditions were basic to staff-line struggles: (1) the conspicuous ambition and "individualistic" behavior among staff officers; (2) the complication arising from staff efforts to justify its existence and get acceptance of its contributions; and, related to point two, (3) the fact that incumbency of the higher staff offices was dependent on line approval. The significance of these conditions will be discussed in order.

MOBILE BEHAVIOR OF STAFF PERSONNEL. As a group, staff personnel in the three plants were markedly ambitious, restless, and individualistic. There was much concern to win rapid promotion, to make the "right impressions," and to receive individual recognition. Data showed that the desire among staff members for personal distinctions often over-rode their sentiments of group consciousness and caused intra-staff tensions.[7]

---

total strata of the line hierarchy could be almost double that indicated here.

In the staff organizations the order from bottom to top was: (1) supervisor (equivalent to the first-line foreman); (2) general supervisor (equivalent to the general foreman); (3) staff head—sometimes "superintendent" (equivalent to departmental superintendent in the line organization). Occasionally there were strata of assistant supervisors and assistant staff heads.

The term "upper line" will refer to all strata above the departmental superintendent. "Middle line" will include the departmental superintendent and assistants. "Lower line" will refer to general and first-line foremen and their assistants.

"Lower," "middle," and "upper" staff will refer respectively to the supervisor, general supervisor and staff head.

"Top management" will refer to the upper line and the few staff heads with whom upper line officers were especially intimate on matters of policy.

[7] In a typical case in one of the plants, a young staff officer developed a plan for increasing the life of certain equipment in the plant. He carried the plan directly to the superintendent of the depart-

The relatively high turnover of staff personnel[8] quite possibly reflected the dissatisfactions and frustrations of members over inability to achieve the distinction and status they hoped for. Several factors appeared to be of importance in this restlessness of staff personnel. Among these were age and social differences between line and staff officers, structural differences in the hierarchy of the two groups, and the staff group's lack of authority over production.

With respect to age, the staff officers were significantly younger than line officers.[9] This would account to some extent for their restlessness. Being presumably less well-established in life in terms of material accumulations, occupational status, and security, while having greater expectations (see below), and more

---

ment in which he hoped to introduce it, but was rebuffed by the superintendent who privately acknowledged the merit of the scheme but resented the staff officer's "trying to lord it over" him. The staff organization condemned the behavior of its member and felt that he should have allowed the plan to appear as a contribution of the staff group rather than as one of its members. The officer himself declared that "By G— it's my idea and I want credit. There's not a damn one of you guys [the staff group] that wouldn't make the same squawk if you were in my place!"

[8] During the period between 1944 and 1950 turnover of staff personnel in these plants was between two and four times as great as that of line personnel. This grouping included all the non-managerial members of staff and line and all the hourly-paid (non-salaried) members of management (about 60 assistant first-line foremen). Turnover was determined by dividing the average number of employees for a given year (in line or staff) into the accessions or separations, whichever was the smaller.

[9] Complete age data were available in one of the larger plants. Here the 36 staff heads, staff specialists, and assistants had a mean age of 42.9 years. This value would have been less than 40 years, except for the inclusion of several older former line officers, but even a mean of 42.9 years was significantly less (C.R. 2.8) than that of the 35 line superintendents in the plant who had a mean age of 48.7 years. The age difference was even more significant when the staff heads were compared with the 61 general foremen who had a mean age of 50.0 years. And between the 93 salaried first-line foremen (mean age of 48.5 years) and the 270 salaried nonsupervisory staff personnel (mean age of 31.0 years) the difference was still greater.

energy, as well as more life ahead in which to make new starts elsewhere if necessary, the staff groups were understandably more dynamic and driving.[10]

Age-conflict [11] was also significant in staff-line antagonisms. The incident just noted of the young staff officers seeking to get direct acceptance by the line of his contribution failed in part—judging from the strong sentiments later expressed by the line superintendent—because of an age antipathy. The older line officers disliked receiving what they regarded as instruction from men so much younger than themselves, and staff personnel clearly were conscious of this attitude among line officers.[12] In staff-line meetings staff officers frequently had their ideas slighted or even treated with amusement by line incumbents. Whether such treatment was warranted or not, the effects were disillusioning to the younger, less experienced staff officers. Often selected by the organization because of their outstanding academic records, they had en-

tered industry with the belief that they had much to contribute, and that their efforts would win early recognition and rapid advancement. Certainly they had no thought that their contributions would be in any degree unwelcome. This naiveté [13] was apparently due to lack of earlier first-hand experience in industry (or acquaintance with those who had such experience), and to omission of realistic instruction in the social sciences from their academic training. The unsophisticated staff officer's initial contacts with the shifting, covert, expedient arrangements between members of staff and line usually gave him a severe shock. He had entered industry prepared to engage in logical, well-formulated relations with members of the managerial hierarchy, and to carry out precise, methodical functions for which his training had equipped him. Now he learned that (1) his freedom to function was snared in a web of informal commitments; (2) his academic specialty (on which he leaned for support in his new position) was often not relevant [14] for carrying out his formal assignments; and that (3) the important thing to do was to learn who the informally powerful line officers were and what ideas they would welcome which at the same time would be acceptable to his superiors.

Usually the staff officer's reaction to these conditions is to look elsewhere for a job or make an accommodation in the direction of

---

[10] One might also hypothesize that the drive of staff officers was reflected in the fact that the staff heads and specialists gained their positions (those held when the data were collected) in less time than did members of the line groups. E.g., the 36 staff officers discussed above had spent a median of 10 years attaining their positions, as against a median of 11 years for the first-line foremen, 17 years for the general foremen, and 19 years for the superintendents. But one must consider that some of the staff groups were relatively new (13–15 years old) and had grown rapidly, which probably accelerated their rate of promotions as compared with that of the older line organization.

[11] E. A. Ross in *Principles of Sociology* (New York: D. Appleton-Century Co., 1938) pp. 238–48, has some pertinent comments on age conflict.

[12] Explaining the relatively few cases in which his staff had succeeded in "selling ideas" to the line, an assistant staff head remarked: "We're always in hot water with these old guys on the line. You can't tell them a damn thing. They're bull-headed as hell! Most of the time we offer a suggestion it's either laughed at or not considered at all. The same idea in the mouth of some old codger on the line'd get a round of applause. They treat us like kids."

Line officers in these plants often referred to staff personnel (especially members of the auditing, production planning, industrial engineering, and industrial relations staffs) as "college punks," "slide-rules," "crackpots," "pretty boys," and "chair-warmers."

[13] John Mills, a research engineer retired from the telephone industry, has noted the worldly naiveté of research engineers in that field in his *The Engineer in Society* (New York: D. Van Nostrand Co., 1946).

[14] Among the staff heads and assistants referred to earlier, only 50 per cent of those with college training (32 of the 36 officers) were occupied with duties related to their specialized training. E.g., the head of the industrial relations staff had a B.S. degree in aeronautical engineering; his assistant had a similar degree in chemical engineering. Considering that staff officers are assumed to be specialists trained to aid and advise management in a particular function, the condition presented here raises a question as to what the criteria of selection were. (As will be shown in a separate paper, the answer appeared to be that personal—as well as impersonal—criteria were used.) Among the college-trained of 190 line officers in the same plant, the gap between training and function was still greater, with 61 per cent in positions not related to the specialized part of their college work.

protecting himself and finding a niche where he can make his existence in the plant tolerable and safe. If he chooses the latter course, he is likely to be less concerned with creative effort for his employer than with attempts to develop reliable social relations that will aid his personal advancement. The staff officer's recourse to this behavior and his use of other status-increasing devices will be discussed below in another connection.

The formal structure, or hierarchy of statuses, of the two larger plants from which data were drawn, offered a frustration to the ambitious staff officer. That is, in these plants the strata, or levels of authority, in the staff organizations ranged from three to five as against from five to ten in the line organization. Consequently there were fewer possible positions for exercise of authority into which staff personnel could move. This condition may have been an irritant to expansion among the staff groups. Unable to move vertically to the degree possible in the line organization, the ambitious staff officer could enlarge his area of authority in a given position only by lateral expansion—by increasing his personnel. Whether or not aspiring staff incumbents revolted against the relatively low hierarchy through which they could move, the fact remains that (1) they appeared eager to increase the number of personnel under their authority,[15] (2)

the personnel of staff groups *did* increase disproportionately to those of the line,[16] and (3) there was a trend of personnel movement from staff to line,[17] rather than the reverse, presumably (reflecting the drive and ambition of staff members) because there were more positions of authority, as well as more authority to be exercised, more prestige, and usually more income in the line.

Behavior in the plants indicated that line and staff personnel belonged to different social status groups and that line and staff antipathies were at least in part related to these social distinctions. For example, with respect to the item of formal education, the staff group stood on a higher level than members of the line. In

---

[15] This was suggested by unnecessary references among some staff officers to "the number of men under me," and by their somewhat fanciful excuses for increase of personnel. These excuses included statements of needing more personnel to (1) carry on research, (2) control new processes, (3) keep records and reports up-to-date. These statements often did not square with (1) the excessive concern among staff people about their "privileges" (such as arriving on the job late, leaving early, leaving the plant for long periods during working hours, having a radio in the office during the World Series, etc.); (2) the great amount of time (relative to that of line officers) spent by lower staff personnel in social activities on the job, and (3) the constantly recurring (but not always provoked) claims among staff personnel of their functional importance for production. The duties of middle and lower staff personnel allowed them sufficient time to argue a great deal over their respective functions (as well as many irrelevant topics) and to challenge the relative merit of one another's contributions or "ideas." In some of the staffs these discussions could go on intermittently

for hours and develop into highly theoretical jousts and wit battles. Where staff people regarded such behavior as a privilege of their status, line officers considered it as a threat to themselves. This lax control (in terms of line discipline) was in part a tacit reward from staff heads to their subordinates. The reward was expected because staff superiors (especially in the industrial relations, industrial engineering, and planning staffs) often overlooked and/or perverted the work of subordinates (which was resented) in response to pressures from the line. This behavior will be noted later.

[16] In one of the larger plants, where exact data were available, the total staff personnel had by 1945 exceeded that of the line. At that time the staff included 400 members as against 317 line personnel composed of managerial officers and their clerical workers, but not production workers. By 1948 the staff had increased to 517 as compared with 387 for the line (during this period *total* plant personnel declined over 400). The staff had grown from 20.8 per cent larger than the line in 1945 to 33.6 per cent larger in 1948, and had itself increased by 29.3 per cent during the three years as against a growth in the line of 22.1 per cent. Assuming the conditions essential for use of probability theory, the increase in staff personnel could have resulted from chance about 1.5 times in a hundred. Possibly post-war and other factors of social change were also at work but, if so, their force was not readily assessable.

[17] This movement from staff to line can disorganize the formal managerial structure, especially when (1) the transferring staff personnel have had little or no supervisory experience in the staff but have an academic background which causes them to regard human beings as mechanisms that will respond as expected; (2) older, experienced line officers have hoped—for years in some cases—to occupy the newly vacated (or created) positions.

the plant from which the age data were taken, the 36 staff officers had a mean of 14.6 years of schooling as compared with 13.1 years for 35 line superintendents, 11.2 years for 60 general foremen, and 10.5 years for 93 first-line foremen. The difference between the mean education of the staff group and that of the highest line group (14.6–13.1) was statistically significant at better than the one per cent level. The 270 non-supervisory staff personnel had a mean of 13.1 years—the same as that of the line superintendents. Consciousness of this difference probably contributed to a feeling of superiority among staff members, while the sentiment of line officers toward staff personnel was reflected in the name-calling noted earlier.

Staff members were also much concerned about their dress, a daily shave, and a weekly hair-cut. On the other hand line officers, especially below the level of departmental superintendent, were relatively indifferent to such matters. Usually they were in such intimate contact with production processes that dirt and grime prevented the concern with meticulous dress shown by staff members. The latter also used better English in speaking and in writing reports, and were more suave and poised in social intercourse. These factors, and the recreational preferences of staff officers for night clubs and "hot parties," assisted in raising a barrier between them and most line officers.

The social antipathies of the two groups and the status concern of staff officers were indicated by the behavior of each toward the established practice of dining together in the cafeterias reserved for management in the two larger plants. Theoretically, all managerial officers upward from the level of general foremen in the line, and general supervisors in the staff, were eligible to eat in these cafeterias. However, in practice the mere taking of one of these offices did not automatically assure the incumbent the privilege of eating in the cafeteria. One had first to be invited to "join the association." Staff officers were very eager to "get in" and did considerable fantasying on the impressions, with respect to dress and behavior, that were believed essential for an invitation. One such staff officer, a cost supervisor, dropped the following remarks:

There seems to be a committee that passes on you. I've had my application in for three years, but no soap. Harry [his superior] had

his in for over three years before he made it. You have to have something, because if a man who's in moves up to another position the man who replaces him doesn't get it because of the position—and he might not get it at all. I think I'm about due.

Many line officers who were officially members of the association avoided the cafeteria, however, and had to be *ordered* by the assistant plant manager to attend. One of these officers made the following statement, which expressed more pointedly the many similar spontaneous utterances of resentment and dislike made by other line officers:

There's a lot of good discussion in the cafeteria. I'd like to get in on more of it but I don't like to go there—sometimes I have to go. Most of the white collar people [staff officers] that eat there are stuck-up. I've been introduced three times to Svendsen [engineer], yet when I meet him he pretends to not even know me. When he meets me on the street he always manages to be looking someplace else. G—d— such people as that! They don't go in the cafeteria to eat and relax while they talk over their problems. They go in there to look around and see how somebody is dressed or to talk over the hot party they had last night. Well, that kind of damn stuff don't go with me. I haven't any time to put on airs and make out I'm something that I'm not.

COMPLICATIONS OF STAFF NEED TO PROVE ITS WORTH. To the thinking of many line officers, the staff functioned as an agent on trial rather than as a managerial division that might be of equal importance with the line organization in achieving production goals. Staff members were very conscious of this sentiment toward them and of their need to prove themselves. They strained to develop new techniques and to get them accepted by the line. But in doing this they frequently became impatient, and gave already suspicious line officers the impression of reaching for authority over production.

Since the line officer regards his authority over production as something sacred, and resents the implication that after many years in the line he needs the guidance of a newcomer who lacks such experience, an obstacle to staff-line cooperation develops the moment this sore spot is touched. On the other hand, the staff officer's ideology of his function leads him to precipitate a power struggle with the line organization. By and large he considers himself as an agent of top management. He feels bound to contribute something significant in the form of research or ideas helpful to management. By virtue of his greater education and intimacy with the latest theories of production, he regards himself as a managerial consultant and an expert, and feels that he must be, or appear to be, almost infallible once he has committed himself to top management on some point. With this orientation, he is usually disposed to approach middle and lower line with an attitude of condescension that often reveals itself in the heat of discussion. Consequently, many staff officers involve themselves in trouble and report their failures as due to "ignorance" and "bull-headedness" among these line officers.

On this point, relations between staff and line in all three of the plants were further irritated by a rift inside the line organization. First-line foremen were inclined to feel that top management had brought in the production planning, industrial relations, and industrial engineering staffs as clubs with which to control the lower line. Hence they frequently regarded the projects of staff personnel as manipulative devices, and reacted by cooperating with production workers and/or general foremen (whichever course was the more expedient) in order to defeat insistent and uncompromising members of the staff. Also, on occasion (see below), the lower line could cooperate evasively with lower staff personnel who were in trouble with staff superiors.

EFFECT OF LINE AUTHORITY OVER STAFF PROMOTION. The fact that entry to the higher staff offices in the three plants was dependent on approval of top line officers had a profound effect on the behavior of staff personnel. Every member of the staff knew that if he aspired to higher office he must make a record for himself, a good part of which would be a reputation among upper line officers of ability to "understand" their informal problems without being told. This knowledge worked in varying degrees to pervert the theory of staff-line relations. Ideally the two organizations cooperate to improve existing methods of output, to introduce new methods, to plan the work, and

to solve problems of production and the scheduling of orders that might arise. But when the line offers resistance to the findings and recommendations of the staff, the latter is reduced to evasive practices of getting some degree of acceptance of its programs, and at the same time of convincing top management that "good relations" exist with officers down the line. This necessity becomes even more acute when the staff officer aspires (for some of the reasons given above) to move over to the line organization, for then he must convince powerful line officers that he is worthy. In building a convincing record, however, he may compromise with line demands and bring charges from his staff colleagues that he is "selling out," so that after moving into the line organization he will then have to live with enemies he made in the staff. In any case, the need among staff incumbents of pleasing line officers in order to perfect their careers called for accommodation in three major areas:[18] (1) the observance of staff rules, (2) the introduction of new techniques, and (3) the use of appropriations for staff research and experiment.

With respect to point one, staff personnel, particularly in the middle and lower levels, carried on expedient relations with the line that daily evaded formal rules. Even those officers most devoted to rules found that, in order not to arouse enmity in the line on a scale sufficient to be communicated *up* the line, compromising devices were frequently helpful and sometimes almost unavoidable both for organizational and career aims. The usual practice was to tolerate minor breaking of staff rules by line personnel, or even to cooperate with the line in evading rules,[19]

---

[18] The relative importance of one or more of these areas would vary with the function of a given staff.

[19] In a processing department in one of the plants the chemical solution in a series of vats was supposed to have a specific strength and temperature, and a fixed rate of inflow and outflow. Chemists (members of the chemical staff) twice daily checked these properties of the solution and submitted reports showing that all points met the laboratory ideal. Actually, the solution was usually nearly triple the standard strength, the temperature was about 10 degrees Centigrade higher than standard, and the rate of flow was in excess of double the standard. There are, of course, varying discrepancies between laboratory theory and plant practice, but

and in exchange lay a claim on the line for cooperation on critical issues. In some cases line aid was enlisted to conceal lower staff blunders from the upper staff and the upper line.[20]

Concerning point two, while the staff organizations gave much time to developing new techniques, they were simultaneously thinking about how their plans would be received by the line. They knew from experience that middle and lower line officers could always give a "black eye" to staff contributions by deliberate mal-practices. Repeatedly top management had approved, and incorporated, staff proposals that had been verbally accepted down the line. Often the latter officers had privately opposed the changes, but had feared that saying so would incur the resentment of powerful superiors who could informally hurt them. Later they would seek to discredit the change by deliberate mal-practice and hope to bring a return to the former arrangement. For this reason there was a tendency for staff members to withhold improved production schemes or other plans when they knew that

the condition described here resulted from production pressures that forced line foremen into behavior upsetting the conditions expected by chemical theory. The chemists were sympathetic with the hard-pressed foremen, who compensated by (1) notifying the chemists (rather than their superior, the chief chemist) if anything "went wrong" for which the laboratory was responsible and thus sparing them criticism; and by (2) cooperating with the chemists to reduce the number of analyses which the chemists would ordinarily have to make.
[20] Failure of middle and lower staff personnel to "cooperate" with line officers might cause the latter to "stand pat" in observance of line rules at a time when the pressures of a dynamic situation would make the former eager to welcome line cooperation in rule-breaking. For example, a staff officer was confronted with the combined effect of (1) a delay in production on the line that was due to an indefensible staff error; (2) pressure on the line superintendent—with whom he was working—to hurry a special order; and (3) the presence in his force of new inexperienced staff personnel who were (a) irritating to line officers, and (b) by their inexperience constituted an invitation to line aggression. Without aid from the line superintendent (which could have been withheld by observance of formal rules) in covering up the staff error and in controlling line personnel, the staff officer might have put himself in permanent disfavor with all his superiors.

an attempt to introduce them might fail or even bring personal disrepute.

Line officers fear staff innovations for a number of reasons. In view of their longer experience, presumably intimate knowledge of the work, and their greater remuneration, they fear[21] being "shown up" before their line superiors for not having thought of the processual refinements themselves. They fear that changes in methods may bring personnel changes which will threaten the break-up of cliques and existing informal arrangements and quite possibly reduce their area of authority. Finally, changes in techniques may expose forbidden practices and departmental inefficiency. In some cases these fears have stimulated line officers to compromise staff men to the point where the latter will agree to postpone the initiation of new practices for specific periods.

In one such case an assistant staff head agreed with a line superintendent to delay the application of a bonus plan for nearly three months so that the superintendent could live up to the expedient agreement he had made earlier with his grievance committeeman to avoid a "wildcat" strike by a group of production workmen.[22] The lower engineers who had devised the plan were suspicious of the formal reasons given to them for withholding it, so the assistant staff head prevented them (by means of "busy work") from attending staff-line meetings lest they inadvertently reveal to top management that the plan was ready.

The third area of staff-line accommodations growing out of authority relations revolved around staff use of funds granted it by top management. Middle and lower line charged that staff research and experimentation was little more than "money wasted on blunders," and that various departments of the line could have "accomplished much more with less money." According to staff officers, those of

[21] Though there was little evidence that top management expected line officers to refine production techniques, the fear of such an expectation existed nevertheless. As noted earlier, however, some of the top executives *were* thinking that development of a "higher type" of first-line foreman might enable most of the staff groups to be eliminated.
[22] This case indicates the over-lapping of conflict areas referred to earlier. A later paper will deal with the area of informal union-management relations.

their plans that failed usually did so because line personnel "sabotaged" them and refused to "cooperate." Specific costs of "crack-pot experimentation" in certain staff groups were pointed to by line officers. Whatever the truth of the charges and counter-charges, evidence indicated (confidants in both groups supported this) that pressures from the line organization (below the top level) forced some of the staff groups to "kick over" parts of the funds appropriated for staff use [23] by top management. These compromises were of course hidden from top management, but the relations described were carried on to such an extent that by means of them—and line pressures for manipulation of accounts in the presumably impersonal auditing departments—certain line officers were able to show impressively low operating costs and thus win favor [24] with top management that would relieve pressures and be useful in personal advancement. In their turn the staff officers involved would receive more "cooperation" from the line and/or recommendation for transfer to the line. The data indicated that in a few such cases men from accounting and auditing staffs were given general foremanships (without previous line experience) as a reward for their understanding behavior.

SUMMARY. Research in three industrial plants showed conflict between the managerial staff and line groups that hindered the attainment of organizational goals. Privately expressed attitudes among some of the higher line executives revealed their hope that greater control of staff groups could be achieved, or that the groups might be eliminated and their functions taken over in great part by carefully selected and highly remunerated lower-line officers. On their side, staff members wanted more recognition and a greater voice in control of the plants.

All of the various functioning groups of the plants were caught up in a general conflict system; but apart from the effects of involvement

in this complex, the struggles between line and staff organizations were attributable mainly to (1) functional differences between the two groups; (2) differentials in the ages, formal education, potential occupational ceilings, and status group affiliations of members of the two groups (the staff officers being younger, having more education but lower occupational potential, and forming a prestige-oriented group with distinctive dress and recreational tastes); (3) need of the staff groups to justify their existence; (4) fear in the line that staff bodies by their expansion, and well-financed research activities, would undermine line authority; and (5) the fact that aspirants to higher staff offices could gain promotion only through approval of influential line executives.

If further research should prove that staff-line behavior of the character presented here is widespread in industry, and *if* top management should realize how such behavior affects its cost and production goals—and be concerned to improve the condition—then remedial measures could be considered. For example, a corrective approach might move in the direction of (1) creating a separate body [25] whose sole function would be the coordination of staff and line efforts; (2) increasing the gradations of awards and promotions in staff organizations (without increase of staff personnel); (3) granting of more nearly equal pay to staff officers, but with increased responsibility (without authority over line processes or personnel) for the practical working of their projects; (4) requiring that staff personnel have a minimum supervisory experience and have shared repeatedly in successful collaborative staff-line projects before transferring to the line; (5) steps by top management to remove the fear of veiled personal reprisal felt by officers in most levels of both staff and line hierarchies (This fear—rising from a dis-

[23] In two of the plants a somewhat similar relation, rising from different causes, existed *inside* the line organization with the *operating* branch of the line successfully applying pressures for a share in funds assigned to the *maintenance* division of the line.

[24] The reader must appreciate the fact that constant demands are made by top management to maintain low operating costs.

[25] This body, or "Board of Coordination," would be empowered to enforce its decisions. Membership would consist of staff and line men who had had wide experience in the plant over a period of years. The Board would (*a*) serve as an arbiter between staff and line; (*b*) review, screen, and approve individual recommendations submitted; and (*c*) evaluate contributions after a trial period. Such a body would incidentally be another high status goal for seasoned, capable, and ambitious officers who too often are trapped by the converging walls of the pyramidal hierarchy.

belief in the possibility of bureaucratic impersonality—is probably the greatest obstacle to communication inside the ranks of management); (6) more emphasis in colleges and universities on realistic instruction in the social sciences for students preparing for industrial careers.

The Dynamics of Organizational Behavior

FRANK J. JASINSKI

It seems reasonable to assume that most personnel men have been fairly well indoctrinated by now with the principles of sound human relations and that many line managers are equally aware of the benefits to be derived from greater consideration of the needs and motivations of the individual employee. Yet, as everyone knows, these splendid ideals exemplify what *should be* rather than what *is*. Life in the average industrial undertaking is still a far cry indeed from—in O. A. Ohmann's words—"[that] sociologists' heaven where everybody does what he *has to* because he *wants to*." [1]

Why is there this gulf between theory and practice? Why is it so difficult for enlightened managers to remold the organization in accordance with the doctrines endlessly being promulgated by the social scientists? Why do so many earnest efforts to institute a more desirable way of industrial life wither away at the root?

In an attempt to answer these questions, this article will take a look at organizational behavior from the anthropologist's viewpoint. It will discuss the various and often conflicting demands on the members of the organization to behave in a certain way and show how their responses to these expectations are further modified by the organization's own particular technology and climate. Possibly this analysis may help to underscore the fact that efforts to bring about a "change of heart" go awry, not so much from lack of good intentions on the part of all concerned, as from the failure to take into account all the influences that shape the interpersonal relations of people in a common work setting.

ROLES AND EXPECTATIONS. Most industrial undertakings have to rely on the joint efforts of many people to accomplish their purpose. Accordingly, the over-all task is divided into various "bits" each of which can be handled by one person. A bit can be the only one of its kind, or one of many other identical bits. These bits are traditionally labelled, "Turret Lathe Operator C," "Clerk-Typist A," "Junior Project Engineer," and the like. The tasks they encompass are set forth in job descriptions or position guides which outline, in varying detail, what the organization expects from anyone who accepts responsibility for that segment of the total work of the organization.

To get someone to accept that responsibility, the organization must offer adequate recompense in the way of rights and privileges. In addition to pay, these inducements may include a variety of fringe benefits, from hospitalization insurance to stock options.

The sum total of all the duties and obligations as well as all the rights and privileges of a given position in the organization can be called its *institutional role*. [2] If an employee

From *Personnel*, Vol. 36, No. 2, March–April 1959, pp. 60–67. Reprinted with permission of the publisher, American Management Association.

[1] O. A. Ohmann, "The Leader and the Led," *Personnel*, Nov./Dec., 1958, p. 8.

[2] This term can be roughly equated with Ralph Linton's definition of "Status" in *Study of Man*,

carries out his specified duties and obligations he can expect in return to receive the specified benefits accruing to his particular role.

Now a modern industrial organization does not specify precisely how its workers should behave in every aspect. Its interest in their behavior is confined to those acts which contribute to the over-all purpose of the enterprise —the manufacture of a product or the provision of a service. The individual members, on the other hand, expect more of one another than the organization specifies; and, having a fairly clear idea of the kind of behavior they desire and expect of their colleagues, they will reward, in various ways, those who behave as is expected of them and punish those who do not. The duties and obligations and rights and privileges devolving upon a worker in his relationships with other members of the organization can be called his *ideal-social role*. The behavior expected of him in these relationships may be quite distinct from the behavior stipulated or expected in his institutional role; sometimes as in the case of rate restriction, it can even run contrary to organizational expectations.

Because each member of the organization participates in a variety of relationships, he is subject to a number of ideal-social expectations. Thus, a foreman, for example, may have several ideal-social roles to fulfill. His general foreman may expect him as a subordinate to behave in a manner that goes beyond the specifications laid down in his job description. His work group will have their own ideas of how their superior should behave—another ideal-social role. The foreman's relationships with other foremen, personnel men, inspectors, time study engineers, and so on, will make other behavioral demands on him. It is here that various ideal-social roles may have certain expectations in common. Nevertheless, many may be unique and even in conflict with the others.

Each person's set of ideal-social roles also includes his own idea of what his behavior ought to be—his self-concept, or answer to the question: "Who am I?" Each of us has a picture of the kind of person we want to be and we all try, as far as possible, to behave in such a way as to live up to our picture of ourselves.

WHICH ROLE TO CHOOSE? Confronted by these varying sets of expectations of the way he should behave, the individual may decide to live up to one particular set only, ignoring all the others, or he may vacillate among them, behaving the way he is expected to depending on the immediate pressures of the situation. Alternatively, he can make compromises, trying to meet each set of expectations at least minimally over a period of time.

However he decides to comport himself, his resultant behavior may be called his personal or *actual role*. This is what he actually does, from day to day, as a member of the organization.

How does an individual decide which role he should play?

A highly important factor in that decision is his self-concept. If he perceives his work situation as a place where he can fulfill his self-concept he will behave in a manner that enables him to do so. But if the work situation does not seem to him to offer any means of achieving such satisfaction, he will probably merely put in his time without getting psychologically involved.[3]

In some cases, the individual's self-concept is in harmony with his defined institutional role. Thus, the rate-busters in the machine shop described by Melville Dalton accepted the economic rewards offered by management and produced as much as they could in order to get as many financial rewards as they could; they saw themselves as hardworking, independent people and rejected the informal social group and the rewards it offered.

On the other hand, an individual's self-concept may be contrary to the institutional role yet in keeping with the ideal-social roles imposed by his work group. Thus, the rate restrictors in the Dalton study saw themselves as "good Joes" and responsible members of the social group; they met management's expectations only minimally in fulfilling their institu-

Appleton-Century-Crofts, Inc., New York, 1936. This formulation of rules draws upon several ideas presented by Ruth (Hudson) Rosen in her unpublished doctoral dissertation, *The Role of the Shop Steward*, submitted to the Department of Sociology, Yale University, 1951.

[3] C. Argyris, "The Organization: What Makes It Healthy?" *Harvard Business Review*, Vol. 36, No. 6 (Nov.–Dec., 1958), pp. 107–116.

tional role, but accepted and fulfilled the informal ideal-social roles, as defined by their work group, to the hilt.

Between these two extremes is "the man in the middle." The Dalton study uncovered a number of these workers who had difficulty in resolving the conflict between management's expectations as expressed in their institutional role and the group expectations that shaped their ideal-social role. This conflict was further complicated by the fact that being "good Joes," conscientious workers, and "good providers" were all part of their self-concept. Dalton reports that these particular workers were constantly bumping up against the informally set ceiling rate and that nine of the 50 had had ulcers. None of the rate-busters, who accepted and fulfilled their institutional role, nor any of the "true" restrictors who for the most part rejected their institutional roles had ulcers.[4]

It must not be supposed, however, that actual behavior is determined simply by the response the individual chooses to make to the various roles expected of him. Though he may have a clear idea of how he should behave, other factors may combine to force him into a totally different behavior pattern. Perhaps the best way to illustrate how these other factors affect both expectations and actual behavior is to examine the foremen-worker relationship. The following case material is drawn, for the most part, from the automobile assembly industry, but is no less applicable to other work situations.

The foremen in this particular study[5] were well aware what kind of behavior their workers expected of them. A foreman should, the workers said:

Know the work in his section and the jobs of his workers from a technical standpoint.

Avoid using pressure on his men.

Stick up for his men in dealing with higher management.

Be helpful.

Be friendly and avoid playing favorites.

Understand his men, listen to them, and ask their advice.

On their part, the foremen, in describing how they "should" behave toward their men, seemed to accept much of what their workers expected of them. They described a good foreman's behavior toward his men as follows: [6]

Treat your men as individuals on the job, since each one is different.

Establish a personal relationship with your men, apart from the job relationship.

Teach and promote your own men as far as possible.

Be a shock absorber.

Stand up for your men and interpret their needs and wishes to upper management.

Consult your workers and delegate responsibility to them.

Apart from what was taught in the way of "good" human relations in the foreman training programs, the "ideal" foreman behavior described by both these workers and their foremen themselves went beyond what was formally expected and defined by management—at least it did not appear in the foreman's institutional role. Here, then, was a pattern of behavior which was verbally accepted at both ends of the foreman-worker relationship. Ostensibly, no conflict need have occurred.

Yet, the foremen's actual behavior, especially at one of the plants studied, generally bore no resemblance whatever to the ideal behavior set forth and "accepted" by both groups. Further, far removed though this behavior was from the mutually accepted ideal-social role of the foreman, it was almost impossible to change. As one foreman commented: [7]

You can't treat the men as equals. They take advantage of good treatment. When I used to be a man on the line, I knew the way I'd like to be treated if I were to be happy on the job. When I got to be foreman, I started to treat my men in the same way—

[4] W. F. Whyte, *Money and Motivation*, Harper & Brothers, Inc., New York, 1955, pp. 39–49.

[5] C. R. Walker and R. H. Guest, *The Man on the Assembly Line*, Harvard University Press, Cambridge, Mass., 1952; and A. N. Turner, "What Makes a Good Foreman," *Personnel*, March, 1955, pp. 382–392.

[6] C. R. Walker, R. H. Guest, and A. N. Turner, *The Foreman on the Assembly Line*, Harvard University Press, Cambridge, Mass., 1956, p. 17.

[7] F. J. Jasinski, "Human Relations Training: The Missing Link," *Personnel*, May, 1956, p. 514.

in other words, the way I'd like to be treated—but you just can't do it. *You can't change overnight what's been going on for 15 years,* and these men have been just spoiled by not having too good supervision in the past. . . . They can always quit if they don't like the job.

What are the causes of this deviation?

On the assembly line, at all events, a pervasive factor is the technological environment. As a rule, the men work independently of each other; the technologically interdependent work group is a rarity. For the most part, the work pace is controlled by the moving conveyor; a worker can leave his station only when replaced by a relief man.

Conversation among the workers is minimal not only because of their geographical immobility but also because of the nature of the job. Even workers at adjoining stations interact irregularly and for only a few seconds at a time.

An observation study by the Yale Technology Project showed the average exchange between a foreman and one of his workers lasted about 40 seconds—and the foreman did not speak to each of his workers every day.[8] There hasn't been a training course devised yet that can teach a foreman to cram understanding, friendliness, and fairness toward his employees within the space of 40 seconds.

While admittedly foremen and workers may not be so pressed for time in other work environments, the assembly line furnishes an extreme demonstration of the influence technology can have on this relationship. Although both these foremen and workers wanted better interpersonal relations, they had learned, realistically, to expect and even accept less. This did not, however, increase the social and personal satisfactions of either the workers *or* the foremen. (In a subsequent study, I found that assembly line workers who liked to talk thought that the company did nothing for its employees, and considered their jobs uninteresting even after working 12 or 14 years on the line.[9])

It would seem, therefore, that before em-

barking on a program to improve "human relations," management would be well advised to look to its technology and the behavior it actually *demands.*

THE ORGANIZATIONAL FRAMEWORK. Another factor influencing the foreman-worker relationship is the organizational environment. The continuous assembly of the automobile on an "uninterrupted" conveyor makes the various foremen's sections unusually dependent on one another. In the automobile plants studied, the average foreman had more contacts with people outside his section than with his own workers—another limiting influence on his relationship with his men. And this relationship was further influenced organizationally by the fact that the foreman reported to a general foreman who rated his performance against the requirements of his institutional role. How much weight was attached, organizationally, to the foreman-worker relationship? Analysis of the general foremen's ratings of their foremen's performance showed that only 9 per cent of the comments were concerned with this relationship at all—and of this small percentage almost all emphasized its disciplinary aspects. Actually, only one foreman was specifically criticized for his "uncompromising attitude in dealing with his employees"—a fact that, incidentally, did not prevent him from being given the highest possible rating. Some typical comments which presumably guided the foremen in their behavior toward their employees were these:

> Very aggressive and controls employees well.
> More forcefulness required to increase the efficiency of the operators.
> He is lax in controlling his people.[10]

Obviously, if the organization is set up in such a way that a foreman is required to spend the greater portion of his time with people outside his own work group, it is difficult for him, in any event, to improve his relations with his men. It is even harder for him to do so when he has a boss who regards consideration for the feelings of employees as so much "coddling" and is likely to give him an adverse performance rating on that very account.

[8] R. H. Guest, "Of Time and the Foreman," *Personnel*, May, 1956, pp. 478–486.

[9] F. J. Jasinski, "Technological Delimitation of Reciprocal Relationships," *Human Organization*, Summer, 1956.

[10] F. J. Jasinski, "Human Relations Training: The Missing Link," *loc. cit.*

Here again, management would do well to precede any program for improving its human relations by a study of the organizational influences presently affecting them.

THE INFLUENCE OF ETHOS. A third set of factors affecting interpersonal relations can be classified as ethological. Ethos—an anthropological concept—is the sum total of the varying values placed by members of an organization on the respective satisfactions or dissatisfactions to be derived from the organization.[11] It is akin to "organizational climate" but goes beyond this more common term in that it is shared by most members of an organization and cannot be readily altered by individuals or a management group.

Thus, the newly appointed foreman cited above, who tried to behave the way he and the workers *said* he should behave discovered, to his dismay, that the workers would not really accept this "ideal" behavior. The workers had "adjusted" over time to "poor supervision" and sought to maintain that adjustment. The workers and supervisors who could not accept the values that made up this plant's ethos had left; those who remained had learned to live with it.

(Ethos can be changed, however. My colleague at the Yale Technology Project, Robert H. Guest, is currently writing an analysis of some drastic changes that have taken place in this same plant with essentially the same people. It should be added that the changes required nearly two-and-one-half years of determined but sincere managerial action, and that this action succeeded only because it included improvements in the technological and organizational environment as well as in the ethological. Certainly, it took a lot more than getting the foremen to walk around smiling and saying a cheery "Hello" to their workers.)

Management, of course, does much initially to establish the organization's ethos. The very way individual jobs are designed and the organization is set up shows the worker how much value management attaches to the varying satisfactions he might derive from his participation in the enterprise. The automobile assembly worker who has been tightening the

same series of nuts for 15 years and is aware that he is no more than a cipher in management's calculations is not likely to be taken in by a glad-handing foreman who has just finished a human relations booster course. The behavior of one foreman cannot be expected to alter a worker's perception of the values which he sees overwhelmingly reinforced and maintained by management's actions in the technological and organizational spheres.

SOME IMPLICATIONS FOR MANAGEMENT. In sum, then, we see that organizational behavior is by no means a simple, straightforward matter. It is the outcome of a number of influences, all of them playing their part in the development and maintenance of behavioral patterns, whether "good" or "bad."

Though the organization's demands on the individual, as defined by his institutional role, are limited to the job to be done, the rights and privileges he receives from the organization in return are similarly limited—and if there is no formal provision for the satisfaction of his social and egoistic needs, he tends to seek this in his interactions with other members of the organization. Since these people are, in turn, seeking to satisfy their social and egoistic needs, they expect the individual to behave toward them in a certain way. These expectations, which go beyond the formal, organizational stipulations of behavior, and may vary with different relationships are defined in ideal-social roles.

Nevertheless, actual behavior is limited by technological, organizational, and ethological factors. Technological requirements may circumscribe the degree and nature of the worker's interactions with others, or of the intrinsic satisfaction he derives from his work. Organizational practices, though they may not directly involve the individual employee, may have an effect on the behavior of others and eventually on his own. Finally, the value system or ethos of the organization may be such that the employee sooner or later learns which satisfactions he can realistically expect in his interactions with others and which ones he must forego.

Since these three factors are interrelated in varying degrees, changes in one will have corresponding effects on the others. Yet management, seemingly unaware of this network of dependent variables, often tries to change be-

[11] Cf. J. J. Horigmann, *Culture and Ethos of Kaska Society*, Yale University Press, New Haven, Conn., 1949, pp. 9–27.

havior by concentrating on one side of a reciprocal relationship. Attempts are made to improve foreman-worker relationships, for example, by training foremen to behave differently. The more the other factors in the situation are ignored the more difficult the task of changing behavior becomes.

It seems imperative that more attention be paid to actual behavior—the adjustment made by the members of the organization to the several, and often contradictory demands made upon them and the factors circumscribing their actions. This, in turn, raises the fundamental question, why the particular adjustment has occurred and what sustains it.

To what degree have the institutional and ideal-social roles affected actual ones? What technological, organizational, and ethological factors have influenced employees' present expectations and behavior? What is the organization's ethos—how did it develop and how is it reinforced?

Recognizing and understanding what be-

havior *is* and why it got that way should bring management considerably nearer to the goal of what organizational behavior *should* be.

In conclusion, it may be said that changes can be made in certain interpersonal relationships without remaking the entire organization or revolutionizing its technology. Some attempts that have been and are being made along these lines may be all the more successful because of management's understanding of the other deterrents to change. Certainly, something may be gained, in light of such understanding, by realistically re-adjusting sights and intermediate goals slightly downward instead of always "going for broke"—and repeatedly going broke.

Ideally, of course, an effective, overall program of change should involve the organization's technology, administrative framework, and ethos. If such a program is impracticable today, who knows but that it may yet be attempted tomorrow?